A ME

Christopher Isherwood, among the most celebrated writers of his generation, was born in Cheshire in 1904. He left Cambridge without graduating, briefly studied medicine and then turned to writing his first novels *All the Conspirators* (1928) and *The Memorial* (1932). Between 1929 and 1939 he lived mostly abroad, spending four years in Berlin, and then elsewhere in Europe, producing the novels *Mr Norris Changes Trains* (1935) and *Goodbye to Berlin* (1939) on which the musical *Cabaret* was later based. Following his move to America (he became a US citizen in 1946), Isherwood wrote another five novels, including *Down There on a Visit* and *A Single Man*, a travel book about South America and a biography of the great Indian mystic Ramakrishna. During the 1970s he began producing a series of autobiographical books: *Kathleen and Frank*, *Christopher and his Kind*, *My Guru and His Disciple* and *October*, the text of one month of his diary published with drawings by Don Bachardy. Christopher Isherwood died in January 1986.

KATHERINE BUCKNELL

Katherine Bucknell is the editor of Christopher Isherwood's *Diaries Volume I: 1939 – 1960* and W H Auden's *Juvenilia: Poems 1922 – 1928*. She also co-edits the Oxford University Press series *Auden Studies* and is co-founder of the W H Auden Society.

ALSO BY CHRISTOPHER ISHERWOOD

Novels

All the Conspirators
The Memorial
Mr Norris Changes Trains
Goodbye to Berlin
Prater Violet
The World in the Evening
Down There on a Visit
A Single Man
A Meeting by the River

Autobiography

Lions and Shadows
Kathleen and Frank
Christopher and his Kind
My Guru and His Disciple
October

Biography

Ramakrishna and His Disciples

Plays (with W H Auden)

The Dog Beneath the Skin
The Ascent of F6
On the Frontier

Travel

Journey to a War (with W H Auden)
The Condor and the Crows

Collections

Exhumations
Where Joy Resides

Diaries

Volume I: 1939 – 1960

Christopher Isherwood

LOST YEARS
A Memoir 1945–1951

EDITED AND INTRODUCED BY
Katherine Bucknell

V

VINTAGE

Published by Vintage 2001

2 4 6 8 10 9 7 5 3

Copyright © Don Bachardy 2000
Introduction, editorial apparatus, chronology
and glossary © Katherine Bucknell 2000

First published in Great Britain by
Chatto & Windus 2000

Vintage
Random House, 20 Vauxhall Bridge Road,
London SW1V 2SA

Random House Australia (Pty) Limited
20 Alfred Street, Milsons Point, Sydney
New South Wales 2061, Australia

Random House New Zealand Limited
18 Poland Road, Glenfield,
Auckland 10, New Zealand

Random House (Pty) Limited
Endulini, 5A Jubilee Road, Parktown 2193,
South Africa

The Random House Group Limited Reg. No. 954009
www.randomhouse.co.uk

A CIP catalogue record for this book
is available from the British Library

ISBN 0 09 928324 7

Papers used by Random House are natural, recyclable
products made from wood grown in sustainable forests.
The manufacturing processes conform to the environ-
mental regulations of the country of origin

Printed and bound in Great Britain by
Bookmarque Ltd, Croydon, Surrey

Contents

Introduction

On his sixty-seventh birthday, August 26, 1971, Christopher Isherwood began to write the autobiographical memoir which is contained in this volume, about his life in California and New York and his travels abroad to England and Europe from January 1945 to May 1951. He called the work a reconstructed diary, and he intended it to recapture a lost period following World War II when he had all but abandoned his lifelong habit of keeping a diary. He based the reconstructed diary on his memories and on what he called his "day-to-day diaries," the pocket-sized appointment books in which he regularly noted the names of people he saw on a given day and sometimes, cryptically, what they had done together.[1] He also drew on the handful of diary entries he did make during the lost years[2] and on letters he had written at the time (he asked for some letters to be returned to him for reference), and he consulted a few friends for their own recollections. The reconstructed diary, never completed by Isherwood but also never destroyed, is now published for the first time as *Lost Years: A Memoir 1945–1951*.

Like his earlier autobiography about the 1920s, *Lions and Shadows* (1938), *Lost Years* describes the relationships and experiences which gave inner shape to Isherwood's life during the period it portrays, but in contrast to *Lions and Shadows*, the memoir begun in 1971 is based as closely as possible on fact. Unlike Isherwood's other diaries, kept contemporaneously with the events they recorded, the manuscript of the reconstructed diary shows many alterations, often using white-

---

[1] He had lost his pocket diary for 1946, and he noted in his diary on September 2, 1971 that during the postwar period even his pocket diaries were not kept up every day.

[2] All of these entries have already been published in Christopher Isherwood, *Diaries Volume One 1939–1960 (D1)*, ed. Katherine Bucknell (London, 1996; New York, 1997). In the reconstructed diary, Isherwood usually calls these diaries "journals," thereby distinguishing them from his day-to-day diaries.

out. Moreover, it is heavily annotated with Isherwood's own footnotes, which comment, correct, and elaborate on his narrative. With
a scholarly precision he might have mocked when studying history at
Cambridge in the 1920s, he sharply scrutinized and questioned his
memories, trying to establish exactly what happened and to understand why.

Lions and Shadows had aimed to entertain and was prefaced by
Isherwood's disclaimer that "it is not, in the ordinary journalistic
sense of the word, an autobiography; it contains no 'revelations'; it is
never 'indiscreet'; it is not even entirely 'true.'" Isherwood goes on
to say, "Read it as a novel." But *Lost Years* is the second book in a
major new phase—roughly the final third of his career—in which
Isherwood moved away from semi-fictionalized writing towards
pure autobiography. It does contain revelations; it is highly indiscreet; and it foregoes deliberate artifice in order to try to recapture
actual past events. It should not be read as a novel, although its
aspiration to be true is partly reflected in its effort—deeply
characteristic of Isherwood—to record and account for the way in
which mythological significance arises from real events. In the
reconstructed diary, as elsewhere in Isherwood's work, the play of
fantasy and emotion is recognized and incorporated as a dimension
of real experience.

Isherwood completed *Kathleen and Frank*, his detailed historical
book about his parents, in the autumn of 1970. Having spent several
years in prolonged meditation upon the heterosexual bond between
his parents—they shared a late-Victorian, upper-middle-class
marriage which was perfectly happy until devastated by Frank
Isherwood's death in World War I—he seemed to need to react by
writing about the very different affinities which shaped his own life.
He was no longer motivated by the spirit of rebellion that governed
his youth, but certainly, at first, by a spirit of relief and light-
heartedness. On Thanksgiving Day 1970, thankful that he had
completed *Kathleen and Frank*, he wondered in his diary, "What shall
I write next?" He considered a book about his relationship with his
spiritual teacher Swami Prabhavananda—a book he would only
begin half a decade later—but he knew already that such a book
could not be a novel:

> Surely it would be better from every point of view to do this as a
> factual book? Well of course there is the difficulty of being frank
> without being indiscreet: but that difficulty always arises in one
> form or another. For example, it is absolutely necessary that I

should say how, right at the start of our relationship, I told Swami I had a boyfriend (and that he replied, "try to think of him as Krishna") because my personal approach to Vedanta was, among other things, the approach of a homosexual looking for a religion which will accept him.[1]

For Isherwood, a book about his religious life, when he came to write it, would have to begin by addressing the question of his sexuality. So he went on to propose to himself that he write a book expressly about his sexuality and sketched out a plan for the reconstructed diary which he would, in fact, begin on his birthday the following August:

> Then there is the fairly big chunk of diary fill-in which I might do, covering the scantily covered period between January 1, 1945 and February 1955—or maybe February 1953, when I met Don [Bachardy], because that's the beginning of a new era. This would be quite largely a sexual record and so indiscreet as to be un-publishable. It might keep me amused, like knitting, but I should be getting on with something else as well.

The project which he compared to "knitting"—recreating the sequence and sense of his life during the late 1940s in little, unimportant stitches—did more than just keep Isherwood amused as he had at first imagined. It proved both challenging and absorbing, and for several years he attempted no other work of his own—although during the first half of the 1970s he collaborated with Don Bachardy on a television script of *Frankenstein* (1971), and on three other scripts which were never made: *The Lady from the Land of the Dead*, *The Beautiful and Damned* (both for television), and a film script of Isherwood's novel *A Meeting by the River* (1967), which they had already successfully adapted for the stage. Moreover, Isherwood's "knitting," somewhat like the flow of unselfconscious, free-associative talk in psychoanalysis, evidently set his mind free to delve more directly than ever before into his private life. The very insignificance and confidentiality of the task opened new avenues to self-reflection. And so perhaps without at first realizing it, Isherwood embarked on an entirely new episode of his life's work.

In his Thanksgiving diary entry he had gone on to ask himself whether he would ever again write fiction:

> Have I given up all idea of writing another novel, then? No, not

[1] Christopher Isherwood, Diaries 1960–1983 (unpublished), November 26, 1970.

necessarily. The problem really is as follows: The main thing I have to offer as a writer are my reactions to experience (these *are* my fiction or my poetry, or whatever you want to call it). Now, these reactions are more positive when I am reacting to actual experiences, than when I am reacting to imagined experiences. Yet, the actuality of the experiences does bother me, the brute facts keep tripping me up, I keep wanting to rearrange and alter the facts so as to relate them more dramatically to my reactions. Facts are never simple, they come in awkward bunches. You find yourself reacting to several different facts at one and the same time, and this is messy and unclear and undramatic. I have had this difficulty many times while writing *Kathleen and Frank*. For instance, Christopher's reactions to Kathleen are deplorably complex and therefore self-contradictory, and therefore bad drama.

On the one hand, Isherwood was restating, and perhaps rediscovering, something he had long known: that his reactions to real experience were more vivid, more intense than anything he could invent. On the other hand, he conceded that writing accurate history was a more severe discipline than writing fiction, because he could not alter the facts to conform to his artistic intention. As early as 1953 he had described in his diary his "lack of inclination to cope with a constructed, invented plot—the feeling, why not write what one experiences from day to day?" Then, in 1953, he had attributed the feeling to the fact that he had fallen in love with Don Bachardy: "Why invent—when Life is so prodigious?" And he had added, "Perhaps I'll never write another novel. . . ."[1] Yet he had gone on to write several of his best novels over the twelve or thirteen years following 1953. But eventually the fiction did stop. Isherwood wrote his last novel, *A Meeting by the River*, in 1965 and 1966; by the time it was published in 1967, he was already hard at work on *Kathleen and Frank*, which is based so closely on his parents' letters and diaries that it incorporates long passages from them, "brute facts," which he could not rearrange and which forced him to struggle with the complexity and contradiction of real life. As soon as he finished correcting the proofs of *Kathleen and Frank*, he began reconstructing the lost years of his own life, 1945 to 1951, according to a similar version of the newly established method.

In September 1973, Isherwood at last began to get on, as he had envisioned in the Thanksgiving diary entry, with "something else as well." This was to be an autobiographical book, about his life in

[1] *D1*, pp. 455–6.

America, in which he planned to tell, according to an inspiration derived from Jung, his "personal myth."[1] It would share publicly some of his wartime diaries as well as the fruits of the "knitting" he had done in the meantime, and it would be for him a new kind of book. By late October the American autobiography began to undergo a metamorphosis, because Isherwood realized that he could not explain why he had emigrated to America without first telling about the personal crisis which had occurred when his German lover Heinz Neddermeyer had been turned away from England by an immigration official in January 1934. So he shifted the book's focus backward to the decade of the 1930s, in order to tell the story of the events which drove him away from England in search of what he called "my sexual homeland."[2] Isherwood and Heinz had been forced to wander through Europe in search of a country where they could settle together, safe from Hitler's persecution of homosexuals and from his conscription; finally, Heinz was arrested by the Gestapo in May 1937, just inside the German border. When Isherwood at last published this autobiography as *Christopher and His Kind* in 1976, he overnight became a hero of the burgeoning gay liberation movement. The book sold faster than any other he had ever written.

Isherwood conceded in interviews and letters that he had moved beyond the brute facts in writing *Christopher and His Kind*, because he wanted it to read as a novel rather than a memoir.[3] In earlier works, as the book itself makes clear, he had moved away from facts not only to heighten dramatic effect but also to avoid writing about his homosexuality. But in *Christopher and His Kind* he no longer wished to avoid writing about his homosexuality; on the contrary he wished to tell about it in detail. This new impulse, to reveal rather than to conceal, is a continuation of the impulse according to which he had begun the reconstructed diary in 1971 (indeed, *Christopher and His Kind* incorporates whole passages from the reconstructed diary), and Isherwood's ability in the 1976 autobiography to deal forthrightly with his sexuality, as the underpinning for the trajectory of his life, grew directly out of the confidential and, as it had once seemed, insignificant work he had already done recapturing his postwar life from 1945 to 1951. *Christopher and His Kind* was a relatively shocking book, even as late as 1976. The reconstructed diary is far more

---

[1] Diaries 1960–1983, September 14, 1973.
[2] Diaries 1960–1983, October 29, 1973.
[3] Interview with W. I. Scobie and letter to Isherwood's U.K. publisher (at Methuen) quoted in Brian Finney, *Christopher Isherwood: A Critical Biography* (London, 1979), p. 282.

shocking; even now, some passages have been altered or removed to protect the privacy of a few of Isherwood's friends and acquaintances who are still alive.

Isherwood's reconstructed diary is sexually explicit partly because, for the first time ever, it could be. In 1971, seven years after the publication of his assertively homosexual novel *A Single Man* (1964), two years after the Stonewall riot in New York, and well into the cultural and sexual revolution spawned during the 1960s, he was comfortable committing to paper (though not necessarily for publication) details of personal relationships such as he would for years previously either never have written down or otherwise felt compelled to destroy. Since the end of the 1950s, censorship laws in the United States had been gradually relaxed; court decisions had increasingly required the post office to deliver magazines formerly ruled obscene and had permitted publication and sale of books that might once have attracted a ban. Even the Hollywood Code, governing censorship of films, gave way during the 1960s. Although some of the sex acts which Isherwood describes in the reconstructed diary were still widely illegal, he could without much risk of penalty record the true habits and attitudes of the homosexual milieu in which he had long lived in semi-secrecy.

Lost Years, the reconstructed diary which began for Isherwood as a task of personal recollection and amusement, can now be seen to have a more general significance as a work of social history. For it aimed to recapture the mood and behavior of a little recognized group which was soon to make itself known to the popular consciousness. Isherwood had studied history with enthusiasm and panache as a schoolboy; later, his revulsion from the dry, academic discipline he encountered at Cambridge propelled him toward literature as if it were an alternative to history, and in his case a mightily preferred one. But his autobiographies, travel books and novels—even the early, most genuinely fictionalized ones—all bear the mark of his historical outlook. He had a journalist's instinct for knowing where to go and who to observe and talk to, and he rendered his vivid personal impressions with a historian's sense of the interconnection between the popular psyche and the facts of social and political change. In his best work, Isherwood consistently achieved the task laid out for literature by his schoolmate and lifelong friend, Edward Upward, who believed that imaginative literature could not escape its relation to material reality and that the socially responsible writer ought to portray the forces at work beneath the surface of material reality which will shape the future of society.

Upward became a dogmatic Marxist in the early 1930s, and he explained in a 1937 essay that:

> For the Marxist critic . . . a good book, is one that is true not merely to a temporarily existing situation but also to the future conditions which are developing within that situation. The greatest books are those which, sensing the forces of the future at work beneath the surface of the past or present reality, remain true to reality for the longest period of time.[1]

Isherwood first became seriously involved with political ideas during his years in Berlin; he had strong communist sympathies in the 1930s, but he never joined the party. His regret, and moreover his sense of guilt, at not having been able to commit himself like Edward Upward to the revolutionary cause of the workers in Europe and England, contributes to the bitter tension of his slim masterpiece *Prater Violet* (1945); related feelings about being away from England during the war fuelled his ingenious and somewhat brittle arguments about emigration and pacifism in his wartime diaries and in his next novels, *The World in the Evening* (1954) and *Down There on a Visit* (1962). For most of his life, Isherwood was not politically committed. As an artist, he abstained, and he bore the guilt of turning his back on worthy causes about which he thought and wrote but in which he took no active role. But as he was finally able to write in his reconstructed diary, "Christopher was certainly more a socialist than he was a fascist, and more a pacifist than he was a socialist. But he was a queer first and foremost."[2]

Gay liberation was the only movement for social change to which Isherwood ever felt personally and entirely committed. In July 1971 he noted in his diary that he felt compelled, now, to mention his homosexuality to everyone who interviewed him, and just a few months earlier he had confessed that he was attracted to the idea of himself as "one of the Grand Old Men of the movement."[3] His later work fulfils Upward's principles in a way that Upward could not have foreseen in 1937 (though Upward read and admired virtually all that Isherwood wrote in the 1970s). Upward had written in the same 1937 essay:

> A writer, if he wishes at all to tell the truth, must write about the world as he has already experienced it in the course of his practical

[1] "Sketch for a Marxist Interpretation of Literature," *The Mind in Chains: Socialism and the Cultural Revolution*, ed. C. Day-Lewis (London, 1937), pp. 46–7.
[2] P. 190.
[3] Diaries 1960–1983, April 19, 1971.

living. And if he shares the life of a class which cannot solve the problems that confront it, which cannot cope with reality, then no matter how honest or talented he may be, his writing will not correspond to reality. . . . He must change his practical life, must go over to the progressive side of the conflict. . . .[1]

For Upward, the struggle was a class struggle, and the progressive side of the struggle was the side of the workers. He divorced his own class to join the workers, and even gave up his writing, for a time, to do communist party work. For Isherwood, the struggle proved to be a sexual struggle, and he was already on the progressive side, the side of the homosexuals; but that side had yet to assemble itself. And it took Isherwood several decades to find the way to acknowledge his side openly, both in his life and in his work.

Isherwood never gave up his writing as Upward did; for he was a writer above all, not an activist, even when it came to his homosexual kind. By writing in explicit sexual detail about his intimate behavior and that of his close friends and acquaintances in the years immediately following the war, he was portraying the hidden energies and affinities of homosexual men all over the United States who during that period were gathering increasingly in certain, mostly coastal cities as peace and prosperity returned to a country much altered by vast wartime mobilization. This hidden social group, whose consciousness of itself as a group was intensified by the demographic shifts brought about by the war and then extended throughout the 1950s, was to emerge in its own right as a significant force of change in America and in western culture generally during the final third of the twentieth century. Much of this change began in southern California, and Isherwood was living at its source. His personal myth is part of, and in many ways emblematic of, the larger myth of the group to which he belonged; and his reconstruction of his life during the postwar years foretells much of what was to come.

In *The World in the Evening*, the novel he was working on during the lost years of the late 1940s and early 1950s, Isherwood wrote more explicitly and more sympathetically than ever before about homosexual and bisexual characters. And he manipulated his publishers and compromised with convention just enough to succeed in getting into print two unsensational homosexual love scenes and a few somewhat more subversive ideas and psychological insights. The sentiments he recorded in his reconstructed diary in 1971, about his sense of

[1] "Sketch for a Marxist Interpretation of Literature," pp. 51–2.

political commitment to queers, were already articulated clearly in *The World in the Evening* by his character Bob Wood, who remarks on joining the army, "I can't be a C.O. because, if they declared war on queers—tried to round us up and liquidate us, or something—I'd fight. I'd fight till I dropped. I know that. I'd be so mad I wouldn't even feel scared. . . . So how can I say I'm a pacifist?"[1]

Possibly Isherwood felt emboldened to write more candidly about homosexuals after reading Gore Vidal's novel *The City and the Pillar*, which Vidal had sent to him in manuscript before its 1948 publication. Three other books which he mentions in the reconstructed diary as having made an even stronger impression on him around the same time, and which have forthright and unsettling passages about homosexuals, were John Horne Burns's *The Gallery* (1947), Calder Willingham's *End as a Man* (1947), and Willard Motley's *Knock on Any Door* (1947).[2] American attitudes to homosexuality were changing generally in the postwar period in any case, and 1948 also saw the publication of Alfred Kinsey's massive volume of research, *Sexual Behavior in the Human Male*—begun in 1938 and based on countless interviews which suggested that as many as thirty-seven percent of men had at least one homosexual experience after the onset of adolescence.

Closer to his heart, Isherwood was almost certainly influenced by the defiant personal style of his companion of the late 1940s, the photographer William Caskey, who was fully capable of the sorts of remarks Isherwood put into the mouth of his character Bob Wood. Wood is partly modelled on Isherwood's later lover and longterm friend Jim Charlton, but Isherwood writes in the reconstructed diary that, "Bob Wood isn't a portrait of Jim, however; he is described as a crusader, a potential revolutionary—which Jim certainly wasn't and isn't."[3] Caskey, on the other hand, "declared his homosexuality loudly and shamelessly and never cared whom he shocked. He was a pioneer gay militant in this respect—except that you couldn't imagine him joining any movement."[4]

---

[1] *The World in the Evening* (New York, 1954), p. 66; (London, 1954), p. 79.
[2] Isherwood met Burns in 1947, and records in the reconstructed diary that he wished he had had time to know him better. *End as a Man* he called "an exciting discovery and the beginning of Christopher's (more or less) constant enthusiasm for Willingham's work" (p. 176, n.). Of *Knock on Any Door* he writes, "Christopher was much moved . . . when he read it; this was *his* idea of a sad story. He fell in love with the hero and wrote Willard Motley a fan letter" (p. 140, n.2). Motley's hero, a heterosexual petty criminal who hustles as trade part time, personifies the absolute defiance of authority which so often captivated Isherwood in his real-life acquaintances.
[3] P. 159, n.1.
[4] P. 54.

Isherwood makes clear in the reconstructed diary how greatly he admired Caskey's outspokenness about his sexuality. Sometimes Caskey's belligerence was too abrasive. For instance, he became bitterly angry with the Chilean painter Matta and his wife, when Matta well-meaningly said that he himself had tried sex with men, and Isherwood and Caskey never saw the Mattas again. But on other occasions Caskey was killingly witty about his homosexuality. To Natasha Moffat's friendly insult that she was glad to be seated next to "a pansy" during a dinner party at Charlie Chaplin's house, he replied: "Your slang is out of date, Natasha—we don't say 'pansy' nowadays. We say 'cocksucker.'" Natasha Moffat had a reputation for energetically offbeat behavior, and her sophisticated Parisian past as an intimate of Simone de Beauvoir and Jean-Paul Sartre made her tough enough for such repartee. Isherwood recalls in the reconstructed diary that her remark was loud and silenced the group; Caskey's more shocking reply restored the balance. And Isherwood goes on to write of his younger self, "Christopher, who truly adored Caskey at such moments, sat glowing with pride in him."[1] His own good manners would never permit him to behave as Caskey did, and he was capable, personally, of feeling embarrassment. "Caskey never suffered from embarrassment. He didn't give a damn what anybody knew about him."[2] Isherwood was immensely attracted to Caskey's bold insistence on the truth, his impatience with social nicety, his willingness to startle and disrupt. He recognized a need for such behavior and privately he identified with it.

The rebelliousness in Caskey which Isherwood so adored was among the chief things, in the end, which drove them apart. Their relationship was a constant struggle for power. Neither Caskey nor Isherwood was ever able to admit to the other that he was in love; each held back—guarded, suspicious, unwilling to trust. They often fought violently; Caskey could make Isherwood lose his temper so badly that Isherwood would shout and sometimes hit Caskey, especially when they were drunk. And Isherwood recalls in the reconstructed diary that drunkenness became a prevalent, destructive necessity: "drinking was a built-in dimension of their relationship; while sober, he felt, they never achieved intimacy."[3] With the drinking came bad moods and lethargy, so that Isherwood worked less and less. The psychological conflict in their relationship was mirrored and underpinned by growing sexual incompatibility, and in

[1] P. 235.
[2] P. 182.
[3] P. 53.

contrast to Isherwood's earlier love affairs, they shared no mythology about one another. They lived continually in the plain light of day, with no natural indulgence in fantasy, no artless playfulness, no imaginative games or magical naming. This made Isherwood feel the relationship was more grown-up than his others, but it also made the relationship harder to sustain. Through their mutual distrust and inability to yield, the pair were confined to a routine of selfconscious passion and relied upon forced playacting to fuel their lovemaking. Isherwood gave way to Caskey's aggressiveness almost out of politeness, but eventually certain tasks of role playing grew wearying. He admits that he would have split from Caskey sooner had he not feared to live alone; and indeed his fear of being alone shaped his romantic behavior throughout his life.

Nevertheless, the years with Caskey were Isherwood's first long-term domestic arrangement with a man close to his own age and emotional maturity. He felt genuinely proud of Caskey's social charm and included him entirely in his own social life, introducing Caskey to his various circles of friends—emigré artists and intellectuals like the Viertels, the Huxleys, and the Stravinskys as well as Greta Garbo and other film people in Hollywood; Swami Prabhavananda and his devotees at the Vedanta Society; literary friends like E. M. Forster and Stephen Spender in England, W. H. Auden and Lincoln Kirstein in New York; new friends like Tennessee Williams, Truman Capote and Gore Vidal; and many others. Introducing Caskey so widely contributed to a new and more open sense of himself as a homosexual. During the war years, when Isherwood lived among the Quakers and refugees in Haverford, Pennsylvania, and later when he tried to become a Hindu monk, he kept his sexuality quarantined from his everyday life. In Haverford he had concealed it; as an aspiring monk at the Vedanta Center he had tried during months of celibacy to rise above it. But once he fell in love with Caskey, everything changed; for a time he allowed his sexuality to shape his life as a whole.

During the same period, he became increasingly at home in a circle of close California friends of whom many were homosexual and most were at ease with homosexuality, so that his identity became established with solidity in the community around him. He was at first troubled by the consistency and honesty this began to require of him. As a young man, he had enjoyed the fragmented life which resulted from living in different countries among discrete groups of friends—shuttling between London and Berlin; fleeing through Greece, Portugal, Denmark and elsewhere with Heinz; shipping out to China with Auden; tasting Manhattan on the return journey. Travelling had afforded him semi-secrecy and any number of escape routes from commitment and from himself. He had engaged in simultaneous love affairs and played freely with several personalities and social strategies, just as he played with the characters in his books. But his postwar life in California permitted him no hiding places. As he writes in the reconstructed diary: "Christopher found that his life had become all of a piece; everybody knew everything there was to know about him. In theory, he saw that this was morally preferable; it made hypocrisy and concealment impossible. In practice, he hated it."[1]

The unification of his life and identity brought to the fore with a new seriousness the question of who he really was and wanted to be. Now he could not escape the results of his actions, and he would be forced to live more deliberately, with a new sense of self and responsibility. But it would take some years before he could achieve coherence between his moral outlook and his day-to-day behavior, and even longer before such coherence would be reflected in his writing. At first the fact that he no longer needed to guard his identity from his separate circles of friends and colleagues simply fed the growing undiscipline of his life in the late 1940s. He may have stopped bothering to write in his diary partly because he no longer needed to keep up a private, unifying narrative about his true self, the self at the controlling center of his various, sometimes less than genuine, social lives. But over the longer term, he would continue to need his diary to understand himself, and by the time he began writing in it again—occasionally in 1948, then gradually more often by the early 1950s—he would already be writing about a different person. In the 1970s he would still be trying to achieve, in his reconstructed diary, a coherent account of the changes which had taken place in him during the dissipated personal aftermath of the war.

In August 1949, Isherwood attended an all-night party at the house of Sam From. The other guests whom he mentions in his 1955 outline of the period[2] and in his reconstructed diary were Evelyn Caldwell, Paul Goodman, Charles Aufderheide and Alvin Novak. These were members and friends of The Benton Way Group, a bohemian ménage, mostly from the Midwest, sharing a house in Benton Way, in Los Angeles. They were intellectuals, generally highly educated, and predominantly homosexual. Goodman was a

---

[1] P. 182.
[2] *D1*, pp. 389–94.

philosopher, social critic, published poet, and novelist whose work Isherwood later came to admire; Aufderheide a movie camera technician who read widely and wrote poetry on the side; Novak a philosophy student at UCLA. Sam From himself was a successful businessman. Others who were part of The Benton Way Group at various times—including Isadore From, David Sachs, Edouard Roditi, Fern Maher—were psychoanalysts, philosophers, scholars, social workers, artists.

Evelyn Caldwell, soon to marry and change her name to Evelyn Hooker, was the psychologist specializing in Rorschach techniques who was about to begin what became her life's work: studying the homosexual community in Los Angeles. She attended many homosexual parties where she joined in the revelry but also engaged in long, personal conversations with the other guests, and within a year of the party where she and Isherwood met, she started to circulate extensive questionnaires and conduct scores of interviews and psychological tests. In 1956, at a professional conference in Chicago, she was to challenge widespread opinion among her colleagues when she presented the first results of her research, which demonstrated that expert psychologists could not distinguish homosexuals from heterosexuals on the basis of then standard, widely used personality tests. In fact, her results from these types of tests showed that as high a percentage of homosexuals as heterosexuals were psychologically well adjusted. She, like Isherwood, was to become a hero of gay liberation.

The conversation at Benton Way parties was friendly but also highbrow and wide-ranging, addressing literature, social change, and, as Isherwood recalls of the all-night party in 1949, the nature of homosexual love. That night the "Symposium," as he calls it, "continued until dawn." Then Isherwood returned home with Alvin Novak, the young man he deemed to be the Alcibiades of the group. In the reconstructed diary Isherwood exposes his mixed motives of passion and idealism and even recalls an element of farce: a drunken Sam From came along with Isherwood and Novak, evidently hoping for sex, then politely passed out, eliminating himself from competition. Isherwood writes in the reconstructed diary that "he later looked back upon that night as having been highly romantic. It was unique, at any rate. Christopher never went to a party that was quite like it."[1]

In The Benton Way Group Isherwood had found a small intellectual community seriously and capably examining the predicament of

[1] P. 198.

the homosexual in modern society and at the same time pursuing an experiment in living that offered them some of the benefits of conventional family life without oppressing their sexuality. In a sense, he had found a new version of Magnus Hirschfeld's Institut für Sexualwissenschaft (Institute for Sexual Science) where he had, as he put it in *Christopher and His Kind*, first been "brought face to face with his tribe"[1] in Berlin in late 1929. According to *Christopher and His Kind*, Hirschfeld's respectable, scientific approach to sexuality had at first offended Isherwood's puritanism, but in the end Isherwood was captivated by Hirschfeld's persona as a "silly solemn old professor."[2] Over the years he came to honor Hirschfeld and his personally dangerous campaign to revise the German criminal code so that homosexual acts between men would be legal.

Hirschfeld was homosexual, Evelyn Hooker was not; and yet there are obvious parallels in their work and in their practical style of approach. Isherwood became close friends with Evelyn Hooker, and just as in Berlin he had rented a room from Hirschfeld's sister immediately next door to the Institut für Sexualwissenschaft, so at the beginning of the 1950s he rented the garden house at Evelyn Hooker's property on Saltair Avenue in Brentwood. His interest in the study of homosexuality was far from superficial, and he evidently wished to involve himself with it both officially and personally. For Isherwood, and for his close friend W. H. Auden, sexual emancipation in Berlin had resulted partly from their anonymous access, as foreigners, to willing boys they met easily in bars and on the streets, and partly from the newly dawning self-understanding which resulted from conscious study of homosexuality and, in Auden's case, from a brief attempt at psychoanalysis. At Hirschfeld's institute, sexual love in all its strange and familiar forms was classified, codified, categorized. Along similarly analytical lines, Isherwood and Auden talked endlessly between themselves and with other friends about their relationships, and they read and also talked about Proust, Gide, Corvo, Freud, Jung, Georg Groddeck, Edward Carpenter, and many others. None of these literary and psychological texts offered them a satisfactory account of who they were. In their own work, throughout their careers, each of them continued to consider and address the question in any number of ways—veiled and indirect at first, then, in Isherwood's case, increasingly overt as the years went by. The earnest scientific thoroughness with which Evelyn Hooker, like Hirschfeld, approached her research, lent Isherwood's way of life in California a

---

[1] *Christopher and His Kind* (*C&HK*) (New York, 1976), p. 16; (London, 1977), p. 20.
[2] *C&HK*, U.S., p. 17; U.K., p. 20.

reassuringly dull legitimacy and probably contributed to his increasing openness about his homosexuality in his writing as well as in his personal life.

In the early 1950s when he was living next door to Evelyn Hooker, Isherwood agreed to write a popular book with her about homosexuality. The plan came to nothing, in part because when Don Bachardy moved into the garden house with Isherwood, Hooker's husband became anxious that Bachardy's youthful appearance would cause a scandal, and the Hookers asked Isherwood to move out. This left Isherwood and Bachardy homeless—a tiny echo of the crisis Isherwood had experienced when Heinz Neddermeyer was refused entry to England in 1934—and it caused a terrible strain in Isherwood's friendship with Evelyn Hooker. Two decades later, in December 1970, just as Isherwood was wondering what to write next after *Kathleen and Frank*, she reminded him of the project. But the idea made him anxious, and his reaction was perhaps still colored by resentment at her failure to stand by him in his relationship with Don Bachardy. On December 11 he wrote:

> Saw Evelyn Hooker yesterday. She wants me to work with her on a "popular" book on homosexuality. . . . I am doubtful about the project. It seems that I shall have to read through sixty case histories and then write about them—which really means retell them, and what the hell is the use of that? Non-writers never understand what writers can and cannot do. They think they can tell you what to say and that you will then somehow magically resay it so it's marvellous. However, I didn't want to refuse straight away. I'll read some of the stuff first and try to find out exactly what it is that Evelyn expects. She is a very good woman and her intentions are of the noblest and I would like to help her, if I can do so without becoming her secretary.

Isherwood read through just two of the case histories and felt certain that the language of psychology was not his own language. In February he wrote:

> This morning I also finished the second of the two files I borrowed from Evelyn Hooker. What a plodding old donkey Psychology is! Evelyn's questions are full of phrases like, "his own processes of sexual arousal are on an ascending incline," "I don't have a very clear picture of how much mutual stimulation is going on," "the primary stimulation is on the head of the penis, would that be true?," "while I have asked you many questions about sexual preferences and gratifications, I have not really asked you

questions couched in his terms of the basic mechanics of sex." I really can't imagine myself working with Evelyn on this sort of thing; it would be like having to write a book in a foreign language. But I mustn't prejudge the issue. I must wait until we have had a talk and I have found out just exactly what it is she wants me to contribute.[1]

By March he had decided against the project:

> Yesterday morning I saw Evelyn Hooker and told her that I can't write her book with her. I think I explained why I can't quite lucidly and I think I convinced her. The analogy of *Kathleen and Frank* was very useful, in doing this, because Kathleen's diaries can be likened to Evelyn's files of case histories. The diaries, like the case histories, can be commented on, they can be elucidated and conclusions can be drawn from them; but they can't be rewritten because nothing can be as good as the source material itself. What is embarrassing—and what I think sticks as a reproach against me in Evelyn's mind—is that I told her, in the Saltair Avenue days, I was prepared to write a "popular" book about homosexuality with her. Of course I was always saying things like this, quite irresponsibly, subconsciously relying on the probability that I wouldn't ever be taken up on them. To Evelyn yesterday I said, "Well, you know, in those days I was nearly always drunk"; which, the more I think of it, was a silly tactless altogether second-rate remark.[2]

Indeed, it was during the Saltair Avenue days that Isherwood had made an analogous promise to Swami Prabhavananda: that he would write a biography of Ramakrishna. Swami persistently reminded Isherwood of the promise, and Isherwood fulfilled it, taking more than a decade to write *Ramakrishna and His Disciples* (1965). He had to submit each chapter of the biography to the order for approval, and the project made him into a quasi-official historian of the Ramakrishna movement. Likewise, through his later works and his diaries, he was to become a historian of the homosexual movement, but without professional psychology or any other "official" involvements; instead, he was to tell its history through his own experience. Although Isherwood slighted the idea of rewriting Evelyn Hooker's case histories, he was already reflecting upon a similar project on his own terms. Later that same month he records that he has begun to

---

[1] Diaries 1960–1983, February 22, 1971.
[2] Diaries 1960–1983, March 2, 1971.

take notes about the private behavior patterns of Don Bachardy ("Kitty") and himself ("Dobbin"). Despite his outcry against psychology, his description of his plan is technical, as if he intended to produce a special kind of case history of his own:

> On the 17th, I started a sort of notebook on Kitty and Dobbin—I'll try to write it rather like a study in natural history; their behavior, methods of communication, feeding habits, etc. I had very strong feelings that I ought not to record all this, that it was an invasion of privacy. But where else have I ever found anything of value? The privacy of the unconscious is the only treasure house. And as a matter of fact, Don is always urging me to write about us. I have no idea, yet, what I shall "do" with this material after I've collected it. I'll just keep jotting things down, day by day, and see what comes of it.[1]

Like all of Isherwood's work, this project was to begin with external observation and recording. By invading his own privacy, by being frank to the point of indiscretion, he could unlock what he calls "the only treasure house," the unconscious. Ordinary habits, the routine of daily life, accurately noted, would reveal the inward, original activity of the mind in its rich, dreamy, nonpersonal, eternal existence. Thus, like a scientist—or perhaps like a spy or a thief—Isherwood set out to make himself and Don Bachardy the subject of a domestic field study.

But the notebook of Kitty and Dobbin was also abandoned, and in the end Isherwood left no specific account of his intimate life with Bachardy. Although his diaries from 1953 onward comprise an episodic narrative of their years together, he never fully analyzed their relationship nor explained its mythology. The names alone, Kitty—suggesting a creature soft and vulnerable, quick to purr and quick to claw—and Dobbin—old, strong and steady, but stubborn and a little boring—tell a great deal. None of the other intimate mythologies which Isherwood describes in the reconstructed diary draws upon animal imagery. They are generally more rivalrous and combative—some derived from wrestling and boxing—or more intellectual and literary—for instance, rooted in Whitman's poetry. Isherwood observes in the reconstructed diary that an animal myth can sustain a relationship when there is conflict: "in the world of animals, hatred is impossible; [they] can only love each other. They focus their aggression on mythical external enemies."[2] Moreover,

---

[1] Diaries 1960–1983, March 19, 1971.
[2] P. 60, n.2.

animals have no language; their world of nestling warmth is based upon physical trust, is inchoate, and inaccessible to outsiders. In the great love relationship of his life, Isherwood, a writer, evidently surrendered to a mythology that did not depend upon language; its parameters could not be declaimed, enforced, or justified by words. They simply had to be acted out. For Isherwood, the relationship may well have been too mysterious or simply too important to dissect. In any case, it was still taking shape at the time of his death, and this, too, may have made it, for him, untellable. Isherwood said in his Thanksgiving diary entry of 1970 that he could not write a book about his friendship with Swami while Swami was still alive because "the book couldn't be truly complete until after Swami's death."[1] Swami died in 1976; *My Guru and His Disciple* was published in 1980. Despite Isherwood's own death in 1986, the story of his relationship with Don Bachardy is even now unfinished.

Although he did not continue in the spring of 1971 with the study of Kitty and Dobbin, Isherwood circled around the idea of a factual, explicit record of his most private life until he at last began the reconstructed diary which, through the gradual accumulation of detailed, intimate, and sometimes trivial, day-to-day memories, gained access to the treasure house of the unconscious and its store of mythology. As he repeated in each of his diary entries about Evelyn Hooker, Isherwood was convinced he must write about homosexuality in his own language. The language of psychology was foreign. His "kind," his tribe, were homosexuals; his kind were also writers. And he asserted that a non-writer, like Evelyn Hooker, could not understand this. He identified with writers, admired writers, socialized with writers. In his reconstructed diary, as in *Christopher and His Kind*, his identity as a homosexual is portrayed as being inseparable from his identity as a writer. And he incorporates in both of these personal histories an account of how he drew on his real-life experiences of the 1930s and 1940s for his fiction, telling how he adapted the facts of his life to suit his artistic purpose. Thus, *Lost Years* and *Christopher and His Kind* reveal not only how he had secretly lived as a homosexual, but also how he had secretly lived as a writer, continually reshaping the truth in his work. In both books, he recalls the works he hoped to write as well as the ones which came to fruition, and so measures himself, ruthlessly, against his unfulfilled ambitions as well as his actual achievements.

---

[1] Diaries 1960–1983, November 26, 1970.

In *Lost Years*, the reconstructed diary, Isherwood tells how throughout the late 1940s he started and restarted the book he at first called *The School of Tragedy* and eventually published as *The World in the Evening*. He recalls that he was never sure of his subject, never sure how to tell his story nor how to give life to a narrator of whose identity and sexuality he was uncertain. In a sense, Isherwood had come to a deadlock with himself because, for a time, his identity as a writer and his identity as a homosexual were at odds. He had introduced Caskey to his friends, so that his life became more unified than ever before, but he was unable to achieve the same unity in his work. Although he put homosexual and bisexual characters into his novel, and portrayed them sympathetically, he was not writing from the center of his own homosexual sensibility. In his diary at the time he argued that his main character "has got to be me . . . it must be written out of the middle of *my* consciousness."[1] But in the reconstructed diary he ridicules this younger aspiration: "How *could* he write out of the middle of his consciousness about someone who was tall, bisexual and an heir to a fortune?"[2] There was a kind of apartheid in his work between the writer and the man, and it was stopping all progress.

Paralleling his difficulties in writing as a homosexual were his difficulties in writing as an American. *Prater Violet*, though written in California, is a book about England and Europe, and it is written in Isherwood's prewar style. *The World in the Evening* shows that even by the early 1950s, Isherwood had not yet discovered an American style. And despite his work for the American movies, his ear had not yet adjusted to the American speech patterns he tried to use in *The World in the Evening*; he managed only a phoney blandness. When Isherwood first visited home after the war, in 1947, some of his English friends commented that his accent had changed. To them, he sounded American, though to Americans he sounded English. He had certainly begun to spell words in the American way, a gradual transformation which would continue for many years. But in the late 1940s the change was not yet fully wrought.

By the time he wrote his last three novels—*Down There on a Visit*, *A Single Man*, and *A Meeting by the River*—the wit of the young Christopher Isherwood—the edgy, embarrassable voice, the controlled mania, the half-acknowledged hyperbole—had begun to give way to a plainer, more sedate tone, relying for its humor on circumstance and narrative point of view more so than on heightened mood

---

[1] August 17, 1949, *D1*, p. 414.
[2] P. 200.

and temperament. He could still achieve comic tension; for instance, his description in *A Single Man* of George preparing, like a magician, to teach his morning class, is bursting with the old, barely restrained glee, and even surpasses the similar, earlier descriptions of his own teacher "Mr. Holmes" in *Lions and Shadows*. At the same time, the underlying polemic of *A Single Man* is more prominent than in Isherwood's earlier works. In *A Meeting by the River* the structure and implied argument of the novel, though subtle, are even more prominent, and the epistolary characterizations of the two English brothers seem stiff and unnatural, as if Isherwood could no longer write in the English idiom that had once been his own. In his maturity, Isherwood seemed increasingly impelled to write in his own authentic voice, to write about real events, and to express his opinions and judgements; the transparent, styleless style he cultivated in America was better suited to truth-telling than to fiction. And this was the style in which he would begin to untangle and explain the impulsive, excited, and even neurotic commitments and crises of his youth.

For his autobiographical works of the 1970s, Isherwood's style became even plainer. It was not even noticeably American (as, for instance, it had been in *A Single Man*). It was contemporary, cosmopolitan, without striking local color. When he was struggling to get started with *Christopher and His Kind*, he fretted in his diary that his style had changed for the worse, but he was confident that his subject matter was weighty and worthwhile: "When I reread my earlier work, I feel that perhaps my style may have lost its ease and brightness and become ponderous. Well, so it's ponderous. At least I still have matter, if not manner."[1] In fact, he was noticing the transformation which had begun many years before, and which had continued along the lines of his personal development and according to the needs of his subject matter. Now, he was no longer in the business of making myths, but rather of trying to explain how he had made myths in the past. Despite the explicit sexual revelations in the reconstructed diary, Isherwood's purpose was not, as it had been, for instance, in *A Single Man*, to outrage the procreating middle classes with his portrayal of homosexual anger and the paranoia he felt was characteristic of minorities. The reconstructed diary is neither angry nor apologetic in tone (Isherwood had come to feel his wartime diaries were unduly apologetic). Instead, it has a kind of anthropological matter-of-factness—describing his work, his social life, his memories and fantasies, his many sexual liaisons with friends, strangers, and occasionally lovers much as he might have described

[1] *Diaries 1960–1983*, November 2, 1973.

them for the benefit of a sex researcher like Evelyn Hooker, but in the plain, literary language he had evolved for himself.

His flat, explanatory, almost pedagogic prose in some ways resembles the mature social realism of his friend Edward Upward whose prose models included John Bunyan, Daniel Defoe, William Cowper, and George Gissing. And the transformation in Isherwood's style corresponds to a similar change in Upward's. It can also be compared to changes in Auden's poetic style. All three of them abandoned the fantastic brilliance of their youth for a more earnest style in maturity. The abundance of quasi-mystical imaginative energy in their early writing disappeared as each converted to a set of beliefs which absorbed that energy on a different—higher—plane. Their writing became more understated and more cautious as they became aware they were writing in relation to what they held to be absolute truths. This happened earliest to Upward when he converted to Marxism; he wrote one last feverishly mystical piece, *Journey to the Border* (1938), about his conversion, and then fell silent altogether for several decades. It happened more gradually to Auden after he returned to Christianity and to Isherwood after he took up Vedanta. For the same reason that Isherwood wrote his biography of the mystic Ramakrishna from the point of view of a skeptic and in the short, reiterative cadences of the King James Bible, he wrote his late autobiographical works in heavily ordinary modern prose and incorporated into them whole passages from his diaries, unembellished: he wanted the experiences to shine through the writing rather than to seem to be created by the writing. This unpretentious late prose style was for him the most convincing medium in which to recount, in *My Guru and His Disciple*, the story of his reverence for Swami Prabhavananda, and it differs little from the style of his diaries in which he tells the episodic story of his love for Don Bachardy.

Just as the reconstructed diary tells of Isherwood's repeated failure to get on with his novel, so it also tells of his repeated failure to get on with his life. As with his work, so with William Caskey: Isherwood started and restarted the relationship, never certain whether Caskey loved him, never able to impose order on their increasingly drunken domestic life. Some of their most tender moments were brought on by their shared sense of guilt over how cruel they were to one another; yet guilt also appears to have been a main stumbling block to progress between them. Isherwood observes that "both Caskey and Christopher were entering upon their relationship with powerful feelings of guilt. . . . Neither of them would admit to their guilt, except by the violence with which they reacted against it."[1] Caskey felt guilty that he was not a good Catholic, that he had not had an honorable discharge from the navy, that he did not love his family. Isherwood felt guilty that he had failed to find a way for Heinz to escape permanently from Germany, that he had failed to be a committed social revolutionary, that he had failed to return to England during the war, that he had failed to become a monk. How could either one of them conduct a successful love relationship while shouldering such burdens? Gradually Isherwood became promiscuous with countless others, and as it progresses the reconstructed diary increasingly becomes a Proustian catalogue of all the relationships in which he tried and failed to find, or to be, the ideal companion. Without self-defense, the narrative obliquely reveals, again and again, Isherwood's further guilt over having loved and left so many.

As a form of confession and expiation, the reconstructed diary is presided over by the ghost of E. M. Forster. In the 1970 Thanksgiving diary entry in which he first mentioned his plan to write it, Isherwood had commented: "I have also had the idea that my memoir of Swami might be published with a memoir of Morgan, based on his letters to me. So that the book would be a Tale of Two Gurus, as it were."[2] Forster died just a year before Isherwood began writing the reconstruction, and in the interval Isherwood supervised the publication of Forster's own explicitly homosexual work, *Maurice*, which had lain waiting many decades to reach print.[3] The publication of *Maurice* in 1971 may have been a spur to begin the reconstruction when he did and to make it as explicit as he did.

While Swami gave Isherwood unconditional love, Forster judged. And it was Forster's moral character which made Isherwood feel the need to judge himself. Isherwood writes in the reconstructed diary that "he thought of Forster as a great writer and as his particular master." In the late 1940s, even though he had already known Forster for a decade and a half (since 1932), he was still in awe of him. Somewhat surprisingly, he was not in awe of Forster as a writer: "It was as a human being that Forster awed him. Forster demanded truth in all his relationships; underneath his charming unalarming exterior he was a stern moralist and his mild babylike eyes looked deep into you. Their glance made Christopher feel false and tricky."[4] Forster let Isherwood know, for instance, that he disapproved of the way

---

[1] P. 55.

[2] Diaries 1960–1983, November 26, 1970.

[3] Written 1913–1914; revised 1959–1960.

[4] Pp. 94–5.

Isherwood handled his 1938 affair with the ex-chorus boy Jacky Hewit, and by 1971 when Isherwood wrote the reconstructed account of this prewar episode, he openly conceded that he felt guilty about promising to bring Hewit to America and then never sending for him. Forster's moral influence can be seen reaching forward into many areas of Isherwood's life, providing a standard against which Isherwood implicitly measured other actions, even the many about which Forster knew nothing. By the time he wrote the reconstructed diary, the intensity of guilt had abated, but the need to judge his youthful self as Forster might once have judged him persisted.

If Forster demanded of Isherwood that he come to terms with past actions, Isherwood's other guru, Swami Prabhavananda, offered a style of thought that looked to the future. Swami's unconditional love existed in the context of a philosophy where guilt had no role. The spiritual aspirant in Vedanta aims to leave the concerns of the world behind, and in meditation, which Isherwood practiced every day for many years, to remember was not as important as to forget. By the end of the 1940s, it was time for Isherwood to leave his past and his burden of guilt behind him. The years of turmoil and waste were to be followed by tremendous new achievements.

A new American friend, Speed Lamkin, helped him to find a way forward with *The World in the Evening* by cutting out the part of the book that was most closely connected to Isherwood's old European life and his former, English successes. Oddly enough, Lamkin seems to have hit on his solution through a lack of historical awareness and perhaps even without recognizing why his advice was so useful. He read the manuscript during the spring of 1951 and told Isherwood, "The refugees are a bore."[1] They were based on the real-life refugees, mostly German and Austrian Jews, to whom Isherwood had taught English in Haverford, Pennsylvania, during the early part of the war. Isherwood's determination to write about the refugees—demonstrated by vain years of effort—was evidently fed by the power of his social conscience and by the allure of his former success in writing about the German middle classes. After all, his descriptions of his Berlin acquaintances, to whose shabby and trivial lives he had once been able to give a bohemian glamor of complete originality, had made his reputation. And the moral viewpoint associated with E. M. Forster and with Isherwood's friend Edward Upward, as well as Isherwood's own puritanism, might have urged him to persist with such a socially worthy subject.

[1] P. 284.

Speed Lamkin's moral viewpoint—if he had one at all—was the opposite of Forster's or Upward's. He was unabashedly, vulgarly ambitious. He was a clever boy from a small town in the South who had come to Hollywood to become rich and powerful and famous. He shared none of Isherwood's guilt or anxiety about social revolution, the cause of the workers, pacifism or the war. He was shallow and ruthless, and his ruthlessness was something which Isherwood desperately needed at this point in his life. As with his novels, so with his life: certain themes had to go. The refugees had to go; guilt had to go; and as Isherwood knew and Lamkin kept reminding him, Caskey had to go. Isherwood recalls of Speed's comment on the refugees: "Speed with his ruthlessness had disregarded Christopher's feelings and expressed his own. Christopher could never be grateful enough to him."[1]

Lamkin was quintessentially American, and he beckoned Isherwood forward into Isherwood's chosen new culture, with its easy rewards and its endless appetite for change. For the Isherwood of the 1930s, immersed in and obsessed by Germany, the refugees would have been an ideal subject. But Isherwood was now immersed in and obsessed by America. In *Christopher and His Kind* Isherwood explains that he had learned to speak German "simply and solely to be able to talk to his sex partners." This had given German a powerful erotic significance: "For him, the entire German language . . . was irradiated with Sex."[2] From the start of the 1940s he wanted to have sex with American boys, and it was the American language which became charged for him with erotic energy. As he observed in his Thanksgiving diary entry of 1970, *his* poetry, *his* fiction always consisted of his reactions to real experience; with the refugees, he was trying to force himself to write about something that was no longer intensely real to him. He observes in the reconstructed diary that even Berthold Viertel—a refugee and mentor once commanding the quality of attention from Isherwood which resulted in one of his finest novels, *Prater Violet*—became unimportant when Isherwood's sense of personal identification with the German diaspora faded: "As Christopher became increasingly detached from his own German-refugee persona (which belonged to the post-Berlin years of travel around Europe with Heinz) Viertel had lost his power to make Christopher feel guilty and responsible for him."[3] And some of the Haverford refugees had themselves begun to lose interest in Germany. In contrast to the German and Austrian artists and intellec-

---

[1] P. 284.
[2] *C&HK*, U.S., p. 21; U.K., p. 23.
[3] P. 148.

tuals Isherwood knew in Hollywood, who were proudly nurturing their native cultural heritage until they could return home after the war, the more ordinary refugees in Haverford, despite their sophistication and cynicism, wanted and needed to learn English and to learn what Isherwood's Haverford boss, Caroline Norment, called the "American Way of Life."[1] Unlike many of their Hollywood counterparts, they had lost everything and, in some cases, suffered great physical deprivation and pain. They wanted to forget about their European past, assimilate into American culture and get on with their lives. Many of them did this rapidly and successfully; they virtually evaporated into America. Isherwood needed to do the same. His decision to drop the refugees from *The World in the Evening* is emblematic of his shedding of his old continental affinities along with his burden of guilt; finally he began to accept his new homeland and his unknown, solitary future.

But Speed Lamkin did not persuade Isherwood to abandon his social conscience altogether. The reconstructed diary grinds to an uncadenced, almost shapeless halt in 1951, stranded tellingly upon Isherwood's account of his dealings with a friend of Speed Lamkin, Gus Field. Field is a minor character in Isherwood's narrative, but a minor character whose fate compares suggestively with the fate of the refugees and even with the fate of Caskey. Lamkin and Field, with Isherwood's permission, wrote a stage adaptation of *Goodbye to Berlin*. Isherwood liked it, but his friends Dodie Smith and her husband Alec Beesley (rich through Dodie's talent as a playwright) did not. So the Beesleys connived that John van Druten should undertake the same project. Van Druten's adaptation, *I Am a Camera*, would eventually place Isherwood on the road to fame and relative fortune, despite wrangles when van Druten took the largest share of the royalties. When the time came to make clear to Lamkin and Field that van Druten's version of *Goodbye to Berlin* was to receive Isherwood's imprimatur, Lamkin accepted the new situation cheerfully and offered no recriminations, thereby abandoning his own script and ingratiating himself successfully with the little group behind van Druten's version. Field, though, who behaved just as well as Lamkin, was excluded and ignored. Isherwood writes in the reconstructed diary:

> As for Gus Field, he took the news well, too. Which was more admirable, since he got very little gratitude from Christopher or anybody else for doing so. If he was invited to the Beesleys', it was only once or twice. Speed dropped him. Christopher only saw

[1] *D1*, April 28, 1942, p. 220.

him occasionally. He was treated as a bore and an outsider—and that, from Christopher's point of view, was what he was.[1]

Speed had called the refugees boring; Isherwood calls Gus Field a bore. To be boring was an unacceptable crime in Isherwood's new Speed Lamkin-style drive for success. Perversely, Field became the scapegoat himself for the ill treatment meted out to him by Isherwood and the Beesleys. As with the refugees and Caskey, Field and the guilt he inspired in Isherwood and his friends, had to go.

And yet part of Isherwood brooded over the excluded, marginalized figure of Gus Field, resulting in the strange non-ending of the reconstructed diary. For Isherwood, the Field episode was closed but not resolved. He had originally planned, at Thanksgiving 1970, that the reconstructed diary might carry through to 1955—or at least to 1953, when he met Don Bachardy. But by March 1974, as he was writing about the end of 1950, his ambition had shrunk: "I would like to record the winter of 1951–1952, even if I go no further."[2] In September the same year, advancing slowly, he had again reduced his aims, "I've reached January 1951. I would like, at least, to get the rest of that year recorded, particularly the production of *I Am a Camera*."[3] Finally, in January 1977, with *Christopher and His Kind* already published, he had made only a little further progress, though he still planned to continue: ". . . thus far, I've reached May 1951 and I would like to carry the narrative on until at least the end of 1952."[4] But he never returned to the task, and in the end he never got beyond the shadow of Gus Field—the necessary victim of Isherwood's success. From time to time, Isherwood also mentions in his diary the idea of returning to the subject of the refugees and writing a novel solely about them. But he never did; they, too, were part of the past of which he had to let go. Their story survives only in his wartime diaries, an adequate and important historical account. As for Caskey, his story is contained in the reconstructed diary.

Isherwood would never cease to be aware of the way in which all success, and indeed all art, excludes or marginalizes somebody. In a sense, his art tries to do the opposite, but whatever is brought to the fore must push something else aside. As a schoolboy he had written to his mother: "I have an essay on 'omission is the Beginning of all Art' which it may amuse you to see."[5] And as he explains at some

[1] P. 286.
[2] Diaries 1960–1983, March 28, 1974.
[3] Diaries 1960–1983, September 11, 1974.
[4] Diaries 1960–1983, January 2, 1977.
[5] February 13, 1921, to Kathleen Isherwood, in Christopher Isherwood, *The Repton Letters*, ed. George Ramsden (Settrington, England, 1997), p. 14.

length in *Christopher and His Kind*, much of the difficulty he had with his work, throughout his career, can be understood as his struggle with the question of how the artist decides what to leave out of his art. The subjects not chosen, the themes not addressed, haunt the imagination with the pain of their rejection; for the novelist who feels a strong loyalty to historical fact, the necessity to omit is like the burden of original sin, a crime of neglect which must precede the possibility of artistic creation.

Isherwood was fascinated throughout his life with marginal figures and with minorities. He himself was a member of what was for centuries one of the most oppressed and anonymous minorities in human society: during the first half of his life, the society which raised and educated him also told him that he was a criminal. Thus, he willingly and with eager curiosity associated with others who, for various reasons, were called criminals and were pushed like him to the margin of society. The shady figures of the Berlin demi-monde —Mr. Norris and the like—had once offered him fruitful ground for his art. But Isherwood was not prepared to live his whole life in the shadows. As a writer and a man he wished to move into the mainstream and forward into the future.

Looking back in the 1970s, recalling the struggle to focus his life and his artistic energies by cutting away the boring, the unglamorous, the unsuccessful, he still reflected upon what had been pushed aside. Gus Field, personifying as he did the guilt from which Isherwood wished to free himself, is a figure well suited to claim not only Isherwood's but also the reader's final attention in the reconstructed diary. With Isherwood's mature success as a writer had come the confidence to unveil both those aspects of his character and his past actions of which society disapproved and also those aspects of his character and past actions of which he himself disapproved; they were not generally the same. By reconstructing them explicitly in *Lost Years* he was able to make some of the differences clear. In its portrayal of Isherwood's sexuality, *Lost Years* is a boldly political book. Perhaps much more surprising, it is also implicitly and persistently moral, describing and judging—often with harsh self-criticism—even the minutiae of daily conduct, in order to try to redefine what is genuinely good and genuinely evil in human relationships.

Textual Note

This diary describing the years 1945 to 1951 was written by Christopher Isherwood between 1971 and 1977. It fills a gap of about half a decade following World War II when Isherwood had kept his diary very irregularly. He wrote nothing about his day-to-day life from January 1945 until September 1947 when he began a travel diary—published as *The Condor and the Cows* (1949)—about his trip with his companion of the late 1940s, William Caskey, through South America. After the South American trip, Isherwood began occasionally to write in his diary again, but not until the early 1950s did he reestablish his old routine of writing several times a week. The entries that he did make during the late 1940s and early 1950s are printed in his *Diaries Volume One 1939–1960*, along with an outline he made, probably in 1955, showing some of the main events of those years.

American style and spelling are used throughout this book. English spellings began to disappear from Isherwood's diaries by the end of his first decade in California, although there are exceptions which I have altered in order to achieve consistency with the general trend. However, I have retained idiosyncrasies of phrasing and also spellings which have a phonetic impact in order that Isherwood's characteristic Anglo-American voice might resound in the writing.

I have made some very minor alterations silently, including standardizing passages which Isherwood quotes from elsewhere in his own writings, from other published authors, and from letters. Also, I have spelled out many abbreviations, including names for which Isherwood sometimes used only initials. Otherwise, square brackets usually mark emendations of substance or possible interest. Square brackets also mark information I have added to the text, such as surnames or parts of titles shortened by Isherwood, and editorial footnotes. And square brackets indicate where I have removed or altered material in order to protect the privacy of certain individuals who are still living.

This book includes many footnotes written by Isherwood himself. His practice in making the reconstructed diary was to write on the rectos only of his black ledger books, and to add information on the facing versos. He numbered almost all such additions as footnotes. Had Isherwood himself prepared the diary for publication, he almost certainly would have incorporated all of his footnotes into the text, rewriting as necessary. I have not attempted to do this on his behalf, but have deliberately retained the rough, two-layered effect of the text he left, although I have sometimes moved his footnotes (especially the long ones) to the end of the phrase, sentence or paragraph in which they appear, in order to help readers arrive at a suitable pause, where they might more easily shift their attention. All footnotes in brackets and footnote symbols in brackets are added by me, as mentioned above.

At the back of the book, readers will find a chronology of Isherwood's life and a glossary of people, places, institutions, and terms which he mentions. In contrast to his other diaries, kept contemporaneously with the events they describe, Isherwood generally introduces friends and acquaintances and explains episodes in detail in this reconstructed diary; therefore my notes and glossary only undertake to fill gaps. Many central figures require little or no mention at all in the glossary, and readers should use the index to find Isherwood's own descriptions of them in his text. (Sometimes Isherwood offers his own cross-reference when someone appears again after a long absence.) The glossary gives general biographical information and also offers details of particular relevance to Isherwood and to events or concerns he mentions in the text. A few very famous people—for instance, Greta Garbo, Charlie Chaplin— are not included in the glossary because although Isherwood knew them quite well, he knew them essentially in their capacity as celebrities. Others who were intimate friends—such as Aldous Huxley, Igor Stravinsky—are included even though their main achievements will be familiar to many readers.

Hindu terminology is also explained in the glossary, although unfamiliar non-Hindu words appearing only once are usually glossed or translated in a footnote.

Acknowledgements

I could not have prepared this book without the constant support and collaboration of Don Bachardy. Isherwood's luck in finding such a partner continues to grow more evident, and I feel privileged to share some of that luck.

Many friends of Isherwood have taken a great deal of trouble to answer questions for Don Bachardy and for me, and we are extremely grateful for their tenacity and their forthrightness: George Bemberg, Walter Berns, Stefan Brecht, the late Paul Cadmus, the late Jim Charlton, Robert Craft, Jack Fontan, John Gruber, Michael Hall, Betty Harford, the late Evelyn Hooker, Richard Keate, Robert Kittredge, Gavin Lambert, Jack Larson, the late José Martinez, the late Ben Masselink, Carlos McClendon, the late Roddy McDowall, Ivan Moffat, Alvin Novak, Fern Maher O'Brien, "Vernon Old," Bernard Perlin, Rupert Pole, Ned Rorem, Paul Sorel, Walter Starcke, Barry Taxman, Curtice Taylor, the late Frank Taylor, Edward Upward, Gore Vidal, Swami Vidyatmananda, Tom Wright, Russ Zeininger.

A number of other people have helped with challenging and sometimes eccentric queries as well as practical matters, and I thank them all: Terry Adamson, Robert Adjemian, Peter Alexander, Alan Ansen, John Appleton, Roger Berthoud, Michael Bessie, Vernon Brooks, Sally Brown (Curator of Modern Literary Manuscripts at the British Library), Peter Burton, Sheilah Cherney, Patricia Clark (The British Council), Gerald Clarke, Michael De Lisio, John D'Emilio, Renée Doolley, Philippa Foote, Christopher Gibb, Joyce Howard, Don Howarth, Nicholas Jenkins, Brian Keelan, Jim Kelly, Judy Kopec (Johns Hopkins University), Fredric Kroll, Tanya Kutchinsky, the late Lyle Leverich, Glenn Lewis, Lloyd Lewis, John Loughery, Jeffrey Meyers, Jean Morin (Directorate of History and Heritage, Ottawa, Canada), Karl Müller, Ed Parone, Susan Peck,

Stuart Proffitt, Andreas Reyneke, Dean Rocco, Jennifer Ruggiero, David Salmo, Suzelle Smith, Willie Walker, Robert Weil, George Wilson (Johns Hopkins University).

For permission to quote part of a letter from Dodie Smith Beesley to Isherwood, I would like to thank Julian Barnes; for permission to quote from E. M. Forster's letters to Isherwood, I would like to thank the Society of Authors as agent for the Provost and Scholars of King's College, Cambridge; for permission to quote part of a letter from John Goodwin to Isherwood, I would like to thank Anthony Russo.

A project like this one is not easy without the continual and thoughtful involvement of editors, agents, and nowadays even lawyers; I am grateful, for each of their efforts, to Helena Caldon, Roger Cazalet, Caroline Dawnay, Jim Fox, Daniel Halpern, Douglas Matthews, Anthea Morton-Saner, Harvey Starte, Stuart Williams and especially Howard Davies, Michael di Capua, Alison Samuel, and Geoffrey Strachan.

To friends who spent more time than they should have spent chasing will-o'-the-wisp details, I am, as ever, very much in debt: Thomas Braun, Axel Neubohn, Peter Parker, Polly Maguire Robison, Margaret Bradham Thornton. I came to depend especially on Christopher Phipps, who is as cheerful as he is meticulous; his resourcefulness has contributed many things to this book. Lucy Bucknell and Edward Mendelson have loyally helped me with small questions and big problems, and above all by reading—with characteristic generosity and strictness—anything I asked them to.

At home I have had unconditional support from Jackie Edgar, Vivian Galang, and Michelle Hatfield, and from a merry and inquisitive little gang who worked hard not to disturb me at my desk: Bob Maguire, Bobby Maguire, Lucy Maguire, Jack Maguire. I could not do without them.

Lost Years
January 1, 1945–May 9, 1951

August 26, 1971.

I am writing this to clarify my project to myself, not actually to begin work on it. Before I can do that I shall have to read through my day-to-day diaries for 1944 and 1945, to find out how much explanation is going to be needed before I can start the narrative itself.

This is the situation: I have day-to-day diaries (just saying what happened in a few words) from 1942 to the present day, except for the 1946 diary, which is lost. I also have journals which begin in 1939 and cover the same period.[*] All have time gaps in them. But the biggest gaps occur in one particular area—there are no entries whatever for 1945, 1946 or 1947 (though my life from September 20, 1947 to March 1948 is covered in *The Condor and the Cows*). The 1948 journal has rather less than twenty entries, 1949 around fifteen, 1950 about the same number, 1951 about twelve, 1952 about fourteen. (It's interesting to notice what a small variation there is for these years—my journal keeping seems to follow a predictable wave-movement.) 1953 is perhaps the worst year of all, about eleven, and 1954 isn't much better. Then the journal keeping picks up frequency and has remained fairly adequate ever since.

So this is my project: I am going to try to fill in these gaps from memory—up to the end of 1952 at least and maybe up to the end of 1954.

I shall write, to begin with, on the odd-numbered pages, leaving the even-numbered facing pages for after-thoughts and notes.

Because the "I" of this period is twenty years out of date, I shall write about him in the third person—working on *Kathleen and Frank*

[* Elsewhere, Isherwood also calls these journals "diaries," and they are published under that title. Readers may find Isherwood's references to them by date in his *Diaries Volume One 1939–1960*, ed. Katherine Bucknell (London: Methuen, 1996; New York: HarperCollins, 1997), cited hereafter as *D1*.]

has shown me how this helps me to overcome my inhibitions, avoid self-excuses and regard my past behavior more objectively.

The last entry in the 1944 journal makes it fairly obvious that Christopher has already decided to leave Vedanta Place (on Ivar Avenue, as it then still was—the name was changed only after the freeway was built). Christopher doesn't admit this, but he emphasizes the importance of japam,[*] rather than the importance of being with Swami,[†] or of having daily access to the shrine, or of living in a religious community. You can make japam under any circumstances, no matter where or how you are living.

In the 1944 journal, Christopher says that he finished the revised draft of *Prater Violet* on October 15. In the 1944 day-to-day diary he says he finished revising *Prater Violet* on November 25—so this must have been a revision of the revised draft.[1] Anyhow it must have been finished and sent off to the publishers before the end of that year.

In the journal, November 30, Christopher says, "The X. situation is beginning again."

"X." was Bill Harris.[2] Denny Fouts[‡] met him first. He had been in the army but only for a short while and was now going to college.

---

[1] In the 1944 journal, it says "the final polishing" of *Prater Violet* was finished on November 24.

[2] Bill was the younger of two brothers—the sons of an engineer. Their father had worked in the USSR and had had to leave with his family at a few hours' notice—the Russians accused the American and British engineers of trying to sabotage a dam which they had been hired to construct. Later, they moved to Australia, where Bill and his brother became expert swimmers. Bill's brother was very attractive, an all-round athlete and a war hero in the U.S. Air Force. Bill was the ugly brother (so he said); homely and fat up to the age of fifteen. Then he made a "decision" to be beautiful. After the war, his brother married and became fat and prematurely middle-aged.

Bill was well aware of being feminine—his resemblance to Marlene Dietrich was often remarked on—but he refused to get himself exempted from military service by declaring that he was homosexual. He wanted to be a model soldier. He worked very hard to keep his equipment clean. Then, after he'd been in the service for a week or two, he was bawled out at an inspection, and this discouraged him so much, after all his good intentions, that he burst into tears. The inspecting officer, amazed at such sensitivity, sent him to the psychiatrist, which resulted in his getting an honorable discharge!

[* Repeating a sacred Hindu word; Isherwood used a rosary. For this and all Hindu terms, see Glossary.]

[† Isherwood's religious teacher under whose guidance he had been living at the Vedanta Center and training as a monk. See glossary under Prabhavananda.]

[‡ A close friend since 1940; for Fouts and for others not fully introduced by Isherwood see Glossary.]

The 1943 day-to-day diary, with the maddening vagueness common to all the early day-to-day diaries, records that, on August 21, Denny came down to Santa Monica to visit Christopher, who was staying for a few days at 206 Mabery Road, opposite the Viertels' home, 165—accompanied by "little Bill" and "blond Bill." I don't remember who "little Bill" was. I am almost certain that "blond Bill" was Harris. His blond hair was then the most immediately striking feature of his beauty, especially when he had his clothes on and you couldn't see his magnificent figure. Aside from this, Christopher used to be fond of describing his first glimpse of Bill Harris—how the erotic shock hit him "like an elephant gun" and made him "grunt" with desire, and how, at the same time, he felt angry with Denny for bringing this beautiful temptation into his life, to torment him.[1] Christopher first saw Harris through the window of the bathroom of 206, just as Harris was arriving with Denny in the car. This in itself fixes the date if my memory is accurate, because Christopher never stayed in that house again.

However, Bill Harris has nothing to do with the sex adventure referred to in the 1943 journal as having taken place on August 24. Christopher had gone into the ocean and was swimming with his trunks off; he was wearing them around his neck, as he often did. A man came along the beach—which was almost deserted in those wartime days—saw him, took his own trunks off, came into the water and started groping Christopher. What made the situation "funny and silly" was that the man was deaf and dumb. They both laughed a lot. Christopher refused to have an orgasm but he had been excited, and he jacked off later, when he had returned to the house.

The other sexual encounters referred to in the 1943 journal were with a boy named Flint,[2] whom Christopher met on the beach on September 20, and with Pete Martinez, a few days later.

It is odd that "X." (Harris) isn't referred to at all in the 1943 journal. It seems probable that Christopher saw very little of him after their first meeting on August 21. In the 1944 journal (March 13) Christopher writes, "A few days after this entry, I started to fall in love, with someone whom I'll call X. . . ." etc. etc. The 1944

---

[1] Christopher even accused Denny of deliberately trying to seduce him from his vocation by introducing him to Harris. According to Christopher, Denny didn't want Christopher to become a monk because it made him, Denny, feel guilty.
[2] [Not his real name.] Flint tried to do a blowjob under water and was quite indignant when he began to drown. He seemed to blame the Pacific Ocean, assuring Christopher with apparent seriousness that you could blow someone beneath the surface of the Atlantic while drawing air into your mouth through his cock!

day-to-day diary doesn't mention Bill Harris until April 5, when Christopher saw him in Santa Monica. (He had previously been living out at Pomona or someplace in that area; perhaps he had now moved to the beach.) After this, the day-to-day diary mentions him from time to time—not often, because Christopher was sick quite a bit and in bed. They had sex for the first time while they were both staying at Denny's apartment, 137 Entrada Drive. They were alone together there from June 26 to 29. Denny had gone off to San Francisco telling Bill to paint the living room before he returned. (Denny always saw to it that his guests made themselves useful.)

In the 1944 journal, Christopher pays a tribute to Harris's "decency and generosity." Well he may—for he treated Harris not merely as a convenience but as one of the Seven Deadly Sins, which had to be overcome by temporarily yielding to it. "Let me go to bed with you so I can get tired of you" was basically his approach. Then, later, when Vernon [Old*] reappears on the scene, Harris gets told, in effect, that he, The Carnal Love, is to stand aside because The Spiritual Love is taking over. (Christopher was going to bed with The Spiritual Love too, however; and The Carnal Love was well aware of this!) Finally, when Christopher has first satisfied and then sublimated and then temporarily lost his lust for Vernon, he reopens his affair with Harris. This he ungraciously refers to as "the X. situation beginning again." (There is a faint memory that the two of them had to stand very close together in a crowded trolley car going downtown, and that this was how it started.) What was Harris's attitude to all of this? Just because he wasn't emotionally involved, he probably found it easy to accept Christopher's on-again, off-again, on-again behavior. Besides, he liked sex—the more of it the better—and must have found Christopher quite adequately attractive, as well as amusing to be with. If this relationship had been represented in a ballet, the dancer playing Christopher would be repeatedly changing costumes and masks and his movements would be artificial, inhibited and tense; the dancer playing Harris would be naked and usually motionless—the only sort of tension he would display would be an eager puzzled smile as he reacted to his partner's contortions.

In the 1944 journal, Christopher writes, "I know quite well that I shouldn't feel guilty if I were not living at Ivar Avenue. That being true, my guilt is worthless." Nevertheless, Christopher certainly did feel guilty—or at least embarrassed—throughout the rest of his stay at the Vedanta Center. His position was false, and several people

[* Not his real name.]

knew this—Denny, Bill Harris, the Beesleys, John van Druten, Carter Lodge, etc. The Beesleys probably found the inconsistency of his life as a demi-monk merely amusing and cute—it seemed "human"—it excused them from feeling awed and awkward in the presence of his faith. But for Christopher, their tolerance was humiliating.

Should he have left the center much sooner than he did? Looking back, I find that I can't say yes. It now seems to me that Christopher's embarrassment and guilt feelings were of little importance and his "spiritual struggles" trivial. What mattered was that he was getting exposure to Swami, that his relations with Swami continued to be (fairly) frank, and that he never ceased to be aware of Swami's love. Every day that he spent at the center was a day gained. That he kept slipping away to see Bill Harris wasn't really so dreadful. That he had lost face in the eyes of various outside observers was a good thing—or anyhow it was a hundred times better than if he had fooled everyone into thinking him a saint.

(Remembering Christopher's position at that time makes me feel great sympathy and admiration for Franklin [Knight] at Trabuco nowadays and for Jimmie Barnett at the Hollywood monastery. *Their* position is, or has been, far more embarrassing and humiliating than Christopher's ever was. And they haven't run away from it.)

1945

Day-to-day diary, January 1, 1945: "Started work on my story." What story? Perhaps an early attempt to do something with the material from the journal about Christopher's stay at the Friends Service Committee hostel at Haverford, 1941–1942. Or perhaps another attempt to write about the character called "Paul"[1] (in those days, he wasn't yet altogether Denny Fouts) and his adventures on the Greek island, which later appeared in "Ambrose."[*]

---

[1] My original Paul character had nothing to do with Denny—indeed I thought of him long before Denny and I met. So what I have written [above] is misleadingly phrased. I never, as far as I remember, planned to put Denny into the Greek island story. On the contrary, I cut Paul out of it and used his name for a portrait of Denny in *Paul*. (An unfinished novel featuring the original Paul character is described in *Christopher and His Kind*, chapter eleven.)

[* In *Down There on a Visit* (1962).]

On January 2, Christopher took the manuscript of *Vedanta and the Western World* to be published by Marcel Rodd. Evidently they were still on good terms with Rodd at the Vedanta Center. Marcel is first referred to on June 20 in the 1944 journal, when he took over the distribution of the Gita,[*] which had already been set up by the printer who printed the magazine. Christopher knew him in a sort of backstairs way, as one of Vernon's many former admirers, and Christopher flattered himself that he could do satisfactory business with Rodd and not get cheated, despite Rodd's character. I can't remember that Rodd ever actually cheated the Vedanta Society, but he caused a lot of annoyance and inconvenience in later years— failing to republish but refusing to give up his rights and ignoring the letters written to him by the society's lawyers. And for all this Christopher was responsible because he had introduced Rodd to Swami. (Though I think it was Denny who had suggested that he should do so. Denny's advice was so often sensible but mischievous.)

In the 1944 journal, it is said that Rodd "is terribly anxious to become a respectable publisher." This suggests that Rodd had already been in trouble as the result of his dealings in pornography—maybe while he had the bookshop and was selling it under the counter. But I remember that he was prosecuted, some time after this, for publishing or distributing sex books—one of them was called *We Are Fires Unquenchable*. The judge said, "I understand, Mr. Rodd, that you also publish religious literature? I strongly advise you to stick to that line in future."

On January 3, Swami's nephew Asit [Ghosh] was finally released from the army. (The circumstances of his induction and the legal proceedings which were taken to release him are described in the 1944 journal.) Asit came back to the center and stayed there for a while. Then he left for India.[1]

---

[1] I have a vivid mental picture of Asit saying goodbye to Swami, after coming out of the temple where they had prostrated before the shrine. Right then, in full view of the street, Asit bowed down and took the dust of Swami's feet. It is my impression that I had never before seen anyone do this. Pranams weren't part of life at the center in those days. What makes the picture more exotic is that Asit is in U.S. Army uniform—which seems most improbable, if he had already left the army!

(Note, made June 16, 1977: As I have just discovered from rereading the journal, my memory referred to September 18, 1944, the day Asit was inducted into the army, not the day he was discharged from it. If he hadn't yet been inducted, would he have been wearing uniform? Surely not.)

[* I.e., the Bhagavad Gita, which Isherwood and Prabhavananda had translated; see Glossary under Prabhavananda.]

The Vivekananda Puja was celebrated on January 4, this year. (In 1944, it was on January 17.) The 1944 day-to-day diary mentions it, but I can find no reference to it in the journal. This puja—or rather, the breakfast puja which is the first part of it—became the only ritual worship which Christopher really enjoyed. This was chiefly because he had an important role in it—Swami had decided that he should be the one to read the Katha Upanishad aloud while Swamiji's[*] breakfast was served. He loved doing this; indeed it was (and has remained) for him the highest imaginable act of sacred camp—a little genuine devotion, a feeling of the absurdity of himself in this role, a sense that the performance is a joke shared with Swamiji, and of course his enjoyment of the sound of his own voice—all these elements are combined in the experience. But, quite aside from this, the breakfast puja had a beautiful domestic significance as long as Sister[†] was alive and could personally pour Swamiji's coffee during the ritual. Because Sister was (almost certainly) the only surviving person who had actually served breakfast to Swamiji while he was in the U.S. He had been a guest in her home, at the beginning of the century.

On January 8, the day-to-day diary records that Sudhira[‡] enlisted in the navy. She may actually have done this, or it may have been one of the tall stories she told Christopher. If she did really enlist, I'm pretty sure she was never called up.

Also on the 8th, a journalist named Felton visited the center; he was doing a story for *Time* magazine in connection with a forthcoming review of the Prabhavananda–Isherwood translation of the Gita. On the 11th, he came again and sat in on Swami's evening class; and on the 15th he sent a photographer to take pictures of Swami, Christopher, the temple, etc.[§]

Day-to-day diary, January 19: "To Santa Monica. Saw Bill and Denny. The kite accident."

When Christopher arrived at Santa Monica that morning, he found Denny Fouts making a tail for a kite out of his Christmas decorations. (This sort of play project, undertaken on the spur of the moment, was characteristic of Denny.) When the kite was ready, Bill Harris and Christopher took it out on the beach to fly it. (I don't remember that Denny was with them—perhaps there were two kites and Denny was flying the other one.) The wind was strong but not

[* I.e., Vivekananda's; see Glossary.]
[† An American disciple of Vivekananda; see Glossary.]
[‡ A disciple of Prabhavananda; see Glossary.]
[§ The article by staff correspondent James Felton appeared on February 12, 1945; see p. 22 and n. below.]

steady. Bill and Christopher got the kite aloft, quite high over the Canyon. Then Christopher said, "We ought to tie a banner to the tail, with 'Vernon is a big queen' written on it!" (The point of this remark was that Vernon happened to be staying somewhere in the Canyon at that time so he would perhaps have seen the banner and been embarrassed. Christopher was being bitchy about Vernon because he still harbored a grudge against him for the failure of their life together up at Santa Barbara. In any case, jokes against Vernon were frequent in Denny's circle.)

Christopher had barely finished making this joke when the kite, as if to punish him for it, took a sudden dive—so sudden that he and Bill Harris had no time to save it by running toward the ocean, pulling the string. In less time than it takes to tell, the kite fell limply onto the power lines along the side of the highway. Then, as Christopher watched incredulously, the tail of the kite began to smoke, there was a flash, a dull puff of sound, like air being expelled, and two of the cables parted and fell across the road. (No doubt they were spitting sparks, but Christopher couldn't see this from where he stood.) Cars which happened to be passing swerved wildly. Brakes squealed. Luckily, there were no collisions. The accident, though minor, was awe inspiring. It belonged in the category of disasters and was as disconcerting to watch, on its own tiny scale, as the air raids Christopher had seen in China. You felt that the order of things was being upset. (And indeed, as Christopher heard later, the electric power was cut off throughout the neighborhood.)

Bill Harris was so horrified that he simply ran away, fearing arrest. Christopher didn't resent this; it rather flattered his own vanity that he was left to play the man while Bill panicked like a girl. And he knew Bill would admire him for his behavior, later. Christopher was a bit scared, of course; he fully expected to be arrested. But he was also shrewd enough to know that nothing very bad would happen to him, provided that he admitted his responsibility without delay.

Meanwhile, a crowd had gathered and the police had arrived. But the police merely took charge of the traffic; they didn't attempt to find out who the culprit was. Christopher joined the crowd. Several people in it had undoubtedly seen him flying the kite. Christopher made up his mind to keep quiet for the time being and wait until questions were asked. But nobody asked any questions.

Then the repair truck arrived. The repair men asked no questions, either. But one of them said: "Whoever was flying that kite, he sure as hell was lucky"—and went on to explain that, if the kite string had been wet, the person holding it would have been electrocuted. The short circuit had been caused by the tinsel ornaments in the kite tail.

Christopher later used this incident in *The World in the Evening*.[1]

Day-to-day diary, January 20: "Supper with Carter (Lodge), Don Forbes, Dave Eberhardt[*] and Chip.[†]" I think Chip was a boyfriend of Carter Lodge. He may well be the boy about whom I dimly remember the following story: When the boy was young, his parents were alarmed because he was so effeminate and they felt sure he would turn out to be homosexual when he grew up; he also had a wretched physique. They consulted a doctor, who advised some sort of hormone treatment. The treatment produced dramatic results; the boy became a virile youth without a trace of effeminacy, with a powerful well-made body and masculine good looks—a well-adjusted, one hundred percent homosexual.

Don Forbes was a newscaster on radio; I think his program was sponsored by Richfield Oil. He was quite a star in the news world—maybe he had done some reporting from the battlefronts. I remember being amused by a photograph of him, enshrined like an oracle amidst flags, bursting shells, whizzing planes and bombarding warships. He was handsome, temperamental and very much of an actor.

Dave Eberhardt was [. . .] just discharged from the navy—a pale husky *joli laid* with a crew cut. Soon after Dave and Christopher met, Dave told Christopher that he found him "powerfully attractive." Christopher reciprocated more than sufficiently, and they would neck whenever they were alone together, sometimes for long spells. Since they always had to do this at the apartment which Don and Dave shared—because Christopher was still living at the Vedanta Center—they never went to bed together, however; Dave thought it was too risky. When they did finally make love, years later, at the AJC Ranch, I seem to remember that it wasn't a success.

Dave Eberhardt was a photographer. He later took some exceedingly flattering photographs of Christopher.

Day-to-day diary, January 21: "With Bill to Beesleys'. Saw Barrymore house." January 21 was a Sunday. Sunday lunch with the Beesleys had become a more or less fixed engagement. John van Druten and Carter sometimes came—though Carter was secretly unwelcome because he was allergic to dogs, so the dalmatians had to be shut away somewhere during his visit. (Dodie, of course, disbelieved in his allergy—like many Britishers of her generation, she dismissed allergies as an American superstition, with the single

[1] See chapter six, part two.

[* Not his real name.]
[† Not his real name.]

exception of hay fever. In her opinion, Carter simply hated dogs, which was a permanent bad mark against him.)

The Beesleys were then living in a magnificent house on a hill above Tower Road—much too big for them. It had lawns, a garden, a tennis court and a pool. I think it rented for four hundred dollars a month, which seemed huge, in those days.

I can find no mention of Bill Harris having had lunch with the Beesleys before January 7, 1945; this was probably his second visit. The Beesleys liked him and on later occasions made opportunities for Bill and Christopher to have sex, by going out and leaving them together, or even by suggesting to Christopher, "Wouldn't you like to take a bath?" (This suggestion wasn't quite as shameless as it sounded, because it was a long-established custom that Christopher should be offered a bath when he came to see them. It was like offering a bath to a serviceman who is in camp. At the Vedanta Center, the bathroom was shared by several people, and an unhurried soak in a spotless tub was a real luxury for Christopher.)[1]

The house which had once belonged to John Barrymore was somewhere in that neighborhood. Its most remarkable feature was a very tall totem pole in the garden. My memory is of a building like a cloister, with a row of dark small cluttered rooms which stank; the place was then unoccupied. It may have stood empty since Barrymore's death in 1942. I remember tales of the filthy state it had been in during his later lifetime—the rooms like sties full of drunken guests snoring amidst their shit and vomit. Maybe Alec Beesley had got permission to look around the house by pretending he wanted to rent it. Or maybe they were simply trespassing.

Day-to-day diary, January 22: "Tried to hitchhike north with Bill, and failed." Bill Harris and Christopher waited on the Pacific Coast Highway, at the Channel Road entrance to Santa Monica Canyon,

---

[1] When Christopher later told John van Druten and Carter Lodge about his lovemaking with Bill at the Beesleys', Carter professed to be shocked. He said something to the effect that it was "turning your friends' home into a whorehouse" to do such a thing. Coming from Carter, this seemed a most mysterious piece of hypocrisy, since Carter himself had taken a shower at the Beesleys' with Christopher, only recently, after swimming in their pool, and they had played around together—as they often did when they happened to be alone. Their relationship was intimate but casual—they had been going to bed together at long intervals ever since they first met in 1939. John knew about this—Christopher had told him—and he didn't mind at all.

Why *did* Carter say he was shocked? Perhaps he resented the fact that the Beesleys would never have invited *him* to behave as Christopher behaved. He probably felt (and with good reason) that they didn't really treat him as a friend—only as John's friend.

for several hours, trying without success to thumb a ride. The war was still very much on, despite increasing prospects of peace— gasoline rationing was in force and nonmilitary traffic, other than local, was greatly reduced. Bill and Christopher were presumably hoping to catch a car which would take them to Santa Barbara at least, if not to San Francisco; and these were rare.

I find this episode (or non-episode) curious and puzzling. It doesn't seem to belong to the style of the Bill–Christopher relationship. To set forth impulsively on an unplanned indefinite hobo trip is something which the Christopher of six years earlier might have done with Vernon Old. Their journey across the U.S. by bus was a modified version of the hobo trip—Whitman, "We Two Boys Together Clinging," the "Song of the Open Road," etc. The Vernon–Christopher relationship aspired to be Whitmanesque—at least, Christopher certainly felt that it was or could be. He fell in love with Vernon as an embodiment of The American Boy.

But now, with Bill Harris, as a forty-year-old lapsed monk, Christopher is attempting a different, more mature style. Why did he suddenly decide on this boyish elopement? Was he trying to prove to Bill how young he still was? Was he running away from the Vedanta Center, or from Denny Fouts? If so, how long did he plan to remain out of town? I simply cannot remember.

It is also possible that Christopher already knew about Pancho Moraturi, Bill's Argentine friend, who was urging Bill to come and live with him. In this case, Christopher may have planned the trip up north as a last fling. He can't have wanted to carry Bill off from Pancho permanently. He must have known then what became obvious to him when he was rewriting his journals a year later, that his intentions toward Bill were not and never had been really serious.

On January 23, Christopher and Bill Harris were down in Santa Monica again. (I suppose they made these trips by bus. Christopher cycled sometimes, but only when he was alone.[1] Bill was now living on La Cienega Boulevard; more about this later.) That evening, at Denny's apartment, there was a party—Chris Wood came, and Stef Brecht ([Bertolt] Brecht's son) and Paul Fox, a friend of Chris's, who was a set designer and worked, appropriately enough, at Twentieth Century-Fox. Christopher and Bill spent the night in one of the back rooms of the 137 Entrada Drive building. I

---

[1] In Santa Monica, he sometimes cycled with Denny. Denny had begun to compose a cycling song with Christopher, to the tune of "Take a Pair of Sparkling Eyes," but they had got no further than the first couplet: "Just a pair of cycling queens / No longer in their teens . . ."

remember Stef, in his formal European way, nodding toward Bill and then saying politely to Christopher, "I congratulate you, he is extremely attractive."[1]

I see from the day-to-day diary that John Goodwin was also there. It is odd that I don't have more memories of him, for he was often with Denny. My impression is that Christopher didn't really like John but was hardly aware of this. Christopher and John were outwardly friendly. John had actually encouraged Bill to have an affair with Christopher. And Christopher himself was, not very energetically, on the make for John—John pretended to be flattered by this, but didn't encourage him to go ahead. Nevertheless, I feel that Christopher was constantly being repelled by John's rudeness, selfishness and arrogance. Christopher hated little rich boys in his deepest heart, no matter how talented they were, or how physically attractive.

On January 24, the day-to-day diary records that Bill Harris "had date at Selznick." Probably John Darrow the agent and ex-actor had arranged that Bill should see the casting director at the Selznick Studios. (John Darrow had had an affair with Bill, shortly before Christopher.) Nothing came of the interview, however.

On January 24, it is also recorded that there was Ram Nam in the evening and that Swami returned to the center from a stay at the ashram in Santa Barbara. Christopher still showed up to take part in these ceremonies, still spent time with Swami, but almost no memories remain of his life at the center during this final period. He was obsessed by Denny's Santa Monica world and by Bill Harris; and that is what has left its mark.

On January 27, Christopher went with Bill and Denny to the Follies and the Burbank, two burlesque shows. Here are some notes he made, either about these performances or some others he saw at that time:

> The hard round bellies, the clutching gestures, the bumps, the grinds, the splits. The hair shaken over the face, to suggest lust and

---

[1] I don't remember exactly when it happened, but the story went around that Stef, with his Germanic thoroughness, decided to find out what homosexual sex was like. So he went to bed with one of his friends. It didn't convert him, but he is supposed to have remarked later that the experience was "extremely pleasant"—or, more likely, "wirklich ganz angenehm [really quite agreeable]." (Stef sometimes made you think that Thomas Mann should have been his father, rather than Brecht; he had the sort of urbanity that goes with pince-nez. And yet he was really sexy, in an odd way. I think most of us would have liked to go to bed with him.)

shame. The gesture of masking the eyes—as if afraid to look at her own body. The brutally aggressive forward-jerking G-string. The secret smile as the dress is loosened. The presentation of the breasts. The final sexual challenge.

The horrible toothless old male comics. A world of triumphant women—in which the men are impotent and hideous.

January 28: "Lunch with Beesleys. Katharine Hepburn came in. Vigil 9–10 p.m." Hepburn lived quite close to the Beesleys. She had walked over to see them. They didn't know her well. A link between them was the Swedish married couple who had once worked for Hepburn and now worked for the Beesleys. This man and his wife were nice looking, youngish, spotlessly clean, demure, lazy, expensive and devoted to vicious gossip. They told Dodie and Alec how eccentric, ill-tempered and domineering Hepburn was as an employer. They claimed that she walked about in the woods naked. I myself have no memory of Hepburn at this time, except that her freckles were very prominent and that she seemed friendly and pleasant.

January 29: "Drove with Bill to Robinsons, to leave Gitas. Spent the evening at his place." This is a good specimen day to represent this period in Christopher's life—with one foot in the Vedanta Center and one foot out of it. These were newly printed copies of the Gita, which Christopher was taking to Robinsons department store. (I think there was a devotee employed in their book department who was going to push the Gita.)

The rest of the day was spent at Bill's La Cienega apartment. It seems to me now that La Cienega was perhaps the most romantic street in Los Angeles, in those days. It had an un-American air of reticence, of unwillingness to display itself. Its shops were small and unshowy; its private houses were private. Also—and this was what really appealed to Christopher—it seemed to have a bohemian, self-contained life of its own. It was a "quarter," which didn't make any effort to welcome outside visitors. Many of its dwellers were hidden away in odd little garden houses and shacks, within courtyards or on alleys, behind the row of buildings which lined the street. It was in one of these that Bill lived.

I suppose Christopher was now very much aware of Bill's impending departure and wanted to perform an act of sexual magic which would, as it were, stake out a permanent claim in Bill even after he "belonged" to Pancho. Anyhow, Christopher told Bill that he wanted to fuck him in every room of the apartment. (This probably consisted only of bedroom, living room, kitchen and bathroom.) Bill was quite willing—the idea of "staged" sex excited him. They had often talked of unusual places where one might make love. On this occasion, their only daring move was to go outside the house—the apartment being on the ground floor—and fuck one more time in the courtyard, in the rain. The neighbors may well have seen them doing this. If they did, there were no complaints. When it was over, Bill and Christopher felt very pleased with themselves and each other. Bill even went so far as to say, "You know, if you were three or four inches taller, you might quite easily be Heathcliff." "Heathcliff" was Bill's name for the ideal sex partner. But "Heathcliff" *had* to be at least a couple of inches taller than Bill.

(The word fuck in the above paragraph is perhaps misleading. I don't mean that Bill and Christopher had five distinct orgasms on this occasion; only that there were five stickings-in and pullings-out. Bill later paid Christopher another compliment indirectly, by telling Denny all about it and saying how it had hurt. I think this was Bill's kind of politeness. Bill was a veteran fuckee, and getting hurt is usually due to inexperience.)

January 31: "With Bill to the framer's. He washed shirts, etc. The soldier came in."

I have forgotten to mention that Bill painted, in those days. (Later, he retouched photographs and made various kinds of art objects.) He had done a self-portrait, I believe, that Christopher wanted as a keepsake—perhaps it was this that was being framed. But then again it seems to me that Bill was dissatisfied with the self-portrait and repainted it as a woman, whom Christopher decided to call Santa Monica. It is Santa Monica's picture, anyhow, which we have here in the house today.

I forget what the soldier's name was. He was one of Bill's lovers and he showed up with the obvious intention of getting some sex. Finding Christopher there, he sat down to wait until Christopher left. But Christopher wasn't about to leave. He glared jealously at the soldier and the atmosphere became tense. Suddenly Bill jumped up and ran out of the apartment and into the street. Christopher followed him. The scene was dramatic, because Bill was barefoot and had nothing on him but a bathrobe—however, no one on the boulevard appeared to pay much attention to this. When Christopher caught up with Bill, Bill was rather cross. "All this *love*—" he exclaimed, "I can't stand it!" As far as I remember, Christopher and the soldier ended by leaving the house together and going up to the soldier's place for a drink. By this time, Christopher was definitely interested in him, for he was sexy. But the soldier wasn't interested in Christopher, and nothing happened.

February 3: "Down to Denny's. Tom Maddox,[*] Jeff[†] and Curly[‡] were there. With Denny and Bill to see *Othello*. Bill and I slept at Bobo and Kelley's."

Tom Maddox was a very good-looking young actor, of the type which is classified as "rugged." His career looked promising at that time, but he never amounted to much. He was having a dangerous and exciting affair with Roddy McDowall, who was then in his teens.[1] According to Tom, Roddy was the one who had started it. Tom said Roddy was insanely reckless and got a thrill out of having sex with Tom in the McDowall home, while Roddy's parents were in the next room.

Jeff and Curly were two of Denny's sexual playmates, a pair of highly untrustworthy teenagers who liked pot and blue movies and who would have been quite capable of turning nasty at any moment and resorting to blackmail. This, for Denny, was a large part of their charm. I think they were brothers.[2]

The performance of *Othello* (downtown at the Biltmore) starred Paul Robeson, José Ferrer and Uta Hagen. Robeson looked marvellous in his costume, indeed he was perfectly typecast, but I don't remember that he was more than adequate; he sweated profusely. José Ferrer was a newcomer then, and he probably seemed better than he was. I remember him being tricky and showy in the "Put money in thy purse" speech to Roderigo and getting a lot of applause. I think we were all grateful, out here in the sticks, for any halfway stylish Shakespeare productions. Such events were like signs that the cultural blackout of the war was coming to an end.

Wallace Bobo and Howard Kelley, always referred to as Bo and Kelley, had another of the upstair front apartments at 137 Entrada Drive. So they were constantly in and out of Denny's apartment and were at most of his parties. They were ideal neighbors, easygoing, helpful, ready to go along with any of Denny's schemes; difficult as he could be, he never quarrelled with either of them. Bo was perhaps

[1] The *Information Please Almanac* says that Roddy was born in September 1928—in which case he would have been only sixteen at this time. Since writing the above, I have been reliably informed that Roddy was eighteen when he had the affair with Tom—which means that it can't have happened until the fall of the following year. I still trust my memory as far as Tom's statement is concerned, but no doubt he was bragging a little to impress Denny, that tireless chicken hawk. Tom would want to make Roddy seem as young and as wild as possible, because that would make him more desirable in Denny's eyes.
[2] The day-to-day diary entry of February 24, 1945, refers to "the twins"; these were probably Jeff and Curly.

[* Not his real name.]   [† Not his real name.]   [‡ Not his real name.]

more "the man of the family"; he was the good-looking one, he worked at an outdoor job (it was either landscape gardening or a nursery garden), he was butch (though not excessively). Kelley (I have forgotten what his job was) made most of the decisions and was altogether more practical; later, when Bo became somewhat [unwell], Kelley looked after him. I don't know how long they had already been together—I think they had both been in the service; but you felt that they would never part. They were both full of fun and gossip and took great interest in everything to do with show business. They both loved to get into drag.

February 4: "Swami had lumbago, van Druten lectured. With Bill to Beesleys'. They went to see house. Van Druten to supper. Said goodbye to Bill."

John van Druten's lecture at the Vedanta temple that Sunday morning was probably a version of the article by him called "One Element" which later appeared in our magazine *Vedanta and the West* and was then reprinted in our anthology *Vedanta for Modern Man*. I remember that John wanted to quote directly from *Androcles and the Lion* and wrote to the Shaw estate for permission to do so. This permission was refused; so, in the article, he has been obliged to paraphrase Shaw's dialogue.

Since this was Christopher's last day with Bill Harris, the Beesleys found an excuse to leave them alone together after lunch. This is the significance of, "They went to see house." (The Beesleys really were about to move, however; their house hunting wasn't fictitious.) It was one of those warm California winter days, and Bill and Christopher were able to have sex out on the lawn, near the swimming pool.

Thus their affair ended. When they met again, it was as friends—by which I mean chiefly that their relationship had ceased to be tense, reproachful, embarrassing. Had they ever been lovers? Not really. I much doubt that Bill was ever anything but friendly in his feelings toward Christopher; also a bit flattered, perhaps, by all the fuss Christopher made over him. He found Christopher sufficiently attractive, sexually—but then, he found all manner of people sufficiently attractive. I don't think he was really turned on by anyone who wasn't taller than himself.

As for Christopher, I don't think he was in love with Bill. I think what Christopher felt was a sort of compulsive craze. While Christopher was still intending to become a monk, Bill represented The Forbidden. Also, he was The Blond, an important myth figure in Christopher's life—Christopher had a strong belief that he was, or ought to be, automatically attracted to spectacular blonds. (No reason for this occurs to me at the moment; if I think of one, later, I'll insert it as a footnote [below].)[1] Also—and this is very important—Bill was introduced to Christopher by Denny. For Denny was another myth figure at that period; he was Satan, the tempter, the easy-as-an-old shoe friend who is so comfortable to be with because he knows the worst there is to know about you; the captive audience which holds its entertainers captive, demanding relentlessly to be surprised and amused. Christopher's Satan held Christopher in his power by provoking Christopher to indiscretion. Having dared Christopher to start an affair with someone—"I bet you can't get him," Satan says—he wheedles and flatters Christopher into talking about the new lover. So Christopher finds himself giving a blow-by-blow and word-for-word description of their affair; and thus the affair turns into a theatrical performance. (When the other person involved knows that this is going on, he will object violently

[1] May 14, 1973. An explanation *has* just occurred to me. It sounds ridiculous, but then psychological insights often do, according to the psychologists. (I realize it's possible that I got this out of one of their books and have chosen to forget that I did.)

Is The Blond maybe an archetype peculiar to the British Collective Unconscious? (I'm not using "archetype" in its strict Jungian sense, of course, because the Jungian archetype "can . . . manifest itself [spontaneously] anywhere, at any time." ["A Psychological View of Conscience," *Civilization in Transition, Collected Works*, volume 10.] But it's the most descriptive word I can think of.) The Blond, in relation to a primitive Briton, would be the blond Norseman or Saxon invader of his homeland. The Blond conquers, plunders, rapes. He is the masculine yang to Britain's feminine yin. As an individual Briton, you are free to deny that you are feminine, to fight him and get killed—but that's your own affair. The Blond is unalterably yang. As for Christopher, he was quite ready to be yin.

So much for the archetype theory. It may account for Christopher's feelings about blonds as a group. But the fact remains that many of the blonds in Christopher's life were definitely un-yang—pretty, feminine boys who wanted to be fucked. This compels me to theorize further: maybe Christopher unconsciously took over the role of Invader when he went to live in Germany and later in the States? He couldn't become The Blond (though he did, occasionally, dip his forelock in the peroxide bottle) but, as The Invader, he could fuck yin boys even if they happened to be blonds. If the blond boy was yang, Christopher merely had to stop being an invader and think of himself as a yin Briton!

Still, I can't believe that Christopher literally thought of himself as an invader—that is such a Jewish fantasy. Certainly, he wanted to "possess" Germany and the United States; not by conquering them, however, but by exploring them and learning to love them. He tried to do this by looking for an ideal German and later an ideal American Boy, through whom he could explore and love these countries.

—if he really cares for Christopher. Bill did know and didn't object.)

But why did Christopher need a Satan in his life? The answer can only be that the affair in itself didn't satisfy him; he could neither enjoy it nor even believe in it until his Satan had helped him turn it into a theatrical performance. On the rare occasions when Christopher did become seriously involved, he lost the desire to talk about it, even to a Satan. So the expected performance was cancelled, and Satan's feelings were hurt. (This happened to Denny, when Christopher met Bill Caskey.)

I even suspect that Christopher wasn't greatly attracted to Bill Harris sexually. From Christopher's point of view, The Blond *had* to be possessed "because he was there." His possession was a status symbol, like owning a Cadillac. And the mere fact that a lot of people envied you—or so you liked to believe—was in itself sexually exciting, up to a point. Nevertheless, The Blond, if he was a perfect example, was too beautiful to excite Christopher for long. Christopher was like a Cadillac owner who really wanted a quite different make of car but wouldn't admit it to himself. (Vernon Old continued to excite Christopher partly *because* his figure wasn't perfect.)

Furthermore, Bill Harris was too feminine for Christopher's taste. I write the word and reject it immediately. "Too smooth" suggests itself as an alternative, but that doesn't explain what I mean. Let me put it that Christopher was certainly able to feel violent lust for a feminine type of boy, provided that he had also a certain grossness, coarseness about him—thick curly hair on his chest and belly, for instance; even a roll of fat could be exciting. . . . Enough about this for the present; the subject will keep coming up.

Auden says that it's important, in considering a sex relationship, to say exactly what the partners did in bed. Christopher used to fuck Bill, belly downwards. Bill never fucked him. (In general Bill only liked to be fucked—but on one occasion at least he made an exception; a teenage boy fell for him and Bill used to fuck the boy, telling Denny and Christopher that it made him (Bill) "feel like a man.") Bill set great store by having what he called "a perfect orgasm"—both partners coming simultaneously. This happened the first time he and Christopher went to bed together, which Bill took to be a very good sign of compatibility.

No memory remains of their sex acts, other than fucking. I suppose they sucked cock and rimmed[*] each other. What I do clearly remember is a remark Bill once made: "Really, it's ridiculous how some people think it's unhygienic to share a toothbrush, and yet

[* Stimulated the anus with the tongue.]

they've been licking each other's shitty assholes!"—meaning that he was in favor of doing both. (But I'm sure that Bill's asshole, and everything else about him, was always kept thoroughly clean.)

February 5: "Bill left for New York. Drove down with John van Druten and Tamara to AJC Ranch." Tamara was a Russian lady who worked for a while as John's housekeeper; I think she was, or claimed to be, a duchess or princess in the old Russian aristocracy. John was fascinated by her at first—he would have had the same reaction if she had been a well-known ex-actress, and indeed her behavior could not have been more theatrical; she was full of archness and corny temperament. Later, the relationship soured, I seem to recall, and Tamara left them, feeling rejected and deeply offended.

Christopher stayed at the ranch until February 12, when he drove back to the Vedanta Center with John van Druten and immediately went to bed with one of his inflamed throats. The throat infection had started two days before this, but the visit was probably very enjoyable otherwise. Carter had a birthday on the 7th, and on the 8th they all drove up to the cabin near Idyllwild.

Christopher always enjoyed the climate of the ranch, its dry relaxing heat. He and John would chatter away together, exchanging their British jokes, making up bits of verses, looking up half-remembered quotations in books, lying by the pool or floating in it, under the palm trees, with the flat cultivated fields all around, dotted with Mexicans at work. They entertained each other charmingly, affectionately, like two no longer young ladies, and complimented each other on their writing. Meanwhile, Carter Lodge came stamping in and out, in boots covered with dust, very much the man of the house, and full of ranch problems and local gossip.

Evidently trying to recapture some magical moment of this visit, Christopher wrote in a notebook—the same one in which he made the notes about the burlesque show: "The sun went down behind the mountain in a reek of chicken fertilizer." Also in this notebook, there is a quotation from Proust which must have been written down about this time: "I was not unhappy—save only from day to day." This, Christopher chose to interpret as: I was not unhappy underneath, only disturbed on the surface by temporary unpleasant-nesses—which he felt was a good description of his own mental condition, I suppose. He later made a resolve to read right through *Remembrance of Things Past* before 1945 was over. John Collier was probably responsible for this.[1]

---

[1] John Collier was an ardent Proustian.

The February 12 issue of *Time* magazine contained a review of the Prabhavananda–Isherwood Gita translation, combined with an article about Swami, Christopher and the Vedanta Center.[1] As was to be expected, *Time* got several of its facts wrong—the statement that the Vedanta Society had an "alabaster temple" became a household joke for months, as did the ten-minute meditation and the "dispassionate ceremony." But Christopher found the article more embarrassing than funny—and especially the photograph of Swami and himself which illustrated it; the two of them standing on the steps of the temple, captioned, "In their world, tranquillity."

As for the story that Christopher was the model for Larry, *Time* may not have invented it, but it was certainly responsible for the letters Christopher now began to get, asking was this true. He wrote a letter to *Time*, denying it, and Maugham himself denied it later, but the story lived a long while.

If Christopher had indeed been solidly settled down at the Vedanta Center, resolved to become a monk, he could have taken all this

---

[1] Extracts from the *Time* article:

> Ten years ago Christopher Isherwood was one of the most promising of younger English novelists, and a member of the radical pacifist literary set sometimes known as "the Auden circle." Now, thinking seriously of becoming a swami (religious teacher), he is studying in a Hindu temple in Hollywood, California.

> Much-travelled author Isherwood's early novel, *The Last of Mr. Norris* . . . was a grisly eyewitness account of British pro-Nazis in Berlin. His *Journey to a War* (with verse commentary by W. H. Auden) was a stark, unromanticized look at embattled China. Now this rebellious son of a British lieutenant colonel lives monastically with three other men and eight women in a small house adjoining the alabaster temple of the Vedanta Society of Southern California. He shares his income and the housework with his fellow students, and daily ponders the teachings of his master, Swami Prabhavananda.

> . . . Three times each day Isherwood repairs to the temple, sits crosslegged between grey-green walls on which are hung pictures of Krishna, Jesus, Buddha, Confucius, other great religious teachers. The Swami enters bareheaded, wearing a long, bright yellow robe that sweeps the floor. He too sits crosslegged, pulls a shawl around him and for ten minutes meditates in silence. Then in a ringing bass he chants a Sanskrit invocation, repeats it in English, ending with the words "Peace, Peace, Peace!"

> This dispassionate ceremony is the ritual of a mystical order of which slight, agreeable, cigarette-smoking Swami Prabhavananda is the Los Angeles leader.

> . . . Larry, the dissatisfied young hero of Somerset Maugham's current bestselling novel, *The Razor's Edge*, whose search for faith ended in Vedanta, is said to be modelled on Isherwood.

publicity in his stride, as part of the process of dying to the world. But
here he was, just about to leave! *Time* made his position false—
before, it had been merely insecure. Now he seemed to be posing as
a monk and a saint.

On February 13, Christopher notes that he has started to read
Wilkie Collins's *The Woman in White*, which Warner Brothers
wanted to make into a film. My impression is that they had had
various producers and writers working on it already—indeed, it
seems to me that John Collier had been on the script for a time,
gotten tired of it and suggested Christopher as a replacement.

On the 13th, Christopher was still in bed with his inflamed throat.
The 14th was Ramakrishna's birthday celebration, that year.
Christopher, who hated pujas, remained in bed and only got up for
vespers, after a visit from Dr. Kolisch. Kolisch's attitude toward
Christopher was friendly and hardboiled, which Christopher found
ideal. (On one occasion, while Christopher was still living at the
center, his penis developed a painful constriction around the middle.
Although Kolisch had every reason to suppose that Christopher was
observing chastity, he said the constriction was due to excessive sex
intercourse. He always made such diagnoses with a perfectly straight
face and matter-of-fact manner.) After seeing Kolisch, Christopher
usually got better at once. Next day, the 15th, he went off to
Warner's, to interview James Geller, who was then the story editor,
and Mr. [Louis] Edelman, who was to be his producer.

February 17: "Lunch with the Beesleys at their new house." The
Beesleys had moved into a house on the Pacific Coast Highway,
belonging to Anatole Litvak; it was number 19130, between Santa
Monica and Malibu. Like nearly all the houses in this area, it was
built to look only one way—straight out to sea. The beach was rocky
and narrow and the tide came right up to the house—and under it,
if I remember rightly. But the house was fairly attractive inside,
somewhat nautical in design, with a circular staircase(?)

February 21: "Went to work at Warner's.[1] Lunch with Matthew
Huxley. Supper with Sam." Matthew Huxley had a job in the
readers' department at Warner Brothers; he had to read novels and
make reports on them, so producers could decide if they were
suitable for filming. Matthew scorned this work and made apologetic
jokes about it. He was full of fun and very popular with his colleagues—his pinkness and freshness and his British accent appealed to
a lot of the girls. Christopher went to visit him sometimes in the

---

[1] I see from the day-to-day diary that Christopher was earning six hundred
dollars a week.

office and they played what Christopher refers to as "the category game." I don't remember what this was.

Sam was Sam From.[1]

February 22: "Cycled to and from Warner's. Talk with Edelman."

I think Christopher usually hitchhiked to work at that time; cycling took longer and car drivers were mostly very cooperative— picking up riders was regarded as part of the war effort. Christopher soon found himself taking these rides for granted, as a form of public transportation; once, he heard himself saying curtly to a driver, "Be as quick as you can, I'm late!"

He must have been working alone on *The Woman in White*—if he had had a collaborator, I should remember. Edelman was a pleasant, easily pleased producer, but I don't think he was much help.

Christopher greatly enjoyed working at Warner's. The writers welcomed him warmly. The Writers' Building was very much a club; very conscious of its importance and very ready to defend its rights. It was said that Jack Warner and the other front office executives were afraid to venture into the building. When James Geller got into a fight with the front office, because he was supporting the writers' point of view, and resigned from his job, the writers signed a strongly worded letter approving his action and pinned a copy of it on their bulletin board.

When a writer left Warner's at the end of his assignment, he would give a party to his fellow writers and their secretaries, during office hours, complete with liquor (which was officially forbidden) and dancing. There would be a party almost every week.

Christopher's particular friend at Warner's was John Collier. (I think maybe they had met sometime before this—perhaps at Salka Viertel's.) Everyone who tried to describe John ended by using the same image: a toby jug. He was small and square, with close-cropped

[1] Sam and Eddie From were twins, but they didn't look much alike, because Eddie had kept a huge Jewish nose and Sam had had his bobbed. Both of them were little and skinny and lively. Christopher had met Eddie first, I think, sometime in 1944.

Sam was in business and had made a lot of money. Eddie was inclined to sneer at him for this. Eddie's role was that of the outspoken brother who preferred poverty to selling out; later he became an amateur psychiatrist. (For all I know, he now has a degree.)

Sam and Eddie had friends in common—Charles Aufderheide, who worked at Technicolor, and Sam's lover, George [Bill], and Evelyn Hooker, and an older woman called Fauna(?) [probably Fern Maher], and David Sachs, the baby-faced professor of philosophy. They sometimes called themselves The Benton Way Group, because Sam owned a house there in which most of them lived, on and off.

hair, a bright red face and round bulging blue eyes. His expression was humorous and yet oddly ferocious; in his youth he had been a boxer. He was British, through and through.[1]

Here are some items from the before-mentioned notebook:

At Warner's Studio: Gordon Kahn (one of the writers) very erect and dapper, with his air of an implacable little district attorney. His stories of the executions he witnessed as a newspaper man.

His barter: He owns a valuable statuette which he got in trade for a telescope which he got in exchange for a pig costing four or five dollars.

I lose my shoe and can't find it for ten minutes. We hunt everywhere. "Did you notice if I had it on at lunch?" Collier said: "This is the way men laugh in concentration camps."

Kahn, seeing me with my weekend bag: "There goes Isherwood with his dunnage." Collier: "Oh, valuable Kahn!"

I think Collier was then working on a screenplay of Wilkie Collins's *The Moonstone*. Later, he switched to a picture which was called *Deception*. Christopher used to consult him whenever he had a problem with his own script. One of Collier's favorite techniques was to fill up his scripts with absurdly detailed and beautifully written stage directions (which charmed and awed his producer), all leading up to a couple of lines of the flattest dialogue: "Where is he?" "I don't know."

Collier said that he did all his script writing at night; he couldn't work in the daytime. Since the writers were required to keep office hours (Monday through Friday, and half-day Saturday) Collier passed the time in gossip and occasional drinking. This made him a perpetual temptation to Christopher, to drop work and join him. Collier said that he never worried when his producer required "a new angle" on the story; he relied absolutely on spur-of-the-moment inspiration and would only begin to think about the problem after he had started walking from his office to the producer's.

Collier believed that one should never economize; if you found that you were spending more money than you earned, you must find a way of earning more. Collier lived expensively, and he was paying

[1] His view of England and English politics was thoroughly realistic, however. After the English elections of July 1945, he won hundreds of dollars because he had bet that Labour would get in. His American colleagues were all so sentimental about Churchill that they refused to believe he could lose. Christopher also refused to believe it but for a different reason—he wanted Churchill's defeat so badly that he didn't dare think it was possible.

a great deal of alimony to his ex-wife; although she had a good job as an agent and [. . .] was young, healthy and very attractive. Collier didn't seem to begrudge her the money at all. They met often and were on the best of terms. Collier told Christopher that he wanted to get married again. (Later, he did.) And he added, "I propose to breed extensively."

Collier was modest. He almost never mentioned his own work—as opposed to his movie writing. His favorite author was Proust. He used to say jokingly that he wanted to rewrite the ending of the *Recherche* so as to give the story an entirely different slant. After having been led to believe that Charlus, Saint-Loup, Jupien and the rest of them were homosexuals, the reader would discover that he had been deceived—their real guilty secret was that they were all in show business. They could never admit to this because, in their social world, show business was regarded as the vilest possible way of life. Therefore they pretended to be homosexuals—since homosexuality was tolerated as a harmless eccentricity. When Charlus took a handsome young man into another room at a party, he would *want* the other guests to believe that this was the beginning of a seduction. But the disgusting truth was that Charlus was offering the young man a part in a Hollywood Western. . . . Fantasies like this one never sound very amusing when they are described in brief. But Collier and Christopher had a great deal of fun with it, and kept inventing new scenes and telling them to each other.[1]

March 12: "The strike began." This strike involved some employees at Warner Brothers, but not all. After conferring with the strikers' representatives, the members of the Writers' Guild were told that the union didn't object to their crossing the picket line; so Christopher and his colleagues continued to go to their offices every day—to their disappointment, for nearly all of them would have

---

[1] Another favorite subject of their conversation was the German language. Collier, being a Francophile, found the sound of German funny. Christopher humored him in this, and read him German aloud, making it sound as absurd as he could. Collier laughed till the tears poured down his scarlet face when Christopher read lines from Wilhelm Busch's *Max und Moritz*, which *were* meant to be funny, or from Liliencron's poems, which weren't. Collier adored Busch's use of ejaculations and onomatopoeic words—such as "Schnupdiwup!" "Knacks!" "Plumps!" "Rums!" "Schwapp!" ["Whoops!" "Crack!" "Splosh!" "Bang!" "Whoosh!"] But he was just as much amused by Liliencron's perfectly serious line: "Zum schlanken Fant in blauen Puffenwams." ["To the slender coxcomb in the blue puffed doublet," in "Una ex hisce morieris" ("One of You Here Will Die").] "Puffenwams" became his favorite joke word.

rather worked at home. Matthew Huxley and the reading department were among the strikers, however. Matthew was a militant socialist and took an active part in union meetings and picketing. Months later, after Christopher had left Warner's for good, the strike situation, which had been dragging quietly on, became violent.[1] The pickets tried to stop people entering the studio, and the picket lines were charged. Jack Warner and the other studio heads were turning from reproachful fathers of ungrateful children into frankly ruthless bosses dealing with their wage slaves—communist inspired, of course.

March 22: "Talked to Swami about leaving." This is one of the most infuriatingly reticent entries in the day-to-day diary. What was it that Christopher said to Swami on this occasion that he hadn't said several times before? Had some crisis arisen, which made Christopher feel he couldn't stay at the center any longer? Had there been some gossip about the life he was living? Had some other members of "the Family" objected that he had no business staying on there when he wasn't planning to become a monastic? I can't remember anything at all. But it is obvious that Swami answered any scruples that Christopher may have had by urging him to stay a little longer. Swami must have said (as he had said on other occasions), "Why do you want to go away? This is your home. We all love you here. I don't want to lose you." And Christopher must have protested, "But you won't lose me, Swami, I'm your disciple, I know this is my real home, and of course I'll keep coming here to see you—" All of which was perfectly sincere on both sides. Swami didn't want Christopher to go away (I believe) because he hoped that Christopher, if he stayed, might gradually begin to feel that he had a monastic vocation, after all. Perhaps Christopher suspected that this might happen to him—hence his instinctive animal desire to escape. But he can't have been seriously afraid of getting caught. Otherwise he wouldn't have lingered on at the center, as he did, for another five months.

[1] Aldous Huxley (see *Letters of Aldous Huxley*) wrote to Anita Loos on October 13, 1945: "Matthew was fortunately absent when the violence broke out on the picket line, but he got arrested and spent some hours in jail on the following day. He is going north to Berkeley in another week or so, to take some courses at the U. of C. . . . The reading job is a dead end . . ." Matthew may not have been involved in the worst violence, but I remember a newspaper photograph of him, dodging a car which was being driven to break through the picket line. Matthew had narrowly escaped being hit and was curving his body over the car's fender with considerable grace, like a bullfighter. I am also pretty sure that Aldous himself came to the studio one day and walked with the pickets, as a gesture of solidarity.

(I still think it is possible—just possible—that, if a proper monastery like Trabuco had suddenly come into being at that time, Christopher would have agreed to join it and at least given the monastic life another try. What he wanted, then, was either complete freedom or much closer confinement, far away from Los Angeles, Denny, the Beesleys and the studio. Life at the Hollywood center had nothing whatever to offer him—except Swami's presence; it was so bohemian and permissive that its few rules and restrictions were merely irritating.)

March 26: "Supper with Wolfgang Reinhardts and Iris Tree. To Thelma Todd's with Jay. Stayed night with Denny."

I forget when it was that Christopher first met Wolfgang Reinhardt—it may well have been soon after he got to know Gottfried. But this get-together was probably due to the fact that Christopher was now working at Warner's, where Wolfgang was a producer. No doubt they were already discussing the film Wolfgang wanted Christopher to work on with him, as soon as *The Woman in White* was finished—Maugham's *Up at the Villa*.

This is the first mention of "Jay," who called himself Jay de Laval. (His real name was said to be Earle McGrath.)[*] But Christopher must certainly have met him before this. He was a friend of Denny's and very much a part of the Santa Monica Canyon circle. I think he may already have opened his restaurant on the corner of Channel Road and Chautauqua, but perhaps not.

Jay had a vague reputation for being crooked. Later on, it was said that he had had to leave California to avoid arrest; this was after he had settled in Mexico. But, when you tried to find out exactly what he had done that was illegal, it seemed that he hadn't gone much beyond running up big bills and then failing either to pay them or return the merchandise. He was also, obviously, a bit of a con man. It was easy to imagine him using his considerable charm to get money out of rich old women; his role as the Baron de Laval was probably related to this.

Jay was large and well built, though inclined to plumpness. He was very blond (maybe artificially) and he had big blue eyes. His eyes didn't sparkle like Collier's, they stared. Despite their seeming boldness, they revealed nothing inward. Jay was all on the surface, all smiles and gossip and camp. It was only when he laughed loudly that you got a hint of madness.

He was not only a very good cook but a marvellous host. He could

[* A mistake; Earl McGrath is the name of a different person, who was living in Santa Monica during the early 1950s. See *D1*, p. 454.]

take you into the kitchen and fix a meal for you both without ever losing the thread of the conversation or making you feel awkward because he was doing all the work. He was also, it seems, a marvellous seducer. Christopher knew of this only at second hand, of course; he wouldn't have dreamt of going to bed with Jay and Jay certainly didn't want it. But the testimony of half a dozen boys who had had sex with Jay and then talked about it to Christopher was quite impressive. Most of them had been literally seduced—they hadn't wanted to do it but Jay had made them like doing it. "It was crazy," one of them told Christopher;[1] and another[2] said, "He made me feel beautiful." Jay himself, when congratulated by Christopher on his conquests, said modestly, "It's quite simple—you just have to start doing all kinds of things to them, all at once, before they realize what's going on."

Thelma Todd's was the restaurant up the coast, just north of the Sunset Boulevard turnoff, which had once belonged to Thelma Todd and was the scene of her murder. It was a kind of hideout rendezvous for Hollywood executives who wanted to meet show girls in secret; the tables were in alcoves which could be curtained off. Perhaps Jay went there to do some business in connection with his own restaurant project and took Christopher along as a drinking companion. Denny and his friends all regarded Thelma Todd's as a place for special evenings, celebrations and treats. The food was very good, but it cost more than they would usually pay.

On April 3, Edelman left or was taken off *The Woman in White* and a Mr. Jacobs[*] became its producer in his place. I can remember nothing whatever about him. I don't think he gave Christopher any trouble.

On April 8, Albert Brush, who was a friend of Jay and also of the Laughtons, took Denny and Christopher to visit Walter Arensberg the art collector and Baconian. After this, Christopher paid several visits to him. Arensberg's house was crammed with pictures and art objects, including the boxes and toys made by Marcel Duchamp. Every inch of wall space was covered, every table was laden, and there were stacks of unhung pictures in every corner.

Arensberg remained a charming enthusiastic sane host until you got onto the subject of Bacon; then he became wild-eyed and rather incoherent, with ruffled hair and gestures of frenzied excitement. I forget what Arensberg looked like but I can remember his

[1] Bill Caskey.
[2] Don Coombs, see page 218.

[* Writer and producer William Jacobs.]

manner at such times—it was that of a madman as he reveals to you the existence of international conspiracies and speaks with smiling scorn of the enemies who are trying to outwit him. Arensberg's enemies were all those scholars and other members of the Establishment who were concealing from the world the truth about Bacon. And what was the truth? That Bacon was a reincarnation of Jesus Christ. (I don't think I *can* be making this up.) That he was the son of Queen Elizabeth. And that he had written all the works attributed to Shakespeare. (My impression is that Arensberg thought this last item was of minor importance. He saw Bacon as the great prophet of the Modern Age, a teacher and philosopher who amused himself with literary composition only in his spare time.)[1]

On April 12, President Roosevelt died. That morning, while Christopher was in his office at Warner's with his secretary, there was a phone call from his secretary's husband, telling her the news. On hearing it, she burst into tears, instantly. Christopher was astonished by the quickness of her reaction—it was as if she had been subconsciously expecting the news and was therefore half-prepared

---

[1] Arensberg believed that Bacon had been secretly buried in the chapter house of Lichfield Cathedral. In 1924 he had published an appeal to the dean and chapter of the cathedral to admit publicly that this was so and that they were all of them members of a secret society founded by Bacon himself. Arensberg had visited Lichfield in 1923. His suspicions were confirmed when the verger showed him a picture in Ogilby's translation of Virgil, with the remark, "Curious, isn't it?" For the picture—which showed Aeneas plucking the golden bough that gave him the right of way into *the abode of the dead*—was marked with the Rosicrucian motto "Ex Uno Omnia" [All from One]. And Arensberg recognized "Omnia" as an anagram of the Spanish word *iamon*, which means "a gammon of *bacon.*" [Correct Spanish would be *jamón*.] However, in spite of the verger's apparent hint and other clues that Arensberg imagined he had found, he was unable to get the dean (the Very Reverend H. E. Savage) to admit that their secret society had been covering up the facts. He even accused the dean of obliterating certain signs by which the location of Bacon's grave had been formerly marked. His statement ends: "I have put the truth on record and the truth will make its way." (Arensberg took it for granted, of course, that the grave, if opened, would be found to contain proofs of Bacon's divine nature, his authorship of Shakespeare, etc.)

The dean obviously thought Arensberg was crazy. I'm fairly sure Arensberg showed Christopher a letter which the dean had written him, breaking off all further communications—"After the events of last Thursday, there can be no friendly relations between us." In telling the story, Christopher used to claim that Arensberg had been caught in the act of digging a tunnel under the road between his lodgings and the chapter house; he was trying to get at Bacon's grave. But this was probably just Christopher's imagination.

for it. But Christopher's own reaction was equally quick. He said to himself, "Good—that means we'll get the weekend off." (The 12th was a Thursday.)

Christopher had never felt any personal liking for Roosevelt. (Even back in 1933, when he had first seen Roosevelt's photographs in the European press, Christopher had mistrusted him and found his face repulsive—the face, as John van Druten had later said, of a "faux bonhomme."[*]) But Christopher had to keep his reaction to himself, as long as he was at the studio. Even hard-boiled outspoken John Collier was deeply moved.

The next month passed without any remarkable incidents, as far as I can judge from the day-to-day diary. It sounds crazy to say this, when, in fact, Mussolini and his mistress were killed on April 28, Hitler's death was announced on May 1, Berlin fell on May 2 and the Nazis surrendered on the 7th! No doubt Christopher shared in the general excitement; probably he was better able to picture the destruction of the Third Reich than were most of his friends. But the day-to-day diary merely records that, on the 28th, he took a taxi to the beach and spent the night at Denny's; that, on May 1, he "tried to write Auden article" (don't remember what that was); that, on May 2, he saw *Devotion*[1] in a projection room at the studio and had supper with Vernon Old; and that, on May 7, he had drinks with John van Druten, Dave Eberhardt and Don Forbes, and then had supper with Aldous Huxley.[2]

On May 16, Henry Blanke took over as producer on *The Woman in White*. Beside this, he was producing the picture Collier was working on—*Deception*.[3] He was neat and smiling and military looking; he might have been a German officer; if he was a Jew he didn't look like one. He had a reputation for getting things done and

[1] *Devotion* was a film about the Brontës, with Ida Lupino as Emily and Arthur Kennedy as Branwell. Christopher was able to see it in the projection room because he was friendly with Keith Winter, who had worked on the script.

[2] It may well be that Huxley made some memorable remarks on this historic evening. Perhaps he repeated what he had written to Julian Huxley earlier that same day (see *Letters of Aldous Huxley*): "All the king's horses and all the king's men cannot put Humpty Dumpty together again—and when they [have] succeeded, more or less, his name will be Humpsky Dumpsky and his address, poste restante Moscow."

[3] It was released in 1946, with Bette Davis, Paul Henreid and Claude Rains. Collier got first credit, with Joseph Than. Produced by Henry Blanke, directed by Irving Rapper.

[* Hypocrite.]

was certainly far more efficient than Edelman and Jacobs had been. Perhaps rather too efficient for Christopher, who had got into lazy ways. Unlike Collier, he wasn't prepared to work at night and, under Collier's influence, he did very little work during the day.

Collier's influence—that is to say, Collier's demand to be amused—even made itself felt in Christopher's sex life. Christopher had of course told Collier that he was homosexual. Collier, as a good Proustian, had to take this in his stride; he only maintained that women had better characters than men—aside from this, he wasn't shocked by boy love, it was merely not his cup of tea. At the same time, as a Proustian voyeur, he was curious to get a glimpse of Christopher in actual pursuit of sex; and Christopher was delighted to oblige him. As with Denny, Christopher now prepared to give a theatrical performance for Collier's benefit, and his own.

It conveniently so happened that the mailing department at the studio was just then the center of a lot of gay activity, and had several attractive messenger boys. One of these was having an affair with Helmut Dantine. They were very discreet about it; they had to be—it was risky for an important actor to get involved like this, right under the noses of the front office. Helmut Dantine's messenger was a nice boy, not much to look at, actually, but lively and full of Jewish fun. Christopher got to know him, and he helped Christopher get acquainted with a boy named Steve,[*] whom he fancied.

Steve was dark and pale, with a long bony El Greco type of face. He was altogether an admirable and lovable character, both physically and morally courageous, lively, amusing, honest and capable of strong affection. If he had found an absorbing interest in life he might have achieved something; as it was, he just plodded along from job to job. He did have some ambition to become an actor, but it wasn't strong enough, and he was too small and slight for leading roles, also a bit queeny in his manner. Denny, who rather liked him, pronounced the verdict: "I think he's quite beautiful, but let's face it, he'll always be a department-store queen."

Steve had changed his name, probably for show-biz reasons [. . .]. He called himself [Steve Cooley] at the time Christopher met him. Later, he called himself [something else].

Steve and Christopher had supper together on May 25. This was their first date, I think. Steve told Christopher about his life in Las Vegas, before he came to Los Angeles; he had worked in one of the casinos, and also, as I seem to remember, on a ranch; he loved riding horses. At that time, he was studying acting with some local group, and working on the part of Branwell Brontë in a play called *Moor Born*, which contained the unsayable line, "You are moor born." He

[* Not his real name.]

and Christopher used to repeat this over and over, but it always sounded absurd.[1]

Collier, Steve and Christopher all enjoyed the dramatic aspects of this affair, from their different viewpoints. Collier found it thrillingly Proustian to look out of his office window and watch the discreet flirtations of the messenger boys—the glances and conspiratorial exchanges of dialogue—which Christopher had now taught him to observe and interpret. For him, it was like the discovery of a secret society; he was now prepared to believe that nearly the entire studio was queer. As for Steve, he certainly loved walking briskly into Christopher's office with a big envelope in his hand and telling Christopher's secretary, "These are for Mr. Isherwood to sign, they said for me to wait, they want them back right away"—which was Christopher's cue to shout from the inner office (grumpily, as if interrupted in his work), "Okay, tell him to bring them in here." Then Steve would come in, closing the door behind him, whisper, "Hello, darling," kiss Christopher a few times, whisper, "See you this evening," and make a brisk exit past the secretary, flourishing the envelope with its dummy contents. . . . Christopher enjoyed this playacting too, of course—but probably not as much as Steve did. Steve was quite shameless, in word and in deed. Christopher realized this was admirable but it embarrassed him.

If they went to bed together that first night, it must have been at Steve's apartment. Otherwise, they had no place to go but Denny's, and they didn't visit him together until May 29. Perhaps they drove up into the hills and made love in Christopher's newly acquired car. This was a Packard convertible, old and noisy but still very sturdy, which had recently been given him by Yogi (Mr. Brown), Yogini's husband. Yogi no longer needed the Packard because he had just bought himself a new car. (I think that he and Yogini had already decided to separate—that is, to accept the fact that Yogini really was a nun.) The first mention of the Packard in the day-to-day diary is on May 19.

[1] *Moor Born* is a play by Dan Totheroh, first performed in New York in 1934. It must have remained a favorite piece for amateur actors all these years, for when I asked about it at the Samuel French library today (January 13, 1972) they recognized the name at once and produced a copy.

BRANWELL: I didn't want to go to my grave unsung . . . obscure . . . a nobody. . . . It's too late now . . . too late for me.
EMILY: Perhaps not too late. Strange things can happen to you, for you are moor born, Branwell. Yes . . . moor born . . . and what the moors took from you, they may return.

On May 28, Christopher stopped working at Warner's for one week. I believe that this break marked Christopher's switchover from Henry Blanke and *The Woman in White* to Wolfgang Reinhardt and *Up at the Villa*. I have an impression (but a very dim one) that Christopher felt that Blanke was dissatisfied with his work, but maybe not. Somehow, I don't believe the script they had worked on was finished. I don't know if Blanke dropped the project at that time, or hired another writer.[1]

Christopher spent most of his holiday week staying with Denny. Steve joined him on the 29th and left early on the morning of the 31st—he must have taken two days off from work.

June 2: "Bill Caskey's birthday party at Jay's."

This is the first mention of Caskey in the day-to-day diary, but Christopher must certainly have met him weeks or even months earlier. This was another case in which Denny had played Satan —daring Christopher to start an affair with someone. When Caskey and his friend Hayden Lewis first showed up in the Canyon, Denny had told Christopher that Caskey had been the boyfriend of "a rich old man" (Len Hanna) and that he had been so disgusted by this affair that he had made a vow never again to go to bed with anyone older than himself. No doubt Denny had told Christopher this in such a way as to challenge Christopher's middle-aged vanity. Anyhow, Christopher had met Caskey and had found him attractive, but hadn't done much about it. They had talked at parties and gone for walks together on the beach; that was all.

Meanwhile, Jay Laval *had* done something about Caskey. They had been to bed together—which meant that Caskey had broken his vow—and now Jay was giving Caskey a party for his (twenty-fourth) birthday. This party made the affair official, from Jay's point of view; he was very possessive and unwisely apt to display his new conquests to his friends. No doubt it was the party which aroused Denny's spirit of mischief; he must have egged Christopher on to make a pass at Caskey. That afternoon, Christopher was going shopping and he asked Caskey to come along for the ride. They went into a clothing store and Christopher bought Caskey a shirt, as a birthday present. At the party, Jay drank a lot and fell asleep, as he often did. Christopher returned from the party to Denny's apartment and told Denny that Caskey had promised to follow him as soon as he could get away.

---

[1] *The Woman in White* was finally made and released in 1948, with Henry Blanke credited as its producer. Stephen Morehouse Avery got sole credit as its writer.

Denny bet Christopher that Caskey wouldn't show up—but he probably wasn't either surprised or displeased when they heard the sound of Caskey's sneakers bounding up the staircase. Christopher, of course, was grinning with gratified vanity from ear to ear.

Caskey and Christopher spent the night together and found themselves sexually compatible; Christopher came in Caskey's mouth, which he was very seldom able to do with anyone. But this didn't lead to instant infatuation—for, according to the day-to-day diary, they didn't see each other again for a week. Jay was very cross and hurt, when he discovered what had happened. He accused Caskey of ingratitude, feeling that the guest of honor at a birthday party ought to stay in his host's bed—even if the host has passed out. As for Christopher, Jay said that his behavior was "hardly what I should have expected, after all his talk about Ramakrishna." But Jay didn't bear grudges; he was basically very good-natured. There was a peace meeting, apologies were made, drinks were drunk, Jay soon found another boy and he, Caskey and Christopher became good friends again.

The next day, June 3, was a Sunday, so Steve was able to come down to Denny's. Steve and Christopher drove to Lake Sherwood. When they got back, Denny was giving a party. I am nearly certain that this was the occasion on which a pretty blond naval officer named Willy Tompkins[*] and an army lieutenant were persuaded by the other guests to take off their clothes and have sex on the couch, with everybody watching. This excited [one of the guests] so much that he wanted to do the same with Christopher, but Christopher was embarrassed and wouldn't. (Willy Tompkins and the lieutenant later retired to Jay's apartment and made love in private.)

On June 4, Christopher went back to work at Warner's—almost certainly on *Up at the Villa*, with Wolfgang Reinhardt.[1]

---

[1] Wolfgang wanted to stick close to the Maugham story. His chief deviation from it was to have Rowley plant some clues around the corpse so that the Italian police are tricked into thinking that Karl (called Paul in the script) has been killed by the Gestapo, which makes them hastily drop the case and announce that death was due to heart attack. This was Wolfgang's idea and I think it works very well—culminating in a good cross-purpose comedy scene between the Italian chief of police and the German consul, in which they both deplore the carelessness of the Gestapo's murder methods.

The code prevented Wolfgang and Christopher from making it clear that Mary and Paul actually have sex together before he shoots himself. Rereading the script today, I can't be sure just how much of a disadvantage this would have been, if the film had been made. (It never was.) The scene as Maugham

[* Not his real name.]

This must also have been the day on which Christopher first discovered, or at least suspected, that he had caught the clap. On June 5, he went to a Dr. Zeiler to be examined and on the 6th he spent the day at Dr. Zeiler's office, being given shots of penicillin. The shots cured him right away—he only saw Dr. Zeiler once more, on the 11th, for a checkup. This was Christopher's second dose of clap and its cure was a happy contrast to the first—those burning douches of potassium permanganate which the Brussels doctor squirted up Christopher's smarting urethra, day after day, in December 1938. The very atmosphere in the offices of the two doctors was quite different. The Brussels doctor was breezy but brutal and his office had a certain grimness, appropriate to those days, when even gonorrhea was a serious business and syphilis was sometimes incurable. Whereas Dr. Zeiler's office seemed bright with the dawn of the Penicillin Era, the doctor gave the injections as casually as if they were flu shots and his nurse, when they had finished, smiled archly at Christopher and said, "That'll teach you to be a good boy, won't it?" No, not good, Christopher thought, but careful. Here was yet another situation in which he felt ashamed of himself and, at the same time, contemptuous of his shame. It was shaming to return from a V.D. clinic to a monastery, but only shaming when he imagined Swami somehow finding out. Once again, he told himself that he must abandon his false position by leaving the center at the first possible opportunity.

It wasn't Steve's fault that he had infected Christopher; Steve was quite unaware that he had the clap, it was in his rectum, so there was no burning and no discharge. When they first went to bed together, Steve wanted Christopher to fuck him but added that this probably wouldn't work, someone else had tried to and hadn't been able to get inside. Christopher tried and succeeded. It always excited him to fuck a virgin and he felt pleasantly superior to the "someone else." But the joke was on Christopher, because the "someone else" had had clap and he had at least gotten in far enough to give it to Steve.

Steve was very apologetic. He expressed fears that Christopher would now stop wanting to see him. No doubt Christopher *was* anxious to assure him that this wasn't true—they met four times in the next seven days—but the clap really did draw them closer

---

wrote it is more convincing, but not entirely so. It might have got some wrong laughs. And Maugham's dialogue is hardly to be believed—he makes Karl say things like, "You have shown me heaven and now you want to thrust me back to earth"!

Christopher once summarized the plot to Collier as, "Humped, bumped, and dumped"—referring to the fate of the Karl–Paul character.)

together, for a short while at least; they had something in common, a shared experience. (Christopher couldn't resist telling Collier about it, however. Collier was delighted. He rolled on the floor, laughing. Thereafter, when Christopher came into his office in the morning, Collier would ask, "Well, my boy, what have you to report—of grave or gay?") Steve was treated by a different doctor—a woman, I think—and quickly cured.

On June 7, Christopher went to a party at Rex Evans's apartment; among the guests were Maugham, George Cukor and Ethel Barrymore.

It seems to me that this must have been at the beginning of the time when Willie was staying with George Cukor and working on a script of *The Razor's Edge*.[1] It was quite possibly at this party that Christopher witnessed a truly classic display of unabashed ass licking. Someone—I'm nearly sure it was Charlie Brackett—was talking to Maugham about a film they had watched together, a short while before. This someone said: "Mr. Maugham, I don't know whether you remember—*I* certainly shall never forget it—as we were coming out of that theater, you made one of the most penetrating, one of the most *profound* criticisms I have *ever* heard in my life—you said, *It's not dramatic!*" Willie didn't reply, but he looked at the speaker with his old old black eyes—and the look said all that was necessary.

This was the first time that Christopher had seen Willie since January 1941, when Willie visited Los Angeles with Gerald Haxton. Christopher had lately been told by Bill Caskey that he had been having an affair with Haxton in those days, and that Haxton had invited him to come out to California with him and Willie. Caskey had refused, for some reason, although he had liked Haxton very much. And now Haxton was dead; he had died in 1944. The day-to-day diary doesn't record that Caskey ever went with Christopher to see Willie during his visit. Perhaps Caskey felt Willie wouldn't want to see him, because of the association with Haxton.

June 9: "Saw *The Letter* in projection room. Helped Steve move his things to Rose Garden Apartments."

This was the Bette Davis film version of the Maugham play, with its punishment-murder of Mrs. Crosbie tacked onto the story as a

---

[1] According to Garson Kanin (*Remembering Mr. Maugham*), Willie didn't begin work on his screenplay until November. Kanin says that Willie asked Cukor to show him the existing screenplay and was so horrified by it that he offered to write one himself, for free. I am almost sure Kanin is wrong about the date, however.

(June 24, 1977: Kanin *was* wrong. I have just seen the revised final draft of Maugham's *Razor's Edge* screenplay. It is dated July 25, 1945.)

concession to the censorship code. Maybe Christopher and Willie saw it together. Anyhow Willie did see the film about this time and, on being asked how he had liked it, made the famous answer, "I liked all the p-parts I wrote."

The Rose Garden Apartments was where Christopher and Vernon Old had stayed for about a month in 1939—their first Hollywood home. Perhaps Christopher had recommended it to Steve for this reason. But the room Steve got was dark and depressing, down in the basement, with walls so thin that you could hear whatever was said next door. Sex making was embarrassing and therefore apt to become defiantly noisy or to break up in self-conscious giggles.

June 18: "Supper at Players with Swami and Maugham." This was probably the first of Maugham's conferences with Swami about his screenplay for *The Razor's Edge*. There were other meetings later at which Cukor was present. Maugham and Cukor wanted Swami to tell them exactly what Shri Ganesha would have taught Larry. So Swami wrote it out for them, as concisely as he could. And Maugham put it into his screenplay—presumably.[1]

The Players Restaurant on the Sunset Strip was in those days

---

[1] When Maugham was about to publish *The Razor's Edge*, in 1944, he had written to Swami for an exact translation of the verse from the Katha Upanishad on which the title of the novel is based. Swami (or maybe Christopher) had replied, explaining carefully that the image of a razor's edge is used to suggest a narrow and painful path (the path to enlightenment) and that therefore one should *not* say, "It is difficult to cross," as some translators do, but rather, "It is difficult to tread." Maugham ignored this piece of advice, however. The translation he used in his novel was, "The sharp edge of a razor is difficult to pass over," which is almost as ambiguous as "to cross."

I don't remember that I ever saw a copy of Willie's screenplay. It was never used. Cukor left the picture and it was finally directed by Edmund Goulding, with a new script (or perhaps a revised version of the original one) by Lamar Trotti. Christopher, at Swami's suggestion, wrote to Trotti, offering free technical advice on the Indian sequence. Trotti never answered. And when the picture was made the Indian scenes had several mistakes in them. Shri Ganesha's teaching was idiotically distorted.

Cukor's choice for the role of Larry was a young unknown amateur named John Russell, who had just left the Marine Corps. He was good looking, and Cukor still (June 1972) maintains that the test they shot of him was excellent. Some of the studio executives thought him too tall, however—he was six foot four—and this was one reason why he didn't get the part when the film was taken over by Goulding. John Russell afterwards worked quite a bit in films and in television, but he never really made a hit. Cukor remembers that he met Russell later and that he was drunk and looked terrible.

Prabhavananda doesn't remember that Cukor ever brought Russell to see

almost a club, as the Brown Derby had once been. Christopher went there quite often—particularly with van Druten, who used to refer to it as "*our* place." He also often saw Keith Winter there, very drunk and inclined to be weepy about his life and sorrows. (Not long after this, Keith had a breakdown and then stopped drinking.)

Steve had started going to dramatic classes at Ouspenskaya's school—this is first referred to on June 12. As far as I remember, the classes consisted largely of learning to sway like corn in the wind and to break like sea waves. I don't think Steve persevered in this for long.

At this time, Christopher was interested in consulting clairvoyants. His motive was partly a wish to know what was going to happen to him, but it was also, and to a much greater degree, scientific curiosity. He was, he said to himself, at a point in his life at which the future seemed altogether obscure—all he knew was that he would soon leave the Vedanta Center, and he had no idea what would happen next. Therefore his was an ideal test case for the powers of precognition which a clairvoyant is supposed to have.

I forget who the people were that Christopher consulted—the unfamiliar names which occur in the day-to-day diary at this time give no definite clue. All I remember is one curious episode: A clairvoyant (who otherwise told Christopher nothing memorable) said, "Quite soon, in a few hours, a close friend of yours will get into serious trouble, he will be arrested—but don't worry, everything will come out all right." That same evening, Steve was walking along the street when he was stopped by the shore patrol and asked to identify himself. This happened all the time, for there were a lot of servicemen going around AWOL in civilian clothes. Steve had been in the navy (in an office in Utah or Nebraska) and had received an honorable discharge. He was supposed to carry this discharge with him at all times, but he had left it at home that evening, which was an offense. So he was under arrest for a while, until the discharge had been produced. He was then cautioned and set free. Christopher knew nothing of this until Steve called and told him, next day.

---

him. But Edmund Goulding did bring Russell's successor, Tyrone Power. Swami was, and still is, scornful about Power. He says that he asked Power if he understood what Larry is supposed to believe, and that Power admitted that he didn't. Some versions of the story of their meeting state that Swami said, "Mr. Power, you are not worthy to play Larry!", but Swami denies that he said this. Seeing Swami must have scared poor Power out of whatever wits he possessed, so it's no wonder he made a bad impression. In the last analysis, Power's lack of understanding was the fault of Trotti and the stupidities of his script.

The day-to-day diary records two more Swami–Maugham meetings; on June 29, Willie came to supper at the Vedanta Center and on July 6 Swami and Christopher went to supper at George Cukor's with Ethel Barrymore and Katharine Hepburn also present. I can recall nothing of these. But I do remember, with impressionistic vividness, another, daytime occasion when Christopher was summoned to Cukor's house because Maugham wanted to speak to him. I have a picture of Christopher making his way through a succession of rooms like Chinese boxes, each one smaller than the last and all crammed with paintings and souvenirs and treasures, into the innermost sanctuary, where Willie sits writing and looks up from his work to say, "I think, C–Christopher, you'd b–better warn your friend Denham that his apartment is b–being watched by the p–police." (What I do not remember is, how Willie had heard this bit of information. It seems to me that Denny had been reported to the police because of his association with minors, including probably Jeff and Curly. But nothing serious came of it. Denny was very impressed and pleased that Willie had taken the trouble to warn him.)[1]

On July 26, Christopher had lunch with Miss Dicky Bonaparte, the immigration counsellor who had helped him get his quota visa and take out his first citizenship papers in 1939. This must mean that they were discussing the steps he must take to get his citizenship; he was now eligible for it. At that time, no conscientious objector could become a citizen because no exceptions or reservations were allowed in taking the loyalty oath; you had to swear to defend the country, no matter what your age and sex were. Christopher had been advised that he should apply for citizenship, however—because soon the regulations might be altered and because, if he didn't apply, his application might be refused later. So he applied, and went downtown to talk to someone in the immigration bureau. This official was not merely understanding but really friendly; it happened that he had liked some of Christopher's books. He even urged Christopher to take the oath anyway, "After all, it's just a form of words." Christopher was charmed by such civilized cynicism, but he wasn't about to commit himself to a public lie which might be used against him sometime in the future by a less friendly bureaucrat. So, with an air of modest nobility, he refused.

□

[1] I don't remember that Denny and Willie ever got together during this visit; but it seems to me that Denny used to brag that he had been admired by Willie—at any rate from a distance—when he was in Europe before the war. Curiously enough, Denny and Willie were to die on the same day, December 16; Denny in 1948, Maugham in 1965.

All through July, Christopher had continued to see Steve. The day-to-day diary mentions only one meeting with Caskey—they had spent the night on the beach, July 21. But at the beginning of August, a change is evident. Christopher sees Steve on the 1st and has supper with him on the 3rd. On the 4th, Denny is away in Mexico and Christopher stays at his apartment with Caskey. After that, Christopher and Caskey begin seeing each other regularly and there are no more meetings with Steve—except for a supper with Steve and his mother, probably a duty date, on August 22.

My memories of this switchover are very dim; perhaps incidents and conversations have been censored by Christopher's feelings of guilt. Christopher's guilt, if any, is uninteresting. The only important question is, did Steve mind being dropped? I think he probably did, much more than he showed; but I don't believe he let it upset him for long. He was very self-reliant. It seems to me that Steve once said, "If I had a lot of money and could invite you out, everything would be different." This (if he did indeed say it) was touching but quite untrue. Christopher never minded paying, as long as he was sure his guest wasn't a gold digger—and never for one moment did he suspect Steve of that. Caskey didn't have any money, either.

Caskey or no Caskey, Christopher would have left Steve before long—because Steve didn't fit into the rest of his life. Steve embarrassed him in every way, not only when they were in company but even when they were alone together. When Steve told Christopher that he thought him much better looking than Gary Cooper, Christopher was amused, of course, but he also felt depressed by the absurdity of the comparison. This was the wrong myth, the wrong kind of playacting; he couldn't go along with it. Even while they were screwing, Christopher often felt it was like a scene out of *True Confessions*.[*] And, when other people were there, Christopher always was aware of being on the defensive. He was watching to see how they would react to Steve. Would they decide, like Denny, that Steve was "a department-store queen"? If Christopher had reached any real intimacy with Steve, he would have been ready to defy everybody. But he hadn't and therefore he wasn't. He wasn't prepared to quarrel with his friends if they looked down on Steve, so he avoided taking the risk; he didn't introduce Steve to the Beesleys or to Peggy Kiskadden or to Salka Viertel or to John van Druten.

All this sounds as if Steve swished, lisped, wriggled, wore makeup,

[* The American magazine.]

elaborate hairdos and flaming costumes. But he didn't. He was quiet, pleasant, unsulky, well behaved. It wasn't that he was, socially speaking, *too much*, he wasn't *enough*. Christopher was a sexual snob—like most other people—and he needed a lover who could impress his friends.

Bill Caskey, on the other hand, *was* socially presentable—indeed, to a remarkable degree, if you considered how wildly he could misbehave in public, when he chose. "Earthy," outspoken, crude, vulgar, violent as he could sometimes be, he was also able to project a southern upper-class charm to go with his Kentucky accent. Red-eyed, drunk and unshaven, he looked every inch a Eugene O'Neill Irish lowlife character; washed and shaved and sober, dressed in a Brooks Brothers shirt and suit, he was fit for the nicest homes. Caskey really was a social amphibian, and Christopher was hugely impressed and attracted by this quality in him; he was—as he was later to prove—equally at home talking to the famous, or to little old ladies, or to fellow prisoners in jail, or to shipmates on an oil tanker; and, unless he was in the mood to pick a fight, nearly everybody liked him.

He was small—smaller than Christopher—very sturdily built, with square shoulders and the slightly bowed legs of a horseman. His brown hair was curly and he wore it very short to conceal this as much as possible. ("A crop-headed rascal" was Collier's description of him.) His grey-blue eyes looked sleepy and his voice had a lazy sound. His over large but well-shaped head and his thick lips both had that Negroid quality which is so often apparent in the white Southerner. His body was sexily covered with a close fuzz of curly hair; there was even quite a lot on his back. He had very bad teeth (which he had the knack of hiding even when he smiled), a biggish cock and only one testicle.

Although Caskey was still so young, he wasn't in the least boyish. He had an impressive air of having "been around"—as indeed he had. He was quite without shyness, even in the presence of the old and the wise; it was this freedom from shyness which made him able to treat them so unaffectedly, and to charm them. (Both Stravinsky and Forster were delighted with him; Stravinsky said of him, "He's my type.") He had a domestic quality which made Christopher feel cozy and looked after, in the periods between their blazing home-wrecking rows. From this aspect, Christopher often reacted to him as if to a woman of his own age; he used to say that Caskey and he were like a sophisticated French married couple, the kind who address each other as "dear friend." He also saw Caskey as a kind of nanny.

Caskey had been in the navy for a while, but not overseas. He had avoided military service as long as he could and had got into some fairly serious trouble with the draft by failing to register or report. His lover, Len Hanna, an elderly and very wealthy man, had used his expensive lawyer to straighten things out. But the navy—in Florida or New Orleans or both—had turned out to be a bore, with lots of office work, which could only be relieved by parties and sex. Caskey had slept around a great deal, and then came one of those big homosexual witch-hunts; a few boys were caught and they named names. Caskey was implicated and so was his friend Hayden Lewis. (Hayden was a civilian employed by the navy in some clerical job. He and Caskey shared an apartment during several months of Caskey's service—they were what used to be called "sisters," not lovers.) As Hayden was a civilian, he was merely fired. Caskey got a "blue discharge," neither honorable nor dishonorable. When he met Len Hanna again, he realized that he didn't want to live with Hanna anymore, so he and Hayden decided to come to California.

Many people found Hayden Lewis attractive, and indeed he could then have been described as handsome; he had a pale romantic melancholy face which suggested to Christopher a young nineteenth-century Catholic priest of the Oscar Wilde period. But Hayden wasn't really a romantic, his temperament was peevish, he sighed and whined and shrugged his shoulders and bitched people in a soft voice. He was one of nature's underlings, full of envy; his approach was demure until he had detected your weak points and was ready to play on them. . . . In a word, Christopher disliked him intensely from their first meeting and Hayden undoubtedly felt the same way about Christopher. But Christopher had to get along with Hayden for Caskey's sake, and Hayden had to get along with Christopher.

Christopher worked hard at this, to begin with, even though he knew that Hayden was trying to sabotage his relationship with Caskey by making fun of him. (It got back to him that Hayden called Caskey "Mrs. Reverend," with the implication that Christopher was a sort of swami-curate.) Later on, there were at least two or three yelling scenes with Hayden—all started by Christopher, when drunk. But their association always had to be patched up because it was simply too tiresome for them to refuse to see each other, as long as Caskey and Christopher were living together. When Caskey and Christopher split up, they immediately stopped meeting.

Aside from Denny's apartment, Caskey and Christopher spent much of their time together at The Friendship or at Jay's apartment or in the kitchen of his restaurant.

The Friendship[1] had been doing terrific business throughout the war years and it was still crammed every weekend with servicemen and their pursuers, female and male. It was also the chief neighborhood bar and one of the very few gay bars in West Los Angeles. In other words, if you went in there, you had to be prepared to mingle with all sorts and conditions. I imagine that the more respectable Canyon dwellers had long since decided to stay away.

The noise was stunning, the tobacco smoke was a fog; you always spilled part of your drink as you eased your way through the crowd. There were little tables you could sit at in pairs, your faces close together, yelling intimacies which no one else had a chance of hearing. This was the scene of Christopher's courtship of Caskey; they seem to have felt more at ease with each other in such a state of public isolation than when they were actually alone together.

It must have been at this time that Caskey was earning some extra money washing dishes at Jay's restaurant. Christopher used to come down in the evenings and help, for free. There was always plenty to drink and Christopher quite enjoyed dishwashing; he had done a lot of it while he was with the Quakers and at the Vedanta Center. Jay and his waiters (who were usually also his boyfriends) darted back and forth between the kitchen and the tiny dark dining room, from

[1] The Friendship at this period is described in *A Single Man* as "The Starboard Side." The sentence about "Girls dashing down from their apartments to drag some gorgeous endangered young drunk to safety and breakfast served next morning in bed . . ." refers to Jo Lathwood's capture of Ben Masselink. Jo was living at her apartment on West Channel Road ("Las Ondas"), only a few doors from The Friendship, throughout this period, but Christopher didn't get to know her until later.

Peter Viertel writes about The Friendship and its owner, Doc Law, in his first novel *The Canyon*. He calls Doc Law "Doc Winters" and The Friendship "The Schooner Café." He also mentions the pharmacy which Doc Law ran, right next to the bar. (The wall between them has been broken down now, and the extra space is sometimes used for dancing.)

Doc Law spent most of the daytime in the pharmacy, drunk. His drugs looked as if they had aged to mere dust in their glass jars. Christopher used to say that one could have gone in there and swallowed spoonfuls from all the jars marked "poison" without coming to the slightest harm. Here are two items about Doc from the notebook [mentioned pp. 14-15, 21, 25] (date unknown):

Doc Law, on the oil strike in New York: "They're a long way from Christ." . . . I go to Doc Law to plead for some toilet paper, during the shortage. Doc is in a good mood. He is printing an announcement—something about "a large assortment"—on a long roll of paper, with a rubber stamp and a ruler to keep the letters in line. "Sure," he answers, "you can wipe your ass with me any time you want to, kid."

which they would return with whispered gossip. The place had already become well known to columnists; there would be at least one movie celebrity among the customers nearly every evening. The chief attraction was Jay's rich gooey French food. And the dimness of the lighting and the depth of the alcoves appealed to well-known people who wanted privacy. I remember much gossip about Charles Laughton's visits there with young men. Jay was a perfect host. He knew how to recognize and flatter without making an indiscreet fuss.

On August 14, Japan accepted the Allied terms of surrender. I can't remember if this was the day on which gasoline rationing was officially stopped, but I do remember a great outburst of automobile driving—just driving for driving's sake—about this time. The result was that the Coast Highway was littered with black chunks of wartime recap rubber which flew off people's tires as soon as they started speeding.

On August 23, Christopher finally moved his things out of the Vedanta Center and into the chauffeur's apartment (so called) which adjoined the house the Beesleys were living in, on the Coast Highway. It was understood that this was to be only a short visit, for Christopher was already planning to set up housekeeping with Caskey in the near future. (I don't remember any farewell scene with Swami, and I have no doubt that Christopher did everything he could to make their parting seem temporary and without any particular significance.)

"The chauffeur's apartment" was simply a bedroom and a bathroom. It was right on the highway and the rumble and rattle of trucks at night would have been hard to get used to if it hadn't been balanced and thus cancelled out by the roar of the waves on the shingle. Christopher found it very snug and he revelled in its complete privacy; it was altogether separate from the house and no noise he could have made would have been loud enough to reach the Beesleys' ears or make their dogs bark. He could even go in swimming after dark without their seeing him. What a change, after two and a half years of semipublic community life!

Caskey and Christopher now saw each other nearly every day and often Caskey stayed the night at the chauffeur's apartment. They spent a lot of time together with Denny, Johnny Goodwin, Hayden Lewis and the Beesleys. (The Beesleys liked Caskey and Denny; Johnny and Hayden they saw only very seldom.) Caskey also met Peggy Kiskadden, Iris Tree and Vernon. As far as I remember, Peggy behaved quite graciously, though she did momentarily enrage Christopher by bitchily pretending to think that Caskey was the reason why Christopher had left the Vedanta Center. (She knew perfectly well that this wasn't true, for Christopher had told her repeatedly that he was going to leave, long before Caskey had even arrived in California.) Iris welcomed Caskey without reservations, as she welcomed all her friends' lovers, and they remained on good terms thenceforward. Vernon, now a confirmed heterosexual, endorsed this new affair of Christopher's with condescending amusement, saying, "He's about your speed."

On September 21, Christopher finished work at Warner's (apparently) and celebrated this by buying a secondhand Lincoln Zephyr convertible, a flashy car which was much better suited than the Packard[1] to his show-off role of Uncle to the Denny–Johnny–Caskey gang. One amusing quirk of the Lincoln was that its speedometer would get out of whack at high speeds; if you were doing 80, it would sometimes climb to 110. When this happened with Denny on board, he would pretend that they were all a bunch of pleasure-mad teenagers of the 1920s, drunk on bathtub gin, and yell "Let 'er rip!" and "Flaming youth!"

On September 25, Christopher was called back to Warner's, but only for a few days' work; there was some polishing to be done on the *Up at the Villa* script. On September 29, it was finished.

This was also the day on which Denny left for New York—the day-to-day diary notes that he did so "by air," this being still regarded as a chic and rather daring way to travel.[2] Christopher and Caskey took over his apartment from him, moving in that same day. Christopher never returned to the apartment at the Beesleys'.

Also on the 29th, a visit to a Dr. Williams is mentioned. I think

---

[1] Christopher didn't trade the Packard in, when he bought the Zephyr. The allowance on it would anyhow have been tiny. Instead, he decided to give it to Hayden Lewis—thereby pleasing and greatly impressing Caskey, as was his intention. This started a tradition, that the Packard must always be given away; to sell it would bring terribly bad luck. And so, during the next few years, the Packard changed owners for free at least half a dozen times. It was a very tough car and lived long.

[2] Sometime before this, Denny must have had the Picasso (see April 13, 1944 [in *D1*]) crated and removed from his apartment to be shipped east. While he was away in the East—in New York, I think—he sold the Picasso to a private buyer, someone he met at a cocktail party, I believe. Denny was very pleased with himself for having arranged this, and said that the sum of money he got for it was far more than the dealers had offered him. Fact and fiction mingle at this point—I can't now be sure if $9,500, the figure I give in *Down There on a Visit*, is correct or not. Anyhow, the picture was eventually resold for something like $40,000. I think it's now in Chicago, in one of the museums. [It is in New York, in the Museum of Modern Art; see Glossary under Fouts.]

this was due to a recurrence of the penis trouble referred to on page 23 of this volume but I can't remember what the symptoms were exactly, except that they were painful. The constriction, or whatever it was, continued, on and off, until the beginning of 1946, when Christopher had the operation which will be described in due course.

On October 1, Caskey and Christopher started on a long motor trip in the Lincoln, which lasted nearly three weeks. Their itinerary was as follows:

October 1. They drove to Santa Barbara, stayed with Denny's sister, Ellen Bowman. October 2. They drove to Carmel. October 3. They visited Monterey. October 4–7. They drove to San Francisco and stayed there three days, at the Hotel Richelieu. October 7. They drove to Fresno. October 8. They drove into Yosemite and back. October 9. They drove through Sequoia Park to Bakersfield. October 10. They drove to Las Vegas, and visited Boulder Dam from there on the 11th. October 12. They drove to Phoenix, stayed at the Hotel Adams. October 13. They drove to El Centro and had supper in Calexico. (Caskey wanted to drive across the border to Mexicali but Christopher wouldn't; as he was still a British subject, he was afraid there might be difficulties when he tried to reenter the States.) October 14. They drove to Johnny Goodwin's ranch, near Escondido. (This was a house called Armageddon, which Johnny had had built for himself. From outside, it looked rather like an Egyptian temple, massive and secret, with a great pillared portal and very few windows. When you entered, you found that the rooms all opened onto an interior courtyard. Johnny had valuable furniture and pictures—including a very striking Miró, one of the few Mirós I have ever really liked.) October 15. They drove to Palm Springs, stayed at the Estrella Villa. October 16. They had dinner with Carter Lodge at La Quinta. October 17. They drove back to Johnny Goodwin's ranch. October 18. They drove to Laguna Beach and had supper with Chris Wood and Gerald Heard. They drove back to Santa Monica and Denny's apartment on October 19.

Oddly enough, I remember almost nothing about this trip; my memories of the places they went to are connected with earlier or later visits. I remember that their stay with Johnny Goodwin was passed largely in playing guessing games and charades. In one of these, Caskey gave himself the name "Miss Bijou Slyboots"—did he invent it? At Laguna, Gerald Heard was rather cool to Caskey and Christopher; he disapproved of their relationship on principle, regarding it as a betrayal of Swami's trust in Christopher. (Maybe Peggy had been talking to him about this.) Chris Wood had no such scruples. He approved of Caskey. But, with his usual frankness, he asked Christopher, "Surely he hasn't got the kind of legs you like, has he?"

On their return to Denny's apartment, Hayden Lewis moved in with them. This must have been understood from the beginning to be a temporary arrangement—until, presumably, Hayden could find another place to live, or a job. But the fact that Christopher agreed to it at all shows that his relations with Caskey were still in the honeymoon stage. The apartment consisted of two rooms only, and he must have hated having Hayden around. The day-to-day diary doesn't say when Hayden left, but he can't have stayed long—maybe not more than two weeks.

On November 17, they had another visitor, the Willy Tompkins who had publicly fucked on Denny's couch at the party in June. He was out of the navy, now, and determined to enjoy himself. Not that he had had such a bad time in the service. Willy belonged to that amazing breed of hero-queens who are able to see war itself as camp. According to him, the battles of the South Pacific were primarily erotic events; all members of the crew who weren't actually firing guns would pair off in corners for high-speed sex. Between explosions, you would hear someone gasp out, "Kiss me, quick, I'm going to come!" Even if they were exaggerated, Willy's stories were none the less beautiful; they were so magnificently death-denying.

One night while Willy was with them, Christopher lay awake (but pretending to be asleep) listening to a conversation about himself between Willy and Caskey. Willy was evidently a bit skeptical about Christopher as a lover, considering his age. But Caskey, more than somewhat drunk, assured Willy, "He's the best lay on the Pacific Coast!" This testimonial must have impressed Willy, for next day, when the three of them were at the then bare-ass Riviera Beach and Caskey had gone off for a stroll, Willy made a pass at Christopher. Christopher would have responded with pleasure, but Caskey reappeared unexpectedly.

On November 22, Caskey, Hayden, Willy Tompkins and Christopher drove down to Johnny Goodwin's ranch for a four-day visit. On November 28, Willy left.

Early in November, *Prater Violet* was reviewed by *Time*, which said it was "a fresh, firm peach in a dish of waxed fruits." Also by Diana Trilling, who really and truly liked it; and by James T. Farrell, who discovered it to be so fraught with political irony and analysis of contemporary culture that it couldn't have been better if it had been written by James T. Farrell himself—as indeed it almost was, by the time he was through describing it. Nearly all the reviews were favorable, and the book sold quite well.

The *Time* reviewer reported that he had been told Isherwood was "now at work on a novel about physically and spiritually 'displaced persons.'" On January 13 of 1946, Philip K. Scheuer published an interview with Christopher in *The Los Angeles Times* in which Christopher tells him that *Prater Violet* was the first of three novelettes about refugees: "They will cover the whole period of immigration between Hitler and the war." Christopher said that he was then at work on the second of these novelettes. One of them must have been about Haverford, I suppose. Maybe the other was about the Greek island, or about the adventures of the girl who is called Dorothy in *Down There on a Visit*—I can't remember. I'm inclined to suspect that Christopher was bluffing when he made these reports. I doubt if he wrote anything much, as long as he was living in the Entrada Drive apartment. One memory of any living place (no matter how temporary) which I nearly always retain is the memory of the spot where I worked. At Entrada Drive I simply cannot picture it. And besides it seems to me that Caskey and Christopher spent most of their time entertaining, and drinking, and having hangovers in the mornings.

Christopher did do one small writing job at home, however. Apparently, it took him only one day—December 28. This was a short film outline. It was based on a ghost story which had been told him by a young man named Lynn Perkins. Christopher had met Lynn Perkins on March 7 of that year; the day-to-day diary doesn't say where. I think Perkins had wanted Christopher to write this story for him right from the start of their acquaintanceship; he was not only very persistent but quite pretty (though unqueer), which was no doubt why Christopher agreed to do so. Later, Christopher went with Perkins to at least one studio (maybe two or three) and made a sales pitch for the story. I have the impression that someone very nearly bought it.

The Beesleys had left their house on the Coast Highway on November 11; Christopher and Caskey helped them move into another one, on the old Malibu Road, just beyond the Colony.[*] The Malibu Road had few houses along it in those days and Alec was able to take the dalmatians out unleashed and let them run on the long empty beach. The house itself was comfortable though rather small, built of wood with shingles, Californian-British cottage style. Christopher and Caskey saw the Beesleys several times during the month of December and ate Christmas dinner with them. They must have also had Dodie and Alec up to the apartment, though the day-

[* The Malibu Colony, a gated beach community.]

to-day diary doesn't mention this; their visits would anyhow have been brief because they would have had to leave the dalmatians in the car and take turns at visiting and dog-sitting—the dogs were seldom allowed in anyone else's home. (Even when they were politely urged to bring the dogs in with them, Dodie and Alec would usually decline, saying that, if they did so, the whole place would be wrecked. They said this with a certain pride—indeed, they liked to think of the dalmatians as being even more violent than they actually were.)

During December, Christopher and Caskey did a lot of entertaining.[1] The day-to-day diary mentions the following guests: Johnny Goodwin, Don Forbes, Dave Eberhardt (see page 11), Bo and Kelley (see pages 17-18), Helen Kennedy (Sudhira), John van Druten, Carter Lodge, Chris Wood, Aldous and Maria Huxley, Peggy and Bill Kiskadden, Salka, Peter and Tommy Viertel, Dick LaPan, the actress Ludmilla Pitoëff and her daughter Anita, Vernon Old (who was [going out] with Anita), Natalia Pascal (who was interested in the Lynn Perkins story), Lynn Perkins, John Cowan and Rob Cartwright,[*] Jay.

John Cowan had been Jay's boyfriend for a short while; then he left Jay because he had fallen in love with Rob Cartwright, and the two of them started living together. But John had been a familiar figure in the Canyon for some time already—a year at least. He was a big blond boy with an extraordinarily beautiful body. Even Bill Harris acknowledged his beauty and jokingly accepted him as a rival, calling him "The Imposter." This nickname had been shortened to "Poster." Christopher called him "the last of The Great Boys."

John Cowan was admirably narcissistic. On the beach, he would sunbathe with his trunks off, squeezing them into a ball and placing them so that they just covered his cock, but not his bush. He then would fall asleep or pretend to, make some movement and thus dislodge the trunks, leaving himself stark naked. There was usually a circle of Cowan watchers lying around him on the sand. John got himself watched after dark, as well, for he strolled around all evening

[1] They also went to see the Ballet Russe de Monte Carlo three times during its visit to Los Angeles—on November 30 (the opening night) with Hayden Lewis, on December 4 with John Goodwin and Hayden, on December 7 with Bo and Kelley. Among the stars of that season were Leon Danielian (who danced *L'Après-midi d'un faune*), [Alexandra] Danilova, Maria Tallchief, Nicholas Magallanes, Herbert Bliss. Balanchine's *Ballet Imperial* was on the program.

[* Not his real name.]

in his trunks. If the weather was cold and he was wearing a sweater he would always take it off as soon as he got inside his friends' homes and sprawl in an armchair with his gorgeous legs wide apart. You couldn't take your eyes off them.

John had a sister named Rita; she was pretty but loud [. . .]. John and she had terrific fights, they were both as strong as apes and John was often the only person able to remove her when she misbehaved at a party.

Rob Cartwright was dark and fairly nice looking but no one could quite understand what John Cowan saw in him. As a pair, they were known as "Poster and Rattles," because Rob Cartwright talked a lot. So, as a matter of fact, did John.

I think I remember that Peggy, when she visited the Entrada Drive apartment, was slightly shocked—for two of the pictures Denny had put up were conversation pieces, to say the least. Both were army posters, warning against the dangers of venereal disease. One of them showed a whore, with a beret over one eye and a cigarette drooping out of a corner of her mouth, standing under a lamppost. This was captioned: "She may be a bag of trouble." The other was simply a diagram of a penis, with dotted red lines to show the spreading of gonorrheal infection up the urethra and into the bladder.

On New Year's Eve, Christopher and Caskey gave a party. This isn't recorded in the day-to-day diary, and I don't remember who was invited—only that, while Caskey made preparations, Christopher sat compulsively skimming through the last pages of *The Past Recaptured* because he had vowed to finish Proust before the end of 1945.[1]

---

[1] Here are [a] few other books read during 1945—from a list in the 1945 day-to-day diary: Cyril Connolly's *The Unquiet Grave* (a book I have never stopped dipping into, because it contains the essence of Cyril's enthusiasms and lovable faults—his literary snobbery, his rash generalizations based on misinformation, his confessions of angst and ill health, his Francophilia—it is amazing how readable he is, and in an area where nearly everybody else is intolerable). George Moore's *Evelyn Innes* and *Sister Theresa*. (These appealed enormously to Christopher at that time, with his then vivid memories of the horrors of monastic life. I still find the ending of *Sister Theresa* tremendous. About the work as a whole, I'm not so sure that it is the masterpiece I once thought it.) Edmund Wilson's *The Wound and the Bow* (I still find the essay on Dickens very exciting). *Brideshead Revisited* by Evelyn Waugh. (At that time, Christopher found something moving in Waugh's sentimentality and the daringly nauseating phrases he uses, both sexual and religious; they seemed to express a special kind of sincerity. A rereading not long ago rediscovered nothing but the nausea.) Christopher was fascinated by G. N. M. Tyrrell's *Science and Psychical Phenomena* (this tied in with his phase of interest in clairvoyants, see page 39). He was

1946

Since there isn't any day-to-day diary for 1946, I shall have to describe the happenings of that year much more vaguely and impressionistically. But before I get on to that, I'll write something about the early stages of the Caskey–Christopher relationship.

As has been said already, Christopher got involved with Caskey partly because Denny had dared him to do it. A bit later, when Caskey and Christopher were already going together, Christopher got another kind of dare—from Hayden Lewis. Hayden warned Christopher, in his soft-voiced mocking way, that Caskey was "a bad boy," implying that he didn't think Christopher would be able to handle him. As Caskey's best friend, Hayden could speak with authority; his warning was impressive, even if bitchily intended. Christopher must have known, even in those early days, what Hayden meant by calling Caskey "bad." But the challenge excited Christopher far more than it deterred him. Caskey's temperament, with all its unpredictability, offered Christopher a new way of life. Part of the polarity between them was that of Irishman[1] and Englishman.

Their relationship demanded violence. Christopher found that, in certain situations, he could only relate to Caskey by losing control of himself, and getting really angry—which he hated doing because it rattled all the screws of his English self-restraint loose and made him feel humiliated and exhausted for hours afterwards. During these scenes, he would yell at Caskey and occasionally hit him. Caskey, who was stronger than Christopher, very seldom hit him back.[2] To have provoked the blow was, for Caskey, a kind of triumph. Even when he got a black eye or a bloody nose, his face would betray a deep sensual satisfaction.

These clashes took place when they were both drunk, but their drinking together didn't necessarily lead to violence. Much more

---

thrilled by Nigel Balchin's *The Small Back Room*, with its harrowing bomb-detonation scene. He also read with interest and admiration James's "Lady Barberina" and "The Author of Beltraffio," Gide's *Lafcadio's Adventures*, John Collier's *His Monkey Wife*—but they haven't made any lasting impression.

[1] Christopher always thought of Caskey as being much more Irish than American. Actually, Caskey was also part Cherokee Indian. He himself believed that this strain was dominant.

[2] When Caskey did hit Christopher, Christopher seldom hit him back, either. One such occasion is mentioned in *The Condor and the Cows*—at Trujillo, Peru, on December 12, 1947.

often, it made them lively and noisy or intimate and quiet. From Christopher's point of view, at any rate, drinking was a built-in dimension of their relationship; while sober, he felt, they never achieved intimacy. Christopher spent their first months together trying to get Caskey to make a real unequivocal declaration of love. But Caskey was cagey—perhaps because he instinctively realized that this was actually, underneath all Christopher's sweet-talking, a conflict of wills. Christopher felt himself becoming seriously involved and he didn't want to be, until he was certain that Caskey was involved, too. He was willing Caskey to give way. When Caskey had done so and become his declared lover—well, then Christopher would be able to relax, take his time and decide finally if he wanted Caskey or if he didn't. Probably he did. He merely wanted to be able to make his decision from a position of strength. He was saying, in effect, "Just because I don't trust you, that's no reason why you shouldn't trust *me*."

(Looking back on the situation, it seems to me that Caskey never did *quite* commit himself. Later on, he told Christopher that he loved him, but these declarations were nearly always followed by actions which seemed meant to contradict them; he would neck with someone at a party in Christopher's presence, or he would go out and stay away all night.)

The furthest Caskey would go, during these first months, was to say, "I like you *enough*." But Christopher wasn't discouraged; he had reason to believe that Caskey cared for him a good deal more than he would admit. Hayden reported to Christopher that Caskey had said, speaking of their relationship, "It's so wonderful to be liked." This doesn't sound wildly enthusiastic, but Christopher was well aware how embarrassing it must be for Caskey to confess to *any* feeling for Christopher in Hayden's presence; Christopher was certainly an improvement on Len Hanna but, still and all, he was seventeen years older than Caskey! Christopher thought he could read, in Hayden's manner toward him, a grudging admission that Caskey had fallen for him, and that Hayden, much as he deplored the fact, could do nothing about it.

Caskey was fond of telling Christopher teasingly, "You've got nothing left but your reputation and your figure"—to which Christopher retorted that this was more than a lot of people could claim, at his age. Once, after they had been to an all-male party, Caskey said, "You know, I looked around and it was amazing—I realized I'd rather go to bed with you than anyone else in the room!" At the end of some heavy sex making in the Beesleys' chauffeur's apartment, Caskey was gracious enough to declare, "That's the best queer fuck I've had in ages!" His compliments nearly always contained such qualifications.

Caskey made a strict distinction between queer and straight fucks. If you were homosexual, you couldn't hope to be graded 1A; his greatest sexual pleasure was in going to bed with basically heterosexual men. He picked them up without difficulty and usually blew them. If he could get to fuck them, that was best of all. He used to say that straight bars were far better than queer bars for pickups. Caskey's preferences for heterosexual men irritated and frustrated Christopher throughout their relationship. Caskey went to bed with far more queers than straights, but he never let Christopher forget that this preference existed. Christopher sometimes suspected that it was Caskey's way of keeping him in line.

If you started to analyze Caskey's sexuality in psychological terms, you ran into paradoxes. On the surface, he was the most normal, most uninhibited of homosexuals; he seemed very tough yet very female. He loved getting into drag. He loved straight men. But, when you looked deeper, contradictions were revealed. Caskey despised queens and didn't think of himself as one. Never, never would he have dreamed of referring to himself as "Miss Caskey." His attitude to heterosexual men wasn't at all passive, he wanted to fuck, not be fucked by them. He never approached them with the mannerisms of a homosexual. Indeed, he told Christopher that, when he was out to make someone, he always dressed "very tweedy, with a tie." And yet he most certainly couldn't be described as a closet queen; he declared his homosexuality loudly and shamelessly and never cared whom he shocked. He was a pioneer gay militant in this respect—except that you couldn't imagine him joining any movement.

Since Caskey refused to regard himself as a queen, one might have expected him to prefer a somewhat effeminate homosexual sex-partner. But not at all. He was seldom attracted by feminine men. In a moment of enthusiasm, he once told Christopher that he was the most masculine person he had ever met—within grade 1B, of course. This pleased Christopher, although Caskey modified the statement later and then denied it altogether.

Caskey had a love–hate relationship with Catherine, his mother, and a hate–hate relationship with his two sisters. He regarded the American Woman as a man destroyer. Sometimes, only half-jokingly, he would say that he regarded himself as a substitute—no, "alternative" would be a better word—which he offered to the American Man. Years later, when Caskey was working on oil tankers and often crossed the Pacific, he found that he had no objection to having sex with Asian girls. But this didn't make him any less homosexual.

To judge from a photograph taken in his early twenties, Caskey's father had been very attractive and very like Caskey. Now (according to Caskey) he was an alcoholic miser with an ugly disposition. He and Caskey quarrelled whenever they met, but Caskey didn't altogether hate him—since he was an American Man and Catherine's victim. I seem to remember that Caskey's father had made a lot of money by breeding horses. Caskey himself had ridden since he was a child. He loved horses, and perhaps this was the only interest that he and his father had in common. I think Caskey's father and mother were now living apart.

The question arises, had Caskey been subconsciously on the lookout for a substitute father and was he now casting Christopher in this role? Yes, I think he was, to some extent. In Caskey's case, however, the father figure wasn't to be merely a stand-in for Mr. Caskey Senior; it was also a father confessor. The Caskeys were Catholics with a streak of black Irish Catholicism, and Bill Caskey, just because he had "lapsed," was the blackest of the lot. He betrayed this when he declared that he couldn't stand converts; the only Catholics he had any use for were born Catholics. Once, Caskey came near to asking Christopher right out to be his father confessor —when he muttered (drunk but nevertheless still embarrassed) that he wished Christopher would tell him whenever he did anything wrong.

Christopher was touched by this. And he was very happy indeed to find that Caskey was religious; it made him realize that he couldn't have lived with a boy who wasn't. He didn't at first mind at all that Caskey took no interest in Vedanta; it was enough that they both recognized the function of a shrine and could therefore kneel down together in any Catholic church.

The trouble was that both Caskey and Christopher were entering upon their relationship with powerful feelings of guilt. Caskey felt guilty not only as a lapsed Catholic but also as a dishonored navy man. (He had a tattoo on his arm which he had acquired during his days in the service, and he wore it as an emblem of nostalgia and a badge of shame. Later, he had another one added to it.) Christopher felt guilty as a failed monk. Neither of them would admit to their guilt, except by the violence with which they reacted against it. Their guilt feelings were self-regarding at first. But by degrees they began to involve each other in them. . . . There will be much more to say about this, further along in the story.

Nevertheless, despite growing tensions, they managed to have a good time together. Christopher enjoyed being with Caskey as long as the two of them were alone. Even the entertaining he enjoyed sometimes, at any rate after the guests had left and the strain was relaxed. And his sex life with Caskey was certainly enjoyable, within its limits.

"Limits" seems a strange word to be using, for they did everything in bed which normal homosexuals do—cocksucking, rimming and fucking. Rimming was the most satisfactory, from Christopher's point of view, because of its grossness. Caskey had a coarse animal smell which Christopher found exciting, when he was dirty and full of liquor and his fuzzy body was rank with sweat. Licking his sweaty armpits and belly fuzz and dirty asshole brought back memories of the Berlin hustlers—but Christopher had been much more fastidious in his youth, nowadays he was able to enter into the spirit of the thing. (How lucky they both were not to get hepatitis!) Caskey insisted on fucking Christopher, if Christopher was to fuck him. Christopher was thoroughly in favor of this, in principle; he believed (had, in fact, just then decided) that the true beauty of homosexuality lies in a balanced active-passive relationship. In practice, Caskey didn't really like being fucked. So Christopher let himself be fucked more and more often, until the time came when he stopped fucking Caskey altogether. Christopher could enjoy being fucked only if he found it possible to reverse gear psychologically and feel that he was giving himself and being possessed. He couldn't ever quite feel this with Caskey, who was smaller than himself and anyhow, from Christopher's point of view, unalterably female. Caskey might be tougher than any bull dyke but Christopher still couldn't see him as a stud. So the two of them were forced to playact. (They both were aware of this—no longtime sex partners can deceive each other—though of course they never discussed it.) Caskey would strip and put on a pair of cowboy boots. "You want to get the shit fucked out of you?" he would ask. Christopher would press the sole of one boot against his erection as Caskey greased Christopher's asshole and his own cock. But, at this point, something was missing and had to be faked—for Christopher must now roll over onto his belly and relax to let Caskey's cock into him. What was missing was some sort of token (at least) of violence and resistance, some hint of rape. And this was unthinkable. To try it would have been ludicrous. They just had to ignore the gap and get on to the fuck scene as quickly as possible—like actors covering up a joint in a crudely cut script.

Back in Berlin, in 1929, Dr. Magnus Hirschfeld of the Institut für Sexualwissenschaft had classified Christopher as "infantile," sexually speaking. This was perceptive. For Christopher then was and has since remained very much under the spell of his prepub[escent] sexual experiences at St. Edmund's School.[1] If he wasn't quite infantile he was definitely inclined to be small-boyish. At St. Edmund's, all of his orgasms with other boys had been while wrestling. (The other boys were probably having orgasms too, but he couldn't be sure because

[1] The statements made in this and the following paragraph raise, but do not answer, the question: *Why* is wrestling a feature of the Whitmanesque relationship? Here is an attempt at an answer, made after much introspection. It sounds corny and is embarrassing to put into words—which suggests that it may come fairly near to the truth.

Whitmanesque homosexuality is concerned with the mating of two completely masculine males. One of these males may be younger than the other, but both must be real men—no effeminate intergrades need apply. A Whitmanesque male must have acknowledged another male to be a real man before he can accept him as a lover. First, they must test each other's virility. Therefore they have to fight. A sex duel is the necessary prelude to sex play. But the sex duel isn't really a fight. The would-be lovers are in no sense trying to destroy each other. They wrestle naked, without weapons. There need not even be a winner and a loser. Wrestling is an isometric exercise; it makes both wrestlers stronger than they were before. And, as they wrestle, they discover and learn to love each other's bodies.

Sex making can be accompanied by all kinds of pretenses, concealments and theatrical performances. But in the utter nakedness of the sex duel there is no room for a lie; this is basic physical contact. So it can be claimed that you reveal more of yourself and find out more about your partner while you are wrestling with him than while you are making sex. That was how Christopher often felt. To him, the experience of the sex duel seemed so intimate that he was usually shy about admitting to other people how much he desired it. Among the German hustlers he lost all his shyness, however; that was what made his sex life in Berlin so wonderful. Stripped and locked body to body with one of those sturdy shameless youths, he felt strong and free and uninhibited as never before in his life.

Boxing also could be a form of the sex duel, though the pleasure Christopher got from it was of a different quality, tinged with sado-masochism. At St. Edmund's, there were regular boxing sessions, supervised by a member of the staff. Anybody who wanted to fight could volunteer and an opponent would be chosen for him. Christopher found a sexual thrill in the very idea of being *matched* with another boy—even if it was with a boy who didn't attract him physically. There was an atmosphere of solemn exciting ritual as your gloves were tied on and the two of you stepped out into the cleared space and faced each other. You were like a wedded pair, joined to fight in the presence of these witnesses. Christopher regretted having to fight in shirtsleeves. He would have much preferred to be naked or at least stripped down to gym shorts. And the fight itself was spoilt by the formalities of competition. The master who supervised the boxing was himself homosexual and no doubt got his kicks from watching it. But he was obliged to keep up the pretense that this thrilling sex ritual was just another good-sport schoolboy game. There were rules and

they always had some clothes on.) Auden and Christopher must have wrestled, during their sex acts. (Detailed memories of sex with Auden—which went on intermittently from 1926 to 1938—are strangely dim, perhaps because Christopher had to make a mental blackout, switching himself back from a grown-up man to a twelve year old, before getting into bed with him.) When Christopher entered the world of the Berlin hustlers in 1929 and found himself able to act out any sex fantasy which appealed to him, he always wanted to wrestle naked; nothing else excited him as much. Boxing excited him, too; he had a fetishistic attitude to boxing gloves. Many of his obliging young sex partners found all this perfectly natural. (This sort of sub-sadistic sexual violence—which also includes mild nonbrutal beatings with a leather strap—seems to suit the German temperament.) A boy who was basically heterosexual would sometimes suggest wrestling of his own accord, get violently aroused during the fight and have more than one orgasm. Later, he would excuse his pleasure by saying that it was something you couldn't do with a girl, something for men only—and therefore, he implied, the only nonperverse homosexual act. When Christopher was taken to Matty's Cell House[*] in New York in 1938, he asked to be introduced to a German-American boy—meaning that he hoped for a reasonable facsimile of a Berlin hustler. Thus he met [one boy who,] oddly enough, despite his hang-ups and considerable sexual selfishness, [. . .] did prove to be "German" in his tastes. He was always eager to wrestle and box. But Christopher now wanted to be fucked or fuck after wrestling, and [the boy] refused to do this. He only liked fucking teenagers. With Christopher, he wanted to lie on top, belly to belly, and come with his cock between Christopher's greased thighs. This wasn't ideal for Christopher, but he

---

scoring—at the end of the bout, you had lost or won on points. Christopher was lacking in competitive aggression and he disliked getting hurt. So he usually lost.

[Only one person] ever really shared Christopher's mystique about boxing. Both of them were deeply aroused by the shape and smell of boxing gloves and the feel of leather on their bare flesh. [This boy] got excited by the mere mention of the word "fight." Unlike Christopher, he wanted to punch and be punched hard; if his nose was bloodied, so much the better. Christopher has a vividly erotic memory of sparring with him, early one morning, in [his] living room on Amalfi Drive. [The boy] has nothing on his naked body but the big leather gloves. ("That's all you ever ought to wear," Christopher used to tell him.) As [the boy] jumps back and forth, punching and dodging and grinning at Christopher, his erect cock keeps slapping against his belly.

[* Also known as Matty's Whore House; it supplied hustlers to such well-known clients as Cole Porter and the character actor Monty Woolley.]

enjoyed it because [the boy] excited him terrifically. He was, in Christopher's eyes, a genuine teenage stud. (Looking back, I get the impression that [this boy] jumped from adolescence to middle age without ever pausing to be a young man.)

Wrestling and other forms of erotic violence are a feature of what I call a Whitmanesque relationship (see page 13). But Caskey was most definitely not a Whitman character. The love duels of naked camerados had no place in his fantasies. When Christopher suggested wrestling, Caskey was amused, in a grown-up way; he referred to it as "prep school stuff" and Christopher was so embarrassed that he never mentioned it again—though he sometimes pretended to himself that Caskey and he were wrestling, in the middle of a sex act. (The violence between Christopher and Caskey (see page 52) was grown-up violence, full of love–hate—quite unlike affectionate immature Whitmanesque violence. It resembled the fighting of married heterosexual couples.)

When Caskey and Christopher were getting along well—which was most of the time, during 1945–1946—their domestic life was placid and curiously polite. They entertained each other with stories and jokes.[1] They were very much on their best behavior. They were considerate. They contrived to flatter each other subtly. (I'm trying to describe the impression they would have made on someone who

---

[1] Some specimens of Caskey's humor (taken from the notebook or from memory): Carlos McClendon (pages 65–66) had been talking about a rich man he knew, saying what an unpleasant person he was. Caskey: "Why, Carlos, I'm afraid you only dislike him for his money!"

Caskey (looking out of the window at 4 a.m., into thick icy fog): "It's going to be a scorcher!"

At one of the beach restaurants, there was a notice on the back of the check which asked the customer to state his opinion of the portions, the cooking and the service, choosing an adjective to describe each. The adjectives from which the customer was to choose were—*portions*: too large, enough, too small; *cooking*: delicious, satisfactory, fair; *service*: excellent, adequate, poor. Caskey suggests that the waitresses themselves should be classified as: delicious, satisfactory or too small.

Christopher had been to a puja at the Vedanta Center and been given a whole cake as prasad. At their next party, they served it to the guests. Caskey said: "*Do* try some, it's delicious—Chris brought it from heaven."

Caskey's humor, like most people's, depended largely for its effect on the way he delivered his lines. He made jokes with an air of great enjoyment, giggling as he spoke. He pronounced words like "delicious" mockingly and campily. He seldom said anything bitchy. His fun was nearly always good-natured. In fact, he was the very opposite of the sourly witty, deadpan comedian.

watched them while they were alone together and sober.) Their relationship when sober seems to me now to have been a surface relationship; they make me think of children playing at being grownups.

Down below this relationship, on the deeper level of drunkenness, two individuals confronted each other who were neither considerate nor polite. Neither trusted the other. Both were ruthlessly alert to find an opening, a letting down of the other's guard. Nevertheless, this was intimacy of a sort. It wasn't playacting. And I think that Caskey and Christopher felt that this confrontation was what really mattered to both of them; it was what held them together.

Taking a relationship apart and finding out what made it work (or not work) is so exquisitely difficult that I shall only be able to do it by slow degrees and ultimately by lucky guesses—if at all. One more idea occurs to me at the moment—namely that the Caskey–Christopher involvement lacked an element which was present in all Christopher's similar involvements; it lacked a myth.

What do I mean by a myth? I mean an abstract, poetical concept of the person you are having a relationship with which makes you able to regard him in double focus, either as a private individual or as a mythical representative figure, whichever you like. For example, Christopher saw Vernon Old as Vernon Old but also as Whitman's American Boy. The contrast between these two aspects was ridiculously great—the hardboiled twentieth-century city youth and the sweet innocent nineteenth-century prairie comrade. Yet it was this myth which made him able to feel romantic about Vernon Old as Vernon Old.[1]

A myth relationship has to be reciprocal, obviously, if it is going to work for long.[2] Did Vernon have a myth about Christopher? I

---

[1] [Another boy Christopher knew] had had one adventure in the classic Whitman style—at the age of fourteen, he had left the city and taken to the road, wandering away down into the deep South. One day, out in the country, several blacks had taken a fancy to him and had forced him to strip and have sex with them by threatening him with their knives. [The boy] admitted that this had excited him, even though he was terrified. He had had an erection throughout the "rape."

[2] There is a demonstration of how a myth can keep a marriage going, at the end of Osborne's *Look Back in Anger*. When Jimmy and Alison find it intolerable to go on being themselves and still relate to each other, they change focus and become The Bear and The Squirrel in their private myth world. And instantly they are happy and safe, because, in the world of the animals, hatred is impossible; The Bear and The Squirrel can only love each other. They focus their aggression on mythical external enemies.

believe he did, for a while—and one which wasn't quite so farfetched. I believe he saw Christopher as a romantic literary world-wanderer. (R. L. Stevenson, sort of.) And of course, Christopher's glamor was enhanced by the fact that, when Vernon met him, he was just back from China and a war.

Anyhow, Christopher didn't have a myth about Caskey. I doubt if he ever realized this at the time. Or, if he did, he regarded the lack of one as an advantage. He used to think of the relationship between himself and Caskey as being more down to earth and therefore more mature than any other he had previously experienced. The nearest he got to a Caskey myth was in regarding him sometimes as a nanny figure. But a nanny isn't romantic. . . . Enough about this for the present, however.

I doubt if Caskey had any kind of myth about Christopher. But he did definitely have one about himself. He was constantly aware of himself as a Gemini. Christopher once overheard him murmuring to himself, "You're a Gemini!" as he gazed at his face in the bathroom mirror. By this, Caskey meant that he was double-natured and that he delighted in his doubleness; that he reserved the right to switch natures at any moment, without warning.

Early in January 1946, Christopher's penis trouble either got much worse or he got impatient with it—for he switched from Dr. Williams (see pages 46-47) to a surgeon named A. D. Gorfain. (Dr. Gorfain isn't mentioned in the 1945 day-to-day diary, so this must have been their first contact.)

I remember Gorfain as being young and strikingly handsome, with a supermasculine manner. But Christopher evidently felt at ease in his presence—or was it merely defiant?—for he quite unnecessarily wrote "homosexual" when filling out a medical questionnaire at Gorfain's office. Gorfain took this calmly enough. He merely asked, "A *strict* homosexual?"—which made Christopher smile. Gorfain then diagnosed Christopher's trouble as a median bar at the top of the urethra, inside the bladder. He assured Christopher that this was nothing unusual and absolutely nonmalignant; it could be removed without difficulty. The date of the operation was set for January 12, at the Santa Monica Hospital.

My memory is that Christopher received this news with relief and also with a certain satisfaction. The relief is easy to understand, for he must have been worried. The satisfaction had a much odder and deeper cause—unless I am inventing this, and I don't think I am. Christopher was satisfied because he felt that he *deserved* some ritual penalty for his failure to remain a monk, and now the penalty had been imposed and it was such a comparatively light one. (How perfectly suitable, though—a penis operation for a breach of celibacy!) It wasn't, I believe, that Christopher felt any actual repentance. No—it was more like one's uneasiness over a traffic ticket which hasn't yet been taken care of.

At that period of his life, Christopher still had a tendency to turn his illnesses into social occasions. He "invited" Sudhira to come to the hospital during the two or three days he would have to be there, and act as his private nurse. Sudhira, of course, was delighted to do this. She spent the nights at the Entrada Drive apartment. She and Caskey drank and were shamelessly Irish together. But Caskey strongly disapproved of the operation, of Christopher's attitude toward it, and indeed of all illness. He was, as Christopher used to say, one of nature's Christian Scientists. His influence on Christopher was excellent in this respect, throughout their relationship, and he did succeed in curbing Christopher's besetting tendency to hypochondria.

Christopher arrived at the Santa Monica Hospital on the 11th, and was given the usual tranquilizing drugs. He was already all doped up when Dr. Gorfain appeared, greeted him saying, "Hi, skipper!" and then asked him, "You aren't planning on becoming a parent, are you?" The reason for this question was as follows—it was Gorfain's practice to guard against infection during this operation by tying the patient's sperm tubes, thus making him sterile. Gorfain was about to ask Christopher's permission to do this. No doubt he explained the situation clearly enough, but Christopher was dopier than he realized. Christopher misunderstood Gorfain to say, "You aren't planning on becoming a *parrot*, are you?" The question seemed to him, in his condition, to be funny but not at all strange. He replied, smiling, "Well, Doctor, whether I planned it or not, I couldn't very well become one, could I?" Gorfain found Christopher's answer perfectly sensible— psychology was not his department, so he probably took it for granted that "a strict homosexual" would be incapable of impregnating a woman, and that this was what Christopher meant by not being able to become a *parent*. Thus the misunderstanding was made mutual.

In Christopher's notebook, the approach to the operating room is described: "The bed floated down the corridor and up the elevator, like a boat in a water lock." He had been given sodium pentothal as well as a local anesthetic, and when he became conscious again, back in the ward, he was not only ecstatic but actually hallucinating. He saw a parrot[1] flying around the room. He could also see Sudhira and Caskey standing beside the bed. It was clear to him that they were real and that the parrot wasn't—indeed he could control its movements by his will. He demonstrated this to himself, with roars of laughter, making it perch on different objects.

In a day or two, he left the hospital, drove back to the apartment, put on his trunks and went swimming. There was no relapse. Two or three times, he got a scare, because he passed blood when he tried to pee; but Dr. Gorfain told him not to worry about it. There was an unpleasant series of visits to Gorfain during which the urethra was probed and disinfected, and that was all. The wound ached now and then, in the course of the next four or five years, and when it did Christopher would feel mildly nauseated. Dr. Kolisch assured him later that the operation had been entirely unnecessary. Possibly this was true. But, as a ritual penalty, it had served its psychological purpose.

Now that Christopher had been sterilized, he could no longer ejaculate sperm—at least, not until several years later, when a few drops would, very occasionally, work their way through the tied tubes as the result of an exceptionally violent orgasm. Otherwise, his sensations were the same as usual. And there was one notable advantage; if he was tired or not really interested, he could now fake an orgasm—since there was no ejaculation anyway, his sex partner could never be certain if he had come or not.

Kolisch also told Christopher that sterilization would make him extra potent sexually for a while and then leave him completely impotent. The second part of this prediction didn't turn out to be true. But Christopher was indeed very horny during the weeks following the operation, maybe because his urethra tickled as a result of the disinfection.

Being horny, Christopher took to visiting what were known as The Pits, on State Beach. The Pits were hollows in some sand dunes which lay far back from the tide line, right below the wall which bounded the yard of the Marion Davies beach house. The shelter of the wall and of the pits, which had been deepened by their occupants, made a trap for any available sunshine on winter days; this was a perfect place for sunbathing. Since the beach was anyhow chiefly the domain of queers at that time of year, it was not surprising

---

[1] The parrot may have been suggested to Christopher's imagination by the "parent–parrot" misunderstanding of the previous day. But it's curious to remember, in this connection, Christopher's vision of the parrotlike bird which is recorded on November 12, 1940 [in *D1*].

that the pits were used by them exclusively. Everybody was stark naked and many had erections. At your approach, heads emerged. You took your pants or trunks off in full view of the audience. There wasn't much privacy even in the bottom of a pit, for your neighbors were apt to peep over. If you weren't a bit of an exhibitionist, this was the wrong spot for you.

It was quite the right spot for Christopher. Indeed, he enjoyed the exhibitionism more than the sex he got there. Much of this was with middle-aged men whom he wouldn't have even considered under any other circumstances. Only one memory remains of sex with an attractive young man; Christopher blew him, while several other people looked on.

The pleasures of exhibitionism were mildly spiced with risk; The Pits weren't as sheltered as they seemed. They could be overlooked from the top of the wall. The Marion Davies beach house was then unoccupied, but gardeners looked after the plants in its yard and kept its swimming pool clean. At least one of these gardeners was both inquisitive and prudish. He would appear without warning on the wall—which bordered the pool—and yell abusively at anyone he saw making sex or even merely lying naked below. It was said that he had once called the police; a futile gesture—for of course his intended victims had run away long before they arrived.

Caskey had been told by Christopher of his visits to The Pits and made jokes about them with indulgent amusement. He would never have gone there himself—The Pits belonged in the category of Christopher's immature sexual tastes. (Not that Caskey ever used the word "immature"; he probably didn't even think it consciously. But he felt it, and his feeling was expressed by his behavior.) Christopher accepted Caskey's attitude; I think he himself was embarrassed by his fondness for The Pits and covered this by talking of his visits to them as sexual slumming. Like Caskey, he called the pit occupants "Pit Queens," without including himself. He and Caskey made up scenes for an imaginary movie: *Pit Queen for a Day*.[1]

Although there is no reference to Caskey's photography in the 1945 day-to-day diary, it's probable that he had started working at it before the year ended. Soon after he and Christopher had begun living together, Caskey decided to become a professional

---

[1] According to Caskey (in a letter written twenty-five years later and therefore not absolutely to be relied on) The Pits had disappeared by the fall of 1948, when he and Christopher returned to California. Their site became part of the grounds of a beach club, which also owned the Marion Davies lot. Her beach house was torn down but her swimming pool is still in use.

photographer; it was one of those "good resolutions" you make on entering upon a new relationship or a new year. So Caskey took a course in developing, printing, enlarging, etc., and bought the necessary equipment. I believe the course was at Santa Monica City College and that it lasted about two months.

Christopher was surprised and delighted to discover that Caskey had a great deal of talent; everybody who saw his work—and that later included several famous photographers[1]—agreed that this was so. Soon he was taking portraits and doing all his own darkroom work, at home.

Among the people who came to the Entrada Drive apartment during the spring of 1946 were:

George Platt Lynes. He took photographs of Caskey and Christopher in the apartment and also amongst the big wooden piles on the beach near the Lighthouse Café.

Bob Stagg, a friend of Caskey's from the pre-navy New York days. Bob was still in the navy and he was badly worried because he thought he might be sent out to the Marshall Islands for the A-bomb tests on Bikini Atoll which were to take place later that year. In those days nearly everybody except (?) the scientists believed that the results of an atomic explosion were quite unpredictable—maybe all the onlookers would be destroyed, maybe the Hawaiian Islands were in danger, maybe a tidal wave would travel clear across the Pacific and swamp Santa Monica. But Bob wasn't sent to the tests after all. He soon returned to civilian life, working as an architect in New York. He was a good-looking lazy friendly young man who drank a great deal.

Carlos McClendon and Dick Keate. They were the season's most attractive pair of lovers; both sweetly pretty boys. Carlos, though a blond, was partly Mexican and had a lot of Latin charm. Dick had been a major (I think)[*] in the air force and had flown many missions over Germany. (Christopher used to call him "The Angel of Death.") There was a story about his demobilization: Dick, while still in uniform, used to frequent the bar of the Biltmore Hotel, downtown,[†] and was accustomed to be treated by the bartenders with the respect due to his rank and his combat ribbons. A short while after leaving the service, Dick returned to that same bar, wearing the [. . .] clothes which expressed his fun-loving peacetime personality. One of the bartenders, not recognizing him, exclaimed,

[1] George Platt Lynes, Cartier-Bresson, Cecil Beaton, Horst.

[* He was a captain.]
[† Keate recalls it was the Hollywood Biltmore, not the one in downtown Los Angeles.]

"Get that [kid] out of here!" and Dick was refused a drink. . . . Carlos and Dick were then very much in love—Carlos perhaps even more so than Dick—and they simply couldn't keep their hands off each other for long. At a party, they [were inseparable].

(The word "party" reminds me of the songs people played on the record players of those days. There have been only two periods in Christopher's life in which he was acutely song conscious, though for different reasons: his life with Caskey in 1945–1946, and his early life in Berlin. Christopher was aware of the Berlin songs of the thirties because they were in German, which he was eager to learn, and because they expressed for him the glamor of this city he had fallen in love with. He felt the glamor of the American songs also, but the effect they had on him was far more painful than pleasant. "It wouldn't be make-believe / If you believed in me . . ." "My sweet embraceable you . . ." "Ev'ry time we say goodbye, / I die a little . . ."[1] Sinatra creating his tremendous pauses: "Why does its flight make us *stop*———in the night, and *wish*———as we all do?" Even today, I can recapture something of Christopher's sensations as he heard them, a sweet but sickening sense of being bewitched, entrapped, unable to escape. He wanted to escape from this party, these people, this life he was leading—the kind of life which these songs seemed to describe. Did he really want to? Yes, but not enough. For the songs were the incantation of a spell which made him helpless. He hated them for that. And he copied into his commonplace book a passage from Proust which might have been written expressly to relieve his own resentment:

> . . . these tunes . . . offered me their secrets, ogled me, came up to me with affected or vulgar movements, accosted me, caressed me as if I had suddenly become more seductive, more powerful and more rich; I indeed found in these tunes an element of cruelty; because any such thing as a disinterested feeling for beauty, a gleam of intelligence, was unknown to them; for them, physical pleasures alone existed. *Within a Budding Grove*. "Seascape."[*])

Ivan Moffat—Iris Tree's son by her American husband—came back from the war about this time, to start working on films in Hollywood with George Stevens. He had just married a girl named Natasha [Sorokine] who had lived for some time with Sartre and

---

[1] For some reason which I can't recall, Christopher associated this song particularly with Caskey. Another Caskey theme song, in Christopher's mind, was "When Irish Eyes Are Smiling."

[* "Seascape, with Frieze of Girls" from C. K. Scott Moncrieff's 1924 translation, vol. 2.]

Simone de Beauvoir, as a sort of erotic stepdaughter.[1] Natasha was Franco-Russian, large and beautiful and sulky; later she became lively and crazy and a public nuisance. Ivan was then extremely cute and very like Dirk Bogarde. More about them both later.

Michael Hall. He was then an actor, in his early twenties, pretty in a sly, sugary way, almost certainly Jewish though he wouldn't admit it. 1946 was the year in which he appeared as the son of Fredric March, in *The Best Years of Our Lives*. Michael didn't do anything to distinguish himself in the picture. He continued to act after this but never with much success. Later he became an extraordinarily successful, almost clairvoyant collector and seller of antiques; he could find real treasures in a thrift shop. . . . Christopher met him at a party sometime in the winter of 1945–1946. Michael made a dead set at Christopher, coming up to him and murmuring, "I'm extraordinarily attracted." (Christopher later heard that Jay de Laval had encouraged Michael to do this, presumably because Jay still owed Caskey a grudge for walking out on him.) Caskey was present at the party, I think, but he certainly didn't mind. Michael's friend (I forget his name) was present also, and did. Christopher knew he was behaving badly, but Michael's attention flattered him, and he took Michael back to the Entrada Drive apartment. When they got there, Christopher found he hadn't a key. Michael climbed in through the fanlight and opened the door, a feat which appealed to Christopher as being sexily athletic. Michael had a plump, creamy white, extremely fuckable body. [. . .] they had an enjoyable time together. And Christopher continued to have sex with Michael from time to time, good-humoredly and without emotional involvement, for about twenty years [. . .].

Lennie Newman. He made his appearance in the Canyon, as Jay's boyfriend, sometime in 1946. He was small, blond, cute, full of giggles and screams, a hard worker, a hard drinker, a defector from the Mormons in Utah. Everybody liked him. He had absolutely honest bleary blue eyes and was so naturally friendly that he even got along with the cops; they didn't arrest him when they caught him driving drunk. Jay took him on as assistant chef at the restaurant and taught him all his secret sauces. Lennie was probably the only one of Jay's "lovers" who really loved him.

---

[1] Simone de Beauvoir had been one of Natasha's professors at a college, when Natasha was seventeen or eighteen. Natasha, who could be very witty at times, later described her as "an alarm clock inside a frigidaire." De Beauvoir can't have been all that frigid, however, for she had had an affair with Natasha before passing her on to Sartre.

Katherine Anne Porter. I am very vague about dates here but it seems to me that Christopher and Caskey got to know her while they were still at Entrada Drive. Perhaps she was visiting Los Angeles because of some projected movie. The image she presented was that of a senior southern belle (she would have been fifty-two), extremely gracious and rather ridiculously ladylike—her "beauty" and her "breeding" were qualities to which she firmly laid claim and you had to accept them as real if you wanted to associate with her. Beneath these airs and graces, Christopher saw a tough coarse frontier woman, pushy, ambitious, fairly good-natured if handled with proper deference. Christopher and Caskey played up to her and for a while the three of them were almost friends. Katherine Anne treated them like favorite nephews; she even cooked meals for them. Unfortunately, however, beneath Christopher's deference and flattery, there was a steadily growing aggression. By her implicit claim to be the equal of Katherine Mansfield and even Virginia Woolf, Katherine Anne had stirred up Christopher's basic literary snobbery. *How dare she*, he began to mutter to himself, this vain old frump, this dressed-up *cook* in her arty finery, how dare she *presume* like this! And he imagined a grotesque scene in which he had to introduce her and somehow explain her to Virginia, Morgan and the others. . . . If Christopher hadn't been drinking so much at this time, he would almost certainly have been able to hide his feelings from Katherine Anne—especially since he knew they were unreasonable and unkind to a middle-aged silly woman who had never done him any harm and who, after all, did have quite a bit of talent. But one evening his tongue got loose and out popped his aggression, accompanied by a drunken laugh: "You know who you are, Katherine Anne? You're the Joan of Arc of Texas!" Real, biting insults often have an element of impressionism in them; they convey far more than they actually say. Katherine Anne undoubtedly understood all the implications of Christopher's phrase, with the mockery and contempt and hostility behind it. Her first reaction, however, was to treat it as a merely impertinent joke; she pulled Christopher's hair hard, till he yelled. (This reaction now seems to me rather sympathetic.) After this, they said goodnight—as they would have, anyway, for Christopher had spoken just as she was about to enter the house where she was staying. . . . Next day, Christopher apologized and tried to explain everything away, thereby making the situation worse. Katherine Anne never forgave him. Years later, when they were actually on the same college campus, she refused to meet him. Mutual friends urged her to pardon Christopher. She replied that she had even forgotten what it was that he had said—which may well have been true; what she had not forgotten was what he had *meant*, and for that, apparently, no pardon was possible. . . . Thus Katherine Anne became the first of an oddly assorted collection of people who, for various reasons, made up their minds that they would never see Christopher again. The others: Charlie Chaplin, Benjamin Britten, Cole Porter, Lincoln Kirstein.

Two other acquaintances of that period come to mind. I have forgotten their names. What I remember about them relates to the nearly fatal auto accident in which they were both involved. I think it happened on New Year's Eve—which would explain why they were drunk enough to drive out onto the Coast Highway from West Channel Road without noticing that a truck was bearing down on them. (It seems incredible, now, but in those days there were no stoplights at the intersection, which must always have been dangerous.) When they were brought into hospital, the doctors supposed that both men—I'll call them A. and B.—were dead. Both responded to stimulants, however. A. had a broken neck and a broken leg; B. had a fractured skull and several broken ribs. They needed transfusions, so Christopher and Caskey volunteered as blood donors. B. recovered fairly quickly, A. more slowly. When A. was convalescent, he asked Caskey to photograph him in drag—sitting up in bed wearing a picture hat, with a feather boa draped around the cast on his neck. Christopher greatly admired A. for doing this—he regarded it as conduct befitting a hero-queen. Years later, he seriously considered using this incident in *The World in the Evening*, when Stephen Monk is recovering from *his* accident. But it didn't ring true. Stephen is no kind of a hero; he would be incapable of such behavior.

Sometime in the spring of 1946, Denny Fouts returned from New York. I don't remember if he intended staying long on Entrada Drive; if he did, it is obvious that the apartment would have been too small for him, Caskey and Christopher, however harmoniously they might have been living together. But that problem didn't arise, because Denny and Caskey started quarrelling almost at once, and so Caskey and Christopher had to get out. No doubt there was jealousy on both sides, chiefly on Denny's. It must have irritated Denny to discover that Caskey and Christopher were now seriously involved with each other and that he had therefore lost most of his power as Christopher's "Satan." As for Caskey, he had probably sensed, from the beginning, that Denny regarded him with fundamental contempt —as just another boy, another pawn in the sexual chess game. And now Denny, that sly old chess player, had made a crude amateur mistake; he had challenged Caskey from a position of weakness. Caskey saw his advantage and pushed their quarrel to the point at which Christopher had to choose between them.

Thus it was that Christopher's friendship with Denny ended. Christopher was sorry, of course. Denny may have been sorry, too—yes, I'm sure he was. But he accepted the situation with his usual arrogant show of indifference. He was in one of his self-destructive moods, ready to break with anyone who wouldn't submit to his will. Christopher, who was also capable of such moods, understood this perfectly. Though he had sided with Caskey, his sympathies remained with Denny. Looking back on the two relationships, it seems to me that Christopher and Denny came closer to each other than Christopher and Caskey ever did.

My impression is that Denny soon left the Entrada Drive apartment, subletting it to someone else, and went back East again, on his way to Europe. He never returned to Los Angeles.

Meanwhile, Caskey and Christopher hunted around for a place to live. They were very lucky. Almost at once, Salka Viertel offered them her garage apartment. It had just become vacant and they could have it cheap. The apartment was on top of the garage, in a white wooden building which was next to but somewhat behind the house, so that the apartment windows overlooked the garden and had a glimpse of the ocean.

It was small but cheerful and full of light—one long narrow bed-sitting room, plus a bathroom and a balcony on which you could sunbathe without being overlooked, provided you lay on its floor. This balcony greatly appealed to Christopher, who loved having sex out of doors.

The Mabery garage apartment had other more important advantages over 137 Entrada Drive, as far as Christopher was concerned. Unlike Entrada Drive, it was relatively private because it was too small to hold a party in and because it was part of an impressive-looking home on a respectable street—beach acquaintances and other near strangers were scared of wandering in there uninvited. On the other hand, if you were in the mood for company, you could get it by merely walking downstairs and into the main house; Salka was always glad to see you and she usually had visitors. Salka was the most perfect landlady-hostess imaginable. Caskey and Christopher were free to visit her at any time, to use her kitchen, to borrow her books. She welcomed any friend they brought with them. Yet she would never dream of coming over to the garage apartment without first phoning to ask permission; and she tactfully avoided confrontations with the people Christopher and Caskey didn't choose to introduce to her.

Salka's "salon" was still in full operation. All sorts of celebrities came to the house, not because Salka made the least effort to catch them but because they wanted to see her and to be with their own friends, who were also her guests. Actually, Salka was a somewhat self-effacing hostess. She greeted newcomers warmly and got them involved in conversation with earlier arrivals, then she disappeared into the kitchen to see how things were going. I remember her most vividly at this moment of greeting; she was strikingly aristocratic and unaffected. Her posture, the line of her spine and neck, was still beautiful; you could believe that she had been a great actress. I think most of her visitors were sincerely fond of her but perhaps they tended to take her for granted. It is slightly shocking to find that, in the indexes to the collected letters of two of her "stars," Aldous Huxley and Thomas Mann, Salka's name isn't mentioned.[1]

Christopher liked living next door to the "salon," as long as he was free to take part in it or leave it alone. A party anyhow lost some of its horror for him when he didn't have to use a car to get to it and could escape from it so easily. He found many of Salka's guests really interesting and he enjoyed introducing them to Caskey. Also, by doing so, he was promoting Caskey's new career—for Caskey usually made a good impression on them and thus got to photograph them.

Garbo seldom if ever attended the "salon" and Caskey never got to photograph her, but she was in and out of Salka's house a great deal, during the daytime. (I think she and Salka continued to discuss film projects, although it was now becoming evident that she didn't seriously intend to make another film.) Once Garbo had gotten used to seeing Caskey and Christopher around the place, she was absolutely at her ease with them. And, if Salka happened to be out when she arrived, she accepted them as substitutes. Being unemployed, with the whole day on her hands, she was ruthless in her demand to be talked to and walked with. Unlike Salka, she hadn't the least hesitation in shouting up to the garage apartment and even climbing the stairs, to find out if they were home or not. At first they both quite enjoyed her visits; she was lively and campy and easily entertained. Then she became a nuisance. And one day, Christopher found himself whispering to Caskey: "Imagine—if someone had told

---

[1] To be fair, I must add that Salka herself, in her autobiography *The Kindness of Strangers*, mentions Christopher's move into her garage apartment but says nothing about Caskey. Is this discretion or snobbery? Probably a mixture.

us, six months ago, that we'd be hiding under this bed, to avoid going for a walk with Garbo!"

Christopher valued his privacy all the more because he had started working again,[1] on a project which he found absorbing, even though it involved a great deal of copying. During the summer and fall of 1946, he made a typescript of the handwritten diaries which he had kept from the beginning of 1939 (his arrival with Auden in the States) to the end of 1944. There had been big gaps in his diary keeping; these he now filled with bridge passages of explanatory narrative. He also revised and expanded many of the diary entries. This produced a typescript of at least 130,000 words—a very conservative estimate.[*]

Christopher found the work absorbing because it was, in fact, a review of his life in America and an apology for his actions and the decisions he had made during those six years—his involvement with Vedanta and the movies and pacifism, his decision not to return to England, his work with the Quakers, his move to the Vedanta Center and his decision to leave it. The apologetic parts of the journals embarrass me now, but Christopher certainly got some important insights in the process of writing them. And the journals as a whole have been an invaluable quarry of material for books I

---

[1] There was another literary project on which Christopher must have worked during 1946—a translation of Shankara's *Crest-Jewel of Discrimination* which Swami Prabhavananda made and Christopher polished. The book was published in 1947, which means that Christopher must have finished work on it before he left for England in January. I'm sure he didn't take it with him.

When I think of Christopher at work on the language of Shankara's brutally uncompromising opening statements, I realize what a profound conflict they must have stirred up in his own subconscious mind:

> Only through God's grace may we obtain those three rarest advantages —human birth, the longing for liberation, and discipleship to an illumined teacher.
>
> Nevertheless, there are those who somehow manage to obtain this rare human birth, together with bodily and mental strength, and an under-standing of the scriptures—and yet are so deluded that they do not struggle for liberation. Such men are suicides. They clutch at the unreal and destroy themselves.

Shankara points his finger straight at Christopher. And what could Christopher reply, by way of an excuse? Nothing. What can he reply now? Only that he *has* begun to struggle—very little and very late. (See also page 121 [note], for mention of yet another 1946 project.)

[* "The Emigration," in *D1*.]

have written since then. It was always Christopher's intention that they should be read by at least a few other people, so his sexual memories are almost entirely censored. I am filling in some of those blank spaces as I write this book.[1]

This period at Salka's garage apartment now seems to me to have been the happiest in Christopher's whole relationship with Caskey— I mean, the happiest for Christopher. Caskey may well have felt

[1] One episode occurs to me which I may as well record right away, because it has no connection with anybody I shall be mentioning in this book. It happened while Christopher was working at MGM, probably sometime in 1940.

In the men's washrooms in the Writers' Building, the partitions between the cubicles which contained the toilets didn't come all the way down to the ground. In the open spaces between partition and floor, spittoons were placed, filled with water. I doubt if people spat into them, but they were convenient for putting out your cigarette. They also performed a function which certainly hadn't been intended for them. When you were sitting on the toilet seat, you were able to see (dimly) the person who was sitting on the seat in the next-door cubicle. The water in the spittoon reflected him—or rather, a small section of him.

One day, when Christopher was thus seated, he glanced down at the spittoon to one side of him and saw the reflection of a naked erect cock, standing up out of its bush against a strip of bare belly. As he watched, a hand appeared and began patting it lightly, then stroking it, then gripping it and jerking it.

Instead of just watching and maybe jerking off too, Christopher gave way to curiosity. He wanted to see the face of the unknown masturbator. So he leaned forward until its reflection indistinctly appeared—quite forgetting that, as soon as he could see the stranger's face, the stranger would be able to see his. The stranger did see it. For some moments, the two of them regarded each other—as wild animals might, on suddenly becoming aware of each other's presence while drinking from a jungle pool. It was a subhuman confrontation, which excluded all possibility of pretense. It was also a marvellous opportunity. Christopher might have said, "Let's jack off together," or he might at least have reassured the stranger by laughing or making a joke. Instead of which, he sat and stared. The other face withdrew its reflection, and then Christopher saw the reflected cock, no longer hard, being stuffed back into its trousers. Both of them sat perfectly still, listening.

At last, Christopher adjusted his clothes and left the cubicle. But he was still curious. He loitered in the passage, just outside the men's room. About five minutes passed. Then the door swung open and the stranger came out. He recognized Christopher instantly, turned and hurried away. Christopher had a good look at his face. It was youngish, pale, unmemorable. They must have seen each other many times after this. But Christopher was never able to identify him for sure.

inhibited there, because he loved entertaining and cooking. But Caskey was busy, too. There was a second, downstair bathroom in the garage building, attached to a room which Peter Viertel had used as a "den." Salka let Caskey have this bathroom for his darkroom. Caskey was taking a lot of photographs, including pictures in Venice, Ocean Park and waterfront Santa Monica which were to be illustrations in a book which Christopher and he were planning to do about The Beach. (This book never got finished—bits of its narrative appeared in a magazine article by Christopher called "California Story"—later, "The Shore"—but with pictures by Sanford Roth, much inferior to Caskey's.[1])

Christopher must have visited The High Valley Theatre sometime this year. He wrote an article about it which was published in *Theatre Arts*, June 1947.[*] The theater was in the Upper Ojai Valley and was run by Iris Tree and Alan Harkness. Here are some notes which Christopher must have taken during his visit—of dialogue between the teacher (either Alan Harkness or Ronald Bennett) and his student actors during a class in "the improvisation of psychological gesture":

TEACHER: Let's have something of a fight. Not physical.
A STUDENT: Something from *Noah*?[†]
TEACHER: Not as outward as that. . . . Yes, and just one other condition—that the woman is separate. . . . Leave the face free. Do it more through the quality through you. . . . Even for the style, the fists are a little too obvious. Let's go away and come together—
A STUDENT: I haven't felt so static since 1943.
TEACHER: Now full tragic style—form a group around the center, with the quality of despair. . . . Now change it to clown style. . . . Now a fairy tale—once-upon-a-time style. A wonderful little creature is beginning to take shape, right before your eyes. . . . (*To a student*) Now, you be like Cornwall in *Lear*, who very darkly, thickly opposes. No, don't *act* it. Yours is a warm powerful will. (*To another student*) Yours is thinner, but somehow withdrawing from it.

Caskey and Christopher both tended to be promiscuous sexually, but this didn't, as a rule, upset the balance of their relationship. Their only problems were that they had one car between the two of them and that, if one of them wanted to use the garage apartment for sex, the other had to clear out. This could generally be arranged without inconvenience.

---

[1] This article was published in *Harper's Bazaar*, January 1952.

[* "High Valley Theatre," Vol. 31, No. 6, pp. 64–6.]
[† Translated from *Noé* (1931) by André Obey.]

Christopher was much more prone to jealousy than Caskey was, but Caskey's sex mates were usually casual pickups and he was always tactful when speaking of them to Christopher; he never made them seem important. As far as I can remember, Christopher only got seriously jealous once, during this period—and even then he had to admit that Caskey was behaving as well as he possibly could, under the circumstances. This was when a sailor named Jack Keohane[*] showed up unexpectedly from Long Beach, on shore leave. Jack Keohane and Caskey had been in the navy together in Florida and had had a passionate affair. (Hayden Lewis told Christopher with teasing bitchiness how, when he came home from his own job there, hungry for supper, he would find Caskey and Keohane in bed together already, and how they would make love all evening till they fell asleep, without eating anything at all.) What had made Keohane extra desirable in Caskey's eyes was that he had then only just "come out"; Caskey was his first male lover. He could therefore be classified 1A, a Real Man, and, by definition, hopelessly Christopher's sexual superior. And The Past now gave him added glamor; he was like The Stranger in [Ibsen's] *The Lady from the Sea.*

There is no doubt that Caskey was deeply stirred, at first, by Keohane's reappearance. They went off together to a steambath downtown, after an evening of drinking. Later, there were trips down to Long Beach to visit Keohane there. Once or twice, Christopher went along and tried to behave well, on the lines of "any friend of Billy's is a friend of mine . . ." but, when alone again with Caskey, he sulked. Caskey took Christopher's jealousy as something tiresome but neutral, he didn't attempt to reassure Christopher; he was frankly under Keohane's spell and made no secret of the fact that they were having sex together. Keohane himself was pleasant to Christopher but not particularly friendly; he seemed unaware of the situation which his presence created. He was a slim, well-built young man, a bit on the skinny side, fairly good-looking, with a mustache. Christopher found him neither charming nor amusing and quite unattractive sexually. As Christopher might have foreseen if he could have looked at the affair objectively, Caskey soon lost interest in Keohane, deciding that he had changed since the old days and was now turning into a queen. As for Keohane himself, this reunion with Caskey probably hadn't meant all that much to him, even at the beginning, and he could get all the sex he wanted elsewhere. The two of them parted on friendly terms.

But, if Keohane had deflated Christopher's ego, it was soon

[* Not his real name.]

reinflated by John Cowan. All of a sudden, Cowan began to show a desire for Christopher's company. The two of them would lie talking on the beach, passing back and forth a bottle of mixed gin (or was it vodka?) and fruit juice. Christopher liked being with Cowan. Quite aside from his physical beauty, he was very entertaining, a hippie born before his time, a great talker, full of quotations from books he had read, stories of people he had met, charmingly irresponsible and cheerful. He flattered Christopher, asking him questions about Life, Eternity and God—treated him, in fact, as a guru. And then, one day, when they were at least halfway through their bottle, Cowan announced that there was someone in the Canyon he could really fall in love with, someone he would like to live with, if only that person were free. "Who is it?" Christopher asked. Cowan answered, "You."

Christopher was overwhelmed, dazzled, delighted. To him, Cowan was now The Blond—more completely so than Bill Harris had ever been. And The Blond had chosen *him*! It was a mythic kind of honor, like being chosen by a Greek god as his human lover. Without doubt, Cowan was full of blarney and capable of saying anything which came into his beautiful head; Christopher knew this, but it didn't spoil his pleasure. For Cowan hadn't spoken as Cowan but as The Blond; and, in the myth world, the words of a god must always come true. It was in the myth world only that Christopher wanted Cowan; the idea of leaving Caskey and setting up house-keeping with Cowan in the everyday world was ridiculous. This Cowan probably understood, as clearly as Christopher did. They went to bed together once—in the garage apartment, one night when Caskey was out on the town. I think Christopher fucked Cowan, but I'm not sure. What remains is simply the sense of having taken part in a magic act, an act of intense excitement and delight— which nevertheless didn't ever have to be repeated, because it was essentially symbolic.

Sometime in 1946, Hayden Lewis started what was to be a long-lasting relationship with a young man named Rodney Owens. Rod was tall, dark, slender and very good-looking. He was also quite intelligent, funny, campy, charming and eager to be friendly. He and Christopher took to each other from the start—indeed, Rod used to tell Christopher later that he would have wanted to have an affair with him if he hadn't met Hayden first. The arrival of Rod improved relations between Hayden and Christopher, though it didn't remove their underlying antipathy. And Christopher had to admit that, for a while at least, Rod made Hayden nicer; they were desperately in love with each other and, during the first months, couldn't bear to be parted even for a couple of days.

As far as I remember, Hayden and Rod went into business to-gether quite soon after they met. They made ceramics—chiefly or entirely ashtrays—first in their home and later at a small workshop with several assistants. Rod proved to be an efficient businessman. In the course of a few years they became comparatively well-off.

Christopher and Caskey sometimes visited the Manns during 1946, at their Pacific Palisades house. I have a clear memory of Thomas holding forth with his urbane pedantry and good humor, smoking one of his big cigars. The extremely serious operation on his lung—Christopher was given to understand that it might be cancer, but apparently it wasn't—seemed merely a momentary interruption of Thomas's work—an interruption which Thomas refused to take seriously. By early June, he was back home safe from the Chicago hospital, still shaky, no doubt, but very much his former reassuring cigar-smoking self. Christopher loved him for his toughness. He had simply made up his mind not to die before his novel was finished. In fact, he lived for another nine years, finished *Dr. Faustus* and wrote three more novels.[1]

Toward the end of the summer, the question of Christopher's citizen-ship came up again. I believe there had been a test case related to citizenship for pacifists which was decided favorably by the Supreme Court—anyhow, the regulations had been to some extent relaxed. So Christopher was examined and his case investigated, for the second time. I remember a hearing at which he was asked if he would be prepared to load ships in wartime. "Yes," he said, "if they were carrying food." "But not if they were carrying arms?" "No—not if they were carrying arms." "Suppose, for the sake of argument, the cargo was entirely foodstuff except for one rifle?" Christopher looked at the questioner for a moment and then said, "*Honestly!*" This made them all laugh. Later, it was decided to grant his application—the decisive point in his favor being that he had actually volunteered for noncombatant service in the Medical Corps while the war was still on; he was over military age at the time and knew that the age limit was most unlikely to be raised again, but that didn't matter!

[1] December 20, 1975. Since writing the above, I have read Katia Mann's *Unwritten Memories*, in which it is stated that Thomas did indeed have a malignant growth; the specialist told this to Katia, who did not tell Thomas. Thomas never had any subsequent trouble with his lung, although one and a half lobes had been removed from it. He had no recurrence of cancer. He died of arteriosclerosis.

So, on November 8, Christopher went to the court downtown to be made a citizen. Peggy Kiskadden insisted on coming with him, as a sort of godmother. They found themselves part of a crowd of several hundred people—a number of them presumably pacifists, since this was (I'm fairly sure) the first opportunity for a pacifist to become a citizen, in the Los Angeles area. Because of the crowd, Christopher couldn't see the judge and could hardly even hear him. And now, after all his protests and explanations, he found himself required to take the ordinary oath of allegiance, without any modification whatever. He did so, reflecting that his objection to it was already a matter of record. After the ceremony, he used the privilege of a newly made citizen of the U.S. to rid himself legally forever of his two middle names.

This day, November 8, was also the sixth anniversary of Christopher's initiation by Prabhavananda. And it was to be the day of the first opening of *I Am a Camera*, out of town, at Hartford, Connecticut, in 1951.

Late in December 1946, Christopher and Caskey flew down to Mexico City to spend Christmas and New Year's Eve. They visited the pyramids of Teotihuacán, Cholula, Puebla and a little town called Tepoztlán (maybe it's big and well known, nowadays) on a side road off the main highway to Cuernavaca. Tepoztlán impressed Christopher more strongly than any other place he saw on that trip. They arrived at sunset and went up onto the roof of the church, from which there was a long descending view through a gap in the hills to the coastal plain. Christopher experienced a moment of stillness and calm, sitting on the roof, which he can still dimly recall. He was drunk, as usual, but neither too much nor too little, and he had "that sense, which comes so seldom and so mysteriously, of having reached the right place at exactly the right moment." (I quote from a magazine article—too slick to be worth reprinting in *Exhumations*—which Christopher published in *Harper's Bazaar*, June 1947. Caskey's photographs to illustrate it were rejected. Without consulting Christopher, the editors substituted for them an idiotic would-be-elegant art-posed picture of some gesturing boys and girls on a staircase, which had nothing to do with anything.)

While in Mexico City, Christopher and Caskey spent a good deal of time with a young painter [. . .] and his friend, an architect, whose name I have forgotten. [The painter] had a brother, [. . .] whom Caskey had known in New York. [The painter] was attractive, good-natured and "gay in a melancholy way" as so many Mexicans are. One night, when they were all drunk, Caskey kissed him and Christopher got suddenly jealous and slapped Caskey's face. [The painter] was delighted. He embraced Christopher, exclaiming, "That's what we Mexicans are supposed to do—you are a real Mexican!" Back at the hotel, Caskey and Christopher made it up in a highly emotional scene and Christopher fucked him, which was unwise, because Caskey was having an attack of La Turista. This is the only occasion I can remember in my life when, as they say, I hit the jackpot.

I don't remember that Christopher got La Turista on that trip, but he suffered at first from the altitude. He had palpitations, which he cured with some drug he was sold by a chemist—I think it was digitalis. Soon after, to his dismay, he felt definite symptoms of an attack of flu. Not wanting to succumb until he had to, he went along with the others to visit the church of the Virgin of Guadalupe. Christopher stood for some time watching the worshippers who hoped to be healed of their sicknesses, as they approached the shrine inch by inch on their knees, up the nave from the west door. The look on some of the faces moved him profoundly and his eyes filled with tears, but he could never have joined them; he didn't even feel that what they were asking for was right—according to his own beliefs. . . . It was only much later, when they had gone on to Teotihuacán and were climbing a pyramid and Caskey was saying, "*We* don't have to worry about those human sacrifices—they only use virgins!" that Christopher suddenly realized his flu symptoms had completely disappeared.

On New Year's Eve, they didn't go to bed at all, since they were to leave early next morning. They drank and danced at a succession of bars, ending up in one which was called The Paricutín.[*] ("As explosive as its name," Christopher says politely in his article, but I don't remember that anything dramatic happened there.)

1947

The 1947 day-to-day diary records that Caskey and Christopher left Mexico City by plane at 6:00 a.m. on January 1; I'm not sure how long the flight to Los Angeles would have taken, according to schedule. Their first stop was at Guadalajara. On the way there, they

[* After the volcano; see below.]

got a glimpse of the real Paricutín, then a very young and notorious volcano (not quite four years old), smoking furiously. Between Guadalajara and Mazatlán, the plane was caught in a thunderstorm over the mountains and tossed about. I don't know how much danger it really was in, but the situation seemed very alarming— because of the flashes of lightning, the bumps and sideslips, the glimpses of rock through the clouds, immediately below, the cries of passengers and the falling of baggage from the racks (in which it should never have been stowed, anyway). At first, Christopher was only anxious—thanks to the dullness which remained from last night's drinking and to the presence of Caskey beside him. (For Caskey was a seasoned veteran of the air. While in the navy, he had gone out on weather planes as an observer and had once circled down over a hurricane.) But now, glancing at him for reassurance, Christopher saw that he too was anxious and maybe even scared—it made him look sulky. Immediately, Christopher became terrified. And, after this experience, he lost confidence permanently. He has never felt at ease in any plane from that day to this.

When they reached Mazatlán, they were told that the plane had engine trouble—presumably because of the beating it had taken in the storm—and that there would be a delay. They stayed there most of the day, then made a slow calm flight up the western coast, stopping at Hermosillo and Mexicali. They didn't arrive at Los Angeles till midnight.

Christopher now had less than three weeks before his departure for England. I imagine that he must have been in a considerable flap about this trip and more than half dreading the prospect of it. But such emotions are quickly forgotten. The day-to-day diary is full of names of people he saw—I no longer remember who some of them were. [Bertolt] Brecht (whom he now definitely didn't like) is mentioned, Hayden and Rod Owens, van Druten and Walter Starcke, the Beesleys and their friend Phyllis Morris,[1] Cyril Connolly (who

---

[1] Phyllis Morris, an English character actress, was a friend of the Beesleys. They had invited her to come over and stay with them, to recuperate from the wear and tear of the war years. Phyllis was eager to come but she dreaded the journey because she was subject to seasickness. Finally, she decided to fly, reasoning that her agony would be much shorter than on a boat. Once airborne, she discovered however that she was capable of an airsickness so acute that it made the Atlantic flight seem longer than a voyage. When they put down at Gander she was beside herself and felt she could go no farther. So she ran away and hid behind a hangar. They found her there before takeoff. Phyllis begged them hysterically to let her stay where she was and freeze to death, or

must then have been almost at the end of his visit to the U.S.), Charles and Oona Chaplin, Chris Wood, Aldous and Maria Huxley, Jay, Bo and Kelley, Iris Tree, Peggy and Bill Kiskadden, the van Leydens, Tim Brooke, Nicky Nadeau, John Mace. There was also Swami, whom Christopher visited several times, taking part in the Vivekananda Puja on January 13.

Sometime toward the end of 1946, Christopher started working with Lesser Samuels on a treatment for a movie story. The story was originally Samuels's idea and I don't think Christopher contributed much to it—it wasn't at all his sort of subject matter. But Samuels was fond of Christopher and evidently got some kind of psychological support from collaborating with him. The story was about a young iceman who invents one of the first automatic refrigerators and a girl art student who falls for him and does a painting of his head attached to a nearly nude body she has copied from a Michelangelo print, thus causing a scandal. Period, the early nineteen hundreds. Samuels gave it the title *Judgement Day in Pittsburgh*. They finished it on January 6.

On January 17, Salka gave a farewell dinner for Christopher, to which the Huxleys, the Kiskaddens, John van Druten, Phyllis Morris and Garbo came. Garbo may have made this social appearance as a gesture of friendship toward Christopher, or because Aldous and Maria were invited. I don't remember anything about the evening— no doubt Aldous gave his expected performance, Peggy was bright with Maria, Bill was courtly with Salka, Phyllis was thrilled to be in such grand company, John was watching Garbo and wondering what she was thinking and what *he* was thinking about her.

Among the final preparations for Christopher's journey was a visit to the British Consulate downtown, also on the 17th. Although Christopher had already travelled on his U.S. passport to Mexico, he still couldn't quite see himself as an American citizen. He found it strange and slightly disagreeable to face the fact that he now needed a visa before he could set foot in England.

January 18: "Saw Swami for breakfast. Tea with Beesleys. Supper with Bill at Romanoff's." These were, so to speak, the last rites. Christopher had to get Swami's blessing—all the more so because of the guilt which he still felt toward him (and would feel for many years to come). He had to see the Beesleys, because they were to be his "audience" on this trip—far more than any of his other friends,

---

else to give her a general anesthetic to knock her out for the rest of the journey. Refusing to do either, they dragged her back to the plane. Needless to say, she survived, but I believe she was later trainsick, all the way from New York to Los Angeles.

they could imagine how he would feel on his return to England, they would identify with him in his adventures there and wait eagerly to hear about them. He and Bill Caskey had to have their Last Supper at Romanoff's because it had become their luxury symbol during the past months. They very seldom indulged in the extravagance of eating there, but they would sometimes drink at its bar and watch the celebrities.[1]

January 19 was the anniversary of Auden's and Christopher's departure for China in 1938 and of their departure from England for the U.S. in 1939. It's possible that Christopher deliberately fixed this same date for his return journey—I'm not sure, but it would have been like him to do so; that was his kind of superstitiousness. Salka shed her easily provoked Jewish–Slavic tears when they said good-bye.[2] Christopher cried too. And at the airport there was another big goodbye scene. He hugged Hayden and Rod as well as Caskey and strode away with restrained pathos to board the plane. But there was a hitch. For some reason, the passengers were told to leave it again; so Christopher came back and rejoined the others. He fancied, rightly or wrongly, that this anticlimax pleased Hayden—that Hayden enjoyed his slight embarrassment at having to stick around talking until the plane was ready and then make a hopelessly un-dramatic second exit. By the time he took off, it was about 5:30 p.m.

   This was the first and shortest of three delays on Christopher's journey. The second was caused by bad weather; Christopher's plane had to land at Buffalo and Christopher had to travel down to New York on the train. He finally arrived there at 8:45 p.m. on the 20th. Auden and Chester Kallman put him up for the night at their apartment. Next day, he left New York at 1:00 p.m. for England, via Gander and Shannon airports. At Shannon there was a third delay of

[1] On one of their visits to Romanoff's bar, Christopher had met John O'Hara. As I recollect it, the bartender pointed O'Hara out to Christopher and Caskey, and Christopher rashly decided to introduce himself and offer O'Hara a drink. O'Hara was gracious at first and even paid Christopher some compliments on his work; then, turning suddenly aggressive, he snarled, "I suppose you're going to write about us—and you'll get it all wrong—you people always do—" ("You people" may have meant The English, or possibly The Queers.) Thus unfairly glimpsed, O'Hara seemed a very usual sort of red-faced alcoholic Irishman, spoiling for a fight. Christopher sincerely admired *Pal Joey* but it's possible that O'Hara found his praise somehow patronizing, especially since it was offered with a British accent.
[2] The goodbye was extra tragic for Salka because Christopher and Caskey had already decided to settle in New York, for a while at any rate, when Christopher returned from England.

about six hours. He reached London (Bovingdon Airport) at 5:00 in the evening of January 22, and it must have taken him at least another two hours to get to John Lehmann's house in South Kensington.[1]

Christopher wrote an account of this journey a few weeks later in letter form, calling it "A Letter from England." He sent it to *Harper's Bazaar* but they didn't want to publish it. Ten years later, he revised it, for a series of articles John Lehmann had planned, called *Coming to London*. "Coming to London"[*] was reprinted in *Exhumations*.

My memories of the reunion with Morgan Forster, Bob Buckingham, Joe Ackerley, William Plomer etc., at John's, that first evening, are dim—I'm not even sure who was actually present, for more meetings took place during the days following and all are blurred into each other. I do remember[2] Peter Viertel being there (with Jigee, I think)—and that Christopher was keenly aware of his presence as the only outside observer of Christopher's welcome home. Lehmann, in *The Ample Proposition*, says that Christopher was "nervous about the way he would be received." This is probably true, up to a point—but it is also true that Lehmann would tend to overestimate the degree of Christopher's nervousness. Lehmann, in his heart, felt that Christopher *ought* to be nervous *and* penitent, because he hadn't stayed in wartime England—and, incidentally, been available to help Lehmann with his publishing projects.

[1] 31 Egerton Crescent:
[2] Or do I? Strangely enough, the day-to-day diary doesn't record that *anyone* was at John Lehmann's to greet Christopher, on January 22. A meeting with Forster is mentioned on the 23rd and a party on the 24th, to which Peter and Jigee Viertel did come, as well as Henry "Green" Yorke, William Plomer, Alan Ross, Keith Vaughan, Joe Ackerley, William Sansom, William Robson-Scott and no doubt many others. Also on the 24th was a lunch party, which included Rupert Doone, Robert Medley and Louis MacNeice—who presumably weren't able to be at the cocktail party later.

My guess is that Forster, Bob Buckingham, Joe Ackerley and William Plomer really *were* there on January 22, but that the Viertels maybe weren't—in which case, my memory could easily have transferred them from the party on the 24th and superimposed them on the earlier scene. Anyhow, Peter Viertel was greatly impressed by the welcome that Christopher got from his old friends, and he later told Berthold Viertel so. Had Peter been half-expecting that Christopher would be spurned by them? Ridiculous as this sounds, it's just possible that he did expect it—as a Jew and as a disciple of Hemingway (who had repaid his devotion by fucking Jigee, so it was said) Peter had an exaggerated view of the shame and horror of being a "deserter" from your tribe. I think he really liked and even admired Christopher, but that he also felt, deep down, that Christopher was "dishonored."

[* As Isherwood retitled the piece for Lehmann's book.]

Lehmann now obviously saw himself as having been a quite important part of the war effort on the home front—and Christopher was willing to offer him all the respect he demanded, being now doubly a guest, in Lehmann's house and on Lehmann's island. Lehmann was, and always had been, a bit of a pompous ass with delusions of importance, but Christopher saw how vulnerable he still was, how insecurely assertive of his mediocre talent. Christopher remembered how Auden had once parodied Yeats's line, "Had even O'Duffy—but I name no more—"[*] as "Had even Lehmann—" As long as he could laugh at Lehmann—and that would be always—Christopher could go on being fond of him.

None of Christopher's other friends showed the least sign of requiring his penitence. If they thought of him as having deserted them in their hour of need, they never let him guess it. Neither then nor at any later time was Christopher aware of receiving any insult or snub, direct or indirect, from anybody he met in England.

After Lehmann had shown Christopher to his bedroom, that first night, and left him to undress and go to bed, a strange thing happened; Christopher became aware that he was quite violently homesick. This wasn't a disguised longing to be with Caskey and it wasn't specifically related to California or any other part of the States that he knew—it was simply a sudden hunger for the taste of something American; even a hamburger might have satisfied it—except that he couldn't stand hamburgers. As it was, Christopher hunted around Lehmann's bookshelves and found a book which seemed to be exactly what he had been hungry for: *An American Tragedy*. For hours he lay greedily rereading Dreiser and loving, as never before, the look of American place-names and words. . . . This experience was never repeated. While in England on this and later visits, Christopher felt homesick now and then, but in a different, more usual way; he simply wished he were back in Santa Monica.

On January 23[1] Christopher went to the branch of the West-

---

[1] I don't know if Alexis Rassine had been at the party, the night before. The day-to-day diary only mentions him on the 23rd, when he, John and Christopher went to see the film of Gide's *Pastoral Symphony*. Alexis was living with John; he had the top floor of the Egerton Crescent house as his own self-contained flat. John was fond of telling how, when Alexis came to see John there for the first time—they had known each other for at least five years before this—he had looked around and declared, "I want to stay here always"; "And, as you see," John would add, leering at his audience, "*he has!*"

Alexis spoke English without any trace of Polish accent—I think he had spent much of his boyhood in South Africa—but he had a graciousness which

[* "Parnell's Funeral."]

minster Bank at which he had had an account since the 1930s. To his delight and amazement, he found that the interest on his deposit had built it up, through these eight years, to a total of more than a thousand pounds. The bank manager was worried about this, because the account now belonged to a citizen of a foreign country and ought to be declared as such to the Bank of England, in accordance with new regulations. The manager frankly didn't want to be involved in so much paperwork. And he took it for granted that Christopher would rather not be billed for delinquent income tax. He therefore urged Christopher, in tactful roundabout language, to please withdraw and spend his money as quickly as he conveniently could—so that he, the manager, might officially forget it had ever existed.

Christopher was quite ready to do this. Since he wasn't allowed to take the money out of the country and put it into an American savings account, it could only be used for entertaining and giving presents to himself and others. This was enjoyable. Christopher's friends were pleased and amused by his extravagance but not embarrassed—for after all he was a Yank now and one expected Yanks to be rich and generous. But, with the best will in the world, Christopher couldn't get rid of his money as fast as the bank manager would have liked; the last of it wasn't spent until his third visit to England in 1951.

Speaking of Christopher as a Yank gets me onto the subject of his accent. Lehmann writes (in *The Ample Proposition*) that Christopher perhaps didn't realize how much his accent and some of his mannerisms had changed, since they had last seen him. Christopher says nothing about this in his "Letter from England" article, although he dwells on the absurdity, to his ears, of the British accent: "Surely, I thought, they are doing it on purpose?"

It now seems clear to me that it was Christopher who was "doing it on purpose." I suppose he had tried, more or less consciously, to adapt his speech to western American, ever since his arrival in California. But he hadn't succeeded in doing much beyond altering his vowels; his speech rhythms remained British. When he spoke in public, ladies would beg him never to lose "that lovely English lilt"—which annoyed him, of course. The only result of his efforts to acquire a "new voice" was that Americans often took him for an Australian! As the years passed, and Christopher settled down in his

---

seemed foreign. He was very much mistress of the house. He didn't appear to be what is actually described as effeminate but rather to belong to a third, intermediate sex. He and Christopher got along well together from the start and even flirted a little, in a polite heterosexual way.

adopted environment, he had gradually relaxed and stopped caring how he sounded.

But the return to England presented another kind of challenge. In California, Christopher had felt challenged to conform; now he felt challenged to be different. He had to prove to the English that his emigration had been a serious action, that he had put down roots and become, at least partially, American. (To prove, in other words, that he had deliberately changed countries, not merely run away from home.) Christopher, being what he was—a born playactor—could only express all this by thinking himself into an Anglo-American persona, expressly designed for his English audience, complete with accent and mannerisms. This persona was usually accepted at its face value by strangers during Christopher's first postwar visits to England. Shopkeepers would often ask him, "Staying over here long, sir?" A girl at the office where he got his food-ration coupons said sweetly, "It seems so silly to have to call Americans *aliens*." Friends tended to be amused or slightly skeptical, however. Lehmann notes that, "These changes did not [. . .] show themselves continuously," and adds, "I had the impression [. . .] that he was, in spirit, being pulled to and fro across the Atlantic all the time." Forster used to laugh at Christopher affectionately for pronouncing Bob Buckingham's name as "Barb."

In the article, Christopher writes about London's shabbiness—the peeling plaster, the faded paint on buildings, wallpaper hanging in tatters from the walls of the Reform Club, pictures still absent in storage from the National Gallery, a once fashionable restaurant (Boulestin's[*]) reduced to "a dingy squalid hash joint." But I don't think "shabbiness" is an adequate word. It now seems to me that Christopher's impressions went in much deeper. Indeed, he quotes William Plomer's remark, "This is a dying city." Plomer was wrong, historically speaking, but he was right in suggesting that postwar London gave you a sharp reminder of mortality—all the more so if you had just arrived from Los Angeles.

On January 25, Christopher left Euston at 12:20 p.m. for Stockport. In "A Letter from England" he writes: "I travelled on an express train which was very fast, admirably punctual, horribly dirty and so old that it was probably unsafe. Several times, I thought we should leave the tracks. There was practically no heating except in the dining car, and we all kept our overcoats on." This was, as it turned out, the first day of a snowstorm which thickened into a long-drawn-out series of

[* Le Boulestin, Southampton Street, Covent Garden.]

blizzards. England was to be paralyzed by them for weeks to come—and by the coal shortage and the rationing of gas and electricity which they caused.

I am almost certain that Richard [Isherwood] didn't meet Christopher on the platform at Stockport station. Perhaps Christopher had asked him not to; perhaps he was feeling hostile toward Christopher. (There were many exhibitions of Richard's hostility on later visits; the two brothers only became friends after Kathleen [Isherwood] was dead.) Christopher arrived at four in the afternoon and took a taxi out to Wyberslegh Hall.

Kathleen didn't seem to him to have grown much older, but Richard's appearance shocked him. Richard's face looked mad and somehow psychologically *skinned*, all its protective coverings stripped away down to the raw, the quick of defenseless misery. He didn't look his age; he was fresh faced and bright-blue eyed, with thick curly hair—a once beautiful boy who had deliberately (as it seemed to Christopher) made himself ugly by refusing to have the gaps in his yellow teeth filled and by playing the village idiot, staring and grimacing and muttering and breaking into screaming laughter. His clothes were aggressively dirty, stained with food and smeared with coal dust. He took so many laxatives for fear of constipation that he would sometimes shit in his bed. His red nose dripped constantly and he kept snorting back mucus. Also, he had a hacking smoker's cough. His cough and snorting were undoubtedly exaggerated in order to embarrass Kathleen and claim her attention. When she tried to tidy him up, he submitted to her like a child. But he was neither childish nor mad; he was a sensitive, intelligent soul in torment.

Christopher embraced both of them when they met. He had seldom if ever done this with Richard before—he hadn't known in advance that he was going to do it; yet hugging Richard was beautifully "in character" for the 1947 Vedantic-American Christopher whom he had travelled six thousand miles with, to present to them. Richard reacted with shyness, pleasure and irony. "A *very* warm welcome!" he exclaimed, to nobody in particular. Kathleen later wrote in her diary (which Christopher would not read until twenty-three years later) that Christopher's face looked "so *kind*."

Little old Nanny sat by the kitchen fire, bright-eyed but infirm, chuckling at Kathleen's novice attempts at cookery. Kathleen and Richard waited on her. Nanny seemed unaware of American Christopher; she treated Christopher exactly as she had treated him in the 1920s, as the young man fresh from college who had bossed her and accepted her service and her flattery as a matter of course.

Nanny adored Christopher. Kathleen she perhaps hated, deep down. Richard she rather despised. It was sad that she was now ending her life with them, in this uncomfortable house, but where else was she to go?

Christopher had written to Kathleen, shortly before this visit, saying, "You will find me quite domesticated," and promising to give her a hand with the housework and the cooking. But Christopher thought of housework in terms of American kitchens and labor-saving devices. The dirt of Wyberslegh appalled him. And soon he was paralyzed by the cold. The snow lay deep all over the hills; many of the lanes were blocked. The gas pressure was kept so low by the authorities during daylight hours that it was scarcely worth lighting the gas fire. The kitchen was the only warm place in the chilly old house, but Christopher couldn't work there. He sat shivering in an overcoat in his bedroom, writing his "Letter from England" article and then rewriting his article about the trip to Mexico. (He also wrote a hard-core sex story about a sailor whose nickname was "Dynamite." Getting horny was a way of raising his body temperature—until he lowered it again by jacking off.) It was too cold to sit still, reading. Books numbed your hands when you opened them; they were actually clammy. In his efforts not to freeze, Christopher held his arms pressed against his sides and shuffled about with hunched shoulders like an old man. He probably suffered more than any of them, with his thin Californian blood. Kathleen seemed to thrive on blizzards. And when men and women came into the kitchen from the adjoining farm buildings, stamping their feet and rubbing their hands, as they told how England was "cut in half," how you couldn't get through to Scotland, how the army was using flamethrowers to melt the drifts, Christopher was aware of their deep, almost unconscious delight—that characteristic British delight in a "National Emergency."

Kathleen was violently opposed to the Labour government and ready to blame it for everything from the coal shortage and the lack of cooking fat to the weather itself. Christopher, who was equally violently pro-Labour, had to be tactful about this. He had made up his mind, in advance, to keep his mouth shut when necessary, and I think he succeeded. But this visit must have been quite a strain on him, in many ways. He was at Wyberslegh from January 25 to February 28. Between the two dates in the day-to-day diary twenty-four spaces are empty, suggesting blank claustrophobic snowbound days on which Christopher yearned for a letter from Caskey and occasionally had hysterical spasms of fear that he would get sick and die before he could escape from this prison, his birthplace. On

February 7, he made his first trip into Manchester and booked a ticket on the *Queen Elizabeth* for his return to New York. This was more than two months ahead of sailing, but trans-Atlantic traffic was heavy at that time and he didn't want to take any chances.

Nevertheless, Kathleen and Christopher got along well together. He had so much to tell her and she was as good a listener as ever. At seventy-eight, her mind was clear, her memory excellent and her hearing perfect. She was even prepared to be interested in Vedanta. Through Christopher's letters she had already formed her own mental pictures of many of his friends; she "liked the sound of" Peggy Kiskadden and Dodie and Alec Beesley, the Swami she regarded with respect, Gerald Heard she mistrusted. (Gerald's "second in command," Felix Green, had visited Wyberslegh during the war to bring news of Christopher, and both Kathleen and Richard had been repelled by his slick charm, glibness and religiosity.)

Kathleen and Christopher went twice into Stockport together and once into Manchester, to shop[1] and see the art gallery. (You could get a bus into the city from the bottom of the hill below Wyberslegh, but I remember that, on one of these outings, the bus was late or they had missed it, and that Christopher stood beside the road and thumbed a ride, California style. They got picked up almost at once. No doubt British drivers had become accustomed to the hitchhiking gesture, when it was made by American G.I.s. And then, of course, Christopher was with an obviously respectable old lady. Anyhow, Christopher greatly enjoyed treating Kathleen to this bit of playacting.) On February 1, Kathleen and Christopher had tea with some of the Monkhouse family. Mrs. Monkhouse still lived at the top of the Brow, in the ugly red house which had once been the home of beautiful John, her younger son, whom she called "Mr. Honeypot" because of his thick yellow hair. In those days, John was a long-legged hockey-playing teenager with an adorable heartbreaking grin, and Christopher had a terrific crush on him. In those days, Allan Monkhouse was alive and leaning against the sitting-room fireplace; he looked like a noble old dog and had a

---

[1] In the "Letter from England," Christopher quotes some miscellaneous prices: Twenty cigarettes—2 shillings 4 pence. A hairbrush—38 shillings. A rubber sponge—1 shilling 9 pence. A natural sponge—22 shillings. A pair of lady's walking shoes (very good quality)—39 shillings. A first edition of R. L. Stevenson's *Weir of Hermiston*—10 shillings 6 pence. One hundred sheets of carbon paper—20 shillings. He adds, "In other words, some things are very expensive, others are more or less normal." Presumably, the expensive items are the hairbrush, the natural sponge and the carbon paper.

Shakespearian quotation to fit every occasion. In those days, Rachel, the elder daughter, was mooning around, her big reproachful eyes[1] stuck into a handsome but irritating red pincushion face; she had a terrific crush on Christopher.

Kathleen and Christopher's hosts at the February 1 tea party were Mrs. Monkhouse, Patrick her elder son and Mitty her younger daughter. Mrs. Monkhouse was now getting senile and losing her memory. Patrick had a high-up post on *The Manchester Guardian* and was probably one of the half dozen most distinguished-looking men in England. (Glancing into a mirror at the age of seventeen, he had once joked to Christopher, "No one could call me handsome, but I think I might be described as brutally impressive.") Mitty (Elizabeth) was the youngest member of the family; she had been a small child during Christopher's adolescence, so he had never taken much notice of her. Now she seemed to him to be an unusually intelligent and charming girl. He wanted to get to know her better. I don't remember that he felt the same curiosity about Patrick, the friend of his youth. Patrick and he still had a great deal to talk about, they were cordial and respectful of each other's achievements; but Christopher (and no doubt Patrick also) was aware of a gulf between them. Quite aside from Christopher's desertion of England, and of the North Country which was still Patrick's home, there was the embarrassing memory of their confidences, in the days when Christopher had told Patrick about his feelings for Mr. Honeypot, and Patrick, who was then an ardent though chaste boy-lover, had shown Christopher his homosexual sonnets. Patrick and Christopher could agree in their liberal politics, but Patrick belonged to the Establishment. Patrick certainly knew about and doubtless accepted Christopher's continued homosexuality—from a distance. But he was solidly a family

---

[1] In 1947, Rachel's eyes were still reproachful with frustrated love—no longer for Christopher but for Wyberslegh. Rachel had lived there as a tenant with her husband, sometime toward the end of the thirties. Then her husband had gone to the war and she had had to move to a cheaper and smaller home. The house had been let (or maybe sublet by Rachel) to an elderly lady who was still there when Henry [Isherwood] died in 1940 and Christopher made it and the rest of the estate over to Richard. I forget exactly what complications followed, but I believe Rachel encouraged the lady to refuse to leave, hoping thereby to make it easier for herself to move back into the house when the war was over. "She behaved as if she owned it," Kathleen told Christopher indignantly. Rachel had no legal case whatever. Richard, as the owner, had merely to wait until the elderly lady had found another place to live. In 1941, he and Kathleen took possession of Wyberslegh. But the feud with Rachel continued. (This may explain why she wasn't at the tea party.)

man. He might have hesitated to let Christopher meet his sons (if any) unchaperoned.

On February 27, Christopher got a cable from Lesser Samuels in Hollywood to say that his agent Meta Ries(?)[*] had sold their movie story, *Judgement Day in Pittsburgh*, for $50,000.[1] This news seemed all the more marvellously improbable because it came to him from the tiny stone post office in High Lane village. Christopher plodded down through the snow to send his reply. "Kiss Meta passionately from me," he wrote. He was aware, as he handed in the cable form, that he had wanted to amuse the people in the post office, just as much as Samuels. They smiled as they read it, but were they really amused? Christopher's joke was in an idiom quite foreign to them. What made them smile, probably, was their pleasure in the glow of wealth and success given forth by Mr. Richard's Brother—who was, after all, still their property, a local boy born within the village bounds, despite his eccentric self-exile amongst the weird two-dimensional creatures of the cinema screen.

On February 28, Christopher travelled down to London. After being shut up in Wyberslegh for more than a month, the prospect of spending two weeks in London—even a ruined and frozen London —seemed wildly exciting. It was like the beginning of the holidays, when he was at school.

Christopher stayed the night of the 28th with Stephen and Natasha Spender. They saw Ben Jonson's *The Alchemist* and had supper at The White Tower. I remember that the performance, with Ralph Richardson, was excellent. The White Tower, known in prewar days as The Eiffel Tower, had been a favorite haunt of Christopher's; his memories of it went back to the time when he was the Mangeots' secretary, and Augustus John used to eat there and draw on the tablecloths. It was crammed, now, and expensive and chic. The food was probably of inferior quality but the restaurant was still cheerfully brilliant with lights and mirrors—and Christopher was anyhow in a mood to enjoy himself to the utmost.

Stephen was immensely entertaining, as always, and bitchier than ever—an amused spectator of Christopher's social comeback. Christopher was very much aware of his own role and he played it with enthusiasm. Even the cold merely gave an edge to his appetite

---

[1] The film was made by RKO and released in 1949, with the title: *Adventure in Baltimore*. Its leading players were Shirley Temple, Robert Young and John Agar.

[* Meta Reis, wife of film director Irving Reis (1906–1953).]

for company. I think most of the people he met were sincerely pleased or at least curious to see him. The wartime military Americans had long since gone back home. There were almost no tourists. Christopher was a New Face. They could tell him their old air-raid stories and he listened goggle-eyed. He admired or was suitably shocked by everything they showed him. Toward the end of his visit, Stephen told him, with typical malicious hyperbole, "You're the most popular man in England."

March 1. Christopher had lunch with Jack Hewit at the Café Royal. Then he met Forster and shopped for books. He had supper with Benjamin Britten and Peter Pears. He went to stay with Forster at his flat in Chiswick.

Christopher's lunch with Jack Hewit must have been embarrassing —at the beginning, at any rate. Christopher had behaved very badly to Jack in 1939—going off to the U.S. and leaving him under the impression that he would soon be sent for. It's impossible now to be quite certain, but I would say that Christopher never had any intention of sending for Jack. I think Christopher had grown tired of him before leaving England and was merely afraid to tell Jack so because Jack was so much in love with him and so emotional and potentially desperate. At most, he thought of Jack as a kind of understudy who might conceivably be called upon in the event of a highly improbable crisis—that is to say, if Christopher was unable to find himself an American boyfriend. But Christopher had Vernon Old already waiting for him in New York. And, very soon after his arrival, he and Vernon became seriously involved with each other. This was partly because Christopher realized that Vernon had taken it for granted that they would live together as lovers, whenever Christopher returned.[*] He couldn't possibly disappoint Vernon, who was so young and pretty and who thrilled him sexually. It was much easier to disappoint not-so-young, not-nearly-so-pretty, tiresome, devoted Jack—who was now on the other side of the Atlantic and whose steamship ticket would cost a lot of money. So Christopher felt guilty but let the months go by—either not writing to Jack at all or writing evasively. In May he travelled out to California with Vernon on a bus. In June, they moved into a house in the hills, 7136 Sycamore Trail. It was here that a shameful long-distance phone call with Jack took place. I think Christopher must already have hinted to Jack in a letter that he must stop expecting to

[* Vernon Old calls this a convenient but inaccurate memory. He says that he never assumed, nor even thought, that he and Isherwood would live together on Isherwood's return to New York.]

join Christopher in California. Anyhow Jack called Christopher, in tears. I can remember that Christopher took the call lying on the bare floor—the house was scantily furnished—writhing about in guilty embarrassment. Jack sobbed that he was frightened, that there was going to be a war, that Christopher had made him a promise, that Christopher had got to help him. And Christopher told him no.[1]

Shortly after this scene, or maybe even before it, Guy Burgess—by virtue of his status as ex-lover—went into action to defend Jack's rights. He made a bad mistake, however, in trying to pressure Christopher through Forster—as a letter from Forster to Christopher (dated June 17, 1939) shows.[2] This was the last Christopher heard of Jack Hewit for several years. I don't remember how or when contact

[1] When Christopher first met Jack Hewit—or Jacky, as he was usually called—Jack was having an affair with Guy Burgess. Jack flirted with Christopher and Christopher responded and suddenly found that Jack was very serious about it. He ought to have pulled out then but he didn't. Instead, he committed himself to taking Jack with him to Brussels, where he and Auden were spending the Christmas and New Year's Eve of 1938–1939. Guy Burgess made a show of minding about this—Christopher was sure he didn't really, for Guy was surrounded with boys. (Christopher himself found Guy attractive and would have preferred him to Jack Hewit as a sex partner, any day, but Guy didn't reciprocate.) Guy asked Christopher if he was in love with Jack, so Christopher had to assure Guy that he was—though he doubted it, even then. (Although Christopher was a born flirt—like Kathleen, but with the difference that he always followed through sexually—and although he was vain of his conquests, the experience of finding himself loved without being able to respond always reduced him to panic.) I remember that he felt this panic in Brussels about Jack, and confessed it to Auden. Nevertheless, he let himself be nudged and coaxed by Jack into promising, or more-than-half promising, that they would live together in America. Auden greatly approved of Jack as a lover for Christopher, saying that Jack had a "truly feminine soul" and would make Christopher settle down and be properly domestic. I think Auden identified with Jack, a little. For he too had been in love with Christopher.

[2] Dearest Christopher,

At a Cambridge commemoration dinner this week, Guy Burgess, supported by Anthony Blunt, came fussing me because you had behaved so badly to Jackie. As I dare say you have, and they then wanted me to read a letter from you to him which they had brought to the banquet. This I declined to do, to their umbrage. I could not see why I had to, when neither you nor J. had requested me to do so. G.B. was insistent I should write to you, which I should have done in any case. He is a most cerebral gangster.

I wrote not long ago to J. suggesting a meeting, but had no answer and now understand why and am glad he did not answer. I guess the situation and feel very sorry for the boy. This much I will say, that now you know you can miscalculate, you will be more careful another time. Have you to provide for him at all?

between them was re-established. Maybe Christopher phoned Jack after his return to England. Maybe he had been asked to do this by a mutual friend. Anyhow, Christopher came to the lunch date on March 1 knowing that Jack had forgiven him.

Christopher found that Jack (who must now have been in his middle thirties) had aged a good deal. In 1938, Jack had had a sturdy but fairly slim body; now he was plump and piggy faced. Jack was painfully aware of this; his humility about his lost looks was touching but also off-putting, sexually. He flattered Christopher by declaring that Christopher hadn't changed at all. (This may well have been more or less true. In 1938, Christopher had already passed through the phase of deterioration which begins around thirty. In 1947, he still hadn't reached the next phase, which begins in the late forties.)

I am inclined to feel irritated by Christopher, because the memories he has chosen to pass down to me are chiefly of compliments paid him, of sex encounters and suchlike, while his meetings with (so-called) valued friends seem to have left only faint impressions. Christopher undoubtedly thought of himself as being capable of strong and loyal friendships, and he has been so described by others (e.g. Forster and Stravinsky). But the fact that he can't remember more of what Forster and the rest of them said, implies a basic inattention, and inattention implies indifference. Of course, Christopher himself must have been doing much of the talking— answering questions about his life in California. All that he remembers about Forster's Chiswick flat is Eric Kennington's exciting pastel of Mahmas with his fierce eyes and naked dagger—the original of one of the illustrations to [T. E. Lawrence's] *Seven Pillars of Wisdom*.

Forster was sweetly affectionate, gay and funny. He hadn't changed since Christopher had first met him, in the early thirties.[1] Neither had their relationship. Christopher was still a little in awe of him. Not because he thought of Forster as a great writer and as his particular master—he did, but this didn't make him uneasy in Forster's presence; Christopher, who spent so much of his life playing the teacher, found it pleasant and relaxing to become a disciple, now and then. It was as a human being that Forster awed him. Forster

---

[1] The first of Forster's letters in my collection is dated October 12, 1932. Forster and Christopher must have met while Christopher was in England that year—between August 4 and September 30. I think they were introduced by William Plomer. In the first letter, Forster calls Christopher "Isherwood," adding, "we do drop 'Mr.,' don't we?" But it isn't till 1935 that Forster starts calling him "Christopher."

demanded truth in all his relationships; underneath his charming unalarming exterior he was a stern moralist and his mild babylike eyes looked deep into you. Their glance made Christopher feel false and tricky. Christopher reacted to this feeling by trying to make Forster laugh. He usually could; the uneasier he felt, the more sparkling his comedy act became.

On March 2, Christopher was driven around town to see some of the bombed areas, by Benjamin Britten and Peter Pears. At this time, there was still a special kind of rapport between them and Christopher because, at the beginning of the war, they had been in America and had discussed with him the possibility of staying there; they were both pacifists. At length they had decided to go back to England, however, because neither of them wanted to settle in America permanently.[1]

I remember nothing about the visit to the bombed areas—or rather, my memories can't be disentangled from memories of photographs I've seen. For instance, St. Paul's and its surrounding ruins is largely by Cecil Beaton. My only clear personal memory doesn't belong to that visit—it is of ringing the doorbell of a house, one night, for a long time, and then peering in through a window and seeing the moon, shining down into the roofless empty shell. From the street, as I approached, it had looked as solid and lived in as any of its neighbors.

On March 3, Christopher went with Forster to supper at the sadly down-at-heel Reform Club and then saw *Les Enfants du paradis*, which was having a big success. I can't remember what either of them thought then of this hateful film.

On March 4, Christopher moved to John Lehmann's house. He had lunch with Brian Howard and Sam Langford, Brian's lover. Brian had met Sam during the war, so Christopher hadn't seen him before this. (Brian's previous lover Toni, whom Christopher had seen such a lot of in the thirties, in Holland and Portugal, was now in the States, married to a rich woman.) The lunch was lively and

---

[1] I forgot to mention that Christopher had supper, that evening, with Bob and May Buckingham. This was probably the first time that they had an opportunity to talk much, although Christopher had seen Bob and possibly also May immediately after his arrival in England. I remember Bob, with tears of laughter running down his cheeks, describing how funny May had looked, being blown down the passage of their house by bomb blast during an air raid. May laughed too, though in a more ladylike way. Their fun about this, and other such experiences, was beautiful. Bob himself had won some decoration for his bravery in saving people, at the time of the Blitz. He was a hero of the most lovable and admirably no-shit sort.

drunken. Christopher nearly always got along well with Brian; and he found Sam cute and refreshingly uncomplicated, after sulky Toni. I'm pretty sure that this was the occasion on which Brian impulsively decided that he must give Christopher a precious stone—or at least a semiprecious one; I remember it as being golden yellow, so it may have been a topaz. The gift seemed princely and somehow characteristic of Brian's Jewish-Oriental persona. Since their lunch had been late and long, they arrived at the jeweler's just at closing time. The iron curtain-gate was being lowered in front of the door. But Brian ducked under it and insisted, with his usual high-handedness, on being served. Christopher had no earthly use for the stone; later he gave it to Caskey, who carried it around for a while in his billfold. I don't know what finally happened to it.

That evening, Christopher had supper with Cyril Connolly and his wife—this was his second wife I suppose, the successor to Jean; anyhow Christopher hadn't seen her before.[*] Not one word remains to me out of what must have been a brilliant display of Connolly talk, literary in-jokes, literary scandal, and the latest literary ratings of contemporary writers. No doubt Christopher was drunk as usual. What I do remember, that night, is a blizzard. (There must have been *some* snow all the time Christopher was in London, but the memory of it is attached only to two or three events.) Christopher had great difficulty in finding a taxi, and, when he did, the driver announced that he refused to venture north of Regent's Park; Christopher got the impression that the center of the city was surrounded by a vast snowdrift. Luckily for himself, he wanted to go south. I remember he later described to John Lehmann how the taxi driver had burst forth into a sort of Shakespearian soliloquy, addressing the blizzard and defying it to do its worst—but I don't remember the taxi driver actually doing this. It was probably one of Christopher's fantasies. Lehmann was very easily entertained by such talk—which was one of the reasons why Christopher liked being with him, despite his phases of pomposity.

On March 5, Christopher went to look at Keith Vaughan's paintings, which were in a gallery where Keith had just had a show. Christopher admired them greatly and was planning to buy one. In the evening, Lehmann took him to see Alexis Rassine dance in *Les Patineurs* at Covent Garden.

On March 6, Christopher had lunch with Gerald Hamilton. This was at a flat which Gerald had rented in Glebe Place. Their reunion was strange and comic. When Christopher entered, Gerald embraced

[* Lys Lubbock; see Glossary under Connolly.]

him hastily and said, "Before we talk, I want you to read those—" and he indicated a pile of papers set out in the middle of the dining table, "It's all in there—you'll see when you read them—I've been accused of being favorable to the enemy—it's the most utter libel and I was able to prove it—the first casualty in any war is Truth—all I did was try to stop the war—"

I forget how much Christopher knew about Gerald's case beforehand. The facts (according to Gerald's book, *Mr. Norris and I*) were that Gerald had tried to leave England without an exit permit in 1941 and go to neutral Ireland in order to persuade the Vatican through its representatives in Dublin to negotiate a peace.[1] His letters were intercepted and he was arrested and interned by the British, in the same prison (Brixton) as Sir Oswald Mosley the fascist leader. After a few weeks, he was released, however, because the authorities decided that the terms he had suggested as a basis for a peace conference were not "favorable to the enemy," and that he had therefore not been guilty of "an act prejudicial to the defense of the realm."

I'm sure Christopher only pretended to study the case for Gerald's defense. In his eyes, Gerald was *always* guilty—and the seeming nobility of his motives on this occasion only made his behavior look more suspicious. Christopher didn't care whether or not Gerald had intended to commit high treason—if you were going to associate with Gerald at all, you had to wink at much worse crimes than that. So Christopher declared himself convinced of Gerald's innocence and made only one reservation—he refused absolutely to meet Sir Oswald Mosley, who was now at liberty and Gerald's good friend. Gerald found Christopher's scruple quaint. When Christopher called Mosley a fascist, Gerald said gaily that he hadn't heard that word in a long while; it was now only used by *Pravda*, when attacking British liberal left-wingers.

Gerald Hamilton had a young man with him, as usual. [. . .] He seemed charming and simple and quite devoted to Gerald. Christopher said to Gerald, "I always say to myself there *must* be *some* good in you, or you wouldn't be able to get such nice boys." Gerald was delighted; he loved being talked to in this tone. He repeated Christopher's remark to [his companion], who grinned.

John Hayward lived in a flat in a house on Cheyne Walk, which is only a short distance from Glebe Place. Christopher went on there

---

[1] *Mr. Norris and I* says that Hamilton had considered escaping to Ireland with a party of Catholic sisters, disguised as a nun. Ronald Searle made a drawing of him in nun drag for the book.

after his lunch with Hamilton. John Hayward had been at Cambridge at the same time as Christopher, but I don't think they had met then. Christopher knew Hayward as a friend of Auden. Shortly after coming down from Cambridge, Hayward got some rare paralytic disease. The doctors told him he would die of it within a year or two, but he didn't. The paralysis somehow arrested itself, leaving Hayward in a wheelchair, very thin, with twisted limbs, a rigid torso and spasmodic puppetlike movements. Just the same, he had his own charm and dignity; he was distinguished looking, despite his big slobbery lips, because his large grey eyes were so intelligent. He was a scholar (among other things, he had edited a book of selections from Swift), a critic, a great talker and a close friend of T. S. Eliot, with whom he was then sharing this flat. When he went out to dinner parties, as he often did, he would be lifted into a taxi seated in his chair. He was said to be quite a ladies' man and heartless in dealing with his girlfriends, jilting them one after the other. It was supposed that he managed to fuck them somehow.

This was the first of Christopher's postwar visits to John Hayward. Thereafter, until Hayward's death, they met whenever Christopher came to England. Hayward was very good company and loved exchanging gossip. He had one extraordinary and embarrassing characteristic; he nearly always spoke of himself as though he were a normally able-bodied person. He once told Christopher, "Well—at least you and I can congratulate ourselves that we've kept our figures." Telling a story, he would begin, "As I was strolling down Bond Street—" Talking about the flu, he said, "And then, after feeling miserable for weeks, there comes that marvellous morning when you wake absolutely tingling with health and you jump right out of bed—"

On March 7, Christopher had lunch with William Robson-Scott, his close friend in the 1930s—especially during the miserable time in 1937 after Heinz's arrest and imprisonment. (It was in gratitude for his moral support that Christopher had dedicated *Lions and Shadows* to William, the following year.)

But now, to everybody's amazement, William had gotten married; his wife had several children by a previous husband. I'm assuming that this had already happened before Christopher's return to England, although I can't be certain. I only remember that people later said of Robson-Scott that he had started to avoid his former friends—maybe because his wife disapproved of queers. So the conversation between him and Christopher was probably constrained; Christopher longing but not daring to ask: "Does she whip you like your boyfriends used to?" No memory of it remains.

That evening, Christopher had supper with Jack Hewit and then went to stay with him at his flat. My recollection is that Jack wanted Christopher to spend at least several days there, and that Christopher, because he still felt guilty about his treatment of Jack, had agreed to do so. But, as it turned out, Jack's flat had only one bed and it was very small. Christopher had made up his mind to have sex with Jack, if Jack wanted it; and Jack did. I can't actually remember what happened that night. I'm almost certain that Christopher managed to get an erection and to fuck Jack. But Jack didn't excite him at all, now, and he was well aware that Jack would get a crush on him all over again if he stayed around. So he made the excuse that he couldn't sleep with another person in such a small bed—actually Christopher could sleep anywhere, in the right company—and told Jack he was moving into a hotel. To make up for this, he saw Jack as often as he could manage, during the rest of his stay in London.

On March 8, Christopher got a room at Oddenino's Hotel, just off Piccadilly Circus. That night, he had supper at the Reform Club with Guy Burgess. What actually happened during their meeting will remain a mystery—unless Christopher's letter about it to Forster survives and is produced by his executors.[1]

---

[1] In answering Christopher's letter, Forster wrote (on March 21): "I saw that wisp(?) in the distance, Guy Burgess. His meeting with you seems to have gone as I expected it would." (If Forster did indeed write "wisp"—the handwriting is unclear—his description of Burgess seems so unfitting as to be perhaps ironical. Burgess was solidly built, even sexily plump. But perhaps Forster meant that Guy's nature was treacherous and capricious, and therefore like a will-o'-the-wisp.) [The question mark is Isherwood's, but his reading, "wisp," appears to be correct.]

In the same letter, Forster refers to the gigantic volume of *Don Quixote* with illustrations by Gustave Doré which Christopher had just given him. It was so bulky and heavy that it couldn't be mailed; it had to be sent to Cambridge by railway express (or whatever that service was called in England). Forster *had* remarked to Christopher that he admired these particular Doré pictures, but Christopher's gift of it to him was really a kind of practical joke. It was accompanied by a note which began: "As a souvenir of our last meeting, I am sending you this tiny volume. . . ." I suspect that Forster found the joke just a trifle vulgar. Christopher's extravagance didn't amuse him, as it amused Christopher's other friends. On another occasion, he mildly reproved Christopher for overtipping at a restaurant.

Forster himself was just about to leave for the United States on the first visit of his life. He ingeniously used the *Don Quixote* to evade the currency regulations, making Christopher the following proposition: "Can I give you a cheque for fifty pounds? . . . The fifty pounds would be, you understand, payment for a copy of *Don Quixote*, illustrated by Gustave Doré, which you sold to me." Christopher must certainly have agreed to this, and given Forster the equivalent of fifty pounds in U.S. dollars when they met again in New York.

All I remember of the evening is that Christopher was very drunk—so drunk that he had no idea how he finally got back to his hotel. After the Reform Club, he and Guy and a young man named Peter Pollock went to several pubs and nightclubs. My impression is that Guy was friendly at first and then hostile—I don't know if this had anything to do with Christopher's treatment of Jack Hewit or not; probably it was just plain hostility. Maybe Guy saw Christopher as a potential convert to communism who had lost his nerve and sold out to pacifism and religion. (When Christopher had met Guy in 1938, Guy had admired Christopher as an orthodox revolutionary writer—on the strength of "The Nowaks"![*] As for Christopher, he had never taken Guy seriously as a communist, and was even more amazed than most people when the Burgess–Maclean scandal broke, in 1951.) Sometime late that night, Christopher fell down a fairly high flight of stairs when leaving an upper-floor club. He told Forster that he suspected Guy had pushed him, but I don't think he believed this. Anyhow, Christopher was drunk enough to fall properly and avoid getting hurt. Burgess and he never met each other again.

On March 9, Christopher had lunch and supper with the Upwards. This was an altogether happy reunion. With Edward and Hilda, Christopher and Kathy, Christopher felt completely accepted. He was their friend, and that was that. What Christopher valued in both Edward and Hilda was their simplicity; Hilda was certainly intelligent, Edward had one of the subtlest, clearest, most perceptive minds that Christopher had ever come in contact with. But what made Edward different from most of the other people whom Christopher would have described as intelligent was that Edward lacked a certain fashionable urban sophistication; down in their drab little home on Turney Road in Dulwich, he and Hilda seemed quite out of the swim, like country cousins. When Edward talked about London literary figures and their writings and sayings, he seemed to be viewing them from a great distance—although, as a matter of fact, he went into town and met some of them, from time to time.

The Upwards' political life was also an expression of their simplicity. They didn't advertise their activities, didn't use left-wing jargon, didn't make a show of righteous indignation or enthusiasm; they just went ahead with dull routine jobs, attending meetings, selling the *Daily Worker*, etc. (I'm not sure just when it was that Edward and Hilda got into an argument with the British communist

[* First published by John Lehmann in *New Writing* and later as part of *Goodbye to Berlin* and *The Berlin Stories*.]

party and decided to leave it, but I think they were still party members in 1947.)

Their married life was equally simple, or seemed so. They had grown middle-aged together; Hilda was pleasant looking but in a take-it-or-leave-it style and her toilette certainly never went beyond keeping herself tidy; as for Edward, he was losing his hair and had a complacent belly. Edward was a devoted father, but not in the exhibitionistic possessive way that many people are. Christopher and Kathy appeared to be healthy, happy and fond of their parents.

And here was Christopher, their guest and their polar opposite— or so he seemed to himself; queer, Peter Pannish (Peggy Kiskadden's adjective), individualistic, exhibitionistic, liberalistic, fickle, promiscuous and an incurable gadabout. And they didn't condemn him— far from it, they wanted him to be exactly what he was. They were intrigued by his friendship with Garbo, his association with the Quakers and even his adherence to Vedanta. They found nothing to disapprove of in his clothes or his appearance. When Christopher took off his jacket after lunch to help with the dishes, Edward remarked that Christopher still had "a wasp waist," and he did so without the least hint of bitchiness.

And when, after lunch, Edward and Christopher were alone in front of a dim gas fire in the baldly public sitting room (totally visible to everyone who walked by along the street), Christopher lost awareness of everything but their relationship, which hadn't changed in any important respect since Cambridge. What their relationship was and had always been about was the writing of books. They had been writers then, they were writers now. Edward was worried now about his work-in-progress. So was Christopher. Both had reason to be. Christopher's amorphous idea for a novel wouldn't take final shape for another five years; Edward's *In the Thirties* would give him trouble for fourteen, bringing him to the verge of a nervous breakdown. But, as long as they were together, these problems seemed fascinating and exciting; discussing them was an unmixed pleasure.

On March 10, Christopher saw Mr. [Alan] White at Methuen's (with whom he was to become very friendly during the next years) and then had lunch with William Plomer and his friend Charles [Erdmann]. This was the first time Christopher had met Charles, and now I can't remember just what William told Christopher about him. My impression is that Charles came from somewhere abroad, was in fact a refugee. William's attitude toward him was humorously protective; he conveyed the impression that he had somehow got stuck with Charles and must make the best of it, since Charles couldn't take care of himself. And yet it was clear that he was fond of Charles in his own strange way; they had jokes together and sometimes scuffled like children. Charles was small and dark and strongly built, with an odd ugly-attractive face; probably he was very lively in bed. William suggested by the way he treated Charles that he was mentally retarded and I guess he was (is), though I can't remember Charles actually saying or doing anything to demonstrate this. I am deeply fond of William—though I haven't seen him in years. He seems to me to be one of those people who make life more bearable for everybody around them; he would be wonderful in a lifeboat with the survivors of a shipwreck, adrift and uncertain of rescue. What is unusual in William isn't his strength only but his humor, it is the humor of a person who is capable of intense suffering. You are aware of this always, and therefore his fun never jars on you or seems trivial and out of place, no matter what the circumstances are. Some of William's friends complain of his secretiveness, and particularly of his tendency to keep his public and private lives in two clearly marked compartments. This may explain his choice of a lover (or however one should describe him) like Charles, who isn't presentable and doesn't anyhow want to be presented.

At that time, Charles was doing a little private business, dealing in watches—which were then hard to come by. Christopher bought a watch from him, as a present for Christopher Upward. When Christopher was born, Edward had asked Christopher to be a godfather—or the equivalent of one; Edward, as a staunch leftist atheist, refused to use that word.

That evening, Christopher went with Stephen Spender to see *The Winslow Boy*. I still remember it because of Emlyn Williams's magnificent performance,[1] and because of the icy coldness of the theater. The audience was small, and it huddled together in the middle of the stalls, wearing overcoats, mufflers and gloves.

On March 11, Christopher moved from Oddenino's Hotel back to John Lehmann's. He had lunch with Brian Howard and Sam Langford and the three of them went afterwards to look at Keith Vaughan's paintings at the gallery. Christopher had already picked out the one that he thought he liked best, but he wanted a second opinion, so he asked Brian which one *he* would choose. There were (I think) more than twenty paintings available. Brian took his task very seriously—he could be passionately serious about any game, and

---

[1] Particularly at the end of act two, when he reduces the Winslow boy to tears by cross-examining and bullying him, and then tells the Winslows: "The boy is plainly innocent. I accept the brief." [The play is by Terence Rattigan.]

this was one, because Christopher hadn't told Brian which his choice was. After nearly an hour and many hesitations and changes of mind, Brian pointed to Christopher's chosen picture. It was a moment of triumph for them both, and one which somehow strengthened their friendship. Christopher immediately bought the picture. (It was very small—a painting of two bathers (I think that was the title), one of them powerfully masculine, the other a woman perhaps, their bodies lit by an odd apricot light with green shadows.)

After this, Christopher had a drink with Ian Scott-Kilvert[1] and

---

[1] Christopher had first met Ian in 1927, when he was hired by Ian's mother as Ian's private tutor. Ian was then eight years old. Ian had an elder brother, Derek, who was a much prettier and duller boy; he was already at a boarding school and only came home for the holidays. And they had a little sister named Pam who later (I think I was told) became beautiful and wild. Ian's mother had recently remarried. Her husband's name was Lang. Soon after Christopher started work at the house, Mrs. Lang discovered, by means of private detectives, that Mr. Lang was queer. This caused Mrs. Lang to speak her first great memorable line: "Oh, Mr. Isherwood, beware of men!"

Ian appears in *Lions and Shadows*; he is called "Graham." Strangely enough, Christopher had just finished correcting the proofs of this book when he met Ian again, after a ten-year interval, on November 20, 1937.

That meeting and some of the others that followed it are described in my 1937 diary. But a few important details are lacking, including the letter which Ian wrote Christopher on November 21. Christopher calls it "astounding," but adds that he "can't make out, or daren't make out, what it really means." It must certainly have been some sort of a declaration of love, but no doubt it was written in an involved, ambiguous neo-Jamesian style—ambiguity was Ian's way of flirting. The sincerity of the letter itself was never questioned by Christopher, despite its tone. However, I suspect that Ian had fallen in love with a situation, rather than with a live person. To meet your boyhood tutor, whom you'd thought of as a senior if sympathetic adult, and find that he's really not that much older than you are, still lively and sexy and famous into the bargain, and quite prepared to be that groovy incestuous elder-brother figure you've been looking for—wouldn't that seem wildly romantic? Wouldn't the meeting itself seem somehow fated—the work of some power "stronger than either of us," to which you could only surrender? As for Christopher, he must have felt the same way, for he was reminded of James's story "The Pupil." He was also tremendously flattered. I don't think any previous boy had so appealed to his sexual snobbery. Ian was The Blond. He belonged to Christopher's social class (even if his mother *was* vulgar as shit and maybe even a Jewess), he was adequately intelligent, he was an athlete with beautiful legs (he had actually, or very nearly, got a Cambridge blue for running), he was the younger-brother figure Christopher had been looking for since he had lost Heinz. And this young public school and university Adonis had actually fallen for Christopher and made the first move! Christopher's first reaction was: how shall I ever rise to such an occasion? I think he meant this sincerely—and yet—when I ask

then supper with Jack Hewit. Ian was regarded by several people as being a victim, like Jack, of Christopher's heartlessness—but Christopher himself didn't feel at all guilty about Ian. When

---

myself: "Would Christopher have fallen for Ian if Ian hadn't written that letter?" I find, to my surprise, that I doubt it. For Christopher, Love was essentially "the art of the possible." He seldom wanted what he couldn't get, and never wanted it for long.

In the 1937 diary, there is no description of Christopher's visit to Mrs. Lang. He was invited to dinner and Ian assured him that it was very important he should show up in a dinner jacket; Mrs. Lang expected it. Christopher hadn't owned a dinner jacket in years, he regarded them as the livery of the bourgeoisie; but he now overcame his leftist prejudices and bought one for the occasion. (This dinner jacket he later took with him to China, to wear at the British Embassy and elsewhere. Then, in 1941, a Quaker helper at one of the work camps for Okies in the San Joaquin Valley asked Christopher if he knew of a tuxedo they could use for amateur theatricals. So it was there that Christopher's last dinner jacket found its last home—the few he has had to wear since then have always been rented.)

Mrs. Lang received Christopher graciously but rather as though he were a former servant of hers who had since pulled himself up in the world by his bootstraps and *almost* become a gentleman. Her opinions hadn't changed and her heavy makeup didn't look a day older. Christopher was as charming as he knew how to be. He avoided looking at Ian, taking it for granted that he must be half dead with embarrassment. I don't remember that Christopher and Ian ever really discussed Mrs. Lang, at any time during their relationship.

Christopher went with Ian on a honeymoon trip to Paris, from December 9 to 14. The trip was sanctioned and partly financed by Mrs. Lang, who regarded it as a resumption by Christopher of his duties as Ian's tutor—Paris was educational. Mrs. Lang even telephoned Kathleen, perhaps to find out what *her* attitude was toward their sons' friendship. Kathleen certainly realized by this time that Christopher didn't accompany young men to Paris just to show them Notre Dame. And when Mrs. Lang cooed, "After all, your Christopher was the first man in my Ian's life," Kathleen must have smiled somewhat sourly—as she did later, repeating the remark to Christopher himself. This was Mrs. Lang's second, and last, great line.

Christopher and Ian certainly had sex during their stay in Paris, and I suppose they had had it in Cambridge before that. What is significant is that I can't remember anything about it, what they did or how it felt. These memories must have been censored because Christopher found them distasteful, they didn't fit into the love story. I suspect that Ian was passive and rather frigid. I'm sure Christopher never got to fuck him. I even think I recall that Ian admitted that his feeling for Christopher wasn't primarily physical— implying that his feeling for Nik Alderson [a previous lover] *had* been. . . . This is not to say that Paris was a disappointment to either of them. Quite the opposite. The 1937 diary contains the following bit of dialogue (which took place in the bus on the way home from Croydon Airport): "He said that he didn't believe Paris was an episode. 'You've domesticated me already.' I said I

Christopher got back from China in July 1938, Ian hadn't been waiting eagerly, as Christopher had expected, to pick up their affair at the point where it had been interrupted—despite all the long

---

hoped so—but that during the next nine months things might change. 'Why should they?' he said. 'They haven't changed in ten years.'"

After they had been back in London for a short while, Ian reported to Christopher that Mrs. Lang had been quite shocked to learn from him that he and Christopher had shared a room at the Hotel Quai Voltaire. The very fact that Mrs. Lang had questioned Ian about this suggests that she was beginning to suspect that Christopher was having sex with him. (Earlier than this—or was it maybe later?—she had found a love letter from Nik to Ian or from Ian to Nik which had upset her terribly. Finally, Christopher became convinced that Ian's carelessness and indiscretion about his sex life must be partly deliberate, motivated by a subconscious urge to confess everything to his mother. So Christopher asked Ian to destroy all his letters, promising that he would destroy all Ian's. Christopher kept this promise—to my great regret.) From then on, Mrs. Lang began raising obstacles whenever Ian and Christopher tried to arrange another trip together.

(Another detail omitted from the 1937 diary is the fact that Christopher had at least one, perhaps several meetings alone with Nik Alderson. Unfortunately I can't remember anything about this—except that the atmosphere was fairly friendly. Nik could hardly blame Christopher for what had happened. And indeed he and Christopher couldn't be regarded as ordinary rivals in love, they weren't competing; what they were and what they had to offer differed too widely. As for Christopher, he was sad to have caused pain, even indirectly, to such a beautiful creature. If he could have soothed Nik's hurt feelings by going to bed with him, he would have done so most enthusiastically.)

The 1937–1938 diary stops on December 30 and the next entry is on July 30, after Christopher's return to England from China and the U.S. So there is no record of Christopher's final days in London or of the huge party given on January 18, the night before his and Auden's departure (at which Brian Howard got into a fight with somebody or other, exclaiming, "I *refuse* to have my friend insulted by the *worst* painter in England!"). I don't remember when, or under what circumstances, Christopher and Ian said goodbye to each other. But I know that Christopher was playing it very big indeed as the departing hero. Christopher had been a departing hero throughout most of the previous autumn. On November 19 he had written: "I must recognize the possibility (quite apart from any pleasing romanticism) that I may die in China. I must live these next two months as if I were certainly condemned to death, quietly, sensibly, working hard, making my preparations. . . ." It was as a departing hero that Ian met him and was able to fall in love with him—which only goes to show that the posturings of which one is later most ashamed can seem endurable or sympathetic or even lovable to another person. On November 29, Christopher agreed to go with Auden to Spain, before going to China, as members of a delegation of writers and artists. But this visit was postponed, so they couldn't take part in it.

In the 1938 diary there are several descriptions of Christopher's feelings

romantic letters Christopher had written him during the journey. In fact, he had gone off for a holiday in Greece. Ian remained lukewarm until the late autumn, when he suddenly regained his interest in Christopher and wrote to him, quoting from the poem by Yeats, "Oh! Solomon! let us try again."[*] But Christopher wasn't in the mood. He had met Jack Hewit, for one thing; for another, he was still thinking about Vernon Old in New York and including him in plans to return to the States. When Christopher went down to visit Ian at Cambridge, shortly before leaving to spend the 1938 Christmas holidays in Brussels with Auden and Jack Hewit, he had definitely decided not to get further involved. Ian may have sensed this, for he came on very strong, rolling about with Christopher on the sitting-room floor and urging Christopher to come up with him to bed. Christopher wouldn't, and I don't think they had sex again. Perhaps Christopher did tell Ian some love lies before he sailed for New York in January 1939, or perhaps he didn't. Anyhow, after Christopher had gone, Ian seems to have played a big public scene as the deserted heartbroken lover. And, since he was so young and pretty, he got a lot of sympathy from various people, including Benjamin Britten and Peter Pears.

Their reunion was friendly but cagey and polite. Ian was married now, to a girl he had known a long time; she was an American named Elizabeth—I think that Christopher had met her, after he arrived in the States. When Ian announced his marriage in a letter to Christopher, Ian said of her that she was the only person who really

---

about the cooling-off between Ian and himself. Christopher seems to think that their attitude toward their relationship was at fault: "We built a wonderful sham cathedral around our friendship." He also blames the influence of Mrs. Lang. And he writes, "I must remain free, I must be ready for Heinz if he needs me"—which sounds like rank hypocrisy, considering how large Vernon Old already loomed on the horizon. No, the simple truth was, Christopher had realized that Ian wasn't the right lover for him.

Presumably, Ian was making the same discovery about Christopher, though more gradually, because he was young and inexperienced. Suppose he hadn't made it? Suppose he had been there to meet Christopher on the dock at Southampton and had convinced Christopher that he still loved him? Would Christopher have been so dazzled that he would have silenced his own doubts? Would they have remained together through the Munich crisis and the next eleven months, right up to the outbreak of war? It's improbable but just possible. In those days, Christopher's plans were all provisional. If he had had someone to stay in England for, he might never have gone to America.

[* From "Solomon and the Witch": her last line after the lovers realize their union has not been perfect enough to bring about the end of the world.]

deserved to have him—no, I can't have got that correctly, but it was the sense of whatever phrase he used, meaning that she had waited longer than anybody else. And now they had a son.

Christopher didn't feel guilty in Ian's presence, but he did feel somewhat intimidated by him. For Ian was doubly a hero. As a conscientious objector, he had gone to Africa with the Friends' Ambulance Unit, where he had narrowly missed being killed. (Nik Alderson, his beautiful young lover whom Christopher succeeded, had been in the same unit and had been killed by a bomb.) Later, Ian had lost his pacifist convictions, joined the army and been ordered— because of his classical education—to act as a liaison officer with the Greek guerillas, fighting behind the German lines in Greece. "How did you get there," Christopher asked Ian respectfully, "did you jump with a parachute?" "I was dropped," Ian answered, casually, yet with a certain note of reprimand, as if correcting an error in phraseology by Christopher. He was no longer pretty but rather beautiful; he looked austere and repressed. He told Christopher, "I can't see that you've changed in the least." This too sounded like a reprimand, as though Ian were telling him that he was uncured and perhaps incurable. But all this was below the surface. Their conversation was largely literary, and Ian was polite about *Prater Violet* and enthusiastic about writing in general. He didn't appear to feel that he'd outgrown the taste for it. They also exchanged several nervous jokes, at which Ian laughed in the way which used to charm Christopher. But there was no communication and couldn't have been any, unless they had taken off their clothes. Which—as Ian kept signalling, rather too insistently—was absolutely absolutely absolutely out of the question.

On March 12, Christopher saw Gerald Hamilton again for lunch —one of the props of Gerald's newly rediscovered Catholicism, Monsignor Barton-Brown, was with him—and Edward and Hilda Upward again for supper. In between these meals, he was reunited with Eric Falk. Like Ian, Eric found Christopher's appearance unchanged, but he chose a much more pleasing way of saying so; "My God!" he cried, "have you made a pact with the Devil?" Christopher, not surprisingly, decided that Eric *had* changed very much, for the better. (He later told Olive Mangeot that he had seen in Eric's face something he had never seen there before—real goodness.) Not being in with the Devil had cost poor Eric something, however; he already looked like an old man, bald and wrinkled.

On March 13, Christopher went to Cheltenham, to stay with Olive Mangeot. She was living there with Hilda [Hauser] and Hilda's granddaughter, whom they had named Amber because that was her color. During the war, Hilda's daughter Phyllis had gone out dancing a lot with American soldiers. A black G.I. had raped her, outside a dance hall. Phyllis was prepared to go to the base and identify the man. But, as she was on her way there, the American officer who was escorting her told her that the wartime punishment for rape was death. So, when Phyllis was confronted with the lineup, she said she couldn't recognize the rapist. (No doubt this was what the officer had hoped she would say, and the reason why he had told her about the death penalty.)

Phyllis had the baby but she also had a violent revulsion against it—maybe its appearance triggered a delayed shock reaction to the rape, maybe she hadn't expected it to be so obviously Negroid; Amber looked far less than half white. Phyllis refused to have anything to do with her. It seemed that Amber had been lucky. Instead of a whining, complaining, self-centered mother, she had got an adoring fat dimpled grandmother who was a marvellous cook—not to mention a charming home and an equally adoring "great aunt," Olive.

Hilda herself didn't seem to have changed one bit since the old days at 21 Cresswell Place. (In *Lions and Shadows*, she is called "Rose.") Altogether, this was a very happy family, with Olive contributing just a faint breath of communistic priggishness—only a breath, because priggishness was so deeply against Olive's nature. Olive and Christopher didn't get into any political arguments during his visit, but he was obliged to refuse to contribute to some party fund and tell her he couldn't support the party in any way, as long as it sanctioned the disgraceful treatment of homosexuals in Russia.

Another not entirely convincing communist, Sally Bowles now become Jean Cockburn, was either staying in the house or living nearby (I forget which) with her daughter Sarah. Christopher found Jean also very little changed in looks, though much in manner; she was a bit of a red bore, until you got her off the party line. Gerald Hamilton had told Christopher that Jean had once said of Claud [Cockburn], Sarah's father: "He's the only man in the world I couldn't possibly go to bed with." But that was long, long ago, before the Spanish Civil War and Jean's political enlightenment and her stay in Madrid, where she was said to have shown remarkable courage during the bombardments.

On March 14, Olive Mangeot and Christopher had lunch with Wogan Philipps and his wife Cristina. Wogan had once been married to Rosamond Lehmann. He was a handsome powerfully built man, quite wealthy, with a charmingly open, enthusiastic temperament. He had been wounded in the Spanish Civil War, while driving an ambulance (I think). He and Cristina had a farm somewhere in the neighborhood. Like many farmers at this period, they were employing prisoners of war, German or Italian, to help out. From the point of view of the prisoner, such a job was extremely desirable; he got paid for it and he didn't have to go back at night to the prison camp if his employer would give him room and board.

Wogan and Cristina told Christopher at lunch that they had been employing a young German POW (whom I'll call Kurt; I forget his real name). They had become very fond of Kurt; he was a good worker, always cheerful, simple, innocent, sweet natured, a typical German peasant boy—or that was how he had seemed to them. Then, a short while ago, the camp authorities had ordered Kurt to leave the farm and return to them. When Wogan protested, he was told that they had discovered that Kurt had a very bad record; as a member of the S.S., he had taken part in a massacre of civilians, somewhere in Russia. The camp authorities told Wogan that it wasn't their job to try war criminals; their position was simply that farm work outside the camp was a privilege only to be granted to prisoners of good character. Kurt obviously didn't deserve this privilege, so Wogan would have to pick someone else. Wogan had answered that he and Cristina couldn't believe this about Kurt; they had got to know him well, he was incapable of such a crime, there must be some mistake. All right, the authorities had told him, if that's how you feel, you may be present at Kurt's hearing; he will be given every opportunity to prove he's innocent.

The hearing had been set for that afternoon. Wogan asked Christopher to come with him to the camp, saying that the hearing would be in German, which he didn't understand well; he wanted Christopher to translate for him when necessary.

When Christopher first saw Kurt, he appeared to be exactly as Wogan had described him, a sturdy smallish peasant youth with a pretty face and apple cheeks, innocent and healthy. If there was any slyness about him, it would be merely sexual, Christopher thought; he would probably be good at slipping noiselessly out of his room at night and sliding into someone's bed. At the moment, he looked subdued and sad, as was only natural, but not guilty or anxious.

The examiner had come down from London. He was an Englishman but he spoke German fluently. He impressed Christopher as being a real expert at his job. He talked quietly, he didn't bully, he made no show of moral indignation—if anything, he seemed faintly amused, though his face remained unsmiling. Obviously, he had studied Kurt's case in the minutest detail. He asked Kurt if he had ever been a member of the S.S. Kurt admitted that he had, but added that he hadn't volunteered for it, he had been drafted. "Where were you inducted?" the examiner asked. "In Dresden." (I'm using names that come into my head; I don't remember the actual ones.) "Where was the barracks that you had to report to?" "On the Wilhelmstrasse." "You're quite sure?" "Yes, I am sure." "Because that was where they took the volunteers. Draftees went to the barracks on the Kaiserplatz." Thus the examination proceeded, step by step. The examiner appeared to know every move Kurt had made; every lie he had told. It became steadily more obvious that the accusation against him was true. Kurt denied everything at first. Then he turned sullen. Two or three times, his face showed a glimpse of rage, like a defiant, cornered animal. There were no tears, no appeals to Wogan for his sympathy. When the hearing was over, he went out of the room without looking at anybody. Wogan was shaken and upset. Even Christopher had become involved. He felt he had witnessed something ugly and terrible, an unmasking. Just for a moment, the fact of the massacre—and of Kurt's part in it—seemed obscenely present, right there in the room. And yet nothing much had actually happened. The authorities had proved their case, but Kurt would almost certainly never be punished; he was one among thousands. To be shocked that a boy who looked like Kurt could have done such a thing—that was sheer sentimentality. Why shouldn't a murderer be pretty? All that had been demonstrated here was a hideous but homely truth: that most of us live quite comfortably with the memory of our vilest acts; and that, if they are discovered, we are angry and humiliated, we curse our stupidity and are heartily sorry —that we got caught.

On March 15–16, there was a tremendous gale; to Christopher, it seemed the most violent he had ever been in. On the 16th, he went with Olive and Jean to the movies. Being out on the streets was quite dangerous, for tiles were being blown off roofs and, once, a large shop sign came crashing down, close to them. Inside the cinema, the noise of the storm was so loud that it distracted your attention from the screen; it even began to seem possible that the building itself might be in danger. Olive was scared. To make her laugh, Christopher said, "Try to pretend it's only an air raid."

The storm brought floods which closed roads and railway lines, thus preventing Christopher from going to Stratford to see Beatrix Lehmann, who was appearing there in the Shakespeare season. That uncanny chameleon was playing Viola, Portia and the Nurse in

Romeo and Juliet on successive nights.[1] Instead, Christopher went directly back to Wyberslegh, on March 17.

I have few memories of this second visit, although it was nearly as long as Christopher's first—exactly four weeks. One memory is of a session with Mr. Symonds, the family lawyer, about the drawing up of a formal deed making over the Marple and Wyberslegh estates to Richard; this was at Mr. Symonds's office in Stockport on March 24. Symonds told Kathleen and Christopher—Richard, I'm nearly sure, wasn't present—that Christopher's gift of the estates to Richard couldn't be regarded as absolutely unconditional, because there was always the possibility that Christopher might have a child who would claim a share. In such an event, said Mr. Symonds, the child's claim might well be upheld by the court. It was typical legal teasing— Symonds positively smacked his lips as he spoke—and Christopher was delighted to be able to shut him up. "There is *no* possibility," he said, "of my having a child." And he went on to tell them all about the median bar, and Dr. Gorfain's surgery and his consequent steri- lization. It seems obvious to me now that Christopher hadn't told Kathleen about this earlier because he knew instinctively that it would upset her. If so, it was extra unkind of him to do it in Mr. Symonds's presence. His motive was spite against them both, as representatives of the heterosexual majority. How dared they assume that he should *want* to have a child, anyway? Nevertheless, the violence of Kathleen's reaction took him by surprise. She seemed to regard Christopher's sterilization as a crime quite equal to that of abortion, and she cast all the blame for it on poor Dr. Gorfain. "He ought to be put in prison!" she exclaimed. When Christopher was alone with her on the way home, he tried to talk her out of her indignation—why in the world should she expect him, a well-adjusted homosexual, to switch to women in his old age? What did it matter if he was sterilized or not? To which Kathleen answered, with an obstinate pout which made her look for a moment like a young girl: "But I want grandchildren!" At seventy-eight, with one foot in the tomb, she could say this—without the slightest consideration for the wishes of the two sons she professed to love! But, of course, this wasn't Kathleen speaking, it was the matriarch-cunt, deaf to all decency, demanding that its gross fleshy will be done. Christopher gasped at it, awed and amazed and disgusted. There was nothing more to be said. . . . The deed was signed later, on March 28.

[1] Commenting on these character changes in a letter to Christopher, Beatrix wrote that it was "all done by faith."

Another memory is of some conversations Christopher had with Mitty Monkhouse, while they were out on walks, around the back of Lyme Park and over Whaley Moor. Alone together for the first time in their lives, the two became intimate at once. Even the landscape made them feel close to each other, for they were both children of these damp sad beautiful dark hills—"moor born," in fact. As for the difference in their ages, about seven years, it meant very little now that Mitty was into her thirties. And she evidently needed a confidant.

She told Christopher that she was in love with a man much older than herself. This man loved her too. But he was married and his wife wouldn't divorce him. Furthermore, his health was very bad; he couldn't expect to last long. Mitty was urging him to come away and live with her. He was tempted, but still refused to do this because he feared he would only make her unhappy—first, by involving her in a scandal, then by dying and leaving her alone. Mitty's choice of such an old lover suggested a hang-up on her father, Allan. Which was ironical, because Allan was the most drastic of puritans. He had once forbidden a young man the house because he had playfully kissed Rachel goodnight. And now Mitty had found herself a father substitute whom Allan would have condemned as the vilest sort of seducer and emotional blackmailer!

I don't think Mitty needed Christopher's advice. She had already made up her mind that she wanted to be with her lover, whatever might come of it. But Christopher's sympathy pleased and impressed her greatly. Perhaps it surprised her too; she knew he had never been married and may have supposed him to be frigid or pure or both. Christopher soon found himself confessing to Mitty that he knew a great deal about the hazards and problems of unlawful sexual unions, from his personal experience. This intrigued her, of course. She wanted details—still, apparently, not guessing that he was homosexual. Christopher then began to get cagey, which I now regret, because his caution prevented him from introducing Caskey to her on his next visit to England and thus becoming really intimate with her. After these walks and talks on the moors, they seldom saw each other again. I never knew, or have forgotten, if Mitty and her lover ever did go off together.

I don't think there was much snow during this visit, because Christopher went for many walks. He and Kathleen shopped in Manchester and saw movies. Christopher also arranged to have his books (which he had left at Pembroke Gardens in 1939 and which Kathleen had brought to Wyberslegh) crated and shipped over to the U.S.

On April 14 he returned to London and went to stay with John

Lehmann. John gave a party for him next day—Cecil Beaton, Rose Macaulay, V. S. Pritchett, William Plomer, Rosamond Lehmann and Ian Scott-Kilvert were among those who came to it.[1]

On April 16, Christopher went to an exhibition of tapestry at the Victoria and Albert Museum. He was astonished to recognize one of the pieces as being identical with the Gobelins piece which had hung in the drawing room at Marple Hall. He wondered if it could possibly be the same, on loan from the museum in the North to which it had been sold. But the curator whom he asked explained to him that the Gobelins state factory in the seventeenth century had turned out many copies of each design. Christopher in his ignorance had supposed that every piece of tapestry must be an "original."

In the evening, Christopher went with Jack Hewit to see Webster's *The White Devil*. I think of this as having been one of the most remarkable productions of a non-Shakespearian Elizabethan play I have ever seen—but I can remember hardly any details. My overall impression is of roughhouse lust and gleeful cruelty. The miming of the lust would probably seem nothing unusual, nowadays. But there must have been something truly memorable in Flamineo's glee and ferocious laughter, after he has tricked his sister Vittoria and her waiting woman into trying to kill him with pistols which have no bullets in them.[2] I also remember Vittoria literally spitting in Flamineo's face—which was strangely exhilarating.

Christopher and Jack Hewit had supper afterwards with Tony Hyndman. This must have been the first time that Tony and Christopher had met, since the war. My memories of Tony are disarranged, but I'm fairly sure that he and Stephen Spender were now no longer on speaking terms. Stephen had told Christopher that Tony was drinking heavily and that he was somehow involved with criminals. (Do I remember that Stephen's house had been robbed and that he suspected that Tony knew who had done it?) Tony had been to Australia, as stage manager of a theatrical company, I believe, and had made a mess of the job.

Anyhow, Christopher's meeting with Tony was certainly a happy

[1] This may have been the party referred to in Christopher's "Coming to London" article, at which "an animated discussion of existentialism was interrupted by one of the guests exclaiming piteously: 'Oh, I'm so *cold*!'" I seem to hear Rosamond Lehmann speaking the line. If she did, this may have been a bit of sisterly bitchery, implying that John, with his well-known stinginess, was depriving his guests of coal which he actually had in the cellar and blaming the temperature on the fuel rationing.

[2] Robert Helpmann played Flamineo, Margaret Rawlings Vittoria. [In fact, the play is Jacobean.]

one. They had been on the best of terms when Christopher left for the United States and nothing had happened to disturb their relationship in absence. Tony looked hardly any older and he was cheerful and affectionate as always. Christopher still found him attractive, but I don't think they had sex together that night or indeed until Christopher came back to England in 1948.[1]

[1] Stephen Spender started living with Tony in 1932 (I think) and Christopher must have met Tony soon afterwards. They saw a good deal of each other during the next few years—especially in 1935–1936, when Christopher, Stephen, Heinz and Tony went to Portugal together and took a house in Sintra. As long as Christopher was with Heinz and Tony was with Stephen, relations between Christopher and Tony were apt to become strained. In his journal, Christopher accuses Tony of being a born prig and of taking it upon himself to judge Heinz because he sulked. But, in fact, Tony was only priggish because he was imitating Stephen, and Heinz was only sulking because Christopher was being so gloomy about the political outlook. Left to themselves, both boys had quite happy natures, especially Tony.

In the summer of 1937, Christopher went to stay with Stephen at a house Stephen had taken in Kent, near the coast. Inez Pearn, whom Stephen had married in the previous year, was there; and so was Tony. To Christopher, the marriage seemed absurd; it was the sort of relationship Shelley might have had. Stephen would embrace Inez and then go across the room and embrace Tony. Tony said laughingly: "You're like a man with a couple of spaniels," but he resented Stephen's behavior; and so did Inez, I guess. Christopher didn't care what Inez felt; he found her repulsive. Stephen was aware of this, and he slyly encouraged Christopher and Tony to bitch her. I remember a walk they all took together among some sand hills. Inez slipped and fell in the sand, and Christopher exclaimed, "Stephen, your wife's down!" The tone in which he said this made Stephen giggle maliciously. (Two years later, Inez fell in love with a spotty-faced poet named Charles Madge and left Stephen.)

During this visit to the house in Kent, Christopher and Tony naturally found themselves in alliance. Christopher felt that Tony was being humiliated and therefore tried to build up his ego. Tony felt that Christopher was lonely for Heinz, who had been arrested in Germany that spring, and therefore tried to cheer him up.

One day, the four of them were driving home from the beach in their swimsuits. Christopher and Tony were sitting in the back of the car. They were laughing a lot, a bit drunk maybe, and then they started to become conscious of each other's naked bodies. They groped and jacked each other off. I don't think Stephen and Inez were aware of this. But, that night, Tony came to Christopher's room, and they had sex properly, and next morning Tony told Stephen about it. Stephen couldn't very well object, but he was surprised and displeased—which was, no doubt, exactly how Tony wanted him to react.

Christopher and Tony later agreed that something very odd had happened—two people who have known each other intimately for nearly five years suddenly find themselves taking part in a seemingly unpremeditated sex act. But the act itself now seems easy to explain; it was a spontaneous

On April 17, Christopher saw Tony Hyndman again in the afternoon, after lunching with a young man named Neville King-Page. I think Neville must have been a friend of John Lehmann and that Christopher met him at John's party on the 15th. Neville must have let Christopher know through John that he was anxious to go to bed with him. Christopher seldom turned down offers from strangers and anyhow Neville was quite sexy, though probably a bit crazy. (He later committed suicide.) But this was Christopher's last day in London and he had already arranged to take Bob and May Buckingham and their son Robin to supper at The White Tower. So he couldn't meet Neville again until late that evening. Neville had recently moved into other rooms and didn't feel he could trust his new landlady to be understanding. Christopher went up to ask John if he could spend the night with Neville there. Neville waited out on the street. To Christopher's surprise and disgust, John refused to agree to this, saying that Alexis wouldn't like it. I'm nearly sure John was lying and that he was merely afraid Neville would make noisy sex with Christopher and keep John himself awake, and then gobble up a huge breakfast. Christopher had to go out and send Neville away. They never saw each other again.

---

counterdemonstration against Stephen's marriage. What is much odder is that this pair of old friends were then to discover that they were marvellously compatible sex partners.

In the Portugal days, after some quarrel with Tony, Christopher had written spitefully about Tony's "primly composed rabbit mouth." And once he had said to him sarcastically, "If you were *my* little boy—" to which Tony had answered, "Thank God I'm not!" But now Christopher began to find Tony's face charming and to be hotly excited by Tony's strong coarse-skinned white body and thick curly reddish brown hair. And Tony told Christopher that he was a much better sex mate than Stephen had been, because he knew how to lead down from an orgasm as well as up to it.

During the rest of 1937 and the second half of 1938 (after Christopher got back from China) Tony and Christopher went to bed together whenever an opportunity offered itself—either at Pembroke Gardens or on visits to Cuthbert Worsley and Tony Bower, who were then having a big affair. In August 1938 they stayed for a while at Dover and then went over to Ostende where they saw Gerald Hamilton. They always had a lot to talk and laugh about and became very fond of each other and grateful for so much mutually satisfied lust. But their relationship was absolutely without romance—which only meant that Christopher could spend nights with Tony even when he was in love with somebody else. He always fucked Tony; that was what they both enjoyed most. The first time Christopher did it, he found the act so delicious that he was unwilling to wash Tony's shit off his cock, so he let it stay there till next morning. I think this was the one occasion when Christopher reacted to Tony in a way which could be called sentimental.

Before leaving London next day, Christopher saw Robert Medley and Rupert Doone. The day-to-day diary doesn't say where he saw them or if they had a meal together, nor does it say if Francis Bacon was with them. (Bacon isn't mentioned in the day-to-day diary until 1952, and yet I have a strong impression that Christopher had met him before that.) In the afternoon, Christopher took the boat train to Southampton and went on board the *Queen Elizabeth*.

The *Queen Elizabeth* was much in the news, for she had run aground on a shifting sandbank called the Brambles, as she entered Southampton Water on her previous inbound voyage. Her passengers had been disembarked in launches and she had been towed off, which had delayed this sailing for several days. John Lehmann had jokingly said that this was yet another symptom of the collapse of the British Empire. When she sailed next morning (April 19) everybody was on deck to watch her crawling progress through the danger area. As she grazed the sandbank, the water turned brown; but she didn't stick.

When the seating lists were being made up for tables in the dining room Christopher had hastily cruised around for a tolerable table mate. The young man he picked on proved to be a lucky guess, and every bit as glad to be found by Christopher as Christopher was to find him. His name was John Holmes. During the war he had had an important government job in Canada; I think he had been an aide to the Canadian Prime Minister, Mackenzie King.

Every night after supper, John and Christopher would go up onto the boat deck, where it was cold and windy and pitch dark and deserted. If you leaned against the funnel you were sheltered from the wind, and the funnel itself was pleasantly warm. Here they kissed and groped each other and sucked cock and had orgasms, without even taking off their topcoats. It was fun but frustrating because it made them eager to go to bed together, which was nearly impossible; each was sharing his cabin with somebody else. Their only opportunity was during the first serving of dinner in the dining room, for John's cabin sharer had chosen this, while John and Christopher had chosen the second. One evening, John and Christopher decided to take the risk. They darted into the cabin, tore off their clothes and got in three or four minutes of sex which were wildly exciting because of the haste and danger; then they were interrupted by someone pounding on the door. Christopher grabbed his clothes and jumped naked into the bathroom to dress. It was only the steward, wanting to tidy the beds, but Christopher and John were too badly startled to care to continue.

When they parted in New York,[1] John told Christopher that he was "a very wholesome person." I think John was inclined to be something of a closet queen. When he called Christopher "wholesome" he was envying Christopher's relative freedom from sexual inhibitions.

Caskey was waiting for Christopher on the dock with their car (he had driven it from California to New York). Christopher was delighted to discover how attractive Caskey was to him, after their three months' separation. He felt himself falling in love, all over again. As for Caskey, he appeared to be equally delighted, though in his own very different style. He was at his most sophisticated—urban, well dressed, well groomed, demure, sparkling, flippantly sentimental. His eyes were bright with flattering Irish glances; but the only compliment he paid Christopher was half in joke—he said that Christopher's hair "looked quite glamorous." Then he went on to speak of the charming sailor he had spent the previous night with. Christopher promptly began to brag about the sexiness of John Holmes. Caskey smiled and seemed subtly amused. As they drove off the dock, he pulled the car into a sheltered parking place, threw his arms around Christopher and kissed him.

Caskey had been staying at the Park Central Hotel and had moved from a single to a double room so that Christopher could spend the night there. (Caskey had already had a run-in with the house detective because of the late-remaining guests he had entertained in his single.)

That evening, Caskey and Christopher went to see Ingrid Bergman in *Joan of Lorraine*, which must have been a ghastly play, though I think they were both dazzled into grudging acceptance of it by Bergman's beauty and stage presence. They also had a meeting with James and Tania Stern. The Sterns were leaving for Europe the next day and Caskey and Christopher were taking over their apartment for the summer. (Christopher later discovered that Auden was shocked because the Sterns were charging Christopher a rent far in excess of what they themselves were paying for it—I have forgotten how much this actually was. Jimmy Stern was just being Jewish, of course, but Christopher couldn't say this to Auden in front of Chester Kallman.)

On April 26, Caskey and Christopher spent their first night in the apartment, at 207 East 52nd Street. I don't think they went to bed until after dawn; it was a long sexless night of drinking and dialogue

---

[1] They landed at about 9:00 a.m. on April 25.

—slow drinking and even slower dialogue. It remains vaguely but powerfully in my mind as being a high point in their relationship. The dialogue was about their feelings for each other; that much I'm sure of. But I can't remember a single line of it. This was quite unlike their normal drunken confrontations (see pages 52 and 60). What made it memorable was that neither one of them was harboring a grudge against the other at that particular moment—for the obvious reason that they had been apart for so long. And, on the positive side, I think both of them were pleased and surprised and rather proud that their relationship remained as good as new. Caskey was at heart a pessimist, with a low opinion of himself—I realize that nowadays much more clearly than Christopher did at the time. Therefore Caskey had probably been expecting that Christopher would return from England feeling bored with him and ready to call the whole thing off. . . . One thing I do remember: this night of drinking didn't result in either Caskey or Christopher becoming really drunk or getting a hangover. Which in itself seems to prove that its psychological climate was more bracing than usual.

The Sterns' apartment was just around the corner from Third Avenue, along which the El[*] still ran, in those days. If the noise of the trains could be heard from the apartment, I don't remember it as loud enough to be disturbing. The traffic along East 52nd Street can't have been very heavy, for Caskey was nearly always able to find a parking place for their car, not too far from 207. As long as they were in New York, Caskey did all the driving because Christopher could never grasp the one-way street system—that is to say, he had decided not to grasp it.

It was during their stay in New York that the "nanny" aspect of their relationship (see page 61) began to emerge. Christopher's excuse for letting Caskey drive was that New York City was Caskey's town, not his—for it had been the scene of Caskey's life before he went into the navy. But, in fact, Christopher wanted to relax and surrender his will (in all matters that weren't important to him) to a nanny figure who would wait on him and relieve him from the tension of making decisions. (He reserved the right to sulk and passively resist, just as a child does, when Nanny's decisions didn't suit him.)

The apartment itself was snug and well furnished; it seemed much more of a home for them than their two earlier habitations. And Caskey, as before, was prepared to make it as comfortable as possible, and to cook for and entertain their friends. Caskey had a great many

[* Elevated train.]

friends in New York and Christopher had Lincoln Kirstein, Paul Cadmus, Auden, Berthold Viertel, Tony Bower and others. Nearly all their evenings were social.

On May 1, Christopher had lunch with Bennett Cerf. This must have been to discuss Christopher's plan to go to South America with Caskey and write a travel book about their journey, illustrated by Caskey's photographs. (Promoting Caskey's career as a photographer was Christopher's chief reason[1] for wanting to make the trip; he always dreaded embarking on any travel and only really enjoyed it in retrospect.) Since they now had the money from *Judgement Day in Pittsburgh*, they could easily afford the travelling expenses, even without the advances on royalties they would get from Random House and from Methuen.

The lunch with Cerf must have included a visit to the Random House offices, because I have two vivid memories of that meeting which don't fit into a restaurant. One is of Cerf seated complacently behind his desk, with his yessing assistants around him. They are discussing a possible title for the book. Suddenly Cerf—that incomparable ass—gets an inspiration; he becomes a Jewish prophet passing the word down from God: "The *High* Andes! That's what we'll call it—"The *High*" (a slight but deeply reverent pause) "*Andes*!!" (Christopher never for one instant considered using this, of course.)

The other memory is of being introduced to Truman Capote. (Even at this prepublication stage of Truman's career, it had to be that way around; one couldn't imagine Truman being introduced to oneself.) Christopher was prepared for the honor by one of the Random House partners, who assured him that this young man, whose first novel, *Other Voices, Other Rooms*, was soon to appear, could only be compared to Proust. And then the marvellously gracious little baby personage itself appeared; Truman sailed into the room with his right hand extended, palm downward, as if he expected Christopher to kiss it. Christopher didn't, but, within a few moments, he was quite ready to—having been almost instantaneously conquered by the campy Capote charm. To hell with Proust; here was something infinitely rarer and more amusing, a live Ronald Firbank character! Christopher came home and raved about him to

---

[1] I now realize that another, surprisingly important reason was Christopher's desire to impress Hayden Lewis—that smiling sneering spectator and critic of the drama of his affair with Caskey. Christopher was determined that Hayden should have to admit that Caskey's life was more exciting, more interesting, more glamorous, more fun than it had ever been before he met Christopher.

Caskey. And when Caskey himself met Truman (on May 21) he wasn't at all disappointed. There and then, they accepted Truman's invitation to come and stay with him and his friend, Newton Arvin, on Nantucket in July.

On May 5, Christopher joined a gymnasium which was run by an old German named Pilates. It was somewhere over on the West Side, maybe Seventh Avenue.[*] I think that Caskey had recommended it and that Caskey himself had gone to it at one time, but he didn't rejoin with Christopher. Mr. Pilates was a bully and a narcissist and a dirty old man; he and Christopher got along very well. When Christopher was doing his workout, Pilates would bring one of his assistants over to watch, rather as the house surgeon brings an intern to study a patient with a rare deformity. "Look at him!" Pilates would exclaim to the assistant, "That could have been a beautiful body, and look what he's done to it! Like a birdcage that somebody trod on!" Pilates had grown tubby with age, but he would never admit it; he still thought himself a magnificent figure of a man. "That's not fat," he declared, punching himself in the stomach, "that's good healthy meat!" He frankly lusted after some of his girl students. He used to make them lie back on an inclined board and climb on top of them, on the pretext that he was showing them an exercise. What he really was doing was rubbing off against them through his clothes; as was obvious from the violent jerking of his buttocks.[1]

Pilates was an excellent teacher, however, and Christopher learnt a lot from him, even though Christopher gave up going to the gym early in July.[2] I remember only two small pearls of his wisdom. Once, a party of workmen were handling heavy metal objects on the roof of the building opposite. Pilates watched them and commented disgustedly that their posture and movements were all wrong—if only these men knew how, they could transform their boring work into a scientific workout and build themselves marvellous physiques. And once he told Christopher, "If you'll just touch your toes one single time, every day of your life, you'll be all right"—which made Christopher think of a saint begging some hopelessly worldly

[1] Such behavior sounds scarcely credible, but I'm sure memory isn't at fault here. Pilates was the sort of eccentric character who can get away with murder. I dare say the girls he did this to were lovers or old friends, who were either excited or amused by him. The gym was often almost empty when Christopher was there, and perhaps Pilates knew instinctively that Christopher would be a suitable audience for his exhibitionism.

[2] This may not have been due to Christopher's laziness. It's possible that the gym was closed during the summer.

[* 939 Eighth Avenue.]

householder to please try to remember God for at least one moment during each day.

It was also on May 5 that Christopher saw Forster for the first time in New York. He came to the apartment with Bill Roerick, with whom he had become great friends during the war, while Roerick was in England as a G.I. Caskey cooked supper for them, and the next night he cooked supper for Forster again. The day after that, he drove Forster and Christopher down to Bryn Mawr, where Forster had to give a lecture. Thus Forster came under the spell of Caskey's charm and efficiency as a nanny. He remained fond of Caskey for the rest of his life.

On May 8, Christopher started what he describes as: "*The School of Tragedy*. First draft of a novel."[1] This fragment—nearly twelve pages

---

[1] I have discovered (September 1973), since writing the [above] paragraph, an entry in another diary notebook [$6'' \times 8\frac{1}{8}''$, also containing diary "Holland 1935"], dated Good Friday, April 4, 1947. This begins by stating that Christopher has already worked out a draft of a novel called *The School of Tragedy* sometime during 1946, in Santa Monica. However, Christopher continues, this draft won't do at all. Its central character is Paul (Denny Fouts?). The anecdote is "too funny, too clever, too trivial for the subject matter." (I don't know what this means, unless Christopher is referring to an idea he had of writing a story about Caroline Norment's curious involvement with accidental fires. See the journals, March 1, 1942 [*D1*, pp. 212–14].)

Christopher goes on to describe a new story line for the novel, moving around the partners in three love affairs. Two of these couples survive in the published version of *The World in the Evening*—Stephen (called Charles in this notebook) and Gerda; Charles (called Stephen) and Bob (called Roy). The third couple was to have been Sarah (Caroline Norment) and Dr. Kurt Traube (Carl Furtmueller, on whom, in real life, Caroline had a violent crush, until he got engaged to and married one of the American Quaker helpers at the Haverford hostel—his own wife having died a few months earlier). This "Sarah" would obviously have been very different from the later Sarah! Stephen–Charles is actually working at the hostel. He has given up his life to social work after an unhappy marriage (to a character like Jane). He has a friendly sex relationship with Gerda, to get her through the period of anxiety and waiting until her husband escapes from Germany and rejoins her. Stephen–Charles and Gerda then part as loving friends.

Charles–Stephen is a doctor who has a boyfriend, Bob–Roy, in the navy. Bob–Roy is killed—he never appears "on stage." Charles–Stephen joins the navy too. (Incidentally, it's curious to note that Christopher was planning to make Bob–Roy an architect in civilian life—about fourteen months before Christopher met Jim Charlton (see page 159 [and note 1]). I suppose that, when Christopher chose that profession for Bob-Roy, he was thinking of Bob Stagg (see [page 123]). But, before he met Jim, he had never been interested in a young man *as* an architect. Sarah's romance with Dr. Traube is the only one

of a large (10½″ × 13½″) thin notebook—consists of descriptions of the refugees at the Haverford hostel taken from the 1941–1942 journals and given fictitious names. Its title also comes from the journals. On June 24, 1942, Christopher records that the Schindlers left their room so untidy that Mr. [Josef] Stern remarked severely: "Such people are not fit for the school of tragedy." Christopher had been delighted by this phrase and had probably been intending to use it for a title, ever since he heard it.

This fragment is just flat-footed reporting and its attempts at humor strike a note of smug condescension; no wonder Christopher soon got bored with it. His second draft, begun on June 17, does at least contain a spark of possible interest; it is in the form of Stephen's mental dialogue with Elizabeth during the Quaker meeting, in *The World in the Evening*. But this dialogue, unfortunately, is with the Narrator's Better Self, or God; it must have made Christopher feel queasy, for he dropped it after two and a half pages. After this, he doesn't seem to have done any more work on the novel for nearly two years.

These two fragments are written very neatly; they must be fair copies. I remember the little room at the back of the apartment where Christopher's writing was done, and how he had to keep wiping the side of his sweaty hand (the weather was hot and humid) to stop it from smearing dirt over the page. Dirt fell unceasingly all over everything, even when the windows were shut. Christopher hated having dirty hands when he was writing. He hated the heat, too. The filthy city with its noise and its horrible climate soon began to get on his nerves. He couldn't settle down to his novel so he blamed his surroundings and the life he was leading. How could he work in this apartment? He couldn't even create a literary nest for himself by having his books around him; when they arrived by boat from England, late in May, he had to store them in the cellar of the building because the bookshelves in the apartment were crammed with the Sterns' books. And how could he work, he said, when he was surrounded by so many friends and going out to so many parties and drinking so much? Christopher often enjoyed seeing individuals

---

with a conventional happy ending. They get married after Traube's wife dies. Frau Traube has some lingering disease. Charles–Stephen, who is her doctor, finishes her off and later admits to Stephen–Charles that he has done so.

Christopher made at least three more entries in this same diary notebook—including synopses, lists of characters and seating plans for the hostel dining room. The last dated entry is on June 9, 1947, so they overlap the entries in the large thin notebook.

—parties he never liked unless they were sexy—drinking was his social anesthetic but hangovers were the destruction of his precious private mornings.

Within three or four weeks—at the very most—Christopher had made up his mind that he couldn't, wouldn't settle in New York. His decision dismayed him, for it seemed to threaten his whole relationship with Caskey. Coming to New York had been chiefly Caskey's idea. He was at home there, it suited him perfectly and its discomforts he took in his stride. To attack New York was to attack the values he had grown up with.

But Caskey, to his surprise and relief, took Christopher's decision quite calmly; saying that he was beginning to feel much the same way. Since they were now planning to leave for South America at the end of the summer, they agreed to stay on at the Sterns' apartment till then and put off discussing where they should live until they had returned from the South America trip, sometime in 1948. Looking back, I doubt if Caskey was being quite sincere when he said he no longer liked New York. I think he said it to please Christopher. He certainly enjoyed himself there that summer— much more than Christopher did.

I feel a strong disinclination to write about Christopher's social life that summer. With a few exceptions, which will be dealt with separately, it's just a pattern of names with very few memories attached to them. Well, to be brief—

They saw something of Lincoln Kirstein and Auden, Berthold Viertel, Paul Cadmus, Tony Bower and van Druten[1]—Christopher's friends—but a good deal more of Ed Tauch, Jack Coble, Bob Stagg, Bernie Perlin, Horst, Ollie and Isa Jennings, Ben Baz and Bill Bailey—Caskey's friends. This was because Caskey's friends tended

---

[1] On May 25, Christopher records a meeting with John van Druten's boyfriend Walter Starkey, whom Christopher and Caskey had already met in January (see [Starcke,] page 81). Starkey had played Thad Greelis in John's *The Mermaids Singing*—which ran for only fifty-three performances and was nicknamed by Dodie Smith *The Mermaids Sinking*—in 1945. John once told Christopher that Starkey had caused him to break a previously unbroken professional rule of his—never to have an affair with one of his actors.

Walter's family name was actually spelled Starcke. When he became an actor he changed it to Starkey but switched back to Starcke as the co-producer of *I Am a Camera*, perhaps because he wanted his acting career forgotten. However, John and Christopher went on using the spelling "Starkey" in their letters to each other, as a sort of nickname which interrelated their boyfriends: Starkey–Caskey. They never wrote or said "Walter" or "Bill" to each other when referring to them.

to be much more party minded than Christopher's. Most of them were included in one of two groups, the Tauch group or the Jennings group. Ed Tauch was an architect and he had a big house divided up into apartments which he leased to other architects, all friends of his and all gay. [. . .] Ed Tauch looked after his tenants like an uncle; he was the only one of these architects who knew how to fix the plumbing, gas, electric light and leaks in the roof. He was quiet, friendly and still good-looking. Earlier on, in his navy uniform, he had been a dreamboat to many. I think Caskey himself had been violently in love with him, but only briefly.

Ollie Jennings was very rich, good-natured, fat. He lived in a fine house at Sneden's Landing (during the summer, anyhow). He had a divorced but friendly wife named Isa who lived in an even finer house, not far away. So both of them could offer cool luxurious out-of-town weekends, with lots to drink. Ollie's steady (to use the most unsuitable word possible) was Ben Baz [brother of Emilio, the painter]. Ben was small, red headed, not particularly Mexican looking, extremely lively [. . .]; a commercial artist by profession, quite a successful one. According to Caskey, Ben kept falling in love with people, coming to Ollie and telling him they must part, and then getting tired of that particular person and deciding to stay with Ollie. Ollie took all this in his stride and continued to love Ben— which moved Caskey to describe Ollie as "a kind of homosexual saint." Ben's latest love was a young man [. . .] about whom I remember only that he was good-humored, adequately attractive but beginning to get plump. Ben's affair with [the young man] hadn't split up the household, however. [The young man] came down there to stay, nearly every weekend. He must have been exceptionally tactful.

It was during a weekend at Ollie Jennings's house that Christopher and Caskey went to have supper with the painter Matta and his wife. The evening was made memorable by one of Caskey's outbursts. Matta, thinking no doubt that he was thus putting Christopher and Caskey at their ease, made some casual reference to the fact that he, too, had occasionally had sex with men. This enraged Caskey, who yelled, "I suppose you think there's nothing more to homosexuality than just cocksucking?" The Mattas were scared and humiliated; they tried to placate him. This happened on May 17.

On May 27, Christopher got two paintings by Edward Burra on approval from the British-American Art Center. They were in the same frame, back to back with glass on both sides, so that you could display them in turns. One was a still life of vegetables and/or fruit with (I think) some landscape in the background. The other I can scarcely remember. I believe it included some of Burra's mysterious figures with masked or hidden faces. Christopher and Caskey never made up their minds to buy this and it finally went back to the gallery. They did buy a small painting of carnival figures by Obin, the Haitian artist. Selden Rodman, who had brought back a lot of pictures from Haiti, sold it to them. I forget the price, but it was stiff.

On June 15, Christopher went to a Quaker meeting—perhaps the life he was leading gave him an appetite for it, as a contrast. He met Caroline Norment there. I wish I knew what Caroline's impressions were of this 1947 Christopher. Did she find him as much changed as he felt himself to be from the Christopher of the Haverford hostel? They had lunch together a few days later and worked hard at being friendly, no doubt. And that was the end of it.

On July 3, Christopher and Caskey went to stay with Horst, at his house in the country (I forget where). Horst's friend, Jamie Caffery, was a longtime friend of Caskey's; he had a queer uncle who then was or had recently been the U.S. Ambassador to France. Christopher liked Horst; he was handsome, well preserved, good-humored and good mannered. He had some thyroid pills which made you lose several pounds overnight; no doubt they were terribly bad for you.

On July 11, Christopher and Caskey set out by car to visit Truman Capote. They drove to New London (which strongly reminded Christopher of the industrial architecture of Stockport and Manchester) and spent the night there. The next night they spent at New Bedford. Next day, they took the steamer across to Nantucket.

Truman was staying with his friend Newton Arvin in a small house in the village of Siasconset. When Truman, in New York, had referred to "my friend," Christopher and Caskey had pictured some mighty and potent brute as being the most likely kind of mate for him to have chosen. They were therefore surprised to find that Arvin was an intelligent and sensitive college professor, quite nice looking but definitely middle-aged. Arvin welcomed them hospitably and was no doubt pleased to see them, but he didn't sparkle, didn't get drunk, didn't want to go to parties. When they went out visiting, he stayed home and read. Maybe this homebody character was part of what Truman, the gadabout, wanted in a friend; maybe he needed someone to come back to. (Jack Dunphy, although quite unlike Arvin physically, also avoids party going.) As for the difference in Truman's and Arvin's ages, that apparently appealed to Truman. When he flirted with Christopher, and he did so constantly, he would say, "You're going to be *awfully* attractive when you're a bit older—another five years, *and you watch out!*"

As a host, Truman was like a masterful child leading a gang of children; he knew what *he* wanted, he was determined to enjoy himself, and he took it for granted that the rest of them would follow him. He never stopped to worry about his guests and whether they were enjoying themselves. And indeed it wasn't necessary. Nearly always, Truman's enjoyment swept them along.

Truman leading the outdoor life of Nantucket seemed quite different from the indoor exotic Truman whom Christopher had met in New York. Without his elegant freaky town clothes he looked much less odd and much more robust. He had a squat, sturdy body, golden brown and baby smooth, with surprisingly strong arms and legs.[1] He was a powerful swimmer, and he liked cycling and horseback riding.

Several people Truman knew were staying at a house not far away —it was called Hagedorn House, I think. The host of this house party was Leo Lerman, the magazine editor, an almost classically Jewish Jew, bald, bearded, sly eyed, somewhat rabbinical in his manner, full of hostile mocking flattery, aggressive humility, shrewdness, rudeness, taste, vulgarity, wit and fun. He courted Christopher and charmed him, at first; Christopher felt at ease with his shamelessness. (Later they were to quarrel many times and never quite make it up.)

The other people living in the house were (as far as I can deduce from the day-to-day diary) Andrew Lyndon, Harold Halma, Helmuth Roder and Fritz Mosel.[2] I am pretty sure that there were at least a couple of dozen neighborhood gays who were on call when they entertained.

---

[1] While writing this (July 26, 1972) I heard John Huston in a TV interview say that he'd seen Truman beat Humphrey Bogart at arm wrestling, when they were working on *Beat the Devil*. Huston described Truman as "a power-house."

[2] I don't remember anything about the doings of Helmuth (Hellmuth?) and Fritz during this visit. They are mentioned in the 1939 journal, when they were in Hollywood. Helmuth changed his name from Schroeder to Roder after coming to the U.S. Christopher had had a brief affair with him in the old Berlin days—succeeding Stephen Spender, with whom Helmuth had had a much longer affair which ended badly but at least inspired Stephen's story "The Burning Cactus" and, I believe, his poems beginning "After success, your little afternoon success," and "Alas, when he laughs, it is not he / But a shopkeeper, who scrapes his hands and bows." [Spender added a title, "Helmut," when he later reprinted this early poem; but in letters to Schroeder he spelled the name "Hellmut."] Now I come to think of it, I'm nearly certain that the episode in *The World in the Evening*, when Mariano Galdós says to Elizabeth, "Bleiben Sie liegen," is based on the actual first meeting of Christopher and Helmuth. (See part two, chapter four.)

Andrew Lyndon was a longtime intimate friend of Truman's. They were both from the South; Andrew's hometown was Macon, Georgia. He was slim, soft-spoken, brown eyed, attractively monkey faced, capable of bitchery and probably of cruelty; quite a southern belle. Harold Halma was good looking and well built and much more masculine; a weaker, nicer character. He was a photographer. Andrew worked in a bookshop. They had an apartment in New York. I don't remember how long they had been living together, but their affair was already on the rocks—that is to say, Harold was still very much in love with Andrew but Andrew had lost interest.

Caskey and Christopher saw Leo Lerman and his guests every day (it appears) during their stay in Nantucket. They had meals together or cycled or went swimming. (The current that swept around that part of the island made swimming exciting but safe; you could float and let yourself be carried by it, very fast and as far as you liked, without ever being taken out of your depth.)

Almost instantly, Andrew Lyndon started to get a crush on Christopher. Christopher, as usual, was flattered and didn't discourage him. Truman encouraged Andrew strongly, out of mischief. Leo was voyeuristically entertained. Harold was jealous. Caskey wasn't; he didn't even resent Truman's effort to promote the affair—knowing, no doubt, that Christopher wasn't serious. And indeed nothing much happened between Christopher and Andrew—there was so little opportunity for them to be alone together, even for a minute. One afternoon, Truman, Andrew and Christopher went swimming in a lagoon, where boats were moored. Andrew, maybe hoping to start something, stripped off his trunks and put them on the deck of one of the boats. Truman promptly grabbed them and swam away —but not far enough to allow Andrew and Christopher any privacy. Only on the last night, when Leo gave a party and the lights were turned out so they could play hide-and-seek, did Andrew and Christopher manage to kiss and grope each other in the dark, but even this was quickly interrupted by Harold.

Next day, July 20, Caskey and Christopher returned by steamer to New Bedford, where they had left their car, and started for Cape Cod. They arrived at Provincetown on July 21.

Paul Cadmus and his current boyfriend George Tooker, Jared French and his wife were staying at Provincetown for the summer. So were Don Windham and Sandy Campbell. Caskey and Christopher saw all of them but not, I think, together. Maybe Paul wasn't on speaking terms with Don and Sandy—for Sandy had been Paul's lover and Don had taken Sandy away from him.

All I remember of this visit are two days on the beach with Paul,

Jared and George. It was a beautiful beach and quite secluded; they all swam and lay in the sun bare-ass—until suddenly a sightseeing jeep full of women would come plunging out of the woods, so fast that there was no time to cover yourself with a towel, even; all you could do was roll over on your belly and let them try not to stare at your buttocks. Another, more constant threat on this beach were the stinging flies. The New Yorkers took these as a matter of course, but they made Christopher and Caskey realize how lucky bathers are in California the (almost) Bugless.

Jared French took a lot of nude photographs of Caskey and Christopher. When these were printed, both of them looked ridiculous—partly because their worst physical features (the bandiness of Caskey's legs, the narrowness of Christopher's shoulders) had been unintentionally emphasized; partly because they had been so stupidly posed. Considering that Jared was an artist, he was a surprisingly poor photographer. Or was he merely inhibited by a private misgiving? Having suggested taking these pictures, did he suddenly feel that he didn't really know Caskey and Christopher well enough? This would explain an oddness which was apparent in nearly every photograph; the distance between the two figures was wrong. As a pair of lovers, Christopher and Caskey should have been closer together; as non-lovers who happened to be stark naked, they were too close. And what *were* they up to, why had they taken off their clothes, if not to fuck? They seemed hardly conscious of each other's presence, dully awaiting some cue or command to move, like animals whose actions are discontinuous and unrelated. The funniest picture showed Caskey halfway up a ladder; he looked as if he had already forgotten why he had started to climb it. Christopher stood below, ignoring him, with an expression of irritable uneasiness. . . .[*] Jared apologized for the pictures and blamed the camera. Christopher and Caskey called them "hippos mating."[1]

On July 26, Caskey and Christopher drove back to New York.

[1] The vicious tone of this whole paragraph suggests that there is still some soreness in this twenty-five-year-old wound to Christopher's vanity! But, aside from this, I now see that my condemnation of Jared French as a photographer is unfair by any standards. It wasn't incompetence that made Jared pose Christopher and Caskey in the way he did. He must have known exactly what he was doing, for the figures in many of his paintings of that period are posed in just the same style.

[* This may be the photograph which appears in David Leddick, *Naked Men: Pioneering Male Nudes 1935–1955* (Universe Publishing, 1997), p. 84, and which belonged to Paul Cadmus and John Andersson. Isherwood destroyed his own copies of French's photographs in 1957 or 1958.]

On July 30, Caskey and Christopher had lunch with Anne, one of Caskey's two sisters. I can't now remember if this was the sister he disliked less or more than the other; he was basically hostile to both of them. I suppose Caskey had to entertain Anne as long as she was visiting New York; this would explain why he didn't accompany Christopher and Lincoln Kirstein on a visit to Auden and Chester [Kallman] on Fire Island that day.

Auden had taken a house in Cherry Grove for the summer, and Christopher had already been to see him there twice, with Caskey, during June. The house, like most of the others in Cherry Grove, was just a wooden shack. Its window screens were rusted by the sea air, and, since Auden and Chester were the housekeepers, flies buzzed over unwashed dishes, uncollected garbage, unmade beds with dirty sheets and a vast litter of books and papers. Neither of them was at all interested in the ocean or the beach as such. Auden spent most of his time indoors, Chester went out chiefly to cruise the population, which was wild and barred no holds. The one little hotel was jumping. Every time the ferry boat crossed the sound from the mainland to the island, a big crowd of residents would be awaiting it, on the lookout for new faces. Guitars twanged, wolf whistles and gay repartee were exchanged. The passengers were eager for the adventures ahead; they stared boldly at strangers who had taken their fancy. This was Watteau's Cythera brought up to date—only it was an arrival at, not an "Embarkation for." At night, the noise from the bar could be heard all over the colony, and couples stumbled out of it and threw themselves down to screw on the sand, scarcely beyond the range of the house lights. No doubt the minority of elderly square homeowners objected strongly to all this, but at that time the only curb on sex activity was an ordinance which put the sand dunes out of bounds—not for moral reasons but because, in the hurricane of 1938(?),[*] the dunes had been the only remaining refuge when huge waves washed over that part of the island; if the dunes were to get trampled flat by would-be fuckers and another hurricane were to hit Cherry Grove, all its inhabitants might be drowned.

Lincoln and Christopher spent the night at Auden's house. They had to share a bed. Lincoln, for the first and only time, made a pass at Christopher—a half-joking, tentative pass, which Christopher jokingly declined. Christopher was ready to have sex with most males within reasonable age limits, and he certainly didn't find

[* In late September 1938, the worst storm to hit the north-eastern states in over a century left standing only fifteen or twenty of about two hundred summer houses on Fire Island; there were many deaths.]

Lincoln all that unattractive. But he hated mixing sex with giggles.

On August 3, Caskey and Christopher were at Isa Jennings's country house, to swim and have supper. Garbo was there, with George Schlee. Noël Coward arrived late and made a big theatrical entrance. Christopher had always been rather prejudiced against Coward—whom I don't think he had ever properly met. He watched sourly as Coward moved with the modest graciousness of royalty among the guests. Garbo got a speech of homage which Christopher thought disgustingly phony and even the lesser lights were presented with a compliment apiece; Christopher had to admit that Coward was inventive, he found a different way of flattering each of them, and each one beamed. Just before Christopher's turn came, he said to himself, "I wonder what kind of shit he'll try on me." They were introduced. Coward reacted strongly. Then, in an almost loverlike tone of shyness, he told Christopher, "It's extraordinary—you look so much like one of the great heroes of my youth, Lawrence of Arabia!"

Christopher often told this story later, mockingly. Yet that day was the beginning of a permanent change in his attitude to Coward. Subconsciously, Christopher started finding reasons to admire him and think him sympathetic. Which wasn't difficult, for there are many. Christopher, that shameless flatterer, had had his ass tickled by a master, and had loved it. Characteristically, he didn't bother to remember what compliment (if any) Coward had paid Caskey.

Caskey and Christopher were given a ride back into town by Garbo and George Schlee. (Caskey and Christopher had come out to the country by train because their car was being repaired.) Christopher was fairly drunk and took this opportunity of attacking Garbo. He told her that her custom of addressing him as "Mr. Isherwood"—and of refusing in general to address her old acquaintances by their first names—was sheer affectation and arrogance and egomania. Did she actually think that *he*, *Christopher*, had to be kept at a distance, lest he should take some advantage of her? Was she really so paranoid? Hadn't it ever entered her head that there were *some* people on this earth who didn't give a damn about her fame or her money or even her appearance—who simply wanted to be friendly?

I don't remember that Garbo said anything in reply to this. She was sitting in the front seat with Schlee—a position which made it easy to ignore a backseat scolder. Christopher probably continued until he ran out of breath. Later—no doubt because he felt he had made an ass of himself—he turned his attention to the ever-silent self-effacing Schlee and began to praise Schlee's driving in extravagant terms. (Was this done partly to bitch Caskey, whose speeding terrified Christopher whenever Christopher was sober?) Oddly enough, in retrospect, it is Christopher's corny compliments to Schlee that I feel ashamed of, not his rebukes to Garbo.

After that evening, Christopher didn't see Garbo for nearly a year. But she hadn't forgotten what he had said to her. When they next met, at Salka Viertel's house in California, in July 1948, she gaily told Salka, "Mr. Isherwood was very *cruel* to me, when we were in New York"; as she said this, she arched her eyebrows in an expression of comic anguish. Obviously, she didn't bear him any grudge. She could afford not to, for she was invulnerable, as far as he was concerned. Nothing he could possibly say could get under her skin. He, who had always found her absurd, now had to realize that she found him even absurder. Indeed, she made this quite clear at a dinner party at Salka's about two months later, when she suddenly announced to the guests, "Mr. Isherwood has *such* beautiful legs!" This tribute from a senior love goddess to a queer in his mid-forties seemed farcical. Everybody laughed. Christopher laughed with them, but only he would savor Garbo's compliment as a subtly malicious echo of Noël Coward's. He often quoted this one too, and in the same tone of mockery—nevertheless, his ass had once again been deliciously tickled.

On August 4, Christopher had lunch with Andrew Lyndon and Harold Halma at their apartment. Harold had to go out immediately afterwards, leaving Christopher and Andrew alone together. It was very hot. After several drinks, Andrew asked Christopher if he'd like to take a shower. This was merely a cue for both of them to undress. Christopher fucked Andrew. When it was over and they were lying naked on the bed, Harold arrived back unexpectedly early, his arms full of groceries. Maybe he had hoped to catch them, for he didn't seem surprised. "Oh, excuse me," he said, put down his shopping bags in the kitchen and left the apartment again. Andrew wasn't at all dismayed. "I'm awfully glad we did that," he told Christopher—who got the impression that Andrew's seduction of him was largely a declaration of independence, addressed to Harold. Christopher put his clothes on quickly and left before Harold returned. He didn't feel particularly guilty but he did feel embarrassed. To get caught like that—even if Harold had planned it—was humiliating and lacking in style. And Christopher liked Harold and didn't want to cause him pain. So, three days later—having made sure that Andrew would be away for the evening—Christopher phoned Harold and asked if he might come around. Harold may have felt hostile but he agreed.

They drank together and the tension eased. Christopher began making it clear that Harold attracted him. Although Christopher had an ulterior motive, he was quite sincere in this. The very fact that he had fucked Andrew made him hot to be fucked by Harold; he pictured himself submitting to it as a brutal but exciting punishment, inflicted by the injured party, this muscular sexy young man. In fucking Christopher, Harold would ejaculate the seed of jealousy out of himself and he would no longer feel excluded from the triangle. . . . However, when Christopher finally asked Harold straight out to come to bed with him and Harold refused, Christopher wasn't greatly disappointed—for his mission was accomplished anyway; to have made the pass was as good as having let himself be screwed—he had effectively disqualified himself as a sexual menace in Harold's eyes.

There was a further step to be taken, however. Christopher feared that Harold might tell Andrew about Christopher's pass, to punish *him* by making him feel that he had been just another in a long line of Christopher's lays, chosen merely because he had been easy to get. Therefore Christopher had to talk to Andrew as soon as possible—preferably before Harold told him—and explain why he had made the pass at Harold. In fact, it was several days before Christopher got this opportunity. When he did, he was relieved to find that Harold hadn't told Andrew anything. Christopher's fears had been founded on a knowledge of his own character—"man imputes himself," as Gerald Heard was so fond of saying. But Harold wasn't Christopher. If Harold had been in Christopher's place, I'm sure he would never have boasted to his friends, as Christopher later did, about the affair and the tact he himself had shown in handling it.

At this time, Lincoln Kirstein was going through a phase of tremendous enthusiasm for the sculpture of Elie Nadelman. On August 5, he drove Christopher and Caskey out to a house in the Bronx (maybe it was Nadelman's former home) in which a lot of the work was stored. Lincoln had filled the living room with a selection of the pieces and he came every day to dust and rearrange them, like a priest taking care of a shrine. Indeed, this art cult *was* Lincoln's religion. And how beautiful and noble his half-crazy passionate devotion seemed, compared to the prim knowingness of the ordinary "art lover."

Next day, Christopher and Caskey were initiated into another of the mysteries of Lincoln's religion. He took them down to Washington to see a collection of paintings which had been brought over from Germany. I'm vague about the details, but I think that the paintings had been hidden in a salt mine for safety during the war and that Lincoln himself had been partly responsible for discovering their hiding place. I assume that the paintings had been appropriated from their original owners by high-ranking Nazis like Göring, so that they were now technically stolen property; for Lincoln explained that their presence in the United States had to be kept secret lest the new German government should protest and demand their instant return. The room in which they were hung was guarded by military police, and Lincoln, Caskey and Christopher were escorted into it by an official of the State Department. I remember the thrill of this contact with the world of Classified Material—but not, unfortunately, anything about the paintings themselves, except that they were all by famous masters. Caskey and Christopher were proud of this privilege Lincoln had obtained for them. They bragged about it to their friends and were therefore disgusted when the State Department changed its policy soon afterward for some unknown reason and allowed the paintings to be taken on tour around the U.S. and exhibited publicly in various cities, before being sent back to Germany.

Christopher and Caskey were now beginning to get shots and visas, in preparation for their South American journey. Their last month in New York became increasingly social. At Ollie Jennings's house, Ben Baz had been joined by his brother Emilio and by Luis Creixell from Mexico [. . .]. Then Berthold Szczesny arrived from Buenos Aires with Tota Cuevas de Vera.[1] Then Stephen Spender

---

[1] Berthold Szczesny and Tota appear in the last two chapters of *The Condor and the Cows*, but discretion forced me to leave out some details about Berthold's background and his relationship to Tota.

Christopher first met Berthold when he [went] to Berlin to visit Auden, in March 1929. Berthold was then a hustler in a boy bar called The Cosy Corner which Auden frequented because it was near to where he was living in the Hallesches Tor district. Christopher fell for Berthold instantly—but not because he found Berthold so very attractive sexually. (In bed they were never quite compatible; Christopher felt that Berthold didn't really enjoy it and this inhibited him. I think they only sucked cock and belly rubbed.) Berthold's undoubtedly strong attraction—for both men and women—was that he was so vividly, charmingly, absurdly conscious of his own myth. (In *The Condor and the Cows*, I call it "The Szczesny Saga.") He was thus able to make his lovers see him as he saw himself—as the romantic, homeless, penniless wanderer, the Lost Boy who roams the earth, pushed hither and thither by fate, dreamily passive yet able and willing to take care of himself when in physical danger; a boxer, a cowboy, an able-bodied seaman who nevertheless seems poignantly vulnerable and whom everyone is eager to help and protect.

When Christopher returned to Germany a few months later, to stay with Auden at Rotehütte, a village in the Harz Mountains, he had arranged

appeared; he had been teaching at Sarah Lawrence. Then Chris Wood paid a visit from California. Through him, Caskey and Christopher met John Gielgud. Through Stephen, they met Frank

---

beforehand that Berthold should join them there. But Berthold didn't show up. So Christopher made a flying visit to Berlin and found out from the owner of The Cosy Corner that Berthold was wanted by the police for robbery. Christopher returned to Rotehütte, bringing with him a boy he had hastily selected as a substitute sex mate. (I think he must have been helped in this transaction by Francis Turville-Petre ("Ambrose" [in *Down There on a Visit*]), for at that time he spoke very little German.) The next day, the police appeared at the village inn where Auden, Auden's boyfriend, Christopher and the boy he had brought from Berlin were staying. The police were looking for Berthold—no doubt they had been tipped off by someone at The Cosy Corner that they might find him with Christopher. Not wanting to return empty-handed, they cross-examined the two young Germans and thus found out that Auden's friend Otto [Küsel]—a charming boy who used to wrestle naked with him in a field near the village, to the amusement of the villagers [and about whom Auden wrote two poems, "Upon this line between adventure" and "Sentries against inner and outer"]—was an escapee from reform school. So they took him away with them, under arrest; which caused Christopher's boy to decide that Christopher was dangerous to know and that he wanted to be sent back to Berlin immediately.

This was Christopher's first experience as an honorary member of the criminal class. And it was made more thrilling by a coincidence: while the police were still in the house, the mailman arrived with a letter from Berthold. Christopher read it under their very noses. Berthold wrote that he was in Amsterdam and hoped that Christopher would send him some money. Being now eager to play a part in The Szczesny Saga, Christopher proposed to Auden that they should go at once to Amsterdam. Auden agreed, though he wasn't feeling very kindly toward Berthold, who had been responsible for disrupting his life at Rotehütte and getting his boyfriend into trouble. (Nevertheless, Auden made his own important contribution to The Szczesny Saga; his poem "Before this loved one . . ." refers to Berthold.)

Auden and Christopher got to Amsterdam within a day or two, and had the good luck to run into Berthold at once, right outside the post office at which Christopher had just left a letter *poste restante*, announcing their arrival. They could spend only a couple of days together because Berthold had no permit to stay in Holland. (Boys would say, "My papers aren't in order," and, "My stomach isn't in order," in the same plaintive tone, as if both were ailments!) So, after a real romantic German farewell (Berthold was wonderful at them) he shipped out. This was probably his first voyage to South America. Many years later, he told Christopher that he had once jumped ship at Punta Arenas, earned money there as a boxer and then made his way across the frontier and up north to Buenos Aires. Perhaps that was when he met Tota and became her lover. She was a millionairess and a countess and old enough to be his grandmother but as human beings they weren't mismatched, for Tota was as sweetly silly as he was and her silliness made her seem sometimes almost girlish. As for

and Nan Taylor. Through Berthold, they met Victoria Ocampo. And, as if all this wasn't enough, Bill and Peggy Kiskadden happened to be attending some medical conference in New York, and Caskey's mother came up from Lexington, Kentucky, to help him and Christopher get packed. The day-to-day diary mentions several other encounters—notably with Mina Curtiss (Lincoln Kirstein's sister), Henri Cartier-Bresson, Jean Stafford, Harold Taylor (the president of Sarah Lawrence), Jinx Falkenburg, John Hersey, the Countess Waldeck, John Horne Burns.

Christopher's first impression of John Gielgud (September 10) wasn't favourable. Gielgud talked bitchily about Dodie Smith—or rather about Alec Beesley, whom he disliked. This put Christopher off him—which Christopher evidently showed, for Gielgud said at a later meeting (in 1948 in London) that he had been aware he had offended Christopher and that he was sorry for it. Thus they became

---

Berthold, it was part of his vanity as a stud to be able to enjoy sex at both age limits. "With a woman," he once told Christopher, "I get a kick out of being the first one, or the last."

(Aside from Berthold, only one memory of this visit to Amsterdam remains. Auden and Christopher toured the harbor and the canals in a launch. At the end of the tour, the passengers were invited to write their impressions in a guestbook. Auden wrote two lines from Ilya Ehrenburg: "Read about us and marvel! / You did not live in our time—be sorry!")

After this, Christopher didn't see Berthold again for at least two or three years. At their reunion, Christopher found it odd to be able to chatter away with him in German. Christopher felt at ease with him now as with an old friend, but he had to admit to himself that the removal of the language barrier had robbed Berthold of much of his romantic mystery.

Then, in the mid-thirties, after the Nazis had come into power, Berthold started appearing briefly in London. He was working on a freighter (either Dutch or Belgian) which plied between London and some North Sea ports. Berthold told Christopher and his friends that they were smuggling refugees into England. They brought only one refugee at a time, and they docked far up the river at a dock which wasn't carefully patrolled. In the evening, after the customs officials had been on board, Berthold and the captain would get their refugee out of his hiding place and walk him on shore and away from the dock as though he were another member of the crew, coming with them to take a look at the town. After that, he was on his own. Sooner or later, I suppose, he would have to give himself up to the British authorities and appeal for asylum.

Sometime in 1939 or 1940 Berthold managed to return to Argentina. And then Tota and [a male friend] (another of his lovers) set him up as part owner of a factory. Shortly after Christopher and Caskey visited Buenos Aires in March 1948, Berthold got married to an Argentine girl of good family with some money of her own—thus trading in his own myth in exchange for a future of middle-class respectability.

friends. Perhaps Christopher had been too hard on Gielgud to begin with. But it is still my opinion that Gielgud got nicer as a person—*and* better as an actor—as he grew older.

Frank Taylor was a publisher—I think, at that time, he was still with Random House. Nan was his wife. I won't describe them yet because Christopher didn't really get to know them until they came out and lived in Hollywood in 1948 and after. This year, Christopher met Frank only twice. I seem to remember that he had a violent crush on Stephen and that they'd been to bed together.

Victoria Ocampo appears in *The Condor and the Cows*. She is described fairly, I think, though a bit too politely. What a bullying old cunt!

It was probably in the latter part of August that Berthold Szczesny told Christopher the ghost story which is printed in *The Condor and the Cows*. "Told" isn't the right word; it would be more accurate to say that Berthold performed it. He hammered on the door of the apartment early one morning, staggered in and dropped limply into a chair, muttering that he had been lying awake all night, too scared to be able to sleep. Then he let Christopher draw the story out of him, bit by bit—how he had walked into the El Morocco and seen a young man who looked vaguely familiar, a young man in a dark blue suit, rather pale-faced but quite ordinary; how this young man had come over to him from the bar and Berthold had said, "I believe we know each other," and the young man had answered, "Certainly we know each other; you buried me in Africa"; how Berthold had recognized him then, as a shipmate on a German boat, who had died of malaria and been buried on the bank of the Gambia River; how the young man had added, "But don't tell anyone, because I'm here on leave," and how Berthold had felt as cold as ice all over and had run out into the street.

Berthold certainly did look badly shaken that morning, but he kept smiling apologetically, as much as to say that he didn't expect Christopher to believe all this. The smiles were curiously convincing.

He then told Christopher that he had made up his mind to go back to the El Morocco that evening. "If he's there I'll walk right up to him and hit him as hard as I can, right in the face. And if he's got a face—if there's anything there, you understand—then I'll pay damages, a hundred dollars, five hundred dollars, a thousand dollars —what does it matter? Only I have to hit him—to be sure . . ."

The next day, Berthold reported what had happened: "I go back to El Morocco and there he is. Just the same as last night, sitting at the bar. And so I come up, all ready to hit him. I think he doesn't see me. But just when I get quite close, he turns around and I see that he's very angry. He says: 'I told you already—I'm on leave. I don't wish to be disturbed.' He says that very quietly, and he sits there looking at me. I can't do anything. My arms are weak, just like a baby's. I turn around and go out of the bar . . ."

After this, Berthold told Christopher that he had visited El Morocco several more times but that the young man was never there.

I'm not sure if Christopher ever fully believed the story. I think he did almost—though he knew that Berthold could lie with great inventiveness. (The story as Christopher tells it in *The Condor and the Cows* is itself faked, up to a point—that is to say, it is presented as a single unbroken narrative, because Christopher couldn't be bothered to explain to the reader that he had heard it in installments.) Some years later, Christopher learned from Maria Rosa Oliver that Berthold had confessed to her he had made up the whole thing. Christopher was hugely impressed by all the trouble Berthold had taken; his playacting seemed to show a genuinely disinterested wish to entertain, which is the mark of a real artist.

I don't remember anything worth recording about Cartier-Bresson, Jean Stafford, Harold Taylor, Jinx Falkenburg (whose guest Christopher was on her radio interview show) or John Hersey. The Countess Waldeck was a friend of Jimmy and Tania Stern, an amusing vivacious attractive little woman with (I suspect) a deeply shady side to her character, a sort of female Mr. Norris. I think she was some variety of Balkan Jewess but she had been tolerated by the Nazis and even entertained by a few of them. Under the name of R. G. Waldeck she had written an extremely perceptive book of memoirs centering around a hotel in Bucharest (?) called *Athene Palace*.[*] John Horne Burns was then quite famous as the author of *The Gallery*, a book which Lincoln Kirstein admired extravagantly and even Hemingway had a kind word for. A faint darkish cloud hangs over the memory of this meeting; my impression is that Burns got drunk and became hostile and tiresome. But he and "Rosie" Waldeck remain in my mind as two people I wish Christopher had gotten to know better.

[* *Athene Palace Bucharest: Hitler's "New Order" Comes to Rumania* (1943); Waldeck was a Rumanian journalist settled in the USA from the end of the 1920s. Returning to Europe in wartime, she found that in Bucharest she could intimately observe the Nazi style of establishing power. As she writes in *Athene Palace*, "she had nothing to gain and everything to lose from the victory of an order of which anti-semitism was an integral part" (p. 6). She felt semi-protected by her status as a U.S. citizen, and reveals that she was sometimes duplicitous in order to achieve friendships useful to her journalism. She gave her book an epigraph from Stendhal to protest her underlying integrity: "Shall I be accused of approving these things because I describe them?"]

Caskey and Christopher went out to the beach fairly often, during this period. There was Long Beach,[*] where they met up with Ollie Jennings and Ben and Emilio Baz. There was a beach I don't remember the name of, where people fucked quite openly in the dunes—Christopher once had to step over a couple who were doing it right across the footpath. (You could go to this beach by bus; the driver, when he stopped at the entrance to it, would shout: "All out for Fairyland!") And there was Fire Island—a long drive plus a ferry crossing but you could do the round-trip in one day.

One of their visits to Fire Island was on Christopher's birthday. Christopher had got drunk the night before and passed out. He woke to find himself in the car, with Caskey driving. They were already a good distance out of New York. "The last thing you said last night was, 'Take me to Wystan,'" Caskey told him. "So I'm taking you." Christopher was delighted. This was Caskey in his aspect as the perfect nanny.

There is an unusually vivid memory attached to one of the Fire Island visits, probably this one. In the late afternoon, as the time approached for them to leave, a storm was building up. After a heavy stillness, the first gusts of wind began whipping the dry grass of the dunes. These gusts were uncannily strong, they made the grass hiss with a sound exactly like drops of water falling on a very hot skillet. Christopher remembered the stories he had heard about the hurricane and was apprehensive. Auden, calm as usual in this sort of situation, insisted on playing a literary guessing game; one of them had to quote a line of verse or prose and the other had to identify its author. I remember that Christopher surprised himself by doing well at this, although his attention was elsewhere. I don't think there was a storm after all, certainly not a big one.

Their final visit to Fire Island was on September 13. They went down there for one day only, with Lincoln Kirstein, Stephen Spender, Chris Wood and Berthold Szczesny. Caskey took a lot of pictures of this historic occasion, including a trio of Wystan, Stephen and Christopher posed just as they had posed for Stephen's brother Humphrey on Rügen Island, fifteen or sixteen years earlier.[†] This was probably the first time that Wystan had seen Berthold since the Berlin days. It was certainly the first time that Wystan, Stephen and Christopher had all been together since 1939. I remember that Chester took a great fancy to Berthold. They were able to communicate fairly well, because Chester could speak Yiddish.

[* On Long Island.]
[† In the Baltic Sea, during the first two weeks of July 1931.]

At least two of the group photographs shot that day cannot be Caskey's, since he is in them; they may have been taken by Stephen, since he isn't. This would explain the ridiculous and yet (I am sure) characteristic pose in which the photographer has caught Christopher; Stephen's malicious eye would have been quick to notice and take advantage of it. Eight of the eleven people in the picture are lying on the sand, all fairly relaxed. Caskey stands behind them, smiling and striking a campy attitude. Next to him stands Chris Wood, looking down, lost in his own thoughts. Next to Chris stands Christopher. His legs are apart, his fists are clenched, his plump little figure is rigid with self-assertion. He looks at the others as if he were demanding their submission to his will, but in fact no one is paying him the smallest attention.

When one glimpses Christopher off guard like this, it seems astonishing that more people didn't find him totally absurd. I do remember that there was a boy—a friend of Ed Tauch's—who burst out laughing at Christopher when they were on the beach together. Christopher asked him what he was laughing about and he answered, "It's the way you keep *strutting*!"

On September 16, Caskey's mother had supper with Caskey and Christopher. (I'm not sure if this was their first meeting; it's possible that Mrs. Caskey had been out to California to visit them in 1946, but I don't think so.) Catherine Caskey was very like her son Bill in certain ways; she was pretty, flirtatious, campy and quite unshockable, and she had the South in her mouth. She was also a nonstop, indiscreet irrelevant talker, and this embarrassed Bill and drove him into rages. Catherine never thought about what she was saying and she would often repeat reactionary ideas she had picked up in Kentucky and didn't even believe in. For example, she once told Bill that one of his sisters was refusing to have sex with her husband because she didn't want any more children and wouldn't use contraceptives. "Poor little Catholic wife!" Catherine kept repeating fatuously, until Bill hit the ceiling. That Catherine was an utter hypocrite as far as Catholic morality was concerned was proved by her acceptance of Bill's relationship with Christopher. She and Christopher got along together splendidly.

On September 19, Christopher and Caskey sailed for South America on the *Santa Paula*, of the Grace Line. Mrs. Caskey, Matthew Huxley, Chris Wood, Tony Bower, Berthold Szczesny and Paul Cadmus came to see them off. I believe it was Tony Bower who brought them a big bottle of champagne. For some reason, they didn't get around to drinking it, and, after a couple of days, when the ship was rolling, the bottle exploded like a bomb. Christopher narrowly escaped getting his face cut.

Caskey and Christopher had had a heavy night of drinking before they embarked, and had left the apartment looking as if it had been searched by the police. Mrs. Caskey spent a couple of days tidying up after them and packing up the things they hadn't wanted to take with them on their journey.[1]

□

[1] The day-to-day diary's list of books read in 1947 includes: *Back*, Henry Green. *The Good Soldier*, Ford Madox Ford. *The Shadow Line*, Joseph Conrad. *Knock on Any Door*, Willard Motley. *The Gallery*, John Horne Burns. *Kaputt*, Curzio Malaparte. *Le Livre blanc*, Cocteau. [Attributed to Cocteau who did the preface and illustrations for this anonymous book.] *Williwaw* and *The City and the Pillar*, Gore Vidal. *The Member of the Wedding* and *Reflections in a Golden Eye*, Carson McCullers. *The Rock Pool*, Cyril Connolly. *The Stranger*, Albert Camus. *Other Voices, Other Rooms*, Truman Capote. *Manservant and Maidservant*, Ivy Compton-Burnett. (There are a number of others—including some quite distinguished works: *On the Marble Cliffs* by Ernst Juenger, *Dirty Eddie* by Ludwig Bemelmans, *Memoirs of a Midget* by Walter de la Mare, *The Moonlight* by Joyce Cary, *The Death of the Heart* by Elizabeth Bowen and *The Thinking Reed* by Rebecca West—about which I can remember absolutely nothing.)

I remembered nothing about *Back* when I opened it just now (December 6, 1972), and yet I find that it has an ending in Henry's best and most characteristic manner; no one else could have written it. *The Good Soldier* (since reread) has left nothing in my memory but its claim to be "the saddest story I ever heard"—which seems to me absurd and perhaps even deliberately campy; Ford's disingenuousness is part of his charm. *The Shadow Line* is another unmemorable work by a beloved writer; Conrad combines startlingly realistic moments of physical experience (the tropical raindrop falling on his face in the midst of the spooky calm) with the artificiality of a cultured foreigner talking English at a literary tea. Christopher was much moved by *Knock on Any Door* when he read it; this was *his* idea of a sad story. He fell in love with the hero and wrote Willard Motley a fan letter. *The Gallery* has left me with a strong sense of the Italian wartime atmosphere, which is certainly something—but that trashy, traitorous liar Malaparte has left me with a series of myths about the war which still haunt me as though they were great art. *Le Livre blanc*? Christopher had heard about it long before he read it, and was a bit disappointed. Cocteau's love act with the boy through the transparent mirror is the only image which has remained with me. Christopher wrote a blurb for *The City and the Pillar*, but he didn't really like it, even then; he much preferred *Williwaw*. Capote's books have always seemed to me to be mere skillful embroidery, unrelated to himself and therefore lacking in essential interest. Christopher never truly appreciated McCullers until he worked on a screenplay based on *Reflections*, in the sixties. It is, in many ways, like a French novel and owes a lot to Faulkner. But McCullers has something that Faulkner and the French haven't—fun. *The Stranger* is a French novel and nothing but a French novel; one of the classic bogus masterpieces of this century. Christopher had been put onto Compton-

And now *The Condor and the Cows* takes over. The doings of
Christopher and Caskey are described in it, more or less, up to March
27, 1948, when they left Buenos Aires on a French ship called the
Groix, bound for France, via Montevideo, Rio de Janeiro and Dakar.

1948

The 1948–1956 journal[*] begins with an entry on April 11, 1948,
written on board the *Groix*, the day before they landed at Dakar.
It is a pity that Christopher didn't begin earlier and include a
description of April 1, the day they spent ashore in Rio as the guests
of [some acquaintances]. I still faintly remember the first glimpse of
that fantastic coastline—Christopher's delighted incredulity as the
harbor mouth and the Sugar Loaf came into view and he said to
himself, "It's not true, I don't believe it!" (Five years later,
Christopher felt the same thing when he got his first sight of
Monument Valley.[1]) [One of the acquaintances] was an obsessive
sexualist; he kept a chart showing the number of boys he had sex
with each month and how many orgasms he had with each. He
and [his companion] were superhosts; after driving Caskey and
Christopher all around the city and giving them a magnificent lunch,
they brought them back to [his] apartment where an incredibly
handsome youth was waiting. I think he was Japanese-Irish-Negro,
such blends being fairly common in Rio. Christopher and Caskey
had a hasty conference, since it was obvious that good guestmanship
required one of them to go to bed with him. Caskey said Christopher

Burnett by the Beesleys, who adored her. Christopher admired her then as I
admire her now—neither more nor less. It is delightful to visit her in her
elegantly, ironically furnished literary mansion; but she never lets you see what's
outside it. Christopher had hated *The Rock Pool* when he first read it, in the
thirties. Rereading it in 1947 he loved it, and has loved it ever since. His early
dislike of it was probably due to left-wing snobbery. He was quite certain that
he knew what kind of a book Connolly *ought* to write, and this wasn't it. It
wasn't socially conscious—or rather, it didn't deal with the kind of characters
you were supposed to be socially conscious about.

[1] Nevertheless, the two experiences were essentially different. Rio inspired an
aesthetic excitement, Monument Valley [in northeast Arizona and southeast
Utah] a primitive religious awe.

[* "The Postwar Years" in *D1*.]

should do it. Left alone with the boy, Christopher was embarrassed at first, chiefly by his fixed though not necessarily hostile scowl and his disinclination to talk even Portuguese (of which Christopher remembered anyhow only a few words). Christopher tried to excite him by sucking, licking and biting but without apparent success —until the boy suddenly turned Christopher over, greased his ass, got an entirely convincing hard-on and fucked him slowly and most satisfactorily.

The journal entries of April 11, 12, 13, 17, 19, and 20 describe the increasing discomforts of the overcrowded ship and Caskey's and Christopher's consequent Francophobia. Caskey was even more emphatic than Christopher about this; his attitude was so evident that the French passengers didn't dare kidnap him, as they did Christopher, to take part in the line-crossing ceremony and get daubed with flour and water and dunked.[*] But Caskey nevertheless condescended to go up on the boat deck every night with a French beau. They only kissed, because the Frenchman was so afraid of being caught if they started any serious sex making.

On April 22, they disembarked at Le Havre and went on by train to Paris, where they stayed a week—visiting Denny Fouts, running into Auden and Chester Kallman and also meeting Gore Vidal for the first time, quite by chance. These happenings are pretty well covered in the journal. Relations between Denny and Caskey were adequately polite but tense underneath—I dimly remember a semi-quarrel between Christopher and Denny on their last evening (the 29th); I think it was because Denny had casually suggested that Caskey should take some money and pick up a packet of opium from a "connection" who was waiting outside the restaurant. Christopher found this outrageous and refused to let Caskey go, saying that the police might well be watching the pusher, in which case Caskey would get arrested. If my memory *is* correct, Denny's suggestion was an entirely characteristic act of aggression. (An altogether different but recognizable version of this scene appears in "Paul."[†])

This was their last meeting with Denny; he died at the end of that year. Shortly after Christopher had left Paris, Denny sent him one of his sour-sweet little letters, saying, "I hope you and Billy will go on being as happy as you seem to be." Denny obviously didn't hope it.

Christopher's journal entries don't betray the fact that he found Gore Vidal sexually attractive, and that Gore was flirting with him.

[* Travellers crossing the equator for the first time are tried at a mock "Court of Neptune" and subjected to joke punishments.]
[† In *Down There on a Visit*.]

On April 29, Gore asked Christopher to come and have breakfast with him at his hotel. (I don't remember how Gore avoided inviting Caskey but he did, and this was probably one of the causes of the hostility which soon developed between them.) Just as Christopher was walking along the corridor toward Gore's room, its door flew open and a young man ran out, collided with Christopher and dashed past him to the staircase. Gore laughingly explained that there had been a misunderstanding. When Christopher's arrival was announced on the house telephone, Gore had told the young man —with whom he had spent the night—"Mon ami vient."[*] The young man had taken it for granted that the "ami" was an enraged lover, so he had jumped into his clothes and tried to escape. Gore received Christopher sitting in bed in his underclothes. Later, when he got out to go to the bathroom, Christopher saw that he had very sexy legs. They flirted all through breakfast, but neither was about to make the first move, so nothing happened.

On April 30, Caskey and Christopher crossed to England. In London, they stayed first at John Lehmann's house and later in a Kensington hotel, the Tudor Court. The journal describes a big champagne party given at the offices of *Horizon* on May 7, at which they met Arthur Waley and Lucian Freud, a supper with Henry and Dig Yorke on May 9 and a lunch with the Cyril Connollys, Rose Macaulay and Raymond Mortimer on May 11. On May 13, Christopher went up to stay at Wyberslegh. Caskey remained in London, where he had already made himself popular with several of Christopher's friends, particularly the Yorkes, Keith Vaughan, John Minton[1] and Alexis Rassine. Later, Forster invited him to come and stay at Cambridge.

---

[1] Caskey was more Minton's friend than Vaughan's. Indeed Minton was an ideal playmate for Caskey, with his wild high spirits, fondness for the bottle and generally erratic behavior. I think he found Caskey attractive. He did a drawing of him which is very flattering. Vaughan certainly liked Caskey too, but Vaughan was always shy and taciturn—all the more so when Minton was around. Christopher, at that time, would have loved to go to bed with Vaughan, but Vaughan definitely wasn't interested. No doubt Christopher's enthusiasm for his paintings pleased Vaughan, but I believe he rather despised Christopher as a human being. There is a coldly contemptuous reference to Christopher in Vaughan's *Journal and Drawings*, as he appeared to Vaughan during a dinner party at John Lehmann's on February 25, 1952: "C.I. casual, rather rasping in speech, sentimental, looking like a dehydrated schoolboy. Enormously interested in the superficialities of life." [The dinner was February 24, 1952.]

[* "My friend is coming."]

In the journal, on May 17, Christopher remarks that he hasn't yet seen Richard, who had gone off to stay with the caretakers at Marple Hall, just before Christopher's arrival. According to Kathleen, Richard had worked himself into a fit of jealousy of Christopher. I can't remember that Richard had shown any signs of jealousy during Christopher's 1947 visit, but he undoubtedly did remain jealous of Christopher as long as Kathleen was alive.

On May 18, Caskey came up to Wyberslegh. He was on his best behavior and helped Kathleen in the kitchen. His easy southern manners impressed her favorably, but I don't think she really warmed to him. She was shrewd enough to be suspicious of his campy politeness, which now and then became a send-up of everything female. When Richard returned to Wyberslegh on May 20, Caskey tried hard to make friends with him too. Richard responded, up to a point; but he too was suspicious, merely because he regarded Caskey as Christopher's ally.

Caskey and Christopher were at Wyberslegh until June 6—except for a two-day trip to London (May 22–23) to see Truman Capote, presumably because Truman was in England only on a brief visit. Caskey took a lot of photographs during his stay—of Lyme, of Marple Hall, of Wyberslegh and of the Stockport viaduct, which he greatly admired. One day he went into Stockport alone and began shooting the viaduct from various angles, running up and down flights of steps which lead to the river that flows beneath it. His movements must have seemed eccentric—photographers do often behave very oddly when they are at work—for he was stopped and questioned by police officers who were on the lookout for an escaped criminal lunatic. This was probably John Edward Allen, "the mad parson." Christopher's journal refers to him on May 29, but without mentioning Caskey's adventure.[1]

On June 7, the day after their return to London, Christopher and Caskey travelled down to Aldeburgh in Suffolk for the festival. This was the first year it was held. Forster and William Plomer lectured and Celia Johnson and Robert Speaight gave a poetry recital. But the stars were Benjamin Britten and Peter Pears. Ben played the piano, Peter sang, and Ben's opera *Albert Herring* had its first performance.[*] This was their hometown and they were putting it on the map.

---

[1] This entry is the last one made during their stay in England. After it, there is a gap of more than five months in the journal. [John Edward Allen had escaped from Broadmoor the previous July; see *D1*, pp. 405–6.]

[* In fact, *Albert Herring* had premiered at Glyndebourne the previous June and been performed at Covent Garden and abroad.]

Christopher still felt warmly toward both of them and would continue to do so. No doubt Ben was already beginning to assume the airs of royalty, even then, but Christopher had spent so much time among musicians that he took their grandeur for granted—he would have been far less tolerant of such behavior from a fellow writer. Did he regard musicians as a slightly inferior artistic caste? Maybe. He certainly claimed the right to be friends with them without showing any particular interest in their work. And, in Ben's case, Christopher's attitude had been very much that of an elder and wiser being, when they were both young, although the difference in their ages was only nine years. Perhaps Ben had always resented this condescension. If so, he took an awfully long time to show it. During their days together at Aldeburgh, Ben made himself charming to Christopher and to Caskey whenever he had a spare moment amidst his many responsibilities.

Aldeburgh itself left vivid impressions in Christopher's mind: the embattled look of the houses along the pebbled beach, confronting the menace of the sea which will one day swallow them; the rugged old martello towers, built to confront Napoleon, a menace who never materialized; the strong smells of boats and fish and the hard brightness of the flat land in the windy east-coast sunshine.

On June 10, Christopher and Caskey returned to London and went to stay with Cuthbert Worsley. They were there for the rest of the month, meeting friends and going to parties, plays and films. On June 16, Caskey went down to Brighton and spent the night; someone had probably invited him. Christopher had supper with Tony Hyndman and this was most likely the night (or one of the nights) when they had sex together. The sex was as enjoyable as it had been in the old days, only now it was Tony who fucked Christopher. On the 16th, Christopher also saw Gore Vidal, who had just arrived in England, at John Lehmann's. Lehmann was publishing an English edition of *The City and the Pillar* and was trying to get Gore to agree to some expurgations—which he finally did, under protest.

Tennessee Williams must have arrived at almost the same time. Christopher and Caskey saw him and Gore at John Lehmann's on June 18. This is the only mention of Tennessee in the day-to-day diary for that month—yet I have a memory of Tennessee, Caskey and Christopher together in a cab at night; it is foggy, and Tennessee exclaims, "We are the dreaded fog queens!" and utters his screaming laugh. Whereupon, all three of them begin to elaborate on the fantasy—how the respectable citizens shudder and slam their shutters and cross themselves as the dreaded fog queens ride by, and how one darling little boy disregards their warnings and looks out of the window and sees the fog queens and they are *absolutely beautiful*, so he shouts to them and begs them to take him with them, and they do, and he is never heard from again.

A day or two later, Tennessee Williams and Gore Vidal decided to pay a visit to Forster at Cambridge. Neither of them had met him. In a letter to Christopher, dated June 25, Forster writes: "Tennessee Williams got up too late to reach Cambridge. Vidal arrived and I wish hadn't, as I disliked him a lot." It appears that Forster took great pains to show Vidal the sights of Cambridge and that Vidal, far from displaying the proper enthusiasm, seemed totally uninterested; all he would talk about was his own career and his rivalry with Truman Capote. The climax of Forster's indignation was reached in the Great Court of Trinity, when Vidal glanced around him and condescendingly commented, "Pretty!"[*]

Caskey and Gore Vidal had their inevitable clash. It was at a party. Caskey got drunk and told Gore that he was a lousy writer—which was unfortunate, because Gore naturally suspected that this must be Christopher's private opinion which Caskey was merely echoing. I'm not sure what happened next. Caskey certainly said many other nasty things. I think Gore hit him.[1] The quarrel was patched up, but the ill feeling remained.

On June 20, Cuthbert Worsley gave a party. I am only guessing but I believe it was during this party that Christopher got a phone call from Gottfried Reinhardt at MGM. Gottfried wanted to know if Christopher would be willing to come back as soon as possible and work on a film about Dostoevsky called *The Great Sinner*, which he was producing. Christopher said yes; the only condition he made was that he wanted to travel by boat and train, not by plane. Gottfried agreed to this extra delay. What I can clearly remember is Christopher's enjoyment of the dramatic moment when he returned to the room in which the party was being held and casually told Cuthbert and his guests: "That was Hollywood. They've offered me a film job." Sensation!

A genial but basically unpleasant society queen named David Webster took up Christopher and Caskey in a big way; I think he

---

[1] It may seem odd that I can't remember such simple visual facts more clearly, but no doubt Christopher was stupid drunk on this as on so many similar occasions.

[* According to Vidal, he and Williams *had* met Forster—at a party John Lehmann gave for the two Americans—and the visit to Cambridge was made at Forster's invitation; Vidal published his own account of the episode in *Palimpsest: A Memoir* (1995), pp. 190–1.]

was the business director of the Covent Garden opera house. He invited them to two parties and a lunch within the space of five days. At the first party, on June 27, a cute radio and nightclub entertainer named Cliff Gordon gave a really brilliant black comedy act: Churchill's speech on the day England lost the war. (Christopher had met Cliff Gordon about ten days previously and gone with him to the steam bath in Jermyn Street, where they had had exhibitionistic sex in front of an excited old man; on another occasion they had fucked at Gordon's flat—after which Gordon, who was a hypochondriac, had become worried because Christopher didn't take regular syphilis tests, as he did, and had talked Christopher into being examined by his doctor. This doctor, who was the coy type, later informed Christopher of the negative result of the test by cabling to him in Los Angeles the single word, "Congratulations.") Webster's second party, on July 1, was a very grand affair, full of theatrical and ballet stars. Introducing Christopher and Caskey to Alicia Markova, Webster said, "I don't think you've met the Isherwoods?" which was characteristic of his would-be-daring vulgarity. But he failed to amuse or startle Markova; she behaved as if he had said nothing unusual. (Or did she merely assume that Caskey was Christopher's son?) Further along in the evening, Christopher was sitting on a couch holding forth to a couple of fellow guests about Anton Dolin's performance in the ballet *Job*, which he had seen the day before. Dolin, said Christopher, was amazing—nearly stark naked, he had executed great leaps up and down a flight of steps; he was as agile as a boy and his body looked magnificent—"And to think," Christopher added, "he was born the same year as me!" At the other end of the couch, slumped and silent and seemingly in deep depression, was a grey-faced withered man who might easily have been in his sixties. Looking at him closely now for the first time, Christopher recognized him with a shock of embarrassment. It was Dolin himself.[1]

On July 2, Christopher went up to Wyberslegh again, for a short

---

[1] Christopher had had a slightly different kind of shock at the end of the same ballet matinée. The other ballet on the program with *Job* was *The Clock Symphony* and Christopher had been dazzled by a young dancer in it named Alexander Grant, whom he hadn't seen before. Grant's solo had seemed to him to express the very essence of joy. As he jumped and twirled, joy flew from him in sparks, igniting the audience. As soon as the curtain came down, Christopher hurried to Webster and asked to be introduced to this magic creature. After some delay, Alexander Grant appeared, deathly pale, on crutches. He had turned his ankle right after his first entrance, and every step he had danced had been in agony.

farewell visit. The day-to-day diary doesn't say that Caskey came along, and probably he stayed in London. On July 5, Christopher returned. He and Caskey spent their last few days in England staying at John Lehmann's house with Alexis Rassine. John was in Paris but came back before they left.

On July 6, Christopher and Caskey travelled down to Trottis-cliffe(?)[*] to see Graham Sutherland; Caskey wanted to photograph him. I don't remember who gave them an introduction to him; I'm pretty certain they hadn't met before. He was dark and handsome and friendly and his wife was charming. (I remember hearing, maybe much later, that their otherwise happy marriage was saddened by the fact that she was unable to have children and they therefore as strict Catholics felt bound to refrain from sex. This was probably sheer fiction.) While Sutherland was showing them his studio, they noticed a watercolor landscape lying, along with other discarded work, on the floor. They offered to buy it. Sutherland told them they could take it, saying, "If I ever come to the States and run short of money, you can give me a hundred dollars." (This never happened.)

That evening, back in town, they had supper with Morgan and Bob Buckingham. It was perhaps on this occasion that Forster took Christopher aside and asked him gently not to drink so much. "You always seem a bit dazed, nowadays," he said.

On July 7, Christopher had lunch with Berthold Viertel. This was the fifth time Christopher had met Viertel in London; and they had met about the same number of times in New York—sometimes with Elisabeth Neumann, whom Viertel married in 1949. There has been nothing to say about him here, for he was no longer an important figure in Christopher's world. As Christopher became increasingly detached from his own German-refugee persona (which belonged to the post-Berlin years of travel around Europe with Heinz) Viertel had lost his power to make Christopher feel guilty and responsible for him. On Christopher's side, strong affection remained. But Viertel's huge old-fashioned ego, his demand to be respected as a German Poet and Thinker, his masochistic Jewishness—"I wanted only to keep the wound open," he had declared in one of his poems—had made it hard for Christopher to go on being intimate with him; it was just too much trouble.[1]

---

[1] If this sounds brutal, here's what Beatrix Lehmann wrote to Christopher many years earlier (1938?) while she was having a sort of love affair with Viertel: "Absence of poor old B.V. for a few days—really like coming out of a madhouse into a green field." [Almost certainly January 1938.]

[* A village in Kent; pronounced "Trosley" by locals.]

This was to be their last meeting. Though Viertel didn't suspect it yet, he was about to begin enjoying the five most successful years of his life—directing plays in Zürich, Berlin and Vienna, among which were translations made by himself of *The Glass Menagerie*, *A Streetcar Named Desire* and *The Rose Tattoo*. During that period, Christopher came back to Europe only once, and then their paths didn't cross. Viertel died on September 24, 1953.

On July 9, Christopher and Caskey sailed on the *Queen Elizabeth* for New York. They landed on July 14. Caskey had decided to stay in the East for a while before returning to California. He was going to visit his mother in Kentucky. Christopher left next day for Chicago on the *Twentieth Century*.

The eight hours you had to spend in Chicago between trains were always a challenge to adventure. This time, Christopher determined not to waste them wandering around the Art Institute. So he looked up steam baths in the phone book, chose one whose name, printed in extra black letters, suggested that it would be big and busy, and called a cab to take him there. The cab driver, a fatherly type, asked him if he wasn't a stranger in town. Christopher said yes, he was. The driver said that was what he'd guessed—because the bath Christopher had mentioned wasn't the kind of place he'd care for; all manner of bad characters hung out there. "I'll take you to a nice quiet place," he added, "where you'll be comfortable."

To Christopher, the driver's meaning seemed obvious; the bath Christopher had picked was queer. So he hadn't the courage to insist on going there. Cursing his luck, he let himself be taken to the nice respectable quiet place the driver recommended. It was called The Lincoln Baths and was in the midst of a residential district. When Christopher entered, he was a little surprised to find a very obvious (black) queen who took his money, grinned archly and told him to "have a good time." But far bigger surprises followed. The "bath" could hardly be described as a bath at all—for there was no steam in the steam room. It was just a shabby dirty warren of cubicles, nearly pitch dark and quite crowded; everybody was cruising. Christopher didn't have much of a good time because the clients were mostly his own age. But this, at least, was an adventure—and an utterly mysterious one. What had been in the taxi driver's mind?

At six that evening (July 16) Christopher left on the *Super Chief*, after having seen and fallen for Montgomery Clift in *The Search*. On July 18 he arrived back in Los Angeles. I think Hayden Lewis and/or Rod Owens must have met him at the depot downtown. They were now living in the Santa Monica–Ocean Park area, which was probably why Christopher decided to take a room at a tiny hotel called the El Kanan, on Ocean Avenue, quite near them.[1] Relations between Hayden and Christopher were much better now that Caskey was absent. But Hayden couldn't resist making put-down personal remarks. "You're fat as a pig!" he exclaimed, on first seeing Christopher. A couple of weeks later, when Christopher was feeling proud of having lost weight, Hayden told him, "My dear, you look like a scarecrow!" Rod Owens was always friendly.

Christopher's room at the El Kanan was dark and small—all the smaller because Christopher had to keep his bicycle in it; there was no other safe storage place. He used it only for going to bed in.

Christopher reported to MGM for work the morning after his arrival; it happened to be a Monday. It was delightful to have Gottfried Reinhardt as his producer again. (Looking back, I can still say that Gottfried has been my favorite boss—leaving Tony Richardson out of the running, because the relation between a writer and his director is different.)

The Great Sinner[2] is listed in its credits as having been based on an original story by Ladislas Fodor and René Fueloep-Miller. I'm pretty sure that Christopher never saw this story, if indeed it ever existed in writing. What he was required to start working on was an already-completed first-draft script which had been put together by Reinhardt and Fodor. (René Fueloep-Miller never appeared—for all I know, he was in Europe or dead.)

The story idea was basically nothing more than an adaptation of *The Gambler*—putting Dostoevsky himself in place of the story's narrator.[3]

---

[1] Caskey had the Lincoln Zephyr convertible with him in the East, if he hadn't already sold it and bought the station wagon in which he later drove back to Los Angeles. Did Christopher rent a car until his return? I don't think he did. So maybe Hayden and Rod let him use the old Packard. Their business was already doing well, and no doubt they now had at least one other car of their own. Aside from this, Christopher could get to MGM on the trolley car which, in those days, ran right past the El Kanan and along Venice Boulevard. And there was a bus which shuttled between MGM and Hollywood. Two days after his arrival, he bought a bicycle. This was useful for getting around Santa Monica and sometimes he rode to the studio on it.

[2] This title was later to provoke sneering smiles from many of Christopher's acquaintances; they all assumed, when they first heard it, that this was a typical piece of Hollywood vulgarity. Actually, *The Life of a Great Sinner* was Dostoevsky's own title for a series of autobiographical novels—a project which he never carried out.

[3] In *The Gambler* he is called "Alexey Ivanovitch." In the screenplay the name Dostoevsky is almost never mentioned; he is called "Fedor" or "Fedja." Polina is called "Pauline."

Thus it is Dostoevsky who falls in love with Polina and becomes a gambling addict through her influence. Finally, after descending to the lowest depths of addiction and even (this was Gottfried's addition) planning—though not actually committing—the murder of the old woman pawnbroker out of *Crime and Punishment*, Dostoevsky cures himself by writing a story about his experiences, which is presumably *The Gambler*.

It's possible that Christopher wouldn't have accepted this assignment so lightly if he had had time to find out more about it and think it over. But the glamor of a job offer by long distance phone was powerful in itself. And then there was the salary, and the free transportation home—and the immense satisfaction of having been remembered and wanted and asked for.

The reunion with Gottfried was like being welcomed back into a cozy Jewish-Viennese club; Christopher felt absolutely at his ease. Ladislas Fodor also belonged to the club, he was a Hungarian Jew who had spent much of his youth in Vienna. But Gottfried and Fodor were very different. Gottfried was intelligent, sad-humorous, idealistic, basically honest and capable of frankness. Fodor was full of smiles and schmaltz, smoothly witty, crafty and capable of ruthlessness. Sometimes, with his slanting, almost oriental eyes and heavy sleek mustache, he looked like a comic Stalin. Christopher didn't trust him for one instant, but that was unimportant. They skated gaily together on the thick ice of professional politeness.

Christopher was given to understand by Gottfried that he was free to rewrite the dialogue of the first-draft script and to reconstruct its story line in any way he wanted. Gottfried also told Christopher that Fodor wouldn't interfere with him, and indeed Christopher *was* left alone when he was working in his office. But Fodor was meanwhile in conference with Gottfried, unpicking Christopher's work of the previous day and restoring the script more or less to its original form. Fodor even fought to preserve his creaky foreign-sounding dialogue; Christopher was merely allowed to polish it. All this was done tactfully and smilingly and with charm; there were never any quarrels. Christopher argued sometimes, but he usually had to agree that this rewriting of his rewrite was necessary, under the circumstances. They were short of time—the picture was due to start shooting early in October—and the first-draft script was at least shootable; it was corny and slick but it made cinematic sense.[1]

If Christopher had had several months and complete freedom to handle this story idea in his own way, he would have tried to create

[1] Fodor got first credit on the completed film, and justly so.

a more lifelike Dostoevsky character—a role for a character actor, not a romantic lead—eccentric, ugly, violent, shameless, farcical. He would have tried to make the love affair with Polina an enslavement, a bizarre addiction, instead of a cool-blooded pretty Viennese romance. He would have thrown out the neat little Fodor–Reinhardt triangle with the casino director, who ends up behaving like an English gentleman. But, alas, he knew already that the Dostoevsky character was to be played by Gregory Peck!

Christopher had always been a model employee. He despised amateurs like Brecht who, when they condescended to work at a film studio, whined and sneered and called themselves whores or slaves. Christopher prided himself on his adaptability. Writing a movie was a game, and each game had a different set of rules. Having learned the rules, Christopher could play along with enjoyment—especially if he had a fellow player like Gottfried Reinhardt who was enjoying himself too. Once Christopher had accepted the fact that this game was to be played according to the Viennese code, he became almost as Viennese as Gottfried and Fodor. I have no doubt that some of the script's most Viennese touches were contributed by him, though I can't remember which they were.[*]

[* Isherwood left the following note nearby but unnumbered:] On July 20, 1948, a well-known herpetologist named Mrs. Grace Wiley was being interviewed by a photographer (from *Life* magazine?), at her home, which was somewhere in the Los Angeles area. She was showing him her pet cobras. One of them, newly arrived from Sumatra, became annoyed by the clicking of the camera. Mrs. Wiley decided to put it back in its box. As she reached out to do this, the cobra bit her in the hand. She remained calm, forced the snake to release its hold, put it into its box and told the photographer where he could find the serum which she kept in the house. But the photographer was so nervous that he dropped the vial containing the serum and broke it. He then took Mrs. Wiley to a hospital in Long Beach. However, the only snake-bite serum available at the hospital was rattlesnake serum. Rattlesnake venom destroys the red blood cells; cobra venom attacks the nerve centers. So this serum couldn't help Mrs. Wiley. She died, ninety minutes after being bitten.

This tragedy made a strong impression on Christopher, because of the fascination–aversion he felt toward snakes and because he had once met Mrs. Wiley, at a snake show to which Vernon Old had taken him, several years earlier. He remembered that she had exhibited two black cobras in a cage, which also contained her purse. Wanting to take something out of the purse, she had put her hand into the cage and casually pushed the cobras aside, giving them light smacks on their noses.

Gerald Heard had known Mrs. Wiley quite well and had visited her at her house where, with his usual sangfroid, he had sat drinking tea while the cobras crawled freely about the room. Gerald reported to Christopher that Mrs. Wiley had assured him she never had any trouble with her snakes because, "You see,

Christopher's first four weeks on *The Great Sinner* were busy but uneventful. He worked all day at the studio, Mondays through Fridays, and sometimes stayed on there with Gottfried and Fodor till nearly midnight. Gottfried would get food sent up from the commissary and they would drink and talk in his office or watch films in the projection room. (One evening, they ran two costume pictures, because both were set more or less in the same period as *The Great Sinner*. During the Vivien Leigh version of *Anna Karenina*, Christopher closed his eyes for what seemed like a couple of seconds. When he opened them again, he was shocked to discover what liberties the director had taken with Tolstoy's story; there seemed to be several unfamiliar characters. . . . He had slept right through into the middle of Max Ophuls's *Letter from an Unknown Woman*!)

In the evenings, Christopher had supper with Hayden and Rod more often than with any of his other friends. They were his nearest neighbors, their company was relaxing and their interest in studio gossip was unfailing. (Like most people who are in the midst of a project, Christopher found it easier to talk about *The Great Sinner* than about anything else; all other topics required extra concentration.)

Christopher also saw Peggy and Bill Kiskadden, Salka Viertel, Lesser Samuels, Vernon Old, Klaus Mann, Chris Wood, van Druten, Tito Renaldo,[1] Carlos McClendon, Jay de Laval and a

---

they know I won't hurt them." Much earlier in her life, as a teacher of natural history, she had been afraid of all snakes. To overcome her fear, she had made pets of the nonvenomous species and had later begun to handle rattlesnakes and cobras. She had been bitten several times. Gerald rightly praised her as a great exponent of nonviolence. But it must be admitted that she was sometimes unprofessionally careless. A lady who works at the Santa Monica Public Library has just told me (January 12, 1973) that Mrs. Wiley got fired from a job in the East because she let some venomous snakes out of their cages in a laboratory, with the result that they escaped from the building and terrified the neighbors.

[1] I don't remember when Christopher first met Tito—but it was before he left California in January 1947. From now on, they saw each other fairly often. Caskey had known Tito longer than Christopher had—in New York, before Caskey went into the navy. Tito, when young, had a well-made exciting brown body and dark Mexican good looks. In those days his air of sadness—the sadness of the *Indio triste* [sad Indian]—was charming; later it turned to obstinate pathological melancholy [. . .]. Tito, when Caskey met him, was going around with Cole Porter—perhaps as a sex mate but more probably as one of the decorative nonsexmaking attendants with whom Porter liked to surround himself. Caskey told Christopher that once, one rainy afternoon when there was nothing else to do, he and Tito had gone to bed together and

few others. Peggy—like Berthold Viertel—already belonged to Christopher's past, but she didn't realize this yet, and neither did Christopher, altogether. So she still had a certain power over him. Even while Christopher was entertaining Peggy with anecdotes about his South American trip, he felt himself becoming involuntarily apologetic. He hated this but he couldn't help it. What was he apologizing for? His defection from the Vedanta Center, and his life with Caskey. He wasn't really apologizing to Peggy, though. He knew very well that she disapproved of Caskey and of all his other boyfriends, past and to come. But that was neither here nor there, for she also disapproved of the Vedanta Center—and for the same reason. Christopher's sexual and religious associates embarrassed her equally; both groups, from her point of view, were shoddy, second-rate, not to be mentioned in nice society. . . . Christopher rejected Peggy's moral judgements in advance, yet he perversely went on seeing her and telling her about himself. Because his life made him feel guilty, he needed disapproval of it by a dogmatically stupid woman, a woman whose disapproval would reassure him. Poor Peggy! Christopher had given her an ungrateful role to play—a role which was very bad for her own character, for it brought out all her self-righteousness. When Christopher got cured of his guilt, several years later, he stopped seeing her altogether. She was well rid of him, and he of her. They were both of them remarkable and even admirable people, but their relationship had been founded on falseness from the start; they could only have acted sincerely as declared enemies. I must blame Christopher far more than Peggy. For years, he had been using her

---

made sex for several hours with great enjoyment.

As for Christopher, he felt much sympathy, even love for Tito, despite Tito's tiresome moodiness, which sometimes expressed itself in attacks of asthma. During August and September, Christopher twice stayed the night at Tito's apartment; the two of them wanted to make love to each other because of their mutual affection. The memory of it is pleasant though the sex acts themselves weren't satisfactory.

Tito was an actor. About that time or a little later, he played the part of Jennifer Jones's young brother in John Huston's *We Were Strangers*. In the movie, Tito gets shot and dies in Jennifer's arms. I have a memory of another evening (I think, in 1949) which Christopher spent with Tito, while Tito was suffering from asthma. Christopher pretended to be Jennifer Jones. Embracing Tito, he murmured in a would-be Cuban accent: "Manolo, Manolo—don't die!" which made Tito laugh in the midst of his choking.

The strongest bond between Tito and Christopher was that Tito was religious. He became a follower of Vedanta and a disciple of Swami. More about this later.

for his convenience and involving her in his neuroses; if he had had an elder sister, he would have used her in much the same manner. Well—enough of that.

Thomas Mann, in a letter to Dr. Theodor Adorno (reprinted in Mann's *Letters*), writes on July 12, 1948, that Klaus is "physically restored" after an attempt at suicide[1] and is staying at Bruno Walter's house along with his sister Erika, "who is giving him spiritual care." Thomas continues:

> I am somewhat angry with him for having tried to do that to his mother. She is understanding about everything—and so am I. That has spoiled him.
>
> The situation remains dangerous. My two sisters committed suicide, and Klaus has much of the elder sister in him. The impulse is present in him and is favored by all the surrounding circumstances—except that he has a parental home he can always rely on, although naturally he does not want to be dependent on it.
>
> It is a good sign that he curses the *publicity* that followed the incident on the grounds that "this makes it so hard to start over again."

I don't know just what Thomas Mann meant by "all the surrounding circumstances" which "favored" Klaus's impulse to suicide. Did these include Klaus's homosexuality in general and his boyfriend Harold Fairbanks in particular?

I don't think Klaus had known Harold Fairbanks very long before Christopher met Harold; the three of them had supper together for the first time on July 27. Harold was a merchant seaman. He was well built (though in danger of fat) and quite good-looking. He drank a lot. He could be very amusing or sullen or aggressive or sentimental, switching his moods suddenly and often. When he was drunk and encountered one or more sexy young studs in a bar, his favorite challenge was, "Fuck or fight!"—he didn't seem to mind being beaten up, at all. He was definitely homosexual [. . .].

If Klaus talked to Christopher about his suicide attempt, I don't remember what he said. Obviously, Klaus must have found the subject embarrassing. I imagine that one could only talk freely about one's own attempted suicide to someone who had tried it himself. Christopher, on the other hand, was a confirmed self-preserver.

On the surface, as always, Klaus was bright, witty and seemingly interested in what was going on in the world around him. He had a lot of courage and he tended to keep the melancholic side of his

[1] Klaus had slashed his wrists but his condition wasn't serious.

nature hidden. I don't think that he got much moral support from any of his love affairs. Certainly not from Harold Fairbanks, who was fond of him no doubt but much too unstable to be able to take a lasting interest in other people's problems.

How seriously did Klaus feel himself involved with Harold? I don't know. But I'm sure that Klaus's realistic pessimism convinced him there was no future in their relationship. He did however make a scene of jealousy when he found Harold sitting drinking with Christopher in Christopher's room, late at night. (Harold also had a room at the El Kanan and Klaus used to come and sleep with him there sometimes.) Christopher and Harold weren't, in fact, doing anything sexual, but Christopher rather wanted to go to bed with him and Harold realized this and would probably have said yes if Klaus hadn't shown up. He and Christopher weren't really attracted to each other, merely compatible; they got along well together from the start. Between them, they calmed Klaus down—it was easy to convince him that his suspicions had been false, especially since he had been drunk at the time. Next morning, he and Christopher were friends again.

Harold Fairbanks used to spend a lot of time on the beach. Christopher often joined Harold there when he could get away from the studio, which was of course only on weekends. I think it must have been on Saturday, August 14, that Christopher first met Jim Charlton. They met on the beach, I'm fairly sure, but it wasn't a pickup. Maybe Jim already knew Harold.[1] Anyhow, they got talking and that evening they had supper together.

When Christopher met him, Jim Charlton must have been about twenty-seven years old.[2] But he still seemed boyish. He was larger than Christopher but not above medium American size. He had a white smooth-skinned body, strong though not heavily muscled, with little hair on it. Big shoulders, sturdy arms and legs, very small buttocks. He couldn't have been described as handsome but he was funny looking and cute. He had a long, oddly turned-up nose, big teeth, a ready grin, blue-grey eyes with a mistrustful look in them, and

[1] No, says Jim (July 3, 1973), he was with Jo and Ben Masselink, not Harold, when he first met Christopher. Ben Masselink and Jim had been fellow students at Taliesin West; and Jim had had an unrequited crush on Ben.

[2] Twenty-seven was my own guess. Since I wrote it, Bill van Petten has told me he once saw Jim's passport and it stated that he was born in 1917, meaning that he was already thirty-one in August 1948 (his birthday was on April 8).

Later (July 1973), Jim himself told me he was born in 1919. Which of them was telling the truth? A passport is impressive, but Bill is perhaps unreliable.

a deep growly voice. He wore his brown hair short but not cropped or crew-cut. His clothes were of the army surplus type, cords, a blue work shirt, a leather jacket, sneakers. He always seemed very clean. At the same time, he had an unusually strong, musky body odor, which Christopher was soon to find delicious and intensely sexy.

I suppose that Christopher must have discovered, on the day of their meeting, the following basic facts about Jim—that he was an architect[1] and at present employed on a fairly large job, the building of about a dozen houses in the Brentwood area; that he had been trained as an architect at Frank Lloyd Wright's two centers, Taliesin North in Wisconsin and Taliesin West in Arizona; that he had joined the air force during the war and had been sent to England but not until the fighting was nearly over; that he was the only child of a widow and was unmarried and homosexual.

Jim knew about Christopher's writing and had read some of it, I think; I forget which book or books. He wasn't an ardent Isherwood fan, however, and Christopher had the impression (later confirmed) that their immediate rapport was a here-and-now affair; it had nothing to do with previous literary admiration, as far as Jim was concerned. This pleased Christopher, of course. And, as that evening progressed with the discovery of more and more topics and tastes in common, Christopher was finally moved to a drunkenly frank statement, "You know, I really like you!" Jim grinned and gave Christopher a mistrustful but pleased look, then turning his head aside, he growled, "You'll find I'm a lousy lay." Christopher was amused but taken aback. He hadn't meant this as a pass. (If he had wanted to get Jim in the hay, he would have led up to it much more gradually; indeed he almost never made a direct pass until he was certain of success, because it embarrassed him to be turned down.) He had had no reason to think that Jim would agree to go to bed with him—Jim had been talking romantically about a long-ago love for a teenage boy—and Christopher had felt no particular desire to go to bed with Jim. However, now that the whole situation had changed within a couple of seconds, Christopher found himself intrigued, curious and quite prepared to follow through. For some reason, Jim couldn't come back with Christopher to the El Kanan then and there; they agreed to meet again the next night.

[1] At that time, Jim hadn't actually got his diploma; he didn't get it until several years later. My impression is that he was an absolutely competent designer and draftsman but that he perhaps, in those days, had to rely on one of his colleagues or a builder with practical experience to tell him if his projected house would stand up and keep the rain out.

Jim's statement that he was "a lousy lay" may have been meant as a flirty come-on; however, Christopher found that he had had surprisingly little sex experience for his age. He had had almost no serious involvements, either with men or women. Since moving to California, his only contacts had been while cruising the coast highway in his car; he picked up hitchhiking servicemen and bought them drinks, after which they sometimes let him blow them. Jim was extraordinarily persistent in his cruising—if necessary, he would pick up half a dozen prospects in the course of one night—but he was also strangely shy when he had to make the pass, so every score cost him a maximum effort.

While staying in Arizona, Jim had met Max Ernst the artist. Ernst had told him that he was the kind of boy who ought to be fucked every day. I don't know if Ernst had meant literally fucked by another man or merely that Jim should get himself laid by a person of no matter which sex. Anyhow, Christopher did literally fuck Jim, for the first time in Jim's life. ("You took my cherry," Jim later growled.)

I have only one clear memory of Christopher's first sex encounter with Jim—the uncoy, entirely matter-of-fact way Jim took off his clothes, almost before Christopher had had time to close the door of his room at the El Kanan. He was like an athlete eager to start playing a game. Having undressed, he threw himself naked into bed, as if plunging into a swimming pool. Nakedness made him seem very young, almost babyish; a baby who was also a puppy.[1] He giggled, bit, kissed, licked, sucked and bounced up and down on the mattress. He wouldn't even pretend to be serious. While Christopher was inclined to verbalize the situation, paying his partner compliments, uttering erotic words and generally talking up the orgasm, Jim said nothing. He came easily, without fuss—after which he would usually make some nearly inaudible wisecrack.

Jim was highly potent. He could have two or more orgasms (as he later demonstrated) with anybody who wasn't altogether repulsive. Many of his subsequent sex mates told him that he was "insatiable." But Christopher nevertheless got the impression that his behavior in bed was affectionate rather than lustful. He loved kissing. He would kiss and hug you almost indefinitely, if you didn't insist on going further. He was never in a hurry. Jim's childlike affectionate playfulness was touching and curiously innocent—it made him delightful to go to bed with. But Christopher had to admit to himself that, as far as he was concerned, Jim lacked one important sexual virtue; he

[1] Christopher decided, very early in their relationship, that Jim was a Dog Person. Indeed, it was impossible to think of him as being any other animal.

was too wholesome to be really exciting, his sex making was vigorous but bland. (Here, I am trying hard to be objective— which Christopher ceased to be, after the first time they had sex together. Thenceforward, Christopher's reason for wanting to continue going to bed with Jim was simply that Christopher had fallen violently in love with him.)

What had made Christopher fall in love with Jim? The most comprehensive answer I can think of is that Jim appealed to him as The American Boy, a boy out of Whitman's poems. Jim was in many ways a much better specimen of a Whitman American than Vernon Old. Jim, like Vernon, was a twentieth-century town dweller, but it was easier to imagine Jim living in the country and the nineteenth century. Jim had a much more poetical feeling for landscape than Vernon had—though Vernon cared more for animals. Jim's descriptions of western canyons and deserts and forests were graphic and full of poetry for Christopher. And Jim, despite all his hang-ups, seemed more spontaneous and therefore more like a Whitman boy than Vernon—at any rate in bed, which was where it counted most. You could imagine Jim as a "Tan-Faced Prairie-Boy" lying all night out of doors kissing Whitman under a blanket. Whereas Vernon would have soon started to complain that he was getting sleepy and that Whitman's beard tickled.

Self-reliant solitude is one of the chief characteristics of Whitman's wandering American Boy. Christopher saw this characteristic in Jim and it moved him deeply. Later, he tried to describe it when writing about the character he called Bob Wood[1] in *The World in the Evening*:

> What struck me chiefly about him, always, was his quality of loneliness; and this was even more apparent when he and Charles came to visit me together. When, for example, Bob was fixing our cocktails, his slim figure with its big shoulders bending over the bottles would look strangely weary and solitary, and he seemed suddenly miles away from either of us. He was like a prospector preparing a meal in the midst of the wilderness.[*]

For Christopher, born on an intimate little island, The American Boy embodied his country's fascinating and challenging aloofness. Christopher felt challenged to break through this aloofness and make

---

[1] Bob Wood isn't a portrait of Jim, however; he is described as a crusader, a potential revolutionary—which Jim certainly wasn't and isn't. But Bob *is* described as being one of the Dog People.

[* Part three, chapter three.]

a closer contact with Jim—and yet he didn't really want to, for that would have destroyed much of Jim's romantic appeal.

Even after Christopher had known Jim for years, he remained deeply impressed by Jim's self-reliance. He was always able to look out for himself and keep himself occupied—he was never at a loose end. When Christopher came to visit, he would find Jim drafting plans for a house, or making a model of a plane, or drawing nude teenage boys, slim, crop-headed and snub-nosed, who grinned as they played with each other's cocks. (Christopher called them Charlton Boys; they all looked a bit like Jim.) Jim was also an efficient cook and a neat housekeeper. Whenever he moved into a new apartment, no matter how shabby and temporary, he would make it recognizably personal—painting it in amusing colors, fixing up odd lamps and covering the walls with striking pictures and clippings from magazines. If Jim felt restless, he would take off in his car and explore some remote stretch of country, all on his own. Once, when he had gone swimming in an irrigation ditch in the desert, miles from anywhere, he had discovered that he couldn't climb back up its concrete walls and had been trapped there for hours until someone happened to come by. On another occasion, he had been climbing a cliff by the seashore and had fallen. He had had to drive himself home with his leg broken.

Jim had been born in Reading, Pennsylvania. But he preferred to recall the fact that he had been conceived at Love Field in Dallas, Texas—since both the name and the state sound more romantic. Jim's parents had been living near Love Field at that time because his father was a pilot in the Army Air Corps. When air postal service began, he flew mail. He was killed in a crash while Jim was still very young.[1] The example of Jim's father may possibly have predisposed

---

[1] Here are some additions and corrections, based on conversations I had with Jim in December 1972, since writing the paragraphs [above].

Jim's father flew into a mountain during a storm. His dead body showed almost no external injuries, only a bruise on its chin. Jim is apt to talk as if his father's accident had been a subconsciously willed suicide—because he was bored with his wife, Jim implies—and a peculiarly inconsiderate one, since it made Mrs. Charlton so afraid of losing her child as well as her husband that she kept Jim at home with her and tried to prevent him from making friends with other boys. Jim blames his mother for his early shyness and inhibitions.

"When I was at Wright's, I was going crazy," Jim says. "I used to wander around the desert behind Taliesin with a copy of Wolfe's *Of Time and the River*. At night, the moonlight was pink." The planes he saw, on the day he decided to join the air force, appeared out of a wash [i.e., a dry stream bed]. They weren't in formation. They were flying very low, each following

Jim to join the air force, but that wasn't the way Jim told it. He described how he had seen two planes appear suddenly out of a canyon, in Arizona, and soar up into the sky doing aerobatics, and how he had decided, then and there, that he must fly too. In other words, Jim's enlistment had been for aesthetic reasons—it had nothing directly to do with admiration for his father, and nothing whatever with patriotism.

In his flying stories, Jim always made fun of himself. He told how, soon after he had started to solo, he had decided that it would be beautiful to fly over a neighboring lake and dip first one wing tip and then the other in the water, so as to leave ripple-rings right across its surface. He hadn't managed to do this, however, and had come to his instructor for advice. The instructor had told him he was an idiot and very lucky—if he had succeeded in touching the water with his wing tip he would have wrecked his plane.

When Jim was finally sent to England, he flew several times over Germany, but the Luftwaffe was by then practically nonexistent and he was never in combat.[*] Once, however, while he was over Berlin—he found he wanted to pee. You had to do this into a special container and it was awkward because of the lack of space. Jim somehow got himself entangled in his machine guns and unintentionally fired them—which brought several of his fellow pilots whizzing down out of the clouds, thinking he was being attacked.

If Jim had been just another good candidate for the role of Whitman American Boy, Christopher would have fallen for him anyway; but what made Christopher really love Jim, and go on doing so long after his feelings had ceased to be romantic, was his view of Jim as an essentially ridiculous character, even a bit of a fake.

---

its individual course, hopping over rocks and clumps of cactus.

At that time, Wright was feuding with the draft board, trying to stop it from taking away his pupils. He declared that their work with him was of far greater national importance than fighting. As a result, some of them ended up in prison. And Wright himself lost several clients, who thought him unpatriotic.

When Jim joined the air force, it was because he wanted to fly, not to fight. He avoided being sent overseas for a long time. He moved from one base to another, flying all kinds of different planes and enjoying himself enormously. Then Jim's great friend became depressed, thinking he was losing his looks and getting old; so he grew careless and crashed. He was found lying dead in a relaxed attitude, without external injuries, like Jim's father.

Jim's father had an identical twin brother. They were both great athletes in school, but the brother was the smaller of the two. Jim's father was nicknamed "Horse" and Jim's father's brother was nicknamed "Colt."

[* But see Glossary under Charlton.]

For one thing, Jim was apt to talk like a male impersonator, in a voice which was too deep for his physique and too butch for his I.Q. He must have worked on this voice a lot when he was younger and eager to adjust to the air force. Also he had a pseudomasculine mannerism which he often affected while telephoning; he would ring your number, say hello so that you knew who was calling and then remain silent until you said something in reply. Christopher (and many others) had the impression that this was a game; Jim's silence was a challenge. When two tough guys confront each other, it is traditionally the weaker who starts talking first. Jim was playing the hero in a western movie.

Although Christopher made affectionate fun of Jim's male impersonations, he privately found them sexually attractive. But he couldn't admit this even to Jim. He would have liked Jim to play the stud in bed, but Jim never playacted there; he dropped his affectations with his clothes. He would fuck Christopher as readily as he would let himself be fucked, but neither of the two positions was symbolic, as far as Jim was concerned—this was simply a matter of give and take. So Christopher was reduced to indulging his fantasy in secret, during the act. With Jim's cock inside him, he told himself: "The big fighter pilot was naked on top of him, raping him, fucking the shit out of him . . ." etc. etc.

When Christopher met Jim, Jim had already been worried for a long time by the shape of the tip of his nose. He had wanted to have it altered, but the plastic surgeon whom he had consulted had pooh-poohed the idea, telling him that he would do better to go to an analyst and find out why he disliked his nose. Jim had followed the surgeon's advice and consulted a number of analysts, without getting any definite answers.

Jim's current analyst—a Jewish family-father—kept urging him to take up family life, with all its responsibilities and joys. He represented homosexual life as being irresponsible, immature and wretched, by contrast. He drooled over the satisfaction he got from washing his baby's diapers. Jim related this to Christopher, obviously wanting him to speak up for the opposition. Christopher did so, with enthusiasm. He poured scorn on the analyst and refuted his statements, and Jim was delighted. What Christopher didn't realize until much later was that Jim was far more disturbed by the analyst's propaganda than he would admit. Jim secretly felt that he *ought* to get married and support a family. And he certainly *wanted* to have a son—who would grow up to become a Charlton Boy. Maybe Jim had fantasies of going to bed with him. (A few years after this, Jim begot a male baby and married its mother, thereby [also] acquiring stepsons. [. . .])

But, for the time being, Jim accepted Christopher as his mentor. He was much impressed by the number of people Christopher had been to bed with—Christopher could no longer state an exact figure but he guessed at one, I think it was somewhere in the four hundreds. Jim immediately vowed to beat this, and, within two or three years, he reported that he had done so.

Throughout the rest of August, Christopher and Jim met whenever they could. Sometimes, Jim stayed the night at the El Kanan. Christopher introduced him to Hayden and Rod, who were flatteringly envious. Hayden said, "Where on earth did you find him?" Rod made a pass at Jim in the men's room of the restaurant where they were celebrating Christopher's birthday.

On the first weekend of that September, the 4th and 5th, Jim and Christopher went on a trip. They drove down to Laguna Beach, where Christopher had reserved a room at a motel. The room had a double bed in it. "I'd thought it was to be for a man and wife," the motel manager said, eyeing them suspiciously. They assured him it didn't matter, and started undressing as soon as he had left. "Let's go to Laguna and fuck," Christopher had said, and fuck they did for the rest of the afternoon, until it was time to have supper with Chris Wood.

Next day, Sunday the 5th, they drove all day, visiting the Capistrano Mission, Lake Elsinore, the Observatory on Mount Palomar and Warner Hot Springs before returning to Laguna Beach. In a note in the journal, when he is restarting it on November 6, 1948, Christopher describes September 5 as having been "one of the happiest days of my life." Why?

Christopher used to be fond of saying, at that time, that happiness is simply the breaking of contact with pain, since it is in our nature to be happy whenever the reasons for being unhappy cease to exist. A highly subjective statement which smells of Disneyism, it is perhaps true in this particular instance. If Christopher was especially happy that day, it was basically because he had no immediate woes or worries. He was in perfect health. He was earning plenty of money at the studio. He had the clear conscience of a wage earner on holiday who knows that his work is up to schedule and is giving satisfaction to his employers. He was released from all the anxieties which arose whenever he was with Caskey. At the same time, he had no reason to be anxious about Caskey in his absence, for Caskey wrote regularly and would soon be returning to California.

But all this was on the negative side merely; the negating of causes for unhappiness. On the positive side was Jim himself. On this day and for this kind of outing, he must have seemed to Christopher to be the absolutely ideal companion. Christopher was fascinated by Jim's conversation and by his stories about his life. He found Jim romantic, ridiculous and delightful. He was hot for Jim and knew that Jim would have sex whenever he wanted it. Above all, he realized instinctively, even then, that Jim wouldn't present any problem in his relations with Caskey. Christopher felt he could let himself go and indulge his crush on Jim to the utmost, because there were no strings attached to him.

Jim probably felt very much the same way about Christopher.[1] While they were together at Lake Elsinore that day, Jim muttered, "No wonder people fall in love with you!" The way he said this made it sound like an accusation—but that was as near as Jim could get to sentiment. He certainly found Christopher exciting to be with. And he enjoyed going to bed with him. As for the existence of Caskey, I'm sure that didn't worry Jim. Being a Dog Person, he could attach himself to a couple just as readily as to an individual. Which is what he later did.

The next weekend, Christopher got three whole days off from the studio, September 11–13. On the 11th, Jim and Christopher drove to Laguna Beach again; this time, they stayed with Chris Wood. On the 12th, they drove down to Mexico and stayed at the huge old Hotel Pacifico in Ensenada. They had some drinks and then decided to take a shower before supper. Under the shower, Jim grabbed Christopher and began kissing him. They must have kissed for at least half an hour without stopping. Then they dried themselves, fucked and fell asleep. Several hours later, Christopher awoke and, as he did so, had a minor psychic experience. It is described in *The World in the Evening* (part two, chapter three):

There was a night . . . when I'd woken from heavy dreamless sleep after making love with Jane, and hadn't known who or where I was. I'd seemed to be looking down, from some impersonal no-place, at our two bodies lying in each other's arms on the bed. I could swear that I'd actually hesitated, then, like a guest at the end

---

[1] What I wrote here may well be more or less true. But, years after writing it (July 26, 1977), I came upon this entry in my 1960 diary (August 17); it puts our 1948 meeting in a slightly different light:

A rather wonderful evening with Jim Charlton last night. We got nearer to our old relation than in a long while—largely because he didn't whine and complain so much of Hilde. . . . He says that when he first met me—when I assumed I was cutting rather a glamorous figure—I was forever complaining about my age and failing powers. Now he finds me much more active and less sorry for myself, and even better looking!

of a party who looks at two overcoats, not sure for a moment which is which, before I'd decided, "That one's mine."

(There is, of course, one falsification here. Stephen, in the novel, is said to be looking down on a male and a female body—not on two male bodies, as Christopher was. Could one actually be in doubt as to one's sex? I suppose it's possible. But that wasn't Christopher's experience.)

Next morning, they went on the beach—huge and (in those days) deserted. Christopher admired Jim's powerful swimming. (He was also a daring surfer.) As they drove back toward the border, Jim suggested stopping near the edge of a big cliff overlooking the sea. Jim had explored this cliff on a previous visit and said that its slope was full of small hollows where you could lie hidden and sunbathe—in other words, fuck. Christopher vetoed this idea—I forget why, but I am sorry he did, because this would have added another happy memory to his memories of their trip. Making love with Jim in the open air always seemed particularly suitable; he was not only a Whitman Nature Boy but also a disciple of Frank Lloyd Wright, who opened his houses—including their bedrooms—to the outdoors.

This was the period in which the Wright Revolution was making its influence visible at the grass roots level; all over the Los Angeles area, soda fountains and hot-dog stands began to appear which were crude but recognizable distortions of Wright's style. Until Christopher met Jim he had known nothing about the Wright philosophy and would probably have dismissed it as pretentious double-talk if it had been explained to him by an academic outsider. But with Jim it was different. He was an authentic disciple. At the Taliesins he had seen a vision, and Christopher could respect visions. Wright's slogans and phrases didn't repel Christopher when Jim repeated them; they seemed part of Jim's lovable absurdity. Christopher sometimes accused Jim of not wanting people to live in the houses he designed—because people were so messy, they choked the rooms with furniture, cluttered them with cooking pots and books and violated the purity of their wall spaces by hanging pictures. Jim grinned, half admitting that this was how he felt.

At the same time, Christopher admired Jim enormously, just *because* he was a truly dedicated architect. Jim made Christopher understand, for the first time, the interrelation of landscape and architecture and taught Christopher how to look at architecture in a new way, as an expression of various philosophies of life. (When they drove back from Mexico, that day, Jim showed Christopher the dining room of the old Coronado Hotel.) Jim even dreamed architecture. Often, when he and Christopher had been sleeping together, he would wake up and describe in great detail some vast building and its adjoining gardens in which he had been dream-wandering, drawing pictures to show Christopher exactly how it had looked.

Part of the fun and excitement of being with Jim was that he felt free to inspect any building which was under construction. If people were at work on it, he would enter with such an air of authority that he was very seldom questioned. He would climb all over it, occasionally uttering scornful grunts or exclaiming, "*Jesus!*" or kicking disgustedly at its walls. Sometimes he would go so far as to knock over an insecure partition, saying indignantly, "What's this goddam thing supposed to be for?" or, "Who do they think they're kidding, for Christ's sake!"

The next weekend, Saturday the 18th and Sunday the 19th, was the last that Christopher and Jim spent together. They didn't leave town. On Monday the 20th, Bill Caskey arrived. He had bought a station wagon (secondhand) in the East and had driven it out to California. The station wagon had been christened "The Blue Bird" by its former owner, and its name was painted on it. (Later, when people asked Caskey what "The Blue Bird" meant, Caskey would answer with his southern grin and drawl, "Honey, *we* bring happiness!")

Caskey had found a driving partner to come with him, a boy named Les Strang.[*] In his first enthusiasm, Caskey had written to Christopher that Les was "like a blond German discus thrower." Whereupon, Christopher had become jealous and had written back to Caskey that he didn't want to meet Les, if Les and Caskey were still having an affair by the time they arrived in Los Angeles. Christopher's jealousy seems quite sick, considering his own involvement with Jim—even now, I'm at a loss to explain it. However, Caskey replied reassuringly—from some town on their route—that he had already lost his romantic interest in Les, who was "behaving like a mad queen." I seem to remember that one demonstration of Les's mad queenishness was that he had [shat] in the corner of a motel bedroom!

Christopher took a larger room at the El Kanan for Caskey and himself, until they had chosen a house to rent. Their first night together, Christopher found that he couldn't make love to Caskey at all; his memories of sex with Jim were still so powerful. Caskey took

[* Not his real name.]

this very calmly. Either he minded but was determined not to show it, or he knew instinctively that Jim wasn't a real rival. If the latter, he was absolutely right. When he and Jim met, a few days later, they became friends at once. Indeed, it was as if Caskey had established, there and then, a ménage à trois agreement with Jim. That winter, whenever Caskey wanted to go out for the night, or to bring in someone to sleep with, he would say to Christopher, "Why don't you spend the night with Jim?" I don't think that he and Jim had sex together—at least not often. Jim wasn't his type. As for Caskey and Christopher, their sex life was resumed almost immediately, without any further hang-ups.

The house which Caskey and Christopher decided to rent was 333 East Rustic Road,[1] down in the bottom of Santa Monica Canyon. It belonged to Lee Strasberg, the director, and his wife Paula, and was fairly adequately furnished. I don't remember how much the rent was, but undoubtedly Paula Strasberg drove a hard bargain; she was a real Jewish landlady—who, at the same time, kept protesting that she was an artist and didn't understand business. There was a sagging bridge over the creek; it was the only entrance to the house and Caskey and Christopher were obliged to get it repaired. Mrs. Strasberg avoided paying for this by ignoring the letters Christopher wrote her about it. She also ignored the problem of a rust-eaten old car which a young actor friend of hers had abandoned on the creek bank beside the house. Christopher had to pester him for months before he bothered to find its pink slip, and then someone had to be persuaded to tow it away. (A teenager finally did and then proceeded to spend several hundred dollars, making it driveable.)

Caskey and Christopher moved into the house on September 28, and at once started receiving visitors. That same night, they had Jim Charlton, Hayden Lewis and Rod Owens to supper. Caskey was happy to be cooking and entertaining again.

Next day, Lesser Samuels came down, to discuss an idea he had had for another film story. The day-to-day diary doesn't give a title, but I think this must have been *The Easiest Thing in the World*. More about it later. Christopher was still working on the script of *The Great Sinner* but only intermittently; it needed just a few finishing touches.

On October 1, the day-to-day diary says vaguely that Christopher went "to see [a friend], with Phil Curry." I think Phil Curry was a lawyer and that this must have been a visit to the downtown jail, where [the friend] was under arrest. He had got into trouble because

---

[1] The house is described in *A Single Man*; Rustic Road is called "Camphor Tree Lane."

a teenager he had had sex with had later denounced him. The teenager was, in fact, no innocent rosebud but an experienced hustler who had been picked up by the police and had got himself off the hook by naming names. Frau Mann rose magnificently to this occasion. She too went downtown to see [the friend], and declared to all and sundry that she found the idea that he ought to be punished absolutely ridiculous. "*Absolutely ridiculous!*"—I can still hear the brisk indignant tone in which she said it—this famous and highly respectable old lady defiantly heckling the Los Angeles police on behalf of her son's [. . .] friend. However, despite her efforts, [the] poor [man] got sent to a prison camp. Christopher and Klaus Mann visited him there on December 19. He was released on February 12.

On October 6, shooting began on *The Great Sinner*. On the 9th, Christopher temporarily finished work at MGM. Stephen Spender stayed that night with Christopher and Caskey, so this may have been the day when he came out to the studio to watch the shooting. It was a scene in Gregory Peck's attic room. He is lying asleep, exhausted after an epileptic fit. Ava Gardner (Pauline) enters, rearranges his bedclothes, then becomes aware that the desk is piled with pages of manuscript. To quote from the screenplay: "In happy surprise she whispers under her breath: 'Fedja . . . you've written.'"[1]

Admittedly, Ava Gardner's diction left something to be desired. Stephen bitchily pretended that he thought she said: "Fedja . . . you're rotten."

During the early days of the shooting, Christopher spent a lot of time on the set. At first, he and Gottfried both had high hopes of Robert Siodmak, a director they greatly admired. But it soon became evident that Siodmak felt somehow ill at ease making this costume picture. He didn't seem to understand the style of the period or the kind of acting that should go with it. Even his lighting was wrong, it suggested one of his modern thrillers. When the doctor came into Peck's attic, the set was so dark that you couldn't see it. And then the doctor spoke his line, "I need more light"—which made everyone who watched the rushes roar with laughter. The scene had to be reshot.

---

[1] Some of the stage directions in the screenplay have obviously been written by Fodor. Here are three samples: "These are the 1860s, an age when gaslight is young, as is the melody that brightly fills the scene. The fashions are charming, the décolletés daring, but the shape of a feminine leg is still a secret." "And once more his whole army of gold is thrown into battle. . . . The silence is ghostly. The whirling ivory ball carries destiny." "Near the windows is the Baccarat table. . . . Surrounded by a wreath of empty chairs, it looks expectant —as though waiting to welcome the return of its nightly guest."

Christopher had had such misgivings about Peck before the film started shooting that he now reacted in the opposite direction, simply because Peck didn't immediately disgrace himself in his first scenes. Christopher tried for a while to believe that Peck was going to be very good, and he said so to all his friends. Ivan Moffat had soon perfected a fiendish imitation of Christopher describing Peck's performance: "It's really wonderful, you know, because he does it so simply. He opens his eyes and he says, 'I've seen Christ'—just like that."

I should write something about Frank Taylor (see pages 134–136) at this point. Frank Taylor had now settled in Los Angeles and was working as a producer at MGM. He was tall, skinny, boyish. His hair was very short and he dressed neatly, in Ivy-League-college-kid style, usually wearing a bow tie. He had professionally sincere blue eyes and lots of Madison Avenue charm. He was quite desperately enthusiastic about everything which he believed to be "in," at any given moment. A positive thinker, he abounded in money-making schemes so grandiose that one kept expecting him to become a millionaire. His sexuality was compulsive and rather scary, he pursued his (always male) prey like a spider and seized it with his long, obscenely thin arms and legs. His wife Nan tried desperately to keep up with [. . .] him. She was small and (I guess) cute. [. . .] They had, at that time, three or four small children, all boys. [. . .]

I have tried to say the worst things about Frank Taylor first, so as to get them off my chest. Having said them, I can admit that Christopher very often enjoyed being with Frank and found him intelligent and amusing; very often agreed with him politically, for he was a model liberal; very often felt his charm. On two occasions, while drunk, he actually had sex with Frank[*]—though it isn't an experience I care to dwell on.

What really repelled Christopher—and what repels me today— about Frank was something which was none of Christopher's business; his dishonest, tricky bisexual posture. Frank bragged about his homosexual affairs and even sometimes demanded that they should be respected as serious love dramas. At the same time, he became maudlin over his marriage and his responsibilities as a father. Stephen Spender is deeply false in the same way, but not nearly as disgusting as Frank, because he is too shrewd to parade his senti- mentality in public. They are both utterly untrustworthy—but then, one should know better than to trust them. On the positive side,

[* Frank Taylor stated that they never had sex and that he did not find Isherwood physically attractive.]

they were useful to Christopher as partial models for one of his worst and one of his best literary characters—Stephen Monk in *The World in the Evening* and Patrick in *A Meeting by the River*. I believe Frank Taylor took Stephen Monk personally and was offended. He never spoke of this to Christopher, but, after the book was published, they gradually lost contact. Stephen Spender wouldn't have been offended—he isn't petty in that way—though he may well have been hurt. But the bond between Stephen and Christopher was and still is too tough to be broken—whatever they may write and say about each other.

On October 14, Christopher brought Frank Taylor an outline for a movie he had written with Klaus Mann; it was based on the life of Han Van Meegeren, the painter-forger, and his dealings with the Nazis. This project was entirely Klaus's idea; he had studied Van Meegeren's career while he was in Holland. Frank wasn't interested; or, if he was, he failed to interest the front office. On November 12, Thomas Mann (see *Letters of Thomas Mann*) wrote to Klaus, "The starry-eyed one seems to have failed—anyone who counts on the movies is throwing himself on Satan's mercies." ("The starry-eyed one" was evidently a family nickname for Christopher. Whether it just meant that his eyes were bright, or whether it referred to his supposedly excessive optimism, I don't know.)

On October 18, Christopher says in the day-to-day diary that he worked on *The Condor and the Cows*. He had already written some of this—the first two chapters were finished on board the *Groix*, but probably little or nothing since then.[1] Christopher didn't finish chapter three until November 15.

On November 6 and 7, there are two more entries in the 1948–1956 journal—the first since May 29. They refer to a party given by Caskey and Christopher on November 4 and to the marriage of Vernon Old and Patty O'Neill[*] on November 5, with Peggy Kiskadden and Christopher in attendance. The guests at the party were Jay Laval, Bill Bailey, Hurd Hatfield, Roy Radebaugh (better known as Richard Cromwell the actor), Lennie Newman (see page 67), Hayden Lewis and Rod Owens, Roger Edens (who was a high-up in the music department at MGM) with [a friend] Don Van Trees, and Jim Charlton. Jim now came to the house regularly,

---

[1] There were however at least six articles covering different phases of the trip which Christopher had written while he was still in South America. These he quoted from directly or rewrote when he worked on the book itself. The articles appeared in various magazines during 1948 or the early part of 1949.

[* Not her real name.]

often bringing a boyfriend with him and later screwing him in one of the two upstair bedrooms. Sometimes he showed up without having been invited; freeloading is a characteristic vice of Dog People. At thirty-eight, Radebaugh still had some of the cuteness which had made Richard Cromwell one of the homosexual pinup boys of the thirties.[1] Now he had given up his movie career and taken to sculpting. He was a touching, sweet-natured tragic character who drank too much. He had a violent unrequited crush on Rod Owens. He was to die of cancer in 1960. Lennie Newman was still cooking for Jay Laval at his restaurant. Lennie had become Caskey's favorite drinking companion. They spent many evenings out on the town together.

Vernon Old and Patty O'Neill had been living together for some time already. I seem to remember that Christopher actually urged them to get married—or rather, urged Vernon to marry Patty, who needed no urging. If Christopher did indeed do this, his motives must have been largely malicious. He must have been harboring a grudge against Vernon, who picked up lovers and dropped them again with no regard for anything but his own convenience. Christopher must have wanted to see Vernon hog-tied, for once, by marriage.[*] And this suggests that Christopher himself was feeling hog-tied and therefore envious and resentful of other people's freedom.

In the journal entry of November 6, Christopher writes that, "Caskey is endlessly busy, home building. . . . He never ceases to carpenter, sew, paint, cook." Christopher adds, "Sometimes I ask myself uneasily, what will happen when the home *is* built?" Christopher says nothing against Caskey here but he goes on to express a lot of guilt and self-defensiveness about their way of life: "I'm being confronted, at last, with the problems of the Householder —and who ever dares to say they are less than the problems of the Monk? . . . No doubt the life in Santa Monica Canyon is empty, vain, trivial, tragic, indigent of God. But that's no reason not to live here and try to do the best you can." The best Christopher could do was to make japam (not very regularly), see Swami now and then, and keep assuring himself that he would restart his novel as soon as

---

[1] I particularly remember a general fluttering of English hearts over him in *Lives of a Bengal Lancer*, 1935.

[* According to Vernon Old, Isherwood remembers wrongly. Old recalls that Isherwood derided marriage as "an old-fashioned and bourgeois thing to do, and couldn't imagine why we wanted it. Yet, he arranged a tiresome reception at Salka Viertel's which everyone dreaded, but went through with to please him. I remember that Caskey fell asleep."]

his bread-and-butter chore, *The Condor and the Cows*, was finished. Meanwhile he continued to drink too much and his guilt pressure continued to build up.

Christopher also refers in this entry to the surprise victory of Truman over Dewey in the elections—which took place, that year, on November 2. Like Salka, and many many others, Christopher rejoiced in the discomfiture of the pollsters even more than in the defeat of Dewey.

On November 19, Brad Saurin[*] is mentioned for the first time. Brad was a very tall blond, amusingly attractive, more than somewhat crazy young man who had served with distinction as a pilot in World War II. He was queer, sexually wild, [. . .] and a joker. He looked deceptively "nice" and upper-class, especially when his pretty gold hair was smoothly brushed and he was wearing a uniform—he was still in the air force, or at any rate [in] the reserve. His father was (I think) a general, a good grey career soldier, courteous, intelligent. Brad's brother,[1] a handsome heterosexual dark boy, was an avowed communist. His existence was a serious blot on Brad's military record, but one of the most impressive things about the Saurin family was that neither Brad, nor his father and mother, would express even a formal disapproval of his doings. They saw him frequently—I believe he had an academic job in San Francisco—and they publicly defended his right to his own political opinions.

At that time, Brad was having an affair with Jay Laval. On November 25, Brad invited Christopher and Caskey and Jay to a party at his parents' house. So I guess General and Mrs. Saurin were as broad-minded about Brad's queerness as they were about his brother's communism.

On November 29, Christopher finished chapter four of *The Condor and the Cows*.

On December 9, he finished chapter five.

On December 16, Denny Fouts died in Rome. I don't remember exactly when or how Christopher got the news. A letter written to Christopher by John Goodwin from Agadir, Morocco, on January 9, 1949, refers to a cable Christopher has sent him—so Christopher must have heard about Denny earlier than this. In his letter Goodwin says that he last saw Denny in Rome in November.[2] Denny had had

---

[1] Named Henry(?)

[2] About this visit, John Goodwin writes: ". . . once I told him very brutally that why he had lost all his friends (as he constantly complained of it) was that he was not himself any more. He asked in his strangely rational and yet hazy way just in what way was he different. It was hard to tell him for I meant really saying that he was not at all rational, that his habits of lying abed and living a

[* Not his real name.]

a friend with him, Tony Watson-Gandy. It was Tony who later came to Paris, met John again and told him about Denny's death. "He had found Denny dead in the john and immediately rushed him to a hospital in case he should still be alive. There was an autopsy and it proved to be his heart. He apparently had had a bad heart for a long time and since I had left Rome he also had had a bad case of flu. It was *not* suicide nor *drugs*. Of course people will say so and it really makes no matter. Tony said that his face showed no pain so that it must have been a sudden attack without agony."[1]

On December 18, Christopher finished chapter six—and was therefore more than halfway through the book.

Gian Carlo Menotti is mentioned in the day-to-day diary as having come to supper that night. Menotti and Christopher had met each other for the first time back in July or August, when they were both working for MGM. Christopher was charmed by Menotti's vitality and they saw each other often. When Caskey arrived home, Menotti promptly made a pass at him, unsuccessfully. Christopher was a little annoyed by this but then decided that Latins will be Latins and must be excused.

On December 22, Ben Bok and his girl Coral were married, and Christopher was at the ceremony. Peggy disapproved of Ben's marriage even more than she had disapproved of Vernon Old's. She told Christopher in a tone of deep distaste that Ben and Coral were only getting married because they wanted sex so badly. Peggy also found Coral's family [not to her liking].

On December 23, Christopher went to Swami's birthday lunch at the Vedanta Center. In the evening, he had supper with Jim Charlton at the Santa Inez Inn. This may just possibly have been the

---

kind of Poe existence made it difficult to share anything of the world with him. But he seemed to see finally what I meant and for a week until I left, though his habits didn't change, he wanted to live, which was something he hadn't cared one way or another about for a long time. He was seriously considering going to England or America to a psychiatrist which I was all for, even though I admitted to him and he agreed that they were only a very last resort."

[1] A sequel to Denny's death was described to Christopher much later—it may be partly untrue: Tony Watson-Gandy was said to have adored Denny and to have done his best to look after him as long as Denny was alive; but Tony refused absolutely to take drugs. However, after Denny's death, Tony found a hypodermic syringe and some heroin in Denny's suitcase. In his misery and grief, Tony decided to try it. As a result he became a dope addict. He went back to England and died a few years later.

Tony took Denny's dog Trotsky back with him. And so that adventurous dog life, which began in a conscientious objectors' camp in the California mountains, ended in one of the stately homes of England.

occasion of a scene which Christopher later adapted for *The World in the Evening*[1]:

While Christopher and Jim were drinking at the bar, before supper, they attracted the notice of two large drunken men. The men had probably guessed that Jim and Christopher were queer. They were intrigued and aggressive. One of the men said to Christopher, "How about us throwing you in the pool?" Christopher told them to go ahead, adding that he was in the mood for a swim. He wasn't at all afraid of the men, for their attitude was basically flirtatious; little as they were aware of this. The pool was heated, and Christopher was drunk enough himself to welcome the prospect of a dip and a mild scandal. One of the men picked him up in his arms, and began walking out of the bar. Christopher didn't offer the least resistance. He was showing off for Jim's benefit. Jim tried to interfere, but the other man blocked his path. Everybody in the bar was watching. A bartender uttered a ridiculously ineffectual warning that the pool was closed for swimming after sunset. Now, however, the manager or some other authority figure appeared and boldly told the man who was carrying Christopher that he was causing a disturbance. This was Christopher's opportunity to dominate the situation. Loud and clear and British, he said, "This gentleman is not annoying me." This wasn't bar-room humor, so it failed to get a laugh from the bar guests—it merely puzzled them. It also puzzled and somehow deflated the high spirits of Christopher's would-be ducker. He put Christopher down and staggered off.

On December 28, there was a party on Stage 15 at MGM to celebrate the end of shooting on *The Great Sinner*. I don't remember anything about this party. Christopher probably got drunk to deaden his embarrassment at having to project optimism amidst his fellow members of this losing team—for it must surely have been evident by now that *The Great Sinner* would be a loser, or at best a nonwinner.

On December 31, Christopher saw the New Year in at Salka Viertel's. I think Montgomery Clift was there among others and that this was the night when Clift insisted on drinking blood brotherhood with Christopher. They had met several times already—Clift having been introduced into the Viertel circle by Fred Zinnemann who had directed him in *The Search*. Whenever Clift and Christopher met, they playacted enthusiasm for each other, but they were never to become real friends. Maybe Clift found Christopher cold and standoffish. Christopher found Clift touching but ugly minded and sick.

---

[1] Part three, chapter one.

It seems strange that Caskey and Christopher spent this New Year's Eve apart—and ironic that Caskey spent it with Jim Charlton. Maybe Caskey was going bar crawling and Christopher just didn't want to come along. It doesn't seem likely that they had actually quarrelled because, on New Year's Day, they drove up to Ojai, taking Jim with them, and all three stayed the night at Iris Tree's ranch.

1949

On January 4, Christopher's books arrived from New York.[1] All this while, they had been stored in the cellar of 207 East 52nd

---

[1] The day-to-day diary's list of books Christopher read in 1948 includes:

The Autobiography of Lincoln Steffens, *The Bostonians* (James), *The Mint* (T. E. Lawrence), *Nostromo* (Conrad), *Le Sabbat* (Maurice Sachs), *The Loved One* (Evelyn Waugh), *Hindoo Holiday* (J. R. Ackerley), *End as a Man* (Calder Willingham), *Portrait of the Artist as a Young Dog* (Dylan Thomas), *Ape and Essence* (Aldous Huxley), *I Capture the Castle* (Dodie Smith), *Cry, the Beloved Country* (Alan Paton), *The Seven-Storey Mountain* (Thomas Merton), *The Plague* and *Caligula* (Camus), *The American People* (Geoffrey Gorer), *No Exit* (Sartre), *A Treasury of Science Fiction* (edited by Groff Conklin). There are more thrillers listed this year than usual, probably because Christopher did so much travelling and therefore required travel reading.

Christopher got interested in Steffens through knowing Ella Winter and her terrifically sexy son Pete Steffens. He found the *Autobiography* very curious; there is something a bit fiendish and inhuman in Steffens's personal liking for the men he exposed and ruined. *The Bostonians* is still my favorite long novel by James—indeed, the only one I really like. Christopher read *The Mint* while staying with Victoria Ocampo at Mar del Plata (see *The Condor and the Cows* [chapter ten]); it hadn't yet been published. It was a bit of a disappointment to him, since he had been expecting something prodigious, but it left many vivid new impressions of demure, humble-arrogant, masquerading Lawrence—about whom Forster, after hours of reminiscence, had sadly delivered the verdict, "One didn't altogether like him." Christopher found *Nostromo* noble and masterly but unmemorable. *Le Sabbat*, which he noticed by chance in a Buenos Aires bookstore, appealed to him as sex gossip about people who interested him. He had never heard of Sachs before and liked his shamelessness. He read the book in French; there was then no English translation. He passionately hated *The Loved One* for its condescending attitude toward California. Later readings, while working with Tony Richardson on the film, have convinced me that this is a mean-minded, sloppily written production,

Street. The Sterns had long since reoccupied their apartment there, and Jimmy Stern had written Christopher a letter telling him that the cellar had somehow been flooded and that he was afraid some of Christopher's books were damaged. So Christopher was prepared for a shock, but not sufficiently. When he saw several of his especially beloved volumes stained and crinkled and cracked, he shed tears. Later he got a few of them rebound, but this seemed to destroy their identity.

On January 6, Christopher went back to MGM for additional work on *The Great Sinner* and stayed there till January 13. During this week, he saw a rough cut of the whole film. I don't remember what

---

probably Waugh's worst and utterly unworthy of his talent. *Hindoo Holiday* must have been a rereading. I wish I could remember what Christopher thought of it in the light of his now increased knowledge of things Indian, but I don't. *End as a Man* was an exciting discovery and the beginning of Christopher's (more or less) constant enthusiasm for Willingham's work. He loved *Portrait of the Artist*, particularly the chapter called "One Warm Saturday." He was shocked by *Ape and Essence*, feeling that Aldous's besetting distaste for the world and the flesh had gotten quite out of control here and produced something cheap and nasty. Against his will, he had to agree with Peggy Kiskadden on this. Peggy, as usual, had no qualms about expressing her opinion unasked for; she told Aldous exactly what she objected to. Christopher kept his mouth shut. But he was forced to say something complimentary to Dodie Smith about *I Capture the Castle*, though it seemed to him mere magazine writing. *Cry, the Beloved Country* was recommended to Christopher by James Stern. The opening seemed so technicolored that Christopher nearly put the book down, but he read on and was tremendously moved. In the November 6 journal entry, Christopher says that he is reading *The Seven-Storey Mountain* and that he is repelled by Merton's Catholic arrogance. But he was also attracted by the very grimness of the Trappist death to the world—which is admittedly far more terrifying but also perhaps easier than trying to be a monk at the permissive Vedanta Center. Christopher admired *The Plague*; it seemed to him altogether different from Camus' fakey *Stranger*. He read into it an antiheroic, anti-Hemingway message—that suffering and death are not romantic and that even a brave and noble doctor would much rather not have to fight a plague. *Caligula* is dimly remembered for one funny scene in which the emperor holds a poetry competition. Christopher thought *No Exit* as phoney as *L'Étranger*. He was delighted with Gorer for saying that, while the European male fears that the homosexuals will seduce his children, the American male fears that they will seduce him. Groff Conklin's science fiction anthology was recommended, I think, by Gerald Heard. (Gerald's story, "The Great Fog," is in it.) The Conklin anthology Christopher read first was the one published in 1948; later he got an earlier one, published in 1946. The story which made the greatest impression on Christopher was Lawrence O'Donnell's "Vintage Season." These books were his introduction to the new school of science fiction writers.

work he did—some of it may have been on passages of narration, in which "Fedor" is presumably quoting from the novel he has just written about the experiences shown on the screen.

On January 14, Jay Laval and Brad Saurin left for the Virgin Islands. Jay had been hired to organize and open a chic restaurant there and he took Brad along as his assistant. Meanwhile, Jay's restaurant in the Canyon stayed open, with Lennie Newman doing most of the cooking. I believe the Virgin Islands restaurant was a success; but Jay's association with Brad wasn't. They quarrelled, and their affair was over by the time they returned to California.

On January 25, Christopher was called back again to MGM. He worked there for three days.

On January 29, he finished chapter seven of *The Condor and the Cows*.

On February 4, he worked at MGM for one day only. I think this may have been a day on which they were recording the narration passages. These, of course, had to be spoken by Gregory Peck. But there was one scene which required a different male actor's voice over the shot. Fedor, down and out, goes into a church to pray. Then he becomes aware of the sound of coins being dropped into the poor box. He is tempted to steal from it and is just about to do so when he thinks he hears a voice, coming from the carved figure on a nearby crucifix. It shames him, and he withdraws his hand from the box.

This voice was to have been Frank Morgan's; he had played a part in the film—Pitard, a ruined gambler who shoots himself and later appears to Fedor as a ghost—but Morgan didn't show up that day because he was sick. (He was to die a few months later.) Since Christopher happened to be in the recording studio and this was an emergency, someone (maybe Gottfried) suggested that he should speak the lines. And so, more or less in a spirit of fun, Christopher took on the role of Christ at five minutes' notice.

In order that his voice should reverberate spookily, they made him stand in a small concrete passageway which led to one of the exits. He was given a hand mike at the end of a long cable, like an announcer. Since he couldn't see into the studio and watch the screen on which his scene was being projected, they rigged up a signal light to let him know when to begin. Whenever the light went on, he was to speak his lines—until they got the reading they wanted.

For some reason, the keep-out sign outside the exit door hadn't been switched on, so Christopher was in constant danger of interruption. Once, just as his signal light flashed, the exit door opened and a young carpenter came in. There was no time for explanations.

Christopher fixed the carpenter with an authoritative glare and told him accusingly: "And they divided my garments among them—and they cast dice for my robe." When telling this story later, Christopher used to say the young man looked panic-stricken, fearing that he was confronted by a religious maniac. I doubt this. What does strike me now, as I write it down, is—how beautifully suitable it was that the young man should have been a carpenter!

On February 12, Christopher finished chapter eight.

On February 21, he went to the Good Samaritan Hospital, to watch Bill Kiskadden operate. Christopher's relations with Bill had always been somewhat strained. He sensed (and was later told definitely by other people) that Bill didn't like him. I think Bill was even physically repelled by Christopher, finding him creepy, unnatural, a faggot. But Bill and Christopher had to keep on polite terms with each other as long as Christopher went on seeing Peggy. They both worked quite hard at this, and they found a topic for communication in Christopher's amateur interest in medicine. So Bill invited Christopher to come and see him at work. It was a challenge maybe, from Bill's point of view; he may have thought that Christopher would either back out or turn squeamish and have to leave the operating room. Christopher had no such qualms. Having seen a leg amputated, an abdomen slit open and a skull trephined, he was convinced that no surgical sight could upset him.

But there is something uncomfortably personal about plastic surgery on the face; it is only too easy to identify with the patient. So Christopher did feel squeamish two or three times that morning, though he didn't give Bill satisfaction by showing it.

The patient was a truck driver—Bill Kiskadden didn't as a rule do cosmetic operations; he repaired the victims of industrial accidents and car wrecks. This man had been driving his truck somewhere up in the mountains when an emergency arose which forced him to choose between colliding with a small car full of people and swinging his truck off the road into a steep slope. He swung off the road and the truck turned over and his face was smashed against the steering wheel. Now Bill Kiskadden was working to get his nose back into its proper position; it had been knocked crooked. The patient was completely conscious. Christopher felt a qualm as Bill took a hypodermic and very slowly and deliberately sank its needle into the tip of the truck driver's nose. The truck driver uttered a groan and exclaimed that it hurt. "I know it hurts," Bill told him, "it hurts like hell. That's what you get for being a brave man." Bill said this in a nice friendly doctor-to-patient tone—and yet there was something about the look on his face which convinced Christopher that what Gerald Heard had always maintained was true: Bill was a sadist.[1]

At this point there is a group of four more entries in the 1948–1956 journal, on February 20, March 1, March 2 and March 3. They refer to the Ramakrishna birthday puja at the Vedanta Center which Christopher attended and a party he and Caskey went to at Thomas Mann's house (both on March 1). Also (March 2) to Christopher's difficulties in starting chapter ten of the South American book—he had finished chapter nine on February 24. There is also a reference to Peter Watson who was then in Los Angeles with his friend Norman Fowler; Christopher and Caskey had been seeing a lot of them.

Christopher doesn't say anything in the day-to-day diary about his work with Swami on Patanjali's yoga aphorisms—translation and commentary—which was later to be published as *How to Know God*. However, in the March 2 entry in the journal, he writes: "Swami's way ahead of me," which shows that they must have been working together for some time already.

The only really significant feature of these entries is that they twice mention the difficulties Christopher is having with Caskey. This is the first time that Christopher has even admitted in writing that there *are* any difficulties and his tone suggests that he is trying hard to minimize them. Indeed he presents the whole problem as though it were a mere lack of consideration by Caskey for Christopher's comfort and convenience. Christopher complains that Caskey stays up, from time to time, playing the record player all night—it seems that this usually happens when they have had a party and Caskey is drunk. Christopher writes:

> It is a most curious deadlock—arising, apparently, out of an emotional blind spot in Caskey. He absolutely cannot understand why I mind being kept awake. And I absolutely cannot understand how he can keep me awake, even if he doesn't understand why. However, I freely admit that I am kept awake by a kind of

[1] Gerald Heard used to tell how, while he was visiting the Kiskaddens, Bill had noticed a wart on his finger and had told him, "I can cure that right away." He had then produced several needles and had stuck them into Gerald's wart. Then he had heated the needles with a match. The pain, Gerald said, was extreme—adding that Bill had watched his face all the time, waiting for him to betray his suffering. But Gerald, being Gerald, didn't—so Bill was foiled.

Bill must have had much more fun when he cut out Christopher's pile (see the journal entry of April 24, 1944) because Christopher "yelled clear around the block."

obstinacy—just as it is obstinacy which makes him play the records.

It is only in the last sentence that Christopher hints at the basic hostility between Caskey and himself; the clash of their wills. The standing argument over Caskey's midnight record playing was simply one expression of this. Caskey's and Christopher's wills had always clashed (see pages 52–53) but the clash was now becoming much more destructive. Now that they had settled into a relatively permanent home, they had no prospect of change or travel to divert them, no move to New York or trip around South America. Neither of them could say to himself, "I'll put up with this, because it won't be for long." Now they had to face the question, "What kind of a life are we going to have together—for the next five, ten, twenty years?"

As far as Christopher was concerned, the answer was, "I want to have a comfortable, predictable, fairly quiet daily life, in which my mind will be as free from anxiety as possible and I shall be able to work. I want sex, of course, with Caskey but I won't be unreasonably jealous if he runs around with other people—especially if he does it elsewhere, because then I'll be able to bring my own boys back here and screw them comfortably at home. I don't care much for parties but I'm prepared to give them from time to time, especially if Caskey makes all the arrangements and does all the cooking and we don't have to stay up too late. Oh sure, I'll help with the dishwashing if necessary. As for Caskey himself, I want him to be happy and busy (at something, never mind what) and to go to bed and wake up at the same time I do."

Caskey didn't see things in this way, at all. He didn't want his life to be predictable. He wanted surprises, unexpected guests, parties which snowballed into roaring crowds, out-of-town trips taken on the spur of the moment. He would tidy the house one day and drunkenly wreck it the next. He was ready to work for hours on any project which interested him, but he hated the concept of work for work's sake and he couldn't understand Christopher's compulsive need to be busy. He may well have begun to feel, already, that by coming back to live with Christopher in California he had walked into a trap.

Christopher's reasonableness, the justice of his case, the moderation of his demands upon Caskey were a bit *too* convincing—and he knew it. Relations between two human beings who are supposed to love each other—and perhaps actually do, from time to time—cannot be regulated by a code of rules. The truth is that Christopher was no more reasonable than Caskey; he merely had a knack of maneuvering himself into positions in which he was, technically, "in the right"—whereupon Caskey, with his passive obstinacy, would not only accept the counterposition of being "in the wrong" but would proceed to make the wrong as wrong as he possibly could. He always behaved worst when there was no conceivable excuse for his behavior. That was his kind of integrity.

Maybe Caskey never quite realized the dimensions of Christopher's arrogance—for Christopher was usually careful not to reveal them. In his inmost heart, Christopher thought of himself as an art aristocrat or brahmin, a person privileged by his talent to demand the service (he preferred to call it "the cooperation") of others. In his youth, he had felt this even more strongly, and had often told Nanny, when she grumbled about the housework, that she ought to feel proud that she was helping him finish his novel—by taking domestic chores off his hands. (In the Soviet Union, he added, this principle was recognized—so that only artists and other leading brainworkers had servants.) Once, in an outburst of frankness, he had confided to the Beesleys—who thoroughly approved of his attitude—"What I really want is to be waited on hand and foot." Vernon Old (of all people!) in the innocence of his early enthusiasm for Christopher, had read *Goodbye to Berlin* and exclaimed, "It makes me feel I ought to drop everything and cook for you and look after you—so you can go on writing!" (This declaration brought tears to Christopher's eyes. It still touches me—even though I now know that Vernon was describing the attitude which he would later expect his various girlfriends and wives to take toward himself. . . . Incidentally, the journal entry of March 3 mentions that Christopher has heard "Vernon isn't getting along at all well with Patty.")

Since his return to California, Christopher had reestablished relations with the Vedanta Center but he only went there when he felt that he absolutely had to. His guilt feelings were very strong. He hated having them and he was inclined to blame Caskey for them. He was aware that both Huxley and Heard had made remarks about his way of life which had reached Swami's ears, directly or indirectly. (This was bitchy of Gerald and Aldous, to put it mildly, for neither of them had disdained to accept Christopher's and Caskey's hospitality.) Swami had so far said very little about this to Christopher, but Christopher felt that Swami regarded Caskey as a bad influence and that Caskey knew this and defiantly enjoyed the situation. The two seldom met and made no contact when they did. If Caskey had been a professed or prospective Vedantist, much would have been forgiven him—but Caskey was clearly unconvertible. A lot of Christopher's guilt was actually embarrassment—it wasn't that he was ashamed of his drunkenness and sex but he hated having Swami know about it. He would have preferred to lead a double life with a clear-cut division between the two halves, but he couldn't, and Caskey was the reason why he couldn't. Just because Caskey was so socially presentable—up to a point—and could mingle with the Huxleys, the Kiskaddens and the rest of Christopher's respectable friends—Christopher found that his life had become all of a piece; everybody knew everything there was to know about him. In theory, he saw that this was morally preferable; it made hypocrisy and concealment impossible. In practice, he hated it.

Caskey never suffered from embarrassment. He didn't give a damn what anybody knew about him. He would take pains to be polite and agreeable, but he was always capable, in any company, of turning loud and nasty. As for his guilt, it was the inspiration of his religious feelings. He had the black Catholic belief that it is only when you feel guilty that you are in a state of grace. He couldn't imagine an approach to God other than as a penitent. So it was continually necessary to do or be something he could be penitent for.

Christopher and Caskey still had poignant moments of tenderness, when their guilt became mutual. For a little while they would be drawn together by realizing how unkind they had been to each other. Then their eyes would fill with tears. Both of them asked for forgiveness and were forgiven; yet forgiveness in itself seemed of secondary importance. They clung together with a feeling that they were two helpless victims of some external power—a power which forced them to be enemies. Caskey enjoyed these moments of reconciliation much more than Christopher did, I suspect. Caskey's Catholic mind and Irish heart revelled in suffering for its own sake, equating love with pain. Christopher, cooler hearted and more practical, was impatient of suffering—was shocked at himself for liking it even a little; he accused himself of masochism. He wanted to tune their whole relationship up, remove all causes of friction and get it running smoothly.

When clashing with Caskey, Christopher often thought of himself as The Foolish Virgin (Verlaine) and of Caskey as The Infernal Bridegroom (Rimbaud) in Rimbaud's *A Season in Hell*. But this was self-flattery. Neither Christopher nor Caskey was wicked enough or desperate enough or daring enough to create an authentic Hell around himself. Their guilt and their suffering was miserably half-assed. Which is why—leaving aside all question of talent—it was eventually commemorated by a miserably half-assed novel, *The World in the Evening*.

No—I won't accuse Caskey. What do I really know about his

deeper feelings? When I call Christopher half-assed, I know exactly what I mean. He had, so to speak, too many dishes on the stove and not one of them was being properly cooked. He made japam, when he remembered to. He went to see Swami, but only out of duty. He worked on the Patanjali translation, but only to placate Swami. He visited paraplegic patients at Birmingham Hospital (this began later in the year) so that he could picture himself as being engaged in social service. He wrote *The Condor and the Cows* compulsively and without enjoyment, claiming that he was doing it to promote Caskey's career as a photographer—and thereby making Caskey responsible for Christopher's forced descent into journalism.

What a martyr he felt himself to be! How put upon! He saw himself as a toiler, Caskey as a lounger—yet Caskey worked just as hard as Christopher when he had something to work on; it was simply that Caskey had the natural gift of being able to relax in his work and Christopher hadn't. Did Christopher ever relax? Yes—in the ocean, plunging his hangover headaches into the waves— drinking, especially if Caskey wasn't around—naked in bed with Jim Charlton or some other sex mate—but such respites were short. Most of the time, Christopher was under tremendous strain. In the March 2 journal entry, he writes that he keeps bleeding from the rectum and thinks that this may be a strain symptom. Two months later, he believes that he may be on the verge of a nervous break-down (May 22).

Now I must mention a feature of life at 333 East Rustic Road which seems to me to have been somehow interrelated with Christopher's psychological condition—the unpleasant psychic atmosphere in the house. I have no way of fixing a date on which this first became apparent to Christopher and Caskey. I can only remember some incidents and impressions—

Quite soon after they moved into 333, Christopher talked to Paula Strasberg (on the phone, I think). In the course of their conversation, she said, "It's a very lonely house." At the time, her choice of adjective seemed merely odd to him—how could 333 be described as lonely, when the next-door house on one side nearly touched it and when there was a continuous line of houses facing it from across the road? However, by the time he next talked to Mrs. Strasberg, eight months later, he thought he understood what she had meant. He said to her: "When you told me that this house is lonely, were you trying to warn me that it's haunted?" Mrs. Strasberg denied this emphatically, she laughed aloud at the very idea. But Christopher wasn't impressed. He told himself that this old Jewess would naturally refuse to admit to a ghost, since it was one of those disadvantages which lower property values. Then why had she let drop that word "lonely"? It must have been a slip—perhaps she had been badly scared at 333, and the impression had remained so strong that she had referred to it in spite of herself. Christopher never found out the truth about this. And now Mrs. Strasberg is dead.

Chris Wood, always a highly credible witness, told how he decided to drop in on Christopher and Caskey, one morning, unannounced. When you crossed the bridge over the creek, the house was on your right. Downstairs were the living room and the kitchen, upstairs were a bathroom and two bedrooms. One of these bedrooms opened onto a glassed-in porch which Christopher used as a workroom. Chris Wood crossed the bridge and approached the house. As he did so, he saw a figure upstairs moving behind the windows of this porch. Taking it for granted that this was Christopher, Chris went to the front door and knocked. No answer. Chris then opened the front door and entered. No one in the kitchen or living room. Remembering the figure he had seen upstairs, Chris wondered if it could be a burglar. But he nevertheless bravely climbed the staircase and looked in all the rooms. They were empty. And there was no other exit from the upper floor.

One evening, Caskey, Carlos McClendon and a few others tried using a Ouija board in the living room of 333.[1] At first the board spelled out words like fuck, cunt, shit—probably with a good deal of encouragement from Caskey. Then they began to question it— "Who are you?" It gave a woman's name. "Are you dead?" "Yes." "How did you die?" "Murdered." "Who murdered you?" "Myself." "Where did you die?" "Here."

On January 1, 1950, Bill Harris came to stay with Christopher (Caskey was away in the East). Bill slept in the bedroom adjoining the glassed-in porch; Christopher slept in the other bedroom, beyond it. One night, Bill woke and saw someone he took for Christopher, in the nearly total darkness, come out of Christopher's bedroom, cross the bedroom Bill was sleeping in and start going down the staircase—which led directly out of that bedroom to the ground floor. Lying in bed, you could watch a person go downstairs until his head

---

[1] No, says Carlos McClendon (December 8, 1972), he wasn't at the Ouija board party, though he does remember Caskey telling him about it. However, Carlos describes an experience he had which was very like Chris Wood's. Approaching the house, one day, he looked up at the glassed-in porch and saw a woman. Bill Harris was downstairs—this must have been in January 1950—and Carlos asked him who the woman was. Bill was alone in the house.

sank below floor level. Just as this was about to happen, the someone who seemed to be Christopher turned and looked at Bill and said, with intense hatred, "You son of a bitch!" Then he disappeared. At first, Bill was merely astonished. "Chris must be terribly mad about something," he said to himself. Then he reflected that he had never seen Christopher get mad like this before. Then he began to wonder, "*Was* that Christopher?" Then he got out of bed, went across to Christopher's bedroom and looked in, to find Christopher in bed, snoring peacefully. Then Bill was scared. Nevertheless, with a considerateness which was typical of him, he didn't wake Christopher.

In themselves, these happenings made no great impression on Christopher. He didn't have to be convinced by any more evidence that "hauntings" (whatever they essentially are) do occur. What did impress him was the intensity of the unpleasant psychic atmosphere at 333. Ever since his boyhood at Marple Hall, Christopher had taken it for granted that one's awareness of such an atmosphere is just as valid as one's awareness of a strong unpleasant smell. He believed that he himself was particularly sensitive to it,[1] and he was rather proud of

---

[1] For example, on May 19, 1948, while Christopher and Caskey were up at Wyberslegh, staying with Kathleen and Richard, they visited Lyme Hall and went round the house on a conducted tour. They managed to keep ahead of the main body of sightseers and thus got an independent first impression of each room before they were caught up with by the others. When Christopher and Caskey went into one of the rooms, Christopher exclaimed at once that it had a horrible atmosphere and must surely be haunted. A few moments later, the guide arrived with the rest of the party and announced that this was The Haunted Room. (Of course it's quite possible that Christopher had been told about this room when he came to Lyme as a boy.)

But this reminds me of a far stranger experience which, for some reason I failed to record in the 1939–1944 journal. It must have happened sometime in 1939 or 1940, during one of the trips that Christopher and Vernon Old took up into northern California—I am sure Vernon was with Christopher at the time, though he wasn't involved in the experience.

They were in their car, driving through the Sequoia forest. It was late afternoon, always a time which Christopher found rather sinister in the big woods—the feeling that night is about to fall seemed to him far more menacing than night itself. Suddenly, the road led them around the edge of a large clearing—a cup-shaped hollow which was grassy and swampy. In the middle of this clearing stood a shack. It was a store, and it looked like the stores of pioneer days; maybe it had survived from the period before Sequoia became a national park and private dwellings were forbidden. Anyhow, there it was—and Christopher was happy as well as surprised to see it. He wanted to buy some cigarettes and had despaired of being able to until they were out of this area.

Vernon stopped the car and sat at the wheel waiting while Christopher ran down into the hollow and entered the store. He found the store empty. It

this. However, his experience at 333 was different from any of his others, not only in intensity but in kind.

This atmosphere made itself more strongly felt on the upper floor and particularly in the front bedroom around the top of the staircase, but Christopher was aware of it everywhere. The smallness of the house seemed to compress it and thus add to its power. 333 was dark in the daytime, because of the neighboring hillside and the over-hanging sycamore trees; at night, a guest who saw it brightly lit and full of people would often describe it as snug. But it never seemed snug to Christopher. It seemed secret, unhomely, *unheimlich*.[*]

Often, when he was working in the glassed-in porch (where there was at least plenty of daylight) he would feel, almost catch a glimpse of, someone at his elbow and turn quickly, but never quickly enough to confront the shadowy presence. At night, when Caskey was out and he was alone in the house, he would sometimes wake thrilling with fear. For a few moments after waking, he would be afraid but not panic stricken. His very belief in the objective existence of the phenomenon reassured him—for him, it wasn't The Unknown. It was a manifestation of the psychic world, and the psychic is always subject to the spiritual. Christopher was a devotee (despite all his backslidings) of Ramakrishna. So how could any psychic phenomenon possibly do him harm?

However, Christopher's experiences in this house did differ from all the others he had had elsewhere, because they had a second aspect or dimension—so it seemed to him. The longer he lived there, the more

---

wasn't dark inside and it looked quite as he had expected it would look—stocked with all the usual goods. After Christopher had waited a short while, a man came out of a room at the back. He asked, "What can I do for you?" Whereupon, Christopher ran out of the store, dashed up the slope to the car and jumped in, gasping to Vernon to drive away quick.

Even at the time, Christopher found it impossible to explain his panic. Nothing like this had ever happened to him before. It has never happened to him since. His impression was that his panic had nothing to do with the atmosphere of the place; it was caused by the man himself. Trying to give Vernon some idea of how he had felt, Christopher said that it was as if that man had been in the midst of doing something unspeakably evil in the back room when Christopher's arrival had interrupted him. Part of the horror was that he was able to come straight from that unspeakable act and ask a customer, "What can I do for you?" in a quiet ordinary voice. Christopher was certain that he hadn't been frightened by the man's appearance; indeed he couldn't remember anything definite about it. So the man must have somehow projected the terror which Christopher felt. Either that, or the man himself was only a projection of an evil ambience in the store—that is to say, not a man at all.

[* I.e., not snug, not comfortable.]

he felt that its psychic atmosphere was *both* something which had belonged to the place before he came there *and* something which was a projection of his own disturbed, miserable, hate-filled state of mind.

On February 24, Christopher finished chapter nine of *The Condor and the Cows*, and on March 15 chapter ten.

On March 12, Glenway Wescott arrived and spent a week in the Canyon. He didn't stay at 333 but at a motel on Entrada Drive, perhaps because he wanted privacy to work. However, he was with Caskey and Christopher most evenings. He was wonderfully cheerful, silly and energetic, and brightened everybody up. He cooked meals for Caskey and Christopher, read Christopher's 1939–1944 journals and praised them to the skies, and went to bed with Jim Charlton. He left in a glow of popularity.

On March 22, there was a sneak preview of *The Great Sinner* at the Criterion Theater in Santa Monica. Christopher had long since given up trying to convince himself that the film was any good. Peck was awful. He did his best but he was hopelessly miscast. In the big emotional scenes he made an ass of himself. Ava Gardner looked beautiful but she was as completely un-Russian as Peck, her voice was ugly and her acting was awkward—they were an uninspiring pair. Walter Huston, as her father, made every scene come to life in which he appeared; but his part was far too small. Ethel Barrymore was excellent in her two gambling scenes. Melvyn Douglas behaved with charm and discretion as Armand de Glasse, the unconvincing character who runs the casino. And the total effect was mediocre, Hollywoodish, saccharine. The preview cards were lukewarm.

Gregory Peck took his failure deeply to heart; it must have hurt his vanity. As a result of this, he developed a distaste for Christopher—having decided, I suppose, that Christopher's script was responsible for his humiliation. Although they had gotten along well during the shooting,[1] Peck henceforth avoided talking to Christopher when

---

[1] Christopher's relations with Ava Gardner, Walter Huston, Melvyn Douglas and Robert Siodmak had been good, too—partly because they were all left-wing liberals. He would have liked to know Gardner better—but that would have meant taking her out in the evenings, and Christopher always avoided tête-à-têtes with beautiful well-known women—either they thought you were making a pass or suspected you of only seeing them because you yourself were trying to pass. (Incidentally, one of the camera crew remarked about Ava to Christopher—"You wouldn't believe it, but I hear she stays home most evenings, longing for the phone to ring. Seems like she's one of the gals that guys never try to date, because they're sure she's all booked up.")

Robert Siodmak was the friendliest of them all. Several people told

they met at parties. It wasn't until years later that he became gracious again—and even helped Christopher become a member of the Academy.

Fodor may well have been partly responsible for Peck's attitude. As soon as it became evident that *The Great Sinner* had laid an egg, Fodor started a subtle propaganda campaign to convince all who were concerned that it was Christopher who had spoilt the script by his revisions. I'm sure Fodor didn't convince Gottfried Reinhardt, and I doubt if Fodor managed to do Christopher any serious harm professionally, but the ill will must be taken for the deed.

On March 26, Christopher went with Tito Renaldo to see Swami. I don't know if this was the day that Tito first met Swami—it may have been much earlier. But I think that Tito probably asked Swami on this occasion if he could go and live at Trabuco as a monk, as soon as it was opened as a monastery. Gerald Heard had already talked the trustees into handing over the property to the Vedanta Society. Trabuco opened officially on September 7, 1949.

On April 2, Christopher finished writing *The Condor and the Cows*.[1] On the 4th, he and Caskey mailed the manuscript and the photographs—two copies of each—to Methuen and to Random House.

Caskey had worked really hard on the photographs, developing, enlarging and cropping them himself and making a dummy of the illustration pages which showed the exact relative sizes for each picture to be printed. He had also designed a photographic montage for the jacket—the two ceramic bulls they had brought back from Pucará in Peru superimposed on a view of the marble column topped by a carved condor (in Puerto Cabello, Venezuela) which commemorates the foreigners who came to South America to fight for Bolívar. And he had done a pen-and-ink drawing of Cuzco as a frontispiece for the book.

On April 5, David Kidd (one of Christopher's [friends]) brought Sara Allgood to the house. Christopher had the advantage of being one of the few people in Los Angeles who had seen her in the

---

Christopher that Siodmak was queer. Christopher never saw any definite evidence of this, but he did sometimes wonder if Siodmak fancied him.

[1] Although Christopher had complained so much about the boredom of this project, he began to enjoy himself while working on the final chapter and was later rather proud of the purple passage with which it closes—particularly: ". . . Atahuallpa baptized and strangled, Alfaro torn to pieces, Valencia translating Wilde above a courtyard of violets—" The rhythm of this seemed to him extraordinarily exciting and he made excuses for quoting it to his friends—in a tone of humorous apology for its melodrama. But no one ever protested that it was beautiful.

original London production of *Juno and the Paycock*. So he was able to delight her by saying (ninety percent sincerely) that her "Sacred Heart o' Jesus" speech was one of his favorite theatrical memories. She loved his flattery, and the little onions which Caskey kept for the martinis—indeed, she ate nearly a whole jar of them. Christopher loved her ladylike airs and her wonderful rich voice—indeed, he found himself talking to her with a slight Irish accent. Their meeting was a huge success and was repeated.

On April 6, Caskey photographed Thomas Mann—this was one of his best sets of portraits.

On April 7, Christopher sent a reply to an invitation to take part in a conference for world peace which was being held in Los Angeles under the auspices of the National Council of the Arts, Sciences and Professions. He refused to attend, on the grounds that this wasn't a genuine peace conference but a political demonstration with a pro-Russian slant. Christopher's letter is very well constructed, it makes telling points and its main accusation is really unanswerable.[1] (Before

---

[1] Some extracts from Christopher's letter:

> Strict pacifism is total and neutral. . . . You do not pretend to be total pacifists, and I'm not going to try to convert you to that position. What I am now concerned with is your neutrality. . . . I am . . . basing my opinion . . . on your own leaflet, your "call" to the conference . . . a whole paragraph is devoted to Washington's misdeeds and mistakes. I agree with much of what is said. . . . But where is the paragraph which ought, in fairness, to follow it . . . dealing with the misdeeds and mistakes of Moscow? You imply or seem to me to imply—that the "cold war". . . must be blamed entirely on the U.S. government. This is simply not true. . . . If we invite guests from overseas, we should not greet them with accusations. We should be humble and dwell most upon our own shortcomings. I take this to be your intention. Nevertheless, I must suggest that such politeness hopelessly confuses the issue . . . by refraining from criticism of Soviet militarism and aggression, you imply that your guests are associated with it and that, therefore, you mustn't hurt their feelings. Isn't this . . . an accusation? A well-founded accusation, I fear. Consider the facts. The greatest police state on earth permits some of its prominent citizens to come over to this country and take part in a peace conference. Such a conference . . . ought to imply a condemnation of all the governments whose nationals are involved[,] since these governments have failed to establish peace. . . . If these Russian delegates had come with genuinely neutral, pacifistic aims, they would be condemning Soviet militarism. Their lives would be in danger. They could never return to their own country. . . . I am forced to believe that the Russian delegates were permitted to come . . . because the Soviet government intends to exploit . . . your whole conference for propaganda purposes. . . . I fear that its findings and resolutions . . . will inspire militarists within the Soviet Union with the most dangerous confidence that the

sending off his letter, he had gotten in touch with the local Quakers and found that they entirely agreed with his stand.) What makes me a bit uncomfortable, rereading it today, is to remember that it was written in the midst of the McCarthy era. The senator and his committee were attacking these people for holding the peace conference, and what they were saying against it was more or less what Christopher was saying—that it was red. Christopher loathed the Soviet government for disowning the attitude toward the private life prescribed by Marx, and for persecuting its homosexuals. He somewhat disliked the Jewish parlor-communist intellectuals who were members of the National Council of the Arts, Sciences and Professions. But he also loathed McCarthy and the red-hunters—and it is humiliating to reflect that they might have approved of his letter or at least decided that it showed he was rather more on their side than the other. (Christopher was certainly more a socialist than he was a fascist, and more a pacifist than he was a socialist. But he was a queer first and foremost. I remember a discussion he had with Caskey and some others around that time on the question: "If you could produce positive proof that McCarthy is queer—would you use it to ruin his political career?" Their unanimous verdict was, "No—because all queers would be harmed if it became known that he was one."

On April 8, Christopher and Caskey had a birthday party for Jim Charlton. And Christopher restarted *The School of Tragedy* for the third time, after an interval of twenty-two months. This opening is perhaps the most promising one he ever made. Stephen is writing a letter—or maybe a journal in letter form—addressed to someone called Edward. I have no idea, now, if Edward was to have been a major or a minor character; but the tone of voice of this extract suggests the literary tone of Edward Upward, and Stephen seems to be much livelier, more amusing, less sentimental and self-pitying than the character he will later become.[1]

---

intelligentsia of the United States are actually on their side; that the cold war . . . should therefore be pressed to the uttermost. . . . Such confidence . . . might well lead to the outbreak of armed hostilities. . . .

[1] Christopher made another start on May 2—this, like the first three, was set in the refugee hostel. On May 9, he tried again—beginning, this time, with the flight east from Los Angeles following Stephen's breakup with Jane (Anne, as she was then called). This may have been another false start—it is certainly very bad; it reads like inferior Scott Fitzgerald—or it may have been revised and then added to later; for the day-to-day diary entry of June 27 records that Christopher finished chapter one of *The School of Tragedy* on that day. I dare say the manuscript of this chapter is stored away somewhere, but I can't be bothered to look for it now.

On April 11, Christopher worked at MGM on what the day-to-day diary describes as "retake changes." I can't remember what these were.

On April 19, Christopher saw Dodie and Alec Beesley, who had recently moved into a house on Cove Way, behind the Beverly Hills Hotel, just off Benedict Canyon. This was to be the last of their Californian homes.

On April 29, he drove with Swami to Trabuco, for the day. This probably means that some monks from the Hollywood Vedanta Center were already living there, cleaning the place up and getting it ready for its official opening.

On May 3, the day-to-day diary notes that Rita was "released." I think this refers to Rita Cowan's release from prison—for I dimly remember that her husband or boyfriend, a black man, was shot dead by the police and that Rita regarded this as a murder and made some kind of [. . .] protest scene which ended with her being locked up.

On May 20, Christopher had another contact with the National Council of the Arts, Sciences and Professions. The writer Paul Jarrico had previously written him about the blacklisting of Albert Maltz, who was under prosecution by the U.S. government for refusing to testify before the Committee on Un-American Activities. As a result, Twentieth Century-Fox had decided not to produce a film based on Maltz's novel *The Journey of Simon McKeever*. Jarrico had asked Christopher to write a letter in support of Maltz which could be read aloud at a meeting of the film division of the council on May 25. Christopher wrote and sent them a letter—he couldn't do otherwise.[1] But, as before, his anti-Soviet sentiments showed between the lines. Also, his resentment at having been made to read Maltz's boring and insipid novel—*why* did the vast majority of these literary martyrs have to be without talent?

On May 21, Klaus Mann killed himself in Cannes. I can't

May 20.

[1]Dear Mr. Jarrico,

Thank you for your letter about Albert Maltz [one of the Hollywood Ten]. I'm sorry that I can't be with you on the platform on May 25 when you hold your meeting, but I shall certainly be there in spirit. I loathe all censorship—no matter whether it comes from the Right or the Left. Luckily, as a rule, it defeats its own object.

As for *The Journey of Simon McKeever*, it seems to me a charming novel, which couldn't hurt a baby, politically or otherwise. If anyone could possibly object to it, I should have expected the communists to do so. Isn't it what they call "liberal romanticism"?

With best wishes for the end of this, and all other witch-hunts,

Sincerely. . . .

remember how soon Christopher got the news; probably almost at once, because of being in touch with the Mann family. I do remember that Christopher had to tell Harold Fairbanks, and that Harold was obviously much more upset than he would admit.

The day-to-day diary records that Christopher finished writing, on that day, a foreword to Luise Rinser's novel *Die Stärkeren*. I think he did this for an English translation of the book which Bill Kennedy was trying to get published in the States—as far as I know, it never actually was. Although Christopher did the job for money, he really liked the book, partly because it made him feel nostalgic. He very seldom read anything in German, and the language itself brought back unexpected memories.

On May 22, there is another isolated entry in the 1948–1956 journal. And in it, for the first time, Christopher discusses the possibility of leaving Caskey. This possibility he rejects because (1) there is no one else to go to and (2) he isn't prepared to return to live at the Vedanta Center. In other words, Christopher is definitely not prepared to face the prospect of living alone.

After writing this, Christopher makes resolutions:

. . . staying together means accepting Caskey *exactly as he is*. I *must* remember this. I must renounce *all* attempts to change Caskey's attitude, behavior or habits. I must accept him, and thereby renounce my whole possessive attitude towards him.

This does *not* mean that I shouldn't give my honest opinion and advice—if asked.

And it doesn't mean that I shouldn't insist on a few simple rules—like the business of making a noise at night. That's all right, because it's no more than anybody would ask, even in the most casually polite relationship.

I *must* stop trying to subdue Caskey, to shame him, to make him feel guilty.

Oh dear—is this possible?

It is not possible if it's done as an act. It is not possible if you are all the time watching to see the effect of your new technique on Caskey. It *is* possible if you build up your inner life of prayer, meditation, artistic creation, physical exercise and routine, and simply let Caskey do as he pleases—always welcoming any advance on his part.

Well—go ahead. You have plenty of work: your novel, the story with Samuels. Take it easy. Don't get tense.

There is one sentence which exposes the futility of Christopher's resolutions: "It is not possible if it's done as an act." But how else could it possibly have been done? Relations between Caskey and Christopher could only have been improved if one of them had made an unconditional surrender, and left it up to the other to be as generous or ungenerous as he chose. But Christopher didn't dream of surrendering. He was merely proposing to adopt a strategy, and a strategy must necessarily be some kind of an act; it can never produce behavior which is spontaneous.

Christopher and Caskey still loved each other, up to a point—but not nearly enough to make their relationship work. In this May 22 entry, Christopher compares the state of affairs between them to "the mood of 1940, in which I was bubbling with resentment against Vernon." This calls attention to a weakness which Christopher showed on both occasions—he found it almost impossible to break off a relationship even when it was making him miserable. It was Vernon who finally had to leave Christopher (on February 17, 1941), though it was Christopher who had prodded him into doing so. And it was Caskey who finally had to force Christopher to leave him; Christopher always hesitated to take the decisive step. He was to go on hesitating for two more years.

How about Caskey? Was he miserable too, at this time? He certainly didn't seem so, to Christopher. But then I am only now beginning to realize how little Christopher knew—bothered to know—about Caskey. Caskey wore a mask of frivolity, camping and wisecracking, which Christopher never saw behind. Their occasional drunken scenes of emotional contrition and forgiveness actually revealed nothing. Christopher never got a glimpse into Caskey's reverie or his fantasies. I don't believe he ever tried to find out what Caskey was thinking about, what kind of myths he was celebrating, as he drank and danced for hours, alone, in the dead of night, to his favorite records.

I now believe that Caskey *was* suffering—but in a way that was only indirectly related to Christopher. He was suffering from guilt because he didn't love his father and sisters and was maddened by his mother, because he had broken with their religion, because he found it a terrible strain to play the unrepentant queer black sheep of the family. All that Christopher offered him was another sort of family life, which didn't work. Caskey was being forced to face the fact that the only security for him was in complete independence. Christopher would never help Caskey achieve this, for Christopher himself was afraid of being alone. Lennie Newman and Caskey's other playmates would never help him, even if they could, for they wanted him to keep on playing his role of the madcap hostess, and for that Christopher's money—and therefore his presence—was necessary. So, sooner or later, Caskey would have to take the initiative and make his own move. In the meantime, Christopher sulked and Caskey danced.[*]

On May 29, 1949, Catherine Caskey arrived, to begin a visit which was to last into the middle of August. The day-to-day diary entries make it seem clear that she didn't sleep at 333 East Rustic, even to start with. But she had a room somewhere nearby, and Caskey and Christopher felt a constant obligation to entertain her.

Christopher could afford not to mind this, because Catherine had no power to embarrass him, and because Caskey resented Catherine's presence so violently that Christopher was obliged to play the opposite role and be her advocate. It was Christopher who suggested that the U.S. edition of *The Condor and the Cows* should be dedicated to Catherine; the British edition was being dedicated to Kathleen. This put Catherine and Kathleen into a relationship with each other, of which Catherine was coyly aware. They were an unsanctified pair of mothers-in-law. The dedication delighted Catherine. It gave her a share in this South American project which had launched Caskey as a photographer—a thoroughly respectable career, of which the whole Caskey family could approve. Whether any of them can possibly have approved of the Caskey–Christopher relationship is more than doubtful, but Catherine was determined to pretend that they did. She even quoted a male relative as having said, "It was a lucky day for Sonny when he met Christopher Isherwood." ("Sonny" was a family nickname for Caskey which Catherine persisted in using; it made Caskey wince and grind his teeth.)

On May 30, Christopher had a visit from a young Canadian named Paul Almond. I suppose he was an admirer of Christopher's work. Paul was blond and apple cheeked and tall, an all-Canadian boy who played championship ice hockey and belonged to a rich family. He returned to the house three or more times during June, and was exposed to the camping of Caskey and the double-meaning jokes of Stephen Spender (who came to stay two nights, June 14 and 15, bringing with him the young writer Bill Goyen, on whom he had a crush, and Goyen's friend Walter Berns). But Paul was either very innocent or very self-absorbed; he saw only what he had come to see, a nice middle-aged celebrity and his charming friends. Later that same year, Paul went over to England, taking with him a letter of introduction from Christopher to John Lehmann. John, on the make for Paul, started dropping arch hints about Christopher's way of

[* Here Isherwood came to the end of his manuscript book and began a new one.]

life—as Christopher had fully expected that he would. Paul was incredulous and indignant. He wrote to warn Christopher that John Lehmann was a false friend who was spreading horrible lies, accusing Christopher and his companions of being "homosexualists."

(Many years later, Paul married the actress Geneviève Bujold and directed her in a film, *Act of the Heart*. They are now divorced.)

On June 1, Christopher bought a Tarascan statuette, dug up in the Mexican state of Colima; a seated figure with its right hand covering its mouth. Christopher paid Stendahl's (an expensive dealer who sold a lot of pre-Columbian art to Charles Laughton) about eighty dollars for it; it would probably now cost at least a thousand. The statuette was a present for Caskey, on his twenty-eighth birthday, next day. But Christopher ended by owning it, when he and Caskey split up and divided their possessions, a few years later.

On June 11, Christopher and Caskey, the old actress Aileen Pringle, Jay Laval, a friend named Leif Argo, Catherine Caskey and Jo and Ben Masselink all drove down to have supper at Charpentier's in Redondo Beach. (This is the first time that the day-to-day diary mentions a meeting with the Masselinks but they, Christopher and Caskey had become acquainted long before this, probably at The Friendship bar.) Charpentier was a famous old French chef whose reputation was such that he cooked suppers by appointment only and always had a long waiting list. He lived in a small ordinary house on the Pacific Coast Highway and the room where you ate was just a typical, rather depressing parlor. Charpentier received you with a fulsome spiel about the cuisine of *la belle France*. You had to bring your own wine. The food was no doubt excellent—Jay thought it was—but Christopher never got to taste it. He was drunk already when they arrived, and went to sleep in a hammock on the front lawn. They woke him when it was time to leave.

There is very little to be said about the rest of June. The day-to-day diary records three parties given by Frank and Nan Taylor—one for Stephen Spender (on another of his visits), one for Robert Penn Warren, and one which included Penn Warren, Chaplin and Edgar Snow. I can remember nothing of interest about Warren, except that Christopher and Caskey both liked him a good deal and that Caskey photographed him. I can remember nothing at all about the meeting with Snow—whom, I suppose, Christopher hadn't seen since the late thirties. Christopher's chief occupations during this period: working with Lesser Samuels on their new film story, *The Easiest Thing in the World*; drinking; lying on the beach. Christopher must also have been working on his novel occasionally, for he records that he finished chapter one on June 27. He still called it *The School of Tragedy*.

On July 5, the proofs of the U.S. edition of *The Condor and the Cows* arrived from Random House. The proofs of the British edition arrived from Methuen's on July 12.

On July 6, the day-to-day diary mentions Jim Charlton's mother. She was then staying with Jim in Santa Monica and Jim took Christopher to visit her. I can't remember what she looked like. Jim thought her half crazy and an obsessive hypochondriac. Mrs. Charlton was convinced that she had cancer and kept going to doctors for examinations and tests. At that time, the tests always proved to be negative. Nevertheless, she died of cancer, not long after this.

On July 9, Caskey and Christopher set off by car at 7:00 a.m. to visit Carter Lodge at the AJC Ranch. (John van Druten wasn't there.) Their car broke down in Redlands, with radiator trouble. They didn't get to the ranch until 6:30 that evening. On July 10, Carter's friend Dick Foote[1] came down to see them for the day. On the 11th, Caskey and Christopher returned home.

---

[1] I don't know when Carter Lodge and Dick Foote first met each other, but I do remember that Carter described their meeting more or less as follows: Carter was waiting somewhere (on a street corner, I think) when a young man walked past him. The young man looked so miserable that Carter found himself saying, "Cheer up!" The young man walked on a little way, as though he hadn't heard; then he turned and came back to Carter and asked him, "Did you say what I think you said?" Thus they became lovers. Dick had been a complete stranger in town, lonely, jobless and desperate—and Carter's kindness so overwhelmed him that he fell for Carter then and there.

This sugary story was all the harder to believe because Dick himself seemed so full of baloney. He was an incurably absurd character. Even his powerful body and his nice-looking face had a quality of caricature about them. His big muscles didn't go with his professed vulnerability and neither did his sentimental dark eyes with his impudence. He was a singer of throbbingly mournful cowboy ballads and a payer of outrageous compliments. He would sidle up to Christopher and mutter: "Jeez, that sexy little ass of yours makes me hot! I'd like to fuck the living shit out of you!" This was his approach to most of the queers and many of the women that he met. He claimed that he had talked like this to Garbo and that she'd loved it. Christopher never knowingly heard Dick utter a sincere word. And yet it was easy to enjoy the silly cheerfulness of his company and even to become fond of him, for he was quite without malice. Christopher became fond of Dick, and so did the Beesleys, up to a point. Alec described him as looking "like a coal heaver."

Christopher and Caskey probably met Dick Foote for the first time on February 5, 1949. This is the first mention I can find of Dick in the day-to-day diary. On that day, Christopher drove down to the AJC Ranch to stay with John and Carter, and remained till February 8. The day-to-day diary doesn't actually name Caskey or say "we drove," so it's possible Christopher was alone.

What did John van Druten think of Dick Foote? Most of the time, he

On July 20, Christopher drove up to Santa Barbara by himself, to see Sister (Mrs. Wykoff) who had been seriously ill with pneumonia and an attack of uremia. She then seemed to be recovering. But she died on the 23rd. On the 26th, Christopher went to the Vedanta Center to attend her funeral. This and his visit to Santa Barbara are described in the 1948–1956 journal. Christopher was much moved by Swami's description of Sister's death and his statement that "she was a saint." Christopher writes that he arrived at the temple in a bad state of mind, because "I'd been horrible and unkind to Caskey before I left the house, because I'm worried about our money and I keep feeling he ought to help us earn some more." But the effect of the funeral (or rather, the part of the ceremony which was held at the center) and of talking to Swami about Sister, was that he came away "in a calm happy 'open' mood which lasted for several days—and I felt a real horror of my unkindness to Caskey—or of any unkindness to anyone." (This latter quote is from the journal entry of August 17.)

On August 6, Caskey made one of his weekend trips to Laguna Beach (probably with Lennie Newman). Christopher went to have supper with The Benton Way Group (see page 24 [note]) at the house on Benton Way. Sam From, his friend George [Bill], Charles Aufderheide, Paul Goodman, Evelyn Hooker (who, in those days, was still Evelyn Caldwell), David Sachs and Alvin Novak were there. Paul Goodman was the Socrates of the group. (At that time, he had already written *The Breakup of Our Camp* and many articles and poems. I don't think Christopher had a high opinion of his work, however. It wasn't until fifteen years later that Christopher was greatly impressed by Paul's novel *Making Do*.) That night, Goodman, David Sachs and Christopher probably did most of the talking. I think that the nature of homosexual love was discussed at enormous length, and that they quizzed Evelyn on her knowledge of gay slang and kidded her, saying that they were going to smuggle her into a gay male bathhouse.[1]

---

probably accepted Dick because he felt he had no right not to, as long as Starcke was around. But Dick certainly got on John's nerves. As for Carter, he loathed Starcke and used his always powerful influence upon John to undermine Starcke's position and get rid of him—which he ultimately succeeded in doing.

[1] On June 8, 1974, Evelyn Hooker reminded me of an extra detail in this story. Christopher and the others said that they would smuggle her into the Crystal Baths, a notorious old bathhouse which then stood on the edge of the beach in Ocean Park. This building had several floors and on the top of it was a sun deck for nude sunbathing. Evelyn says that Christopher told her that he could get her onto the ground floor and maybe the second but that she'd undoubtedly be caught if she ventured higher, and that the queers would then put her to death instantly. (A typical specimen of Christopher's antiwoman fantasies!)

Evelyn had begun her researches into the social structure of the homosexual subculture, and she was an energetic and daring field-worker who had ventured into many rough bars and orgiastic parties.

Sam From had been among the first who volunteered to answer Evelyn's exhaustive questionnaires. He and Evelyn had also been to bed together.[*] At the moment, Sam had a slight crush on Christopher. But Christopher wasn't interested. Besides, he was dazzled by Alvin Novak, the Alcibiades of that evening's Symposium, whom he was meeting for the first time. Alvin was a dark handsome boy. Christopher immediately decided that he resembled Titian's painting of the young man with the glove.[†] No doubt he told Alvin this repeatedly. Alvin must have felt flattered, for his eyes gave Christopher encouraging signals. In true Platonic style, the Benton Way Symposium continued until dawn, and then Christopher drove back to Santa Monica with Alvin Novak. Sam From came along too, perhaps hoping to get into bed with Christopher. My impression is that Christopher either avoided this altogether or that he played around with Sam until Sam, who always got very drunk on these occasions, passed out. Anyhow, Christopher ended up making sex with Alvin, and he later looked back upon that night as having been highly romantic. It was unique, at any rate. Christopher never went to a party that was quite like it.

On August 9, Lesser Samuels and Christopher finished the rough draft of the treatment of *The Easiest Thing in the World*.[1]

On August 10, Christopher had lunch with Igor and Vera Stravinsky, Aldous and Maria Huxley and Robert Craft at the Farmer's Market. This was Christopher's first encounter with the Stravinskys and Craft. Craft has described it at length, in *Retrospectives and Conclusions*. I myself remember little or nothing about it; my first distinct memories are of our second meeting. Craft uses the surprising adjective "lovelorn" to describe Christopher. Can he have meant that Christopher somehow showed that he was unhappy in his

---

[1] "Everybody loves scandals . . . and witch-hunts . . . and smears. It's the easiest thing in the world to make us believe evil—of anything—a play, a book, a person, a faith." This quotation [from the script] sufficiently explains the title. I can't bring myself to summarize the story itself. It is one of the least distinguished pieces of film writing in which Christopher was ever involved; a liberalistic, goody-goody drama about the awful effects of slander on the inhabitants of a small town.

[* Near the end of her life, Evelyn Hooker said they had not.]
[† "The Man with the Glove" (c. 1520), in the Louvre.]

homelife? If so, this doesn't jibe with Craft's statement that, "His sense of humor is very ready. He maintains a chronic or semi-permanent smile . . . supplementing it with giggles," etc. Craft goes on to relate how Christopher told them "a story of why he is no longer invited to [Charlie] Chaplin's: 'Someone had said I had peed on the sofa there one night while plastered.'" This one detail makes me suspect that this alleged diary entry may in fact have been reconstructed by Craft quite a long while after the event. For Christopher *was* actually still being invited to the Chaplins'. He went on seeing them for another ten months.[1]

On August 14, Catherine Caskey finally left—for San Francisco, on her way back to Kentucky. Christopher writes about her on August 17, in the 1948–1956 journal, saying that Caskey has admitted that "his drinking and neurotic laziness [were] largely due to her being here." Christopher adds that Catherine is determined to regard Caskey as a model son and that "her obviously excessive (and insincere) praises" make him "frantic with guilt." (Christopher suspects that Catherine is subconsciously trying to spite her husband by praising her son.)

In this entry, Christopher states that, "All [that] stuff I wrote about leaving him is beside the point. I can't. I must not. At least not now.

---

[1] As far as I can recall, the accusation that Christopher had passed out at a Chaplin party and then peed, while unconscious, on one of his sofas was reported to Christopher by Iris Tree or Ivan Moffat. Caskey, who was with Christopher that evening, was certain that it was untrue. Iris and Ivan obviously believed that it *was* true, which hurt and annoyed Christopher a good deal. Personally, I'm pretty sure that Christopher was innocent, simply because he had never done such a thing before and has never done it since. The intoxicated body is apt to have a predictable pattern of behavior. Christopher's bladder and stomach were both strong; it was no more likely that he would pee involuntarily than that he would throw up—and he never threw up.

Still, the fact remains that Chaplin did stop inviting Christopher. He was reported to have said, "I can't stand a man who can't hold his liquor." Many years later, Christopher tried, through Salka Viertel, to arrange a reconciliation with him. Salka went to Oona Chaplin, who went to her husband; but Charlie was firm—so firm, that Oona told Salka she believed Charlie must have some other, much more serious motive for his refusal. The mystery is still unsolved.

(Talking of making messes in public—or rather, of *not* making them— reminds me of a scene which took place sometime in 1951, while Christopher and Caskey were living at Laguna. They had gone to a queer party at the home of an excessively houseproud male couple and Christopher had fallen asleep, drunk, on the floor. One of the hosts saw this and begged Caskey to remove Christopher "before he throws up all over the carpet." To which Caskey—as Christopher was later told—replied with blazing scorn, "What do you think he is—*a queen*?")

The day may come when I ought to. I don't know. I certainly don't want to."

There are also some "good" resolutions. Christopher counts his blessings and reminds himself that, "Prayer, meditation, thought, creation are the *only* refuge and stronghold. Without them, I am nothing. Without them, life is really an agony." (I have no right to sneer at Christopher's soul searchings, just because they were conducted amidst bottles and boys—but they do embarrass me.)

Then Christopher refers to his novel, which he is trying to restart, and to its chief character, whom he calls "Stephen Monkhouse." "Stephen Monkhouse has got to be me—not some synthetic Anglo-American. The few circumstances can so easily be imagined—his ex-wife, his Quaker background, etc. But it must be written out of the middle of *my* consciousness." These remarks now seem astonishingly naive to me. Didn't Christopher realize that what he calls "the few circumstances" must of necessity alter everything? How *could* he write out of the middle of his consciousness about someone who was tall, bisexual and an heir to a fortune? Christopher's trouble (which he never recognized until it was too late) was that he was trying to create a fiction character with three dimensions and a life of its own and then use it as the observer figure Christopher Isherwood is used in the Berlin stories and elsewhere.

A journal entry on August 18 merely describes a visit to the Down Beat Café on Central Avenue. Christopher was taken there by Bernie Hamilton and his girlfriend Maxine, on the night of the 17th. I can't remember who Bernie was, except that he was black. I can't remember anything about the evening, except the embarrassment Christopher felt when Bernie took him into an all-black restaurant for supper before they went on to the Down Beat. It seemed to Christopher that he ought not to be annoying these people by his presence, since there were hundreds of restaurants in this same city where *their* presence would be unwelcome.

On August 19, Christopher went with a screenwriter named George Bradshaw to visit Birmingham Hospital in the San Fernando Valley. At that time, it was an armed services veterans' hospital and a lot of its patients were paraplegics and quadriplegics. Bradshaw had started a project; he wanted to get some of the patients interested in writing stories and articles, and to find fellow writers who would give them professional advice. After this visit, Christopher agreed to join Bradshaw's project.

On August 20, Christopher and Caskey had supper with the Stravinskys at their house on Wetherly Drive. (It was probably Bob Craft who got Caskey included in the invitation, for he had visited

Rustic Road alone on the 17th and had met Caskey there.) Stravinsky welcomed Christopher by saying: "Shall we listen to my Mass before we get drunk?"[1] By the end of the evening, Christopher was very drunk indeed and utterly enslaved by the Stravinsky charm, by Vera's quite as much as Igor's.

Here are Christopher's earliest impressions of Igor and of Vera, insofar as I can recapture them: His cuddly animal smallness,[2] his

[1] In the Stravinsky–Craft *Dialogues and a Diary*, Igor is quoted by Craft as saying: "On Christopher's first visit to my home, he fell asleep when someone started to play a recording of my music. My affection for him began with that incident." Igor's memory (or Bob's) may be inaccurate here, but I can easily believe that Igor found Christopher sympathetic because (a) he was always ready to get drunk and (b) he offered Igor a friendship which was quite uncomplicated by maestro worship. On the same page of *Dialogues and a Diary*, Igor is quoted as saying, with reference to Christopher: "We have often been drunk together—as often as once a week, in the early 1950s, I should think." This is, to put it mildly, a wild exaggeration, but the note of approval is clear. Christopher's appetite for good wine and liquor and food, his lack of pretense about his sex life and indeed also his preference for a devotional form of religion may well have seemed to Igor agreeably "Russian." Much as he loved and admired Huxley and Heard, Igor must sometimes have found their intellectual power chilling and their Britishness alien. With Christopher, he could be more relaxed. As for Christopher's deficiency in musical appreciation, Igor was too great a king in his art to feel the lack of one extra courtier. Christopher actually did like a lot of classical music, including some of Stravinsky's, but he never told the Stravinskys so—the gross compliments of their courtiers disgusted him. Maybe Igor understood this about Christopher and respected him for it.

[2] It was this quality which caused Christopher to begin to think of Igor as belonging to a trio with Prabhavananda and Forster. Both Igor and Swami had an animal smallness which made Christopher want to touch and hug them protectively. Forster was larger and less animal, but he had something in him of the ageless, innocently trustful baby, so it was natural to want to hug him too. Christopher did frequently hug Stravinsky and Forster. His reverence for Prabhavananda as his guru inhibited him, but he was deeply happy when Prabhavananda occasionally hugged *him*. In most of Christopher's dreams about Prabhavananda, there were situations of physical (but altogether asexual) closeness—for example, they would be sharing a bedroom in a hotel, or Christopher would be helping Swami dress.

Christopher was never conscious that his familiar behavior toward Stravinsky caused any offense. But Lillian Libman suggests that perhaps it did, to a slight extent. (She was his press representative and personal manager from 1959 onward.) In her book, *And Music at the Close*, she claims that Christopher's customary greeting, "Hi, Igor" (according to her, Christopher pronounced it "Eager," but he didn't), brought to her ears, and Bob Craft's, "an echo of disrespect," and that "it always startled the composer as much as it did the rest of us." She adds that Christopher and Don Bachardy (who was of

spontaneous warmth and unembarrassed kisses, his marvellous multi-lingual conversation, his wit (which sometimes seemed wry Jewish, sometimes epigrammatic French, sometimes punning German), his joy in eating and drinking, his Russian-peasant devoutness and superstitiousness, his royal dignity, his aristocratic humility, his accurately and deeply cutting contempt for his enemies, his beautiful modest love for Vera, his acute nervousness.

Her great beauty and her even greater poise. Moving and breathing so easily within the atmosphere of worldly fame, she was Igor's only imaginable consort. And yet she often seemed as vulnerable as a child. She too loved the best of wine and food, but she didn't demand that it should be served to her; she was capable of shopping at the market and cooking delicious meals, herself. She also found time to paint pictures and to help run a boutique. She complained constantly of her troubles and problems, always with charming humor. Everything she did and said seemed simple and spontaneous. She was naturally hospitable and extravagant.

(The word "extravagant" reminds me of a characteristic for which Igor was well known, his avariciousness. Auden, who had had business dealings with him when writing *The Rake's Progress*, complained of it often. Christopher was never exposed to it, which is why it isn't mentioned in the above list of Christopher's impressions. It always appeared to him that Igor accepted and enjoyed the considerable luxury in which they lived. But Vera certainly was extravagant, and maybe this was compensatory role playing, to balance Igor's penny pinching. As Bob Craft's influence in the household increased, he came down heavily on the side of extravagance, encouraging the Stravinskys to spend their money lavishly—not on him but on themselves.)

Bob Craft, when Christopher first met him, was about twenty-five—he had then been associated with the Stravinskys for less than eighteen months. He appeared to Christopher to be an outstanding specimen of the American disciple type. He obviously adored the Stravinskys and was quick to show off his knowledge of every aspect of The Master's music. He was pale, boyish, eager, pedantic, cute

---

course merely following Christopher's example in this) were in a tiny minority; only two or three other people called Stravinsky by his Christian name. These statements by Libman may be mere bitchery. If true they are interesting as a demonstration of two opposed mental attitudes. From Christopher's point of view, calling Stravinsky "Igor" expressed loving respect, just as continuing to call him "Mr." or "Sir" or "Maestro" (Christopher *never* could have used that word except in fun) would have expressed a polite refusal to become more than an acquaintance, and hence a *lack* of respect and of love.

[. . .]. Christopher was later flattered to discover that Bob also knew a great deal about *his* work. Bob even asked a book collector's technical questions about different editions of *The Memorial*—questions which Christopher himself couldn't answer. He was in fact a whiz kid by nature. Once his mouselike shyness had been overcome, he would get smart-alecky and tactless. On one occasion at least, he went so far as to correct a statement made by Huxley. And he was right!

Craft's cleverness didn't annoy Christopher, because they weren't in competition. Christopher had an entirely different set of pretensions—to intuition, psychological insight, sensibility, etc.—which Bob was prepared to respect. At that period, Bob greatly admired Christopher's work.[1] Christopher felt drawn to Bob and would have liked to become his close friend. But the circumstances of Bob's life apparently didn't permit this. In the years to come, they very seldom met each other alone, outside of the Stravinsky household.

Christopher was charmed not only by the Stravinskys themselves but also by their house—or rather, by the atmosphere they had created in it. The Stravinskys had a number of valuable pictures, including several Picassos. Any art gallery or wealthy individual can own such artworks, but Igor's pictures had their own different kind of value and magic because they were all related to his own life, they were souvenirs of people he had known, not just items in a collection. Being souvenirs, they didn't seem out of place amidst the many photographs by which they were surrounded—groups of to-be-famous young faces on the beaches and in the concert halls and restaurants of the nineteen hundreds, the tens, the twenties.

At the end of the house was Igor's studio, doubly a sacred place, since it contained an icon to which he prayed. One wasn't forbidden to enter it, but Christopher seldom did more than peep in, respectfully, from its threshold. At the back of the house, steps led up to a small overgrown garden which was often invaded by neighborhood children. Christopher was enraged to think that the wealthy thick-skinned hog neighbors should allow their children to disturb Igor in the midst of his composing—but Igor didn't seem to mind the noise they made. All he complained of was that they would turn

---

[1] On September 29 of that year, Craft wrote to Christopher from Kingston, New York, where he was staying with his parents. Christopher had just sent him a copy of *The Condor and the Cows*: "It is radiant, full of love and peace. There is a new quality in you in these last three years. After three rapid readings it seems to be the best writing I know, whatever." This suggests something more than literary admiration [. . .].

on the garden hose and flood the hillside, making mud. He remarked mildly, "They are not always prudent."

On August 24, Christopher paid his first visit to Birmingham Hospital alone. He was terribly self-conscious. It seemed tactless and tasteless to have brought his relatively able body into this retreat of the disabled. His self-consciousness was soon cured, however. The day was hot and the hospital passages were very long. By the time he had reached his first patient's bedside, Christopher heard himself exclaim (to his subsequent huge embarrassment), "My feet are killing me!"

Christopher soon found that he could do what was required of him easily enough. Some of the patients were indeed interested in writing; others just played along with it out of politeness, because Christopher had taken the trouble to come to see them and because this was the official purpose of his visit. What all of them wanted was to have visitors who would gossip with them about the outside world, and specifically sports and show business. Christopher was no good at the former but better than average at the latter. It was also important that the visitor should be reliably regular, so that his visit could be looked forward to without fear of disappointment. Christopher wasn't quite regular, but he did manage to visit Birmingham Hospital at least once and nearly always three or four times a month from then on until the end of May 1950, when the patients were transferred to a hospital near Long Beach. Sometimes he went alone. Sometimes he took friends with him—either attractive young actresses or people who could talk easily and amusingly. (Caskey was marvellous at this.)

The paraplegics weren't sentimental about themselves. Their humor when speaking to each other was brutal. They said "cripple" in the tone that blacks say "nigger." They had no use for the sympathy of able-bodied outsiders, though some of them were probably prepared to exploit it. A visitor was on dangerous ground if he referred to the war. All these men were technically veterans, but that didn't mean that they had all got their injuries in battle or even that they had seen combat. Those who had been paralyzed as the result of a car wreck in the States or of diving into an empty swimming pool at night while drunk were not charmed if you treated them as heroes or suggested that they had sacrificed themselves to save democracy.

The quadriplegics were, I guess, all hopeless cases; there was nothing they could do to alter their condition. But the paraplegics could do a lot, provided that they persevered—laziness was their deadly sin and living death. Christopher talked to patients who had been developing their upper bodies doggedly, day by day, for years—first merely *imagining* the movement of a finger and sending out commands to it from the brain, again and again and again; then making the finger actually bend; then, months later, achieving a clenched fist; then, after more months, the raising of an arm. They had produced beautifully muscular golden-skinned torsos which Christopher often felt a lust to touch and kiss. They could swing themselves lithely into and out of cars and wheelchairs; cars with specially designed hand controls enabled them to drive around town independently. Sometimes they would even regain their sexual potency; this had been known to happen when a patient started to go to college and found himself amongst girls who attracted him.

Nevertheless, beneath all this brave activity there lay the squalid basic fact of paralysis. You might move out of the hospital into a home of your own but you couldn't move very far. You had to go back to the ward for periodical checkups, and you might need to be rushed there if you had a sudden relapse due to some toxic condition which could easily be fatal. And then came periods of depression, when you thought, "Who's kidding who?" and were apt to drop your bodybuilding and studying and drink a lot and grow fat and dull. I remember that there was an American Indian boy who decided that he couldn't endure this state of medical slavery any longer. His family came for him and took him back with them to their reservation. The doctors at Birmingham warned him that he was probably going to an early death, but he didn't believe them or didn't care. I never heard what became of him.

Shortly before Christopher began visiting Birmingham, the paraplegics had been involved in the shooting of a film about themselves. This was *The Men*. Its script had been written by Carl Foreman. Fred Zinnemann directed it, Stanley Kramer produced it; its stars were Marlon Brando and Teresa Wright. Quite a lot of the paraplegics appeared as extras in the film and one of them, a beautiful young man named Arthur Jurado, had a speaking part, as "Angel." The head doctor of the paraplegic section, Dr. Bors, gave Zinnemann technical advice and was represented in the film by a character called "Dr. Brock," played by Everett Sloane.

The actors who played paraplegics—Brando, Richard Erdman, Jack Webb and maybe a few others—all had to learn the techniques of getting into and out of their wheelchairs and of steering and propelling the chairs at racing speed along the hospital corridors. They also used to visit the bars in their chairs with the genuine patients and pretend to be paraplegics throughout the evening. Christopher longed to know how the patients themselves felt about this (to him) slightly indecent playacting. As far as he could tell, they regarded it as merely amusing—with perhaps an underlying pleasure in being, for once, on terms of physical equality with able-bodied young men who were celebrities into the bargain.[1]

On September 4, Christopher went to a party given by [. . .] a visiting French journalist who had already interviewed him.[*] The party (all boy) was in a shacky old house in the Canyon. After things had got going, a young man danced nearly nude to a record of Ravel's *Boléro*. His writhings and yearning gestures seemed ridiculous to Christopher, who rudely laughed. At the end of the dance, the young man announced that he was going into the bathroom and that all were welcome to join him there—"Except that old bag," he added, with a venomous glance at Christopher. Most of the guests did go into the bathroom, where (presumably) they lined up to fuck the dancer. But the orgy was brief. Something went wrong with the water heater. There was an explosion, followed by yells from the scalded guests and their reappearance in various states of nakedness.

On September 6, Lesser Samuels and Christopher checked a final typescript of *The Easiest Thing in the World* before handing it over to

---

[1] There was a story about one of Brando's bar visits which later found its way into gossip columns and became famous. It was certainly true in substance; Christopher heard it from a patient who had been present. Here is, more or less, the patient's version:

While they were in the bar, a woman came in who was a fanatical evangelist—and maybe drunk, as well. She started haranguing the wheelchair boys, telling them that, if they had faith in the Lord and would pray to Him with her, they could arise out of their chairs and walk. The paraplegics at once realized the comic possibilities of the situation. They waited eagerly to see how Brando would handle it.

Brando began by disagreeing violently with the woman: "That's a lot of bullshit! I don't buy that crap!" Then, gradually, he let himself be persuaded —okay, he still didn't believe, but she could pray over him if she wanted to. So the woman started to pray. For a long time, Brando remained absolutely still. Then he began to writhe, twist, strain, groan and try to heave himself out of his chair. He half succeeded, slumped back, tried again, staggered to his feet, seemed about to fall—then suddenly became his normal self, dropped all pretensions, did a short buck and wing routine and ran out of the bar. The woman fainted.

There was another version of the ending to this story—untrue but better: The woman didn't show the least surprise at Brando's apparent healing. Turning to the paraplegics, she said: "What did I tell you, boys? All you need is faith! Come on now, who's next?"

[* The man was Argentine, not French; he says that he was not a professional journalist and does not recall the interview.]

be mimeographed. During the next week, copies were sent out to the studios—to be rejected by all of them.

On September 7, Christopher went down to Trabuco for its official opening as a monastery of the Vedanta Society of Southern California. The day-to-day diary says that Christopher drove there with the van Leydens and drove back with Iris Tree and Ford Rainey. I have no memories of this occasion.

I can skim over the next two months fairly quickly. There are few outstanding events:

Christopher did very little work during this period. Right at the end of it he notes, in the journal, that he has only got as far as page eighteen of his novel. He was steadily but very slowly revising Swami's commentary on the yoga aphorisms of Patanjali. According to the day-to-day diary entry of September 12, he wrote a foreword on that day to Swami Vividishananda's *A Man of God*, which is a life of Swami Shivananda. (Considering the slowness of Christopher's writing, it's hard to believe that he finished this job in a single day, even though it only runs to two and a half pages—but maybe Swami was pressuring him.) In the day-to-day diary there are also four references to talks about unspecified movie stories—with Lesser Samuels on October 7 and 24, with Lesser and Aldous Huxley on October 20 and with Aldous on November 3. These were almost certainly just discussions, without anything being put down on paper.[1]

Meanwhile, Christopher saw quite a lot of people, with or

---

[1] Christopher's talks with Huxley must have been about the Latin American film story which they later wrote and named *Below the Equator.* I suppose Christopher called Samuels in as a consultant on this, but he can't have thought much of their idea for he didn't collaborate. As for Samuels himself, one of the stories he discussed with Christopher was almost certainly *No Way Out.* My memory is very weak on this point, but my impression is that the story had been entirely invented by Samuels and already partially written. Nevertheless, Samuels urged Christopher to work on it, saying that he liked having Christopher as a partner. Christopher was discouraged by the failure of *The Easiest Thing in the World* and altogether in a lazy pessimistic state of mind. So he refused, excusing himself by pointing out that Lesser didn't need him and could easily finish the story outline alone. Lesser agreed that this was true but he renewed his offer and added that of course he would split fifty-fifty with Christopher in the event of a sale, as before. Again, Christopher refused. Not long after this, *No Way Out* was finished and promptly sold for a good sum—I believe $75,000 or over. Christopher cursed his stupidity and vowed that, in future, he'd collaborate on any story Lesser proposed. *No Way Out* was shot and released in 1950, with a screenplay by Lesser Samuels and Joe Mankiewicz, its director. Linda Darnell and Richard Widmark were its leads, but it is chiefly remembered as the film which made Sidney Poitier (like it or not) a star.

without Caskey. These included Iris Tree and Ford Rainey, the Beesleys, Jim Charlton, Hayden Lewis and Rod Owens, Jay Laval, Jo and Ben Masselink, Gerald Heard, Michael Barrie, the Huxleys, Chris Wood, Salka Viertel, Frank and Nan Taylor, Peggy Kiskadden, John van Druten. In the day-to-day diary, there is no mention of the Stravinskys; they were probably out of town a good deal.

Christopher and Caskey were still having sex together, despite their strained relationship. But Caskey often went out for the night and he spent weekends at Laguna Beach. Christopher would then spend the night with Jim Charlton or with a young man named Russ Zeininger. Russ had originally been picked up by Caskey, late in August. But Russ didn't at that time want to be fucked, so Christopher took him over—at first out of mere politeness. Later Christopher became quite fond of Russ, who was a friendly, intelligent person. Their sexual relations weren't thrilling but were adequate. Russ had an unusually small cock. Christopher was no size queen and this didn't bother him unduly. Russ has remained a friend to this day—though seldom seen.

Tennessee Williams came to Los Angeles at the end of September, to talk to Irving Rapper and others at Warner Brothers about the forthcoming filming of *The Glass Menagerie*. Tennessee had Frank Merlo with him. Christopher and Caskey saw them on the 23rd and again on the 25th. Christopher was certainly meeting Frank for the first time. I have an idea that Caskey had met him already, sometime in August or September of 1948, while Caskey was still in the East. Caskey liked Frank from the start, he indeed said that he liked him even better than Tennessee. Christopher also took to Frank at once and soon became deeply fond of him—as nearly all of Tennessee's friends were. Frank's racial background was Sicilian. He was small, lithe, muscular, sexy, with a long pale face and black hair. You could imagine him taking part in a vendetta; he was capable of rage, loyalty to the death, enduring passion. And, at the same time, he was campy, funny, gay, quite as ready to dance as to fight. Frank looked after Tennessee in every way, arranging his travels and his parties, cooking, coping with hustlers, agents and unwelcome callers, giving him shrewd business advice. He was the ideal nanny; the truest friend and lover Tennessee could ever hope to have. Tennessee was well aware of this. He loved Frank dearly, though he often behaved badly to him. They had shattering Latin quarrels which were usually short.

On October 3, an FBI man named Roger Wallace[*] came to talk

[* Not his real name.]

to Christopher about Agnes Smedley. (FBI men are apt to visit in pairs and I have the impression that Wallace had a colleague with him. If so, his name isn't mentioned in the day-to-day diary.) Wallace had read *Journey to a War* and knew of Smedley's meetings with Auden and Christopher in Hankow, in 1938. He asked if Christopher could add any details to that account. Christopher could remember none. Then Wallace put a question which seemed to Christopher so ridiculous that it must be a joke: "Do you think Agnes Smedley is a communist agent?" Christopher retorted: "Do you think Stalin is a communist agent?"—and went on to say that the word "agent" suggests undercover activity; how could it be applied to Smedley, who bombarded the U.S. government every week with public denunciations of its crimes against the people of the communist world? Wallace smiled at this, and the interview was soon concluded in the most friendly manner, without the faintest hint of any accusation against Christopher himself for having associated with a notorious Red. (Christopher thought he could detect, in Wallace's attitude, the sophisticated contempt of an FBI professional for the crude standards of the McCarthy amateurs—but maybe this was wishful thinking.) Then why had Wallace taken the trouble to visit Christopher at all? Christopher was inclined to believe that his name had been merely one of many on a list of routine checkups to be made, and that Wallace had chosen him because he lived near the beach and could therefore be used as an excuse for Wallace to spend a couple of extra hours away from the office, sunbathing and swimming.

On October 10, the day-to-day diary records that Christopher went with Jay Laval to court—this would have been the West Los Angeles police court—to be present at Caskey's trial. Since Jay accompanied Christopher and since the 10th was a Monday, I assume that Lennie Newman was also involved and that their arrest was the result of some offense they had drunkenly committed during that weekend. Whatever it was, they didn't get sent to jail. No doubt they were fined.

Also on the 10th, Christopher went to the Vedanta Center to say goodbye to Swami. He left for India next day, taking three of the nuns with him—Sarada, Barada and Prabha. This was Swami's second return visit since his arrival in the States in 1923. His first visit, with Sister, had been in 1935.

On November 8, after a lapse of nearly three months, Christopher made an entry in the journal. After noting that this is his personal Initiation Day—initiation by Swami in 1940, becoming a U.S. citizen in 1946—he resolves to keep up the journal more regularly, to write three articles he has promised, to get on with the Patanjali book and with his novel.[1] "This summer has been really disgraceful. I don't think I can ever remember having been so idle, dull, resentful and unhappy. . . . I feel sick, stupid, middle-aged, impotent. . . . I bore myself beyond tears."

Christopher also records that, "My life with Bill has reached such a point of emotional bankruptcy that he is leaving, by mutual consent, in a day or two, to hitchhike to Florida to see his sister." What Christopher calls "emotional bankruptcy" was actually boredom on Caskey's side and frustration on Christopher's. They were weary of being together—though Christopher, as usual, wouldn't quite admit this and left it to Caskey to make a move. One symptom of their weariness was that they had stopped quarrelling. No doubt most of their friends thought they must be getting along quite well together, and were surprised by Caskey's sudden departure. In the journal, Christopher comments: "Will this solve anything? It didn't with Vernon. Well, anyhow, we have to try it." I don't think that either of them regarded this as the beginning of a permanent separation. But maybe Christopher was half-consciously hoping that now they might gradually drift apart, painlessly and without fuss.

Caskey left on November 11. I can't remember any details of a parting scene; no doubt it all happened very quietly. What I do remember is that that night, after Christopher had returned from a party and gone to bed, he was wakened out of a doze by Jim Charlton. Jim came bounding up the stairs in the darkness, stripping off his clothes, and jumped naked upon Christopher, panting and laughing. Christopher was amused, sexually aroused and deeply touched—the dog had sensed that his master would be needing him. Their lovemaking was the perfect prelude to a happy holiday from Christopher's domestic life.

On November 15 there is a journal entry, complaining of a spell

---

[1] In actual fact, Christopher only managed to make six journal entries during the remaining fifty-three days of that year. Of the three articles he mentions, only one was written at that time; his contribution to the Klaus Mann memorial volume, which he finished on December 1. He did write about Santa Monica Canyon in the article called "California Story," but not until 1951. (*Harper's Bazaar* got it, not Lehmann.) The projected article for Gerald Heard on Vedanta and Christianity was never written. I can't even remember why Gerald wanted it. The novel continued to give Christopher trouble and he couldn't make any real progress with it. I suppose he kept the Patanjali book going, at its customary snail crawl, because he had to produce installments of it for the Vedanta magazine.

of hot weather which is making Christopher lazy, of a sore throat which sometimes almost prevents him from swallowing, and of the cost of entertaining people in restaurants while making "infinitely cautious overtures to prospective affairs." The only "prospective affair" I can identify was [. . .] a very good-looking young actor, who flirted with Christopher over a considerable period but never put out. Christopher's complaints about wasting money in restaurants are actually an indirect compliment to Caskey. For Caskey—despite all his wild outings—had remained a strictly economical housekeeper and a fairly regular provider of excellent home-cooked meals.

The next journal entry, November 18, is mostly about Jim Charlton. Christopher had spent the previous night sleeping at Jim's apartment, down on the beach near the pier. This was a domestic, not a romantic evening. Christopher, who had just given up smoking, felt "somewhat dumb and dazed" and his sore throat "was closed, it seemed, to an aperture the size of a pinhole." After supper (and plenty of drinks, no doubt) both he and Jim dozed off, waking at 3:00 a.m. just long enough to get into bed. In the morning, Christopher felt happy and peaceful. He adds that his thoughts about Caskey are still resentful "—with a kind of wondering horror: how did I ever stand it? The great thing, now, is to relax."

Here, for the first time, Christopher tries to describe Jim as a character. I have quoted some of the description already (see page 156).[1] Its tone suggests that Christopher is still rather in love with Jim—and yet this romantic, sexy, amusing, intelligent and considerate lover–friend evidently isn't enough for Christopher. He complains that Jim can't be exclusively loved, because he is a Dog Person and therefore everybody's property. But the truth is that Christopher found Jim too restful, too easy to be with, too predictable to be all absorbing. Sometimes, by way of a change, Christopher would deliberately provoke Jim to anger and once or twice Jim even hit him. But there was never any real tension, never any deep jealousy or clash of wills between them. And Christopher's nature needed tension, much as he hated it when Caskey created it for him.

On November 18, Christopher had supper with James Whale, the film director, his friend David Lewis, and two young makers

---

[1] Additional details: "He has the weary face of a young officer—a boy prematurely saddled with responsibility. When women are around, he puts on a knitted wool tie and laughs with his front teeth. He grunts in the morning—surly. But likes it when I say, 'You old cow' or, 'Okay, Miss Nosey.'"

of "underground" films, Ken Anger and Curtis Harrington. Christopher could remember Whale as a young cute redheaded actor in a revue at the Lyric, Hammersmith, back in the twenties, but I don't think they had ever met before, either in England or in California, although Whale lived near the Canyon, on Amalfi Drive. Ken Anger (whom Christopher had known since he was a strikingly attractive boy named Angermayer, fancied by Denny Fouts) showed his soon-to-become-famous film, *Fireworks*, which was later praised by Cocteau. Christopher didn't like it and said so, after getting aggressively drunk on Whale's strong martinis. He thereby offended Anger and also (to his great regret) Whale. Curtis Harrington—also destined for celebrity, if not fame—[. . .] had made a short film called *Fragment of Seeking*, which Christopher called *Fragment of Squeaking*.

On November 20, Christopher had supper with Benjamin Britten and Peter Pears, who had just arrived in Los Angeles to give two or more concerts. The reunion was most cordial. Indeed, they both treated Christopher as the one real friend with whom they could relax from the strain of official hospitality. Christopher at once arranged to give a party, at which, he promised, they would meet as many attractive boys as he could manage to collect. The party was held on November 22. A journal entry, made earlier that day, refers to preparations for it. Christopher is jittery—chiefly because he is in the throes of nicotine disintoxication; this is his sixth day without smoking. He still fears that he will have to smoke in order to be able to write, and there is his article on Klaus Mann to be finished, as well as his current installment of Patanjali. Christopher was also jittery about the party, though without much reason, for, as usual, he had shifted the responsibility for organizing it onto someone else—Leif Argo, assisted by another friend, David Robertson. Christopher's only legitimate worries were that he had maybe invited too many people and that he wouldn't be able to remember all their names.[1] He kept repeating them, to reassure himself.

[1] In the journal, Christopher writes: "Names—Waldo Angelo, Hank Burczinsky, Hanns Hagenbuehler, Nicky Nadeau, Victor Rueda, Leif Argo, Russ Zeininger, Ted Baccardi, Amos Shepherd. American names." In *The World in the Evening* (part two, chapter five) this list is partially repeated, with Nadeau changed to Naddo (probably to make it sound more exotic) and Baccardi corrected to Bachardy (in 1949, Christopher didn't even know how to spell the name which in 1953 was to become his household word!)

It must have been quite a long time before this that Christopher first noticed Ted Bachardy on the beach—maybe the previous spring, maybe as early as the fall of 1948. Ted was then in his late teens; January 16, 1949, was his nineteenth birthday. He was a dark good-looking boy with a well-made brown body;

The party wasn't an unqualified success. The house was certainly crammed with young men who were most of them fairly attractive. They danced together or went upstairs and necked. When invited, many had told Christopher that they were eager to meet the guests of honor, Britten and Pears—but, having done so, they quickly lost interest in them. In this gay setting, where celebrity snobbery was replaced by sex snobbery, Ben and Peter were just a pair of slightly faded limey queens, who were, furthermore, too shy and too solidly mated to join in the general kissing and cuddling. The party wasn't really for them, though they politely pretended to believe that it was.

In the November 22 journal entry there is also a reference to an event which isn't mentioned in the day-to-day diary: "It's shameful and petty to have to confess it—but I despise Jim just the least bit for his behavior the other evening. Anyhow, I despise his self-pity over it. Also, he looks so silly, all banged up. But that's unkind, and I must be very careful not to show it."

On either November 18 or 19, quite late at night, Jim Charlton brought three or four boys over to Christopher's house. They were

---

Christopher found his legs outstandingly sexy. Ted had many admirers, but he didn't flirt, didn't eye other people. If you talked to him, he didn't snub you but he didn't open up. He had quiet modest good manners.

By November 1949, Christopher knew two things about Ted. One was that he now had a lover, a self-assertive [. . .] young man named Ed Cornell. The other was that he had recently had a severe mental breakdown, from which he had now apparently recovered. During the breakdown, Ted had become violent and had had to be hospitalized. Christopher had been shocked when he heard the news; he now saw Ted as a touching, threatened figure—all the more so because Ed didn't show much sympathy for him (though, as a matter of fact, Ed had behaved quite well while Ted was sick). Christopher wasn't seriously interested in Ted, however—merely a bit sentimental about this attractive boy menaced by insanity, and merely eager to have sex with him if this could be arranged without drama or too much exertion.

A few days before November 22, Christopher happened to meet Ted on the beach and impulsively invited him to the party. If Christopher hoped he would thus get an opportunity to date Ted alone later, he was disappointed. Ted arrived with Ed (whom Christopher had been obliged to invite also) and remained close to him throughout. When the two of them danced together, Christopher could see that Ted was very much in love. Christopher never asked Ted to the Rustic Road house again; no doubt because it seemed wasted effort to go on pursuing him. During the next three years, they saw each other only occasionally. Nevertheless, a weak link of acquaintanceship had been formed between them—a link which was just barely strong enough to draw its attached chain of beautiful and incredible consequences into Christopher's life—the first of them being Christopher's meeting with Ted's four-years-younger brother, Don.

all (I think) marines in civilian clothes. After a few drinks, Jim got into an argument with one of them (whom I'll refer to for convenience as Red) and called him, quite casually and without venom, a son of a bitch. Red was sexy, well built and pugnacious. He declared that no one ever called him son of a bitch and got away with it, because that word was an insult to his mother. So he was going to beat Jim up. Jim said they couldn't fight in the house, because of the furniture, or in the yard, because of the neighbors. Christopher tried to calm Red down. The other boys took no sides and didn't seem to care what happened. But Red said that he'd either fight or go to the police and tell them that Jim had propositioned him. Finally they all drove up the hill to the Ocean Avenue park. Here Red hit Jim, who was bigger than himself, again and again until Jim's face was bloody. Jim didn't attempt to defend himself. He later insisted that he had done the only sensible thing. If he had fought back, the fight might well have gone on until a police car drove by, in which case they would all of them have been in trouble. Jim was right, and Christopher was right to feel ashamed of his own reactions. Nevertheless, there *was* something slightly repulsive about Jim's masochistic attitude to Red when they met again in a bar, some days after this. Jim said admiringly: "You certainly beat me up!" Red, like the silly boy he was, didn't unbend. He replied grandly that he'd do the same thing any time to anyone who called him son of a bitch because that word etc. etc.

On November 24, Christopher ate Thanksgiving lunch with the Beesleys and Phyllis Morris. That evening, he and Jim went to a concert given by Britten and Pears, downtown. I believe it was after this concert that Ben and Peter told him that they longed to get away to the country for a couple of days and be quiet. So Christopher arranged to take them on a short trip and he asked Jim Charlton to come along. On the 26th, they drove to Palm Springs and then on to the AJC Ranch, where they saw John van Druten. They spent the night at the Rancho Mirage, ten miles outside Palm Springs. On the 27th, they drove southwest to Mount Palomar (the day-to-day diary doesn't actually say they visited the observatory but I assume they did), then out to the coast at Oceanside, then up to Laguna Beach, where they had supper with Chris Wood and slept at a motel nearby. On the 28th, they drove back to Los Angeles.

I don't have many memories of Ben and Peter during their visit or of this trip Christopher and Jim took with them. Once, when he was alone with Ben, Christopher asked (I suppose in a more or less tactful manner) if Ben ever had sex with other people. Ben said no, he was faithful to Peter, adding, "I still feel the old charm." Another memory is of Ben requesting Christopher, quite pleasantly, to stop singing. Christopher would do this for hours on end when he was by himself, repeating the same song over and over. A great favorite was Cole Porter's "Ev'ry time we say goodbye . . ." because he loved attempting the transition in, "But how strange / The change / From *major to minor*." This was what Ben must have found particularly painful, because Christopher had almost no ear. Also I remember that Jim asked Ben how he composed—maybe he didn't put the question so crudely. Anyhow, Ben didn't snub him but replied: "Well—I think I'll begin with some strings, and then I think I'd like to bring in some woodwind, and then I think I'll put a bit of percussion under that. . . ." (This may well be inaccurately reported and nonsense musically, but it conveys the effect which Ben's practical, unromantic attitude had upon Christopher—who had seen so many Hollywood films about composers that he had lapsed into accepting the notion that they get their ideas by hearing a lark, or church bells, or waves on the shore.)

The trip itself was undoubtedly a success. Ben and Peter loved the desert and the mountains. They became quite schoolboyish, laughing and joking. By the time they had got to Laguna Beach and had had supper with Chris Wood, they were so relaxed that they went over to his piano of their own accord and played and sang for a couple of hours. They both liked Jim. Peter may have found him physically attractive. Anyhow, I suspect that Christopher thought he did—for, when Peter knocked on the door of their two-bed motel room next morning, Christopher exhibitionistically called to him to come in (despite Jim's embarrassment) so that Peter should see Jim and himself naked in Christopher's bed, where they had just finished having sex.

On November 30, Jim and Christopher went to another concert given by Ben and Peter, at the University of Southern California.

On December 1, Christopher finished his article on Klaus Mann. He was quite pleased with the article—and so were Thomas and Erika Mann when they read it. But, in order to finish it, he had started smoking again.[1]

On December 2, Christopher had lunch with Ben and Peter, just before they left Los Angeles.

---

[1] Writing in the journal on July 3, 1951, Christopher notes that he has started another attempt to give up smoking, ten days previously, and he recalls this earlier failure: ". . . last time I quit I ran into what seemed a hopeless block—I had to get the article on Klaus Mann finished, and I just couldn't. So I restarted smoking, and it came like magic."

Nicky Nadeau had taken up with an immensely rich young man named [Karl] Hoyt. Hoyt had a big house in Bel Air. On December 3, he called up and asked Christopher if he would care to come around that evening. Hoyt's casual tone made Christopher suppose that he was being invited over for a few drinks with the two of them, and possibly a snack in the kitchen, later. So he didn't change his clothes or even put on a tie. But, when he drove up to the house, he was staggered to find himself in a line of cars which were being directed to parking places by several uniformed cops. Inside, a band was playing, and there were crowds of elegant guests, including some movie stars—the first person Christopher set eyes on was Hedda Hopper. Christopher was embarrassed and furious—especially when Hoyt and Nadeau greeted him in tuxedos. But he couldn't, wouldn't retreat—and very soon he was unembarrassed, drunk and talking to Gloria Swanson. I remember that evening as a prize specimen of the Hollywood social booby trap.

On December 4, Christopher had supper with Jim. Afterwards they went into a bar called the Variety which was on the Pacific Coast Highway, not far from Jim's apartment. They had visited the Variety many times before this; hitherto it had [been] a mixed bar, chiefly heterosexual but with a tolerated minority of homosexual customers. That night, however, Christopher and Jim realized at once that it must have changed managements or adopted a new policy, for it was completely and obviously homosexual. Shortly after their arrival, the bar was raided. The cops went around taking the names of the customers. Christopher gave his name, then asked, "What's this all about?" He was at once told he had to come along to the police station. Jim had to come with him.

The police sergeant who was in charge of the raid proved to be a foulmouthed bull of the old school. The other cops were younger and nicer—or at least more sophisticated. The sergeant declared that he recognized Christopher from the "faggot bars" downtown. Christopher assured him that this was impossible because he never went to them. When they got to the Santa Monica police station, the sergeant phoned headquarters to ask if Christopher and Jim had criminal records and was told, to his disgust, that they hadn't. This made him even more aggressive. He asked Christopher and Jim, "Are you two having a romance?" Then he had Christopher and Jim taken into separate rooms and questioned. Both of them were asked, "Are you a queer?" Jim said, "You must ask my psychiatrist." When the question was repeated, he answered, "No." Christopher also said, "No." While the sergeant was out of the room, some of the other cops apologized, more or less, for his behavior, saying, "He's always like that." They asked Christopher how many times a week he did it. They weren't bullying now but giggly and teasing, like sexually inquisitive little boys. Christopher answered, "I don't have to tell you that," but, when they laughed and agreed that he didn't have to, he did give them some kind of jokey answer, I forget what it was. After this, Christopher and Jim were let go, with warnings not to visit that kind of bar again. It's just possible that the cops had decided that Christopher and Jim weren't queer, after all, and were warning them lest they should be doped or made drunk by the fiendish faggots and then raped!

This actually not very dreadful ordeal has haunted Christopher ever since. Even as I write these words, I feel bitterly ashamed of him for not having said that he was queer. And yet I'm well aware of the counterargument: why in hell should you give yourself away to the Enemy, knowing that he can make use of everything you tell him?[1]

On December 5, Christopher had supper with Tito Renaldo. (He refers to this in the journal entry of December 6.) Tito had recently left Trabuco after a short try at being a monk. Christopher writes that, "Tito feels sad and lost between two worlds. He sits in his horrid *moderne* little apartment, waiting for the call to work at the studio, and drinking [. . .]. Soon he'll start having sex again, then asthma." Poor Tito's life became, from then on, increasingly unhappy [. . .]. He returned to live at Trabuco later, but he couldn't settle there. He developed dark resentments against some of the other monks and revealed them in outbursts [. . .]. And yet he yearned for the Vedanta Society whenever he turned his back on it. "He clings to me," Christopher writes, "as the only person who can understand the particular kind of mess he's in. But I can't really help him."

The December 6 journal entry also contains a passage about getting up early and going down to the kitchen for breakfast which Christopher echoed, fifteen years later, in *A Single Man*. And there are a couple of paragraphs about his decision (made after talking to Dodie Smith at lunch on the 4th) to write the novel in the third person, because "I simply cannot believe in Stephen Monkhouse, or

---

[1] In the next journal entry, December 6, Christopher writes:

The utter brutality of those cops, the night before last, and my guilt that I didn't handle them properly—wasn't wonderful and poised and mature. I ought to have called their bluff, insisted on being locked up, hired a lawyer, taken the case to the Supreme Court, started a nationwide stink. Why didn't I? Because I'm cowardly, slack, weak, compromised. My life at present is such a mess.

any other fictitious character, as the narrator," and because "I can't narrate this myself."[1]

On December 9, the day-to-day diary records that Christopher had supper with Don Coombs and that he stayed the night. Don Coombs taught English at UCLA. Christopher had first met him at a party at Jay's. Maybe Jay had recommended him to Christopher as a good lay; it was Coombs who later told Christopher that he had enjoyed going to bed with Jay because "he made me feel beautiful" (see page 29). Anyhow, Christopher had kissed Coombs at that party and it had been agreed that they would soon have a date together.

Coombs was a pretty blond with big lips. He looked much better naked than in his demurely faggy clothes. His smooth cream-skinned body was well built. He was lively and shameless and he loved to be fucked. He had big firm, hotly inviting buttocks. (The day-to-day diary also records that Christopher had been visited that afternoon by [. . .] a tall muscular good-looking young man [he] had met on the beach. [The young man] had flattered Christopher by saying he wanted to fuck him and I believe this was the occasion on which [he] did it. Christopher was excited to be playing the passive role for a change but he didn't much enjoy the fucking; [the man's] cock was too large and it hurt him.)

After Coombs's uninhibited behavior in bed that night, Christopher was greatly surprised when he later confessed that he had been horribly nervous about meeting Christopher. He had arrived

---

[1] In a journal entry on December 13, Christopher writes that he is stuck again, because "Stephen can't narrate, and yet, if he doesn't, I can't say half the things I want to."

However, Christopher was continuing to work on the novel from another angle. In the large thin notebook (first referred to on page 121) there are some notes which Christopher made that same day, concerning his minor characters. He was still intending to describe Sarah's house, "Tawelfan," as a hostel for European refugees, whose characters would be based on some of the real refugees at the Haverford hostel. He lists thirteen of them. He also gives a list of the bedrooms at Tawelfan with their occupants and a diagram showing where they all sat at the tables in the dining room. (Christopher much enjoyed this kind of planning.) The large thin notebook contains two drafts of openings for the novel, both probably written on December 21 though only one of them is dated. Both are fragments of a letter to Jane which Stephen is writing or composing in his head as he flies east from California to visit Sarah. The narration of the first fragment is in the third person. The second fragment is all letter, but its narration would probably have been in the third person also, if Christopher had continued writing. I'm pretty sure of this because the next two fragments, written on January 4 and January 20, 1950, are both in the third person.

much too early for their appointment, gone into a nearby bar and downed several martinis to fortify himself, thrown up, and then managed to pull himself together so successfully that Christopher had noticed nothing strange in his manner when they finally met.

Coombs and Christopher met and fucked often after this. Coombs was prepared to admire Christopher and be amused by his jokes; he once said that Christopher had more vitality than anyone else he had ever known. Christopher had only one fault to find with Coombs; he was inclined to be stingy and never even offered to pay his share at a restaurant. Christopher finally spoke to him about this. Coombs took the rebuke in good part and afterwards told Christopher that he had been right.

On December 10, Christopher gave a party for some of the patients from Birmingham Hospital. I don't remember anything about this party, as distinct from my memories of other such parties later. There was always the problem of getting the quadriplegic patient—my impression is that Christopher only knew one of these personally—out of the car and into the house. And there was always a polite awkwardness until the patients were sufficiently drunk to be able to relax. The day-to-day diary says that this party included George Bradshaw and Fred and Renée Zinnemann; these were obviously invited because of their suitability as cohosts. I don't know how many patients came to the party, but there can't have been more than ten at the very most, considering the smallness of the living room and the extra space required for the wheelchairs.

Christopher's last journal entry for 1949—on December 14—is full of self-scoldings.[1] Christopher has decided that he is going

---

[1] "Certainly, my mind is softening, weakening. I have so little coordination that I putter around like a dotard. . . . Then there is this constant sexual itch, which never seems to be satisfied, or very seldom, because it is accompanied by a certain degree of impotence." (I'm not sure what Christopher means by this last sentence. As a result of his 1946 operation, Christopher had developed an idiosyncrasy; he could get a more complete orgasm if he pressed his thumb against a nerve at the root of his penis while he was jerking off. But this didn't mean that he couldn't have an orgasm during sex with another person. And if that orgasm wasn't as complete, it could be (obviously) far more satisfactory, psychologically. When Christopher talks about his impotence, he may merely be saying that his compulsive mental "itch" drives him to attempt more sex acts than his body really "wants," with the consequence that his sex organs refuse to cooperate.)

. . . there is a hyper-tension, worse, I think, than any I have ever experienced.
    And so I fail to write. I put it off and put it off, and I do nothing about getting a job, and I drift toward complete pauperism, with nothing in

through the "change of life"; he says that Gerald Heard put the idea into his head. About Caskey, Christopher writes that he hates being alone but that he doesn't "exactly" want Caskey back "—at least, I certainly don't want him the way he was when he left."

On December 17, Christopher drove down to the AJC Ranch with Russ Zeininger. John van Druten and Carter Lodge were both there and Dave Eberhardt (see page 11) was staying with them. Dave and Christopher hadn't seen each other for a long time. No doubt they picked up their flirtation where they had dropped it, which would explain why Christopher went round to Dave Eberhardt's place in Los Angeles two days later, to have supper with him. (I believe Dave and Don Forbes had now [stopped sharing an apartment].) At Dave's, that evening, was a youth named Michael Leopold. There was a lot of talk and drinking, at the end of which Christopher decided to stay the night; perhaps he was too drunk to drive home. I'm almost certain that he didn't go to bed with either Dave or Michael Leopold on this occasion. It could be that Dave and Michael had sex with each other. Anyhow, Michael came to visit Christopher at Rustic Road on December 23 and they started what was to be an on-and-off but longish affair.

Michael was then about eighteen; a Jewboy with thinning hair, a high forehead, spectacles (his sight was very poor), a cute cheerful face (resembling Anne Francis, a starlet of the period), a hideously ugly Texan accent (which Christopher tried to persuade him to modify) and a pair of long sturdy legs (of which Christopher thoroughly approved). He was intelligent, ardently literary, a tireless talker and sex partner. He had a wild laugh. He amused Christopher and flattered him outrageously and excited him considerably. Christopher later discovered that he was a pathological liar. His taste in males was catholic—ranging from boys of his own age to men in their sixties, so Christopher had no reason to feel embarrassed by the

---

sight. I am lazy and dreamy and lecherous. . . . And I am fundamentally unserious in my approach to other people. I don't believe in myself or my future, and all my "reputation" is just a delayed-action mechanism, which only impresses the very young.

At the end of this negative verdict—which Christopher, as usual, is evidently making as black as possible in order to cause a counterreaction and thus cheer himself up—Christopher resolves to "keep right on trying and struggling."
 I can tell that he wasn't really worried, however. Paradoxically, despite his uneasy guilty nature, Christopher had learned to live with himself—indeed, he says as much in this same journal entry: "One of the chief benefits that remain to me from the Ivar Avenue days is that I have learned *not* to be alarmed by any mental symptoms, however violent or odd." [*D1*, p.419.]

age gap. Besides, Michael was evidently drawn most strongly to elder brother and father figures. He often talked of a marine sergeant who had taken him up to a hotel room and kept him there several days a prisoner, well fed and well screwed. (This may of course have been one of Michael's many fantasies.)

Christopher often found Michael exasperating but nevertheless became very fond of him. It was easy to love Michael in bed, he enjoyed himself so heartily, he gave his body so completely to the experience—kissing, wrestling, rimming, sucking, being fucked and fucking with equal abandon. (Once, when Christopher had got drunk and passed out, Michael greased Christopher's asshole and fucked him—or so he later claimed.) When Michael was reaching an orgasm, he would utter screams of lust which could surely be heard by the neighbors.

Michael stayed with Christopher at the Rustic Road house from December 26 through the 28th and returned on the 31st to spend the night—or what was left of it, by the time Christopher had got back from two New Year's Eve parties—at Salka Viertel's and Gottfried Reinhardt's.[1] (Despite all the pleasure he had had with Michael, Christopher's loneliness or his mental itch caused him to get Don Coombs to come and have sex with him on December 29—either for variety or because Michael wasn't available.)

But Michael had more than sex to offer. He was also eager to become Christopher's literary disciple. He asked Christopher endless questions about writing. He dipped into the books on Christopher's shelves and then wanted to hear Christopher's opinion of them. He brought a story with him which he had begun to write and worked on it down in the living room while Christopher was working upstairs in the glassed-in porch.[2] Thus their brief acquaintance was

---

[1] As I remember it, Michael didn't come with Christopher to these parties —either because he had parties of his own to go to or because Christopher feared that it would be embarrassing to bring him. As a homosexual, Christopher had long since made a discovery about his "understanding" heterosexual friends; having once brought themselves to "accept" their queer friend's "official" boyfriend, they are sincerely shocked if he shows up with other boys, even when the boyfriend is out of town. Christopher had some-times found himself in the ridiculous and humiliating position of explaining the other boy's presence and even apologizing for it—"He's a friend of Billy's," etc.

[2] On January 2, Christopher made an entry in the journal, headed "Some ideas for stories." The first of these ideas is the life of the film dog Strongheart—or rather, an improved version of it which that seldom reliable but always magically memorable fabulist Gerald Heard had told to Christopher: ". . . the

already taking on an aspect of domesticity. Christopher was under no illusions that he and Michael could set up housekeeping together. Christopher wasn't in love with him, wasn't at ease with him when he chattered and showed off, didn't believe that he had much, if any, literary talent. And yet, Christopher and Michael came close to each other; Christopher felt an unwilling kinship with this freaky young creature. They were somehow two of a kind.

On December 20 and 23, Christopher sat for the artist Nicolai Fechin. Fechin lived in a big dark old redwood house which was rather like the inside of a sailing ship—at the back of the Canyon. He was a friend of Jo Lathwood and Ben Masselink; an amiable Russian genius. He drew Christopher in charcoal. At the end of the first sitting, the drawing looked so wildly romantic—a kind of Nordic hero—that Christopher protested. When it was finished it had become one more in the series of Fechin's anthropological portraits—a typical specimen of Intellectual Man—angry looking but also flattering, in a different way. I still have a photograph of it. I don't know what Fechin did with the original.

On December 30, Christopher had supper with the Stravinskys and Robert Craft at their house. Aldous and Maria Huxley were

---

very mean dog who is trained, given a wonderful disposition, so that it turns into a canine saint and finally dies trying to understand" its master and mutate into a human being.

The second idea is the story of Denny Fouts and Tony Watson-Gandy (page 173, note 1) told from the viewpoint of a fictitious character who is in love with Tony and hates the evil influence of Denny upon him.

The third idea is obviously suggested by Christopher's relations with Michael Leopold:

A middle-aged, "established" writer and a very young writer, still unpublished. The middle-aged writer is going through a period of complete impotence, but the young one doesn't know this. He is tremendously impressed by the older man and quite overwhelmed when the latter asks him to stay. Every morning, the young man sits down joyfully in the living room, thinking, "We are working under the same roof," and writes as never before, in a fever of inspiration. Meanwhile, the older man goes up to his study and stays there all day, pretending to work. Does the young man unconsciously "cure" him? Perhaps.

What strikes me as remarkable here is the speed with which Christopher's creative metabolism has functioned. Barely ten days after their first meeting, Michael has been "assimilated" and transformed into a fiction character. This was the sincerest compliment that Christopher—being Christopher—could possibly have paid him and their relationship. Michael had somehow touched the nerve of Christopher's imagination.

there. I have a memory—which, I believe, belongs to this occasion —of Christopher lying on the floor, dozy with drink. Christopher looks up and sees Aldous towering skyscraper-tall above him— ignoring Christopher with English tact, as he talks aesthetics to Igor in French.[1]

[1] The day-to-day diary's list of books Christopher read in 1949 includes: *The Blood of the Martyrs* (Naomi Mitchison), *The Servant* (Robin Maugham), *Concluding* (Henry Green), *The Season of Comfort* (Gore Vidal), *The Narrow Corner* (Maugham), *The Heat of the Day* (Elizabeth Bowen), *The Tower of London* (Ainsworth), *The Ides of March* (Thornton Wilder), *Nineteen Eighty-Four* (Orwell), *Two Worlds and Their Ways* (Compton-Burnett), *A Long Day's Dying* (Frederick Buechner), *Love in a Cold Climate* (Nancy Mitford), *The Oasis* (Mary McCarthy), *Herself Surprised* (Joyce Cary), *The Sheltering Sky* (Paul Bowles), *The Lottery* (Shirley Jackson).

Christopher had reread *The Narrow Corner* that year because Fred Zinnemann was considering remaking it as a film. (It had already been made in 1933, with Douglas Fairbanks Jr.) Dipping into it before writing this (August 6, 1973) I feel again what Christopher felt then, that it is Maugham's one really magic novel—by which I suppose I merely mean that it is the novel I would have vaguely yearned for if he *hadn't* written it, the Maugham book which is custom-created for Christopher and his particular fantasies. I love its setting in the Spice Islands, its dreamy languid equatorial atmosphere, its romantic queerness. I love Dr. Saunders (the most sympathetic of all Maugham's doctors) and Ah Kay (the most adorable of his Chinese boys) and Captain Nichols (for being so wonderful at the funeral of the Japanese pearl diver). Erik, with his goodness, is rather a bore, and so is Fred with his sulks and the stilted dialogue Maugham gives him to speak. But the poetic *idea* of Fred, under the curse of his own sex appeal, is terrific. I think this could be an unforgettable film, if it was directed by the right man—not Zinnemann. Zinnemann soon dropped the project.

The Tower of London was another book that Christopher reread that year. It had been one of his childhood favorites and, as far as I remember, it didn't disappoint him at all—he still felt the magic of the Cruikshank illustrations, smelt the smell of the period and was aware of a privately perceived relationship between the Tower of London and Marple Hall. (I think this was created by Ainsworth's narrative technique, which is absurd and yet curiously effective: in the midst of a melodramatic scene, Ainsworth will unexpectedly turn his novel into a guidebook. For example: the Spanish Ambassador, Renard, has been muttering threats against the life of Lady Jane Grey and resolves that Mary shall have the throne. Suddenly he stops to look at the White Tower, and Ainsworth describes it, ending with a couple of sentences which bring us out of the period and right up to the date when they were written: "The round turret, at the north-east angle, was used as an observatory by the celebrated astronomer Flamsteed, in the reign of Charles the Second. The principal entrance was on the north, and was much more spacious than the modern doorway, which occupies its site." Christopher, during his boyhood at Marple Hall, had guided visitors around and lectured them on the

1950

On January 1, Bill Harris arrived to stay with Christopher. He had come from New York to California to visit his mother, who was living in La Jolla. Bill was greatly excited about Jack Fontan, his new lover. Jack had a small but prominent part in *South Pacific*, which had opened in New York the previous April. The character Jack played was called Staff Sergeant Thomas Hassinger on the program, but he was already known to hundreds of queers as "The Naked Sailor." Wearing nothing but a pair of the shortest shorts, without underwear, Jack sprawled in the midst of the group which sang "What ain't we got? We ain't got dames"—displaying nearly all of his large and magnificent body, including glimpses of his genitals. Bill had a reclining photograph of him stark naked; it had had to be shot in three separate sections because of Jack's great length. Bill proudly displayed it on a shelf in the bedroom where he slept during his visit.

Bill Harris and Jack Fontan had met each other in the late fall and

---

history of the building; he had thus developed a double-image awareness of past and present. So Ainsworth's Victorian guidebook voice didn't seem anachronistic to him. Quite the reverse. In the midst of these long-ago Tudor treasons and head choppings, it was Ainsworth's voice which made history credible, and the rooms of the Tower—even its dungeons and its torture chamber—familiar and almost cozy. . . . Of course it must be added that, although Ainsworth is a painstaking antiquarian, the *tone* of his melodrama is unmistakably nineteenth century, not sixteenth.)

When I saw *The Ides of March* on the 1949 list, I couldn't remember anything about it, except that it had been Christopher's favorite among the new books he read that year. Now (August 19, 1973), having just finished rereading it, I admire it very much—partly because it is the kind of historical novel I would like to have written, if I were a historical novelist. Wilder is a bit too elegant for my taste, and too arch, and too much of a name-dropper—such a scholarly closet queen. But his method of telling the story through fictitious documents seems to me the best imaginable, when you're dealing with a character as remote from us in time as Caesar is. In fictitious documents, you can stylize dialogue acceptably because the reader isn't being asked to believe that this is *exactly* how the character talked. In direct narrative, the same dialogue would sound hopelessly artificial, because direct narrative makes an implicit claim to be realistic.

The Sheltering Sky was Christopher's first experience of Paul Bowles's writing. He felt that he liked the book—particularly its evocation of North Africa—much better than he liked its author's tone of voice. Bowles has an air of only just barely tolerating the presence of the reader. "Don't stick around on *my* account," he seems to be saying, "you're going to loathe this place"

Bill had immediately moved in with Jack, who was living in an abandoned synagogue. When the cold weather began, their waterpipes froze. Bill had to fetch water in pails from a shop below—he spoke of himself as being "like Rebecca at the well." The cold was so intense that they couldn't get warm even when holding each other in bed. Bill and Jack tried to remedy this by lifting the bed onto two chests of drawers—one at each end—over the gas oven, but, when they climbed into bed, the bed broke in half. Since they couldn't use the toilet, they had to shit into newspapers and then leave their shit packages outside on the windowsill until they froze solid and could be carried downstairs and left in a trash can. . . . Bill described these hardships to Christopher with the sentimental relish of an infatuated lover.

(To return to the subject of Jack Fontan's shorts in *South Pacific*, Jack tells me—August 4, 1973—that, when rehearsals started, the minor characters were given a pile of military garments and told to pick out the ones that fitted them. So Jack got himself a navy work-shirt, pants and a pair of shoes. When Joshua Logan, the director, arrived to inspect the costumes, he promptly ordered Jack to take off his shirt and his shoes. He then called for a pair of scissors and snipped

---

(indicating the Sahara desert) "and you'll never understand these people" (meaning the Arabs). Christopher felt, and I still feel, that Bowles's arrogance is peculiarly Frog—you could call him an English-speaking French anti-novelist. But, still and all, he's readable and few of the Frogs are.

Christopher liked *Two Worlds and Their Ways* as much but no more than he had liked *Manservant and Maidservant*. However, *Two Worlds and Their Ways* contains a tremendous passage which Christopher has been quoting ever since he read it: "We think our little failings have their own charm. And they have not. And they are great failings." *The Blood of the Martyrs* disappointed him. Mitchison was suffering, he thought, from leftist Christianity—which is the dreariest kind of leftism, and of Christianity. . . . *Concluding* disappointed him too: it seemed rather dull. . . . Being almost invariably bored by satire, he wasn't disappointed in *Nineteen Eighty-Four*—merely bored by it. . . . *The Servant* is mere closet-macabre—one of those novels in which queerness is equated with Evil and loss of class status with Degradation. . . . Christopher thought *The Season of Comfort* better than Gore Vidal's earlier novels—excluding *Williwaw* —but that wasn't saying much. . . . In a journal entry of March 2, 1949, Christopher quoted an arty-farty phrase from *The Heat of the Day*, which he hadn't yet finished. "Quite exciting," he adds, "and some good charac-ters"—but my memory assures me that it was trash. . . . Christopher recommended *A Long Day's Dying* in a blurb. I can't remember why. I have never been able to get through any other book by its author; when you open them, moths fly out. . . . As for the other books on the list (by Mitford, McCarthy, Cary and Jackson) Christopher found them charming, entertaining, clever and altogether worthy of praise—by *The New Yorker*. They weren't, any of them, his dish.

away the legs of Jack's pants, just above the knee. This didn't satisfy him, however. He kept snipping higher and higher, until Jack's legs were left bare right up to the crotch. Logan then decided that Jack could put the shoes on again.

Jack wasn't in the habit of wearing underwear. So he came on stage on the first night with nothing under his shorts. After the show had been running a few days, the stage manager told him there had been complaints from ladies sitting in the front rows. Jack was to put on jockeys. When Logan heard of this, he was very angry. The jockeys were prohibited. Logan's instructions to the box-office were: "If they don't want to see his balls, they can have their money returned.")

Bill Harris stayed at the Rustic Road house during most of January—from the 1st to the 11th, from the 17th to the 28th and from the 31st to February 3, when he returned to New York. The visit was a success, from Christopher's point of view; Bill was a model guest, helpful with household chores, always ready to make himself agreeable to callers and to keep himself occupied when Christopher had to work or go out. Aside from this, he was a cheerful, responsive companion. He showed an interest in all Christopher's doings and concerns which seemed feminine in the very best way. I think Bill enjoyed his visit too—even including his unpleasant psychic experience which is described on pages 184-185. This was anyhow a happy period in his life, because of Jack Fontan—and there is a peculiar pleasure in talking about a current love affair to a sympathetic ex-lover. Bill and Christopher shared pleasant memories of sex with each other. Bill knew that Christopher's interest in Jack Fontan was therefore more than merely polite; it had a quality of identification. But Bill also knew that Christopher wasn't in the slightest degree jealous, wasn't carrying even the last ember of a torch. So the two of them could be perfectly relaxed together.

On January 3, there is a journal entry about *The School of Tragedy*. Christopher is still bothered by the problem of narration—shall it be told in the third person or in the first? Christopher obviously wanted to write in the first person, through Stephen's mouth, but he saw two difficulties if the story is told retrospectively, "I fear the necessarily indulgent tone, the wise smile over the mistakes of the past"; but if, on the other hand, the story is told from day to day, in a diary, "This seems too contrived. Why should he be taking all this trouble to present his experiences, to make them into an aesthetic performance, if he is really suffering?"

So Christopher returns to a consideration of a narrative in the third person, "I . . . hear a very simple tone of voice. Something inside me keeps saying *Candide*. . . . When I want him to be articulate, analytical, he must express himself in conversation. Ditto when he tells anything about the past. But when we're listening to his mind, we should really only get his *feelings*. Very important, this."

In this entry, Christopher also tries to state the theme of the novel—that Stephen, who is chronically guilty because he is torn between a Quaker background and an urge toward bohemianism, discovers how to overcome his guilt "by understanding the lives of those who aren't guilty—Sarah, [Gerda,] Dr. Kennedy and the best of the refugees."

Looking back, I feel that a novel written by Christopher with this subject matter was foredoomed. Because Christopher didn't—and I still don't—understand the kind of guilt which would make such a story credible. To a writer of my temperament, prolonged guilt is distasteful and boring as a theme for fiction. The character of Stephen Monk doesn't come to life because Christopher was bored by him. At the very end of the book, Stephen says, "I . . . forgive myself from the bottom of my heart," but his tone rings false. The words were actually Christopher's; he had once said them to Iris Tree, but in a quite different, campy, playacting tone, with a deep comic sigh, when they were talking about sin: "God knows, Iris, I forgive myself —from the *bottom* of my heart." After which they had both roared with laughter. When Stephen speaks the line one doesn't laugh. One is embarrassed.

On January 5, there is a charming anecdote about Bo and Kelley (see pages 17-18) in the journal. For reasons of discretion, presumably, they are referred to in the journal by initials only, and nothing is said about why Kelley was in jail at that time. As far as I remember, he had been arrested on the Riviera Beach near Point Dume. This beach was perfectly safe for bare-ass swimming and sex making in 1945 (see page 48) but more and more houses had been built on the headland since then and their builders thought they had bought the view as well. So they proceeded to edit it to their liking. Those tiny figures in the far distance, away down there amongst the dunes—you couldn't see if they were nude or make out what they were doing, unless you used binoculars. So the police were called in and given binoculars and told to watch. And so there were roundups of view spoilers—one of which included Kelley. (In those days, when a queer had served a jail sentence and his straight friends asked him what he had been in jail for, he would reply, with a wry, suggestive smile, "Making a U-turn." Such is the humor of a persecuted tribe, which isn't allowed even to speak openly of its sufferings.) This is the anecdote: Bobo took Howard Kelley a sweater to wear in jail.

Kelley spent a whole afternoon, with another prisoner, cleaning it by picking off hairs belonging to Bo and Kelley's three cats. Kelley was able to identify the hairs of each cat. They sorted the hairs into three piles and put each pile into a separate matchbox.

On January 13, Christopher had Norman Mailer to dinner, with Salka Viertel (who probably helped cook). The day-to-day diary also mentions "Ted and Mrs. Anderson, John and Mrs. Hamlin" as guests. I'm pretty sure that Ted Anderson and John Hamlin were paraplegics, and that it was Ted who had given Fred Zinnemann and Carl Foreman (see page 205) a lot of advice while *The Men* was being written and filmed. Indeed, I think the character played by Brando in the film was to some extent based on Ted Anderson. In the film, Brando marries Teresa Wright and they go through the problem of an impotent paraplegic married to a sexually potent and physically active woman. At the end of the film they are still together, however. Ted and his wife finally split up, but that was after a fairly long marriage.

Norman Mailer was in town (I think) because of a project to film his novel *The Naked and the Dead*. (There were many delays and the picture wasn't actually made and released until 1958.) Norman and Christopher got along well together. Norman, in those days, was a deceptively quiet and polite young man who amused Christopher by his sudden outbursts of candor. They didn't meet often, but I am unable to put a date—unless it is this one—to my memory of Norman entertaining a fairly large group of paraplegics at Christopher's house.[1] According to my memory, Christopher had asked his paraplegic guests in advance if there was any available celebrity they would like to meet. All had agreed on Mailer. He arrived on time, neatly dressed, demure and sober. The women present were obviously reassured. Then he began to tell stories about his army life—perfectly harmless funny little stories, with no horrors in them, no sex, no venereal disease. All that was startling was the dialogue. "By that time, the sergeant was beginning to get a little bit impatient, so he said to me—" Mailer kept the same nicey-nice party smile on his face as he continued, without the least change of tone, "Why, you mother-fucking son of a bitch, another word out of you and I'll ram this mop right up your ass!" The male guests roared. The women blinked and tried to smile—reflecting, no doubt, that they had read talk as rough as this in Mailer's novel; coming from

[1] If Mailer had been at the party on December 10, the day-to-day diary would surely have mentioned him. On March 10, 1950, Mailer visited Christopher with his wife but nothing is said about any other guests.

his mouth, you couldn't call it vulgarity; it was practically literature.

On January 17, Aldous Huxley and Christopher met and talked about their film story *Below the Equator* (see page 207 [note]). On the 23rd, they met again, this time with John Huston. I think it was Huston who had originally suggested that they should write a story for him to direct. Meanwhile, on January 19, the day-to-day diary records that Christopher saw Lesser Samuels about a movie story. This must have been *The Vacant Room*, a ghost story set in a Los Angeles bungalow court. I think the original idea was Lesser's, but Christopher was particularly interested in showing that a "haunting" can take place in an unremarkable small modern building.

On January 22, Russ Zeininger, Curtis Harrington, Bill Harris and Christopher drove to The High Valley Theatre in the Upper Ojai Valley (see page 74) to see a performance of *Ethan Frome*. It had been adapted by Iris Tree (who was later sued by the owners of the authorized adaptation, which Ruth Gordon had played in New York). Iris, Ford Rainey and Betty Harford played Zeena, Ethan and Mattie. Oliver Andrews, Betty's future husband, designed the set —which is the only part of the production I remember, because it was so absurdly arty. Oliver decided that the bobsled was the symbol of the whole tragedy and that it therefore ought to dominate the stage throughout. So there it was at the back of the set, standing on its end and looking like an expressionist war memorial. This in itself would have been stupid rather than absurd. But then the moment came when Ethan and Mattie had to convert the symbol into a stage prop. Placing the sled in a horizontal position on top of a steep structure which represented a hill, they climbed onto it and rode it offstage. The hazards of this ride were ridiculously realistic. The heavy sled shook the lightweight hill to its foundations and, a moment later, it could be heard and felt hitting a bank of cushions behind the scenes with a force which seemed sufficient to carry it straight through the wall of the theater. The whole audience gasped—but it was the wrong kind of gasp, expressing concern for the fate of Ford Rainey and Betty Harford, as if they had been circus acrobats risking their lives. At that instant, they ceased to be Ethan and Mattie. This farcical stunt annihilated their characters and nullified the rest of the play.[1]

Throughout February, Christopher worked on the two film

---

[1] These negative impressions are all that remain now. But maybe Christopher liked the acting at the time when he saw it. Either that, or he was being very polite when he gave a quote which *The Los Angeles Times* printed: "The best acting I have ever seen this unusually talented group do." (Betty Harford showed me the clipping, October 1973.)

stories, with Huxley and with Samuels. Mike Leopold came down to stay with him several times; Christopher also saw Russ Zeininger and Don Coombs. He had supper with the Stravinskys, Jo and Ben Masselink, the Kiskaddens, the Zinnemanns. The Zinnemanns often showed their guests a film, after supper. On February 25, Dr. Bors (from the Birmingham Hospital, see page 205) was one of the Zinnemanns' guests. He proudly announced that he had brought a film of his own which he was going to run for them. It turned out to be a documentary of an unusually bloody operation, shot in color. Some of the ladies present were so revolted that they nearly vomited. But Dr. Bors was happily unaware of this. He left under the impression that he had provided everybody with a delightful evening's entertainment. (A few days before this, *The Men* had been screened for the patients at Birmingham Hospital. Christopher had gone there to see it.)

On March 5, Samuels and Christopher finished *The Vacant Room*. Christopher continued to work with Huxley on *Below the Equator* and Samuels was asked to give them his advice—they met three times. When Samuels and Christopher turned in a copy of their story to Christopher's agent, Jim Geller, Christopher typed a special title page for it: "*The Vacant Room*. A Masterpiece." The joke fell flat, because Geller couldn't get anybody interested in the story.

Christopher saw Mike Leopold only four times that month. I think Christopher must also have been going to bed with Jim Charlton, because only one other sex mate (Zeininger) is mentioned in the day-to-day diary and because Christopher and Jim had supper together often.

On the 16th, Christopher had supper with the Huxleys. Gerald Heard and Michael Barrie were there, also a hypnotist named Leslie LeCron[1] and his wife. On the 22nd, the LeCrons invited Christopher to have supper at their house. There were no other guests. I think it had been more or less agreed in advance that LeCron would try to hypnotize Christopher. Christopher himself was skeptical. Several people had tried to hypnotize him already and had failed. He told LeCron this, and LeCron replied that the failure had probably been due to Christopher's attitude. Christopher expected a hypnotist to overpower his will. "That's the wrong attitude," LeCron told him, "you have to cooperate. I can't make you do anything as long as you think of me as an opponent and keep bracing yourself to resist me. My will isn't stronger than yours. You mustn't think like that."

[1] The word "hypnotist" always sounds slightly derogatory. Aldous, who greatly respected and liked LeCron, refers to LeCron in his letters as a psychotherapist.

LeCron certainly didn't look as if his will was stronger than Christopher's, or anybody else's. From Christopher's point of view LeCron's amiably harmless appearance was reassuring and it undoubtedly contributed to the success of their experiment. As far as I remember, LeCron told Christopher to fix his eyes on one of LeCron's eyes and begin to count backwards from one hundred. Very soon, Christopher found himself relaxing from an upright to a horizontal position on the sofa. He lay there in a comfortable sprawl, feeling, as he said, like a puppet with all its strings loose. He was quite conscious and rather amused by his condition. He told LeCron that he knew he could assert his will but that he simply didn't want to. He remained in this light hypnotic trance for several minutes, until LeCron roused him by snapping his fingers.

Christopher's relaxation had been even deeper than he had realized. This only became evident to him after he had left LeCron's house and was driving home. He experienced a state of euphoria so intense that I can recall it as I write these words. Christopher was no longer an individual driver, keeping a wary eye on other drivers— alert for possible drunks, slowing down to force tailgaters to pass him, pulling out to avoid being trapped behind slowpokes. He was part of the traffic, moving in perfect harmony with all the other cars, like a dancer in a ballet. Never once, that evening, did he have to brake or accelerate abruptly; when he changed lanes, he described faultless curves, slipping into his new position with exactly the right amount of spare distance between himself, the car ahead and the car behind. Christopher thought of himself as being a well-adjusted driver. He was seldom consciously nervous even in bad weather and heavy traffic. But now he realized how tense he ordinarily was.

At the end of the hypnotizing, LeCron had given Christopher a posthypnotic suggestion: "You're going to sleep better tonight than you've ever slept before." When Christopher got into bed, he did indeed fall into a profound sleep, from which he woke next morning unable to remember who or where he was for several seconds. This moment of amnesia wasn't in the least alarming. It was accompanied by a sense of calm joy.

On April 2, Christopher had supper with Mr. and Mrs. Richard Brooks. Christopher probably first met Brooks when they were both working at MGM in 1948. I may be wrong but I think that this supper party was at a house the Brookses were living in on the slopes of the Hollywood Hills looking out over the Valley. Anyhow, Christopher did visit them in such a house and later used it for the setting of the first scene of *The World in the Evening*. I remember that they kept their bedroom immaculately neat, with all their clothes and

superfluous belongings stored away in adjoining closets or bath-
rooms. When they entertained, the guests were free—were indeed
almost challenged—to wander through this bedroom as though it
were an extra living room. The Brookses seemed to be saying: "Go
ahead—search! You won't find any clue to our private life, or to
what sort of people we really are."

There was, nevertheless, one damning clue to Richard's character
which lay hidden in the house—and which Richard, characteristically, couldn't resist the temptation to reveal—the living room
was wired for sound. At the end of the evening, Richard would play
back the tape to any guests who cared to listen—thereby, I suppose,
making at least a few permanent enemies at each party. I remember
a recorded murmur of unintelligible drunken conversation, out of
which Christopher's voice arose, embarrassingly clear and precise,
saying: "*King Lear* really *is* a most extraordinarily *silly* story!"

On April 9, Christopher had supper with Speed Lamkin. I guess
this must have been their first meeting. I have no idea who brought
them together. Possibly, Speed simply phoned Christopher and
introduced himself; that would have been like him. I don't recall
how Christopher then reacted to this bold sexy naughty niggery
young man,[1] with his mischievous eyes and "aw, c'mon—you *know*
you want to" grin. Speed's first novel, *Tiger in the Garden*, was being
published that year, and his self-confidence was overwhelming.
Probably Christopher was a bit overwhelmed, a good deal amused
and intrigued, but very much on his guard. I say this because he took
Speed after supper to see Jim Charlton—which suggests that he
wanted to park Speed in Jim's bed, rather than face three or four
more hours of Speed's sparkling dialogue. Speed was really funny,
but his name-dropping soon got to be a bore and his tale telling was
so indiscreet that you became afraid to open your mouth lest you
should provide him with more gossip fodder. . . . All in all, I'm sure
Christopher would have been very much surprised if he had been
told, then, that he would one day become really fond of Speed and
even take Speed's opinions seriously.

On April 10, fairly early in the morning, Christopher got a call
from Dylan Thomas, whom he had never met. Dylan was downtown at the Biltmore and due to give a reading at UCLA that
afternoon. The UCLA English department had made no arrangements for his transportation out to the campus, merely told him to
take a bus. Christopher found this outrageous and volunteered to
drive down and pick him up.

[1] Speed was then twenty-two.

The events of that memorable day were recorded in the journal—not at the time but much later, on December 8, 1953, about a month after Dylan's death. (Stephen Spender had asked Christopher to contribute to some obituary article on Dylan and Christopher had declined, saying that his memories involved other people, who might be offended—he meant chiefly Majal Ewing, head of the UCLA English department. But it was Stephen's request which prompted Christopher to make this journal entry.)[*]

The journal records only Ivan Moffat's account of Dylan's visit to Charlie Chaplin, that evening—which is that Dylan was drunk and that Chaplin was therefore offended. But I remember another version of the story (by Frank Taylor?) which sounds truer and is certainly funnier: when Chaplin was asked if Dylan might visit him, he said, "Yes, but don't bring him unless he's sober." Dylan's escorts, including Ivan and Christopher, agreed to this. However, when they all arrived, the escorts were stumbling drunk and it was only Dylan who made a perfect gentlemanly entrance, saying in bell-clear tones, "It's a great honor to meet you, Mr. Chaplin."

On April 19, Caskey returned to Rustic Road, after an absence of just over five months. Since I don't have any of Caskey's letters belonging to that period, I don't know what the atmosphere of their reunion was. Had they discussed their difficulties and resolved to make a fresh start? Or had they avoided discussion, just hoping for the best? I strongly suspect the latter. In a journal entry made on April 24, Christopher doesn't mention Caskey at all. This may mean that Christopher is superstitiously afraid of writing anything optimistic about the prospects for their life together.

They started seeing people at once—Hayden Lewis, Rod Owens, Jim Charlton, Lennie Newman, the Beesleys and Jay Laval, who was now in charge (I believe) at the Mocambo. On April 23, they went to dinner with the Chaplins. Emlyn and Molly Williams were there too. I'm pretty sure that they had never met Chaplin before.

Toward the end of dinner, as I remember it, Christopher went out of the dining room to pee. When he returned to the table, he found that Emlyn was questioning Chaplin, while the other guests sat silent, listening. Emlyn is a shockingly frank questioner. His manner is at once authoritative and playful, never in the smallest degree apologetic. He questions you with the air of a doctor, who has the right to ask his patient absolutely anything and who is teasing the patient for being embarrassed and reluctant to answer. Chaplin was

[* See *D1*, pp. 458–63.]

certainly embarrassed. As Christopher entered, Emlyn was asking:

"*Mr*. Chaplin,[1] tell me—did *Mr*. Hearst really murder *Mr*. Ince?"

Charlie wriggled in his seat: "No—no of course not. That story's ridiculous—absolutely untrue."

"But *Mr*. Chaplin, you *were—involved* with *Miss* Marion Davies?"

This time, Chaplin glanced quickly down the table to be sure that Oona wasn't present—she too had left the table. "Well yes, yes I was."

"But didn't *Mr*. Hearst know that?"

"Yes. I suppose so. He must have known. Yes, I'm sure he did."

"And didn't he object?"

"Oh yes, he certainly objected. But, after all," Chaplin was still acting embarrassed, only now it was obvious that he was beginning to enjoy Emlyn's cross-examination, "there wasn't much he could do about it."

"*Mr*. Chaplin—did you have an affair with *Miss* Pola Negri?"

"No. Oh no. Absolutely not. Quite out of the question. Wasn't my type at all."

Who knows what else Emlyn might have asked! Alas, right after Chaplin's reply, Oona came back into the room and that page of Hollywood history was blotted forever.

On May 13, Christopher and Caskey went to the Chaplins' again—for what was to be, unless the day-to-day diary has omitted to record a later meeting, Christopher's last visit. (Caskey went to lunch with them next day, alone.) So it would appear that this was the evening on which Christopher is alleged to have passed out and peed on a sofa—see page 199 and [note].[2]

There was another dramatic incident at the Chaplins' which I can't put a date to exactly—it may well have happened earlier that evening. All I am sure of is that it was at a dinner at which Natasha

[1] In this dialogue, Emlyn Williams very slightly accented the *misters* and the *miss*. The effect was mocking, but the mockery was so subtle that Chaplin would only have made himself ridiculous if he had taken offense at it.

[2] Since writing this, I discovered from the day-to-day diary for 1951 that Christopher and Caskey went to a party at the Chaplins' on March 24. This seems to prove that the alleged peeing incident took place then, and not on May 13, 1950. Still, it should be noticed that ten months elapsed between the two meetings. So it could be argued that the alleged peeing *did* take place (seemingly or actually) on May 13, 1950, that the Chaplins were angry with Christopher for a long while but then decided to give him another chance, that he was invited on March 24, 1951 but behaved badly, and that therefore they struck him off their guest list forever. In any case, March 24, 1951 *does* seem to have been their last meeting.

Moffat (see pages 66-67) was present—which means that Ivan was probably there too.

When the guests took their places in the dining room, Natasha and Caskey found that they were to sit next to each other. Whereat Natasha exclaimed, loudly and clearly: "Oh good, Billy! I always like sitting next to a pansy." Natasha was now entering her lively, crazy phase, in which she would often behave in this "spontaneous" style. This was no intended bitchiness. From her point of view, she was being friendly. She quite liked Caskey and she was implying that he, like other pansies, was an entertaining dinner partner. That was all.

It was more than enough. The deathly silence which followed her remark proved that everybody at the table had heard it.

In the midst of that silence, with the utmost good humor, in his laziest southern drawl, Caskey replied: "Your slang is out of date, Natasha—we don't say 'pansy' nowadays. We say 'cocksucker.'"

I don't think anybody ventured to laugh. Such words were still genuine shockers in those days. But there was a surge of grateful relief. A member of the insulted minority had spoken up, thereby saving the majority from the embarrassment of trying to defend it and him—or from the guilt of failing to do so. No doubt the several Jews present were especially conscious of this. Natasha herself, amused but not in the least abashed by Caskey's retort, began talking to him about something else. Christopher, who truly adored Caskey at such moments, sat glowing with pride in him. But Christopher's pride can't have been visible to others—at least, not to the lady who sat at his side. She, kind soul, evidently supposed that his feelings had been deeply wounded. In a muddle-headed attempt to console him for being what he was, she told him, "You mustn't feel too badly about this." Then, lowering her voice and glancing over at her husband, she added, "You know something? Bob and I can't have children *either*!"

On May 15, Christopher went to the NBC studios to listen to a radio performance of *Prater Violet*. I can't remember who was in this, but it seemed fairly effective.[*]

Also on May 15—and again on the 17th and 23rd—Christopher visited Leslie LeCron. I think this was to take lessons in auto-hypnotism, which was one of LeCron's specialties. LeCron claimed (and Aldous Huxley confirmed this) that it is possible to put yourself into a light hypnotic trance, for the purpose of overcoming anxiety, relaxing and sleeping. According to LeCron, this kind of trance is

[* Fritz Field, Whitfield Connor, Eileen Erskine, Ramsay Hill; adapted by Richard E. Davis, directed by Andrew Clore. The one-hour broadcast was on May 14 with Don Rickles announcing and a commentary by Irwin Edman.]

never dangerously deep—if the house were to catch fire, you would regain normal consciousness at once. Christopher never mastered the autohypnotic technique—maybe he was afraid of using it, despite LeCron's reassurances. But he did sometimes use, with good effect, a method of autosuggestion which LeCron had also taught him. First you lie on your back on the floor. Then you successively tense and relax the muscles in every part of your body, from head to feet. Then you tell yourself a story about yourself, *in the third person*. The story varies, according to the kind of result you want to produce. You could say, for example: "His energy was amazing. People said that he ran up and down stairs like a young man. His sitting posture was perfect, so he was able to write hour after hour without tension. Then he could run on the beach for a mile or more, dismissing all worries from his head and enjoying the strength of his own body, like an animal. When night came, he was all ready for fun, parties, entertainment, sex—" Or you could say: "He was exhausted—absolutely worn out and happy to rest, knowing that he had done his work well and earned his repose. Tired, relaxed, content, his mind quite calm, he lay waiting for sleep—"

On June 5, Aldous Huxley and Christopher finished their film story, *Beyond the ~~Horizon~~ (Equator?)*[*]

On June 7, Christopher went for the first time to the Long Beach Veterans Hospital. Many, if not all of the paraplegics he had been visiting at Birmingham (see page 204) had just been transferred there. This was a much longer drive and in those days, before the freeways had been built, it took a lot more time than it would now. Christopher was probably unwilling to admit to himself, at first, that the extra distance would gradually deter him from going there. He would have done better to break off his visiting at once. As it was, he impressed and pleased the paraplegics he knew by seeming to have remained faithful to them. Later, when he stopped coming to Long Beach, they must have felt that he had let them down.

The day-to-day diary also records that on June 7 Christopher began a rough draft of *The School of Tragedy*. The large thin notebook has a June 7 entry which Christopher probably wrote to get himself into the mood to start work. Characteristically, Christopher begins with a pessimistic statement: "Now, after all these delays and indecisions, I must admit to myself that I still don't see my way clearly." He is subconsciously trying to use negative suggestion here—to make himself write by saying, "Don't—you're not ready."

On June 12, Christopher saw LeCron again. I may be wrong but

[* The screenplay was first called *Below the Equator* and later retitled *Below the Horizon*.]

I believe this was the occasion on which LeCron began urging Christopher to practice the techniques of Dianetics. Ron Hubbard's book had just been published and LeCron took it very seriously.[1] He wanted Christopher to "restimulate his engrams," and specifically to try to reexperience his own birth. Christopher didn't want to try. He decided that LeCron was crazy, as far as this one subject was concerned, and he got himself out of LeCron's office as quickly and politely as he could. LeCron didn't take offense at this. He and Christopher continued to see each other socially.

June 14. Swami had an operation—I'm nearly sure it was for hernia—at the Queen of Angels Hospital. In the large thin notebook Christopher writes that he has roughed out the opening of the novel but that he feels that he has only a beginning and an end, very little

---

[1] Here is an outline of Hubbard's theory, taken from *Inside Scientology* by Robert Kaufman, published in 1972. Kaufman is admittedly hostile but probably not too unfair:

> The single source of our grief here on earth is found to lie in *engrams*, recordings of overwhelmingly painful events which, unbeknownst to us, were imprinted on our reactive minds over the years whenever the analytical mind *shorted-out* due to stress.
>
> . . . One has only to locate these incidents on the patient's time track and have him *relive* them in all their grisly detail. Several *relivings* are generally sufficient to *erase* an engram and its harmful effect. A person who gets rid of all his engrams in this manner is called a *Clear*. He is then completely free from neuroses and psychosomatic symptoms, gifted with total recall, and possessed of an almost superhuman I.Q. . . .

However, I don't believe that Christopher's refusal to try Dianetics was simply due to skepticism. Christopher had—and I still have—a deep-seated reluctance to try tinkering with his own psychological mechanism. When Christopher was young, he would have explained this reluctance by saying that he was afraid of inhibiting his creative process; while at Cambridge, he had been told of a young Georgian poet who was unable to write a single line after having been "successfully" psychoanalyzed. Nowadays, I would say I believe that the unconscious must by its nature remain unconscious. It doesn't belong to me. It is my means of communication with what is nonpersonal and eternal. All attempts to meddle with it are therefore attempts to impose my will and my ideas of what is good for me upon the infinitely greater wisdom of the nonself. As such they can only be self-damaging and anyhow doomed to failure. (To do Ron Hubbard justice, it must be said that he can have had no such qualms —for, in those days at any rate, he didn't believe that there is any such thing as the unconscious. According to him, man has only a conscious *analytical mind* and a *reactive mind* which is, to quote from Robert Kaufman, "a stimulus–response mechanism, a moronic, miasmal carryover from caveman days"— utterly inferior to the conscious mind, in other words, and an obstacle to our development as human beings.)

to put in the middle. Also he is worried that he won't be able to make his characters interesting—there are so many of them. He tries to find an "experience" for each of the principal characters—something from which each one of them can learn his or her lesson in *The School of Tragedy*. He makes a list of these experiences. And then draws one of his not very illuminating diagrams.

June 15. Gerald Heard, Margaret Gage (at whose house Gerald was living), Michael Barrie and Mr. and Mrs. LeCron came to 333 East Rustic Road after supper, bringing with them a medium named Sophia Williams. My impression is that Christopher and Caskey had also invited a few people—maybe Hayden Lewis, Rod Owens, Lennie Newman, Carlos McClendon.

Sophia Williams had been "discovered," I think, by the Huxleys. She displayed her powers in the interests of psychic research, not for money. Exactly what her powers *were* was a question which interested Gerald particularly. It was probably he who had arranged for this sitting.

As I remember, the party sat down on a semicircle of chairs in the living room, facing towards its windows which overlooked the creek. Sophia Williams sat more or less in the middle of the semi-circle. She wasn't isolated from the others. She could easily have touched either of her neighbors. One of these was Gerald.

Sophia made no attempt to create a "spiritual" atmosphere. She said that the electric lights could be left on and that people could smoke and drink if they wished. She herself took a Scotch. I believe she smoked too, but I won't swear to that.

After a short period of silence, a sound was heard—at first it seemed like the whine of a mosquito. The sound came out of the empty space near the windows; it was definitely localized. As they all listened, it became louder or more distinct and was recognizable as a tiny voice.

If only Christopher had written down in his journal at least a few of the things it said. Why didn't he? Because, as usual, he was too lazy. Because, no doubt, his next morning's memory was fuddled with drink. However, I do remember that he and Caskey and their guests were much more impressed by the voice itself than they were by its statements, which seemed to them to be rather ordinary séance talk. Questioned by Sophia, the voice said it was Christopher's father. I'm pretty sure that Christopher had already told Sophia that his father was dead—and this seemed anyhow to be a suspiciously conventional act of politeness, that the Spirit World should choose to address Sophia's senior host. The voice certainly wasn't Frank's voice, even allowing for psychic distortion and "long distance," and it told Christopher nothing that Sophia couldn't have known or guessed at.

Next day, Caskey and Christopher discussed the séance with Gerald Heard. He was inclined to believe that Sophia Williams had produced the voice ventriloquially, perhaps without being conscious that she was doing so. While the voice was speaking, Gerald had watched her and seen that there was great tension in the muscles of her neck and back. He agreed that the production of the voice at this distance from the ventriloquist would anyhow be a remarkable feat.

Quite aside from the voice, Sophia managed to astonish them all, that evening. While they were sitting there, the frogs in the channel outside the windows set up a concerted croaking. This was usual at that time of the year—it was so loud that it could be heard right across the Canyon. Someone said jokingly to Sophia that she should make the frogs be quiet. She answered, in a matter-of-fact way, that she would try. Almost at once, the frogs stopped croaking and were silent from then on.

On June 17, Christopher went to visit Swami at the Queen of Angels Hospital—he was the pet of all the nuns. Probably their enthusiasm for his cuteness and sweetness was complicated by a sense of guilt; under the pretext of nursing him, they were associating with a preacher of a heathen cult, and not even trying to get him to see the Light!

On June 18 and 20, there are entries in the large thin notebook which show that Christopher is worried about the great number of characters in his novel. But he hasn't yet seriously considered the possibility of getting rid of them, because he is still determined to write about his life at the Haverford refugee hostel. Instead, he plans to change the character of Sarah (Caroline Norment) and make her "a happy-go-lucky, the-Lord-will-provide kind of person." By doing this, he reasons, the hostel will become "much more of a mess . . . and . . . the more of a mess it is, the more opportunities I obviously have for being interesting and amusing about it." (When one watches a writer—especially if he is oneself—floundering about like this, one begins to dream of a computer which would present his material to him in terms of all the conceivable ways it could be handled—thereby saving him from wasting months, even years. Or are these flounderings of some ultimate value?)

On June 21, Caskey and Christopher went down to Long Beach Veterans Hospital.

On June 25, Christopher had breakfast with Swami, who must have returned to the center from the Queen of Angels, and then gave a reading at the temple, as he sometimes did when there was no one available to give a proper lecture.

On June 28, Christopher went to Long Beach Hospital alone. At Long Beach, for some reason I don't remember, he found himself visiting T.B. patients as well as paraplegics. Before he visited the T.B. ward, it had been explained to him that he ought to take two precautions against infection—he should wear a white hospital gown over his clothes and he shouldn't come too near the patient or sit on his bed. No doubt the doctors themselves thought these precautions were exaggerated and only passed them on to visitors because the hospital insurance regulations so required. But Christopher couldn't resist milking a little melodrama from the situation. He pointedly *didn't* wear a hospital gown and *did* sit on beds. He also called his friends' attention to the fact that he was behaving in this way, saying that self-protective precautions only raised a barrier between you and the patients—you couldn't talk to them naturally if you were treating them as unclean. Which was true. Still, the fact remained that Christopher was posing as a fearless Francis of Assisi.

A journal entry on June 29 is prompted by the Korean War, which had begun on June 25 and had already caused Truman to send air and naval units to fight the North Koreans. Christopher quotes two sentences from a diary which he had been keeping during the Munich Crisis of 1938: "From now on, I'll try to write every day. It will be a discipline—and these messages from the doomed ship may even be of some value, to somebody, later." Applied to the Korean War by an overage civilian sitting in safety thousands of miles away, this sounds fairly hysterical. But Christopher wasn't alone in fearing that the Korean crisis might possibly lead into World War III. And he was quite justifiably afraid that he might swing over from alarm into thick-skinned indifference.[1]

---

[1] "The great effort I [must] make is to realize that this fighting is actually taking place, that people are being killed, that the fighting may spread into a general war . . . even that Los Angeles and other cities may be bombed—perhaps with atom bombs. It is very hard to realize the horror of all this—precisely because I have already spent most of one war right here in this city and so the prospect seems deceptively familiar and scarcely more than depressing. The danger of taking the war unseriously is a truly hideous spiritual danger. If I give way to it, I shall relapse into the smugness of the middle aged, who have nothing much to fear because they won't be drafted, or the animal imbecility of queens who look forward to an increase in the number of sailors around town.

"To see Jo and Ben Masselink this morning. Both are worried. . . . Told Ben how much I liked his travel-book manuscript, which delighted Jo; she

Then there was the threat to Christopher's younger friends. It seemed unlikely that Caskey would be drafted, because of his "blue discharge" from the navy (see page 43). Jim Charlton, Ben Masselink and Bob Craft were veterans, so they wouldn't be called immediately. (As it turned out, none of them were ever called. Indeed, I can only remember one person Christopher had previously known who took part in the Korean War, and he had to do so because he was an air force reserve officer and an experienced World War II pilot—Brad Saurin, see page 172.)

A publisher named Bill Kennedy had come into town from New York on June 27. Christopher and Caskey already knew him—maybe through Eileen Garrett the medium. They picked him up at the airport. Mrs. Garrett, whom Christopher knew through the Huxleys, had control of the magazine *Tomorrow* and Kennedy, I believe, was helping her reorganize it. *Tomorrow* had previously been devoted to psychic matters only; now it was to include short stories, assorted articles and reviews. Kennedy was urging Christopher to review books for the magazine and offering what then seemed generous terms—four hundred dollars per review. Christopher was definitely interested, for he was feeling hard up. So he was ready to be pleasant to Kennedy, whom he would otherwise have avoided. Kennedy was well-meaning but irritating and a bit of a murderee. On June 28, Caskey and Christopher took him to dine at the Holiday House, a restaurant up the coast above Malibu, romantically situated with a view over the ocean, which Christopher sometimes used for seduction suppers. Here Caskey and Christopher got drunk—Kennedy was on the wagon—and Caskey (to quote the journal) "denounced Kennedy for belonging to the entrepreneur class, staying at the Miramar, etc." On June 30, Christopher took Kennedy for a drive, to patch things up.

Long talk about Billy's accusations. Kennedy had been much hurt, had even considered leaving this morning. He is full of guilt and

---

embraced me several times. In this time of anxiety, one sees how motherly she is. Her Baby may be taken away from her. And this is really heartbreaking, because they so deserve to be happy. They have built up such a charming, yet modest life together. Jo is so industrious, and clever, making swimming suits for her customers. Ben works so hard at his writing. They are gay and bright-eyed and grateful for every instant of pleasure, and yet they demand so little in order to enjoy it.

"With their example, I ought to be unfailingly kind and thoughtful in my dealings with Billy (Caskey). How can I ever be otherwise? Especially at a time like this." [*D1*, pp. 423–4.]

self-depreciation (sic) and takes us all far too seriously. Billy doesn't like him. I don't feel much either way. But his proposals for me to work on the magazine *Tomorrow* may open a way out of this whole movie mess into a more serious literary life.

The June 30 journal entry also describes a performance given by the Peruvian singer and dancer, Yma Sumac, at Salka Viertel's house. It had been arranged as a sort of informal audition, to expose Sumac's talents to Hollywood. Charlie and Oona Chaplin, John Huston, Iris Tree ("in a converted sari"), John Houseman, Hedy Lamarr, Ella Winter, Friedrich Ledebur with "a bored tennis-playing maharajah" and Ivan Moffat ("poker-faced, appalled by all the imitations he would have to give") were among those present. Christopher describes the performance carefully.[1] He is playing one of his literary tricks on himself—using his declared "private State of Emergency" to make himself write in his journal, not only about the war but about anything that appeals to him.

On July 2, Christopher had supper with Peter Darms.[*] Peter was a young man he had met on the beach, two or three months previously. Christopher had been running, and when he passed the ruin of the wooden breakwater, Peter had been sitting on top of it, swinging his strong handsome legs. He was a big boy with thick blond hair, darkly suntanned. He had made some remark and Christopher had been only too willing to stop and talk to him; he had an attractively scowling good-natured face. Christopher was surprised and delighted when the young man made a shamelessly direct pass at him, rubbing his thigh against Christopher's. They had lain down together in a sheltered place and rubbed off against each other. Christopher hadn't seen him since then.

Luckily, he had remembered the young man's name and recognized it when he heard it repeated by Paul Fox, who had been going to bed with Peter Darms. Fox wasn't particularly interested in the affair and he willingly gave Christopher Darms's phone number. When Christopher called, Darms didn't seem surprised. He accepted Christopher's invitation to dinner and Christopher took it for

---

[1] "The slant-eyed Yma and her cousin, balancing so lightly on their little feet, and uttering sudden wails of mimic despair. And the boy behind them, very close, and thrusting forward with his guitar; so that they seemed to be continually advancing upon us with the compactness and drive of a little military formation. . . . The dances had an airy uncanny birdlike authority: you got the feeling of the uncanny jungle and the discontinuous, abrupt movements of the birds. . . ." [*D1*, p. 425]

[* Not his real name.]

granted that Darms remembered who he was. They met, ate, got along well and ended the evening in bed. When sex was satisfactorily completed, Peter Darms began to laugh. "My God," he said, "I've just realized who you are—how we first met! I've been trying to figure it out all evening!"

Peter and Christopher had sex many times after this—Christopher always fucked him. Thus they formed a pleasant uncomplicated friendship. Later, when Peter found himself a steady, serious lover, Christopher complimented the lover in the words of Lady Windermere to Lord Augustus: "[Y]ou're marrying a very good woman!"[*]

On July 8, Caskey and Christopher drove to Sequoia and back with Igor and Vera Stravinsky and Bob Craft. The trip is described in a journal entry next day.[1] (Christopher had already failed in his resolve to keep a day-to-day record of the Korean crisis and this was to be his last entry that month.) The only reference to Korea is that Bob Craft is said to be worried about being drafted and that Stravinsky is quoted as saying that he doesn't expect World War III, only an indefinitely prolonged border struggle between the two empires.

On the drive to Sequoia, as they were crossing the San Fernando Valley, Igor asked them all to excuse him: "I have to think about my opera for ten minutes." So everybody kept quiet. While Igor meditated on *The Rake's Progress*, Christopher meditated on his novel. And, just as he had often found it helpful to meditate in the

---

[1] Shortly before they entered the Sequoia park, Christopher told Igor—who had never been there before—that he would find the landscape strangely out of perspective, because at first you are surrounded by very small trees, birches, while at the same time you look up and see the giant trees on the skyline, thousands of feet above you. Igor seemed to understand what Christopher meant. He answered promptly: "Just like Shostakovich at the Hollywood Bowl."

Later they visited the General Sherman Tree, which is supposed to be the largest living thing on earth—274 feet tall, 101 feet around at the base, and between three and four thousand years old. When Igor stood looking up at it, Christopher didn't feel that it made him seem smaller, as it does most people. This was a confrontation of two great stars. Igor said of the tree: "That's very serious."

Igor, then sixty-eight, still had a trim well-coordinated figure. At that time, he was exercising every day. He showed a lot of energy, walking about, scrambling over rocks. He had a huge appetite and complained because they weren't able to get a meal exactly when he wanted one.

While they were looking at the view of Mount Whitney from Moro Rock, Igor said that Derain had told him that a mountain is the most difficult of all objects to paint.

[* Oscar Wilde, *Lady Windermere's Fan*, act four.]

presence of his spiritual guru, Swami, so now the presence of this artistic guru, Igor—not *his* guru but certainly a very great one— apparently inspired him. He had several insights which he records on July 9 in the large thin notebook.[1] This is the only occasion in my life on which I have deliberately practiced "artistic meditation."

On July 9, Christopher had lunch with the Beesleys. I have said little about them in this diary because their meetings with Christopher don't usually "make news." But they were one of Christopher's most important contacts throughout this period. Dodie was indeed the only person within the area of his daily life who had the authority to encourage him to keep on writing—in the sense that Swami had the authority to encourage him to keep on meditating and making japam. Christopher didn't greatly admire Dodie's work but that was unimportant. She was a real writer, a professional; therefore she had the authority—every bit as much as if she had been Henry James. And she was an excellent critic—even of work which wasn't at all to her taste. Christopher discussed his novel with her whenever they met. (It wasn't merely Christopher's egotism which prevented them from also discussing Dodie's writing-in-progress. Dodie was always superstitiously secretive about it.) An

---

[1] Briefly put, these insights were all about the character of Stephen. Christopher decided—for the first time, I believe—that Stephen should be bisexual. ("The degree to which this notion scares me only proves that I'm on the right track.") Stephen has revolted from Quakerism as a young man but hasn't escaped from the puritanism which goes with it—so his occasional homosexual affairs have been guilty. Because he feels guilty, he has behaved irresponsibly toward his male lovers. Then he takes refuge in marriage to Elizabeth Rydal. But she can't satisfy him sexually. After her death, he marries Jane, who can. But Jane herself is promiscuous, and Stephen finds that he is jealous both of her lovers and of her. And Jane sometimes (as in the scene at the Hollywood party) deliberately takes a boy because she knows Stephen is attracted to him.

Then, at the hostel, Stephen has his first serious homosexual relationship. He falls in love with the doctor, Charles Kennedy. It is Charles who makes the first advances, forcing Stephen to admit to his homosexuality.

Stephen's bisexuality "—i.e., flirting because one can't make up one's mind —has to be exposed spiritually, economically, politically, socially, as well as sexually. Stephen has to find adjustment on all levels before the book ends."

"Stephen's conflict: he can't subscribe to Quaker mysticism or Quaker pacifism because he hates Quaker puritanism. And yet he is by nature a mystic and a pacifist. . . . If Stephen's 'conversion' means anything, it means that he can accept an apparent paradox—i.e., he still believes in God—or more than ever believes in God—while doing something the God-mongers condemn —that is, loving another man."

entry in the large thin notebook (on July 11) refers to this particular meeting. It begins: "Dodie was quite right when we talked this over on Sunday. I am starting at the wrong place. . . ."[1]

On July 10, Christopher was visited by Anaïs Nin and her very handsome and much younger husband—or lover, they may not have gotten married till later—Rupert Pole. I don't remember anything about this meeting. I'm nearly sure it was Christopher's first with Anaïs. Maybe he had met Rupert before—because I have the impression that Rupert later claimed that Christopher had made a pass at him, which irritated Christopher greatly. (Christopher didn't like to think of himself as a maker of hopeless passes; it was something that senile queens did.)

What I do know is that Anaïs had sometime previously sent Christopher a copy of her novel *Children of the Albatross*, inscribed: "Our mutual friend Bill Kennedy tried to have us meet but you were not home. This is a preface to a future meeting. Anaïs." Christopher had read the novel and been seriously impressed. Nevertheless, he had laid it on far too thick in his note of thanks, telling Anaïs that she had made him feel, as never before, what it is like to be a woman —and adding, "Since one could hardly say more than this to Flaubert about Bovary, I conclude that your novel also is a masterpiece." Anaïs, being regally accustomed to courtly language from her admirers, took this tribute quite as a matter of course.

On July 13, the day-to-day diary notes that Christopher went to the Huntington Hartford Foundation for tea. I think that Frank

---

[1] Dodie's suggestion was that the novel should start with the scene at the Hollywood party and the discovery of Jane and her lover fucking in the doll's house. So Stephen leaves for Sarah's home, where he finds Gerda but no other refugees. He tells Gerda about Jane and she laughs, making Stephen see the funny side of the situation. Then the Traubes arrive and Dr. Kennedy comes to attend Miss Traube, who is very sick. The first time Charles Kennedy is alone with Stephen, he refers to a character in *The World in the Evening*. The character is female but is actually a portrait of Stephen himself—this was Elizabeth's way of hinting to Stephen that she knew about his homosexuality. Stephen has long since realized this, and now Kennedy has guessed it. He is flirting with Stephen by asking him about this character. It is Gerda who finally tells Stephen (after he has been to bed with her—they get drunk to celebrate the news that her husband Peter has escaped from the Nazis) that he, Stephen, is in love with Charles Kennedy. So then Stephen goes to Charles and tells *him*. And, after that, they get together.

There is another big entry in the notebook on July 12, which is a rough short draft of the first chapter, not too unlike the chapter which finally appeared in the printed book. On August 9, there is a redrafting of the opening paragraphs. Then no more entries in 1950. But Christopher evidently went on working during the fall.

Taylor was probably with him. Frank did go with him to see the Hartfords on July 19 at their house in Hollywood—this is recorded in the day-to-day diary—and the reason for their visit was that Frank was urging Christopher to become one of the trustees of the foundation. My impression is that Frank himself had already become a trustee and no doubt he wanted to control the board through his nominees. Although Frank was for the time being a film producer at MGM, he still kept up his connection with the New York publishing world, and it is advantageous for a publisher to be in a position to promote literary fellowships for his authors. Hartford was full of conservative artistic opinions but fundamentally lazy and gullible; an operator like Frank could manage him easily and charmingly, without ever having to get tough. As for Christopher, he was intrigued by the idea of becoming a trustee. This was a new role for him, and the foundation, as he increasingly discovered, could be an ideal place of escape from his homelife with Caskey.

It was a ranch house surrounded by a good deal of land, near the end of a dirt road which straggled along part of Rustic Canyon, north of Sunset Boulevard. The canyon was very hot in summer and an obvious firetrap, but it had the charm of sleepy old-Californian remoteness, although it was so near suburbia; and Hartford had fixed up the swimming pool and had several attractive cottages built in the surrounding woods, all ready to be filled with writers, artists and composers.

On July 15—Caskey having gone off to Laguna Beach with Lennie Newman—Christopher drove up to the top of Mount Wilson with Peter Darms. On the way back, they stopped at the Clear Creek Forest Station, where Rupert Pole was living and working as a forest ranger. Anaïs was staying there with him—in defiance of the regulations, since no wives or girlfriends were permitted and there was no accommodation for them. Anaïs and Rupert had to sleep together in one large room which was shared by the other rangers; their only means of privacy was a screen. Anaïs was obviously enjoying herself as the queen of this male community, and Christopher admired the style and charm of her behavior and her foreign gaiety. The other men all seemed respectfully impressed by her and also amused by the naughtiness of her presence among them. But Christopher suspected that Rupert was horribly embarrassed. Not that that made any practical difference to the situation, for Rupert was humbly and lovingly under Anaïs's thumb.

From July 21 to July 23, Christopher stayed at Trabuco with John van Druten. At this period John was wondering if he shouldn't perhaps become seriously involved in Vedanta. He never did, because Vedanta didn't really "speak to his condition," and because Swami didn't altogether appeal to him as a guru. (He once outraged Christopher by remarking, quite innocently, that he was sure Swami was "a very good little man.") Although John had formally broken with the Christian Science Church, he remained a Scientist at heart and he was deeply infected by the heresy that goodness is more real than evil—meaning that there is no reason why a human being shouldn't enjoy an unbroken spell of health, wealth and success throughout his life. The kind of guru John was drawn to would usually be a Christian Scientist who had broken away from the Mother Church, such as Joel Goldsmith, whom John already knew (I'm almost sure) at that time and with whom he was in constant correspondence, even while he was discussing Vedanta with Swami.

I have only one memory which may be related to this Trabuco visit—or did it happen later? John van Druten gave Michael Barrie money to buy an organ for the choir he had organized at Trabuco. But Michael then left Trabuco without having bought the organ and John asked for his money back. He got it, of course, but a slight coolness had been created. People at the Vedanta Center felt that John should have told them they could use the money for something else. Swami ruled that henceforth no gifts would be accepted which had conditions attached to them.

On July 25, the day-to-day diary notes that Christopher has finished his review of Ray Bradbury's *The Martian Chronicles*. Sometime earlier that month, Christopher had run into Ray Bradbury, whom he knew only slightly, in a bookshop. Bradbury promptly bought a copy of the *Chronicles* and presented it to Christopher. According to Bradbury (in a letter written twenty-three years later to Digby Diehl, the book editor of *The Los Angeles Times*), "His face fell." As well it might! How often in a whole lifetime does an author give you a book of his, unsolicited, which you can honestly say you love? This, however, was one of the times. Furthermore, by a blessed coincidence, Christopher was wondering what should be the first book he reviewed for *Tomorrow*—and here was an ideal choice, a discovery, a near masterpiece (well, why not say boldly a masterpiece) produced by an almost unknown author! In his 1973 letter, Bradbury says handsomely, "His review turned my career around, that year." I would love to think this is true but I doubt it, because *Tomorrow* didn't have that kind of authority or circulation.

On August 11 Christopher set out with Peggy Kiskadden and her baby son Bull on a drive to New Mexico, to visit Georgia O'Keeffe. Caskey, meanwhile, was planning to drive down south and join a party of friends—including Jay Laval, I believe, and Lennie New-man. They were going to Baja California.

The New Mexico trip is partly covered by entries in the journal—two big ones and a much shorter one, made on August 13, 15, and 19.

They spent the night of August 11 staying with Bob and Mary Kittredge at their house in Oak Creek Canyon. The Kittredges were from the East but they had lived out in Arizona for twenty years, on and off. Jim Charlton was living with them while he and Bob built a house Jim had designed. They were doing it all themselves, including the plumbing. For Jim, this was a secular-monastic "retreat" from his life in Los Angeles.[1]

Did Christopher and Jim make love that night? Apparently not, since Christopher writes in the journal: "I have no right to feel hurt or slighted, and I really don't. I shall keep his friendship if I endorse this venture, wherever it may lead him." Looking back on this episode, it seems to me that Jim was cockteasing Christopher outrageously. And the cockteasing was most effective, for Christopher found himself getting an absurdly violent crush on Jim, all over again. I think the romantic pioneer setting had a lot to do with it. In Oak Creek Canyon, Jim became The Whitman Nature Boy, almost as good as new.

Peggy, meanwhile, was disapproving of the Kittredges and of their way of life.[2] Christopher caused a crisis in the middle of supper by remarking that he had always longed to visit Monument Valley. Bob Kittredge was ready to close the house and leave next morning on a three-day trip there and back. (He had taken a strong fancy to Peggy, partly sexual, partly sentimental, because he had discovered that they

---

[1] "Jim lost no time in telling me that he misses nothing and nobody in Santa Monica, is perfectly happy here, and looks forward to staying through the winter. (Just the same, he was obviously very pleased to see me, and had even bought a special bottle of rum for us to drink after we went to bed at night in the house where he sleeps.) . . . Jim is now drinking very little, having no sex, making no trips to Flagstaff, even." [For this and ensuing quotes from journal in text and in notes, see *D1*, pp. 427–31.]

[2] "Peggy was pained by the untidiness in which the Kittredges live. . . .Mary Kittredge, Peggy pointed out, is a typical slovenly Southerner, and, said Peggy, there is a far wider gap between New Englanders and Southerners than between New Englanders and British. . . .

". . . (They gave us venison for dinner. Peggy heroically ate some.) . . .

"Peggy says Bob Kittredge is the type of Easterner who was born one hundred years too late. He should have been an Indian guide; and now, though he comes out to the West and learns all about camping and hunting and wild life, he is really lost and isolated in the middle of the twentieth century."

were distant cousins.) "But Peggy was greatly alarmed. She wanted to get on to Georgia's, she disliked haphazard camping, she was somehow jealous of the Kittredges' Arizona as against Georgia's New Mexico." So Christopher, of course, had to decline the invitation. Jim urged him to stop off on the way home and make the trip with them then.

Next morning, August 12, Peggy, Bull and Christopher set out on the second half of their drive via Gallup and Santa Fe to Abiquiu, the village where Georgia O'Keeffe lived.[1]

Abiquiu is northwest of Santa Fe, on a road which branches off the road to Taos, at Española. In those days, Abiquiu was an almost entirely Spanish-speaking community and it might as well have been in the heart of Old Mexico, except that its plumbing was probably superior. It would have been safer in Old Mexico, however. Here,

---

[1] Christopher later described the psychological atmosphere of this drive, in the journal: "Peggy's guilt at having been allowed to get her own way—" i.e., by refusing to visit Monument Valley—

(and I see she will get nothing else throughout this trip) occupied us with the most elaborate self-justifications and generalizations during most of yesterday's drive. But I didn't really care. I was . . . in a fairly well-balanced mood of happiness–unhappiness . . . thinking of the misery of the mess at Rustic Road . . . and of the slowly maturing war situation; and, at the same time . . . happy to be out on the endless blue levels of the plateau. . . .

What Christopher doesn't mention in any of these journal entries is the ambivalence of the relationship between himself and Peggy. On the one side, he is observing her and criticizing her rather bitchily. On the other side, he is playing the protective elder brother, looking after her and little Bull—who, incidentally, behaved like an angel throughout the trip. Even at this late date—they had known each other for more than ten years—their brother–sister relationship was slightly incestuous—that is to say, flirtatious. They would remind each other that they made a handsome couple and that they looked young for their ages. When they stopped that day to eat at a roadside restaurant, it amused and pleased them both that the waitress took Christopher for Bull's father. (Why in the world shouldn't she have?) Peggy had the impertinence to assure Christopher that nobody would ever suspect him of being homosexual, because he seemed one hundred percent masculine. And no doubt, in the innocence of her arrogance, she sincerely believed she was paying him a compliment!

In the journal, Christopher notes that,

Peggy is much concerned with the change of life and anxious not to try to be attractive any more. (She will, though.) She is transferring her sexual vanity to her children, as bankers transfer money from a city which may be bombed. . . . Peggy goes on and on about her children until one could scream.

it was less than thirty miles from Los Alamos and therefore presumably in danger of some atomic accident which could devastate the whole area. Los Alamos—referred to locally as "The Mountain" —employed thousands of people and had made Española a boomtown.

In the journal, Christopher describes Georgia O'Keeffe as "that sturdy old beautiful weather-beaten cedar root." He admired her —even liked her at times—but they were natural enemies from the moment they met. Maybe Georgia would have been the natural enemy of any man who was escorting Peggy, and maybe the knowledge that Christopher was queer merely added contempt to her hostility. I'm not saying that Georgia was a dyke—I mean, yes, sure she was, but that wasn't the point about her. She was first and foremost an archfeminist, a pioneer women's libber. According to Peggy, Georgia had had a very handsome, much-spoilt elder brother and had thus begun telling herself, "Anything you can do, I can do better."

Georgia had perhaps had a crush on Peggy once. Now she was certainly very fond of her still, but in a spirit of grown-up amusement. One evening, Georgia and her secretary, Doris Bry—just arrived back from New York—had an argument with Peggy about women's rights. Peggy, needless to say, was antilegislation and in favor of women getting their way *through* men. Later, Georgia and Doris told Christopher that Peggy simply didn't understand such problems, because she had always been so attractive and had never had to earn her living. Christopher describes Doris Bry as being "pale, tall, thin, exhausted; just a trifle murderee."

Georgia, says Christopher, kept "apologizing, half humorously, for being 'cruel.'" She was certainly masterful. Her house represented a way of life which you just had to adopt as long as you were living in it.[1] You ate what Georgia ordained—sternly simple vegetarian fare. You got up at dawn. You had supper before it was even dark and were then supposed to retire to your room.[2] There were also

---

[1] "Georgia O'Keeffe's house. The massive adobe walls—big round pine beams with cross rafters of aspen or cedar. In some rooms, old cedar has been used; it looks like bundles of firewood. The pastel colors of New Mexico—pinkish brown or grey of adobe, pale green of sage. The black modernistic chair sitting like a spider in a corner of the hot patio."

[2] It was then that Christopher wrote in his journal and read F. M. Ford's *Parade's End*, another book he was reviewing for *Tomorrow*. The character of Sylvia Tietjens made him think of Caskey and the quarrels at Rustic Road:

We cannot settle anything by bargaining. We have to live this through, with great patience, but without any of that "neither-do-I-condemn-thee"

various compulsory and somewhat sacramental amusements—quite aside from the outings which Georgia organized daily. For example, she would call her guests out in the middle of the afternoon to watch the almost invariable summer thunderstorm over the Sangre de Cristo mountains; she had already arranged the chairs on the patio as if for a theatrical performance. Or she would sit Christopher down in front of a portfolio containing a couple of hundred classical Japanese paintings of bamboo, every one different but all nearly identical. Acutely conscious of Georgia standing over him and sardonically watching his face, Christopher examined each painting with care and tried to find a comment for each, or at least a special appreciative grunt.

Visiting an art guru such as Georgia is like visiting a monastery. In both cases, you are being forced to slow down your normal life tempo, to concentrate your usually scattered attention and renounce your habitual distractions. This experience is painfully uncomfortable while it is going on. You merely long for it to be over. But later —years later—you find yourself recalling it vividly and with satisfaction.

(I should mention that Georgia wasn't at all eager to show her own paintings; indeed she seemed touchingly modest about them.)

Another sacramental amusement—far easier to enjoy than the bamboo paintings—was looking at the photographs taken by Alfred Stieglitz, Georgia's late husband. Stieglitz and his theory of photography[1] were certainly impressive and Christopher could have been far more enthusiastic about both if only Georgia had presented them to him less sacredly. (As for Peggy, she had known Stieglitz too, and she used him to put Christopher down whenever Christopher ventured to praise Caskey's talent as a photographer.) Chiefly to placate Georgia, Christopher bought three numbers of the magazine *Camera Work* which Stieglitz had published in the early 1900s. They were then already collectors' items. As I remember, Georgia charged him quite a lot for them.

On August 13, Georgia took them up to a ranch she owned in the

---

stuff. Oh, I shall never, never get out of this rut until I do that, once. The funny thing is—it's exactly the subject of my novel (which looks promising, at present).

[1] Stieglitz used to maintain that the artist only needs a minimum of subject matter to work with. A vast number of his best pictures were all taken within a radius of a few yards, inside and outside his house on Lake George, New York—the interior, the exterior, the view from the porch, the poplars, the clouds.

hills, The Ghost Ranch. All I remember about it is a collection of strangely colored and shaped stones on a table outside the front door. And the emptiness of the uplands, the parklike clearings, the hills covered with piñon and weeping cedar (not that I even recall what a weeping cedar looks like, but Christopher liked the name for its own sake and wrote it down). My actual memory is of the feel of the emptiness—quite a different feel from that of a countryside which has been recently deserted; this was really, utterly empty. It made Christopher uneasy.

On the 14th, they visited the Indian cliff dwellings at Puye. Christopher had been rather dreading this and had tried to resign himself, since at least one cliff dwelling is a must for the tourist in New Mexico. As far as Christopher was concerned, cliff dwellings meant ladders; tall, vertical, vertiginous. The Puye ladders were probably not nearly as tall as some others, but they were quite tall enough for Christopher. Indeed he was surprised that the forest rangers let visitors of all ages scramble up and down them unaided. Georgia, though in the pink of condition, was nevertheless a woman in her sixties; little Bull was too young to be able to climb alone; Peggy, girlish as she looked, was no chicken. And here was Christopher, condemned to be the Man of the Party. Halfheartedly, he offered to carry Bull, but Peggy wouldn't hear of it. . . . They got up to see the cliff dwellings without trouble. Christopher felt giddy at moments but he didn't freeze on the rungs. His chief concern was that he knew it would be much worse for him going back down. Georgia, becoming unexpectedly feminine, declared that she had hated the climb. Wasn't there some path which would bring them over the hill and around to their car by a safe ladderless route? There wasn't, it seemed. So Georgia said she would climb down last, with Christopher immediately below her to catch her if she slipped. This put Peggy in the lead, with Bull riding on her shoulders. She too was nervous but tensely brave. A strong breeze started to shake the ladders and blow sand into their faces. Bull, clinging around Peggy's neck, announced: "I'm frightened!" . . . When it was all over, Christopher felt fairly pleased with himself. At least he hadn't panicked.

On the 15th, Georgia drove them up into the hills behind Abiquiu. Here they saw, from a respectful distance, the shrines which were visited by the local Penitentes on their Holy Week processions. Each shrine represented one of the Stations of the Cross. Georgia, as a respected resident of Abiquiu, even though non-Spanish and non-Catholic, was always invited to join the procession, but only as far as the third or fourth station—I forget which. At that point, she was expected to turn back and go home, while the rest of the procession moved forward, station by station, until it reached a secluded place where the crucifixion ritual was performed. (Georgia said that this ritual wasn't as bloody and dangerous as some of the rituals performed in Old Mexico. The Christ actor was whipped but he wasn't beaten nearly to death; his hands weren't nailed to the cross, he was tied by the wrists.) The only Spanish Catholic in Abiquiu who didn't take part in the procession was the priest. He was ordered not to do so by his bishop, who regarded the Penitentes as heretics. So the priest tactfully left the village that week. Officially, he didn't even know that the ritual was being performed.

On the 16th, Carl Van Vechten and a friend of his named Saul Mauriber came to lunch. The day-to-day diary, as so often, expresses itself ambiguously, but I deduce from it that Christopher then drove Carl and Saul back to Santa Fe in Peggy's car. (But, if they hadn't got a car of their own, how did they reach Abiquiu?) In Santa Fe, Christopher had drinks and/or supper with Witter Bynner and his friend Bob Hunt. Plenty of drinks, certainly, for he left Santa Fe drunk, late at night. As he swung off the Taos road and whizzed through Española, two cops stopped him. For a moment, things looked serious. The cops put on stern faces. Then one of them said, "Do you want to stand trial, or settle this right away?" When Christopher told them meekly that of course he wanted to settle it, they took him into a smallish wooden hut at the side of the road. Inside the hut was a desk. One of the cops produced a gavel from a drawer in this desk and struck the desk with it three times, saying, "The Court of the State of New Mexico is now in session." He then told Christopher the amount of his fine—I think it was thirty dollars—and Christopher paid him, without even venturing to ask if he might have a receipt. No doubt the cops kept the "fine" for themselves. I suppose they had noticed that he had sufficient ready money on him when he took out his billfold to show them his driver's license.

(I don't remember anything about Christopher's conversations with Van Vechten and Bynner, except that they were pleasant. Maybe he and Bynner talked about Bynner's book on Lawrence. *Journey with Genius*. When it was published, the next year, Bynner inscribed a copy to Christopher as "its godfather"—which probably means that Christopher read it in manuscript sometime in 1950 and made some encouraging comments on it. It now seems to me an extremely interesting but rather bitchy, envious book.)

On the 17th, Georgia, Peggy and Christopher drove to Taos, where they saw Frieda Lawrence, her husband Angelo Ravagli and Dorothy Brett. With Brett they went up to the Del Monte Ranch and spent the night. Next morning, they came back down to Taos, met Mabel Dodge Luhan, then returned to Abiquiu. All this is described in the journal.[1]

On the 21st, Peggy, Bull and Christopher started on the drive

[1] "Shrill, blonde-white witchlike Frieda, who is very sympathetic, and Angelino, who is rather too sleek and suave. Also, his Latin sex act bores me. He picked Peggy up in his arms, and this excited little Bull so much that he bit her in the buttock—'the haunch,' Peggy calls it."

Christopher says in the journal that the Del Monte ranch was "exactly as Lawrence described it in *St. Mawr*." But he contradicts himself immediately by referring to the new house which Angelo had built since Lawrence's death,

blocking out the view from the old Lawrence house behind it; from jealousy, probably. It has a very squalid atmosphere, whereas the older house seems strangely joyful. The dead bees on Lawrence's bed, and the yellow *santo* [saint's image] and the string mat Lawrence made to sit on by the fireplace. A reproduction or small copy of the awful Lawrence painting Frieda has down in her house—the great tortured German frau dragging a factory after her by a harness of ropes and straining up towards a bearded Lawrence figure, who is rolling his eyes with horror and apparently fighting off another frau with a sword, maybe, or a radioactive rolling-pin. . . . Brett says she and Lawrence did all the work, while Frieda lay on the bed smoking cigarettes. But you can't believe a word these women disciples say of each other.

Christopher took to Brett very strongly (was this partly because of her utter Britishness?): "I really love her, with her hearing aid and her enormous ass and absurd bandit's jacket. I said how good I always feel in the mornings, and she said, 'Yes—but by the afternoon one has worried oneself into a fit.'" Christopher admired Brett's Indian paintings—and also "a very beautiful Union Jack, faded to rose pink" which she had on the wall of her house. (On her garage door she had painted the arms of her family.) But he thought her portraits of Stokowski were ridiculous and rather like the original paintings by Van Meegeren—the ones that *aren't* forgeries.

That night, up at the Del Monte Ranch, Brett and her dog slept in Angelo's new house, while Georgia, Peggy, Bull and Christopher lay out of doors under the pines. Brett's dog set up a howl of the kind that dogs are supposed to utter when their master or mistress dies. So Christopher went into the house to investigate (playing the Man in Charge again) and found Brett peacefully snoring. Then Georgia told Christopher to recite poetry to put them to sleep but Christopher could only remember his basic repertoire of murder and ghost scenes from *Macbeth* and *Hamlet*. Bull loved every minute of it, because he was going to bed at the same time as, and with, the grown ups. They slept fairly well but awoke looking frowsy and crumple-faced. Christopher said, "Bull looks six, at least." Georgia got up and went striding off through the morning woods, "walking the ditch" (as she called it), to keep the irrigation ditch clear of undergrowth. She triumphantly found that some animal had died in the tank, making the water stink. Christopher meanwhile visited Lawrence's tomb, which he describes as "amateur-dauby." Nevertheless, this place was for him home. I have a vividly unpleasant memory of a thunderstorm which was moving in the same direction and bombarded them for at least fifteen miles. The lightning kept striking quite close to the road, now on one side, now on the other, now behind them, now ahead. Peggy got really scared and finally screamed at Christopher not to drive so fast, when he wasn't driving fast at all. Their route led them through Oak Creek Canyon, and of course Peggy had to start urging Christopher to stop off at the Kittredges' and make the trip with them and Jim to Monument Valley while she and Bull drove on to Los Angeles alone. Christopher knew perfectly well that this was one of Peggy's tests of his character. If he *did* stop, he would never hear the last of it and Bill Kiskadden would never be allowed to forgive him. A Real Man never under any circumstances deserts the women and children. Peggy's bitchery annoyed him so hugely that he told her with shameless frankness how much he loved Jim and how bitterly he regretted—and would regret for the rest of his life— having missed this marvellous experience. At the same time, he kept repeating that nothing would induce him to leave her. This reduced Peggy to a temporary state of meek submission.

They stayed the night at the Hassayampa Hotel in Prescott. About this, I have an odd memory. Having washed himself in his room before supper, Christopher went into Peggy's adjoining room still naked to the waist, with the towel in his hand. There *was* something he wanted to ask her, but it's possible also that Christopher was in a macho show-off mood. Anyhow, he realized at once that Peggy was displeased and slightly shocked. She had seen Christopher seminaked dozens of times,

a very sacred shrine—perhaps the most sacred of any in his literary myth world. When he later happened to mention to Peggy that he had signed the guest book in the chapel, she was shocked; she found this touristy. So he didn't tell her that he had also taken two red flowers from the hillside in front of the chapel and pressed them in his billfold for relics.

When they had returned to Taos, Peggy and Christopher visited Mabel Dodge Luhan

—a great disappointment, after all the stories about her witchlike fiendishness, jealousy and ruthless egotism. Such a dowdy little old woman—as Peggy said, "She's reverted to Buffalo." She looks like a landlady. And her house is full of the stupidest junk. It was very sad; the feeling of the old days gone—John Reed gone—Lawrence gone—and this old frump stuck with her fat Indian man, building houses and drinking whiskey in the morning. And yet the stories persist. The woman who lent Mabel a jacket. Mabel wore it all summer, then returned it. One night, the woman was out riding in the jacket, and a bullet whizzed past her. She dismounted, ran to the nearest bush, where a young Mexican, whom she knew, was crouching with a gun. "Forgive me," he gasped, "I thought you were Mrs. Luhan."

in the days when he stayed at her house. But this was different. Here they were together *in a hotel*. Someone might come in and suppose that they were *unduly intimate*. Or was Peggy afraid that little Bull might talk about this later to his father? Who could tell? Peggy's reactions on such matters were absolutely unpredictable.

She was in for a much greater shock next day, and so was Christopher. It must have been late in the afternoon of the 22nd that they reached Los Angeles. Peggy made a detour into Santa Monica Canyon to drop Christopher off at 333 East Rustic Road before going home. Together they entered the living room and stopped short in astonishment.

Evidently, Caskey had given a party after Christopher had left. There were glasses all over the room with the remains of drinks in them and plates with the remains of food. The place was in a wild mess. But what made this mess special and a bit spooky was its antique appearance. There were spider's webs on some of the glasses and drowned insects in others. The food, in that damp atmosphere, was already furred with mold. And there was an odor of decay in the air.

After the first moment of surprise, Christopher considered the situation fairly calmly. It was clear that Caskey had given this party *before* leaving for Baja California, since the mess must be at least several days old. It was very unlike him to go away without tidying things up, but Christopher could understand why he had done so; he had expected to return before Christopher. . . . Well, he must have changed his plans, that was all. No doubt he was enjoying himself and had decided to stay on.

But Peggy was horrified. Since she equated dirt and disorder with Evil, she shuddered at the sight before her. It must have appeared to her as a physical manifestation of what was spiritually rotten in the Caskey–Christopher relationship—like the transformation of Dorian Gray's picture. "Let's get away from here, darling," she said urgently and in a hushed voice, "you can come and stay with us—for as long as you like." Christopher thanked her, but said, no, he'd be all right. "But you *can't* stay here!" she cried in dismay. It took him a long time to convince her that he was in earnest. After she had gone, he called Jo and Ben Masselink, telling them what had happened. They came over at once and the three of them soon got everything cleaned up, laughing and joking as they did so. Jo and Ben's complete, affectionate acceptance of Caskey, along with all his exploits and outrages, made Peggy's puritanism look sick and silly. Henceforth, Christopher began to regard Jo and Ben as intimate friends in whom he could confide and with whom he felt at home. As for Peggy, this trip to New Mexico had finally convinced him that he couldn't afford to be intimate with her. At least, not as long as he was living in any kind of homosexual relationship. She would always try to undermine it and make Christopher feel guilty. She couldn't help herself—she was a compulsive ball cutter.

Next day, when Christopher went to pick up the mail which the post office had held for him while he was away, he found a letter from Caskey. It was written from the Santa Ana jail.

This, as well as I can remember, is what had happened to him:

On August 11, approximately, Caskey had given the party of which Christopher and the Masselinks had had to clear up the remains and had then set off alone and drunk, fairly late in the evening, to drive down to San Diego or wherever it was that the others were waiting for him. At San Clemente, he had stopped at a filling station, where they had filled his car with gas, accepted his money, let him go on his way again without any protest or warning—and then called the police, giving his number and telling them to watch out for a very drunk driver. San Clemente, in those days, was a notorious traffic trap; the community needed all the fines it could collect. The judge who tried Caskey offered him the option of a fine. When Caskey refused this, the judge turned nasty and sentenced him to three months.

When Christopher saw Caskey in jail on August 26—the next permitted visiting day—and heard the details of the case, he wanted to hire a lawyer at once. Even now, he said, Caskey could almost certainly get himself released, with the aid of some discreet bribery. But Caskey wouldn't hear of it, saying that he refused to let Christopher throw his money away on such crooks. He was so vehement about this that Christopher finally gave way. By then, it had become obvious that Caskey actually *wanted* to stay in jail and serve out his sentence. His Catholic conscience imposed this penance, to some extent; he felt that it was time for him to be punished for his drunkenness. Also, he wanted to keep away from Christopher for a while, knowing that Christopher's martyred forbearance would make him feel more guilty, as well as hostile. Also, he was quite enjoying being in jail; the life brought out his good-humored toughness, which Christopher always greatly admired. He could hold his own among his fellow prisoners, amusing them by drawing sex pictures and telling them sex stories, while making it clear that he wouldn't let himself be pushed around. When a prisoner had accused a weak timid youth of being queer, Caskey had told him sassily, "Well, honey, it takes one to know one," and had nearly got into a serious fight.

Christopher and Caskey parted affectionately. Christopher promised to come down and visit him every Saturday (which he faithfully did, until Caskey was released). Then he drove over to have tea with Chris Wood in Laguna. Though Christopher didn't admit this to any of his friends, he felt a great deal of relief. The Caskey problem was shelved for at least two months—assuming that Caskey would get time off for good behavior. And Christopher didn't have to feel guilty; he had done what he could. So, since this *was* his birthday, he decided to celebrate the rest of it with Mike Leopold. They had supper and spent the night together, very happily, and Christopher gave him one of the red flowers he had brought back from the Del Monte Ranch.

And now began a social, sexy period, during which Christopher enjoyed himself a good deal and I suppose got on with his novel. He also at last finished work on Patanjali's yoga aphorisms (October 5). And he started writing a review of Antonina Vallentin's *H. G. Wells, Prophet of Our Day* for *Tomorrow*.

In addition to Mike Leopold, he had several sex partners, old and new—Russ Zeininger, Don Coombs, Peter Darms, Brad Saurin, Keith Carstairs,[*] Barry Taxman, Bertrand Cambus,[†] Donald Pell,[‡] Mitchell Streeter.[§]

Brad Saurin had reappeared in the Canyon. I think he had been in Korea. Christopher found him more interesting than before— partly because he had written some quite talented, self-revealing poems;[1] partly because he had become altogether more attractive.

---

[1] The Self-Sufficient Seagull

> There was a wounded bird,
> Who, like an awkward aeroplane,
> Flew with one gear down.
>
> It was a smooth-feathered seagull,
> Swimming in slow circles,
> Limping when aground.
>
> He was no fishing frolicker,
> Screeched not nobly
> Reached no mate.
>
> He made no cackling congress
> At the prancing place, just
> Sat in state,
>
> Or swooped softly,
> Quietly, along the leeshore—
> Lonely.

[* Not his real name.] [† Not his real name.] [‡ Not his real name.] [§ Not his real name.]

It seemed natural that the two of them should start going to bed together and they both enjoyed it greatly. As Brad once remarked in the middle of a sex act, "It's a hell of a lot nicer doing this when you really like the guy!" But Brad's true love was Jim Charlton. This love affair developed later, after Jim had returned from Arizona, and it lasted a long time. Brad was very serious about it, and Jim was flattered that Brad kept suggesting they should set up housekeeping together. Jim had no intention of doing so, of course, though he admired Brad and was fond of him; they both belonged to the fraternity of crazy pilots and had much in common temperamentally. Brad was far crazier than Jim had ever been, however.

Keith Carstairs was just a very nice boy with a very sexy body. He and Christopher met from time to time and always made love. There was no drama about it. Keith and Christopher weren't at all involved emotionally; Keith had a steady boyfriend he saw on weekends. They made love because they liked each other and were compatible. It was a contact sport; good wholesome exercise. I still remember Christopher holding Keith in his arms and thinking, "How can anybody call this unnatural—it's the most natural thing in the world!"

Mitchell Streeter and Bertrand Cambus were both one-night stands, but for different reasons—Streeter wasn't interested in repeating, Bertrand would have been interested but his visit to Los Angeles was over. Streeter had the kind of physique you see in magazines; not heavily muscled but almost perfect. He displayed it when he first came to the house wearing nothing but his swimming trunks. (I forget who he came with and why.) Christopher was suitably impressed and hinted that he should return, alone. This he did, fully dressed but obviously ready for action. They had a couple of drinks, kissed and went upstairs. Christopher fucked him and then blew him. Satisfaction seemed mutual. When they next met, however, something was wrong from the start. Streeter sat there without giving the go-ahead signal, so Christopher, not wanting to make a pass and be rebuffed, invited him to come out to a restaurant—only to find, when they arrived, that he had brought too little money with him. They had to go Dutch. Streeter showed that he thought this was a cheapskate trick. Christopher couldn't blame him, but resented his thinking so, nevertheless. They didn't see each other again.

Christopher met Bertrand Cambus through a Texan queen [. . .] who liked to be called by his initials D.J.[*] After their first meeting, D.J. acted as go-between, telling Christopher that Bertrand found

[* Not his real initials.]

him very attractive and had particularly admired his legs. Christopher was flattered and delighted—for Bertrand was a dark handsome charming boy, athletically built and quite unlike Christopher's image of a wispy French faggot. (He was on a business trip to the States, representing one of the French automobile firms.) Christopher told D.J. to assure Bertrand that his lust was reciprocated. With the result that Bertrand and Christopher had supper and spent the night of September 3 together. Bertrand then had to return to France, whence he wrote Christopher a politely affectionate note, saying, "Happy times won't let themselves be forgotten." Speed Lamkin later told Christopher that he and Bertrand had been having an affair during Bertrand's stay in Los Angeles, and that it was he who had encouraged Bertrand to go to bed with Christopher.

Donald Pell was so pretty that Christopher was dazzled into thinking him sexy. Actually, he wasn't quite Christopher's type. They went to bed together without either of them really wanting to. Donald was busy pretending to himself that he wasn't queer, but only, as he put it, "trade." This pretense (which he later gave up) forced him to do his best to ignore the sexual aspects of his relationships. So he was apt to say things which made you stare at him incredulously. For example—one day, Donald and Christopher were eating a meal in Christopher's kitchen and Donald, who hoped to become a professional actor, was telling Christopher about the director of a play he had been in. This director had kept dropping into Donald's dressing room and giving him advice about his part. "But," said Donald, "I don't think it was my *acting* he was interested in—" and he gave Christopher a playful nudge in the ribs, "*if you get what I mean*, Chris." Donald wasn't trying to be funny. He was perfectly, squarely serious. No one who heard him could have suspected that Donald and Christopher had been having sex with each other, only half an hour before.

On August 27, Don Coombs telephoned to ask if he might bring two friends down with him, when he came to supper with Christopher, that evening. Christopher agreed, ungraciously. He had been expecting to have Coombs to himself, in bed, and he didn't want to sit up talking to strangers. However, when the three of them arrived, Christopher was placated, because both of the friends were attractive. One was called Fred;[*] I don't remember anything else about him. The other was a Jewish composer and teacher of music named Barry Taxman; very good-looking, slightly queeny, in his middle twenties.

[* Not his real name.]

As soon as they had arrived, Coombs took Christopher aside and asked if Fred and Barry might spend the night together in the back bedroom. Ordinarily, this would have annoyed Christopher, who hated being pressured into hospitality which he hadn't been prepared for. But, under the circumstances, he was amused, because he saw through Coombs's plan. Fred was obviously an ex-lover whom Coombs was planning to win back in one or both of two ways— (A) by making Fred jealous of Christopher, and/or (B) by making Barry take a fancy to Christopher and walk out on Fred.

Christopher would have liked the plan better if it had included getting him into bed with Fred, whom he fancied most, but that wasn't to be hoped for; Fred ignored him. So he concentrated on making Fred jealous. When Christopher woke with Coombs in the front bedroom next morning, they united in an energetic fuck— both of them grunting and moaning with pleasure but neither admitting to the other that this was mostly noisy playacting meant to be heard by the couple in the back bedroom.

Before long, Barry came out, without Fred. Coombs, now contentedly fucked, pretended to be asleep. Barry suggested to Christopher that they should go down and take a prebreakfast swim. Christopher agreed. On the way to the beach, Barry said, "Last night I kept wishing you were in bed with me, instead of Fred." Christopher was surprised, and also pleased, for Barry looked unexpectedly masculine, as well as handsomer, in trunks. They agreed to meet again, alone, at the earliest opportunity.

So Coombs's Plan B had succeeded. And also, as it later turned out, his Plan A. When Christopher and Barry got back to the house, they found Fred and Coombs deep in intimate conversation—no doubt assuring each other that they didn't, respectively, give a damn about Barry and Christopher.

Barry and Christopher finally got together on September 4. (The delay was due to Christopher's wooing of Bertrand Cambus.) When Barry arrived, all dressed up in his somewhat faggy best,[1] they were

---

[1] When Barry had a date with Christopher—or any other sex partner, presumably—he would bathe, shave, shampoo his hair and dress with extreme care. Christopher used to kid him about this, saying, "Five minutes after you arrive, you strip all those clothes off and toss them on the floor, and then we roll around till we're slippery with sweat and stinking like pigs, and then you, having carefully brushed your teeth and washed out your mouth with antiseptic, lick my ass and get shit on your tongue, and then I fuck you till my cock's smeared with shit which afterwards gets rubbed off on your belly—so why take all this trouble with your toilet?" [Taxman states that this passage is of doubtful authenticity and is extremely offensive and distasteful to him.]

both awkwardly conscious that this was a sex rendezvous. There seemed nothing else to talk about, and the atmosphere of embarrassment thickened, until Christopher said, "Look, why should we wait? Let's get into bed for a little while. Then we can have supper, knowing that everything's okay and there's going to be more sex later and so we needn't be tense about it." Barry agreed.

As they undressed, Barry told Christopher that he could get a hard-on but that he was unable to come; he hadn't had an orgasm in a long while. Christopher answered that Barry was to relax and not worry. Privately, he felt confident that he could get Barry over his inhibition. Christopher knew from experience that boys who told you this were often subconsciously challenging you to arouse them. This challenge excited Christopher, and he did his best to bring Barry to a climax. But he couldn't. Aside from this, their lovemaking was a success. Barry wanted Christopher to fuck him and he was very exciting to fuck, he really loved it.

(A few months after this, Barry fell in love with someone. Immediately, he was able to have orgasms again, not only with his lover but with anyone he found physically attractive. He was so delighted that he went around having sex with all his former partners, to prove to himself and them that he had been completely released. It was at this time that he had his first orgasm with Christopher.)

That first evening in bed together, Barry said, "How extraordinary this is! Here am I, a Russian Jew, making love with Christopher Isherwood!" His remark jarred on Christopher; it seemed indecent, masochistic, sexually off-putting. But, as Christopher got to know Barry better, he found a different significance in it. When Barry thus called attention to his Jewishness, he wasn't really demeaning himself. He wasn't at all a humble person. Indeed, he had that Jewish tactlessness, argumentativeness and aggressiveness which always aroused Christopher's anti-Semitic feelings. Only, in Barry's case, Christopher's anti-Semitism quickly became erotic. It made him hot to mate Barry's aggressiveness with his own, in wrestling duels which were both sexual and racial, Briton against Jew. Barry's aggressiveness became beautiful and lovable when it was expressed physically by his strong lithe body grappling naked with Christopher's. As they struggled, Christopher loved him *because* he was a pushy arrogant Jewboy. But he never talked to Barry about his feelings. They were too private.[*]

[* Taxman finds this passage to be apocryphal and extremely offensive and distasteful to him.]

Barry soon desired these duels as much as Christopher did, though for a different reason—at least, that is my guess. Barry had never wrestled with any of his other lovers. And his approach to sex had been from the yin side only; he wanted to be possessed. But now Christopher had, without consciously meaning to, made him aware of his yang self. When he wrestled with Christopher, he was all boy and he seemed to delight in his own virility. Switching back to yin again, after the fight, was a new sensation for him; the contrast between the two selves may well have made him enjoy being fucked more than ever. He and Christopher were always hot for each other.

At this time, Christopher saw a good deal of Gerald Heard[1] and Michael Barrie, also of Frank and Nan Taylor—of Frank rather than Nan, because Frank turned his queer friends into sexual conspirators against his own marriage, telling them all about his affairs with other men, and Nan hated them for it. It was at the Taylors' house that Christopher saw a showing of the semiprofessional film of *Julius Caesar* which had been shot on locations in and around Chicago, with Charlton Heston, then almost unknown, as a beautiful Mark Antony. As far as I remember, the scenes of Caesar's murder were played in a neoclassical bank building and the battle of Philippi took place among the sand dunes of Lake Michigan. On September 6,

---

[1] I wish I had at least some record of Christopher's talks with Gerald at this period. I remember only that his chief interest was in the many sightings and alleged sightings of Unidentified Aerial Objects—flying saucers. Gerald believed in them wholeheartedly and would soon publish *Is Another World Watching?*, in which it is stated that June 24, 1947 (the Kenneth Arnold sighting near Mount Rainier) "may prove to be one of the most important dates in history." Gerald told Christopher that, "Liberation is my vocation, the saucers are my avocation." He expressed the wish that one of the objects would land and require a human go-between to explain the ways of earth men to their people and to be instructed in their own culture, as far as that was possible. Gerald longed to be this go-between. I think he had elaborate fantasies about the role he would play—including the brilliant, epigrammatic lectures on Earth history he would deliver and maybe even the splendid space costumes he would wear. I remember Gerald as being very cheerful in those days. Yes —now a memory comes to me. It belongs to August 30, when, according to the day-to-day diary, Gerald, Michael Barrie and Christopher, "Picked up Harold's Rolls." The Rolls belonged to Harold Fairbanks—that much I'm sure of—but how Harold had acquired it, where they were taking it and for what purpose, I don't know. It was a handsome old car, and Gerald enjoyed its faded grandeur. They were all three laughing and chattering, and suddenly Gerald exclaimed, "What good talk!" I can still picture his face as it looked at that moment, lit up with the vivid pleasure of a connoisseur. And I can hear the tone of his voice, so melodiously Irish. At such moments one glimpsed him as he must have been when he was young and unholy.

Frank and Christopher had supper at the Hartford Foundation with its manager, Michael Gaszynski, a Polish nobleman who also had a cheesecake concession at the Farmer's Market. Michael was all smiles and politeness in those days—later on, when Christopher became a trustee and began staying at the foundation, they were forced into being enemies.

On September 5, Christopher drove with Sam From to spend the evening in Santa Barbara. I think this was the occasion on which Sam was so drunk that he made a swerve off the Pacific Coast Highway just after they had left the Canyon and very nearly turned his open convertible right over. Christopher was lucky—for Sam was a frequently drunk driver and this might well have been a fatal wreck. Sam finally got killed in a collision which was agreed to have been entirely his fault.

On September 14, the day-to-day diary records that Bob Craft, Eduard Steuermann (Salka Viertel's brother) and someone named Dahl "went through" the text of Schoenberg's *Pierrot lunaire* with Christopher. I do remember that Bob had proposed to Christopher that he should speak the "speech-song" at a performance some-where, and Christopher had agreed. But the performance never took place. Maybe the musicians decided that Christopher's voice wasn't right for the part.[*]

On the night of either September 16 or 17, one of the sycamore trees near the house suddenly fell. I remember that Christopher woke abruptly, about half a minute before this happened. Later—maybe in order to intrigue Gerald Heard, who loved all things extrasensory—he ascribed his waking to precognition; but it is more likely that Christopher had been woken by a preliminary cracking sound; such a sound, in the dead of night, could be quite as loud as a gunshot. The tree narrowly missed the house. If it had hit, it would probably have staved in the roof.

Mentioning the fall of the tree reminds me that the sycamores quite often dropped their limbs and occasionally did serious damage. It must have been about this time that Christopher happened to be looking out of the window when a big branch fell from one of the trees on the other side of the road. Its fall was broken by some lower branches, otherwise it would have hit the house below it. Even so, it was a serious menace, because the next strong wind would almost

[* Robert Craft conducted *Pierrot lunaire* in New York the following October, but recalls asking Isherwood for help only with possibly improving the translation made by Ingolf Dahl (1912–1970), a composer and refugee who was a close friend of Stravinsky. According to Craft, the speaking part for Isherwood would have been in Stravinsky's *The Flood*, much later, in 1962.]

certainly shake it loose. Christopher therefore immediately crossed the road and rang the doorbell of the threatened house. The woman who lived there opened the door and he explained to her what had happened. This was the first time he had ever spoken to her. She didn't seem at all grateful to him. On the contrary, her manner was hostile and suspicious, as if she were thinking, "*Why* is he telling me this? What's he *really* want?"

Some weeks later, Christopher was visited by one of his neighbors, who told him that this woman was psychotic and a threat to the whole community. "I'm going to get something on each one of them," she was alleged to have said, and she kept reporting her suspicions to the police. She had gone all the way down to Balboa in the hope of discovering that a man she knew was keeping a sailboat there without a license. She had accused Mrs. Macdonald of running an unauthorized insane asylum, because Mrs. Macdonald had a son who was mentally retarded. She had complained that an orgy was going on in a nearby house; when the police arrived, it turned out to be a child's birthday party. "As for you, Mr. Isherwood," Christopher's informant added, giggling nervously, "she claims you are a *homosexual*! There was a police car watching your house for a couple of hours, the other night." "They'll have to watch a lot longer than that," Christopher said, grinning feebly but turning very pale. He willingly signed a petition which the neighbors had drawn up, appealing to the district attorney to ignore this woman's accusations.

Not long after this, she suddenly left the neighborhood.

On September 18, the day-to-day diary makes its first mention of a project undertaken by Speed Lamkin and Gus Field; an adaptation of Christopher's *Sally Bowles* for the stage. Gus Field was a screenwriter. I think Christopher had met him while they were both working at MGM. He was youngish, curly haired, and not bad looking; Jewishly self-assertive, full of stories about himself in the air force and himself in bed with girls, but anxious to be friendly and helpful. He was a fairly competent writer, but he cluttered his scripts with instructions about shots and camera angles which were nothing but show-off and must have irritated his director. He and Speed made an odd couple. Probably Gus, who must have been snubbed by many of his colleagues, liked associating with queers because he felt that they were lower than himself in the pecking order. He could treat them with indulgent amusement. But he was also smart enough to realize that Speed was smarter and that Speed could introduce him to some celebrities. As for Speed, he had accepted Gus as a professional who could teach him the tricks of dramaturgy. Aside from this, he looked down on Gus as a kike.

The two of them now came to Christopher to discuss their ideas about the play. Speed, of course, did most of the talking and assumed credit, without actually claiming it, for all the ideas. Of these, I remember only two—one of them truly daring and symbolic in the best theatrical sense, the other minor but amusing. Christopher was amazed when he heard them. He hadn't been taking the Lamkin–Field collaboration seriously; now he was forced to respect it and encourage it.

The major idea was as follows:

When the curtain rises, Christopher is discovered in his Berlin room. It is a narrow set occupying only the front part of the stage. From behind the wall at the back of this set we hear the sounds of a large noisy party. They annoy Christopher, who is trying to work. Then Sally, whom he hasn't met before, comes in, introduces herself as the party giver and his next-door neighbor and asks if he can lend her any glasses. Christopher is quickly charmed out of his hostility. They are joined by some of Sally's friends. Christopher is given drinks. Then Sally points out that her room and his room are actually the halves of one big room which has been divided by a somewhat flimsy partition wall. There'd be more space for them all to dance, she says, if they could have the whole room as it originally was. Christopher is getting drunk by this time and he declares that he'll tear the wall down. Sally and her guests volunteer to help him and they start to do so as the curtain falls.

In the next scene, Christopher wakes out of a drunken sleep to find that the wall is down; nothing is left of it but a pile of rubble. Sally lies in her bed on the other side of the big room. Christopher is horrified at first, then amused. Sally tells him that they're both going to be much happier this way and Christopher accepts the fact that he is now irrevocably involved in Sally's life.

The minor idea was that at some point well along in the first act, after Sally and most of the other important characters have been introduced and a dialogue between several of them is in progress, there is a knock on the door. Christopher crosses to it and opens it. A girl stands there. We haven't seen her before. Christopher looks embarrassed. "Look," he tells her, "I'm terribly busy. In fact, I'm going to be busy for quite a while. I'll give you a call, as soon as I can." The girl nods and turns sadly away. Christopher shuts the door. "Who was that?" Sally asks. "Oh—that's my girlfriend." "But, Chris, I never knew you had a girlfriend! Why didn't you tell me? You're so mysterious. You never tell me anything about yourself."

Christopher smiles: "I've never had a chance to. You've been telling me about *your*self ever since we met!" Throughout the rest of the play, the girl never reappears. She isn't even referred to.

Tennessee Williams and Frank Merlo had arrived in town and were staying at the Bel Air Hotel, because Tennessee was polishing the script of *A Streetcar Named Desire* which was about to start shooting, with Marlon Brando and Vivien Leigh. Christopher saw Tennessee and Frank several times—they came by for drinks on September 17, they gave a party at their hotel on the 21st, Frank Merlo went with Christopher to visit Caskey at the Santa Ana jail on the 23rd, they came by for drinks again on the 24th, they gave a supper on the 26th which included Kazan, Brando, William Saroyan and Christopher. The next day, Christopher drove them to the airport. This was a visit of which I have very happy memories. Tennessee and Frank were at their best. The party at the hotel was wildly lavish, because Tennessee had contracted with the studio to do this polishing job for expenses only. The studio probably ended by regretting its bargain. Not only did the drinks flow in torrents but each guest was urged to take whole cases of liquor away with him.

Christopher also enjoyed meeting Brando, although his first impressions were bad. Brando seemed to Christopher to be just another young ham giving himself airs. He was talking about Vivien Leigh, with whom he'd spent the whole afternoon, waiting to be called onto the set for a take. And now he gravely announced: "I don't think she's very sincere." This was too much for Christopher. "My God, Mr. Brando," he exclaimed, "how sincere do you think *you'll* be, when you've been in this business as long as she has?!" But, to Christopher's surprise and pleasure, Brando wasn't either offended or crushed. He grinned at Christopher appreciatively, as much as to say, "Good for you—we understand each other!" What Christopher understood at that moment—or thought he did—was that Brando was capable of high camp and that most of his public behavior was probably camping. As for Brando's private behavior and his private self, I'm no wiser about that now than Christopher was then; I've never gotten even a glimpse.

Brando did confer a mark of his favor upon Christopher—or maybe it was merely a test. A few days later, Christopher returned home to find Brando sitting in the living room with a girl; they were eating sandwiches they had made from food in Christopher's kitchen and drinking his beer. Christopher was astonished but also flattered by this bold act of intimacy, and he did everything to make them feel at home. But the visit wasn't repeated, and it was quite a long time before he saw Brando again.

On October 3 and again on October 6, Christopher went with James Agee to John Huston's ranch in the San Fernando Valley where Huston was directing *The Red Badge of Courage* for MGM. On the 6th, Frank Taylor and Donald Pell came along too. Audie Murphy was starring in the picture. Christopher got to say only a few words to Murphy but watched him a lot of the time. Murphy fascinated Christopher, not only because he was still boyishly attractive but because he appeared to be such a mixed-up and potentially dangerous character. Christopher liked to imagine that Murphy had won all his decorations for bravery as the result of his fury and shame at being The Prettiest Boy in Texas. No doubt his buddies had kidded him about his baby face, and Murphy, being too small to lick them, had gone into action and killed every German within sight. But this, and the subsequent honors, hadn't made him feel any better, apparently; for he was still amazingly aggressive. Whenever he wasn't actually in front of the camera, he kept playing practical jokes on his fellow actors. These jokes weren't fun, they were full of hostility and the object of them, clearly, was to provoke their victims to fight. Since Murphy was The Star, and also smaller, the other actors were unwilling to tangle with him; but he usually managed to annoy them into doing so. When they did, Murphy fought back in deadly earnest. His face was grim, and he looked capable of pulling a knife. Most people seemed a bit afraid of him. Christopher got the impression that he was thoroughly unpopular.

John Huston was Murphy's opposite—large, charming, popular, relaxed. (He was also a far greater and deadlier monster than Murphy could ever be.) On this picture, Huston was so relaxed that he actually sat chatting with Christopher under a tree while his assistant director shot one of the battle scenes.

Everybody agreed that he was wonderful with the actors, especially the bit players. Christopher himself witnessed an impressive demonstration of his patience with one of them—I have probably got the circumstances of the script story wrong here, but this is what happened: The troops have just succeeded in driving the enemy from a position on a wooded hill. They are feeling very pleased with themselves, especially those of them who have been in action for the first time. And then a soldier comes out of the woods. He is dazed and shaken. They tell him that he just missed the battle. He answers that the real battle was on the other side of the hill. They are amazed and disappointed.

When Huston directed the first take of this scene, everything went well until the actor who played the soldier appeared. He blew up on his line. Huston told him not to worry, to take his time. They shot the scene right through again. Again the actor blew up. He apologized profusely. Huston said never mind, they had the whole morning. He suggested a simplified version of the line. The actor assured Huston that he could do it. He was trembling and sweating. He blew up for the third time. Huston remained imperturbable. They did a fourth take. The actor managed to get the line out correctly, though in a strangled, unnatural voice. Huston put an arm around his shoulder and led him away, soothing him as though he were a frightened horse.

As an expert horseman, Huston had a specially close relationship with the stunt riders on the picture. They were extra eager to please him. Christopher was standing at Huston's side, near to the camera, when one man had to mime being shot dead at full gallop. The cameraman had drawn a smallish circle with a stick in the dirt, only a few yards away from where they were standing; this was where the stunt rider's body was to hit the ground. It was a breathtaking performance. Christopher had to restrain himself with a conscious effort of will from instinctively jumping aside as the horse came thundering toward them. Then Huston gave the signal. The rider registered the impact of the imaginary bullet and rose in the stirrups, clutching himself; his well-trained horse swerved to avoid the camera. The rider crashed from the saddle and landed with stunning force—only just outside the circle. The next instant, he had jumped to his feet, breathless and apologetic: "Sorry, Mr. Huston—it won't happen again—I slipped!"[1]

In addition to Audie Murphy, there was another famous war veteran acting in the picture: Bill Mauldin the cartoonist. Like Murphy, Mauldin was still boyishly cute, in a charming monkeyish way. Unlike Murphy—perhaps because he had never had to be a hero—he was relaxed and friendly. He spent most of his free time with his wife. When he was looking for her, after a take, he wandered around exclaiming, in a theatrical southern accent, "Where's ma bride?"

Christopher watched a big scene in which Murphy and Mauldin were in the center of the front line during an attack. The whole area over which they were to advance was mined with small explosive charges wired for detonation. It was the assistant director's job to see that these explosions occurred as near as possible to the actors without injuring them. (If you were right on top of an explosion

---

[1] Someone, I forget who, recently told me at a party that stunt riders often make bad falls deliberately, because they are paid a prearranged amount for each fall, good or bad. Huston undoubtedly knew this. He probably tolerated such cheating good humoredly, unless the stuntman overdid it.

you could get burned.) When the cameras started to turn, Murphy and Mauldin, with the caution of seasoned soldiers, advanced very slowly, keeping their distance from the mini-mines which were bursting ahead of them. The nearest extras on either side naturally followed their example. But, meanwhile, the extras out on the wings —not near enough to the stars to realize what they were doing and aware only that they themselves were attacking under the eye of John Huston—rushed forward recklessly. So the front line became an in-curving crescent. This annoyed the assistant director. He yelled to the center to catch up. Murphy and Mauldin ignored him. The assistant director was obliged to detonate charges immediately *behind* the two of them, as near as he dared, to get them running.

(The memory of this absurd situation didn't prevent Christopher from being moved deeply and shedding tears when he saw the photographed and edited scene, long afterwards, on the screen.)

Jim Agee, big, handsome, sentimentally alcoholic, terribly anxious to be liked, was around most of the time. He made a hero of Huston and eagerly, indeed desperately, tried to keep up with Huston in any activity or amusement which he proposed. It was said that Huston would be the death of Agee, who had a weak heart and a poor constitution generally; Huston was always getting him to come riding or play tennis or sit up drinking half the night. Actually he didn't die until 1955.

Also present at the filming during Christopher's visits was Lillian Ross, a journalist on the staff of *The New Yorker* who had come out to California to cover the production of the picture. Christopher was already strongly prejudiced against her because of the profile of Hemingway she had written for her magazine, earlier that year. Rereading it now (March 1974), I find it only mildly distasteful—it was an early specimen of a style of journalism to which I have since then become accustomed. Lillian Ross, in her preface to the profile when it was published in book form, says that, "I attempted to set down only what I had seen and heard, and not to comment on the facts or express any opinions or pass any judgements. . . . I liked Hemingway exactly as he was, and I'm content if my Profile caught him exactly as he was during those two days in New York."[*] What Ross means by catching Hemingway exactly as he was is that she has attempted an absolutely faithful reproduction of Hemingway's dialogue, gestures and physical appearance. But the written word is inadequate if you try to use it in this way—writing is impressionistic, subjective, conceptual—and the effect that Ross was trying for can

[* *Portrait of Hemingway*, 1961.]

only be achieved with a movie camera. What I get from her profile now is boredom, irritation. Everything she tells about Hemingway is irrelevant. She never comes near him. But Christopher, reading it in 1950, felt that Hemingway was being sneered at and cheapened by a creature of the New York gutter.

He was therefore coldly polite to Ross when he met her. Ross melted him somewhat by her intelligence and considerable charm but he didn't altogether relent, even when he found that she was one of his fans and had brought a book of his to be signed. He wrote in it, "For Lillian Ross, on condition that she never writes about me." This startled, hurt and also intrigued her. Later they talked about many things and got along well together. But she kept returning to the subject of the profile and defending herself energetically. Finally, at a party given by Tim Durant on October 8, Christopher got drunk and condemned her in the words of the St. Matthew Gospel: ". . . it must needs be that offenses come; but woe to that man by whom the offense cometh!"[*] They parted as fairly good friends, however.

On October 21, after visiting Caskey at the Santa Ana jail, Christopher drove with Donald Pell to stay at the AJC Ranch (I imagine John van Druten must have been there, though the day-to-day diary doesn't say so); the next day, they visited the mud pots on the Salton Sea (these are described in *Down There on a Visit*) and returned to Los Angeles via Julian and Mount Palomar. Christopher was taking Donald Pell around with him quite a lot, just then, so I suppose he must have found him an amusing companion. But I remember nothing that Donald did or said. The only incident which remains with me from their trip happened on the road to Lake Elsinore, en route for the AJC Ranch. A dead sidewinder was lying across the road. Christopher stopped the car, got out and was about to pick the snake up by the tail and toss it into the ditch—chiefly to impress Donald, who was timid. But now another car stopped and a young man and a girl got out. The young man—probably wanting to impress *her*—picked up the sidewinder by its neck, squeezed its poison glands so that the poison squirted out onto the road, then produced a pocket knife and removed its fangs from its jaw, wiping them clean on his pants leg, then put the fangs into his billfold, remarked to Christopher and Donald, "They bring good luck," got back into his car followed by the shuddering girl, and drove away.

The Sadler's Wells Ballet was then in town. Christopher went to see it on October 19, with Iris Tree and Ivan and Natasha Moffat. On the 23rd, Moira Shearer, Freddy Ashton, Alexis Rassine and

[* Matthew 18:7.]

Moira's husband, Ludovic Kennedy, came to see Christopher, and then they all went to a party given for the ballet by the van Leydens. I think this was the season the ballet did *The Sleeping Beauty*, in which Freddy played the Wicked Fairy in marvellous drag. He was carried onto the stage in a sedan chair, by two dancers dressed as mice. Freddy told Christopher that it never mattered how drunk he was—as soon as the mice had helped him out of the chair and onto his feet, he could always get through his dance. If he fell down, the audience loved it and laughed all the harder. And, if he showed signs of passing out altogether, the mice would simply bundle him back into the chair and remove him. Freddy was a wonderfully happy person. He loved his life.

On October 27, Caskey was released from the Santa Ana jail. Christopher drove down there and brought him home.

Two days later, Christopher became ill. He was sick in bed for seven days—from October 30 through November 5 (when Swami visited him). At that period of his life, prolonged illness was very unusual for Christopher—so unusual that I suspect a psychosomatic cause. Was Christopher trying either to punish Caskey for his past behavior or to appeal for sympathy to Caskey's nanny persona? Maybe both. I can't now even remember what his physical symptoms were, but I think one of them was a numbness in the legs. John van Druten had suffered from a similar numbness and had been told by his doctor that he had "senile polio"—that is to say, a variety of polio which only afflicts elderly people and is never severe enough to cause paralysis. Christopher was a copycat with regard to his friends' ailments. Later on, he used to reproduce Jo Masselink's.

Before taking to his bed, Christopher had seen Dr. Kolisch on October 24, and Kolisch came to see him again on November 1. It may have been on one of these occasions that Kolisch gave Christopher the most memorable piece of medical advice he has ever received: "You have the kind of constitution which is capable of simulating every species of pathological condition. So I would urge you, never consult a doctor again, as long as you live. It will only be necessary once—and then it will be too late."

On November 7 and again on November 10—after spending another day in bed in between—Christopher went househunting with Caskey. I suppose that Mrs. Strasberg had refused to renew the lease of 333 East Rustic Road. Evidently they didn't like any of the houses they saw in the Santa Monica area. I can't remember how it came about that they decided, later that same month, to leave Los

Angeles altogether and settle in Laguna Beach. On November 25, they drove down to Laguna and were shown houses by Alan Walker, a friend of theirs, who was a real estate agent. I think they must have made up their minds about one of them, that same day—for they signed a lease on it three days later.

On November 30, Speed Lamkin and Gus Field came to talk about their Sally Bowles play. Later, Speed took Christopher and Caskey to have dinner with Marion Davies. This visit is described in the journal. Christopher was impressed by the prisonlike atmosphere of the house—your drinks were served to you by uniformed, armed cops; by the gold plate on the sideboard; by the heavily felt presence of nonpresent Hearst, now bedridden and referred to as "the Man Upstairs"; by the paranoid-fascist conversation of two men from the New York headquarters of some Hearst publication; by the little office dominated by a portrait of General MacArthur—from which, according to Speed, the whole Hearst empire was controlled; and also, most of all by Davies herself.[1]

After supper, when the New Yorkers had been called upstairs to see Hearst, Davies took Christopher, Speed and Caskey into the office. She was very drunk now and wanted to dance. She did the splits, over and over again, to the music of "Baby, It's Cold Outside." Her legs parted without effort, like an open banana skin, but, once down on her sacrum, she was helpless and had to be hauled giggling to her feet by her partners. They kept this up until 3:30 a.m., when her nurse, who had been reading, all this while, in a dressing room adjoining one of the downstair toilets, appeared and led Davies off to bed.

Speed revelled in all this. Christopher says in the journal:

He adores this smell of power, in a sort of Balzacian way. With his vulgarity, snobbery and naive appetite for display, he might well become a minor Balzac of Hollywood. There is something about him I rather like, or at any rate find touching. He is so crude and vulnerable, and not malicious, I think. He reminds me of Paul Sorel, but he is much more intelligent; and he has energy and talent.

On December 5, Caskey and Christopher drove to Laguna and spent their first night in the new house. It was in South Laguna, actually—number 31152 on Monterey Street, which wound around

---

[1] "Marion Davies, thin, pink, raddled, with luxuriant dead-looking fair hair, very innocent blue eyes, came in drunk. One wanted to say, like a Shakespearian character: 'Alack, poor lady. . . .' She stumbled a little and had to be helped to her chair; but she made a lot of sense, and talked seriously to the two men about business." [*D1*, p. 432.]

the hillside above the Coast Highway, looking down on Camel Point and the beach below it. You could get to the beach much more directly on foot, by a narrow downhill trail. High above was the modernistic house built for Richard Halliburton, the madcap explorer, shortly before his death. This part of Laguna was sleepy and sparsely inhabited in those days especially during the winter months.

Number 31152, like its neighbors, was built in country-cottage style, with a disproportionately long garden sloping down rather steeply to the road. (The houses on the opposite side of Monterey Street stood so much lower that you could see right over them, out to the ocean horizon.) During World War II, several whores had lived at 31152 and had entertained service men there. Caskey felt that this had given the place "a party atmosphere."[1]

The rest of December was spent in moving into the Monterey Street house. This required several trips back and forth. On December 15, they brought Christopher's books down to Laguna in the station wagon; the books were so heavy that a tire blew out, near Newport Beach. On the 22nd, they rented a truck and brought down the furniture. (This was chiefly furniture given to Caskey by his mother. 31152 was partially furnished by its owner, as 333 had been.) After this, Caskey made two more trips to Santa Monica, on the 27th and the 29th, to collect the last of their belongings from 333. So they weren't completely established at 31152 until just before New Year's Eve. Hayden Lewis and Rod Owens came down to spend it and New Year's Day with them.[2]

---

[1] Christopher wrote in the journal on December 11:

> I like this house, despite its knotty pine walls, because it fits into a picture I have of the atmosphere of "Old Laguna"—the original colony of third-rate watercolorists, mild eccentrics, British expatriate ladies who ran "Scottish" tea shops, astrologers, breeders of poodles, all kinds of refugees from American city life. Also, this whole area of small houses, gardens of flowering shrubs and sheltered winter sunshine, sandy lanes winding up and down the steep hillside, takes me back to early memories of Penmaenmawr [Wales] and Ventnor [Isle of Wight]. I have an agreeable feeling of having come to the very last western edge of America, looking out over the pale bright Pacific—much cleaner than at Santa Monica—with nothing between me and Catalina but mist and a huge telephone pole.

(The islands of Catalina (opposite) and Clemente (to the south) figured largely in the seascape. You could also see the Palos Verdes headland (to the northwest) on a clear day, and beyond it, on a clear night, some of the lights of Los Angeles.)

[2] Among the books Christopher read in 1950, I chiefly remember the ones he reviewed and/or was reading for the second time: *The Martian Chronicles*;

1951

The December 11 journal entry, from which I've already quoted [in note 1, page 274], contains resolves by Christopher to make a new start with Caskey. And Caskey himself was working hard to fix up the house. I have one endearing memory of him at this time: they had brought down an icebox from somewhere and there it stood outside the back door, seemingly too large to be moved into the

---

F. M. Ford's *Parade's End* (he had read only part of this before); [Spender's] *World Within World*; *H. G. Wells—Prophet of Our Day*, by Antonina Vallentin; Masefield's *Multitude and Solitude*. Out of the rest of them, Calder Willingham's *Geraldine Bradshaw* made a dazzling impression, it seemed a masterpiece of comedy, but I haven't yet reread it. *Nothing*, by Henry Green, isn't among my absolute favorites; I prefer *Living*, *Loving* and *Doting*. Eliot's [The] *Cocktail Party* slightly nauseates me, good as it is. I find *Venus Observed*—and the few other Christopher Fry plays I've read—piss-elegant posing. Christopher enjoyed [Thor Heyerdahl's] *The Kon-Tiki Expedition*, but mostly because it is about the South Pacific. *Homage to Catalonia* (which I think Christopher must have read before) is certainly a noble book; I honor grim old Orwell far more than I enjoy him. The same with Lowell Naeve's *A Field of Broken Stones*. *Miss Lonelyhearts*—that's a different matter; I neither honor nor enjoy Nathanael West. William Goyen's *The House of Breath* and Donald Windham's *The Dog Star* are both of them remembered as crypto-queer trifles, though I believe Christopher wrote blurbs for them. James Barr's *Quatrefoil* is at least honest fag-trash. [Tennessee Williams's] *The Roman Spring of Mrs. Stone* is trash too, but of the sort which can only be produced by a great dramatic poet. *A Drama in Muslin* is very minor George Moore, but I love Moore now as Christopher did then, dearly. I remember liking William Cooper's *Scenes from Provincial Life* quite a lot but not quite enough; it was typical of the sort of novel the Beesleys really loved. They had recommended it to Christopher. Christopher admired Gerald Sykes's *The Quiet American* [sic, Sykes's book was *The Nice American*; Graham Greene's more famous title appeared in 1955] and wrote a big blurb for it—but something tells me I'll never reread it. And then there was Connolly's *The Unquiet Grave*—this must surely have been Christopher's second reading of it. Connolly's most maddening, snobbish book and, for that very reason, his most fascinating and self-revealing. And it contains a passage which I keep quoting to myself:

> . . . the true function of a writer is to produce a masterpiece . . . no other task is of any consequence. Obvious though this should be, how few writers will admit it, or having made the admission, will be prepared to lay aside the piece of iridescent mediocrity on which they have embarked! Writers always hope that their next book is going to be their best, for they will not acknowledge that it is their present way of life which prevents them from ever creating anything different or better.

house through that entrance. Caskey sent Christopher away, saying, "I have to get furious with it before I can do it." He looked very small and the icebox looked very big. But, when Christopher returned half an hour later, there it was in position, inside the kitchen.

During the first two weeks of January, Christopher worked on a review [for *Tomorrow*] of the Robert Louis Stevenson omnibus published by Random House. On January 12, they bought a Ford Anglia and sold their station wagon. The Anglia seemed cramped at first, but it was sturdily built and never gave them any trouble. Christopher later described it to Iris Tree as "a very loyal little car."

On January 13, [a friend] came down to stay, bringing with him an actor [. . .] with whom he was having an affair. [This actor's] chief claim to fame was that he looked very much like [a certain film star]. When [the star] died [. . .] leaving his role in the film [he was then making] unfinished, [the little-known actor] was used to represent [the star]—mostly with his back to the camera—in the scenes which remained to be shot.

That evening they probably all drank a lot. Hangovers often gave Christopher a kind of feverish vitality. Waking up early, he ran down to the beach and swam in the ocean for the first time that year. When he got back to the house, he went into the guest room and found [his friend] and [the actor] naked in one of the bunk beds, making love. [The friend] suggested that Christopher should strip and climb in too. The ever-randy [friend] was all ready for more sex, although he had just had an orgasm with [the actor]. [The actor] excused himself, saying that he was pooped and couldn't come again. He was very much in love with [Christopher's friend], so maybe he was jealous that [the friend] should want to have Christopher. [The friend], no doubt, was just showing off. Christopher found [his friend] unattractive but he fancied [the actor] and it made him wildly excited to do this in [the actor's] presence. The bed was narrow, and Christopher, as he writhed naked in [his friend's] arms, kept managing to rub against [the actor's] naked body lying beside them. (I don't quite trust this memory. I suspect that it may be partly fantasy. It's much more probable that [the actor] retired to his own bed before [Christopher and his friend] started doing whatever they did to each other.)

On January 17, the day-to-day diary notes that Caskey and Christopher "got air raid information." I don't know exactly what this was. Instructions for taking shelter, cutting off the gas at the main, laying in a supply of food suitable for sustaining life during a period of fallout? Anyhow, it is a reminder of those H-bomb-minded, Russian-menaced times.

On January 21, Speed Lamkin and Gus Field came down for the day. They and Christopher discussed their play *Sally Bowles*. The first draft of it was finished.

On January 28, Christopher finished his review of Spender's *World Within World* for *Tomorrow*.

On February 1, Christopher drove to Los Angeles for the day and had another discussion with Speed Lamkin and Gus Field about the Sally Bowles play. During the next eight days, Christopher worked on his novel, lay on the beach, helped Caskey entertain various visitors, was painted by Paul Sorel (so was Caskey) and went to Camille's, the chief local gay bar. On February 10, he drove to Los Angeles, had another play discussion with Speed and Gus and then spent the night at the Hartford Foundation. The day-to-day diary mentions that Mike Leopold, Chester Aarons, Dick LaPan and Leonard Culbrow were there. No doubt Christopher took the opportunity of going to bed with Mike. Next day, Christopher saw his boyhood friend Patrick Monkhouse, who was in Los Angeles on business, probably, for *The Manchester Guardian*. (See pages 90-91.) I don't remember anything about this encounter except the mood of it, which was polite embarrassed goodwill. . . . Oh yes, it comes back to me that Paddy made some remark which he evidently thought was tactless because it might seem to refer to Christopher's homosexuality. He blushed and tried to excuse himself. Christopher, who hadn't detected any such reference, didn't know how to reassure him.

On February 18, while Christopher was in Los Angeles for the weekend, he had lunch with Dodie and Alec Beesley and they discussed the Lamkin–Field Sally Bowles play. Dodie wasn't much impressed by it. She felt that the breaking down of the wall, which Christopher so much liked, would be unworkable in actual performance. It was perhaps at this time that Dodie and Alec began to feel that something must be done to set Christopher free from his commitment to Speed and Gus.

The large thin notebook has its first entry for the year on February 20. Christopher has now written a rough draft of the first four chapters. The opening of the novel is more or less what it will be in the finished version, but Christopher is still planning to include a big group of refugee characters and is still worrying about how he shall relate them to each other and to Stephen Monk.

On February 25, Christopher drove to Los Angeles and spent the night at the Hartford Foundation. Next day, he had tea at the Vedanta Center with Aldous Huxley and Alan Watts. The meeting between Watts and Swami Prabhavananda wasn't a success—at least, not from Christopher's point of view. My memory of it is vague however and Christopher's disapproval of Watts at that time—later, Christopher got to like him—is expressed by a mental picture of Watts's yellow teeth, flavored with bad nicotine breath.

Christopher's first journal entry of the year, on March 6, consists of self-reproaches and complaints. "I'm dull and wretched, so weary of my stupid aging slothful self in its alienation from God. It comes to me, again and again, how I have deteriorated into a dull-witted selfish useless creature. . . . Swami stands ready to help me if I'll even raise one finger. But I won't. I won't go to live at Trabuco." (However, despite this talk about sloth, Christopher had finished chapter four of his novel a few days earlier.) These moanings are followed by the old complaints about Caskey—how he comes home at all hours, brings people home with him and disturbs Christopher's work.

In the middle of March it turned warm and they went swimming, which no doubt temporarily relieved the tension. (Talking of swimming and warm weather reminds me of an incident which I can't date. It happened on a cold day—during a weekend, probably—when Christopher, Caskey and a party of friends had a big drunken lunch and then went for a walk on the beach, fully dressed. Christopher was in a characteristic, half clownish, half hostile mood. He let the others go on ahead, sat down on the sand and stared at the ocean. Then an idea came to him—it might have been inspired by an illustration to some nineteenth-century novel: a shore in winter, cold rough waves, deserted beach, a clothed, drowned body rolling in the surf. . . . When Caskey and their friends returned, Christopher was awash, face downward in the water, in his leather jacket and shirt and corduroys. The guests were suitably startled, but Caskey said with his comical grin, "Ignore him," and led them up the path to the house, leaving Christopher to follow in his drenched clothes. He was warm with alcohol and didn't catch a chill.)

On March 14, Christopher mentions that he is working on a "story about Basil Fry"; this was maybe his first attempt to write what became "Mr. Lancaster" in *Down There on a Visit*. On the 17th Christopher finished chapter two of the annotated translation of Patanjali's yoga aphorisms. On the 18th and 19th, he was in town, staying the night at the Hartford Foundation, where he saw Speed Lamkin, who had just arrived. I think that one of Speed's chief motives for coming to live at the foundation was that he wanted to get to know Christopher better and adopt him as his Elder Friend, which indeed he quickly did.

On the 24th, Christopher and Caskey went to a party at the

Chaplins'. This was the first time they had visited the Chaplins in nearly ten months. It was to be their last meeting. (See pages 233-234.)

On the 25th (Easter Day) Christopher and Bill were back in Laguna. Steve (see page 32) came down to see them with his latest lover, Jack Garber.[*] Steve didn't seem much changed and Christopher still felt affectionate toward him. Jack Garber was a good-looking blond boy, whom Christopher found attractive but a bit pretentious. There seemed to be tension between him and Steve; the relationship didn't look as if it would last long.

After supper they left, to drive back to Los Angeles. Then, very much later, Lennie Newman arrived. By this time, Bill was snoring in bed, drunkenly asleep. But Christopher, also in bed (have I ever mentioned that he and Bill had separate beds in the same room?), heard the knocking and got up to let Lennie in. Christopher had been drinking all evening. Lennie, no doubt, was drunk as usual. As usual, they hugged and kissed. But then the unusual began to happen. Kissing prolonged itself into tongue kissing. Their hands moved down each other's bodies and started to grope buttocks and loins and cocks. Christopher, who slept in the raw, was naked already underneath the bathrobe he had put on to greet Lennie. He merely had to throw it off.

Meanwhile, when already well on his way to Los Angeles, Steve had found that he must have left his wallet behind at Monterey Street—I forget how or why. Back they had to drive. Getting no answer when they knocked, they came in—to find the lights on in the living room and bedroom, Caskey still asleep in one bed, Christopher and Lennie lying naked on the other—Lennie on his belly, with Christopher on top, fucking him. Christopher and Lennie talked to them while they looked for and found the wallet, but Christopher didn't withdraw his cock from Lennie's asshole and continued the fuck in low gear, with deep slow thrusts which Lennie countered with movements of his buttocks. When Steve and Jack Garber had left again, the fuck gathered speed to its climax.

(Christopher's exhibitionism, in making love to Lennie in the presence of Steve and Jack Garber, is strangely paralleled—now I come to think of it—by the party at Denny Fouts's apartment on June 3, 1945 (see page 35) at which Willy Tompkins and the lieutenant had sex in public and [one of the guests] urged Christopher to do likewise with him. I don't know how Steve was affected, if at all, by seeing Christopher fuck Lennie. Jack Garber was rather turned on. He later wrote to Christopher, telling him that he

[* Not his real name.]

was "a Triton amongst the minnows"—which was certainly intended as a compliment and not as a reference to the line in *Coriolanus* III: i.[*])

Lennie was so agreeably surprised by Christopher's performance as a sex partner that he told Caskey and other friends about it. Christopher was equally pleased, but not particularly surprised, to find that Lennie was a marvellous lay. All his natural sweetness, his wholesomeness, even the positive aspect of his Mormon upbringing was expressed in his sex play. As a fuckee, he couldn't have been less passive; he was yin with the maximum of energy and cooperation. He had developed such control of his sphincter muscle that he could massage and milk his partner's cock most excitingly.[1]

Christopher had had a motive for going to bed with Lennie, but he only became aware of this after he had done it. He had always been a bit jealous of Lennie, much as he liked him, because Caskey's friendship with Lennie seemed so exclusive. Lennie was the companion whom Caskey usually chose when he wanted to get away from Christopher and go off on a binge. By going to bed with Lennie, Christopher cured himself of his jealousy in the best possible way. Now Lennie and he had a relationship of their own. This didn't mean that they had to keep having sex together—they only did it once again—or even that they saw much more of each other than before. But now there was a real lasting warmth between them. Caskey didn't in the least resent this.

On March 31, Bill Caskey started a gardening job, according to the day-to-day diary. I don't remember anything about this.

April was a seemingly uneventful month which nevertheless brought Christopher much nearer to the climax with Caskey. He struggled on with the novel—"this horrible bitch of a book," as he

---

[1] In connection with this, I have a memory which is very vivid but which I suspect slightly, simply because I can't find any reference to it in the day-to-day diary. Jim Charlton came to spend the night at Monterey Street, not long after Christopher's fuck with Lennie. In the morning Jim walked into Christopher's and Caskey's bedroom, naked, with a hard-on. Caskey was asleep. Jim grinned at Christopher, lifted him naked out of bed and carried him out of the room and into the guest bedroom. This was a typical specimen of Jim's he-man camp; Christopher found it funny but also sexually exciting. He wanted Jim to fuck him, and, when Jim started to, Christopher began flexing and unflexing his sphincter muscle in imitation of Lennie Newman. It was an amateur performance but it impressed Jim. "Where did you learn that whore trick, for Christ's sake?" he growled. The fuck was a huge success.

[* "Hear you this Triton of the minnows?" with which Coriolanus scoffs at the people's tribune, Sicinius.]

calls it in the large thin notebook on March 28. He drove to Los Angeles on April 21 and stayed two nights at the Huntington Hartford Foundation. He saw the people he usually saw—Jo and Ben Masselink, Peggy Kiskadden (with whom he still maintained a surface friendship although, underneath, they thoroughly disapproved of each other), Dodie and Alec Beesley, Frank Taylor, Speed Lamkin. Caskey, meanwhile, went off on his own. I seem to remember he had a particular buddy amongst the marines and was actually able to spend nights at Camp Pendleton. Maybe they had guest rooms for relatives and friends.

As usual, various acquaintances and sex mates (of Caskey chiefly) came by for drinks or meals or to stay the night. The nicest of the sex mates was a herculean boy [. . .], a navy frogman, stationed at San Diego, who had been over to Korea several times, where he had taken part in dangerous underwater missions, attaching mines to enemy ships in harbor, etc. He had an unusually sweet, gentle nature. His way of introducing himself to you was to get you into bed with him. When he came to the house he went to bed with Bill, Christopher and any of their guests who were available; and he made them all love him a little.

Talking of love—it was probably during this month that Caskey made a declaration to Christopher. I can only recall that it was made in their bedroom. As so often, the memory of Christopher's emotional reaction is related to an object or objects. In this case, Christopher is looking at the bureau and the mirror above it while he hears Caskey say, "I'm not in love with you anymore. I've been in love with you for a long time, but now it's over."

I suppose Caskey meant by this that he no longer felt romantically toward Christopher. He probably said so in order to counteract Christopher's tendency to express insincere sentiments. Christopher, at that time, really rather hated Caskey but he wouldn't admit to it. Whereas Caskey, I think, never wavered—never has wavered—in his love for Christopher. He wanted Christopher to admit, now, that *he* wasn't any longer in love with Caskey. I don't believe he made his declaration in order to cause a permanent break between them, or even to stop Christopher wanting to have sex with him now and then. Caskey, as he later proved, continued to want to have sex with Christopher when he was in the mood. Quite possibly, however, Caskey was beginning to feel that he would like to get right away from Christopher for a longish spell. (Not long after they split up, he decided to go to sea.) After that, he was ready to resume a loving friendship, unromantic but occasionally sexual, for the rest of their natural lives.

I don't remember if Christopher made any reply to this. Most likely he just looked hurt and sulked.

And now a new chapter in Christopher's life opened. That is to say, during May 1951, two of Christopher's immediate problems began to solve themselves. Also, something happened—quite unplanned, unforeseen by him—which was to make a big difference to his literary career and economic future.

The Caskey problem began to solve itself when Christopher left Monterey Street and moved, for the time being, into the Huntington Hartford Foundation. The problem of Christopher's novel began to solve itself, thanks to Speed Lamkin. The unforeseen happening was John van Druten's decision to make a play out of Christopher's character Sally Bowles and some other parts of his *Goodbye to Berlin*.

The domestic break with Caskey was inevitable, I suppose. Yet Christopher will hardly admit this to himself, even in the last of the journal entries (May 6) preceding it. The furthest he will go is to write: "There is absolutely no doubt, I really *ought* to leave Bill. I am only plaguing him. And yet, somehow, to leave—just like that—as the result of a 'sensible' decision—or in a towering rage; both seem wrong."

Writing in the journal, on May 28, about his move to the foundation on May 21, Christopher merely states that, "I moved because life with Billy had become unbearable. It doesn't matter just how, or why; and it is certainly no use passing 'moral' judgements." In other words, Christopher refuses to discuss what happened, even with himself. Later, in another journal entry (August 22), he alludes to "that dreadful party on May 20 when I decided to go to the foundation." But what *was* so dreadful about the party?[1] From the day-to-day diary I see that [the herculean navy frogman] was there, not to mention Peter Darms, of whom Christopher had always remained fond. It's probable that it was Christopher himself who behaved badly, not any of the guests; he must have been in one of his ugly sulking moods and made a scene with Caskey, later—perhaps bringing up old grudges and threatening to leave. If so, Caskey, who

---

[1] Referring to an earlier party (April 27–28) Christopher writes [on May 6]: "All sorts of people came down for the weekend, and I was cheerful and it 'went' very well. But afterwards I felt—well, sort of disturbed in my inmost nest. It was hard to settle down on the eggs again. (The eggs, this week, were a rather stupid review I did of a book on Katherine Mansfield.)" [Sylvia Berkman, *Katherine Mansfield: A Critical Study* for *Tomorrow*, reprinted in *Exhumations*.]

never gave way to threats, would have answered: okay, suit yourself.

Caskey's attitude was negative, almost neutral. He would never have urged Christopher to leave him. Neither would the Masselinks or the Beesleys or Jim Charlton. They merely stood ready to help, if needed—which was, indeed, all that Christopher expected of them. He had had quite enough attempted interference in his life, already, from Peggy Kiskadden and others. Early in May, he had written a letter to Jim—"a cry for help"—and then burned it.

And yet, Christopher *was* open to interference—by the right person. And that person proved to be, astonishingly enough, Speed Lamkin. Speed could influence Christopher because Christopher didn't take him, or his concern for Christopher's future, seriously. It all seemed camp—yet, of course, camp itself must have, according to Christopher's definition, an underlying seriousness. What was one to make of this niggery, flirty, shrewd, frivolous, perceptive young person? Did he mean *anything* he said? Even when he was talking obsessively about himself, boasting of all the things he would accomplish in the world, he couldn't help giggling. And now he had made Christopher one of his projects. Christopher *had* to leave Billy—with whom, however, Speed was on the best of terms—and come to live at the foundation and put his future in Speed's hands. If he did that, Speed guaranteed to make him a Success, the success he ought always to have been. (Speed was unimpressed by Christopher's literary career to date. Christopher had never been properly appreciated, Speed said, because he hadn't known how to promote himself.)

As I shall have to keep repeating, the power of this extraordinary tempter was in his absurdity—combined, of course, with intelligence and considerable sex appeal. An aspect of Speed's camp was to let it be supposed by everybody at the foundation that he and Christopher were having an affair. Well, weren't they? No—not exactly. But they were clowning an affair, and the clowning sometimes became nearly realistic. Occasionally, it climaxed with the two of them naked in bed together; tickling, biting, groping, laughing, kissing. (I don't remember that they ever actually had an orgasm.) Or else, embracing in Speed's parked car, they would imagine a glamorous love life, with a New York apartment and a Bel Air home with two swimming pools. Certainly, Christopher never seriously considered living with Speed for one instant. But he did enjoy their intimacy, and mentally playing house with him.

I think Speed was already working on his second novel, *The Easter Egg Hunt*, although it wasn't published until 1954. They must have talked about this. But Christopher was preoccupied with the difficulties he was having with his own novel. And Speed was eager to deal with them—for this would strengthen his influence over Christopher. Speed had already read and greatly admired the first chapter (which would be published next year in *New World Writing*); now Christopher showed him the rest of the manuscript. Next day, May 29, Speed delivered his verdict: "The refugees are a bore."

The sentence was like an axe stroke, cutting the novel in half; but the operation was life-giving, not destructive. Because, as Christopher now saw, the novel had been two novels, self-destructively, chokingly intertwined—the story of Stephen, Elizabeth, Sarah and Jane was one novel; the story of Sarah and the refugees was the other. They would never form a whole. (It now seems that the second will never be written.)

Nobody had condemned the refugees before. The Beesleys were probably dubious about them but hadn't wanted to upset Christopher by upsetting the applecart. Speed with his ruthlessness had disregarded Christopher's feelings and expressed his own. Christopher could never be grateful enough to him. And how quickly everything now fell into place! The large thin notebook has an entry for June 1 which shows that, after a series of discussions with Speed and the Beesleys, the main outlines of the novel in its final form have already been decided on.

Yet the revised manuscript of *The World in the Evening* didn't go off to the publishers until November 30, 1953!

Meanwhile the Beesleys had been working on Christopher's behalf in a quite different area.

As has been recorded, neither of them liked the Speed Lamkin–Gus Field play based on *Sally Bowles*. Now, while they were driving together to visit John van Druten at his ranch in the Coachella Valley, Alec got the idea that John should be persuaded to take on the project. Dodie writes (August 25, 1975): "I have such a vivid memory of Alec (by arrangement) putting his head out of John's swimming pool and saying, 'Why not make a play out of Sally Bowles'—and then diving down again, leaving me to get John going."

(Dodie's letter was written to correct my misremembered or, rather, invented version of the facts in my introduction to *The Berlin of Sally Bowles*,[*] published in 1975.)

Once John's inventiveness had been challenged, the rest was predictable. John quickly produced a first draft. And now the news

[* *Mr. Norris Changes Trains* and *Goodbye to Berlin* reissued in one volume by the Hogarth Press.]

was told to Christopher. On May 28, John, Starcke and Christopher
had supper together and John read his play aloud. It was then still
called *Sally Bowles*.

I have no memory whatsoever of the impression made on
Christopher by that first reading. I think he disliked the character of
Christopher Isherwood from the beginning and never changed his
opinion. I think he also objected to most of the speeches about the
persecution of the Jews which John had written in, and to several of
John's jokes. But what mattered to him chiefly was that this play
would almost certainly be performed and would probably make
money. And, already, he saw the glitter of footlights ahead of him
and felt the thrill of escaping into the New York theatrical world.

Christopher was obviously the person who had to tell Speed
Lamkin and Gus Field—since it was he, after all, who had to accept
the responsibility of deciding to authorize John van Druten's play
and reject theirs. Speed could not have behaved better. He assured
Christopher that he quite understood the situation. In Christopher's
place, he would jump at this chance. He was happy for Christopher
and knew that the play would be a terrific hit. As for Gus, he would
explain everything to him. It would be easier, Speed said, for him to
do it himself than for Christopher to do it.

So Christopher felt more warmly toward Speed than ever—as did
the Beesleys, partly perhaps because they were suffering from slight
guilt. They invited Speed to their house, several times, with
Christopher. And Speed charmed them; he had nice southern
manners which he could use when he wished. Also, he continued to
create a most peculiar relationship with Alec Beesley. Declaring to
Christopher, in private, that Alec was one of the handsomest men
he'd ever set eyes on and that he'd bet Alec wasn't that hard to get,
he began flirting quite openly but inoffensively with Alec in Dodie's
presence. Neither Alec nor Dodie could object to this because Speed
was such an avowed faggot that his behavior seemed no more than
natural. But it amused Christopher to realize that Alec was not only
slightly embarrassed by it but also coyly pleased. Alec even tried to
learn Speed's language—that is to say, he tried to get Speed to explain
to him what "camp" is. But Speed's teasingly misleading definitions
left him nowhere. Alec ended by deciding that camp is any kind of
irresponsible unmotivated behavior. Therefore, one morning when
Speed and Christopher had been invited to lunch, they found that
Alec had prepared for their arrival by throwing all the garden chairs
into the pool, where they were floating. "It's a camp!" Alec explained, obviously pleased with himself, like a proud pupil expecting
praise.

As for Gus Field, he took the news well, too. Which was more admirable, since he got very little gratitude from Christopher or anybody else for doing so. If he was invited to the Beesleys', it was only once or twice. Speed dropped him. Christopher only saw him occasionally. He was treated as a bore and an outsider—and that, from Christopher's point of view, was what he was.

Chronology

1904 August 26, Christopher William Bradshaw Isherwood, first child of Frank Bradshaw Isherwood and Kathleen Bradshaw Isherwood (*née* Machell Smith), born at Wyberslegh Hall, High Lane, Cheshire, on the estate of his grandfather, John Bradshaw Isherwood, squire of nearby Marple Hall.

1911 October 1, Isherwood's brother Richard Graham Bradshaw Isherwood born.

1914 May 1, Isherwood arrives at his preparatory school, St. Edmund's, Hindhead, Surrey; August 4, Britain declares war on Germany and Isherwood's father receives mobilization orders; September 8, Frank Isherwood leaves for France.

1915 May 8 or 9, Frank Isherwood evidently wounded at Ypres, probably killed.

1917 January 1, Isherwood begins keeping a diary; he records walking with W. H. Auden at school.

1919 January 17, Isherwood arrives at Repton, his public school, near Derby.

1921 Winter, Isherwood joins G. B. Smith's history form, where he meets Edward Upward, at Repton; November, Kathleen Isherwood moves with her mother to 36 St. Mary Abbot's Terrace in West Kensington, London.

1923 October 10, Isherwood goes up with an £80 history scholarship to Corpus Christi College, Cambridge, where he renews his friendship with Edward Upward.

1924 Isherwood and Upward start keeping diaries and begin to invent a fantasy world, Mortmere, about which they write stories.

1925 June 1, Cambridge Tripos exams begin; June 18, Isherwood is summoned to Cambridge to explain his joke Tripos answers and withdraws from university; August, takes job as secretary to André Mangeot's string quartet; December, meets W. H. Auden and renews prep school friendship.

1926 Easter, Isherwood begins writing *Seascape with Figures*, which is the first version of *All the Conspirators* and his fourth attempt at a novel.

1927 January 24, takes first job as private tutor.

1928 May 18, Isherwood's first novel, *All the Conspirators*, is published by Jonathan Cape; May 19, he visits Bremen; June 22, Auden introduces Isherwood to Stephen Spender; October, Isherwood begins as a medical student at King's College, London, and Auden moves to Berlin.

1929 March, Isherwood leaves medical school at the end of spring term; March 14–27, he visits Auden in Berlin where he meets John Layard and begins an affair with Berthold Szczesny; November 29, Isherwood moves to Berlin.

1930 December, Isherwood becomes tenant of Fräulein Meta Thurau at Nollendorfstrasse 17; during 1930, his translation of the *Intimate Journals of Charles Baudelaire* is published.

1931 By early 1931, Isherwood meets Jean Ross and soon afterwards he also meets Gerald Hamilton; in September, he begins teaching English.

1932 February 17, *The Memorial* is published by Isherwood's new publisher, the Hogarth Press; March 13, Isherwood meets Heinz Neddermeyer while living at Mohrin with Francis Turville-Petre; August 4–September 30, Isherwood visits England and meets Gerald Heard and Chris Wood; September 14, he meets E. M. Forster; October, works as translator for a communist workers' organization, the IAH (Internationale Arbeiterhilfe), in Berlin.

1933 March 23, Hitler achieves dictatorial powers; April 5, Isherwood arrives in London with his belongings, preparing to leave Berlin for good; April 30, he returns to Berlin and on May 13, leaves for Prague with Heinz; they travel to Greece for the summer and return to England in September; October, Heinz returns to Berlin and Isherwood begins work as Berthold Viertel's collaborator on a film script for *The Little Friend*.

1934 January 5, Heinz is refused entry into England; January 20, Isherwood meets Heinz in Berlin and takes him to Amsterdam, returning alone to London; February 21, filming starts on *The Little Friend*; March 26, Isherwood joins Heinz in Amsterdam and they travel to Gran Canaria for the summer; June 8–August 12, Isherwood writes *Mr. Norris Changes Trains*; August 26, *The Little Friend* opens in London; September 6, Isherwood and Heinz set off for Copenhagen.

1935 January, Auden visits Copenhagen to work with Isherwood on *The Dog Beneath the Skin*; February 21, *Mr. Norris Changes Trains* is published by Hogarth; April, Isherwood moves Heinz to Brussels; May 9, *The Last of Mr. Norris* (U.S. edition of *Mr. Norris Changes Trains*) is published by William Morrow; May 13, Heinz receives a three-month permit for Holland and they settle in Amsterdam, lodging next to Klaus Mann; also in May, *The Dog Beneath the Skin, or Where Is Francis?*, written with Auden, is published by Faber and Faber; September 16, Isherwood and Heinz return to Brussels; December 21, they move from Antwerp to Sintra, Portugal, where Spender and Tony Hyndman join them.

1936 January 12, *The Dog Beneath the Skin* opens at the Westminster Theatre in London; mid-January, Isherwood completes a draft of *Sally Bowles*; March 14, Spender and Hyndman leave Sintra for Spain; March 16–April 17, Auden visits Sintra to work on *The Ascent of F6*; July 25, Heinz is ordered through the German consul in Lisbon to report for military service, but does not; September 11, Faber publishes Auden and Isherwood's play *The Ascent of F6*; Isherwood works on *Lions and Shadows*.

1937 February 26, *The Ascent of F6* premieres at the Mercury Theatre in London; March 17, Isherwood takes Heinz from Brussels to Paris; April 25, he joins Heinz in Luxembourg; *F6* successfully transfers to the Adelphi Little Theatre; May 12, Heinz is forced to leave Luxembourg and goes to Trier, in Germany, where he is arrested by the Gestapo; July 16–August 4, Isherwood works for Alexander Korda on the film script of a Carl Zuckmayer story; August 12–September 17, he works with Auden in Dover on their new play, *On the Frontier*; September 15, Isherwood finishes *Lions and Shadows*; October, the Hogarth Press publishes *Sally Bowles* (later incorporated into *Goodbye to Berlin*).

1938 January 19, Isherwood and Auden leave for China to write a travel book, *Journey to a War*; during the spring "The Landauers" appears in John Lehmann's magazine, *New Writing*; March 17, *Lions and Shadows* is published by Hogarth Press; July 1–9, Isherwood and Auden, returning around the world from China, visit Manhattan where Isherwood meets Vernon Old; September 19, Isherwood begins writing *Journey to a War*, using his own and Auden's diary entries; September 26, *The Ascent of F6* is televised; October 1938, Faber publishes Auden and Isherwood's last play together, *On the Frontier*; November 14, *On the Frontier* opens at the Arts Theatre in Cambridge; mid-December, Isherwood works with Auden in Brussels on *Journey to a War*, completed December 17; Jacky Hewit accompanies Isherwood in Brussels through the New Year.

1939 January 19, Isherwood sails for America with Auden, arriving January 26 in New York where they settle; March, *Goodbye to Berlin* is published by the Hogarth Press and in the U.S. by Random House; the same month, *Journey to a War* is published by Faber and by Random House; early May, Isherwood applies for U.S. residency; May 6, he sets off for California with Vernon Old; June 9, Isherwood gets quota visa; July, Isherwood begins working with Berthold Viertel again and meets Swami Prabhavananda; early August, Isherwood begins instruction in meditation; October, Isherwood's new story, "I Am Waiting," is published in *The New Yorker*; November, Isherwood gets his first Hollywood film job writing for Goldwyn Studios.

1940 January, Isherwood begins his first writing job at MGM, on *Rage in Heaven* for Gottfried Reinhardt; July 9, Uncle Henry Bradshaw Isherwood dies, Isherwood inherits the family estate and gives it to his brother, Richard; November 8, Swami Prabhavananda initiates Isherwood.

1941 By January 11, Isherwood finishes working on *Rage in Heaven* and then "polishes" other MGM scripts; February 17, he breaks with Vernon Old and, in mid-March, moves next door to Gerald Heard; early May, Isherwood finishes his first year's contract at MGM and leaves the studio; by mid-June,

Denny Fouts moves in with Isherwood; July 15, Kathleen Isherwood returns to live at Wyberslegh with Richard; August 22, Isherwood flies east to visit Auden and meets Caroline Norment at the Cooperative College Workshop, a refugee hostel in Haverford, Pennsylvania; October 11, he moves to Haverford to work in the hostel; also during 1941, Gerald Heard begins to build his monastic community, Trabuco.

1942 June 30, Isherwood has a medical exam at the draft board; July 6, the Haverford refugee hostel closes, and Isherwood returns to California; July 13, he receives his draft classification, 4-E, and applies to Los Prietos Camp to do civilian public service; by October 12, Isherwood begins working on a translation of the Bhagavad Gita with Swami Prabhavananda; October, another story, "Take It or Leave It," is published in *The New Yorker*; November 30, Isherwood starts work at Paramount on Somerset Maugham's *The Hour Before Dawn*; December 31, Isherwood writes "The Wishing Tree" for the Vedanta Society magazine.

1943 January 29, Isherwood finishes at Paramount; February 6, he moves into the Vedanta Center, Ivar Avenue, in preparation for becoming a monk; May, Isherwood begins writing *Prater Violet*; August, Denny Fouts introduces Isherwood to Bill Harris.

1944 February and again in March, Isherwood stays with Aldous and Maria Huxley in Llano where Isherwood and Huxley work out a film story, *Jacob's Hands*; April 17, Isherwood decides he cannot become a monk; during June, Isherwood spends a few days with Bill Harris at Denny Fouts's flat in Santa Monica; Isherwood and Huxley complete draft of *Jacob's Hands*; August, Isherwood and Prabhavananda's translation of the Bhagavad Gita is published; September 25, Isherwood moves to Ananda Bhavan, the new Santa Barbara Vedanta Center in Montecito; November 17, Isherwood leaves Ananda Bhavan and moves to Laguna; late November, Isherwood returns to the Hollywood Vedanta Center on Ivar Avenue.

1945 February 5, Isherwood's affair with Bill Harris ends; February 21, Isherwood starts three months' work on Wilkie Collins's *The Woman in White* for Warner Brothers; June 2, Isherwood attends Bill Caskey's twenty-fourth birthday party; June 4, he returns to Warner Brothers to work on Maugham's *Up at the Villa* for Wolfgang Reinhardt; during the summer, *Prater Violet* appears in *Harper's Bazaar* and New Directions publishes *The Berlin Stories*, containing *The Last of Mr. Norris* and *Goodbye to Berlin*; August 23, Isherwood moves out of the Vedanta Center into the Beesleys' chauffeur's apartment; he begins translating Shankara's *Crest-Jewel of Discrimination* with Swami Prabhavananda; September 25, Isherwood and Bill Caskey move into Denny Fouts's empty apartment, 137 Entrada Drive, Santa Monica; November, *Prater Violet* is published in the U.S. by Random House; towards the end of the year, *Vedanta for the Western World*, edited and introduced by Isherwood, is published by Marcel Rodd.

1946 January 12, Isherwood undergoes surgery to remove a median bar inside his bladder; April, Caskey quarrels with Denny Fouts, and Isherwood and Caskey move into Salka Viertel's garage apartment, 165 Mabery Road, Santa

Monica; May, *Prater Violet* is published in the U.K. by Isherwood's new English publisher, Methuen; during the summer, Isherwood revises his wartime diaries, 1939–1944; November 8, he becomes a U.S. citizen; towards the end of the year, Isherwood works with Lesser Samuels on a film treatment, *Judgement Day in Pittsburgh*.

1947 January 19, Isherwood sets out (via New York) on his first postwar trip to England; March 28, he signs deed of gift passing on Marple estate, including Wyberslegh, to his brother Richard; April 16, returns to New York; during the summer, he lives with Caskey at James and Tania Stern's apartment at 207 East 52nd Street, Manhattan; in August, Shankara's *Crest-Jewel of Discrimination* is published; September 19, Isherwood sails with Caskey for South America to write a travel book, *The Condor and the Cows*; September 28, they arrive in Cartagena, Colombia; October 28, Isherwood and Caskey travel south via Bogotá; November, they continue through Ecuador and reach Lima, Peru, by year end; also in 1947, the first U.S. edition of *Lions and Shadows* is published by New Directions.

1948 January, Isherwood and Caskey travel in Peru and Bolivia; February, they leave La Paz, Bolivia, for Argentina and depart from Buenos Aires by ship in late March; April 1, they stop in Rio, then continue direct from Brazil to North Africa and France, arriving in Paris on April 22; April 30, they proceed to London; late May, Isherwood visits his family at Wyberslegh; June 9, Isherwood and Caskey sail for New York; June 15, Isherwood returns alone to California and on July 19 he starts work on *The Great Sinner* at MGM; mid-August, he meets Jim Charlton; that summer, Isherwood begins translating Patanjali's yoga aphorisms with Swami Prabhavananda; September 20, Caskey returns; September 28, Isherwood moves with Caskey into 333 Rustic Road; October 9, Isherwood finishes work at MGM; November 12, Isherwood's nanny, Annie Avis, dies; December 16, Denny Fouts dies in Rome.

1949 January 6–13, Isherwood works for Gottfried Reinhardt at MGM; April 12, he completes *The Condor and the Cows*; he begins to work intermittently on his proposed novel *The School of Tragedy*; by May, he begins working with Lesser Samuels on *The Easiest Thing in the World*; August 6–7, Isherwood meets Evelyn Caldwell (later Hooker); August, he finishes draft of *The Easiest Thing in the World* with Lesser Samuels; August 10, meets Igor and Vera Stravinsky and Robert Craft; also in August, he works on *Below the Equator* with Aldous Huxley and Lesser Samuels; September 7, Trabuco is dedicated as a Ramakrishna monastery; November 11, Caskey leaves for Florida; also in November, Methuen publishes *The Condor and the Cows*; December 1, Isherwood writes a memorial article on Klaus Mann; during 1949, Isherwood is elected to the U.S. Academy of Arts and Sciences.

1950 Isherwood works on a film script, *The Vacant Room*, with Lesser Samuels; late April, Caskey returns via Kentucky to Rustic Road; June 29, Bill Kennedy proposes that Isherwood begin reviewing regularly for *Tomorrow*; August 11, Isherwood and Peggy Kiskadden leave for Arizona and New Mexico by car; December 10, Isherwood moves with Caskey to 31152 Monterey Street, Coast Royal, South Laguna.

1951 May 21, Isherwood leaves Caskey and moves to the Huntington Hartford Foundation, 2000 Rustic Canyon Road, Pacific Palisades; he works on *The School of Tragedy*; during the spring, John van Druten writes the play *I Am a Camera*, based on *Goodbye to Berlin*; by August 22, Isherwood is back in South Laguna with Caskey; mid-September, he decides to break finally with Caskey and returns to the Huntington Hartford Foundation; October, Isherwood goes to the East Coast for rehearsals of *I Am a Camera*, directed by van Druten; November 8, *I Am a Camera* opens in Hartford, Connecticut; November 28, *I Am a Camera* opens successfully on Broadway at the Empire Theater; December, Isherwood sails for England where he spends Christmas with his mother and brother in a London hotel; Caskey joins the merchant marine.

1952 February 10, Isherwood returns to Berlin after eighteen years and sees Heinz Neddermayer for the first time since Heinz's arrest by the Gestapo in 1937; February 27, Isherwood sails from England for New York; by April 8, he returns to California with Sam Costidy; May 4, Isherwood settles at Trabuco where he completes Patanjali translation and part one of his novel, still called *The School of Tragedy*; May 21, he moves alone to the Mermira apartments in Santa Monica; also during May, Isherwood resigns from the board of the Huntington Hartford Foundation and the first chapter of his unfinished novel is published in *New Writing*; June, Isherwood begins fixing up Evelyn Hooker's garden house at 400 South Saltair Avenue in Brentwood and moves there in late summer; during 1952, *Vedanta for Modern Man*, edited by Isherwood, is published in U.S. and U.K.; Isherwood completes "California Story" (later reprinted as "The Shore" in *Exhumations*) to accompany Sanford Roth's photographs in *Harper's Bazaar*.

1953 January 6, Caskey leaves for San Francisco and ships out again; February 14, Isherwood begins relationship with Don Bachardy; February 20–26, Bachardy's brother Ted has a nervous breakdown and is committed; April 25, Bachardy moves out of his mother's apartment and into his own furnished room in Hollywood; May 16, Bachardy moves into Marguerite and Harry Brown's apartment in West Hollywood; August 5, Isherwood completes *The World in the Evening*; September, Isherwood moves out of Evelyn Hooker's garden house, at her request, and stays at the Browns' apartment with Bachardy; September 19, Isherwood and Bachardy move together into their own apartment; during October, Isherwood's article on Ernst Toller appears in *Encounter*; also in 1953, *How to Know God: The Yoga Aphorisms of Patanjali*, translated with Swami Prabhavananda, is published.

1954 January, Isherwood begins editing an anthology, *Great English Short Stories*, and plans a biography of Ramakrishna as well as various new pieces of autobiographical fiction; January 25, he begins work for Eddie Knopf at MGM on *Diane*; June, *The World in the Evening* is published in the U.S. and the U.K.; August 25, Isherwood completes script for *Diane*; August 26, Isherwood turns fifty; during the spring and summer, John Collier writes a screenplay based on John van Druten's play, *I Am a Camera*, and Julie Harris accepts the lead; November, Isherwood and Bachardy visit Tennessee Williams in Key West to watch filming of *The Rose Tattoo* in which Isherwood plays a bit part;

December, they travel to Mexico with Jo and Ben Masselink and Isherwood has an idea for a new novel which will eventually be called *Down There on a Visit*.

1955 Isherwood gets more work at MGM on *Diane* and writing *The Wayfarer*, a script about Buddha; February 10, Bachardy starts his junior year at UCLA; February 12, Maria Huxley dies; March 18, Ted Bachardy has another breakdown and is hospitalized again; May 2, *Diane* starts filming; May 18, Bachardy's twenty-first birthday party; May 28, Isherwood begins writing his new novel first conceived in Mexico; June 8, he meets Thom Gunn; June 22, Isherwood sees preview of film, *I Am a Camera*; October 12, Isherwood leaves with Bachardy for New York City and on October 20, they sail from New York for Tangier; October 30, they sail for Italy and in mid-December continue on to Somerset Maugham's house in France; by Christmas, they are in Munich; December 28, they arrive in Paris.

1956 January, Isherwood and Bachardy arrive in London; January 30–February 6, Isherwood stays with his mother and brother at Wyberslegh and sees Marple Hall for the last time (it will be demolished in 1959); March 6, Isherwood begins writing his new novel, calling it, for the moment, *The Lost*; March 11, Isherwood and Bachardy leave England for New York and California; during April, they buy 434 Sycamore Road; July 2, Bachardy enrolls at Chouinard Art School; September 24, Isherwood begins work on *Jean-Christophe* for Jerry Wald at Fox.

1957 February 12, Isherwood discovers a lump on the side of his belly; February 15, the tumor is successfully removed and proves benign, but ill health and depression persist; April, Isherwood prepares an introduction for a new edition of *All the Conspirators*, to be published in U.K.; early July, Isherwood and Gavin Lambert begin television project for Hermione Gingold, *Emily Ermingarde*; August 15, *Jean-Christophe* is shelved by Fox; October 8, Isherwood and Bachardy begin around-the-world trip, via Japan, Hong Kong, Singapore, Bali, Bangkok, and Angkor; November 30, they fly to Calcutta and in December continue on to London.

1958 January 30, Isherwood and Bachardy reach Los Angeles (via New York); February 2, Bachardy returns to Chouinard Art School; February 11, Isherwood renews work on his novel and on the Ramakrishna biography; February 25, Bachardy begins taking painting classes from Vernon Old; mid-March, Isherwood begins work on *Mary Magdalene* for David Selznick, until late June; July 5, Isherwood completes a new foreword for U.S. edition of *All the Conspirators*; October, Isherwood and Bachardy begin writing a play, *The Monsters*; during the autumn, Isherwood and Lambert begin revising the film script of *The Vacant Room*.

1959 Mid-January, Isherwood and Bachardy complete *The Monsters*; March 7–April 13, Isherwood writes "Mr. Lancaster," the first part of the final draft of his novel; March 20, he signs on to teach at Los Angeles State College; April, the first installment of *Ramakrishna and His Disciples* appears in the March/April issue of the Vedanta Society magazine; May 1, Bachardy takes his first job as a professional artist; Isherwood begins writing "Ambrose," the second part of his novel; mid-June, Isherwood and Bachardy undertake to buy 145 Adelaide Drive; July 31, Isherwood finishes writing "Afterwards," a homosexual short story; August 18, Isherwood and Bachardy travel to New York and then England where Isherwood visits Wyberslegh and sees his mother for the last time; September, they visit France and return to New York and Santa Monica; September 22, Isherwood begins teaching at L.A. State College; September 30, Isherwood and Bachardy move to 145 Adelaide Drive; October, "Mr. Lancaster" appears in *The London Magazine*.

1960 L.A. State mounts exhibition on Isherwood; during the spring, Isherwood begins working with Charles Laughton on a play about Socrates; April 18, begins writing part three of his novel; May 25, he accepts a job at the University of California at Santa Barbara (UCSB) for the following autumn; June 10, begins writing "Paul," the final part of his novel; June 15, Kathleen Isherwood dies; August 26, Isherwood completes his last handwritten diary; September 22, he begins teaching at UCSB; also in 1960, *Great English Short Stories* is published by Dell.

1961 January 23, Bachardy leaves for London to study art at the Slade; April 6, Isherwood joins Bachardy in London; he works with Auden on Berlin musical, but they abandon it when Auden leaves London in mid-June; October 2, Bachardy's first show opens at the Redfern Gallery; October 15, Isherwood returns to Los Angeles alone; December 11–12, he travels to New York to meet Bachardy.

1962 January 2, Bachardy's first New York show opens at the Sagittarius Gallery; January 25, Isherwood returns alone to Santa Monica and on January 28 begins teaching again at L.A. State; he plans a new novel called, at first, *The English Woman*; February 17, Bachardy returns; early March, *Down There on a Visit* is published by Methuen in the U.K. and by Isherwood's new publisher, Simon and Schuster, in the U.S.; Isherwood's UCSB lectures are broadcast on radio; Isherwood and Bachardy begin remodelling their garage as a studio for Bachardy; Isherwood's novel, *The English Woman*, begins to evolve into *A Single Man*.

1963 During the winter and early spring, Bachardy considers living alone; October, Isherwood finishes draft of *Ramakrishna and His Disciples*; October 21, Isherwood sends final draft of *A Single Man* to both his U.S. and U.K. publishers; November 22, Aldous Huxley dies; December, Isherwood travels via Japan to India with Swami Prabhavananda and thinks for the first time of writing *A Meeting by the River*.

1964 January, Isherwood returns from India via Rome and New York and begins final draft of *Ramakrishna and His Disciples*; February, he starts to gather material for *Exhumations*; March, Isherwood begins working on *The Loved One* with Terry Southern; meets David Hockney; during the summer, Bachardy travels to North Africa, Europe, and London; July–September, Isherwood works on screenplay of *Reflections in a Golden Eye*; *A Single Man* is published in the U.S. by Simon and Schuster and, on September 10, in the U.K. by Methuen; September–December, Isherwood works on screenplay of *The Sailor from Gibraltar*.

1965 January 6, Bachardy leaves for a further long spell in New York, visiting several times during the year; Isherwood finishes *The Sailor from Gibraltar* and *Exhumations*; early February, Isherwood takes up post as Regent's Professor at the University of California at Los Angeles (UCLA); spring, he begins writing *A Meeting by the River*; April 8, *Ramakrishna and His Disciples* is published by Methuen and appears in the U.S. during the summer; November 1, he begins *Hero-Father, Demon-Mother* (*Kathleen and Frank*).

1966 Spring, Isherwood is visiting professor at UCLA; Gerald Heard has the first of many strokes; *Exhumations* is published in the U.S. and the U.K.; May 31, Isherwood completes third draft of *A Meeting by the River*; July, he agrees to work on *Silent Night* with Danny Mann for ABC television, travels with Mann to Austria in September for filming; October, Isherwood visits England and stays with his brother at Wyberslegh where he reads his father's letters; November, *Cabaret*, Fred Ebb and John Kander's stage musical based on *I Am a Camera*, opens in New York, produced by Hal Prince.

1967 January, Isherwood begins working in more earnest on the book which eventually will be called *Kathleen and Frank*; spring, he corrects proofs of *A Meeting by the River* which is published in April in the U.S. and in June in the U.K.; May, he returns to England to look at family papers at Wyberslegh for *Kathleen and Frank*, carrying some back to California with him; also in 1967, Isherwood works with James Bridges on a play of *A Meeting by the River*.

1968 Isherwood adapts Bernard Shaw's novella *The Adventures of the Black Girl in Her Search for God* for the stage, and also adapts Wedekind's *Earth Spirit* and *Pandora's Box*; Bachardy again spends time in London and in New York; spring, Hockney begins work on a double portrait of Isherwood and Bachardy; October, Isherwood again begins writing *Kathleen and Frank*; also during 1968, Isherwood and Bachardy work together on the play of *A Meeting by the River*.

1969 *The Adventures of the Black Girl in Her Search for God* opens at the Mark Taper Forum in Los Angeles; July, Isherwood and Bachardy travel to Tahiti, Bora Bora, Samoa, New Zealand and Australia and begin work on a screenplay of Robert Graves's *I, Claudius* and *Claudius the God* for Tony Richardson; also in 1969, *Essentials of Vedanta* is published.

1970 February–April, in London together, Isherwood and Bachardy continue to work on stage version of *A Meeting by the River*; Isherwood sends final draft of *Kathleen and Frank* to U.S. and U.K. publishers; also in 1970, E. M. Forster dies, leaving Isherwood the rights to *Maurice*.

1971 Isherwood completes revisions to *Kathleen and Frank*; February, Isherwood and Bachardy start work on a TV script of *Frankenstein* for Universal Studios; April 6, Stravinsky dies; August 14, Gerald Heard dies; August 26, Isherwood begins writing reconstructed diary of the "lost years," 1945–1951; October, *Kathleen and Frank* is published by Methuen; also in 1971, Isherwood undergoes hand surgery for Depuytren's contracture.

1972 January, Isherwood sees preview of film *Cabaret*, based on the musical, and the U.S. edition of *Kathleen and Frank* is published by Simon and Schuster; Isherwood and Bachardy undertake another TV script for Universal, *The Lady* *from the Land of the Dead*; April, the Los Angeles premiere of James Bridges' production of *A Meeting by the River*; also in 1972, Isherwood receives an award from the Hollywood Writers' Club for a lifetime of distinguished contributions to literature.

1973 Isherwood and Bachardy travel to London for the filming of *Frankenstein*; they visit Wyberslegh and afterwards go to Switzerland and Rome; summer, they work together on a screenplay of *A Meeting by the River*; Jean Ross dies; September 29, Auden dies; October, Isherwood begins a new autobiographical book eventually titled *Christopher and His Kind*; December, Isherwood and Bachardy's screenplay, *Frankenstein: The True Story*, is published by Avon Books.

1975 Isherwood works with Bachardy on a TV script adapted from Scott Fitzgerald's *The Beautiful and Damned*.

1976 May, Isherwood completes the final draft of *Christopher and His Kind*; July 4, Swami Prabhavananda dies; November, Isherwood's new U.S. publisher, Farrar Straus and Giroux, publishes *Christopher and His Kind*; *Frankenstein: The True Story* wins best scenario at the International Festival of Fantastic and Science Fiction Films.

1977 March, the U.K. edition of *Christopher and His Kind* is published by Methuen.

1979 May 15, Richard Isherwood dies of a heart attack; Isherwood and Bachardy collaborate on *October*.

1980 *My Guru and His Disciple* is published in the U.S. and the U.K.; July 16, Isherwood hears that Bill Caskey is dead; *October*, with drawings by Bachardy, is published.

1981 October, Isherwood learns that he has a malignant tumor in the prostate.

1983 July, Isherwood makes his last diary entry.

1986 January 4, Isherwood dies in Santa Monica.

Glossary

This glossary does not include entries for people adequately introduced by Isherwood himself in his text, nor does it incorporate information from the text. Readers should use the index to locate Isherwood's own descriptions.

Ackerley, J. R. (1896–1967). English author and editor. Ackerley wrote drama, poetry, and autobiography, and is known for his intimate relationship with his dog, described in two of his autobiographical books. He was literary editor of *The Listener* from 1935 to 1959, and published work by some of the best and most important writers of his period; Isherwood contributed numerous reviews during the thirties. Their friendship was sustained in later years partly by their shared acquaintance with E. M. Forster.

Adorno, Theodor (1903–1969). German philosopher. In 1933, he emigrated to Oxford and then to the U.S. where he became friends with Thomas Mann; later, he returned to his academic career in Frankfurt. Adorno was a critic of phenomenology, existentialism, and neo-positivism. He also wrote about music, language, and literature.

Agee, James (1909–1955). American poet, novelist, journalist, and screen-writer; born in Tennessee and educated at Harvard. Agee's first book was a 1934 volume in the Yale Series of Younger Poets. He became famous for his collaboration with the photographer Walker Percy on *Let Us Now Praise Famous Men* (1941), about Alabama sharecroppers during the Depression (an assignment rejected by *Fortune* magazine). Later he wrote two semi-autobiographical novels, *The Morning Watch* (1951) and *A Death in the Family* (1957), the second of which was published posthumously and won a Pulitzer Prize (it won another Pulitzer when adapted for the stage as *All the Way Home*). Agee was on the staff of *Time* as well as *Fortune*, and he became widely known as a film critic. His screenplays included *The African Queen* (1951, with John Huston) and an adaptation of Stephen Crane's *The Bride Comes to Yellow Sky* (1953).

AJC Ranch. Carter Lodge, John van Druten, and the British actress and director Auriol Lee (who had directed several of van Druten's plays) bought the ranch in the early 1940s. They named it "AJC" for Auriol, John, Carter. Lee died in a car accident not long afterwards. Van Druten also owned a forest cabin nearby, in the mountains above Idyllwild.

Allgood, Sara (1883–1950). Irish actress. At the Abbey Theatre in Dublin, Allgood created the part of "Juno Boyle" in *Juno and the Paycock* by Sean O'Casey. Isherwood evidently saw the first London run of *Juno and the Paycock* between November 1925 and May 1926. Allgood repeated the role of "Juno" for Hitchcock's 1930 film, and later settled in Hollywood where she made numerous films.

Almond, Paul (b. 1931). Canadian director, producer, screenwriter; educated at McGill University and at Oxford, where he was president of the poetry society and edited the undergraduate literary magazine *Isis*. On leaving Oxford, Almond joined a British repertory company before returning to Canada in the early 1950s to work as a TV director and later in film. He made *Isabel* (1967), *Act of the Heart* (1970), and *Journey* (1972) starring his first wife, Geneviève Bujold. His second wife, Joan, is a photographer. With a life-long literary friend, Michael Ballantyne, Almond published a memoir, *High Hopes: Coming of Age at the Mid-Century* (1999).

Andrews, Oliver. California sculptor, on the art faculty at UCLA. He died suddenly of a heart attack during the 1970s, while still in his forties.

Angermayer, Ken (Kenneth Anger) (b. 1929). American filmmaker and author. His films include *Fireworks* (1947), *Eaux d'Artifice* (1953), and *Scorpio Rising* (1964). Angermayer grew up in Hollywood. His sensationalist book, *Hollywood Babylon* (1975), exposes the habitual excesses of many stars and the ruthless way in which some stars were exploited.

Arvin, Newton (1900–1963). American literary critic and professor of literature; born in Indiana and educated at Harvard. Arvin taught at Smith College in Northampton, Massachusetts. and published biographies of Hawthorne, Longfellow, Whitman, and Melville. The Melville biography (which he was working on in Nantucket when Isherwood visited in the summer of 1947) won the National Book Award in 1951. He also contributed to scholarly journals and to *The Nation*, *The New Republic*, and, later, *Vogue* and *Vanity Fair*. He was unsuccessfully married for eight years, from 1932 to 1940, to a former student, Mary Garrison. Arvin met Truman Capote at Yaddo in June 1946, and they began an intense love affair which lasted several years. In 1960, Arvin was arrested when his large collection of erotic photographs and stories was discovered by the police; he informed on a number of colleagues and close friends, then had a nervous breakdown and lost his job at Smith. Not long afterwards, he discovered he had terminal cancer.

Ashton, Frederick (Freddy) (1906–1988). British choreographer and dancer, born in Ecuador, raised in Peru, and educated in England from 1919. Ashton studied with Léonide Massine and Marie Rambert. She was the first to commission a ballet from him, in 1926. In the late 1920s, he worked briefly as a dancer and choreographer in Paris. Then in 1935, he joined the Vic-Wells (later Sadler's Wells) Ballet where he spent the rest of his career. The company gradually evolved into the Royal Ballet, and in 1963 he succeeded Ninette de Valois as its director. Sadler's Wells had its first New York season and U.S. tour in the autumn of 1949, with *The Sleeping Beauty* as its centerpiece, and they toured again the following autumn.

Auden, W. H. (Wystan) (1907–1973). English poet, playwright, librettist, critic. Perhaps the greatest English poet of his century and one of the most influential. He and Isherwood met as schoolboys at St. Edmund's School, Hindhead, Surrey, where Auden, two and a half years younger than Isherwood, arrived in the autumn of 1915. They wrote three plays together —*The Dog Beneath the Skin* (1935), *The Ascent of F6* (1936), *On the Frontier* (1938)—and a travel book about their trip to China during the Sino-Japanese war—*Journey to a War* (1939). A fourth play—*The Enemies of a Bishop* (1929)—was published posthumously. As well as doing several stints of schoolmastering, Auden worked for John Grierson's Film Unit, funded by the General Post Office, for about six months during 1935, mostly writing poetry to be used as sound track. He and Isherwood went abroad separately and together during the 1930s, famously to Berlin, and finally emigrated together to the United States in 1939. After only a few months, their lives and interests diverged (Auden settled in New York while Isherwood went on to California), but they remained close friends until Auden's death. Auden is caricatured as "Hugh Weston" in *Lions and Shadows* and figures centrally in *Christopher and His Kind*. There are many passages about him in *D1*.

Aufderheide, Charles. American technician, from the Midwest. Aufderheide came to Los Angeles with Ruby Bell and the From twins. He began working on cameras at Technicolor soon after he arrived, and he continued there for about thirty years. According to a friend, Alvin Novak, Aufderheide's personal qualities were largely responsible for the longterm harmony of The Benton Way Group: he had quick insight into the needs and motives of his circle of acquaintances and friends, liked to entertain, and was able to talk practically on a wide range of sophisticated subjects. The Benton Way Group became a special haven for certain intellectuals who belonged neither to the Hollywood film world, nor to the continental high culture of the refugee community. The Benton Way Group were almost exclusively Americans, apart from the Egyptian-born scholar and intellectual Edouard Roditi (who was evidently attracted to them precisely because they were unlike himself). Aufderheide also wrote poetry, and after he died his friends collected some of his verses in a book.

Avis, Annie (d. 1948). Christopher Isherwood's nanny, from near Bury St. Edmunds, in Suffolk. She was employed by Isherwood's mother in October 1904, when Isherwood was two months old and Avis herself was about thirty, and she remained with the family for the rest of her life. She never married, though she had once been engaged (her fiancé died). Isherwood and his younger brother, Richard, were close to Nanny and, in childhood, spent more time with her than with their mother. When Richard started school as a day boy at Berkhamsted in 1919, he lodged in the town with Nanny, and his mother visited only at weekends; Isherwood by then was at Repton. Richard later felt that Nanny had made a favorite of Isherwood. Isherwood wrote in *Kathleen and Frank* that he loved Nanny dearly; in adolescence he had bullied her, but he had also shared intimate secrets with her. And he recalled that Nanny never criticized him.

Bachardy, Don (b. 1934). American painter; Isherwood's companion from

1953 onwards. Bachardy accompanied his brother, Ted Bachardy, on the beach in Santa Monica from the late 1940s, and Isherwood occasionally saw him there. They were introduced in November 1952, met again in February 1953, and began an affair which quickly became serious. Bachardy was then an eighteen-year-old college student. He studied languages and theater arts at UCLA, then attended Chouinard Art School and, later, the Slade School of Art in London. His portraits have been widely shown, and he has published his drawings in several books including *October* (1980) with Isherwood and *Last Drawings of Christopher Isherwood* (1990). Bachardy figures prominently in *D1*.

Bachardy, Ted (b. 1930). Elder brother of Don Bachardy. After a number of breakdowns, Ted Bachardy was diagnosed as a manic-depressive schizophrenic. When well, he worked at various jobs: as a tour guide and in the mail room at Warner Brothers, as a sales clerk in a department store, and as an office worker in insurance companies and advertising agencies.

Bacon, Francis (1909–1992). British painter, born in Dublin. Bacon worked as an interior decorator in London during the late 1920s and lived in Berlin in 1930, around the time that he taught himself to paint. He showed some of his work in London during the 1930s, but came to prominence only after the war when his controversial *Three Studies for Figures at the Base of a Crucifixion* made him suddenly famous in 1945.

Barada. A nun first introduced to the Hollywood Vedanta Center by Sarada Folling in 1943. Her original name was Doris Ludwig; later, after taking final vows in the Ramakrishna Order, she was called Pravrajika Baradaprana. Barada was interested in music and composed Vedantic hymns. Eventually she became a senior nun at the Sarada Convent in Santa Barbara.

Barnett, Jimmie. American painter and metaphysical teacher. Isherwood knew him when Barnett was a devotee at the Hollywood Vedanta Center; later Barnett settled in the Southwest.

Barrie, Michael. A one-time singer with financial and administrative talents; friend and secretary to Gerald Heard from the late 1940s onward. Barrie met Heard through Swami Prabhavananda and lived at Trabuco as a monk until about 1955. Later, Barrie nursed Heard through his five-year-long final illness until Heard's death in 1971. Isherwood often mentions him in *D1*.

Barton-Brown, Monsignor. British papal chamberlain; an acquaintance of Isherwood's friend Gerald Hamilton from just after World War I, when Barton-Brown was attached to the Vatican. Barton-Brown was Hamilton's priestly counterpart in an attempt, at the start of World War II, to avert the conflict by arranging a meeting between Axis and Allied diplomats on neutral ground (the Vatican was proposed). Barton-Brown and Hamilton contacted various highly placed Catholic officials, and when Hamilton was refused an exit permit to travel from England to Dublin—where he hoped to be able to communicate more easily with Rome—Barton-Brown arranged for him to travel in disguise as a member of a party of Irish nuns. But Hamilton was arrested at Euston station before he could depart, and as Isherwood tells, spent six months in Brixton prison.

Beaton, Cecil (1904–1980). English photographer, theater designer, and author. Beaton photographed the Sitwells in the 1920s and went on to photograph the British royal family, actors, actresses, writers, and many other public figures. From 1939 to 1945 he worked successfully as a war photographer. He was a dandy and a creature of style, and his numerous costume and set designs for stage and screen were widely admired. In Hollywood his most celebrated achievements were *Gigi* (1958) and *My Fair Lady* (1964), for which he won two Academy Awards. Isherwood and Beaton were contemporaries at Cambridge, but became friendly only in the late 1940s when Beaton visited Hollywood (with a production of *Lady Windermere's Fan* which he had designed and in which he was acting).

Beesley, Alec (d. 1987) and Dodie Smith Beesley (1896–1990). She was an English playwright, novelist, and actress, known professionally as Dodie Smith. He was a conscientious objector and an unofficial legal advisor to other conscientious objectors in Los Angeles during the war; he also managed her career. The Beesleys spent a decade in Hollywood because of Alec's pacifist convictions, and Dodie wrote scripts there for Paramount and her first novel, *I Capture the Castle*. They returned to England in the early 1950s. Isherwood met the Beesleys in November 1942, through Dodie's close friend and confidant John van Druten. Some details for the marriage between Stephen Monk and the writer Elizabeth Rydal in *The World in the Evening* are taken from the Beesleys' professional and domestic arrangements, and Elizabeth Rydal's correspondence with her friend Cecilia de Limbour resembles the voluminous letters continually exchanged between Dodie and John van Druten. Isherwood dedicated the novel to the Beesleys. In the summer of 1943, the Beesleys mated their dalmatians, Folly and Buzzle, and Folly produced fifteen puppies— inspiring Dodie's most famous book, *The Hundred and One Dalmatians* (1956), later filmed by Walt Disney. See *D1* for more passages about the Beesleys (and about their dogs).

Bennett, Ronald. American actor, born in New England. A member of Michael Chekhov's Chekhov Theater Studio. Bennett taught drama at Brown University as well as at The High Valley Theatre.

Berns, Walter. American academic. He met Bill Goyen in the navy when they served on the same battleship, and after the war they built an adobe house together in Taos, New Mexico, near Dorothy Brett and Frieda Lawrence with whom they became friends. Frieda Lawrence introduced them to Stephen Spender when Spender visited Taos in 1948 with Leonard Bernstein. At the time, Berns hoped to become a writer, but in 1949, he left Taos to study at the London School of Economics and for a few months he and Goyen lived at the Spenders' house. Berns went on to the University of Chicago where he got a doctorate in Political Science; in 1951 he married, and he and his wife had three children. Berns taught at Yale, Cornell, the University of Toronto, and finally, Georgetown University. When he retired from teaching in 1994, he became a resident scholar at the American Enterprise Institute for Public Policy Research in Washington, D.C. He has published numerous books and articles.

Bill, George. American engineer; he worked in the aerospace industry in Los Angeles, possibly at Lockheed.

Bill, also **Billy.** See Caskey, William.

Bo. Wallace Bobo; see Index and see also *D1*.

Bok, Ben. Eldest son of Peggy Kiskadden and Curtis Bok, a Philadelphia lawyer and judge. Ben became a wolf breeder near Llano, California.

Bower, Tony. American friend of Jean and Cyril Connolly; Isherwood met him in Paris in 1937. Bower's accent and manners gave the impression he was English; his mother became Lady Gordon-Duff through a second marriage, and his sister, Jean Gordon-Duff, was a great beauty. He wrote about film for a New York paper and was drafted into the U.S. Army twice during the war. During the late 1940s he worked at New Directions and eventually became editor of a New York art magazine. He was murdered in his Park Avenue apartment in 1972, evidently by a young man he picked up in a bar, possibly The Klondike, near Fifth Avenue in the West Forties. Bower was the model for "Ronny" in *Down There on a Visit* and there are passages about him in *D1*.

Brackett, Charles (1892–1969). American screenwriter and producer; from a wealthy East Coast family. He began as a novelist, then became a screenwriter, and later a producer, often working with the Austro-Hungarian writer-director Billy Wilder. Brackett was one of five writers who worked on the script for Garbo's *Ninotchka* (1939). He won an Academy Award as writer-producer of *The Long Weekend* (1945), and he produced *The King and I* (1956), as well as working on numerous other films. When Isherwood knew him best during the 1950s, Brackett worked for Darryl F. Zanuck at Twentieth Century-Fox, where he remained for about a decade until the early 1960s. Brackett appears in *D1*.

Brecht, Bertolt (1898–1956). German writer, poet, and dramatist; he was closely associated with the German communist party from the late 1920s onwards, though he never joined it. Brecht used the theater to promote his socialist beliefs, but only a handful of his plays are explicitly didactic, and he theorized and wrote at length about his radical approach both to theme and treatment. He worked for two years in Berlin in Max Reinhardt's Deutsches Theater and collaborated with the composer Kurt Weill on *The Threepenny Opera* (1928) and *The Rise and Fall of the City of Mahagonny* (1929). Among his best known and most widely appealing plays are *Mother Courage and Her Children* (1941), *The Good Woman of Szechwan* (1943), *The Life of Galileo* (1943), and *The Caucasian Chalk Circle* (1948). Forced to flee the Nazis in 1933, he spent part of his exile in California, from 1941 to 1947; in 1949 he returned to East Berlin where he founded the Berliner Ensemble. Isherwood and W. H. Auden were youthful admirers of Brecht, and Isherwood translated the verses for Desmond Vesey's 1937 English version of Brecht's *Dreigroschenroman*, *A Penny for the Poor.* In *D1*, Isherwood records that in August 1943, Berthold Viertel introduced Isherwood to Brecht and his wife, Helene Weigel, and their son, Stefan. When they next met, Brecht harshly criticized Isherwood's spiritual convictions and denounced Aldous Huxley, enraging Isherwood.

They continued a tentative friendship, and in April 1944 Brecht asked Isherwood to translate *The Caucasian Chalk Circle*; Isherwood declined partly because he had come to dislike Brecht for his ruthless and somewhat hypocritical obsession with his own beliefs and ambitions.

Brett, Dorothy. English painter. A daughter of Viscount Esher and sister of the Ranee of Sarawak, she studied painting at the Slade. Brett became friends with D. H. Lawrence late in 1915 and was the only one of his circle to accompany Lawrence and Frieda to America in 1924 to found his utopia, Rananim. The plan soon fell apart, though Brett remained with the Lawrences in Taos and travelled with them in Mexico until she was banished by Frieda. She then lived on her own in Taos, returned to Europe where she saw Lawrence one last time in Italy, tried in vain to consummate their long restrained love, and finally settled back in New Mexico. As he mentions in his diary of the time (*D1*), Isherwood read her memoir, *Lawrence and Brett* (1933), in 1940.

Britten, Benjamin (1913–1976). British composer. At W. H. Auden's instigation, Britten composed the music for *The Ascent of F6*, and Isherwood perhaps first met Britten at rehearsals in February 1937. By March 1937, the two were friendly enough to spend the night together at the Jermyn Street Turkish Baths, though they never had a sexual relationship. Britten also wrote the music for the next Auden–Isherwood play, *On the Frontier*. He went to America with Peter Pears in the summer of 1939, but, as Isherwood notes in *D1*, returned to England halfway through the war, registering with Pears as a conscientious objector. A major figure, Britten composed songs, song cycles, orchestral music, works for chorus and orchestra such as his *War Requiem* (1961), and nine operas including *Peter Grimes* (1945), *Albert Herring* (1948), *Billy Budd* (1951), *A Midsummer Night's Dream* (1960), and *Death in Venice* (1973). Don Bachardy recalls that Britten withdrew gradually from his friendship with Isherwood, and Isherwood sensed it was because Britten associated Isherwood closely with Auden, against whom Britten harbored more particular griefs. But there was a reunion between Isherwood and Britten in 1976, in Aldeburgh, not long before Britten died. Pears had visited Isherwood and Bachardy while performing in Los Angeles and was able to bring about the rapprochement. Britten was frail by then and wept when he saw Isherwood.

Brooke, Tim. British novelist; a contemporary of Isherwood at Cambridge, he later spent time in Los Angeles. His novels, published under the name Hugh Brooke, include *The Mad Shepherdess* (1930), *Man Made Angry* (1932), *Miss Mitchell* (1934), and *Saturday Island* (1935). He was a close friend of the dancer Nicky Nadeau.

Brooks, Richard (1912–1992). American novelist, screenwriter, film director and producer. Brooks was a sports writer and radio commentator before he began writing screenplays in the early 1940s; he then went on to direct and produce. His films include *The Blackboard Jungle* (1955), *Cat on a Hot Tin Roof* (1958), *Elmer Gantry* (1960, for which his script won an Academy Award), *Sweet Bird of Youth* (1964), *Lord Jim* (1965), *In Cold Blood* (1967), and

Looking for Mr. Goodbar (1977). One of his novels, *The Producer*, is about Hollywood.

Buckingham, Bob. British policeman; the longtime friend of E. M. Forster. Buckingham's wife, May, was also friendly with Forster.

Burgess, Guy (1910–1963). British diplomat and double agent. Burgess became a communist while at Cambridge, and he was secretly recruited by the Soviets during the 1930s. He worked for the BBC until joining the Foreign Office in the mid-1940s and was meanwhile employed also by MI5. In May 1951, having been recalled from his post in Washington under Kim Philby, Burgess was warned by Anthony Blunt that he was suspected of espionage. He disappeared with Donald Maclean, also a double agent, and it eventually became clear the pair had defected to Moscow (their presence there was announced in 1956). Isherwood first met Burgess in 1938 in London, where Burgess was also friendly with W. H. Auden and Stephen Spender, and Burgess introduced Isherwood to Jacky Hewit. Hewit had been Burgess's lover until Burgess met Peter Pollock that year. After roughly a decade with Pollock, Burgess lived with Hewit again intermittently during the three years leading up to his defection. See also *D1*.

Burra, Edward (1905–1976). English painter and ballet and theatrical designer; he studied at the Royal College of Art. Burra sought out scenes of low life in French cities and ports during the late 1920s and visited New York in the 1930s and 1940s chiefly to paint subjects in black Harlem. He was somewhat influenced by the surrealists and from about the time of the Spanish Civil War he began to introduce into his paintings masked figures such as Isherwood mentions, along with soldiers, skeletons, and bird-men.

Bynner, Witter (1881–1968). American poet. Bynner and Arthur Davison Ficke launched a spoof literary movement, "Spectrism," to parody Pound's Imagism. *Spectra: A Book of Poetic Experiments* achieved wide recognition, and Bynner went on to write more seriously under the identity he adopted for the hoax, Emmanuel Morgan. Afterwards he translated Tang poetry from the Chinese with the scholar Kiang Kang-hu. He had a tortured friendship with D. H. Lawrence and disliked Lawrence's characterization of him as Owen Rhys in *The Plumed Serpent*, which paved the way for his own bitter book about Lawrence, *Journey with Genius* (1951). Bynner lived in Santa Fe with his friend Bob Hunt, and also had a house in Mexico, at Lake Chapala.

Cadmus, Paul (1904–1999). American painter of Basque and Dutch background; trained by his parents and at the National Academy of Design in New York. He worked briefly in advertising, travelled and painted in Europe at the start of the 1930s, and joined the U.S. government Public Works of Art Project in late 1933. Lincoln Kirstein became interested in Cadmus's work after they met in New York in the mid-1930s, and Kirstein later married Cadmus's sister, Fidelma, also trained as a painter. Cadmus drew Isherwood in February 1942 in New York, where Cadmus lived, and the two became friends as Isherwood tells in *D1*. Eventually Cadmus settled in Connecticut with Jon Andersson, continuing to paint into his nineties.

Caffery, Jamie. American journalist and landscape designer. Caffery's family was from Louisiana; he worked as a researcher for *Fortune* magazine and also had jobs with *Time* and *Life* before moving to England where he took up gardening. In 1950 he went to Tangier with David Herbert and became garden columnist for the *Tangier Gazette*. Eventually Caffery settled on the Costa del Sol as a landscape designer. The uncle Isherwood mentions, Jefferson Caffery (1886–1974), was ambassador to Paris from 1944 to 1949 (he had previously been ambassador to Cuba and Brazil and afterwards was ambassador to Egypt). Jefferson Caffery married at fifty but had no children.

Campbell, Sandy (d. 1988). American stage actor; educated, for a time, at Princeton. He appeared with Tallulah Bankhead in Tennessee Williams's *A Streetcar Named Desire*, and published a book of letters about the production. Campbell was also a fact checker at *The New Yorker* and worked with a number of well-known writers including Truman Capote, who especially requested his assistance in 1964 with *In Cold Blood*. He was Donald Windham's lover for many years, and eventually set up a specialist publishing business with Windham in Italy.

Capote, Truman (1924–1984). American novelist, born in New Orleans. Capote worked at *The New Yorker* in the early 1940s and contributed to other magazines. In 1946 he won the O. Henry Prize for his short story, "Miriam," and then he began to write longer works, including *Other Voices, Other Rooms* (1948), *The Grass Harp* (1951), *Breakfast at Tiffany's* (1958), and the non-fiction novel *In Cold Blood* (1966). In later years, Capote travelled extensively and sometimes lived abroad; drink and drugs accelerated the end of his life. Isherwood also writes about him in *D1*.

Cartier-Bresson, Henri (b. 1908). French photographer. He studied art and literature before starting to take photographs at the beginning of the 1930s, and much later in his career, during the 1970s, he returned to painting and drawing. He also worked in film, as an assistant to the French filmmaker Jean Renoir, towards the end of the 1930s. After the war, around the time Isherwood met him, Cartier-Bresson helped to found Magnum Photos, the independent photographic agency.

Caskey, William (Bill) (1921–1981). American photographer, born and raised in Kentucky. Isherwood and Caskey met in June 1945 and by August had begun a serious affair. They split for good in 1951 after intermittent separations. Later Caskey lived in Athens and travelled frequently to Egypt. As well as taking photographs, he made art objects out of junk and for a time had a business beading sweaters. There are many passages about him in *D1*.

Cerf, Bennett (1898–1971). American publisher. Cerf was the founder of Random House, Isherwood's (and W. H. Auden's) first American publisher. He had persuaded Faber and Faber jointly to commission *Journey to a War*, and in early March 1939, when Isherwood was newly arrived in New York, Cerf gave him a $500 advance on his next (unwritten) novel. Cerf founded the Modern Library and held senior posts at Random House until his death. He is popularly known for his books of jokes and humor.

Charlton, Jim (1919–1998). American architect. During the war, Charlton flew twenty-six missions over Germany including a July 1943 daylight raid on Hamburg. From 1948 he and Isherwood shared a friendly-romantic attachment that lasted through a number of years and a number of other lovers. Isherwood tells more about Charlton in *D1*. Towards the end of the 1950s Charlton married a wealthy Swiss woman called Hilde, a mother of three, and had a son with her in September 1958. The marriage ended in divorce. Afterwards he lived in Hawaii until the late 1980s before returning to Los Angeles. He wrote an autobiographical novel called *St. Mick*.

Cockburn, Claud (1904–1981). British journalist; educated at Berkhamsted and Keble College, Oxford. After a stint as New York correspondent for the London *Times*, Cockburn joined the Communist Party of Great Britain in the early 1930s and began producing a weekly newsletter, *The Week*, about the political state of Europe. He was also diplomatic correspondent for the *Daily Worker*. Later, he became a columnist for *The Sunday Telegraph* and contributed to various English journals. He wrote a novel, *Beat the Devil* (1953), and published half a dozen volumes of autobiography.

Cockburn, Jean. See Ross, Jean.

Collier, John (1901–1980). British novelist and screenwriter. Best known for *His Monkey Wife* (1930), he also wrote other fantastic and satirical tales. Isherwood admired his short stories. Collier was poetry editor of *Time and Tide* in the 1920s and early 1930s and came to Hollywood in 1935. In 1951 he moved to Mexico, though he continued to write films, including the script, deplored by Isherwood in *D1*, for the film version of *I Am a Camera*.

Connolly, Cyril (1903–1974). British journalist and critic; educated at Eton and Balliol College, Oxford. Connolly was a regular contributor to English newspapers and magazines. He wrote one novel, *The Rock Pool* (1936), followed by collections that combined criticism, autobiography, and aphorism: *Enemies of Promise* (1938) and *The Unquiet Grave* (1944). Further collections appeared after the war, displaying his gift for parody. In 1939, Connolly founded *Horizon* with Stephen Spender and edited it throughout its publication until 1950. Connolly was married three times: first to Jean Bakewell, who divorced him in 1945, then to Barbara Skelton from 1950 to 1956, and finally, in 1959, to Deirdre Craig with whom he had a son, Matthew, and a daughter, Cressida. From 1940 to 1950 he lived with Lys Lubbock, who worked with him at *Horizon*; they never married, but she changed her name to Connolly by deed poll. He also appears in *D1*.

Coward, Noël (1899–1973). English actor, playwright, and composer; he also published verse, short stories, a novel, and two volumes of autobiography. Coward became famous in his twenties in his own play, *The Vortex* (1924), and went on to write the witty and sophisticated comedies for which he is known best, including *Hay Fever* (1925), *Private Lives* (1930), *Design for Living* (1933), *Blithe Spirit* (1941), and *Present Laughter* (1942). He put together musicals and revues for which he wrote his own scores and lyrics and sang with stylish nonchalance. One of Coward's wartime films, *In Which We Serve* (1942), won an Academy Award, but his reputation declined after the war. He occupied himself with cabaret appearances in London and Las Vegas until a revival of interest in his earlier plays began in the 1960s.

Craft, Robert (Bob). American musician, conductor, critic, and author; colleague and adopted son to Stravinsky during the last twenty-three years of Stravinsky's life. Craft lived and travelled everywhere with the Stravinskys except when professional commitments forced him to do otherwise. Increasingly he conducted for Stravinsky in rehearsals and supervised his recording sessions, substituting entirely for the older man as Stravinsky's health declined. After Stravinsky died, Craft married, had a son, divorced, and later married again. He published excerpts from his diaries as *Stravinsky: Chronicle of a Friendship 1948–1971* (1972, expanded and republished in 1994), and he often appears in *D1*.

Cuevas de Vera, Tota. Argentine rancher. She was married to a Spanish count with whom she had several children, and she managed an 86,000-acre estancia, El Pelado (The Bald One), near Buenos Aires. Isherwood and Caskey visited her there early in 1948, and in *The Condor and the Cows* Isherwood describes El Pelado as a business large enough to send an entire trainload of produce from its own railway station to Buenos Aires each week.

Cukor, George (1899–1983). American film director. Cukor began his career on Broadway in the 1920s and came to Hollywood as a dialogue director for *All Quiet on the Western Front*. In the thirties he directed at Paramount, RKO, and then MGM, moving from studio to studio with his friend and producer David Selznick. He directed Garbo in *Camille* (1936) among others, and Hepburn in her debut, *A Bill of Divorcement* (1932), as well as in *Philadelphia Story* (1940). Other well-known work includes *Dinner at Eight* (1933), *David Copperfield* (1934), *A Star Is Born* (1954), and *My Fair Lady* (1964). As described in *D1*, Isherwood first met Cukor at a party at the Huxleys' in December 1939. Later they became friends and worked together.

Curtiss, Mina. American writer. As a young woman, she lived in London on the fringes of the Bloomsbury group; later she taught French literature at Smith College and published books on French subjects, including a biography of Georges Bizet and a translation of Proust's letters. She married Harry Curtiss in 1924, and after his death she was the longtime lover of Alexis Saint-Léger (St.-John Perse). Like her brother, Lincoln Kirstein, Curtiss was extremely wealthy. She divided her time between Manhattan and her husband's farm, Chapelbrook, in Ashfield, Massachusetts.

Davies, Marion (c. 1898–1961). The Ziegfeld Follies chorus girl taken up by William Randolph Hearst, who financed her movies and tried to make her into a romantic star. Some of her films were successful, though Charlie Chaplin, with whom she also had an affair, noticed that Davies' real talent was for comedy. Her relationship with Hearst is the basis for the story in Orson Welles's *Citizen Kane* (1941), although Welles's heroine is not a close portrait. She lived with Hearst at San Simeon and at houses in Beverly Hills and Santa Monica until he died in 1951. Ten weeks after Hearst's death, she married Captain Horace Brown, whom she had known for many years.

"de Laval, Jay" (probably an assumed name). Chef; he adopted the role of the Baron de Laval. In the mid-1940s he opened a small French restaurant, Café Jay, on the corner of Channel Road and Chautauqua in Santa Monica. As Isherwood tells in *D1*, another restaurant was established in the Virgin Islands, and in 1950 he was briefly in charge of the Mocambo in Los Angeles. Eventually he left California, settled in Mexico, and opened a grand restaurant in Mexico City in the early 1950s. There he also planned interiors with the Mexican designer Arturo Pani, and advised airlines on food, creating a menu for Mexico Air Lines and crockery for Air France. He divided his time between Mexico City and a condominium in Acapulco. De Laval was a friend of Bill Caskey before Isherwood met Caskey, and also of Ben and Jo Masselink.

D1. Christopher Isherwood, *Diaries Volume One 1939–1960*, ed. Katherine Bucknell (London: Methuen, 1996; New York: HarperCollins, 1997). In *Lost Years*, Isherwood usually calls these diaries his journal, as distinct from his day-to-day diaries.

Doone, Rupert (1903–1966). English dancer, choreographer, and theatrical producer. Founder of The Group Theatre, the cooperative venture for which Isherwood and W. H. Auden wrote plays in the 1930s. The son of a factory worker and originally called Reginald Woodfield, Doone ran away to London to become a dancer, then went on to Paris where he was friendly with Cocteau and met Diaghilev, turning down an opportunity to dance in the corps de ballet of the Ballets Russes. He was working in variety and revues in London during 1925 when he met Robert Medley, who became his permanent companion. Doone died of multiple sclerosis after many years of increasing illness.

Dunphy, Jack (1914–1992). American dancer and novelist; born and raised in Philadelphia. Dunphy danced for George Balanchine and was a cowboy in the original production of *Oklahoma!* For a time he was married to the Broadway musical-comedy star Joan McCracken. From 1948 he was Truman Capote's companion, although in Capote's later years they were often apart. He published *John Fury* and *The Nightmovers*.

Durant, Tim. American tennis player and actor. Durant was a tennis star during the 1930s and afterwards worked as an agent for United Artists. He played the part of the general in *The Red Badge of Courage* (1951). He was good-looking and wealthy, and he married and became a father. His athletic prowess never deserted him; he rode race horses well past middle age, and finished the gruelling Grand National when he was in his early seventies.

Edens, Roger (1905–1970). American film producer, born in Texas. During the 1950s, Eden supervised musicals at MGM, sometimes working with Arthur Freed. He won numerous Academy Awards—including for *Annie Get Your Gun* (1950)—and later produced *Funny Face* (1956), *Hello Dolly* (1969), and others.

Erdmann, Charles (b. 1909). Longtime companion of William Plomer. Erdmann was born in London of a German father and Polish mother. At the outbreak of World War I, the family went to Germany where Erdmann was raised from about age five. He returned to England as a refugee in 1939, and worked as a waiter and a pastry-cook (for which he was trained in Germany) and at other things. He met Plomer in 1944 while working as a cloakroom attendant in a Soho restaurant and lived with him for the next twenty-nine years, until Plomer's death.

Evans, Rex (1903–1969). British actor working in Hollywood from 1930 onwards. He also ran an art gallery.

Falk, Eric (1905–1984). English barrister. Falk, who was Jewish, met Isherwood at Repton, where they were in the same house together, The Hall, and in the History Sixth. He helped Isherwood to edit *The Reptonian* during Isherwood's last term. Falk grew up in London, and often went to films with Isherwood during school holidays. He introduced Isherwood to the Mangeots, whom he had met on holiday in Brittany. He appears in *Lions and Shadows* and in *D1*.

Falkenburg, Eugenia (Jinx) (b. 1919). Spanish-born actress, raised in Chile. She began her U.S. career working as a model and then made comedies and musicals in Hollywood in the late 1930s and early 1940s before becoming a radio personality and hosting her own radio show.

Firbank, Ronald (1886–1926). English novelist; educated for a time at Trinity Hall, Cambridge. His grandfather's railroad contracting fortune enabled Firbank to travel and pay for the publication of his own novels and stories. He was a Roman Catholic and a dandy and his writings are witty, fantastic, and somewhat artificial. Among his best-known novels are *Vainglory* (1915), *The Flower Beneath the Foot* (1923), and *Concerning the Eccentricities of Cardinal Pirelli* (1926).

Fontan, Jack (b. 1927). American actor and painter; educated at New York University. After his appearance in the original New York production of *South Pacific*, he settled in Laguna Beach where he made collages with his longtime companion Ray Unger. The pair worked as professional astrologers during the 1970s and afterwards owned and managed a gym. In 1994 their house was destroyed by the widespread fire which devastated the area, and they resettled in Palm Springs.

Forster, E. M. (Morgan) (1878–1970). English novelist, essayist, and biographer; best known for *Howards End* (1910) and *A Passage to India* (1924). His homosexual novel, *Maurice*, was published posthumously in 1971 under Isherwood's supervision. Forster had been an undergraduate at King's College, Cambridge, and one of the Cambridge Apostles; afterwards he became associated with the Bloomsbury group and later returned to King's as a Fellow until the end of his life. He was a literary hero for Isherwood, Edward Upward, and W. H. Auden from the 1920s onward. He remained supportive when Isherwood was publicly criticized for remaining in America after the outbreak of war in 1939. He is mentioned often in *D1*.

Fouts, Denham (Denny). Son of a Florida baker, Fouts left home as a teenager and travelled as companion to a series of wealthy people of both sexes. Among his conquests was Peter Watson, who financed *Horizon* magazine.

Fouts helped Watson solicit some of the earliest contributions to *Horizon*, and Watson gave Fouts a large Picasso painting, *Girl Reading* (1934). The painting was loaned to the Museum of Modern Art under Watson's name for the exhibition *Picasso—Forty Years of His Art*, November 1939–January 7, 1940, and Fouts later sold the painting in New York (evidently to the Florence May Schoenborn and Samuel Marx Collection, whence it became a gift to MOMA).

During the war, Watson sent Fouts to the USA for safety. Isherwood met Fouts in Hollywood in August 1940 and, although Swami Prabhavananda would not accept Fouts as a disciple, Fouts moved in with Isherwood in the early summer of 1941 in order to lead a life of meditation. Isherwood describes this domestic experiment in *Down There on a Visit*, where Fouts appears as "Paul," and there are numerous passages about Fouts in *D1*.

Fouts, a conscientious objector, was drafted into Civilian Public Service Camp part way through the war; after he was released, he got his high school diploma and then studied medicine at UCLA before settling in Europe.

Fowler, Norman. American boyfriend of Peter Watson from 1949 onward, and heir to most of Watson's estate. He had been in the navy and possibly was an epileptic (he was subject to unexplained fits or seizures from which he sometimes had to be roused); he was evidently psychologically disturbed. When Watson drowned in his bath in 1956, Fowler was in the flat; the police dismissed foul play, but the death remained suspicious. After Watson's death, Fowler bought a hotel, called The Bath Hotel, on Nevis, in the British Virgin Islands, and lived there until he himself drowned in the bath in 1971, within weeks of the fifteenth anniversary of Watson's death.

Fox. See Twentieth Century-Fox.

French, Jared (d. 1988). American painter, from Princeton, New Jersey. He met Paul Cadmus at the Art Students League in New York, became his lover, and travelled with him to Europe in 1931. They lived and painted together in Greenwich Village until French married the painter Margaret Hoening in 1937; afterwards the three continued as close friends and artistic associates, styling themselves the PAJAMA group, for PAul, JAred, MArgaret. French died in Rome.

Freud, Lucian (b. 1922). German-born British painter; grandson of Sigmund Freud. He emigrated to London with his parents at the start of the 1930s, studied at the Central School of Arts and Crafts in London and the East Anglian School of Painting and Drawing in Dedham, and became a British citizen in 1939. During the war, he was invalided out of the merchant navy and turned to art full time, establishing a reputation by the early 1950s. His work is figurative and strikingly realistic; he specializes in nudes and portraits.

From, Eddie and Sam. Twin brothers at the center of The Benton Way Group. Eddie's real name was Isadore, and some of his friends called him Isad. The Benton Way Group began when Ruby Bell, a librarian from the Midwest, inherited some money and encouraged a group of her friends, mostly homosexuals and including the Froms and Charles Aufderheide, to move with her to Los Angeles. There she used her inheritance to acquire the house in

Benton Way where they settled together. The house was called The Palazzo because it looked like an Italian villa, and the name later accompanied the household to other settings. Some of the group were able to find work in the film industry, and Eddie From worked for Technicolor before taking up psychotherapy. According to Alvin Novak, Eddie was once picked up by the police for an offense related to his homosexuality, and Isherwood made a lasting impression by coming to his aid. There are more passages about the Froms in *D1*.

Furtmueller, Carl. Viennese school inspector. Isherwood met Furtmueller and his wife in October 1941 at the Quaker refugee hostel in Haverford, Pennsylvania, and describes them in *D1*. The couple had been interned in a Spanish prison on their flight from Vienna, and Mrs. Furtmueller was mortally ill with lung cancer by the time she arrived in the U.S. She died in late November 1941. The following June, Furtmueller married Leah Cadbury, a Haverford spinster in her fifties who worked in an office during the daytime and volunteered as an English teacher at the hostel during the evenings.

Gage, Margaret. A rich and elderly patroness of Gerald Heard. She loaned Heard her garden house on Spoleto Road to live in from the late 1940s until the early 1960s.

Garrett, Eileen (1893–1970). Irish-born medium. During World War I, Eileen Garrett ran a tearoom in Hampstead which was frequented by D. H. Lawrence and other intellectuals; later she ran a labor hostel in Euston Square, and then a children's soup kitchen in the south of France. In 1941, with the fall of France, she went to New York, founded a publishing firm, Creative Age Press, and launched *Tomorrow*, a monthly review of literature, art, and public affairs. Assisted by Bill Kennedy, she was able to commission work from the likes of Robert Graves, Klaus Mann, Aldous Huxley, Lord Dunsany, and Isherwood, among others; she knew many of the emigré intelligentsia, and Isherwood met her in the late 1940s or early 1950s through the Huxleys.

Geller, Jim. American film agent. Geller was a story editor at Warner Brothers during the 1940s and expressed interest in Isherwood's work, especially the film treatment written with Aldous Huxley, *Jacob's Hands*. Later Geller abandoned his studio career, and by the early 1950s he had become Isherwood's agent. Isherwood moved on to Hugh French about a decade later. Both relationships are traced in *D1*.

Ghosh, Asit. Bengali nephew of Swami Prabhavananda. Ghosh was a student at the University of Southern California and hoped to become a film director. He was a devout Hindu, and lived at the Hollywood Vedanta Center during the early 1940s, but he was not preparing to become a monk. Isherwood tells about this in *D1*. In September 1944 Ghosh found himself inducted into the army even though he was not a U.S. citizen. He was released the following January as a conscientious objector, and soon afterwards he returned to India.

Gielgud, John (b. 1904). British actor and director. Gielgud achieved fame in the 1920s acting Shakespeare's tragedies; he also performed Wilde and

Chekhov before Chekhov was well known to English audiences. During the 1950s and 1960s, he worked with contemporary British playwrights, but throughout his stage and film career he returned to and extended his Shakespearian repertoire. He was late to adapt his career to film, but became a ubiquitous success. Isherwood also tells about their friendship in *D1*.

Goldsmith, Joel (1892–1964). American spiritual teacher and healer. Goldsmith came from a Jewish background in New York, turned to Christianity as a teenager, and was drawn to Christian Science when his father miraculously recovered from a grave illness. He was a Freemason for most of his life, and during the 1930s he took up meditation and studied eastern religions. As a marine during World War II, he had a vision calling him to pray for the enemy. He never saw combat. After the war, the family business collapsed and Goldsmith fell ill with tuberculosis, but like his father he made a miraculous recovery—through Christian Science. After failing as a travelling salesman, he became a Christian Science spiritual reader, advisor and healer, sometimes seeing as many as 135 patients a day. He taught Bible classes in California and gathered students and devotees around him, including John van Druten and Walter Starcke. Van Druten wrote the introduction to *The Infinite Way* (1952), the first of Goldsmith's twenty or so books. In the early 1950s Goldsmith resigned from the Christian Science Church, asserting that healers become so by their own authority. His movement, known as the Infinite Way, was funded partly by the donations of wealthy followers; he also circulated a monthly newsletter to paying subscribers. He urged believers to live by grace alone; his own experience taught him that material success would naturally flow toward those who were spiritually "centered" or "on the path." He was married three times.

Goodwin, John. American novelist. A wealthy friend of Denny Fouts; Isherwood met him probably during the first half of 1943 and often mentions him in *D1*. As well as his ranch near Escondido, Goodwin owned a house in New York. He published *The Idols and the Prey* (1953) and *A View of Fuji* (1963).

Gottfried. See Reinhardt, Gottfried.

Goyen, William (1915–1983). American novelist, playwright, teacher, and editor; born in Texas, where much of his work is set. His novels include *The House of Breath* (1950), for which Isherwood wrote a blurb, and *In a Farther Country* (1955); he also wrote many short stories.

Grant, Alexander (b. 1925). New Zealand-born ballet dancer and director. He spent his whole dancing career with the Sadler's Wells, later the Royal Ballet at Covent Garden.

Green, Henry (1905–1973). Pen name of Henry Yorke, the novelist. Yorke came from a privileged background, was educated at Eton and Magdalen College, Oxford, worked for a time in a factory belonging to his family and then made his way up through the firm to become managing director. His novels draw on his experience of both working-class and upper-class life, and also on his time in the National Fire Service during World War II; best known among them are *Living*, *Party Going*, and *Loving*. Isherwood also mentions Yorke's wife, who was known as Dig.

Greene, Felix. A half-German cousin of Isherwood, on Kathleen Isherwood's side. Greene worked for the BBC in New York, then with Peggy Kiskadden's second husband, Henwar Rodakiewicz, in Rodakiewicz's documentary film unit, and, during the war, for the Quaker Friends Service Committee in Philadelphia. He had a genius for administration and practical arrangements and made himself indispensable to Gerald Heard in founding Trabuco. Greene decided to move to California in the summer of 1941 to be Heard's disciple, and by the following summer he had already completed the building of the monastery, large enough for fifty. Isherwood tells about this in *D1*. Towards the end of the war Greene upset Heard by deciding to marry.

Halliburton, Richard (1900–1939). American explorer and adventurer; educated at Lawrenceville Academy and Princeton. During the 1920s he climbed the Matterhorn and swam various famous bodies of water (the Nile at Luxor, the Hellespont, most of the Sea of Galilee, the Panama Canal). He also flew from Paris to Manila in his airplane, *The Flying Carpet*, in 1931. In 1934 he attempted but failed to cross the Alps on an elephant. He wrote a number of bestselling books about his adventures and lectured widely. After selling the movie rights to his first book, *The Royal Road to Romance* (1925), he settled in Hollywood where he narrated and co-directed a travel film about India, *India Speaks* (1933). Halliburton was homosexual and had relationships with the film stars Rod la Rocque and Ramon Novarro. He was lost at sea in the Pacific.

Hamilton, Gerald (1890–1970). Isherwood's Berlin friend who was the original for "Mr. Norris" in *Mr. Norris Changes Trains*. Hamilton's mother died almost immediately after his birth in Shanghai, and he was raised by relatives in England and educated at Rugby (though he did not finish his schooling). His father sent him back to China to work in business, and while there Hamilton took to wearing Chinese dress and converted to Roman Catholicism, for which his father, an Irish Protestant, never forgave him. He was cut off with a small allowance and eventually, because of his unsettled life, with nothing at all. So began the persistent need for money that apparently motivated some of his dubious behavior. Hamilton was obsessed with his family's aristocratic connections and with social etiquette, and lovingly recorded in his memoirs all his meetings with royalty, as well as those with crooks and with theatrical and literary celebrities. He was imprisoned from 1915 to 1918 for sympathizing with Germany and associating with the enemy during World War I, and he was imprisoned in France and Italy for a jewelry swindle in the 1920s. Afterwards he took a job selling the London *Times* in Germany and became interested there in penal reform. Throughout his life he travelled on diverse private and public errands in China, Russia, Europe, and North Africa. He returned to London during World War II, where he was again imprisoned, as Isherwood records, for attempting to promote peace on terms favorable to the enemy. After the war, Hamilton posed for the body of Churchill's Guildhall statue and later became a regular contributor to *The Spectator*.

Harford, Betty. Irish-born actress; she acted for John Houseman in numerous stage productions and made a few movies, including *Inside Daisy Clover*. Harford was a close friend of Iris Tree. Her son with Oliver Andrews —Christopher, born in the 1950s—was named after Isherwood.

Harkness, Alan. Australian-born actor; director of The High Valley Theatre in the Ojai Valley, where he specialized in teaching and directing the plays of Chekhov. A few members of the group first met in the late 1930s at the theater school at Dartington founded by Michael Chekhov (nephew of the playwright) and followed Chekhov to Connecticut. When Chekhov's school broke up during the war, they went on to southern California, continuing to study and act together while also doing obligatory war work (they were mostly pacifists). Eventually the group was able to purchase a schoolhouse in the Upper Ojai Valley and converted it themselves into a theater. The High Valley Theatre aimed to be a school as well as an acting company. Harkness continued to follow Michael Chekhov's approach to acting, which was derived from the teachings of Rudolf Steiner and the methods of the Moscow Art Theater. He emphasized creating a character from the imagination and from observation and giving autonomous life to this character on stage rather than impersonating. The group frequently worked by improvisation. Harkness was killed in Carpinteria when his car was hit by a train at a railroad crossing.

Harrington, Curtis (b. 1928). American director; he made underground films and then moved on to features and television. At a party in 1954, Isherwood punched Harrington in the face after a friend of Harrington also at the party made advances to Don Bachardy; Harrington sued Isherwood and they eventually settled out of court.

Harris, Bill (d. 1992). American artist. Isherwood met him in the summer of 1943, and they began a love affair the following spring. The relationship lasted only as a casual friendship. Harris later moved to New York where he became successful as a commercial art retoucher. Isherwood refers to Harris as "X." in his 1939–1945 diaries (see *D1*), and he calls him "Alfred" in *My Guru and His Disciple*.

Hartford, Huntington. Grandson and heir of the A&P grocery stores multimillionaire, Huntington Hartford, for whom he was named. He produced films and took an active interest in the arts. He was ultra-conservative, anticommunist, and homophobic. He set up the Huntington Hartford Foundation in 1949 to nurture artists, writers, and musicians. Frank Taylor assembled the board of directors, which included Isherwood, W. H. Auden, Speed Lamkin, Michael Gaszynski, and Robert Penn Warren, among others. Isherwood records more about the foundation in *D1*. The job of board members was to give away fellowships bringing young artists to live and work at the foundation for three months. By 1951 there were 150 people living there —a western Yaddo. The board members resigned one by one as Hartford's views gradually emerged in intolerable forms (for instance, he wanted each of them to submit to a graphology test which he believed would reveal their respective sexual inclinations). Hartford disliked avant-garde art; he also founded a museum of contemporary art in New York to foster his theories, and the building later became his New York headquarters. Isherwood never respected Hartford and found the management of the foundation inefficient and too easily swayed by gossip and favoritism; he resigned in 1952 when a resident writer was ousted from his fellowship for having an unauthorized overnight guest. Eventually the foundation became an arts and crafts colony.

Hatfield, Hurd (1918–c.1998). American actor; from New York City, educated at Columbia. He made his debut on the London stage and later appeared on Broadway. Hatfield began working in films in 1944 and played the lead in *The Picture of Dorian Gray* (1945), but stardom eluded him, and he is mostly admired for his stage roles. Later films include *Joan of Arc* (1948), *El Cid* (1961), and *Crimes of the Heart* (1986), among others.

Hauser, Hilda. Housekeeper and cook to Olive and André Mangeot, and to Olive after the Mangeots divorced. Isherwood first met her when he began working for André Mangeot in 1925.

Hayden. See Lewis, Hayden.

Hayward, John (1905–1965). British editor and scholar. Hayward was crippled by muscular dystrophy and was confined to a wheelchair. He shared a flat in Chelsea with T. S. Eliot from 1946 until 1957, when Eliot remarried.

Heard, Henry FitzGerald (Gerald) (c.1885–1971). Irish writer, broadcaster, philosopher, and religious teacher. W. H. Auden took Isherwood to meet Heard in London in 1932 when Heard was already well-known as a science commentator for the BBC and author of several books on the evolution of human consciousness and on religion. A charismatic talker, Heard associated with some of the most celebrated intellectuals of the time. One of his closest friends was Aldous Huxley, whom he met in 1929 and with whom he joined the Peace Pledge Union in 1935 and then emigrated to Los Angeles in 1937 accompanied by Heard's friend Chris Wood and Huxley's wife and son. Both Heard and Huxley became disciples of Swami Prabhavananda. Isherwood followed Heard to Los Angeles and through him met Prabhavananda.

Heard broke with the Swami early in 1941, and set up his own monastic community, Trabuco College, the same year. By 1949 Trabuco had failed, and he gave it to the Vedanta Society of Southern California to use as a monastery. During the early 1950s, Heard shared Huxley's experiments with mescaline and LSD. He contributed to *Vedanta for the Western World* (1945) edited by Isherwood, and throughout most of his life he turned out prolix and eccentric books at an impressive pace; these included *The Ascent of Humanity* (1929), *The Social Substance of Religion* (1932), *The Third Morality* (1937), *Pain, Sex, and Time* (1939), *Man the Master* (1942), *A Taste for Honey* (1942, adapted as a play by John van Druten), *The Gospel According to Gamaliel* (1944), *Is God Evident?* (1948), and *Is Another World Watching?* (1950, published in England as *The Riddle of the Flying Saucers*; see also UFOs). There were many more books.

Heard is the original of "Augustus Parr" in *Down There on a Visit* and of "Propter" in Huxley's *After Many a Summer* (1939). He also appears in *My Guru and His Disciple* and throughout *D1*.

Heinz. See Neddermeyer, Heinz.

Hersey, John (1914–1993). American writer; born in China, educated at Yale. He was *Time* magazine's Far East correspondent from 1937 to 1946, and during the same period he published his Pulitzer Prize-winning documentary novel, *A Bell for Adano* (1944; filmed the following year). Hersey wrote various other semi-fictionalized books about World War II, and a pamphlet-length, first-hand account of the effects of nuclear explosion, *Hiroshima* (1946). There were many further novels, short stories and works of nonfiction, several of which were dramatized.

Hewit, Jack (1917–1998). English dancer, spy, and civil servant; son of a metal worker. He won a scholarship to ballet school, but his father forbade him to accept it, so he ran away from home and began dancing in revues. He met Guy Burgess while dancing in the chorus of *No, No, Nanette* and became Burgess's lover; Burgess involved him in counterespionage work for MI5. Through Burgess, Hewit also met Anthony Blunt, and became Blunt's lover as well. Burgess and Blunt ran Hewit's spy career for him, passing on his intelligence to the KGB as well as to MI5. Isherwood met Hewit towards the end of 1938 through Burgess and mentions him in *D1*. During the war, Hewit joined the Royal Artillery, but was transferred back to MI5; afterwards, he joined UNESCO. He lived with Burgess at different periods, including the three years leading up to Burgess's defection to the Soviet Union in May 1951. The connections with Burgess and Blunt bedeviled Hewit in later life, though he was able to join the Civil Service as a clerk in 1956 and left as a Higher Executive Officer in 1977. He published one short story, "Tales of Cedric" (1991).

Hirschfeld, Magnus (1868–1935). German sex researcher; founder of the Institute for Sexual Science in Berlin, where he studied sexual deviancy. Hirschfeld wrote books on sexual-psychological themes and dispensed psychological counselling and medical treatment (primarily for sexually transmitted diseases). He was homosexual and campaigned for reform of the German criminal code in order to legalize homosexuality between men. His work was jeopardized by the Nazis and he was beaten up several times; he left Germany in 1930 and died in France at around the same time that the Nazis raided his institute and publicly burned a bust of him along with his published works. Isherwood took a room next door to the Institute in 1930 and first met Hirschfeld then, through Francis Turville-Petre.

Holmes, John (1910–1988). Canadian diplomat, author, and teacher. Holmes was born in Ontario and educated at the University of Western Ontario, the University of Toronto, and the University of London. He held many diplomatic and academic posts in Canada and abroad. When Isherwood met him in 1947, Holmes was completing a three-year post as First Secretary at Canada House in London and preparing to spend a year as the Chargé d'affaires at the Canadian Embassy in Moscow. Later he represented Canada at the U.N. and served as the Assistant Under Secretary of State for External Affairs (1953–1960). When he retired from public service, he became the Director General of the Canadian Institute of International Affairs and was a Professor of International Relations at the University of Toronto. His books include a two-volume work *The Shaping of Peace: Canada and the Search for World Order, 1943–1957* (1979 and 1982) and *Life with Uncle: The Canadian-American Relationship* (1982).

Hooker, Evelyn Caldwell (1907–1996). American psychologist and psychotherapist, trained at the University of Chicago and Johns Hopkins; professor of psychology at UCLA where for a time she shared an office with the Rorschach expert, Bruno Klopfer, who was impressed by her work and assisted and encouraged her. Hooker was among the first to view homosexuality as a normal psychological condition. Encouraged by her involvement with The Benton Way Group and, according to Alvin Novak, inspired in particular by her close friendship with Sam From—to whom, Novak recalls, she was especially drawn, and who was equally drawn to her—she worked with and studied homosexuals in the Los Angeles area for many years. At Klopfer's urging, she first presented her research publicly at a 1956 conference in Chicago, demonstrating that as high a percentage of homosexuals as heterosexuals were psychologically well-adjusted. The paper, entitled "The Adjustment of the Male Overt Homosexual," was later published in a Burbank periodical, *Projective Techniques* (this was the journal of the Society for Projective Techniques and the Rorschach Institute; it later changed its title to *Journal of Projective Techniques and Personality Assessment*). Born Evelyn Gentry, she took the name Caldwell from a brief first marriage, then changed to Hooker when she married Edward Hooker, a professor of English at UCLA and a Dryden scholar, at the start of the 1950s. Isherwood lived in the Hookers' garden house on Saltair Avenue in Brentwood for a time in 1952-1953. He describes the friendship in *D1*.

Hopper, Hedda (1890–1966). American actress and Hollywood columnist. She began in silent movies and went on to act in many sound films, but she was best known for her influential columns. She also wrote several volumes of autobiography.

Horst (1906–1999). German-born fashion photographer. Horst B. Horst (also known as Horst Bohrmann) was a shopkeeper's son, from a small German town; he studied art history in Hamburg, then persuaded Le Corbusier to take him on as an architectural assistant in Paris in the early 1930s. In Paris he became a protégé of the Russian-born, half-American photographer George Hoyningen-Huene with whom he worked for many years. Like Hoyningen-Huene, Horst photographed Parisian and Russian emigré society, and took countless pictures for *Vogue* and other fashion magazines. Another mentor was the American fashion photographer George Platt Lynes. Horst eventually made New York his home, but frequently travelled and worked in Europe.

Houseman, John (1902–1988). American movie producer and actor. Houseman began as a stage producer and founded the Mercury Theater with Orson Welles in 1937. He produced Welles's *Citizen Kane* (1941) and then worked for David Selznick in Hollywood. After the war he worked in theater, film, and, eventually, television. He produced a long string of successful, widely admired films before taking the first of many acting roles in *Seven Days in May* (1964), and he won an Academy Award for his supporting role in *The Paper Chase* (1973).

Howard, Brian (1905–1958). English poet and aesthete of American parentage; an outspoken antifascist. Howard was educated at Eton and Christ Church, Oxford, where he became friends with W. H. Auden. He was exceedingly dissolute, a heavy drinker and a drug user, and he never lived up to his promise as a writer. Evelyn Waugh's character Ambrose Silk in *Put Out More Flags* is modelled on Howard, and Anthony Blanche in *Brideshead Revisited* is also partly inspired by him. Howard lived a vagrant's life, moving from place to place in Europe, and was often in Paris. Isherwood met him in Amsterdam in 1936, during the period when each of them was trying to find a country where he could live with his German boyfriend—Howard's boyfriend throughout the 1930s was a Bavarian known as Toni. At the start of the war, Toni was interned in the south of France; Howard worked for his release evidently in vain, but after the fall of France, Toni escaped to New York via Tangier. He found work loading trucks at night, and soon married a wealthy American woman. Howard worked briefly for British intelligence and then joined the RAF as a clerk and later a public relations writer. After the war he again travelled to and from Europe, with his new companion Sam Langford, struggling with alcoholism and eventually with tuberculosis which propelled him ever faster into drug addiction. When Langford died in their new home in the south of France, Howard committed suicide with a drug overdose.

Hoyt, Karl. A close friend of Chris Wood during the early 1940s. He was drafted into the army during World War II and afterwards settled in Bel Air, the Los Angeles suburb.

Huston, John (1906–1987). Film director, screenwriter, and actor. Huston wrote scripts for a number of successful films during the 1930s and early 1940s before making his directing debut with *The Maltese Falcon* (1941); he directed many more movies during the following fifty years—including *The Treasure of Sierra Madre* (1947), *The African Queen* (1952), *Beat the Devil* (1954), *The Misfits* (1960), *Fat City* (1971), and *Prizzi's Honor* (1985). *The Red Badge of Courage* (1951) was adapted from Stephen Crane's novel about the Civil War. Huston also continued intermittently as a writer and occasionally acted.

Huxley, Aldous (1894–1963). English novelist and utopian. Not long after he arrived in Los Angeles, Isherwood was introduced to Huxley by Gerald Heard. Huxley was then writing screenplays for MGM for a large weekly salary, and he and Isherwood later collaborated on several film projects. Like Heard, Huxley was a disciple of Prabhavananda, but subsequently he became close to Krishnamurti, the one-time Messiah of the theosophical movement. Huxley was educated at Eton and Oxford, a grandson of Thomas Huxley and brother of Julian Huxley, both prominent scientists. In youth he published poetry, short stories, and satirical novels such as *Crome Yellow* (1921) and *Antic Hay* (1923), drawing on life in London's literary bohemia and at Lady Ottoline Morrell's Garsington Manor, where Huxley worked as a conscientious objector during World War I. He lived abroad in Italy and France during the 1920s and 1930s, part of the time with D. H. Lawrence—who appears in his *Point Counter Point* (1928)—and Lawrence's wife, Frieda. In 1932 Huxley published *Brave New World*, for which he is most famous.

An ardent pacifist, Huxley joined the Peace Pledge Union in 1935, but became disillusioned as Europe moved towards war. His *Ends and Means* (1937) was regarded as a basic book for pacifists. In April 1937 he sailed for America with his first wife, Maria, and their adolescent son, accompanied by Gerald Heard and by Heard's friend Chris Wood. Huxley's plans to return to Europe fell through when he tried and failed to sell a film scenario in Hollywood, became ill there, and convalesced for nearly a year. California benefitted his health and eyesight—he had been nearly blind since an adolescent illness—but he was denied U.S. citizenship on grounds of his extreme pacifism. *After Many a Summer* (1939) is set in Los Angeles, and Huxley wrote many other books during the period that Isherwood knew him best, including *Grey Eminence* (1941), *Time Must Have a Stop* (1944), *The Devils of Loudun* (1952), *The Genius and the Goddess* (1956).

Huxley's study of Vedanta was part of a larger interest in mysticism and parapsychology, and beginning in the early 1950s he experimented with mescaline, LSD, and psilocybin, experiences which he wrote about in *The Doors of Perception* (1954) and *Heaven and Hell* (1956). In addition to *Below the Equator* (later called *Below the Horizon*) Huxley and Isherwood also worked together on two other screenplay ideas during the 1940s: *Jacob's Hands*, about a healer, and a film version of *The Miracle*, Max Reinhardt's celebrated 1920s stage production. Isherwood often writes about Huxley in *D1*.

In 1960 Huxley found a malignant tumor on his tongue but refused surgery in favor of less radical treatment; he died of cancer on the same day John F. Kennedy was shot.

Huxley, Maria Nys (1898–1955). Belgian first wife of Aldous Huxley. Isherwood met her in the summer of 1939 soon after he arrived in Los Angeles and mentions her frequently in *D1*. Maria Nys was the eldest daughter of a prosperous textile merchant ruined in World War I. Her mother's family included artists and intellectuals, and her childhood was pampered, multi-lingual, and devoutly Catholic. She met Huxley at Garsington Manor where she lived as a refugee during World War I; they married in Belgium in 1919 and their only child, Matthew, was born in 1920. Before her marriage, Maria showed promise as a dancer and trained briefly with Nijinsky, but her health was too frail for a professional career. She had little formal education and devoted herself to Huxley and to his work. Her premature death resulted from cancer. According to Huxley, she was a natural mystic and had "pre-mystical" experiences in the desert in California in the 1940s.

Huxley, Matthew (b. 1920). British-born son of Aldous and Maria Huxley. Matthew Huxley was brought to America in adolescence and Isherwood met him in Santa Monica in 1939. He attended the University of Colorado with the intention of becoming a doctor, served in the U.S. Army Medical Corps during World War II, and was invalided out of the army in 1943. Much of this is recorded in *D1*. Huxley became a U.S. citizen in 1945. In 1947 he took a degree from Berkeley and later studied public health at Harvard. This became his career, and for many years he worked at the National Institute of Mental Health in Washington, D.C. He also published a book about Peru, *Farewell to Eden* (1965). He married three times, and had two children with his first wife.

Hyndman, Tony. Secretary and companion to Stephen Spender in the early

1930s. Hyndman ran away from his working-class home in Wales at eighteen and spent three years in the army before becoming unemployed and meeting Spender. He split with Spender in the autumn of 1936, became a communist, joined the International Brigade, and went to fight in the Spanish Civil War. In Spain, he was greatly disillusioned and became a pacifist. He deserted and was imprisoned, but eventually Spender, who had followed him to Spain, obtained his release. Hyndman appears as "Jimmy Younger" in Spender's *World Within World* and in *Christopher and His Kind*.

Ince, Thomas (1882–1924). American film director and producer. Ince moved from stage and vaudeville to become an important figure in the early film industry. The studios he built at Culver City in 1916 evolved into MGM and the company, Triangle, which he formed with two other partners, D. W. Griffith and Mack Sennett, eventually became United Artists. His later films were released through Adolph Zukor. Ince became mortally ill while on board William Randolph Hearst's yacht *Oneida*; his death two days later was attributed to heart failure resulting from severe indigestion, but rumor suggested that Hearst shot Ince, either because he suspected Ince of having an affair with Marion Davies or because Hearst suspected Charlie Chaplin, also on board the yacht, of having an affair with Davies and shot Ince when he mistook him for Chaplin.

Isherwood, Henry Bradshaw. Isherwood's uncle (his father's elder brother). In 1924 Uncle Henry inherited Marple Hall and the family estates on the death of Isherwood's grandfather, John Bradshaw Isherwood. Though he married late in life (changing his name to Bradshaw-Isherwood-Bagshawe in honor of his wife), Uncle Henry had no children; thus, Isherwood was his heir, and for a time after Isherwood's twenty-first birthday he received a quarterly allowance from his uncle. The two had an honest if self-interested friendship, occasionally dining together and sharing intimate details of their personal lives. When Henry Isherwood died in 1940, Isherwood at once passed on the entire inheritance to his own younger brother, Richard Isherwood.

Isherwood, Kathleen Bradshaw (1868–1960). Isherwood's mother. The only child of Frederick Machell Smith, a successful wine merchant, and Emily Greene, Kathleen was born and lived until sixteen in Bury St. Edmunds, then moved with her parents to London. She travelled abroad, mostly with her mother, and helped her mother to write a guidebook for walkers, *Our Rambles in Old London* (1895). She married Frank Isherwood in 1903 when she was thirty-five years old. They had two sons, Isherwood, and his much younger brother, Richard. After the second battle of Ypres in May 1915, Kathleen was told her husband (by then a colonel in the York and Lancasters) was missing, but it was many months before his death was officially confirmed, and she never obtained definite information about how he died. Isherwood's portrait of her in *Kathleen and Frank* is partly based on her own letters and diaries (he regarded the latter as her masterpiece), but heavily shaped by his attitude towards her. She was also the original for the fictional character "Lily" in *The Memorial*. Isherwood mentions her throughout *D1*.

Like many mothers of her class and era, Kathleen consigned her sons to the care of their nanny from infancy and later sent Isherwood to boarding school.

Her husband's death affected her profoundly, which Isherwood sensed and resented from an early age. Their relationship was intimate and mutually tender in Isherwood's boyhood, increasingly fraught and formal as he grew older. Like her husband, Kathleen was a talented amateur painter. She was intelligent, forceful, handsome, dignified, and capable of great charm. Isherwood felt she was obsessed by class distinctions and propriety. As the surviving figure of authority in his family, she epitomized everything against which he wished to rebel. Her intellectual aspirations were narrow and traditional, despite her intelligence, and she seemed to him increasingly backward looking. Nonetheless, she was utterly loyal to both of her notably unconventional sons and, as Isherwood himself recognized, she shared many qualities with him.

Isherwood, Richard Graham Bradshaw (1911–1979). Christopher Isherwood's brother and his only sibling. Younger by seven years, Richard Isherwood was also backward in life. He was reluctant to be educated, and never held a job in adulthood, although he did wartime national service as a farmworker at Wyberslegh and at another farm nearby, Dan Bank. In childhood Richard saw little of his elder brother who was sent to boarding school by the time Richard was three. The two brothers became closer during Richard's adolescence, when Isherwood was sometimes at home in London and took his brother's side against their mother's efforts to advance Richard's education and settle him in a career. During this period Richard met some of Isherwood's friends and even helped Isherwood with his work by taking dictation. Richard was homosexual, but he seems to have had little opportunity to develop any longterm relationships, hampered as he was by his mother's scrutiny and his own shyness.

In 1941, Richard returned permanently with his mother and nanny to Wyberslegh—signed over to him by Isherwood with the Marple estate—where he lived, more and more, as an eccentric semi-recluse. There are further passages about him in *D1*. After Kathleen Isherwood's death in 1960, Richard depended upon a local family, the Bradleys. He had become friends with Alan Bradley after the war when Bradley was working at Wyberslegh Farm, and Bradley and his wife, Edna, cared for Richard when Kathleen died. Later, Bradley's brother, Dan Bradley, took over the role with his wife, Evelyn (Richard referred to them as the Dans). Richard was by then a heavy drinker. Marple Hall fell into ruin and became dangerous, and Richard was forced to hand it over to the local council which demolished it in 1959, building houses and a school on the grounds. He lived in one of several new houses built beside Wyberslegh, with the Dans in a similar house next door to him, and when Richard died he left most of the contents of his house to the Dans and the house itself to their daughter and son-in-law. Richard's will also provided for money bequests to the Dans, Alan Bradley, and other local friends. Family property and other money was left to Isherwood and to a cousin, Thomas Isherwood, but Isherwood refused the property and passed his share of money to the Dans.

japam. A method for achieving spiritual focus in Vedanta by repeating one of the names for God, usually the name that is one's own mantra; sometimes the repetitions are counted on a rosary. The rosary of the Ramakrishna Order has

108 beads plus an extra bead, representing the guru, which hangs down with a tassel on it; at the tassel bead, the devotee reverses the rosary and begins counting again. For each rosary, the devotee counts one hundred repetitions towards his own spiritual progress and eight for mankind. Isherwood always used a rosary when making japam.

Jay. See de Laval, Jay.

John, Augustus (1878–1961). English painter, trained at the Slade during the 1890s. His most admired work was produced during the first two decades of the twentieth century, and he is remembered above all for his portraits, especially of literary figures including Hardy, Yeats, Shaw, Dylan Thomas, T. E. Lawrence, Joyce, and Joyce's friend Oliver Gogarty. John knew many other writers, and led a flamboyantly bohemian life involving numerous affairs and children out of wedlock. He is said to be the model for characters in various novels of his period.

Johnson, Celia (1908–1982). British actress, primarily on the stage. She made her film debut in Noël Coward's *In Which We Serve* (1942) and is best known for her role in his *Brief Encounter* (1945). She also appeared in *The Prime of Miss Jean Brodie* (1968) and continued to act on stage and television until near the end of her life.

journal. In *Lost Years*, Isherwood often uses the term "journal" for his earlier diaries which have been published in Christopher Isherwood, *Diaries Volume One 1939–1960*, ed. Katherine Bucknell (London: Methuen, 1996; New York: HarperCollins, 1997). Editorial notes refer to this published volume of diaries by the abbreviation *D1*.

Kallman, Chester (1921–1975). American poet and librettist; companion and collaborator to W. H. Auden. He also appears in *D1*. Auden met Kallman in New York in May 1939, and they lived together intermittently in New York, Ischia, and Kirchstetten for the rest of Auden's life, though Kallman spent a great deal of his time with other friends, often in Athens as he grew older. Kallman published three volumes of poetry and with Auden wrote and translated a number of opera libretti, notably *The Rake's Progress* (for Stravinsky), *Elegy for Young Lovers* and *The Bassarids* (both for Hans Werner Henze).

Kazan, Elia (b. 1909). American stage and film director, born in Constantinople to Greek parents. He studied at Yale and began his career as an actor on Broadway and in Hollywood. Among the plays he directed are Thornton Wilder's *The Skin of Our Teeth* (1942); Arthur Miller's *Death of a Salesman* (1949); and Tennessee Williams's *A Streetcar Named Desire* (1947), *Cat on a Hot Tin Roof* (1955), and *Sweet Bird of Youth* (1959). Kazan brought his production of *A Streetcar Named Desire* to the screen, and he made a number of other celebrated films, including *Gentleman's Agreement* (1947, Academy Award), *East of Eden* (1954), and *On the Waterfront* (1954, Academy Award). He was a founder in 1947 of The Actors Studio, famous for Method acting. In 1962 he moved from The Actors Studio to The Lincoln Center Repertory Company, then turned to writing fiction and eventually his own autobiography, *Elia Kazan: A Life* (1988). He also appears in *D1*.

Keate, Richard (Dick) (b. 1922). American pilot and furniture designer. Keate flew B-17s for the air force during World War II and afterwards became a flying instructor in northern California. From there he often visited Santa Monica Canyon and sometimes took trips with Isherwood and Carlos McClendon to Johnny Goodwin's ranch and to the bullfights in Tijuana. In the late 1940s he was a pilot for Air Services of India (now Air India) and lived in India. When he returned to California, he attended the American School of Dance on the GI Bill and worked as a dancer. In 1956 he moved to New York, planning to take up acting, but instead studied Flamenco guitar; his studies took him to Spain where he became interested in furniture, and he began to import Spanish furniture to New York and then to design and manufacture his own furniture. He opened a shop, Casa Castellana, in Greenwich Village in 1964 and was successful for many years.

Kelley. Howard Kelley; see Index and see also *D1*.

Kennedy, Bill. American editor, magazine publisher, and radio host. Kennedy lived in New York, but Isherwood first met him in January 1949 at Salka Viertel's house. During the 1940s, Kennedy helped the medium Eileen Garrett to relaunch her psychic magazine *Tomorrow* as a literary publication, and he later persuaded Isherwood to write regular reviews for it. He also co-hosted a radio show, "The World in Books," with a friend Vernon Brooks; both Isherwood and W. H. Auden were guests on the show.

Kennedy, Ludovic (b. 1919). Scottish-born writer and broadcaster; educated at Eton and Christ Church, Oxford. He served in the British navy during World War II and worked as a librarian and a lecturer before joining the BBC, where he presented television news and public affairs programs. He was a newscaster for ITN in the mid-1950s. His later television shows also focused on criminal and legal topics, especially miscarriages of justice, and he published books on similar matters. In the late 1950s he ran for Parliament. As Isherwood mentions, he is married to Moira Shearer.

Kennington, Eric (1888–1960). English painter and, later, sculptor. Kennington was born in London, studied at the Lambeth School of Art, and was an official war artist during both world wars. He is best known for his illustrations of T. E. Lawrence's *The Seven Pillars of Wisdom* (1926). The illustration Isherwood saw at Forster's flat, of Mahmas, a camel driver, appears in book 7, chapter 87.

Kirstein, Lincoln (1907–1996). American dance impresario, author, editor, and philanthropist. Isherwood's first meeting with Kirstein in New York in 1939 was suggested by Stephen Spender who had already befriended Kirstein in London. Kirstein was raised in Boston, the son of a wealthy self-made businessman. He was educated at Berkshire, Exeter, and Harvard where he was founding editor of *Hound and Horn*, the quarterly magazine on dance, art, and literature. He also painted and helped establish the Harvard Society for Contemporary Art. In 1933 Kirstein persuaded the Russian choreographer George Balanchine to come to New York, and together they founded the School of American Ballet and the New York City Ballet. Kirstein was also involved in starting the Museum of Modern Art in New York, and in other similar projects. His taste and critical judgement combined with his entrée into wealthy society enabled him to promote some of the great artistic talent of the twentieth century. In 1941 he married Fidelma Cadmus (Fido), sister of the painter Paul Cadmus. He served in the army from 1943 to 1946. Isherwood often tells about Kirstein in *D1*. Don Bachardy blames himself as well as Kirstein for the end of this friendship. Trouble arose between Kirstein and Bachardy in 1966 when Kirstein, without consulting Balanchine, commissioned Bachardy to do portraits of the New York City Ballet stars; Balanchine did not approve of some of the portraits, and the whole project was withdrawn. Kirstein thereafter refused to see Isherwood again, even though W. H. Auden tried to bring about a reconciliation.

Kiskadden, Peggy. Thrice-married American socialite from Ardmore, Pennsylvania; born Margaret Adams Plummer, she was exceptionally pretty and had an attractive singing voice. From 1924 until 1933, she was married to a lawyer and (later) judge, Curtis Bok, the eldest son of one of Philadelphia's most prominent families. In the early 1930s she accompanied Bok, a Quaker, to Dartington, England, where she first met Gerald Heard and Aldous and Maria Huxley. Her second marriage, to Henwar Rodakiewicz, a documentary filmmaker, ended in 1942, and she married Bill Kiskadden in July 1943. She had four children, Margaret Welmoet Bok (called Tis), Benjamin Plummer Bok, Derek Curtis Bok (later President of Harvard University), and William Elliott Kiskadden, Jr. (nicknamed "Bull"). Isherwood was introduced to her by Gerald Heard soon after arriving in Los Angeles; they became intimate friends but drew apart at the end of the 1940s and finally split irrevocably in the 1950s over Isherwood's relationship with Don Bachardy. There are numerous passages about her and her family in *D1*.

Kiskadden, William Sherrill (Bill) (1894–1969). American plastic surgeon; third husband of Peggy Kiskadden. Kiskadden was born in Denver, Colorado, the son of a businessman. He studied medicine at the University of California and in London and Vienna in the late 1920s and eventually established his practice in Los Angeles. He was the first clinical professor of plastic surgery at UCLA and founded the plastic surgical service at UCLA County Medical Center in the early 1930s, as well as holding distinguished positions at hospitals in Los Angeles—teaching, administering, and practicing—and writing articles on particular procedures and problems. Kiskadden became interested in the population problem and with Julian and Aldous Huxley and others founded Population Limited in the early 1950s. He served in both world wars, the second time in the Army Medical Corps.

Knight, Franklin. Vedanta monk living at Trabuco monastery from 1955 onwards; a cousin of Webster Milam, who, as a high school student, lived at the Vedanta Center with Isherwood and others during the war. Isherwood often mentions Milam in his diaries of the period; see *D1*. Webster did not become a monk, but Knight did. After he took his first vows his name became Asima Chaitanya.

Kolisch, Joseph. Viennese physician. Kolisch was a follower of Swami Prabhavananda. Aldous and Maria Huxley, Gerald Heard, several of the nuns and monks at the Vedanta Center, and perhaps even Greta Garbo, followed his advice and were on his vegetarian diets during the 1940s. At the suggestion of Gerald Heard, Isherwood first saw Kolisch in January 1940 for what he thought was a recurrence of gonorrhea. In *D1* Isherwood describes how then and on other occasions, Kolisch tended to attribute his symptoms to Isherwood's psychological makeup.

Lamarr, Hedy (1913–2000). Austrian-born film actress. She appeared nude in a 1933 Czech film, *Extase*, and a few years later Louis B. Mayer brought her to Hollywood where she played various seductress roles. She appeared in *Algiers* (1938), *Comrade X* (1940), *Boom Town* (1940), *Ziegfeld Girl* (1941), *H. M. Pulham Esq.* (1941), *Tortilla Flat* (1942), *White Cargo* (1942), and others. Her career faltered after the war (she turned down Ingrid Bergmann's role in *Casablanca*), though she is still remembered for *Samson and Delilah* (1949). Lamarr married six times.

Lamkin, Speed. American novelist; born and raised in Monroe, Louisiana. Lamkin studied at Harvard and lived in London and in New York before going to Los Angeles to research his second novel, *The Easter Egg Hunt* (1954)—about movie stars, in particular Marion Davies and William Randolph Hearst—and he dedicated the novel to Isherwood who appears in it as the character "Sebastian Saunders." Lamkin was on the board at the Huntington Hartford Foundation. In the mid-1950s he wrote a play *Out by the Country Club* which was never produced, although Joshua Logan was briefly interested in it, and in 1956, he scripted a TV film about Perle Mesta, the political hostess. During 1957, he wrote another play, *Comes a Day*, which had a short run on Broadway. Eventually, when this play failed, Lamkin returned home to live in Louisiana. He appears often in *D1*.

Langford, Sam (d. 1958). Irish-born companion to Brian Howard, from 1943 onwards. Langford liked to sail and commanded an Air-Sea Rescue Launch in the British navy during the war. He was invalided out of the navy with a foot problem and briefly worked for the BBC before travelling and living abroad with Howard. Like Howard, Langford became addicted to drugs. He died in his bath when he was gassed by a faulty water heater at the house he shared with Howard and Howard's mother in the south of France. Howard killed himself a few days later.

LaPan, Dick. A boxer; evidently Isherwood first met him at the Viertels' in July 1943. During the 1950s LaPan moved to Mexico and taught English.

Lathwood, Jo. See Masselink, Jo.

Laughton, Charles (1899–1962). British actor. Laughton played many roles on the London stage from the 1920s onward, and began making films during the 1930s—*The Private Life of Henry VIII* (1934), for which he won an Academy Award; *Les Misérables* (1935); *Mutiny on the Bounty* (1935), in which he played Captain Bligh; *The Hunchback of Notre Dame* (1939); and many others. He also acted in New York and Paris, and gave dramatic readings throughout the U.S. from Shakespeare, the Bible, and other classic literature. He became an American citizen in 1950. Isherwood met Laughton in the late 1950s through

Laughton's wife, the actress Elsa Lanchester, and later the two became neighbors and close friends, as Isherwood records in *D1*; they worked on various projects together, including a play about Socrates.

Lawrence, Frieda (1879–1956). German-born wife of the English writer D. H. Lawrence. She was the daughter of a Prussian army officer, Baron Friedrich von Richthofen, and grew up in Metz; at twenty she married Ernest Weekley, a professor at Nottingham University, and moved with him to Nottingham. There in 1912, aged thirty-two, she met Lawrence, a former student of her husband, and eloped with him back to Germany. They married in 1914 after her divorce, lived in London and Cornwall, and then, persecuted over Lawrence's work and suspected as German spies, left for Italy in 1919. In the early 1920s, they travelled further afield, to Ceylon, Australia, and America, settling intermittently just outside Taos, New Mexico, where Lawrence for a time hoped to found Rananim, his utopian community. They stayed in various properties belonging to Mabel Dodge Luhan, and in 1924 Mrs. Luhan gave Frieda a ranch with 160 acres of land on Lobo mountain. Lawrence named the ranch "Kiowa." In 1925, while travelling in Mexico, Lawrence was diagnosed with tuberculosis, and the pair returned to Taos and then to Europe, persisting in their nomadic life, he writing and painting all the time. He died in France in 1930. Later, Frieda returned to New Mexico with her lover, Angelo Ravagli, an Italian military officer from whom she and Lawrence had rented a villa in Spotorno in 1925. In 1933, Ravagli built a modern house for them at the Del Monte Ranch, where Dorothy Brett lived and where the Lawrences had also lived, about two miles below the Kiowa cabins. Ravagli also built the little chapel where Lawrence's ashes were deposited. Frieda married Ravagli in 1950.

Ledebur, Count Friedrich (b. 1908). Austrian actor; second husband of Iris Tree. The marriage ended in 1955. His films include *Moby Dick* (1956), *The Blue Max* (1966), and *Slaughterhouse Five* (1972).

Lehmann, Beatrix (1903–1979). English actress; the youngest of John Lehmann's three elder sisters. She met Isherwood when she was visiting Berlin in 1932, and they became close friends.

Lehmann, John (1907–1988). English author, publisher, editor, autobiographer; educated at Cambridge. Isherwood met Lehmann in 1932 at the Hogarth Press, where Lehmann was assistant (later partner) to Leonard and Virginia Woolf. Lehmann persuaded the Woolfs to publish *The Memorial* after it had been rejected by Jonathan Cape, publisher of Isherwood's first novel, *All the Conspirators*. Isherwood helped Lehmann with his plans to found *New Writing*, discussing the manifesto and obtaining early contributions from friends such as W. H. Auden. He tells about this in *Christopher and His Kind*, and also writes about Lehmann in *D1*. When he left the Hogarth Press, Lehmann founded his own publishing firm and later edited *The London Magazine*. He wrote three revealing volumes of autobiography, beginning with *The Whispering Gallery* (1955).

Lehmann, Rosamond (1901–1990). English novelist; an elder sister of Isherwood's longtime friend John Lehmann. She made a reputation with the frankness of her first novel, *Dusty Answer* (1927), and her later works—

including *Invitation to the Waltz* (1932), *The Weather in the Streets* (1936), *The Echoing Grove* (1953)—also shocked with their candid handling of sexual and emotional themes. From 1928 to 1944 she was married to the painter Wogan Philipps with whom she had a son and a daughter.

Lerman, Leo. American magazine editor. Lerman was an actor and then a writer, and he held various editorial positions at Condé Nast, eventually becoming one of its most senior managers. During the 1940s he was well-known in New York for his Sunday night parties which attracted writers, actors, and dancers, and for a time, he wrote a gossip column for *Vogue*. He also introduced various new writers into *Vogue*'s pages. He was close friends with his Manhattan neighbor, Truman Capote, from the day of their first meeting in 1945 and attended Yaddo with Capote in 1946. The house Lerman rented on Nantucket, Hagedorn House, which Isherwood mentions, was evidently a converted coastguard station in Quidnet and may have belonged to the poet and biographer, Herman Hagedorn.

Lewis, Hayden (1919–c.1994). Lewis was born in Alabama; his family came from Caledonia, a rural community near a tiny town called Pineapple, and they later moved to Fairhope, not far away, where Lewis eventually retired. As a young man he worked in Chicago, and attended the University of Chicago with a younger brother. Then, during the war, he went to Florida and worked for the navy in a civilian capacity until he and Caskey moved on together to California. After spending several decades building up his successful ceramics business with Rodney Owens, Lewis returned to Alabama where he married a Florida native, Mildred MacKinnon, whom he met at the Marietta Johnson School of Organic Education. He appears frequently in *D1*.

Litvak, Anatole (1902–1974). Russian-born film director. He made his first film in Russia, then worked in Germany, France, and England from the late 1920s before going on to Hollywood in 1937. His films in English include *Confessions of a Nazi Spy* (1939), *All This and Heaven Too* (1940), *Sorry, Wrong Number* (1948), *The Snake Pit* (1948), *Decision Before Dawn* (1952), and *Anastasia* (1956). During the war, Litvak co-directed propaganda films with Frank Capra.

Lodge, Carter (d. 1995). American friend of John van Druten. Lodge was van Druten's lover in the late 1930s and early 1940s. He lived mostly in the Coachella Valley at the AJC Ranch, which he and van Druten purchased in the early 1940s with Auriol Lee, the British actress and director. Lodge managed the ranch, where they grew corn and tomatoes, and handled his own and van Druten's financial affairs very successfully. Isherwood also writes about him in *D1*.

Logan, Joshua (1908–1988). American stage and film director, producer, and playwright; educated at Princeton. In the 1930s he went to see Stanislavsky in Moscow before beginning his career as a producer in London. Usually working with others, Logan wrote, directed, or produced some of the most successful ever Broadway musicals and plays, including *Annie Get Your Gun* (1946) and *South Pacific* (1949). In Hollywood he made musicals into films, and directed *Bus Stop* (1956), *Picnic* (1956), and *Sayonara* (1957), among others.

Luhan, Mabel Dodge (1879–1962). American writer, patron, salon hostess; married four times. Her four volumes of memoirs, begun in 1924 and published during the 1930s, were admired by D. H. Lawrence, who was both attracted and repelled by her. Born in Buffalo, New York, to great wealth, she was sent to Europe in 1901 to recover from a nervous breakdown; there she lived in a Medici villa in Florence, wore Renaissance dress, had lovers, befriended Gertrude Stein, and entertained lavishly. In 1912 she returned to New York where she set up her salon at 23 Fifth Avenue and had an affair with the radical journalist John Reed. Next she moved to Taos, New Mexico, where she met Tony Luhan, a Pueblo Indian whom she married in 1923. The Indian way of life became her religion, and she believed that she and her husband were messiahs by whose leadership white civilization would be redeemed. She brought others to Taos to celebrate her new life, including Georgia O'Keeffe, Leopold Stokowski, John Collier, and Lawrence. During the 1920s and 1930s she worked for land reform, self-determination, and medical benefits for the Indians.

Lynes, George Platt (1907–1955). American photographer; educated at The Berkshire School, where he met Lincoln Kirstein, and, briefly, at Yale. Lynes first photographed Isherwood and W. H. Auden during their brief visit to New York in 1938. In the 1940s, he encouraged Bill Caskey in his efforts to become a professional photographer, and later, in 1953, Lynes befriended and photographed Don Bachardy. He appears in *D1*. Lynes made his living from advertising and fashion photography as well as portraits (his work appeared in *Town and Country*, *Harper's Bazaar*, and *Vogue*), but he is also known for his photographs of the ballet, male nudes, and surrealistic still lifes; he did many portraits of film stars and writers.

Macaulay, Rose (1881–1958). British novelist, essayist, and travel writer; educated at Somerville College, Oxford. She was the daughter of a Cambridge don and published her first novel in 1906. In all she wrote twenty-three novels; the last and perhaps best, *The Towers of Trebizond* (1956), became a bestseller in the U.S. Macaulay also produced various works of nonfiction, including a biography of Milton and a book about the writings of E. M. Forster, and she wrote numerous articles for periodicals.

Mace, John. Los Angeles lawyer. He and Isherwood had a number of mutual friends and sometimes attended the same parties in the 1940s and 1950s. In 1954, Isherwood asked Mace to represent him when Curtis Harrington sued Isherwood for punching Harrington in the face at a party given by Iris Tree. The case was settled out of court and Isherwood paid Harrington $350.

MacNeice, Louis (1907–1963). Poet, born in Belfast. MacNeice was an undergraduate at Oxford with W. H. Auden and Stephen Spender, and he collaborated with Auden on *Letters from Iceland* (1937). He worked as a university lecturer in classics and later for the BBC as a writer and producer, while publishing numerous volumes of verse, verse translation, autobiography, and plays for radio and stage.

Madge, Charles (1912–1996). South African-born sociologist and poet; educated at Winchester and Magdalene College, Cambridge. He became a communist in the early 1930s, worked as a journalist and was a founder in 1937 of Mass Observation. His first marriage, to the poet Kathleen Raine, ended in 1939, and he then began an affair with Stephen Spender's first wife, Inez Pearn, whom he later married. He published only two volumes of poetry, but continued his social and economic research through the war and, in 1950, became a professor of sociology at Birmingham University.

Maher, Fern (b. 1917). American social worker. Educated at UCLA where she became close friends with David Sachs. She lived for some years in the Benton Way house. In 1948 she married Ken O'Brien, a photographer who was an occasional resident at Benton Way, and after some time abroad in North Africa, they eventually settled in Venice, California.

Mailer, Norman (b. 1923). American novelist; born and raised in New Jersey and Brooklyn and educated at Harvard. Mailer was in the army and fought in the Pacific during World War II; he became famous with the publication of his first novel, *The Naked and the Dead* (1948), about an American infantry platoon invading a Japanese-held island. Subsequent books include *The Deer Park* (1955) about Hollywood, *An American Dream* (1965), *Why are We in Vietnam?* (1967), *Of a Fire on the Moon* (1970) about the lunar landings, *The Executioner's Song* (1979) about the execution of a convicted murderer, two books about Marilyn Monroe, and *Oswald's Tale* (1995) about Lee Harvey Oswald. He won a Pulitzer Prize for *The Armies of the Night* (1968), describing the first peace march on the Pentagon—in which he was a participant—during the Vietnam era.

Mangeot, André, Olive, Sylvain and Fowke. Belgian violinist and his English wife and two sons. Isherwood met the Mangeots in 1925 and worked for a year as part-time secretary to André Mangeot's string quartet which was organized from the family home in Chelsea. The Mangeots' warm and chaotic household offered an irresistible contrast to the cool formality of Isherwood's own, and Olive, energetic but easygoing, was an attractive rival to Kathleen in the role of mother. Isherwood brought all his friends to meet Olive when he was in London. She is the original of "Madame Cheuret" in *Lions and Shadows* and Isherwood drew on different parts of her personality for the characters "Margaret Lanwin" and "Mary Scriven" in *The Memorial*. She had an affair with Edward Upward and through his influence became a communist. Later she separated from her husband and for a time lived in Cheltenham with Jean Ross and her daughter.

Mann, Erika (1905–1969). German actress and author; eldest daughter of Thomas Mann. Isherwood first met Erika Mann through her brother Klaus in the spring of 1935 in Amsterdam; she had fled Germany in March 1933. Her touring revue, The Peppermill (for which she wrote most of the satirical, anti-Nazi material), earned her the status of official enemy of the Reich, and she asked Isherwood to marry her and provide her with a British passport. He felt he could not, but contacted W. H. Auden who agreed, and the two met and married in England in June 1935. In September 1936 Erika emigrated to America with Klaus and unsuccessfully tried to reopen The Peppermill in New York. As the war approached, she lectured widely in the USA and wrote anti-

Nazi books, two with Klaus, trying to revive sympathy for the non-Nazi Germany silenced by Hitler. She worked as a journalist in London during the war, for the BBC German Service and as a correspondent for the New York *Nation*. Later, she became increasingly close to her father, travelling with her parents and helping Thomas Mann with his work. She also appears in *D1*.

Mann, Klaus (1906–1949). German novelist and editor. Heinrich Klaus Mann was the eldest son of Thomas Mann; Isherwood became friendly with him in Berlin in the summer of 1931. By then Klaus had written and acted with his sister, Erika, in the plays which launched her acting career, and he had published several novels in German (a few appeared in English translations) and worked as a drama critic. He travelled extensively and lived in various European cities even before he left Germany for good in 1933; in 1936, when his family settled in Princeton, he emigrated to America and lived in New York, continuing to travel to Europe as a journalist, and later settling for a time in Santa Monica. He founded two magazines: *Die Sammlung* (*The Collection*) in Amsterdam in 1933, and *Decision*, which appeared in New York in December 1940 but lasted only a year because of the war. Klaus became a U.S. citizen and served in the U.S. Army during the war. He wrote his second volume of autobiography, *The Turning Point* (1942), in English. Isherwood wrote a reminiscence about Klaus for a memorial volume published in Amsterdam in 1950, *Klaus Mann—zum Gedaechtnis*, and describes their friendship in *D1*.

Mann, Thomas (1875–1955). German novelist and essayist; awarded the Nobel Prize in 1929. Mann was patriarch of a large and talented literary family; he and his wife Katia Pringsheim Mann (whose father was a mathematics professor and Wagner scholar) had six children. Mann's novels and stories are among the greatest German literature of this century. They include *Buddenbrooks* (1901), *Tonio Kröger* (1903), *Death in Venice* (1912), *The Magic Mountain* (1924), *Doktor Faustus* (1947), and *The Confessions of the Confidence Trickster Felix Krull* (1954). Mann lectured in support of the Weimar Republic both in Germany and abroad during the 1920s, and he publicly dissociated himself from the Nazi regime in 1936, taking Czech citizenship (though he had remained in Switzerland since a 1933 holiday). Isherwood first met him in Princeton where Mann was a visiting professor after his flight from the Nazis. Then in 1941, Mann moved with his family to Pacific Palisades and became part of the circle of German emigrés and artists with which Isherwood was intimate; he is sometimes mentioned in *D1*. Later the Manns returned to Switzerland.

Markova, Alicia (b. 1910). English prima ballerina; her real name was Lilian Alicia Marks. She danced for the Ballets Russes in 1924 and afterwards for various companies in England where she was partnered for many years by the British dancer Anton Dolin (also a former member of the Ballets Russes). In 1935, Markova and Dolin founded their own ballet company and toured internationally. Later she became a professor of dance at the University of Cincinnati in Ohio.

Martinez, José (Pete) (c. 1913–1997). Mexican-born ballet dancer; also known as Pete Stefan. Isherwood met him through Lincoln Kirstein in 1939.

Martinez was among the first students at the American School of Ballet (founded by Kirstein and Balanchine), and during the 1940s he danced with the American Ballet Caravan and the Ballet Society, forerunners of the New York City Ballet. He created the scenario for *Pastorela* (1941) and toured in it to Latin America. In 1942, Martinez worked with Isherwood at the refugee hostel in Haverford, Pennsylvania, while waiting to be drafted into the army. Isherwood records their life together in *D1*. Martinez's family then moved from Texas to Long Beach, and Isherwood saw him in Long Beach in 1943 before Martinez left to fight in northern France from 1943 to 1945. Afterwards they met occasionally in New York and California. When the war was over, Martinez danced for two more years: he was in the original cast of Balanchine's *Four Temperaments* (1946), and he created the role of the minister in William Dollar's *Highland Fling* (1947). A knee injury forced him to retire in 1947, and he became a teacher, opening his own studios in Virginia, Ohio and, finally, California where he worked until the mid-1960s and then remained for the rest of his life.

Masselink, Ben (1919–2000). American writer. Masselink was in the marines during the war; one night on leave, he got drunk in The Friendship, the bar in Santa Monica Canyon, and Jo Lathwood took him to her apartment nearby and looked after him. When the war was over he went back to her and stayed for over twenty years. Masselink had studied architecture, and Isherwood helped him with his writing career during the 1950s. His first book of stories, *Partly Submerged*, was published in 1957, followed by two novels about his war experience—*The Crackerjack Marines* (1959) and *The Deadliest Weapon* (1965), the second of which Isherwood admired—and a story for teenage boys, *The Danger Islands* (1964). Masselink also wrote for television throughout the 1950s and in 1960 worked at Warner Brothers on the script for a film of *The Crackerjack Marines*. In 1967, when Lathwood was in her late sixties, Masselink, still in his forties, left her for a younger woman. There are numerous passages about the Masselinks in *D1*.

Masselink, Jo (c. 1900–1988). Women's sportswear and bathing suit designer from Northville, South Dakota; among her clientele were movie stars such as Janet Gaynor and Anne Baxter. She had worked as a dancer and was briefly married to a man called Jack Lathwood (whose name she kept professionally); also, she had a son and a daughter with a North Dakotan, Ferdinand Hinchberger. From 1938 onwards she lived on West Channel Road, a few doors from The Friendship, and by the late 1940s she knew many of Isherwood's friends who frequented the bar—including Bill Caskey, Jay de Laval, and Jim Charlton. She never married Ben Masselink, though she lived with him and used his surname. She appears often in *D1*.

Matta Echaurren, Roberto Sebastián (b. 1911). Chilean-born surrealist painter. Matta trained as an architect with Le Corbusier and began painting in Paris towards the end of the 1930s. During World War II, he worked in New York with other European surrealists who had emigrated there, such as André Breton, Max Ernst, and Yves Tanguy.

Maugham, William Somerset (Willie) (1874–1965). British playwright and novelist. Maugham was married and had a daughter, but for a long time his usual companion was Gerald Haxton, eighteen years younger, whom he met in 1914 working in an ambulance unit in Flanders. Maugham and Haxton travelled, and they entertained on Cap Ferrat at the Villa Mauresque which Maugham bought in 1926. After Haxton's early death, Maugham's subsequent companion and heir was Alan Searle. Isherwood met Maugham in London in the late 1930s and saw him whenever Maugham visited Hollywood, where many of Maugham's works were filmed; later Isherwood also made several visits to Maugham's house in France. Their friendship is described in *D1*. Shri Ganesha (the character about whom Maugham consulted Swami for the film of *The Razor's Edge*) was based on Ramana Maharshi (1879–1950), an Indian holy man Maugham met in 1936. Later, in 1956, Swami and Isherwood both advised Maugham again on his essay "The Saint," about Ramana Maharshi. "The Saint" was published in Maugham's *Points of View* (1958).

Mauriber, Saul. Assistant to the photographer and writer Carl Van Vechten. He was still a student when he met Van Vechten and worked with him for twenty years. Later, Mauriber also became a designer.

McClendon, Carlos (b. 1923). American designer and shop owner. McClendon was born in California and worked as an apprentice set designer at MGM and as a dancer before opening his shop, Chequer, in New York in 1954. He sold clothes of his own design for men and women, furniture, and art objects, and he travelled widely to acquire raw materials and finished goods, including ethnic textiles and folk art from Japan, Indonesia, Mexico and elsewhere. He spent time living in Haiti and in Mexico as well as in New York, and he eventually opened Chequer West in West Hollywood, frequented like his New York shop by theater, movie and entertainment people, and designers and costumiers. Isherwood met McClendon through Denny Fouts and John Goodwin in the 1940s when McClendon often visited the beach in Santa Monica. The friendship continued long after McClendon left Los Angeles in the early 1950s. Eventually McClendon settled in New Mexico.

McDowall, Roddy (1928–1998). British actor and photographer. McDowall began his education at a Catholic school in a south London suburb and made his first movie when he was eight years old. When the Blitz began, he was evacuated to the USA and became a Hollywood star as a teenager after appearing as the crippled boy in *How Green Was My Valley* (1941) and, with Elizabeth Taylor, in *Lassie Come Home* (1943). During the 1950s he took stage and television roles in New York, where he won a Tony Award for his supporting role in *The Fighting Cock* in 1960. He returned to Hollywood in the 1960s and starred in *Planet of the Apes* (1968), most of the sequels, and the television series. Other films include *My Friend Flicka* (1943), *Thunderhead, Son of Flicka* (1945), Orson Welles's *Macbeth* (1948), *The Subterraneans* (1960), *The Longest Day* (1962), *Cleopatra* (1963), *Bedknobs and Broomsticks* (1971), *The Poseidon Adventure* (1972), *Funny Lady* (1975), and *Fright Night* (1985). He published several books of his photographs, mostly of celebrities.

Medley, Robert (1905–1995). English painter. Robert Medley attended Gresham's School, Holt, with W. H. Auden, and the two remained close friends after Medley left for art school at the Slade. In London, Medley became the longtime companion of the dancer Rupert Doone, and was involved with him in 1932 in forming The Group Theatre, which produced *The Dog Beneath the Skin*, *The Ascent of F6*, and *On the Frontier*. Medley also worked as a theater designer and teacher, founding the Theatre Design section at the Slade in the 1950s before becoming Head of Painting and Sculpture at the Camberwell School of Arts and Crafts in 1958.

Menotti, Gian Carlo (b. 1911). Italian-born composer, librettist, and conductor. Menotti emigrated to the USA, where he studied at the Curtis Institute in Philadelphia and began to establish an international reputation with his operas from the late 1930s. He won Pulitzer Prizes for *The Consul* (1950) and *The Saint of Bleecker Street* (1954), and his widely known opera, *Amahl and the Night Visitors* (1951), was the first to be written expressly for American television.

MGM. The preeminent Hollywood studio from the mid-1920s to the mid-1940s; Isherwood began writing for MGM at the start of 1940, his second Hollywood job. Formed by a three-way merger between Loewe's Incorporated (owner of the Metro Pictures Corporation), the Goldwyn Studios, and the Louis B. Mayer Pictures Corporation, the studio was run by Mayer with Irving Thalberg and Harry Rapf. Stars included Garbo, Norma Shearer, Gable, Joan Crawford, the Barrymores, Elizabeth Taylor, Garland, Katharine Hepburn, Spencer Tracy, and Greer Garson; among the directors and producers were George Cukor, Clarence Brown, Victor Fleming, Mervyn Leroy, Vincente Minnelli, Busby Berkeley, David Selznick and Arthur Freed. MGM reached its apogee between 1935 and 1945, then management conflicts gradually developed and enforcement of the Sherman antitrust laws eroded its power. Financial losses and further management upheavals plagued the studio throughout the 1960s, and MGM has been the object of various corporate takeovers since then.

Minton, John (1917–1957). English painter and theater designer. His paintings were admired by Wyndham Lewis, and he taught at several London art schools. He took his life with a drug overdose.

Moffat, Ivan (b. 1918). British-American screenwriter; son of Iris Tree and Curtis Moffat. He was educated at Dartmouth and served in the U.S. military during World War II. Afterwards he assisted the director George Stevens on *A Place in the Sun* (1951), was Stevens's associate producer for *Shane* (1953), and co-wrote *Giant* (1956) before going on to work for Selznick on *Tender Is the Night* (1962). He met his first wife, Natasha Sorokine, in Paris at the end of the war; the marriage broke up at the start of the 1950s, leaving a daughter, Lorna. Moffat then had a series of beautiful and talented girlfriends until marrying Kate Smith, an Englishwoman, whose family fortune derived from the book and stationery chain, W. H. Smith. He often appears in *D1*.

Monkhouse, Allan (1858–1936). English journalist and theater critic; father of Isherwood's boyhood friend, Patrick Monkhouse. Allan Monkhouse also wrote plays and fiction, including a novel, *My Daughter Helen* (1922), in which one of the main characters, Marmaduke, is partly modelled on the adolescent Isherwood.

Monkhouse, Patrick. English journalist. Patrick Monkhouse was raised in Disley, near Marple, and became Isherwood's close friend by the time they were adolescents. He was at Oxford a year or two ahead of W. H. Auden, and edited *The Oxford Outlook*.

Moraturi, Pancho. Wealthy Argentine. Longtime lover, companion, and supporter of Bill Harris. In his April 1949 preface to *The Condor and the Cows* ("To the Reader") Isherwood names Moraturi and Harris among those whom he wishes to thank for helping him and Caskey during their visit to Buenos Aires.

Morris, Phyllis. British actress. She was a student with Dodie Smith (later Beesley) at the Academy of Dramatic Art (precursor to RADA) in London during World War I, and they remained close friends for life. Morris came from a wealthy family. She was a stage actress, but played minor roles in a few Hollywood films after the war—for instance, *That Forsyte Woman* (1949). She also wrote children's books and plays.

Mortimer, Raymond (1895–1980). English literary and art critic; he worked for numerous magazines and newspapers as both writer and editor and wrote books on painting and the decorative arts as well as a novel. Mortimer was at Balliol College, Oxford, with Aldous Huxley and later became a close friend of Gerald Heard, introducing Heard to Huxley in 1929. He was also intimate with various Bloomsbury figures and an outspoken advocate of their work. From 1948 onward Mortimer worked for *The Sunday Times* and spent the last nearly thirty years of his life as their chief reviewer.

Nadeau, Nicky. American dancer. Isherwood had a sexual relationship with him in the late 1940s or early 1950s. Possibly he met Nadeau through Chris Wood's wealthy Bel Air friend Karl Hoyt; Nadeau had an affair with Hoyt and later, towards the end of the 1950s, with Chris Wood. He is mentioned in *D1*.

Nanny. See Avis, Annie.

Neddermeyer, Heinz. German boyfriend of Isherwood; Heinz was about seventeen when they met in Berlin, March 13, 1932. Their love affair, the most serious of Isherwood's life until then, lasted about five years. Hitler's rise forced them to leave Berlin in May 1933 and afterwards they lived and travelled in Europe and North Africa. In a traumatic confrontation with immigration officials at Harwich, Heinz was refused entry on his second visit to England in January 1934, so Isherwood went abroad more and more to be with him. In 1936 Heinz was summoned for conscription in Germany, and Isherwood scrambled to obtain or extend permits for him to remain in the ever-diminishing number of European countries which would receive him. A shady lawyer failed to obtain him a new nationality, and finally Heinz was expelled from Luxembourg on May 12, 1937, and returned to Germany. There he was arrested by the Gestapo and sentenced—for "reciprocal onanism" and draft evasion—to a three-and-a-half-year term: six months' imprisonment, then one year of labour, and two years of military service. Nonetheless, he married in 1938, and with his wife, Gerda, had a son, Christian, in 1940. Isherwood did not see Heinz again until 1952 in Berlin, though he corresponded with him both before and after this visit. Heinz's conscription first turned Isherwood towards pacifism. Their shared wanderings are described in *Christopher and His Kind* and their friendship also serves as one basis for the "Waldemar" section of *Down There on a Visit*. He is sometimes mentioned in *D1*.

Nin, Anaïs (1903–1977). American writer. Nin was born just outside Paris, raised in New York from age eleven, and spent most of the 1920s and 1930s back in Paris seeking out the company of writers, intellectuals, and bohemians. She was a model, a dancer, and a teacher, and later became a psychoanalyst, as well as writing novels, short stories, and literary criticism. She is now best known for her six-volume *Diary* which began to appear in the 1960s and which tells, among other things, about her Parisian friendship with Henry Miller. She had many love affairs and was married twice. Her second husband, Rupert Pole, is a stepgrandson of Frank Lloyd Wright. By the 1970s the pair had settled in the Silver Lake district of Los Angeles in a house designed by Wright's grandson, Eric Lloyd Wright.

Norment, Caroline. American Quaker relief worker and administrator. Norment was director of the American Friends Service Committee's Co-operative College Workshop, the refugee hostel in Haverford, Pennsylvania, where Isherwood worked as a volunteer during the war. She was in her fifties when Isherwood first met her in late summer 1941. She had previously done relief work in Russia and Germany, and she had also served as Dean of Women at Antioch College in Ohio. As he mentions in *Lost Years*, Isherwood wondered whether Norment somehow attracted or unconsciously caused fires. In his wartime diaries he had recorded for April 30, 1942 that there was a bad fire at the hostel, Norment's fifth. In two earlier fires she had lost most of her possessions; later, there were two more near fires also at the hostel (*D1*, pp. 212–14). Norment is the original of Sarah Pennington in *The World in the Evening*; Isherwood took the character's first name from the actress Sara Allgood, whom Norment resembled.

Novak, Alvin (b. 1928). American pianist, born in Chicago. He moved to Los Angeles as a teenager with his family, and his father died shortly afterwards. Novak put himself through college at UCLA, where he studied philosophy and met other members of The Benton Way Group with whom he became closely involved. At twenty-six, when he graduated, he began a new life in New York, developing his gift for the piano into a professional career as a teacher and performer. Later he lived increasingly on Long Island, organizing concerts in the Hamptons as well as teaching and performing there.

Obin, Philomé (1891–1986). Haitian painter. Obin was an important figure in the Haitian art movement and one of the first to apply to the Centre d'Art in Port-au-Prince in the early 1940s. He was a devout Protestant, and reportedly prayed and sang hymns while he painted; among his important works were a *Crucifixion* and a *Last Supper* for the Saint-Trinité Episcopal Cathedral in Port-au-Prince.

Ocampo, Victoria. Argentine writer, critic, editor, and publisher. She owned and edited *Sur* (South), the international literary magazine for which Isherwood had agreed, a few years before he met her, to assemble the work of some modern writers to be translated into Spanish. She also ran her own small publishing house—Aldous Huxley, D. H. Lawrence, and Virginia Woolf were among the contemporary writers she introduced to her Argentine audience. Her background was privileged and traditional, and she was celebrated as a beauty in her youth, but she was bohemian and an outspoken feminist who preferred to write in French rather than Spanish. During the 1950s she was imprisoned by the Perón regime. She was a close friend of Maria Rosa Oliver, who helped her with *Sur*, and of Tota Cuevas de Vera. In early 1948, Isherwood and Caskey visited the three of them in Buenos Aires and in the nearby seaside resort, Mar del Plata.

O'Hara, John (1905–1970). American journalist, short story writer, and novelist, from Pennsylvania. Many of his books were later reworked as movies, including *Butterfield 8* (published 1935, filmed 1960), *A Rage to Live* (1949, filmed 1965), and *Ten North Frederick* (1955, filmed 1958). *Pal Joey* (1940) was adapted for the stage as a musical comedy by O'Hara himself with Rodgers and Hart, who wrote songs for it which are still well-known, such as "My Funny Valentine" and "The Lady Is a Tramp." It was filmed in 1957.

O'Keeffe, Georgia (1887–1986). American painter. Raised on a farm in Wisconsin, she studied art in Chicago and New York early in the century and was a pioneer of American modernism. Her early work was abstract; later she became more figurative, painting townscapes and landscapes as well as the flower and plant forms for which she is most widely known. O'Keeffe married the photographer Alfred Stieglitz in 1924. He had promoted the work of European artists such as Matisse, Toulouse-Lautrec, and Brancusi and later of American artists, including O'Keeffe, in a series of New York galleries from just after the turn of the century. *Camera Work*, which Isherwood mentions, was published from his first gallery and eventually included not only photography, but all the visual arts, as well as criticism, reviews, and new American writing. O'Keeffe wintered in New Mexico from the 1930s and settled there in 1946 after Stieglitz died, although from the 1950s she began to travel widely.

Old, Vernon (not his real name). American painter; raised in New York City and New England and educated partly at Catholic boarding school. Isherwood met Vernon Old in 1938 when first visiting New York, and Vernon featured in Isherwood's decision to return to New York in 1939. They moved to Los Angeles together that spring, but split up by mutual agreement in February 1941. Vernon then lived unsteadily on his own, working on his painting. He could not return to his family as his parents were divorced and he did not like his mother's second husband. During the war, he tried to become a monk, first in a Catholic monastery in the Hudson Valley and later at the Hollywood Vedanta Center and at Ananda Bhavan, another center which became the Sarada Convent, in Montecito. Later, he married and had a son before divorcing. His painting career was increasingly successful, and in the late 1950s he tutored Don Bachardy. He appears in *Christopher and His Kind* and in *My Guru and His Disciple* (as "Vernon," without a surname) and in *D1*.

Oliver, Maria Rosa. Argentine intellectual. Isherwood first met her during the war when she visited Hollywood in August 1944 with an introduction from Lincoln Kirstein. She asked Isherwood to find contemporary writers whose work could be translated into Spanish for her friend Victoria Ocampo's literary magazine, *Sur*. When Isherwood and Caskey saw her in Argentina early in 1948, Caskey photographed her for *The Condor and the Cows*. Oliver's legs were partly paralyzed, and she was confined to a wheelchair.

Ouspenskaya's school. The School of Dramatic Arts founded by Maria Ouspenskaya (1876–1949), a Russian actress who first arrived in Hollywood with the Stanislavsky troupe in 1923.

Owens, Rodney (Rod). Hayden Lewis's companion and business partner for many years from 1946; a California native. He is often mentioned in *D1*. After he split with Lewis, Owens became a sales person for the clothing designer Helen Rose and settled in New York.

Patanjali. The obscure Indian compiler of the yoga sutras, the series of spare, aphoristic statements formulating the philosophy and practice of yoga. Patanjali was a follower of Sankhya philosophy, not Vedanta, and did his work sometime between the fourth century BC and the fourth century AD. In ancient times, the sutras could not be recorded in books and so were repeated from memory and elaborated and explained by a teacher. This is partly why they are so short and, on their own, seemingly difficult. In 1948, Isherwood and Swami Prabhavananda began making a translation of the sutras in which they expanded and paraphrased them for modern, English-speaking devotees and also added a commentary drawing on various earlier teachers. This was published by the Vedanta Society in 1953 as *How to Know God: The Yoga Aphorisms of Patanjali*.

Pears, Peter (1910–1986). English tenor. The youngest of seven children, Pears went to boarding school at six and rarely saw his family. He was sent down from Keble College, Oxford, after failing his first-year music exams, became a prep school master, studied briefly at the Royal College of Music and then joined the BBC Singers in 1934. Pears became close friends with Benjamin Britten in 1937; they shared a flat from early 1938, and began performing together in 1939. That same year, the two travelled together to New York where Pears studied singing further, and they went on to California before returning to England in 1942. Although at first they both had other relationships, their lives became increasingly fused, with Britten writing a great deal of his music for Pears, and Pears singing it expressly for Britten.

Pembroke Gardens. The address of Isherwood's family home in London before the war. Kathleen Isherwood lived at 19 Pembroke Gardens, Kensington, from June 1928 until mid-July 1941, when she and Richard and Nanny (Annie Avis) returned to Wyberslegh.

Perkins, Lynn. American screenwriter. He approached Isherwood for help with a film outline for a ghost story. Evidently he was a writer for a series of action–science fiction films called *The Purple Shadow Strikes* (also *The Purple Monster Strikes*) produced in 1945 by Ronald Davidson for Republic Pictures.

Perlin, Bernard (Bernie). American painter; associated through his work with Paul Cadmus, Jared French and George Tooker. Bill Caskey met Perlin in Miami in 1944 when they were both still in the navy. Perlin had recently survived a German attack in Greece and encouraged Caskey not to fear persecution by the admiral who was conducting a homosexual witch-hunt at their naval air base; the scandal shortly resulted in Caskey's blue discharge. After the war, Perlin lived in Italy from the late 1940s until the mid-1950s, and later he settled in Connecticut.

Philipps, Wogan (1902–1993). English painter and, later, politician; educated at Eton and Magdalen College, Oxford. Philipps was a communist and drove an ambulance for the International Brigade during the Spanish Civil War. When Isherwood saw him in 1947, he was serving as a communist councillor on the Cirencester Rural District Council. He succeeded his father as second Baron Milford in 1962 and became the first communist peer in the House of Lords. He was married three times: first, to Rosamond Lehmann; then to an Italian, Cristina, who was the ex-wife of the Earl of Huntingdon and a daughter of the Marchese Casati; and, after Cristina died in 1953, to Tamara Rust, widow of William Rust, the editor of the *Daily Worker*.

Pilates, Joseph (1880–1967). German-born exercise guru, of Greek ancestry. Pilates was frail in childhood and began bodybuilding in adolescence to overcome fears of tuberculosis; he was also a gymnast, boxer, skier, and diver. He and a brother performed a Greek statue act in a circus which was touring England at the outbreak of World War I. Pilates was interned and passed the time teaching self-defense, bodybuilding, and wrestling to his fellow internees while beginning more systematically to develop his exercise method. By one account he also became a nurse and designed his unusual exercise apparatus by attaching springs to hospital beds for patients who could not move. He returned to Germany for a time after the war and trained police in Hamburg. There, during the early 1920s, he also met members of the dance world who incorporated some of his techniques into their own practices, and who began to teach them to other dancers. Pilates helped train the heavyweight boxer, Max Schmelling, and Schmelling persuaded him to emigrate to the U.S., where Pilates established a studio in New York in 1926. The studio was frequented by dancers from George Balanchine's New York City Ballet, and Pilates' followers included many other prominent dancers and choreographers, as well as numerous actors and musicians. His method (he called it "Contrology") is used increasingly widely today.

Plomer, William (1903–1973). British poet and novelist; born and raised in South Africa. He met Isherwood in 1932 through Stephen Spender. In South Africa, Plomer and Roy Campbell had founded *Voorslag* (Whiplash), a literary magazine for which they wrote most of the satirical material themselves (Laurens van der Post also became an editor). Plomer taught for several years in Japan, then in 1929 settled in Bloomsbury where he was befriended by the Woolfs; they had already published his first novel, *Turbott Wolfe*, in 1926 at the Hogarth Press. In 1937 Plomer became principal reader for Jonathan Cape where, among other things, he brought out Ian Fleming's James Bond novels. During the war he worked in naval intelligence. In addition to his own poems and novels, Plomer also wrote several libretti for Benjamin Britten, notably

Gloriana (1953). A 1943 arrest for soliciting a sailor in Paddington station was hushed up, but led Plomer to destroy early correspondence with homosexual friends and to practice extreme circumspection in his private life.

Pollock, Peter (b. 1921). English steel heir; the family fortune left him with small private means. Pollock was still a public school boy when Guy Burgess met him in Cannes in 1938, and they were lovers for about a decade. Burgess recruited Pollock to help MI5 spy on foreigners in England. In 1955 Pollock and his later longterm companion, Paul Danquah, a lawyer and actor, began sharing their Battersea flat with Francis Bacon, who lived with them until 1961 and became an intimate friend. Pollock and Danquah afterwards settled in Tangier, where, for a time, Pollock ran a beach bar, The Pergola.

Porter, Cole (1891–1964). American composer and lyricist, educated at Yale University, Harvard Law School, Harvard School of Music, and also in Paris. His Broadway hits include *Anything Goes* (1934) and *Kiss Me, Kate* (1948), and many of his individual lyrics, such as "Let's Do It," "You're the Top," and "I Get a Kick Out of You," are permanently lodged in the popular imagination. Isherwood was fond of Cole Porter and, according to Don Bachardy, believed that a third party had made mischief between them, possibly by repeating (perhaps inaccurately) a remark made by Bill Caskey. The friendship ended just a year or two before Porter's death, preventing any reconciliation.

Porter, Katherine Anne (1890–1980). American novelist and short story writer, born in Texas; best known for *Ship of Fools* (1962). She was a good friend of Glenway Wescott who may have suggested she meet Isherwood and Caskey.

Prabha. Originally Phoebe Nixon, she was the daughter of Alice Nixon ("Tarini"), and after taking her final monastic vows, Prabha became Pravrajika Prabhaprana. The Nixons were wealthy Southerners. Isherwood first met Prabha in the early 1940s in the Hollywood Vedanta Center, where she handled much of the administrative and secretarial work, and he grew to love her genuinely. By the mid-1950s, Prabha was head nun at the Sarada Convent in Santa Barbara.

Prabhavananda, Swami (1893–1976). Hindu monk of the Ramakrishna Order. Gerald Heard introduced Isherwood to Swami Prabhavananda in July 1939. On their second meeting Prabhavananda began to instruct Isherwood in meditation, and in November he initiated Isherwood, giving him a mantram and a rosary. From February 1943 until August 1945 Isherwood lived monastically at the Hollywood Vedanta Center, but decided he could not become a monk as Swami wished. (Isherwood invariably pronounced it *Shwami*, as he had been taught phonetically by Prabhavananda.) He remained Prabhavananda's disciple and close friend for life. Their relationship is described in *My Guru and His Disciple*, which is based on the many passages about Prabhavananda in Isherwood's diaries.

Prabhavananda was born in a Bengali village northwest of Calcutta and was originally named Abanindra Nath Ghosh. As a teenager he read about Ramakrishna and about his disciples Vivekananda and Brahmananda, and he met Ramakrishna's widow, Sarada Devi. At eighteen, he visited the Belur

Math—the chief monastery of the Ramakrishna Order beside the Ganges outside Calcutta—where he met Brahmananda and was so affected that he briefly abandoned his studies in Calcutta to follow him. Because he was studying philosophy, Abanindra returned to Belur Math regularly for instruction in the teachings of Shankara, but he still placed greater importance on his political beliefs and became involved in militant opposition to British rule, mostly as a propagandist. After a second peculiarly compelling experience with Brahmananda, he suddenly decided to give up his political activities and become a monk. He took his final vows in 1921, when his name was changed to Prabhavananda.

In 1923 Prabhavananda was sent to the United States to assist the swami at the Vedanta Society in San Francisco; later he opened a new center in Portland, Oregon. He was joined in Portland by Sister Lalita and, in 1929, founded the Vedanta Society of Southern California in her house in Hollywood, 1946 Ivar Avenue. Several other women joined them. By the mid-1930s the society began to expand and money was donated to build a temple, which was dedicated in July 1938. Prabhavananda remained the head of the Hollywood Center until he died.

Isherwood and Prabhavananda worked on a number of books together, including a translation of the Bhagavad Gita (1944), and Prabhavananda contributed to two collections on Vedanta edited by Isherwood. Also, Prabhavananda persuaded Isherwood to write a biography of Ramakrishna, *Ramakrishna and His Disciples* (1964).

pranam. A salutation of respect made by folding the palms, or by touching the saluted one's feet and then touching one's own forehead (i.e., taking the dust of the saluted one's feet), or by prostrating.

prasad. Food or any other gift that has been consecrated by being offered to God or to a saintly person in a Hindu ceremony of worship; the food is usually eaten as part of the meal following the ritual, or the gift given to the devotees.

Pritchett, V. S. (1900–1997). British literary critic, short story writer, and novelist; raised mostly in various suburbs of London. He worked abroad as a photographer and journalist before publishing his first novel in 1929. His short stories began to appear in London magazines such as *The Cornhill* and *The New Statesman* during the 1920s and were later collected in diverse volumes; he also contributed criticism to *The New Statesman* for several decades, and was its literary editor just after World War II, when Isherwood saw him in London. Pritchett's literary-critical books include *The Living Novel* (1946) and studies of Balzac, Turgenev, and George Meredith. He also published two volumes of autobiography.

puja. Hindu ceremony of worship; usually offerings—flowers, incense, food —are made to the object of devotion, and other ritual, symbolic acts are also carried out depending upon the occasion.

quota visa. The U.S. Immigration Act of 1924, known as the Quota Act, dictated that the number of immigrants admitted annually from any one country could not exceed two per cent of the existing U.S. population deriving from that same national origin (as determined by the 1890 census), although a minimum quota of 100 immigrants was permitted to all countries. As the vast majority of Americans at that time traced their ancestry to Great Britain, British nationals could immigrate with ease.

Rainey, Ford (b. 1908). American actor, born in Idaho. Rainey made his professional stage debut in 1932 and had acted on Broadway by 1939, but his roles were small. During the 1950s and early 1960s he appeared in a few Hollywood films, including Westerns, and went on to act for television shows such as *Bonanza*, *Gunsmoke*, and *Perry Mason*. He divorced his first wife in 1950, then married again in 1954.

Ramakrishna (1836–1886). The Hindu holy man whose life inspired the modern renaissance of Vedanta. He is widely regarded as an incarnation of God. Ramakrishna, originally named Gadadhar Chattopadhyaya, was born in a Bengali village sixty miles from Calcutta. He was a devout Hindu from boyhood, practiced spiritual disciplines such as meditation, and served as a priest. A mystic and teacher, in 1861 he was declared an avatar: a divine incarnation sent to reestablish the truths of religion and to show by his example how to ascend towards Brahman. Ramakrishna was initiated into Islam, and he had a vision of Christ. His followers gathered around him at Dakshineswar and later at Kashipur. His closest disciples, trained by him, later formed the nucleus of the Ramakrishna Math and Mission, now the largest monastic order in India. Ramakrishna was worshipped as God in his lifetime; he was conscious of his mission, and he was able to transmit divine knowledge by a touch, look, or wish. Isherwood wrote a biography, *Ramakrishna and His Disciples* (1964), an official project of the Ramakrishna Order.

Ram Nam. A sung service of ancient Hindu prayers which invoke the divinities Rama, his wife Sita, and the leader of Rama's army, Hanuman. In Ramakrishna practice, Ram Nam is sung on Ekadashi, the eleventh day after the new or the full moon, a day generally observed by devout Hindus with worship, meditation, and fasting.

Rapper, Irving (1898–1999). Hollywood film director, born in London. Rapper directed for the stage before becoming an assistant director at Warner Brothers in the 1930s. His films include *Now Voyager* (1942), *The Corn is Green* (1945), *Rhapsody in Blue* (1945), *Deception* (1946), *The Voice of the Turtle* (1947), *The Glass Menagerie* (1950), *The Brave One* (1956), and *Marjorie Morningstar* (1958).

Rassine, Alexis (1919–1992). Ballet dancer; his real name was Alec Raysman. He was born in Lithuania of Russian parents and, from about ten years old, was brought up in South Africa. He studied ballet there and in Paris, joined the Ballet Rambert in 1938, and danced with several other companies before joining the Sadler's Wells Ballet in 1942, where he became a principal and a star.

Reed, John (1887–1920). American journalist. Born in Portland, Oregon, and educated at Harvard. Reed was a radical leftist and began his career covering American textile and mining strikes and reporting on Pancho Villa's role in the Mexican Revolution. He was a war correspondent in Europe during World War I and became involved with the Bolshevik leadership in

Russia. In 1917 he reported on the Bolshevik coup and then returned home for a time to try to establish a communist party in the U.S. He died in Russia and was buried in the Kremlin. Much of his reporting was published or republished in book form: *Insurgent Mexico* (1914), *The War in Eastern Europe* (1916), *Red Russia* (1919), and the work on the Bolshevik take-over for which he is most widely known, *Ten Days That Shook the World* (1919). He is the subject of Warren Beatty's film *Reds* (1981).

Reinhardt, Gottfried (1911–c.1993). Austrian-born film producer. Reinhardt emigrated to the United States with his father, the theatrical producer Max Reinhardt, and became assistant to Walter Wanger. Afterwards he worked as a producer for MGM from 1940 to 1954 and later directed his own films in the United States and Europe. His name is attached to many well-known movies, including Garbo's *Two Faced Woman*, which he produced in 1941, and *The Red Badge of Courage*, which he produced in 1951. He was Salka Viertel's lover for nearly a decade before his marriage to his wife, Silvia, in 1944. Through Salka and Berthold Viertel, Reinhardt gave Isherwood his second Hollywood film job in 1940, and Isherwood worked for him a number of times after that. There are numerous passages about him in *D1*. Reinhardt and his wife eventually returned to Europe and settled near Salzburg.

Reinhardt, Wolfgang. Film producer and writer; son of Max Reinhardt, brother of Gottfried. He produced *My Love Come Back* (1940), *The Male Animal* (1942), *Three Strangers* (1946), *Caught* (1948), and *Freud* (1962), for which he won an Academy Award as co-writer. As Isherwood records in *D1*, Reinhardt and Isherwood tried to work together several times. With Aldous Huxley they discussed making *The Miracle*, a film version of the play produced by Max Reinhardt in the 1920s, but nothing came of it. Reinhardt hired Isherwood to work on Maugham's 1941 novel *Up at the Villa*, but the film was never made. Much later, in 1960, Reinhardt approached Isherwood to write a screenplay based on Felix Dahn's four-volume 1876 novel, *Ein Kampf um Rom* (*A Struggle for Rome*), about the decline and fall of the Ostrogoth empire in Italy in the sixth century, but Isherwood turned the project down. Wolfgang's wife was called Lally.

Renaldo, Tito. Mexican actor. He played the first son in *Anna and the King of Siam* (1946). He was known as an exceptional cook at the Vedanta Center, which he joined and left five times. During the late 1950s and 1960s, he worked for a time in Carlos McClendon's shop in West Hollywood. Afterwards, in the 1970s, Renaldo returned in frail health to his family in northern Mexico and fell out of touch with his Los Angeles friends. He is often mentioned in *D1*.

Repton. Isherwood's public school, near Derby.

Richardson, Tony (1928–1991). British stage and film director. Richardson is most admired for his work in the theater, especially at the Royal Court in London during the 1950s, and he made movies from many of his productions there. His films include *Look Back in Anger* (1958), *The Entertainer* (1960), *Sanctuary* (1961), *A Taste of Honey* (1961), *The Loneliness of the Long Distance Runner* (1962), and *Tom Jones* (1963), for which he won an Academy Award.

He was married for a time to Vanessa Redgrave, with whom he had two daughters during the 1960s. Isherwood became friends with Richardson in Hollywood in 1960, and in 1964 Richardson hired him to adapt Evelyn Waugh's *The Loved One* for film; Richardson then gave Isherwood's script to Terry Southern who wrote most of the dialogue. Later projects with Richardson included a script for *Reflections in a Golden Eye* (which John Huston did not use when he took over the film), *The Sailor from Gibraltar* (based on Marguerite Duras' novel), and adaptations with Don Bachardy of Robert Graves's *I, Claudius* and *Claudius, the God* which were never made because Richardson fell out with his proposed Caligula, Mick Jagger. Richardson appears in *D1*.

Robson-Scott, William (1901–1980). English teacher and scholar of German; educated at Rugby School, University College, Oxford, and in Berlin and Vienna. Robson-Scott was lecturing in English at Berlin University in 1932 when Isherwood first met him. He summered at Rügen Island that year with Isherwood, Heinz Neddermeyer, Stephen Spender, and others, and remained a close friend through the 1930s. When he returned to London, Robson-Scott became a lecturer in German, and later in German language and literature, at Birkbeck College, University of London, where he continued to teach until 1968. He married in 1947 and, with his wife, made a translation of Freud's letters to Lou Andreas-Salomé, published in 1972.

Rod. See Owens, Rodney.

Rodd, Marcel. English bookseller and publisher living in Hollywood. Rodd published Prabhavananda and Isherwood's translation of the Bhagavad Gita and *Vedanta for the Western World* as well as the magazine, *The Voice of India* (later *Vedanta and the West*).

Roder, Hellmut. German emigré; Peggy Kiskadden helped Roder and his friend Fritz Mosel escape from Germany via France and Spain, then onward to Mexico and Los Angeles. Later, the pair moved to New York where they designed jewelry, especially for opera costumes. They also dealt in metal and feathers. Eventually Fritz Mosel committed suicide, and after a time, Hellmut Roder apparently did the same.

Rodman, Selden (b. 1909). American writer and editor; educated at Yale. In the 1930s and early 1940s, Rodman published narrative poems—one about T. E. Lawrence, another about airmen. During the same period, he was co-founder and editor of a review called *Common Sense* and later co-founder of another magazine, *Our House*. He also became a director of the Centre d'Art in Port-au-Prince, Haiti, worked to promote Haitian art, and eventually wrote a number of books about Haiti and about Haitian art, as well as a verse play about the 1791 liberation of Haiti. In later years, Rodman wrote travel and guide books about Central and South America, and he produced various volumes of autobiography and commentary on modern art and poetry.

Roerick, Bill. American actor. Isherwood met him in 1943 when John van Druten brought Roerick to a lecture at the Vedanta Center. His companion for many years was Tom Coley.

Ross, Alan (b. 1922). English poet and journalist; editor of John Lehmann's *The London Magazine* from 1961 onwards. Isherwood probably met him when he returned to London for the first time after the war.

Ross, Jean (d. 1973). The original of Isherwood's character Sally Bowles in *Goodbye to Berlin*. Isherwood met Jean Ross in Berlin, possibly in October 1930, but certainly by the start of 1931. She was then occasionally singing in a nightclub, and they shared lodgings for a time in Fräulein Thurau's flat. Ross's father was a Scottish cotton merchant, and she had been raised in Egypt in lavish circumstances. After Berlin, she returned to England where she became close friends with Olive Mangeot. She joined the communist party and had a daughter, Sarah (later a crime novelist under the name Sarah Caudwell), with Claud Cockburn, though she and Cockburn never married.

Roth, Sanford (Sandy). American photographer; known for his pictures of actors and actresses, and especially of James Dean. Isherwood first met Roth in 1951 when Roth photographed Isherwood with Julie Harris costumed as Sally Bowles.

Sachs, David (1921–1992). American philosopher, born in Chicago; educated at UCLA and Princeton, where he obtained his doctorate in 1953. He taught philosophy at Cornell, Brandeis, Iowa State, Rutgers and Johns Hopkins—he was on the faculty there for many years—and he held visiting posts at many other universities in the USA and in Europe. Sachs lectured widely and published numerous philosophical essays on ethics, ancient philosophy, and philosophy of the mind; his subjects included literature and psychoanalysis, and his work appeared in journals such as *The Philosophical Review* (of which he was editor), *Mind*, *Philosophical Studies*, and *Dissent*. In 1951 he reviewed Walter Kaufmann's *Nietzsche* for Eileen Garrett's *Tomorrow*. He also published poems in *Poetry*, *Epoch*, *Voices*, *The New York Times*, and elsewhere.

Salka. See Viertel, Salka.

Samuels, Lesser. American screenwriter. In 1940 Isherwood was hired to polish dialogue on Samuels's script for a remake of *A Woman's Face*; not long after, Samuels asked Isherwood to help him on Maugham's *The Hour Before Dawn*. Like Isherwood, Samuels had worked for Gaumont-British during the 1930s. In subsequent years they often worked together, sometimes on their own ideas, including *Judgement Day in Pittsburgh* (for which they were paid $50,000), *The Easiest Thing in the World*, and *The Vacant Room*. Samuels was married and had a daughter. There are a number of passages about him in *D1*.

Sansom, William (1912–1976). British writer, born in London. Sansom travelled in Europe during the 1930s and wrote stories about the Blitz when he was in the London Fire Service during the war; these were published in 1944 as *Fireman Flower*. Afterwards he published many further volumes of stories, and he also wrote travel books and novels, including *The Body* (1949) and *The Cautious Heart* (1958).

Sarada. "Sarada" Folling was a young nun at the Vedanta Center when Isherwood arrived in Hollywood in 1939. She was of Norwegian descent, had studied music and dance, and while at the center learned Sanskrit. Her father lived in New Mexico. Sarada later moved to the convent at Santa Barbara where Isherwood occasionally saw her. She was a favorite of Prabhavananda, who gave her the Sanskrit name Sarada, but eventually left the Vedanta Society rather suddenly after becoming interested in men. Thereafter, Prabhavananda forbade her name to be mentioned to him. Isherwood tells about her in *D1*.

Saroyan, William (1908–1981). American writer of Armenian parentage, born in Fresno, California. Saroyan turned down a Pulitzer Prize for his play *The Time of Your Life* (1939). Other plays include *My Heart's in the Highlands* (1939), *Love's Old Sweet Song* (1941), *The Beautiful People* (1941), *Get Away Old Man* (1944), and *The Cave Dwellers* (1957). He also published many volumes of short fiction, and his novels include *The Human Comedy* (1943), *The Adventures of Wesley Jackson* (1946), *Rock Wagram* (1951), *Mama, I Love You* (1956), *Papa, You're Crazy* (1957), *Boys and Girls Together* (1963), and *One Day in the Afternoon of the World* (1964). Some of his novels and plays were made into films: *The Human Comedy* (1943) won an Academy Award. From the 1950s onward, Saroyan turned increasingly to autobiography and memoirs.

Schindler, Mr. and Mrs. German actor and his wife. He had worked with Max Reinhardt in Europe. Isherwood met them when they arrived at the Haverford refugee hostel, via an Italian concentration camp, in March 1942; he records in *D1* that they left Haverford by the end of June.

Schlee, George. New York financier of Russian background. Schlee met Greta Garbo towards the end of the 1930s at his wife Valentina's New York dress shop, and the three became involved in a long-running ménage à trois. In the late 1940s, Garbo bought an apartment in the Schlees' building on East 52nd Street, and when Schlee died in his sleep in 1964, he was in a suite adjoining Garbo's at the Hotel Crillon in Paris.

Scott-Kilvert, Ian. British cultural administrator. He matriculated at Gonville and Caius, Cambridge, in 1936 as a classicist but changed to English and took his B.A. in 1940. Afterwards he became Head of the Recorded Sound Department at the British Council. He appears as "Graham" in *Lions and Shadows*.

Searle, Ronald (b. 1920). English artist and cartoonist. He created the St. Trinian's schoolgirls and achieved more serious recognition for the drawings he made while held as a prisoner of war by the Japanese during World War II. He was for many years a theatrical illustrator for *Punch*, contributed to *The New Yorker* and *The New York Times* among other publications, and had numerous one-man gallery shows. Later he also designed animated films and film sequences.

Shankara. Hindu religious philosopher and saint (of between the sixth and eighth centuries AD), widely recognized as an emanation of Shiva. Shankara wrote commentaries on the Brahma Sutras, the principal Upanishads, and other religious texts, as well as philosophy, poems, hymns, and prayers. Much of his work is not attributed with authority. He probably organized the Hindu mendicant orders.

Shearer, Moira (b. 1926). Scottish-born ballet dancer and, later, actress. She also became a writer, publishing biographies of Balanchine and of Ellen Terry as well as reviewing books. See also Ludovic Kennedy, her husband.

Shivananda, Swami (d. 1934). Hindu monk; a direct disciple of Ramakrishna. Shivananda was originally named Tarak Nath Ghoshal, and his father was legal advisor to a rani. He met Ramakrishna in 1880, when he was about twenty-six, and though he afterwards married, he remained celibate and eventually renounced the world to live as a monk. After Ramakrishna's death, there followed a period of wandering; then Shivananda founded a Ramakrishna monastery at Benares, and in 1922 he became President of the Ramakrishna Order.

Sister Lalita (Sister) (d. 1949). Carrie Mead Wykoff, an American widow, met Vivekananda on one of his U.S. lecture tours and became a disciple of Swami Turiyananda (another direct disciple of Ramakrishna). Turiyananda gave her the name Sister Lalita. In 1929 she invited Swami Prabhavananda to live in her house in Hollywood and within a decade they had gathered a congregation and built the Hollywood temple in her garden. She appears in *D1*.

Smedley, Agnes (1892–1950). American journalist and author; a radical advocate of feminist, communist and nationalist causes. She was involved in Margaret Sanger's birth control movement and was jailed for her role in trying to organize an overseas Indian independence movement. During the 1920s she lived in and wrote about Weimar Germany. Smedley was helpful to Isherwood and W. H. Auden when they met her in Hankow in March 1938. She spent nearly a decade there organizing medical supplies for Mao's Eighth Route Army, writing a book about the army, and writing for German and American newspapers about the antifascist struggle in China. She had many Chinese contacts and she was also a willing go-between for the U.S. government; she was frequently at the U.S. Embassy and was friendly with American officials. Smedley died under the accusation of being a Soviet spy.

Snow, Edgar (1905–1972). American author; born and educated in Missouri. Snow began his career as a reporter. He went to China in 1928 and became correspondent there for several U.S. and British papers. In 1936 he was the first correspondent to interview Mao Tse-tung. During World War II he covered Asia and later Europe, and he was the first correspondent to enter liberated Vienna. Afterwards he travelled widely as a special correspondent for various newspapers and magazines. Snow wrote a number of books about Chinese and Soviet communism; among the best known is *Red Star Over China* (1937). He also made a documentary film about China at the end of the 1960s. Isherwood and W. H. Auden mention Snow in their foreword to *Journey to a War* because he helped them with information and introductions for their China trip.

Sorel, Paul (b. 1918). American painter, of midwestern background; his real name is Karl Dibble. Sorel was a close friend of Chris Wood, and lived with him in Laguna in the early 1940s. He moved out in 1943 after disagreements about money and in 1944 went to New York for a time, then intermittently returned. Chris Wood continued to support Sorel for the rest of Wood's life, though they did not live together at all after 1953. Sorel is also described in *D1*.

Sorokine, Natasha. White Russian intellectual, raised in France where she and her parents were officially stateless. At her lycée, she was taught by Simone de Beauvoir, befriended her and became part of de Beauvoir and Sartre's intimate circle during the war. De Beauvoir described their friendship in her memoirs *La Force de l'âge* (1960) and *Tout compte fait* (1972), thinly disguising Natasha as "Lise Oblanoff." (In fact, de Beauvoir and Sartre called her Nathalie and, according to Ivan Moffat, also addressed her as Sarbakhane—after a West African trumpet of great length and exotic design.) According to de Beauvoir, Sorokine's interest in philosophy led her to pursue a degree at the Sorbonne during the war. During the same period, she became romantically involved with a student of Sartre's, a young Spanish Jew who was arrested and killed by the Nazis near the end of the war, leaving her devastated. Not long afterwards, she met and married Ivan Moffat, joining him in California. They had a daughter, Lorna Moffat, but the marriage did not succeed, and Sorokine struggled to make a living. She wrote, taught French, worked in a kindergarten, waitressed, and studied law. Her fiction was never published. She married a second time, to a physicist Sidney Benson, with whom she had a son and adopted a daughter, but she was plagued by ill health and mental instability. She died in the late 1960s.

Speaight, Robert (1904–1976). British actor and writer; educated at Lincoln College, Oxford. He established a stage reputation by the start of the 1930s and began publishing novels around the same time. Among his many stage roles was Becket in T. S. Eliot's *Murder in the Cathedral* in 1935. During the later part of his career he published scholarly books on Shakespeare and a number of biographies.

Spender, Humphrey (b. 1910). English photographer and designer; brother of Stephen Spender. He was educated at Gresham's School, Holt, Norfolk; at the University of Freiburg, Breisgau, Germany; and at the Architectural Association School, London. During the 1930s he worked as a portrait and commercial photographer from his own studio in London, was a staff photographer for the *Daily Mirror* newspaper, and became the official photographer for Mass Observation. Before the war he moved to *Picture Post* magazine. He trained in the Royal Army Service Corps (Tanks) in 1941, worked for the Ministry of Information, and became a War Office Official Photographer and afterwards a Photo Interpreter for Theatre Intelligence Service. When the war ended, he returned to *Picture Post*, but gradually gave up photography to paint and to design textiles. He had many individual shows in these media during the 1940s and 1950s, and also taught design at the Royal College of Art and at several other schools in London until the mid-1970s. From the late 1970s, a revival of interest in his photographs led to numerous exhibitions of his 1930s work. Spender married twice (his first wife died of Hodgkin's disease) and had one son with each of his wives.

Spender, Natasha Litvin. English concert pianist; she married Stephen Spender in 1941 and had two children with him, Matthew and Lizzie.

Spender, Stephen (1909–1995). English poet, critic, autobiographer, editor. W. H. Auden introduced Isherwood to Spender in 1928; Spender was then an undergraduate at University College, Oxford, and Isherwood became a mentor. Afterwards Spender lived in Hamburg and near Isherwood in Berlin, and the two briefly shared a house in Sintra with Heinz Neddermeyer and Tony Hyndman. Spender was the youngest of the writers who came to prominence with Auden and Isherwood in the 1930s; after they emigrated, he cultivated the public and social roles they abjured in England. He worked as a propagandist for the Republicans during the Spanish Civil War and was a member of the National Fire Service during the Blitz. He was co-editor with Cyril Connolly of *Horizon* and later of *Encounter*. He moved away from his early enthusiasm for communism, but remained liberal in politics. In 1968, at the request of Russian dissident Pavel Litvinov and with the combined support of various celebrated intellectuals (mostly personal friends) and of Amnesty International, Spender helped to found *Index on Censorship* to report on and publicize the circumstances of persecuted writers and artists throughout the world. His 1936 marriage to Inez Pearn was over by 1939, and in 1941 he married Natasha Litvin with whom he had two children. Spender appears as "Stephen Savage" in *Lions and Shadows* and is further described in *Christopher and His Kind* and in *D1*. He published an autobiography, *World Within World*, in 1951, and his *Journals 1939–1983* appeared in 1985.

Stafford, Jean (1915–1979). American novelist and short-story writer. Her much-praised first novel, *Boston Adventure*, appeared in 1944 and her second, *The Mountain Lion*, in 1947, followed by other novels and numerous short stories. She worked on *The Southern Review* and occasionally taught college. In 1966 she published an interview with Lee Harvey Oswald's mother, *A Mother in History*. Her *Collected Stories* (1969) won the Pulitzer Prize. When Isherwood met Stafford in 1947 she was married to the poet Robert Lowell, but this first marriage (for both) ended in 1948; later she was married to A.J. Leibling.

Stern, James (1904–1993) and Tania Kurella Stern (1906–1995). Irish writer and translator and his wife, daughter of a German psychiatrist. He was educated at Eton and, briefly, Sandhurst. In youth, he worked as a farmer in Southern Rhodesia and as a banker in the family bank in England and Europe, then travelled until settling for a time in Paris in the 1930s, where he met Tania Kurella. They married in 1935. She was a physical therapist and exercise teacher, exponent of her own technique, the Kurella method. She fled Germany in 1933 to escape persecution for the left-wing political activities of her two brothers, already refugees. Isherwood met the Sterns in Sintra, Portugal in 1936 through William Robson-Scott and introduced them to W. H. Auden with whom they became close friends, later, in America. James Stern's books include *The Heartless Land* (1932), *Something Wrong* (1938)—both story collections—and *The Hidden Damage* (1945), about his trip with Auden to survey bomb damage in postwar Germany for the U.S. Army. Tania Stern collaborated on some of his translations. Eventually they returned to England and settled near Salisbury.

Stern, Josef Luitpold (1886–1966). Viennese poet, journalist, and editor; identified throughout his career with the cause of the workers. Stern reformed the workers' library in Vienna and was a high-ranking administrator in workers' education both before and after the war. He arrived as a refugee at the Quaker hostel in Haverford, Pennsylvania, where Isherwood volunteered during the war, and Isherwood records in *D1* that they met there in the autumn of 1941. Stern returned to Vienna after the war. He published nearly twenty volumes, including *Klassenkampf und Massenschulung* (1925), *Zehn Jahre Republik* (1928), *Lyrik und Prosa aus vier Jahrzehnten* (1948), and *Das Sternbild, Gedicht eines Lebens*, a collected works in two volumes (1964–1966).

Steuermann, Eduard. Polish-born concert pianist; Salka Viertel's brother and briefly a member of her extended household during the war. He re-established his career in the USA, achieving wide recognition as an interpreter in particular of Schoenberg, Berg, and Webern. Among his students was Alfred Brendel. Steuermann married twice, and had three daughters. His second marriage was to his student, Clara Silvers, thirty years his junior.

Steve, also Stevie. Steve Conway; see index and see also *D1*.

Stevens, George (1904–1975). American film director. Early in his career, Stevens directed Laurel and Hardy. He made a number of successful films in the 1930s and early 1940s, and had a special touch for comedy. His prewar films include *Alice Adams* (1935), *Swing Time* (1936), *Gunga Din* (1939), *Woman of the Year* (1941)—in which he introduced Spencer Tracy and Katharine Hepburn—and *Talk of the Town* (1942). During the war, Stevens headed the Sigma Corps Special Motion Picture Unit in Europe, where, among other disturbing scenes, he filmed Dachau soon after it was liberated. Although he made some of his best-known films after his return, his work became heavier and, eventually, less successful. Later films include *I Remember Mama* (1947), *A Place in the Sun* (1951, Academy Award), *Shane* (1953), and *Giant* (1956, Academy Award).

Stokowski, Leopold (1882–1977). English-born conductor. He studied at Oxford University and at the Royal College of Music. Stokowski began as a church organist in London and then in New York and settled in the USA, becoming a citizen in 1915. He conducted many celebrated orchestras in his long career, in particular the Philadelphia Orchestra from 1912 to 1938, for which he established a superlative international reputation and where he introduced important European works to U.S. audiences—such as Mahler's 8th Symphony, Stravinsky's *The Rite of Spring*, and works by Schoenberg, Berg, and Rachmaninoff—as well as performing new American music. He conducted the Philadelphia Orchestra for Walt Disney's *Fantasia* (1940) and was also involved in several other movies. Afterwards, he conducted leading orchestras all over the world, including the New York Philharmonic and the Houston Symphony, finally returning to London in 1972 where he often appeared with the London Symphony Orchestra.

Strasberg, Lee (1901–1982) and Paula. Lee Strasberg was an American theater director and acting teacher; he derived his approach from Stanislavsky. In 1931, he helped to found the Group Theater (in New York), and in 1950 he became a director of The Actors Studio, where he made his reputation as a leading proponent of Method acting. Paula Strasberg, his wife (Isherwood's landlady on East Rustic Road), became Marilyn Monroe's acting coach.

Stravinsky, Igor (1882–1971). Russian-born composer; he went to Paris with Diaghilev's Ballets Russes in 1910 and brought about a rhythmic revolution in Western music with his *The Rite of Spring* (1911–1913), the most sensational of his many works commissioned for the company. In youth he was greatly influenced by his teacher, Rimsky-Korsakov, but Stravinsky's originality as a composer derived partly from his ability to borrow and rework an enormously wide range of musical forms and styles. He remained continuously open to new ideas, even into old age. Many of his early works evoke Russian folk music, and he was influenced by jazz. Around 1923 he began a long neoclassical period during which he drew on and responded to the compositions of his great European predecessors. After the Russian revolution, Stravinsky remained in Europe, making his home first in Switzerland and then in Paris, and turned to performing and conducting to support his family. In 1926 he rejoined the Russian Orthodox Church, and religious music became an increasing preoccupation during the later part of his career. At the outbreak of World War II, he emigrated to America where he settled in Los Angeles and eventually became a citizen in 1945. Although he was asked to, he never composed for films. His first and most important work to English words was his opera, *The Rake's Progress* (1951), for which W. H. Auden and Chester Kallman wrote the libretto. During the 1950s, with the encouragement of Robert Craft, Stravinsky began to compose according to the twelve-note serial methods invented by Schoenberg and extended by Webern —he was already past seventy. There are many passages about Stravinsky in *D1*.

Stravinsky, Vera (1888–1982). Russian-born actress and painter. Second wife of Igor Stravinsky; she was previously married three times, the third time to the painter and Ballets Russes stage designer Sergei Sudeikin. In 1917, Vera Arturovna Sudeikin fled St. Petersburg and the bohemian artistic milieu in which she was both patroness and muse, travelling in the south of Russia with Sudeikin before going on to Paris where she met Stravinsky in the early 1920s; they fell in love but did not marry until 1940 after the death of Stravinsky's first wife. Vera Stravinsky's paintings were in an abstract-primitive style influenced by Paul Klee, childlike and decorative. She appears often in *D1*.

Sudhira. A nurse of Irish descent; she was a probationer nun at the Hollywood Vedanta Center when Isherwood arrived to live there in 1943. Her real name was Helen Kennedy. She had been widowed in youth, and first came to the Vedanta Center professionally to nurse a devotee. After the war she married for a second time and returned to nursing. Isherwood tells about her in detail in *D1*.

Sutherland, Graham (1903–1980). English artist. Sutherland began his career as an etcher and engraver and took up oil painting by the mid-1930s, producing semi-abstract pictures inspired by the landscape of Pembrokeshire. He was an official war artist during World War II, employed to depict bomb damage. After the war he began painting religious subjects, and in 1949 he painted a portrait of Somerset Maugham, thus embarking on a new phase as a portrait painter. His best-known work is an enormous tapestry, *Christ in Glory*, which he designed during the 1950s for the rebuilt Coventry Cathedral. He also worked with ceramics and designed for the stage. From the late 1930s, Sutherland and his wife lived half the year in France and half in Trottiscliffe, Kent.

Swami. Used as a title to mean "Lord" or "Master." A Hindu monk or religious teacher. Isherwood used it in particular to refer to his guru, Swami Prabhavananda, and he pronounced it "Shwami," according to the Sanskrit phonetics Prabhavananda taught him; see Prabhavananda.

Swamiji. An especially respectful form of "Swami," used in particular as a name for Vivekananda in his later years.

Taxman, Barry. American composer; raised in the Midwest and educated at Yale and the University of Chicago. He was associated for a time with the University of California at Berkeley and his music is regularly performed in Berkeley where he settled.

Taylor, Frank (1915–1999). American publisher and movie producer, born in upstate New York and raised as a Roman Catholic. Taylor was turned down by the draft for health reasons and made a meteoric rise in New York publishing during the war years. He began in advertising at Harper and Brothers, the *Saturday Review of Literature*, and then Reynal & Hitchcock where he was able to move to the literary side during the war and discovered his first bestsellers, *Strange Fruit* by Lillian Smith and, later, *Under the Volcano* by Malcolm Lowry. After the war, he visited England and established literary friendships which helped him expand the list of American and international authors he was already publishing, such as Arthur Miller, Karl Shapiro, Howard Nemerov, Saint-Exupéry, Le Corbusier, and Brecht. He vainly tried to start his own publishing firm, worked briefly at Random House, then in 1948 went to Hollywood to produce movies, first of all at MGM, later at Fox. Despite critical recognition and ubiquitous success on the Hollywood social scene, he was victimized during the McCarthy period for his former associations with the communist party—he was a labor activist throughout his early career in New York—and eventually toward the end of 1951 he returned to New York. There, in 1952, he became editor-in-chief at Dell, achieving huge success during the paperback revolution. But Hollywood beckoned again, and Taylor produced *The Misfits* (1960) with his old friend Arthur Miller. As he records in *D1*, Isherwood worked with Taylor on film ideas in the 1950s—including *The Journeying Boy*, a detective story by Michael Innes, and *I Am a Camera*—and he prepared the 1960 anthology *Great English Short Stories* for Taylor at Dell. During the 1960s and 1970s, Taylor ran the trade division at McGraw-Hill where he published Marshall McLuhan, Eldridge Cleaver, Germaine Greer, and Nabokov, among others.

Taylor, Nan (b. 1915). American radio hostess; born and raised in Minnesota as a Roman Catholic. Her maiden name was Skallon. Taylor trained as an actress at the University of Minnesota and afterwards had a children's radio show in New York. During the war, she worked with Bennett Cerf, presenting a books program. She gave up her career when she moved to Hollywood with her husband, Frank Taylor, and looked after their four sons,

Michael, Mark, Curtice, and Adams. When the Taylors returned east, they settled in Greenwich, Connecticut, where she founded the town's first day-care center and, later, during the 1970s, became head of the Board of Education. She was also president locally of the English Speaking Union. The Taylors divorced in the 1970s and Nan remarried, though she remained close to her first husband.

Thomas, Dylan (1914–1953). British poet, born and raised in Wales, where his father was the English master at Swansea Grammar School. Thomas began writing poetry in childhood, left school early and published his first book, *18 Poems*, in 1934 while working as a journalist. In London he also worked as a scriptwriter and broadcaster for the BBC and wrote stories as well as poems. His marriage in 1937 to Caitlin Macnamara was famously stormy and drunken, but Thomas's work nevertheless attracted critical acclaim and a wide audience. After the pair moved back to Wales together in 1949, he made a series of taxing reading tours through the USA because he needed the money. He died in New York of alcohol poisoning in November 1953. His *Collected Poems* appeared in 1952, and he completed a version of his radio play *Under Milk Wood* not long before he died.

Todd, Thelma (1905–1935). American movie actress. She owned an establishment on the Pacific Coast Highway north of Santa Monica incorporating a restaurant, a gambling casino and a whorehouse, and she was murdered there. Afterwards the restaurant—named Chez Roland after Gilbert Roland with whom Todd was supposed to be in love—remained in business for many years; Isherwood always referred to it as "Thelma Todd's."

Tooker, George. American painter. He became Paul Cadmus's lover after they met at the Art Students League in New York in 1942, and he was friendly with Cadmus's circle. During the 1950s he moved to Vermont with another artist, William Christopher, and continued his career there.

Trabuco. Monastic community founded by Gerald Heard in 1942, on a ranch about sixty miles south of Los Angeles and roughly twenty miles inland. An anonymous benefactor provided $100,000 for the project, and Isherwood's cousin, Felix Greene, administered the practical side, buying the property and constructing the building, which could house fifty. By 1949 Heard found the responsibility of leading the group too much of a strain and Trabuco was given to the Vedanta Society.

Tree, Iris (1896–1968). English actress, poet, and playwright; third daughter of actor Herbert Beerbohm Tree. She published three volumes of poetry and wrote poems and articles for magazines such as *Vogue* and *Harper's Bazaar*, as well as *Botteghe Oscure*, *Poetry Review*, and *The London Magazine*. In youth she travelled with her father to Hollywood and New York and married an American, Curtis Moffat, with whom she had her first son, Ivan Moffat, born in Havana. Until 1926 she lived mostly in London and in Paris where she acted in Max Reinhardt's *The Miracle*; she toured with the play back to America where she met her second husband, the Austrian Count Friedrich Ledebur, with whom she had another son, Christian Dion Ledebur (called Boon) in 1928. Iris Tree had known Aldous and Maria Huxley in London, and they introduced Isherwood to her in California during the war. With Alan Harkness, she brought a troupe of actors to Ojai to start The High Valley Theatre, and she adapted, wrote, and acted in plays for the group, including her own *Cock-a-doodle-doo*. She moved often—from house to house and country to country—and in July 1954 left California for good, settling in Rome where she worked on but never finished a novel about her youth. Her marriage to Ledebur ended in 1955. Isherwood modelled "Charlotte" in *A Single Man* partly on Iris Tree and wrote much about her in *D1*.

Turville–Petre, Francis. English archaeologist, from an aristocratic Catholic family. Isherwood met the eccentric Turville-Petre through W. H. Auden in Berlin in 1929, and it was at Turville-Petre's house outside Berlin that Isherwood met Heinz Neddermeyer in 1932. In 1933 when Isherwood and Heinz fled Germany, they spent nearly four months on Turville-Petre's tiny island, St. Nicholas, in Greece. Turville-Petre is the model for "Ambrose" in *Down There on a Visit*.

Twentieth Century-Fox Film Corporation. One of Hollywood's five biggest studios. It was formed by a merger between Twentieth Century Pictures and Fox Film Corporation. Darryl F. Zanuck ran it from 1935 to 1952 and again from 1962 with his son Richard Zanuck. Alan Ladd Jr. took over in the 1970s, and Twentieth Century-Fox has since been sold and resold, eventually to Rupert Murdoch. Its many stars have included Shirley Temple and Marilyn Monroe, and Fox produced the first widescreen Cinemascope film, *The Robe*, in 1953, followed by other big screen spectaculars, including *The King and I* (1956), *Cleopatra* (1963), and *The Sound of Music* (1965). Isherwood worked at Fox scripting *Jean-Christophe* in 1956 and 1957, but the film was never made.

UFOs. In June 1947 an Idaho businessman, Kenneth Arnold, reported seeing through the window of his private plane, near Mt. Rainier, flying objects which he described to the press as looking like "skipping saucers." So many more "sightings" followed around the country that the U.S. military officially investigated the possible threat to national security. In his 1950 book *Is Another World Watching?* (*The Riddle of the Flying Saucers* in the U.K.), Gerald Heard described many of these early UFO sightings. He believed they were either top secret, ultra-fast experimental aircraft which the government was covering up or, more exciting to him, visitors from Mars. Among the numerous accounts of flying saucers analyzed by the U.S. Air Force between 1947 and the mid-1950s, about ten percent of reported sightings were never accounted for. As the terminology indicates, they remain Unidentified Flying Objects. Official U.S. investigations were abandoned in 1969.

Upward, Edward (b. 1903). English novelist and schoolmaster. Isherwood met Upward in 1921 at their public school, Repton, and followed him to Corpus Christi College, Cambridge. They were closely united by their rebellious attitude toward family and school authority and by shared literary interests. In the 1920s they created the fantasy world, Mortmere, about which they wrote surreal, macabre, and pornographic stories and poems for each other; their excited schoolboy humor is described in *Lions and Shadows* where

Upward appears as "Allen Chalmers."

Upward made his reputation in the 1930s with his short fiction, especially *Journey to the Border* (1938), the intense, almost mystical, and largely auto-biographical account of a young upper-middle-class tutor's conversion to communism. Then he published nothing for a long time, writing only fragments while he devoted himself to schoolmastering (he needed the money) and to communist party work. From 1931 to 1961 he taught at Alleyn's School, Dulwich, where he became Head of English and a housemaster; he lived nearby with his wife, Hilda, and their two children, Kathy and Christopher.

After World War II, Upward and his wife became disillusioned by the British communist party, and they left it in 1948; but Upward never abandoned his Marxist-Leninist convictions. In the face of psychological difficulties of some magnitude, he returned to his writing in earnest towards the end of the 1950s, and eventually produced a massive autobiographical trilogy, *The Spiral Ascent* (1977)—comprised of *In the Thirties* (1962), *The Rotten Elements* (1969), and *No Home but the Struggle*. The last two volumes were written on the Isle of Wight, where Upward retired in 1962, and they have been followed by several collections of short stories. Upward remained a challenging and trusted critic of Isherwood's work throughout Isherwood's life, and a loyal friend. He is often mentioned in *D1*.

van Druten, John (1901–1957). English playwright and novelist. Isherwood met van Druten in New York in 1939, and they became friends because they were both pacifists. Of Dutch parentage, van Druten was born and educated in London and took a degree in law at the University of London. He achieved his first success as a playwright in New York during the 1920s, emigrated in 1938 and became a U.S. citizen in 1944. His strength was light comedy; among his numerous plays and adaptations were *Voice of the Turtle* (1943), *I Remember Mama* (1944), *Bell, Book, and Candle* (1950), and *I Am a Camera* (1951) based on Isherwood's *Goodbye to Berlin*. Many of these were later filmed. In 1951, van Druten directed *The King and I* on Broadway. Van Druten usually spent half the year in New York and half near Los Angeles on the AJC Ranch, which he owned with Carter Lodge. He also owned a mountain cabin above Idyllwild which Isherwood sometimes used. A fall from a horse in Mexico in 1936 left van Druten with a crippled arm, and partly as a result of this, he became attracted to Vedanta and other religions (he was a renegade Christian Scientist). He was a contributor to Isherwood's *Vedanta for the Western World*, and there are numerous accounts of him in *D1*.

van Leyden, Ernst and Karen. Dutch painters and decorative artists. They specialized in painting on glass, and they were responsible for a mural painted on glass in Jay de Laval's restaurant Café Jay. Karen van Leyden also painted screens and panels. The van Leydens had been friendly with Brian Howard in Portugal in 1933 when Howard travelled there with Cyril and Jean Connolly and Howard's boyfriend Toni. During the 1940s and early 1950s they lived on Barrington Avenue in Brentwood, which was then still rustic with open fields, and they converted the large barn on the property into their studio.

Van Meegeren, Han (1889–1947). Dutch painter and perhaps the greatest forger ever; he painted a number of Vermeers and De Hooghs which were accepted as authentic and which hung in the Rijksmuseum in Amsterdam until 1945 when Van Meegeren was arrested as a collaborator because he was associated with the sale of a Dutch master painting to Goebbels. To clear himself of the charge of collaborating, Van Meegeren confessed that the Goebbels painting and certain others were his own work. A two-year scientific study confirmed his claim, uncovering his immensely complex process and also his remarkable talent. He was sentenced to a year in prison and died there of a heart attack.

van Petten, Bill (1922–1989). American film administrator. Van Petten came from a wealthy oil family, read widely, especially in Sufi literature, and eventually converted to Islam. For two years he was assistant to the Saudi Arabian Minister of Information and helped to establish an Imax theater at the royal palace. He also supervised the filming of documentary footage there. He lived in Santa Monica, for many years in the same building with Jim Charlton.

Van Vechten, Carl (1880–1964). American novelist and poet, critic of music and dance, and, late in life, photographer. He was a prolific writer and a figure of New York's bohemia, frequenting Harlem clubs and greatly contributing to popular recognition of black artists during the Harlem Renaissance. He was also an early editor of Gertrude Stein. Among his seven novels are *The Tattooed Countess* (1924) and *Nigger Heaven* (1926). He was married to Fania Marinoff.

Vaughan, Keith (1912–1977). English painter, illustrator, and diarist. He worked in advertising during the 1930s and was a conscientious objector in the war; later he taught at the Camberwell School of Arts and Crafts, the Central School of Arts and Crafts, and the Slade, as well as briefly in America. Isherwood met him in 1947 at John Lehmann's and bought one of his pictures, "Two Bathers," a small oil painting still in his collection. Vaughan's diaries, with his own illustrations, were published in 1966.

Vidal, Gore (b. 1925). American writer. Vidal introduced himself to Isherwood in a café in Paris in early 1948, having previously written to him and sent the manuscript of his novel *The City and the Pillar*. They became lasting friends. Later, Isherwood also met Howard Austen (Tinker), Vidal's companion from 1950 onward. Vidal was in the army as a young man; afterwards he wrote essays on politics and culture as well as many novels, including *Williwaw* (1946), *Myra Breckenridge* (1968, dedicated to Isherwood), and the multi-volume American chronicle comprised of *Burr* (1974), *Lincoln* (1984), *1876* (1976), *Empire* (1987), *Hollywood* (1989), and *Washington, D.C.* (1967). During the 1950s Vidal wrote a series of television plays for CBS, then screenplays at Twentieth Century-Fox and MGM (including part of *Ben Hur*), and two Broadway plays, *Visit to a Small Planet* (1957) and *The Best Man* (1960). In 1960 he ran for Congress, and in 1982 for the Senate, both times unsuccessfully. He described his friendship with Isherwood in his memoir, *Palimpsest* (1995), and there are many passages about him in *D1*.

Viertel, Berthold (1885–1953). Viennese poet, playwright, and film and theater director. Isherwood worked for Viertel in London as a screenplay writer and, later, dialogue director on Viertel's film *Little Friend* made by Gaumont-British. This was Isherwood's first experience in the film business, and he made it the subject of *Prater Violet*, in which Viertel appears as "Friedrich Bergmann." Viertel also appears throughout *D1*. Viertel had settled his first wife and children in Santa Monica in 1928 and returned alone to Europe for long periods to work. His description of the life in California was a glamorous lure to Isherwood; they renewed their friendship soon after Isherwood arrived there in 1939, beginning work on a film vaguely inspired by *Mr. Norris Changes Trains*. At the Viertels' house in Santa Monica Canyon Isherwood met a number of the celebrated European emigrés then in Hollywood, and the friendship with Viertel led to his second Hollywood job (the first of any substance) with Gottfried Reinhardt at MGM. Viertel began his career as an actor and stage director and turned to films in the 1920s. He first made films in Germany, began directing in Hollywood from the late 1920s, and in England from 1933. Towards the end of his life he lived partly in New York and eventually, with his second wife—the German character actress Elisabeth Neumann—he returned to Europe as a theatrical director, staging, among other works, German-language productions of Tennessee Williams.

Viertel, Peter (b. 1920). German-born second son of Berthold and Salka Viertel; screenplay writer and novelist. Peter Viertel attended UCLA and Dartmouth and became a freelance writer. He served in the U.S. Marines during World War II and was decorated four times. He wrote the award-winning screenplay for Hemingway's *The Old Man and the Sea* as well as other Hemingway adaptations, and his own novels are in the Hemingway vein, with subjects such as soldiering (*Line of Departure*, 1947), big game hunting (*White Hunter, Black Heart*, 1954), and bullfighting (*Love Lies Bleeding*, 1964). His first novel, *The Canyon* (published in 1941, but completed when he was just nineteen), gives a compelling adolescent view of Santa Monica as it was around the time when Isherwood first arrived there, and Isherwood mentions it in *D1*. Viertel's first marriage was to Virginia Schulberg, known as Jigee, and in 1960 he married the actress Deborah Kerr. Like his mother and father he eventually resettled in Europe.

Viertel, Salka (1889–1978). Polish actress and screenplay writer; first wife of Berthold Viertel with whom she had three sons, Hans, Peter, and Thomas. Sara Salomé Steuermann Viertel had a successful stage career in Vienna (including acting for Max Reinhardt's Deutsches Theater) before moving to Hollywood where she became the friend and confidante of Greta Garbo; they appeared together in the German-language version of *Anna Christie* and afterwards Salka collaborated on Garbo's screenplays for MGM in the 1930s and 1940s (*Queen Christina*, *Anna Karenina*, *Conquest*, and others). Isherwood met her soon after arriving in Los Angeles and was often at her house socially or to work with Berthold Viertel. In the 1930s and 1940s the house was frequented by European refugees and Salka was able to help many of them find work—some as domestic servants, others with the studios. Among her guests were some of the most celebrated writers and movie stars of the time. By the mid-1940s, her husband had left her; her lover Gottfried Reinhardt had married; Garbo's career was over; and later, in the 1950s, Salka was persecuted by the McCarthyites and blacklisted by MGM for her presumed communism. In January 1947, she moved into the garage apartment Isherwood and Caskey had let from her and rented out her house; then in the early 1950s she sold the property and moved to an apartment off Wilshire Boulevard. Eventually she returned modestly to writing for the movies, but finally moved back to Europe, although she had been a U.S. citizen since 1939. Isherwood tells about her in detail in *D1*.

Viertel, Tommy. Youngest son of Berthold and Salka Viertel. He was drafted into the U.S. Army in February 1944. After the war he lived in Los Angeles where he worked for Los Angeles County. He married twice.

Viertel, Virginia (Jigee). Peter Viertel's first wife, from 1944 to 1959. Born Virginia Ray to working-class Americans ruined by the Depression, Jigee was a dancer in the Paramount chorus and then married the writer Budd Schulberg with whom she shared strong leftist political convictions. She and Schulberg divorced after having a daughter, Vicky Schulberg. Jigee's second daughter, Christine Viertel, was born in Paris in 1952, and Jigee and Peter separated immediately afterwards. Salka Viertel partly raised both Vicky and Christine. After the ruin of her second marriage, Jigee drank increasingly heavily; then in January 1960 she fell asleep with a lit cigarette and died of burns in the hospital. She appears in *D1*.

Vivekananda, Swami (1863–1902). Narendranath Datta (also known as Naren, Narendra and later as Swamiji) was Ramakrishna's chief direct disciple. Ramakrishna recognized him as an "eternal companion," a perfect soul born into the world along with the avatar and possessing some of the avatar's characteristics. Vivekananda led the disciples after Ramakrishna's death and founded the Ramakrishna Math and Mission. He also spent time wandering through India practicing spiritual disciplines and travelling to America and Europe, where his lectures and classes spawned the first Vedanta centers in the West. His teachings and sayings were published in various volumes, and Isherwood wrote the introduction to a 1960 selection from these.

Vividishananda, Swami. Hindu monk, from India. Vividishananda ran the Seattle Vedanta Center; Isherwood met him at the dedication of the new Portland temple in 1943 and afterwards briefly visited his Seattle center. Swami Vividishananda's biography of Shivananda, *A Man of God: Glimpses into the Life and Work of Swami Shivananda, a Great Disciple of Sri Ramakrishna*—for which Isherwood wrote the foreword in 1949—was eventually published in 1957 by the Ramakrishna Math.

Waley, Arthur (1889–1966). English poet and scholar of Chinese and Japanese; educated at Rugby and King's College, Cambridge. Waley lived in Bloomsbury and associated with figures in the Bloomsbury group. He is best known for his translations of Chinese and Japanese literature which he began to publish during World War I. His renderings from the Chinese influenced Ezra Pound and the Imagists, among others, and his major prose translations (*The Tale of Genji*, *Monkey*) along with his scholarly writings on Japanese and Chinese art and culture contributed in England from the 1920s onward to a growing general interest in oriental literature.

Walter, Bruno. German conductor. Walter was a neighbor of Thomas Mann in Munich from before the start of World War I, and they became lifelong friends. Their children were acquainted with one another from childhood. When the Manns first arrived to spend the summer in Brentwood in 1940, the Walters were already settled nearby. Walter also lived in New York.

Warner Brothers. One of the major Hollywood studios, founded in 1923 by the four sons of a Polish shoemaker. Warner Brothers pioneered talking pictures and later became known for realistic, often black-and-white, films. As well as gangster movies and musicals, there were numerous relatively highbrow historical and political films, and the studio was especially successful from the 1930s to the 1950s. It was increasingly run by the youngest brother, Jack Warner, although Darryl F. Zanuck and, after him, Hal Wallis, contributed to Jack Warner's success. Warner Brothers was sold to Seven Arts in 1967 and later taken over by a conglomerate, eventually merging with Time Inc. in 1989.

Warren, Robert Penn (1905–1989). American poet, novelist, critic, and teacher; born in Kentucky and educated at Vanderbilt, Berkeley, Yale, and Oxford. Warren won a Pulitzer Prize for his 1946 novel *All the King's Men*, also his best known, and he wrote numerous other novels and works of non-fiction, mostly preoccupied with the concerns of his native South. He helped to found *The Southern Review* and co-edited it with Cleanth Brooks from 1935 until 1942; with Brooks he also later compiled two volumes of criticism and literary writing which spread the so-called New Criticism into many college classrooms: *Understanding Poetry* (1938) and *Understanding Criticism* (1943). Warren's first volume of poetry appeared in 1935, and he won two more Pulitzer prizes for later volumes of poetry, *Promises* (1957) and *Now and Then* (1978). He also won several other major literary awards and was made America's first poet laureate in 1986. He held university teaching posts throughout his career. For a time he was on the board of the Huntington Hartford Foundation with Isherwood, giving away three-month fellowships for young writers.

Watson, Peter. The financier behind *Horizon*, of which he was art editor and co-founder. Watson was heir to a margarine fortune, intelligent, and idealistically devoted to art. He collected art and befriended many artists. He was close to Denny Fouts in the 1930s and was the officially named owner of Denny Fouts's Picasso when it was exhibited at the Museum of Modern Art in New York. Later, he lived with Norman Fowler, whom he met in New York in 1949. The pair lived together in London until the apparently healthy and sober Watson mysteriously drowned in his bath in 1956.

Watson-Gandy, Anthony Blethwyn (Tony) (1919–1952). British RAF flying officer and scholar; educated at Westminster, King's College, Cambridge, and the Sorbonne. His parents were minor gentry, and his father a soldier like Isherwood's. Watson-Gandy translated from French *The Rise and Splendour of the Chinese Empire* (1952) by René Grousset.

Watts, Alan (b. 1915). English mystic, religious philosopher, author, and teacher. Watts became a Buddhist while still a schoolboy at King's School, Canterbury, Kent, and went on to study all forms of religious thought and practice. His many books include *An Outline of Zen Buddhism* (1932), *Behold the Spirit: A Study in the Necessity of Mystical Religion* (1947), *The Supreme Identity: An Essay on Oriental Metaphysic and the Christian Religion* (1950), *Nature, Man and Woman: A New Approach to Sexual Experience* (1958), and *Psychotherapy East and West* (1961). He emigrated to America at the start of World War II, eventually settling near San Francisco where he became Dean of the American Academy of Asian Studies. He is known as a Zen Buddhist, but was also ordained as an Anglican priest in 1945. He was a close friend of Aldous Huxley, whom he first met in 1943, and he was impressed by Krishnamurti's decision to renounce his messianic role. Krishnamurti greatly influenced Watts's *The Wisdom of Insecurity* (1951). Watts felt that Huxley and Gerald Heard were working toward the same synthesis of Christian and oriental mysticism as himself, and like them he experimented with LSD in the 1950s. He opposed the Hindu emphasis on asceticism: he married three times and asserted that sex improved spiritual presence. He was a figure of the San Francisco beat scene and a model for Kerouac's *Dharma Bums*.

Wescott, Glenway (1901–1987). American writer. Wescott was born in Wisconsin, attended the University of Chicago, lived in France in the 1920s, partly in Paris, and travelled in Europe and England. Afterwards he lived in New York. Early in his career he wrote poetry and reviews, later turning to fiction. His best-known works are *The Pilgrim Hawk* (1940) and *Apartment in Athens* (1945). He was President of the American Academy of Arts and Letters from 1957 to 1961. From the late 1930s, Wescott, his longterm companion Monroe Wheeler, and George Platt Lynes shared a country house in New Jersey.

Whale, James (1886–1957). British actor and stage and film director. Whale's film career began when he arrived in Hollywood in 1930 to direct *Journey's End*, which he had produced for the stage in London and New York. He went on to make other movies, including *Frankenstein* with Boris Karloff (1931) and *Bride of Frankenstein* with Karloff and Elsa Lanchester (1935), *Showboat* (1936), and *The Man in the Iron Mask* (1939). He retired in 1941 to paint, then in 1949 tried to make another film, but it was never released.

White, J. Alan. British publisher. He joined Methuen in 1924, became a director in 1933 and retired as Chairman in 1969. He brought many new writers to the firm (which had already published Conrad and James), emphasizing the importance of taking risks on new talent. During the war, he was exempted from military service even though he was only thirty-five because his boss, C. W. Chamberlain, said he could not run the firm without him. White moved his family to Kent and commuted to London to struggle with paper and labor shortages and wartime printing regulations; at night he served in the Home Guard. *Prater Violet*, published in New York in 1945 but delayed in England until the spring of 1946, was Isherwood's first publication with Methuen. White got the book for his new postwar list simply by offering Isherwood more money than any other English publisher. Methuen remained Isherwood's U.K. publisher for the rest of Isherwood's life, and posthumously, until 1998 when Random House attempted to take over the imprint which by then belonged to a larger group, Reed Books. Methuen achieved independence through a management buy-out, but permitted Isherwood to go to Chatto & Windus at Random House. (Random House was already publishing Isherwood's diaries in a Vintage paperback edition; by chance, Chatto had in any case been the home since 1946 of Isherwood's much earlier publisher, the Hogarth Press.)

Williams, Emlyn (1905–1987). Welsh playwright and actor. Williams wrote psychological thrillers for the London stage, including *Night Must Fall* (1935), and is perhaps best known for *The Corn Is Green* (1935), based on his own background in Wales and in which he played the lead; both of these were later filmed. He acted in many other stage productions, including Shakespeare and contemporary theater. During the 1950s he toured with one-man shows of Charles Dickens and Dylan Thomas (the Dylan Thomas show was titled *Growing Up*). Isherwood first met Williams in Hollywood in 1950 and saw him and his wife Molly again in London and Hollywood in subsequent years.

Williams, Tennessee (1911–1983). American playwright; Thomas Lanier Williams was born in Mississippi and raised in St. Louis. His father was a travelling salesman, his mother felt herself to be a glamorous southern belle in reduced circumstances. His essentially autobiographical play, *The Glass Menagerie*, made him famous in 1945, and soon afterwards he wrote *A Streetcar Named Desire* (1947). Many of his subsequent plays are equally well-known—such as *The Rose Tattoo* (1950), *Cat on a Hot Tin Roof* (1955), *Sweet Bird of Youth* (1959), *The Night of the Iguana* (1962)—and were made into films. Williams also wrote a novella, *The Roman Spring of Mrs. Stone* (1950). When he first came to Hollywood in 1943 to work for MGM, he bore a letter of introduction to Isherwood from Lincoln Kirstein; this began a long and close friendship, with numerous visits on both coasts, often to attend openings of Williams's plays. There are many passages about Williams in *D1*. Williams's longtime companion, Frank Merlo, died of cancer in 1963.

Windham, Donald (b. 1920). Novelist and playwright, from Georgia. Windham was a friend of Lincoln Kirstein and of Glenway Wescott as well as of Paul Cadmus and George Platt Lynes, and wrote a book, *Tanaquil*, based on this circle of artists. Isherwood probably met him in New York early in the 1940s, certainly by 1942. Windham worked for Kirstein at *Dance Index*, and ran the magazine while Kirstein was away in the army during the war. He also collaborated with Tennessee Williams—a close friend—on the play *You Touched Me!* (1945). Isherwood wrote a blurb for Windham's 1950 novel *The Dog Star*.

Winter, Ella. American author and translator. During the 1920s she translated from German *The Diary of Otto Braun with Selections from His Letters and Poems* and Wolfgang Koehler's *The Mentality of Apes*. Her book about the Soviet Union, *Red Virtue: Human Relationships in the New Russia* (1933), was a bestseller. Winter's first husband, Lincoln Steffens (1866–1936), was a journalist and author (she edited his letters), and she later married the American playwright and screenwriter Donald Ogden Stewart. The Stewarts were neighbors of Salka Viertel in Santa Monica.

Winter, Keith. British novelist, playwright, and screenwriter; born in Wales, educated at Berkhamsted and Lincoln College, Oxford. His 1934 play, *The Shining Hour*, was filmed in 1938 with Joan Crawford and Margaret Sullavan (using a script by Jane Murfin and Ogden Nash), and during the 1940s Winter worked on numerous screenplays at MGM and at Warner Brothers, where Isherwood mentions being friendly with him. One of Winter's boarding-school novels, *The Rats of Norway* (1932), was staged successfully in London, but flopped in New York in 1948. Winter also wrote the first movie adaptation of Evelyn Waugh's *The Loved One*, later scripted by Isherwood and Terry Southern.

Wood, Christopher (Chris) (d. 1976). Isherwood met Chris Wood in September 1932 when W. H. Auden took him to meet Gerald Heard, then sharing Wood's London flat. Wood was about ten years younger than Heard, handsome and friendly but shy about his maverick talents. He played the piano well, but never professionally, wrote short stories, but not for publication, had a pilot's license and rode a bicycle for transport. He was extremely rich (the family business made jams and other canned and bottled goods), sometimes extravagant, and always generous; he secretly funded many of Heard's projects and loaned or gave money to many other friends (including Isherwood). In 1937 Wood emigrated with Heard to Los Angeles and in 1941 moved with him to Laguna. Their domestic commitment persisted for a time despite Heard's increasing asceticism and religious activities. Ultimately, the household disbanded as their lives diverged, though they remained friends. From 1939, Wood was involved with Paul Sorel, also a member of the household for about five years. Wood appears throughout *D1*.

Worsley, Cuthbert. English writer, theater critic, and schoolmaster. T. C. Worsley was a friend of Stephen Spender and in 1937 accompanied him to the Spanish Civil War on an assignment for the *Daily Worker*. Worsley returned to Spain soon afterwards to join an ambulance unit. He later wrote about this period for *The Left Review* and in *Behind the Battle* (1939), as well as in a fictionalized memoir published much later, *Fellow Travellers* (1971). During the 1950s he wrote about theater for the *Financial Times*.

Wright, Frank Lloyd (1869–1959). American architect. A preeminent figure in twentieth-century architecture, Wright originated the organic principle that the form of a building should develop naturally from its setting, from its function, and from its materials. He began as a designer in a Chicago firm and eventually opened his own practice, first expressing his genius for spacious, open-plan interiors in his low-standing "prairie" houses. His houses in particular tended to conform to the features of the natural landscape in which they were set, but also, he was trained as a civil engineer, and he was able to apply the principles of engineering to his architectural designs. Thus, he initiated new techniques in offices and other large public buildings—such as concrete blocks reinforced with steel rods, air conditioning, indirect lighting, panel heat, and new uses of glass. In 1910, Wright established Taliesin, near Spring Green, Wisconsin. It was both his home and an architectural school (named after a sixth-century Welsh bard). Later, in 1938, he founded Taliesin West, in Scottsdale, Arizona, where he spent the winter months and where apprentice architects also gathered to work with him. His foundation, the

Taliesin Fellowship, supported both centers.

Wyberslegh Hall. The fifteenth-century manor house where Isherwood was born and where his mother lived with his brother, Richard, after the war; it was part of the Bradshaw Isherwood estate.

Yogi and Yogini. Disciples of Swami Prabhavananda. His real name was Walter Brown, and he was in the army briefly during the war. Isherwood met him in April 1943 when Brown visited the Hollywood Vedanta Center where Mrs. Brown, Yogini, was already a probationer nun. Yogi and Yogini both lived at the center for a time, but eventually Yogi left and Yogini remained there alone as a nun.

Yorke, Henry. See Green, Henry.

Zinnemann, Fred (1907–1997). Viennese-born director; son of a physician. He studied at the Technical School of Cinema in Paris in 1927 and 1928, briefly worked as an assistant cameraman in Berlin, and arrived in the autumn of 1929 in Hollywood, where he was employed as an extra in *All Quiet on the Western Front* and then became Berthold Viertel's personal assistant. He learned about documentary filmmaking from Robert Flaherty during an otherwise fruitless movie project back in Berlin, then filled in for his friend Henwar Rodakiewicz directing a documentary for the Mexican government, *The Wave* (1934). Two years later he was hired to direct shorts at MGM and eventually went on to other major studios, still using the semi-realistic style shaped by his documentary experience. By the early 1940s, when Isherwood met him, Zinnemann was living with his English wife, Renée Bartlett, on Mabery Road, near the Viertels, and Isherwood mentions them both in *D1*. He directed a great many successful films—*High Noon* (1952), *The Member of the Wedding* (1953), *From Here to Eternity* (1953), *Oklahoma* (1955), *A Hatful of Rain* (1957), *The Sundowners* (1960), *A Man for All Seasons* (1966), *The Day of the Jackal* (1973), *Julia* (1977), and others.

Index

NOTE: Works by Isherwood appear directly under title; works by others appear under authors' names.

& n; reading, 23, 51, 140n,
175n, 223n, 274n; hitchhikes to
work, 24; owns cars, 33, 46,
276; takes out U.S. citizenship
papers, 40; sexual snobbishness,
41–2; entertaining with Caskey,
49–51; at school in England,
57 & n; exhibitionism, 64,
279–80; and songs, 66;
antagonizes Katherine Anne
Porter, 68–9; gives blood to
accident victim, 69; occupies
Salka Viertel's garage
apartment, 70–1, 73–4;
promiscuity, 74; jealousies, 75,
79, 166; granted U.S.
citizenship, 77–8, 209;
pacifism, 77–8, 100, 189–90;
fear of flying, 80; plans to settle
in New York on return from
England (1947), 82n;
homesickness for USA, 84;
accent, 85–6; wears dinner
jacket, 104n; attends Pilates'
gymnasium, 120;
photographed by Jared French,
128; photographed on Fire
Island, 138–9; returns to Los
Angeles (1948), 149–50;
bicycling, 150n; moves into
East Rustic Road with Caskey,
167, 183; hospital visiting, 183,
200, 204–5, 219, 236, 239–40;
psychic sensitivity, 185–7 & n;
attends Benton Way Group
meeting, 197–8; gives up
smoking, 211–12; resumes
smoking, 215n; detained in
raid on homosexual club,
216–17; Fechin portrait of,
222; hypnotized by LeCron,
230–1; driving, 231; practises
autosuggestion, 236; attitude to
Jews, 262, 266; encounter with
psychotic neighbor, 264–5;
leaves Los Angeles for Laguna
Beach, 273–5; painted by
Sorel, 276; play–acts drowning,

278; moves into Huntington
Hartford Foundation, 282
Professional activities: film script
writing, 23–5, 28, 32–5, 46,
150–3, 167, 176–7, 191, 195,
207 & n, 229; film outline of
ghost story, 49; works for
MGM, 73n; works with Lesser
Samuels, 81, 91, 167, 195, 198,
206, 229; speaks lines for
Christ's voice in *The Great
Sinner*, 177–8; membership of
Academy of Motion Picture
Arts and Sciences, 188; as
trustee of Hartford Foundation,
245–6, 264
Relationships: with Don
Bachardy, ix–x, xxi, xxiii,
xxvii, xxxii; with Heinz
Neddermayer, xi, xxi, xxx;
with Bill Caskey, xv–xvii, xxv,
xxvii, 20, 34–5, 41–9, 52–6,
59–61, 66, 69, 73–5, 79,
117–18, 163, 166–7, 175, 182,
193–4, 208, 233, 241n, 257–8,
277–8; with Jim Charlton, xv,
156–66, 183, 208, 210–11,
213–14, 216, 230, 248, 280n;
with Jack Hewit, xxix, 92–4,
98–100, 103; with Bill Harris,
4–7, 9–20; with Carter Lodge,
12n; with Steve Cooley, 32–7,
41–2; with Vernon Old, 45,
50, 92, 106, 193; with Auden,
58; friendship with Denny
Fouts ends, 70; with John
Cowan, 76; with Ian
Scott–Kilvert, 103–7 & n; with
Tony Hyndman, 114–15n,
145; difficulties with Caskey,
179–83, 197, 210, 220, 250n,
278; considers leaving Caskey,
192–3, 199–200; Caskey breaks
with, 195, 282–3; with Don
Coombs, 218–19, 221, 258,
260–1; with Michael Leopold,
220–2, 230, 258, 277; with
Peter Darms, 242–3, 258, 282;

Christopher Isherwood

GOODBYE TO BERLIN

'Brilliant sketches of a society in decay'
George Orwell

Christopher Isherwood is the narrator of *Goodbye to Berlin*. His story obliquely evokes the gathering storm in Berlin before and just after the rise to power of the Nazis, as seen through the eyes of a series of individuals: his landlady, Fräulein Schroeder; Sally Bowles, the English upper-class waif; the Nowaks, a struggling working-class family; the Landauers, a wealthy, civilized family of Jewish store owners, whose lives are about to be ruined.

'Isherwood – fresh as ever…The prose is excellent'
Irish Independent

Christopher Isherwood

PRATER VIOLET

'The best prose writer in English'
Gore Vidal

Set in London in the mid-1930s, *Prater Violet* is a consummate and living portrait of one man: Friedrich Bergmann, the film director, for whom Isherwood was hired to write a script.

Prater Violet is the graphic and comic record of the scripting and shooting of a film, a comment on the sterile politics of pre-war England and an analysis of the true role and limits of the artist. But principally it is Bergmann – magnificent, loveable, and emperor, taken captive and 'a tragic Punch'; and it endures as a sophisticated, witty book with a subtle and questing inner depth.

V

VINTAGE

Christopher Isherwood

DIARIES VOLUME ONE: 1939–1960

Edited and introduced by
Katherine Bucknell

'A major literary event...an essential part of his ouevre'
Guardian

In 1939 Christopher Isherwood and W.H. Auden emigrated together to the United States. These diaries describe Isherwood's search for a new life in California and his work as a screenwriter in Hollywood, his pacifism during World War II and his friendships with such gifted artists and intellectuals as Garbo, Charles Chaplin, Thomas Mann, Charles Laughton and Aldous Huxley.

'There is not a page that does not contain a good joke, original insight, deadly accurate description or delicious nugget of gossip...After the self-serving literary memoirs of recent years, it is all very refreshing. A major literary work, the diaries round off the writer both as man and artist. They are intimate and intensely personal'
Independent on Sunday

V

VINTAGE

TITLES BY CHRISTOPHER ISHERWOOD
AVAILABLE IN VINTAGE

☐ LIONS AND SHADOWS	£6.99
☐ GOODBYE TO BERLIN	£6.99
☐ CHRISTOPHER AND HIS KIND	£6.99
☐ A SINGLE MAN	£6.99
☐ DOWN THERE ON A VISIT	£7.99
☐ PRATER VIOLET	£5.99
☐ BERLIN NOVELS	£9.99
☐ DIARIES	£9.99

- All Vintage books are available through mail order or from your local bookshop.
- Payment may be made using Access, Visa, Mastercard, Diners Club, Switch and Amex, or cheque, eurocheque and postal order (sterling only).

☐☐☐☐☐☐☐☐☐☐☐☐☐☐☐☐

Expiry Date:_____Signature:_____

Please allow £2.50 for post and packing for the first book and £1.00 per book thereafter.

ALL ORDERS TO:

Vintage Books, Books by Post, TBS Limited, The Book Service,
Colchester Road, Frating Green, Colchester, Essex, CO7 7DW, UK.
Telephone: (01206) 256 000
Fax: (01206) 255 914

NAME:_____

ADDRESS:_____

_____

_____

Please allow 28 days for delivery. Please tick box if you do not   ☐
wish to receive any additional information
Prices and availability subject to change without notice.